CLOSE THE GAP. LIVE THE PROMISE.

THE DANIEL FAST: CLOSING THE GAP!

A 21-Day Prayer Journey to Wellness

A Complete Biblical Fasting & Prayer Guide for Christian Breakthrough

SPIRITUAL RESTORATION • IDENTITY TRANSFORMATION • PURPOSE ACTIVATION

THE 4-STAGE TRANSFORMATION FRAMEWORK

Nicola McFadden

THE DANIEL FAST: CLOSING THE GAP!
A 21-Day Prayer Journey to Wellness
Copyright © 2020 by Nicola McFadden
First Edition: December 23, 2020
Expanded Edition Copyright © 2025 by Dr. Nicola McFadden-Marvin
Expanded Edition | Transformation Manual: October 2025

Published by Nikimac Solutions Inc.
Ontario, Canada
https://nikimac.com

ISBN-10: 1999417569
ISBN-13: 978-1999417567

All rights reserved. No part of this publication may be reproduced, stored in a retrieval system, or transmitted in any form or by any means—electronic, mechanical, photocopy, recording, or any other—except for brief quotations in critical reviews or articles, without prior written permission from the publisher.

SCRIPTURE REFERENCES

Unless otherwise indicated, all Scripture quotations are from the New King James Version®. Copyright © 1982 by Thomas Nelson.

Used by permission. All rights reserved. Scripture marked (AMP) from the Amplified Bible, Copyright © 2015 by The Lockman Foundation.

Used by permission. www.Lockman.org Scripture marked (NIV) from the Holy Bible, New International Version®, NIV®. Copyright © 1973, 1978, 1984, 2011 by Biblica, Inc.™

Used by permission of Zondervan. All rights reserved worldwide. Scripture marked (NCV) from the New Century Version®. Copyright © 2005 by Thomas Nelson.

Used by permission. All rights reserved. Scripture marked (MSG) from The Message. Copyright © 1993, 2002, 2018 by Eugene H. Peterson.

Used by permission of NavPress. All rights reserved. Represented by Tyndale House Publishers. Scripture marked (ESV) from The ESV® Bible (The Holy Bible, English Standard Version®), copyright © 2001 by Crossway, a publishing ministry of Good News Publishers.

Used by permission. All rights reserved. Scripture marked (NASB) from the New American Standard Bible®, Copyright © 1960, 1971, 1977, 1995, 2020 by The Lockman Foundation. Used by permission. All rights reserved. www.Lockman.org.

MEDICAL DISCLAIMER
PLEASE READ CAREFULLY BEFORE BEGINNING

GENERAL DISCLAIMER
This book provides educational content based on biblical principles and personal experience. It is NOT medical, nutritional, psychiatric, or psychological advice. Always consult qualified healthcare providers before beginning any fasting program or making dietary changes. NEVER disregard professional medical advice or delay seeking it because of something you read in this book.

CONSULT YOUR HEALTHCARE PROVIDER BEFORE BEGINNING
You MUST consult your physician or qualified healthcare professional before starting any fast, especially if you have pre-existing conditions, take medications, have a history of disordered eating, or have any health concerns.

DO NOT FAST IF YOU
- Are pregnant, nursing, or under 18 years of age
- Have diabetes or blood sugar disorders
- Have or are recovering from eating disorders (anorexia, bulimia, binge eating, orthorexia)
- Take medications requiring food intake or that could be affected by dietary changes
- Have cardiovascular, kidney, liver, or thyroid disease
- Are immunocompromised or have gastrointestinal disorders
- Are underweight (BMI below 18.5) or have nutrient deficiencies
- Have been advised by a medical professional not to fast
- Are managing any chronic medical or mental health condition

STOP IMMEDIATELY AND SEEK MEDICAL ATTENTION IF YOU EXPERIENCE
Chest pain, severe dizziness, fainting, confusion, irregular heartbeat, severe headaches, extreme weakness, shortness of breath, severe abdominal pain, persistent nausea/vomiting, dangerously low blood sugar (below 70 mg/dL for diabetics), rapid weight loss (more than 2-3 lbs/week), or any concerning symptoms lasting over 24 hours.

MEDICATIONS
If taking ANY medications (especially blood sugar, blood pressure, blood thinners, or diuretics), consult your healthcare provider before fasting. NEVER adjust or stop prescribed medications without medical direction.

MENTAL HEALT
If you have depression, anxiety, OCD, body dysmorphia, PTSD, or any mental health condition, consult both your mental health provider AND physician before fasting. If you experience suicidal thoughts or mental health crisis, STOP immediately and call 988 (National Suicide Prevention Lifeline) or seek emergency care.

PREGNANCY/NURSING
Pregnant and nursing mothers should NOT fast. If you discover pregnancy during a fast, STOP immediately and consult your healthcare provider.

INDIVIDUAL RESULTS & NO GUARANTEES
Individual results vary significantly. Testimonies reflect personal experiences attributed to divine intervention and individual commitment. These are not typical results. NO SPECIFIC OUTCOMES ARE GUARANTEED. Results, if any, will vary by individual.

ASSUMPTION OF RISK & PERSONAL RESPONSIBILITY

By applying this book's contents, you acknowledge that you: - Voluntarily choose to participate in fasting and spiritual practices - Accept FULL responsibility for your decisions and outcomes - Understand fasting carries inherent risks including nutritional deficiencies, dehydration, blood sugar imbalances, fatigue, dizziness, and other potential health complications - Have been advised to consult healthcare professionals before beginning - Will not hold the author, publisher, or affiliated parties responsible for any adverse effects, injuries, or damages

COMPLEMENTARY, NOT REPLACEMENT CARE

This guidance complements but NEVER replaces medical care. All health conditions must be managed with qualified, licensed healthcare providers. Your SOAP journal documents spiritual transformation, but your physical safety remains paramount.

WISDOM OVER RIGIDITY

Modifying or ending your fast for medical reasons is NOT failure—it is WISDOM. God values your health above rigid religious performance. Listen to your body. Honor medical advice. When in doubt, err on the side of safety.

MEDICAL SAFETY CHECKPOINT

Review the complete Medical Safety Checkpoint at the beginning of Chamber 1 (page [xx]) for detailed guidelines, preparation instructions, and daily monitoring protocols. Maintain open communication with your healthcare provider throughout your journey.

EMERGENCY

Call 911 or go to the nearest emergency room for any medical emergency including chest pain, difficulty breathing, loss of consciousness, or life-threatening situations.

LIMITATION OF LIABILITY

To the fullest extent permitted by law, neither the author (Nicola McFadden-Marvin), publisher (Nikimac Solutions Inc.), nor any affiliated parties assumes liability for adverse effects, injuries, damages, or consequences resulting from use of this book's information. This book is sold with the understanding that neither author nor publisher is engaged in rendering professional medical services. If professional assistance is required, seek competent, licensed professionals.

NOT INTENDED TO DIAGNOSE, TREAT, CURE, OR PREVENT DISEASE

This book is not intended to diagnose, treat, cure, prevent, or otherwise address any disease, medical condition, or health concern. The FDA has not evaluated any statements in this book.

YOUR HEALTH IS PARAMOUNT

When in doubt about any aspect of fasting or your health, STOP and consult your healthcare provider. No spiritual goal is worth compromising your physical or mental health. God created your body as a temple—honor it, protect it, care for it wisely.

DEDICATION

To my mother, who knelt beside my bed in midnight hours when hope felt like a foreign language. You prayed when I couldn't, believed when I wouldn't, and lived to witness every promise fulfilled. Your prayers are woven into every transformation story in this book.

To Nick and Matt, my sons who walked through the valley with me and emerged as men of unshakeable faith. You saw me broken and loved me anyway. You watched me rise and cheered the loudest. Standing with you on the mountain, I see God's faithfulness in flesh and blood.

To John, my husband, who saw the call before the proof and chose to build anyway. Walking with you is answered prayer in human form.

To every reader who whispered "help me" into empty rooms, trusting that Someone was listening. Your breaking points became breakthroughs that changed the world. This book exists because your courage to transform gave others permission to try.

To the One who answered my desperate prayer—line by line, promise by promise, exceedingly abundantly above all I dared to ask or dream. This book is Your faithfulness in print.

ACKNOWLEDGMENTS

This book exists because Heaven mobilized an army on earth. Every breakthrough documented in these pages was birthed through partnership—divine orchestration working through human hands, prayers, and presence.

To the Holy Spirit: You downloaded revelation in 3 AM hours, whispered strategy through desperation, and transformed my breaking into blueprints for thousands. Every framework, every word, every breakthrough—it's all You.

Valley Warriors: The single mother who secretly filled my trunk with groceries when I had nothing. The 5 AM prayer warriors who covered me when darkness felt final and hope felt foreign. Those who spoke life when death seemed certain, who stood in the gap when I couldn't stand at all. You loved me through the lowest valleys. Heaven recorded every act of kindness that kept me standing. You didn't just witness my wilderness—you walked through it with me.

Chayah Club Global Community: You transformed framework into movement, theory into testimony, revelation into revolution. Your courage to fail forward gave others permission to rise. Your vulnerability became someone else's victory. You are the living proof that this system creates lasting transformation. Six continents. Thousands of lives. One relentless pursuit of God. You didn't just apply these frameworks—you became them. Take your seat at the table: https://chayah.club.

Pioneers: You received revelation still warm from Heaven's oven when the ink was barely dry and the frameworks were barely tested. Your trust proved what testing would confirm. Your faith turned theory into testimony, concept into conviction. This expanded edition exists because you dared to go first, documented every breakthrough, and refused to settle for temporary transformation. You built the foundation that others now stand on.

Amazon Reviewers: Your authentic testimonies became endorsements money couldn't buy. Your vulnerability in sharing transformation stories—the raw, real, unfiltered accounts of God's faithfulness—gives hope to countless others standing where you once stood. You didn't just review a book. You testified to a movement. Your words reach people I'll never meet, in places I'll never go. Thank you for making your private breakthroughs public proof.

John: Walking with you is covenant made visible. You looked at a woman carrying Heaven's vision and said, "Let's build this together." You didn't just join a movement in progress—you multiplied what Heaven began. Your partnership expanded ministry beyond my wildest dreams. You saw potential when others saw problems, believed in blueprints when others saw brokenness, and stood firm when the journey demanded everything we had. This expanded edition exists because you held the vision when I held the pen. Every late night, every early morning, every "we can do this"—it's woven into every page.

To every person who will hold this book: Your name may not appear on these pages, but Heaven already recorded what you're about to become. The prayers you're about to pray, the ground you're about to take—it's already changing the world. Thank you for saying yes to the journey. The journey continues. Bring someone with you: https://danielfastclub.com.

WHAT READERS ARE SAYING

"This book is a legacy. It will be passed down to my child, and to her children, and to her children's children. We are generational curse-breakers, glory carriers, Kingdom builders, and faith walkers. This fast is more than abstaining—it is positioning."
— K.M., United States

"Transformation 5.0 is the only way to describe this book. It's like a College Spirituality Class for only the cost of the book. And the weight loss is just the added benefit that comes along with the course."
— B.K., United States

"LIFE CHANGING...TOTAL TRANSFORMATION FROM THE INSIDE OUT! This Book Is One that you want to Forcefully give to EVERYONE you know."
— M.T.E., United States

"If you're embarking on a Daniel fast and looking for the perfect companion, this is the ONLY book I recommend. You can genuinely feel the dedication and hard work that went into every page."
— M.M., United States

"Chains of bondage has broken and continues to break from my life... I have a better understanding of Daniel fast."
— T.S., Canada

"This is my second year doing the Daniel Fast 21 days of prayer with Nicola and there is so much more I am learning and implementing as strategies to achieve my vision."
— K.R., United States

"If you truly want your life to change for the better or if you're in a grave situation like I was then please, I urge you to get this book. And your life will never be the same."
— B.K., United States

"Practical, Insightful, Fruitful and most importantly Faith-Filled! I would definitely recommend this book!"
— J.N., Canada

"Love my book... Having a tangible book this time around made it so much easier to follow my daily fasting and devotional regime."
— Amazon Customer, Canada

"Transformational. I highly recommend...life transforming. I have the kindle and ordered the paperback."
— Amazon Customer, Canada

"This book is anointed to provoke change! It provides reference guides and checklists to help you stay on track. My favorite part is the journaling. A life-changing experience!"
— P.T., United States

TABLE OF CONTENTS

Dedication v
Acknowledgments v
Preface 1

SECTION ONE: THE BREAKING THAT BUILT THE BLUEPRINT 4
Chapter 1: When Heaven Reads Your Email 5
Chapter 2: The Pattern That Breaks You Before It Makes You 11
Chapter 3: The Revolution Born from Ruins 18
Chapter 4: The Wilderness Nobody Warns You About 26
Chapter 5: From My Story to Your Strategy 36

SECTION TWO: UNDERSTANDING THE TOTAL SYSTEM AND PREPARATION 40
Chapter 6: The Daniel Foundation 41
Chapter 7: The Total Transformation System 46
Chamber 1: Prepare: STAGE 1.1 -The I Decide™ 61
Chamber 1: Prepare: STAGE 1.2: Soap Documentation 87

SECTION THREE: CHAMBER 2: TRANSFORM WEEK 1: GROW (7G) 92
- Day 1 - GOSPEL 93
- DAY 2 — GRACE 108
- DAY 3 — GOODNESS 121
- DAY 4 — GIFTS 133
- DAY 5 — GLADNESS 147
- DAY 6 — GREATNESS 161
- DAY 7 — GLORY 179

SECTION FOUR: CHAMBER 2: TRANSFORM WEEK 2: ALIGN (7A) 200

- DAY 8 — ADOPTION 201
- DAY 9 — ABUNDANCE 217
- DAY 10 — AUTHORITY 234
- DAY 11 — ANOINTING 249
- DAY 12 — ADVANCEMENT 267
- DAY 13 — ATTRIBUTES 287
- DAY 14 — AFFIRMATION 315

SECTION FIVE: CHAMBER 2: TRANSFORM WEEK 3: PROPEL (7P) 335

- DAY 15 — PRESENCE 336
- DAY 16 — PROTECTION 358
- DAY 17 — PEACE 374
- DAY 18 — PROVISION 389
- DAY 19 — PROMOTION 403
- DAY 20 — PROSPERITY 420
- DAY 21 — PURPOSE 436

SECTION SIX: CHAMBER 3: INTEGRATE THE LIFESTYLE THAT LASTS 458

STAGE 3.1: DAY 22 - BREAKING THE FAST 459

STAGE 3.2: ARCHITECTING THE CHAYAH LIFESTYLE 467

SECTION SEVEN: CHAMBER 4: MULTIPLY THE LEGACY THAT OUTLIVES YOU 483

STAGE 4: THE MULTIPLICATION MODEL™ (Legacy LIVING) 484

References 494

PREFACE

In December 2020, I published a book on bathroom tiles at 3:47 AM.

Seventeen hours into formatting what should have been professionally edited. Eyes burning. Fingers trembling. Every amateur mistake visible. But God had given me the revelation and a December deadline, and obedience doesn't wait for perfection. I hit "publish" on what readers would later call "Transformation 5.0" and "a College Spirituality Class for only the cost of the book."

That messy first edition has since transformed thousands of lives across six continents.

This expanded edition exists because of what those thousands discovered—and documented—God's manifestation of their answered prayers and the promises of not just breakthroughs but transformations, not just information but revelation for personal reformation and community revival.

WHY THIS EDITION NOW

C.S. Lewis wrote that when God first comes into our lives, we expect a small renovation—fixing obvious faults. But soon He starts knocking the house about in ways that hurt and confuse us. The reason? He isn't making us into a tidy little cottage; He's building a grand palace—adding new wings, putting up towers, laying courtyards—because He intends to dwell there Himself.

That's what happened to this book. And to everyone who applied it.

I did my first Daniel Fast in 2015 and God showed up immeasurably more than I could ask, imagine, or think—with breakthroughs, restoration, and deliverance. But the more you seek God, the more of Him you discover, and the more you know how much He loves you right where you are, but loves you too much to leave you there. So I cried out for more—not just to get my feet wet but my whole body immersed, not just for His help but to be healed and held.

In 2018, God gave me the 21-day framework, the GAP Strategy, during 21 live sessions—21 sermons with declaration, impartation, and spiritual warfare prayer. The 2020 edition documented the GAP Strategy for three weeks of fasting, prayer, and consecration, introducing the conception of four master blueprints.

But God wasn't finished. As I heeded the process, the evolution and revelation continued. Five years of personal transformation and global implementation revealed the palace God was actually creating. I was building, but God was making me. What began as a fasting guide became a transformation manual. What started as personal breakthrough became generational architecture. The latter glory is proving greater than the former—exactly as Haggai 2:9 promised.

I still remember the weight of that first publish button. The nausea of knowing I was releasing something imperfect. The terror that no one would understand. The faith that obedience matters more than perfection. That 3:47 AM decision changed everything—not because the book was flawless, but because God honors availability over ability, obedience over perfection.

This expanded edition preserves the original revelation while adding what five years of breakthrough stories taught us: how to sustain transformation past Day 22, how to multiply frameworks beyond yourself, how to build lifestyle from event. What thousands tested through tears and triumphs, this manual now systematizes for your permanent transformation.

THE DANIEL FAST: CLOSING THE GAP!

THIS IS YOUR BURNING BUSH MOMENT

Isaiah 50:2 confronts us: "Why, when I came, was there no man? Why, when I called, was there none to answer?" God isn't asking if you're capable. He's asking if you're available. The silence of man often delays the display of God.

Whatever situation brought you to this book—that's your burning bush. The crisis isn't the curse. It's the call. Not just for breakthrough, but for transformation. Not just to survive January, but to become someone who lives consecrated every day of the year.

We're living in modern Babylon—a culture systematically targeting your soul, your seed, your purpose, your destiny, your generation, your legacy. Romans 8:19 declares: "For the earnest expectation of the creation eagerly waits for the revealing of the sons of God." This is that awakening.

You weren't made for lukewarm compromise. You weren't called to make God your last resort when He demands to be your first love. Matthew 6:33 isn't a suggestion—it's the architecture of Kingdom living: "But seek first the kingdom of God and His righteousness, and all these things shall be added to you."

WHAT MAKES THIS DIFFERENT

This is not a book about fasting. This is a manual for transformation built on the foundation of fasting—not as an event you complete, but as an identity you become as you fast and consecrate yourself.

The Daniel Fast isn't your goal. **Chayah** [khah-YAH] is your goal. Hebrew for "to live, to revive, to flourish." Ezekiel 37:5 promised dead bones: "Thus says the Lord God to these bones: 'Surely I will cause breath to enter into you, and you shall live.'" Not just survive. Not just exist. Live. Fully. Fearlessly. Faithfully.

That requires dying to your old self and living fully in Christ. Galatians 2:20: "I have been crucified with Christ; it is no longer I who live, but Christ lives in me; and the life which I now live in the flesh I live by faith in the Son of God, who loved me and gave Himself for me." Event thinking says, "I'm doing a Daniel Fast." Identity thinking says, "I'm becoming someone who lives consecrated."

This expanded edition shows you how.

WHAT YOU'LL FIND HERE

Returning readers: You loved the 21-day GAP Strategy (GROW → ALIGN → PROPEL). This edition reveals what happens on Day 22 and beyond—the Chayah Lifestyle framework that sustains what the fast ignites, plus the vision architecture (10-year legacy, 3-year targets, annual goals, quarterly milestones) and daily 8F pillars for permanent integration. Advanced strategies for multiplication show how your personal breakthrough becomes your family's legacy, your community's catalyst, your generation's inheritance. What you experienced in 21 days, you'll now sustain for a lifetime.

New readers: You're receiving five years of battlefield testing distilled into systematic blueprints. The Four-Chamber Transformation Architecture—I DECIDE, GAP Strategy, Chayah Lifestyle, Multiplication Model—forged in fire and proven through thousands of lives across six continents. Not theory. Testimony translated into transferable tools. Not inspiration to admire but instruction to implement.

Both: This manual shows you how God's hand isn't shortened (Isaiah 50:2) and how your latter house will surpass your former. Haggai 2:9 promises: "'The glory of this latter temple shall be greater than the former,' says the Lord of hosts. 'And in this place I will give peace,' says the Lord of hosts." The rubble you're staring at? God's about to crown it with greater glory. Your humble rebuild season? Preparation for weightier presence and deeper peace than before the loss.

PREFACE TO THE EXPANDED EDITION

HOW TO USE THIS BOOK

Don't skim for inspiration. Apply for transformation.

Section One will break your heart open—my 15-year journey from bathroom floor to global platform, from Gmail prayer typed through tears to every impossible promise fulfilled. You'll see yourself in my breaking. You'll recognize your valley in mine. These aren't chapters to read—they're mirrors to look into. Revelation 19:10 declares: "For the testimony of Jesus is the spirit of prophecy." My testimony prophesies over your future. What God did for me, He will do for you.

Section Two gives you the biblical, historical, and scientific foundation Daniel chose for 70 years of consecration. Ancient wisdom validated by modern science becomes your modern architecture. Before you fast, you need to know why it works. Heaven's strategy meets earth's evidence.

Sections Three-Five deliver 21 days of transcendent breakthrough chapters—not devotional thoughts, but systematic revelation you'll return to again and again. Week 1: GROW into intimacy. Week 2: ALIGN your identity. Week 3: PROPEL into purpose. Daily themes. Scripture. Revelation. Prayer. SOAP journaling. This is where bathroom floor desperation becomes breakthrough documentation—and your reference library for lasting transformation.

Section Six shows you how to sustain what 21 days ignites—because breakthrough without maintenance becomes just another January memory faded by February. Day 22 is the most dangerous day of your transformation. This section turns it into your launching pad. Vision architecture. 8F daily rhythm. The Chayah Blueprint. Breakthrough becomes lifestyle. Event becomes identity.

Section Seven multiplies your victory into legacy—your testimony becomes someone else's blueprint, your survival becomes their strategy, your scars become their sermon. C1 through C5. Personal transformation becomes institutional impact. Individual breakthrough becomes generational inheritance.

Read Section One to see the journey. Apply Sections Two through Seven to walk your own.

THE CALL YOU'RE ANSWERING

God is calling. Isaiah 50:2 asks if anyone will answer. Your presence here—holding this book, reading these words—is your answer. You're not here by accident. This is divine appointment. The distance between promise and fulfillment is bridged by obedient agreement.

Your simple, daily "yes"—repentance, prayer, consecration, obedience—becomes the timber the Spirit uses to frame a dwelling for greater glory. Answer the call you already hear. Carry the stone that's already at your feet.

Five years ago, I published imperfect obedience on bathroom tiles at 3:47 AM. Today, that obedience has multiplied across continents, transformed thousands of lives, and proven that God honors availability over ability, obedience over perfection.

This expanded edition is the palace God was building all along. He intends to come and live in it Himself—not just in the book, but in you. Your bathroom floor moment, your burning bush encounter, your desperate prayer typed at 10:23 PM on a Sunday night—it's all preparation for the palace He's building in and through you.

Your transformation begins now.

Dr. Nicola McFadden-Marvin
The Daniel Fast: Closing the GAP
2025 Expanded Transformation Manual

"When preparation meets revelation through fasting and consecration, transformation becomes inevitable."

SECTION ONE
THE BREAKING THAT BUILT THE BLUEPRINT
From Personal Crisis to Global Commission

"He also brought me up out of a horrible pit, out of the miry clay, and set my feet upon a rock, and established my steps." — Psalm 40:2

Your valley wasn't random—it was required education. These chapters reveal how personal breakdown becomes public breakthrough, how private pain transforms into reproducible process, and how one woman's desperate prayers became systematic architecture tested through thousands of lives across six continents.

Every blueprint begins with breaking.

CHAPTERS 1-5: THE JOURNEY
CHAPTER 1: THE BREAKING (2010-2015)
The Gmail prayer. Bathroom floor desperation. When everything falls apart, God collects the pieces.

CHAPTER 2: THE PATTERN (2015-2017)
The breakthrough-fade cycle. The Day 2 prophetic letter. Recognizing the pattern is the first step to breaking it.

CHAPTER 3: THE REVOLUTION (2019-2021)
The 6 PM trauma. The 365: Live Fearlessly download. Day 22 launch. When personal practice becomes community transformation.

CHAPTER 4: THE REFINEMENT (2022-2025)
Success wilderness. Oregon rejection. The Sun, July 6, 2014, 10:23 PM Gmail prayer—fulfilled. Most people survive the valley but die on the mountain.

CHAPTER 5: FROM MY STORY TO YOUR STRATEGY (The Bridge)
How testimony becomes transferable. The three questions that drive transformation: WHOSE you are → WHO you are → WHY you are. New wine requires new wineskins. The only difference between testimony and strategy is documentation.

What you're about to read isn't theory—it's testimony. These five chapters trace the 15-year journey from bathroom floor to global platform, proving God doesn't waste your wilderness. He weaponizes it.

Your breaking is preparation for your building.
Your mess becomes your message.
Your test becomes your testimony.
Turn the page. Your transformation begins.

"Though your beginning was small, yet your latter end would increase abundantly." — Job 8:7

CHAPTER 1
WHEN HEAVEN READS YOUR EMAIL
THE BREAKING (JULY 2010 - MAY 2015)

The tiles had branded my knees with their pattern. July 6, 2014. 10:23 PM. Bathroom floor, fluorescent bulb humming its clinical judgment overhead. I'd been down so long the ceramic had pressed squares into my flesh—physical evidence of spiritual demolition. My laptop glowed from the vanity counter, cursor blinking in an empty Gmail draft like a heartbeat waiting for resurrection. The smell of desperation hung in the air—stale coffee, unpaid bills, and the metallic taste of fear that coated my mouth daily.

How do you write to Heaven when hell has your return address?

The house held that particular silence single mothers know—when the refrigerator's hum becomes judgment, when ceiling creaks remind you this rental isn't home, when the absence of another adult voice becomes a presence that suffocates. My boys slept. Finally. After another day of scrambling eggs with shaking hands while pretending Mommy wasn't breaking. After calculating whether milk would last until Friday. After helping with homework while my mind couldn't focus past tomorrow's impossibilities.

The cursor blinked. Waiting. Mocking. Daring me to believe Heaven had WiFi. "God," I typed. "If You have an inbox..." Delete. Start again. Different this time. Specific. Not begging but declaring—writing the vision, making it plain. Habakkuk 2:2 commanded: "Write the vision and make it plain on tablets, that he may run who reads it." If Heaven had WiFi, I was about to send the most detailed prayer request ever written.

THE EMAIL THAT STARTED EVERYTHING

Let me share with you the exact words that would change everything.
From: Nicola Chambers
Date: Sunday, July 6, 2014, 10:23 PM
Subject: Prayer Request
To: Nicola Chambers
Pray for me and my boys as we are going through a divorce and seeking God for breakthrough in all areas of our lives:

HEALING — Spiritual, emotional, psychological, physical restoration for all three of us.

FAVOR — Open doors for management consultant contract starting September. To provide for my children, build wealth, invest in God's kingdom.

HOME — We lost our home in divorce, now rent. Need: deposit, improved credit score, mortgage approval, closing costs covered.

VICTORY — Divorce settlement must align with 2 Kings 8:6: "Restore all that was hers, and all the proceeds of the field from the day that she left the land until now."

Declaring in Jesus' name: Primary custody of my children. Spousal support I pay: CANCELLED. Child support from father: ACTIVATED. Fair income assessment for father. Equal division of home proceeds. Complete restoration.

BUSINESS — Establish Nikimac Solutions Inc. on God's principles. Contractual opportunities to launch.

GODLY HUSBAND — Future spouse to love me and my boys as Christ loved the church. Partner in ministry. Father figure. Legacy builder.

FINANCIAL BREAKTHROUGH — All debts cleared. Credit score restored. Positioned under Heaven's floodgate.

MY SONS — Healing from trauma. Growing in Christ's image. Academic excellence. Future leaders.

Thank you Lord for answering these prayers. Every detail. Every request. In Jesus' name. Amen. I hit send. To myself. **Sometimes Heaven needs receipts.**

THE PRECISION BEHIND THE PRAYER

Maybe you're reading this from your own floor—bathroom, bedroom, boardroom. Maybe you've typed prayers into phones at 2 AM, whispered them into pillows, screamed them in empty cars. This story is for you. For everyone who's ever wondered if Heaven has a spam folder.

The specificity wasn't random. Matthew 7:7 promises "Ask, and it will be given to you," but James 4:3 warns "You ask and do not receive, because you ask amiss." Every detail precise. Every request measured. This wasn't wishful thinking. This was Jeremiah 33:3 activated: "Call to Me, and I will answer you, and show you great and mighty things, which you do not know." When Heaven's math doesn't match earth's calculator, Heaven wins. Eventually.

But to understand that bathroom floor moment—to grasp why it would take exactly six months for Heaven to answer—you need to know the four years that broke me into position for breakthrough. What I now call my Job season.

THE JOB SEASON

2010 began what Scripture describes in Hebrews 12:27: "Now this, 'Yet once more,' indicates the removal of those things that are being shaken, as of things that are made, that the things which cannot be shaken may remain." Picture this: Director at a Fortune 500 company. Million-dollar home in an executive neighborhood. Boys in private Christian school. Success by every earthly measure. But like Job before his testing, I didn't know the conversation happening in heavenly realms about my life.

2010: The Death That Started Everything. The unraveling began with death—my biological father, the man whose absence shaped me more than presence ever could. Standing at his funeral, I mourned not what was but what never had been.

2011: The Foundation Cracked. Divorce proceedings began. Ten years of marriage dissolving in lawyer's offices. I founded Nikimac Solutions from my dining room table, not knowing I was building the lifeboat for a ship already sinking. Job 1:21 echoed: "Naked I came from my mother's womb, and naked shall I return there. The Lord gave, and the Lord has taken away; blessed be the name of the Lord." Yet even in the dismantling, grace appeared. A former colleague reached out unexpectedly in 2012: "I believe in what you're building with Nikimac. Use me as a reference." That single endorsement would later open doors when every other door was closing. Sometimes God sends ravens before you know you'll need them.

2012-2013: The Systematic Stripping. During the divorce years, my mother flew from Jamaica multiple times, trying to hold together what was falling apart. Each visit, she'd pray over the boys, anoint the doorposts, wage spiritual warfare I was too exhausted to fight. The boys moved from private school blazers to public school anonymity—another loss in the catalogue of losses. Depression had a medical code: "Situational." From Director to medical leave. Six figures to sixty percent. Corner office to kitchen table. The mathematics of collapse. Paying spousal support from disability checks while receiving nothing for my boys. The mathematics of injustice multiplying daily. The million-dollar house sold by court order, proceeds frozen in legal battles. I had a FROM address for the moving company but no TO address.

The Final Descent. Boxes packed. Nowhere to go. Three days before homelessness, through desperate prayer, a rental materialized—the owners literally heading to the airport, accepting below-market rent without credit check. God's provision in the eleventh hour for me, my boys, mom, and dog. New neighborhood. No friends. All comfort zones demolished. Like Job, I sat in the ashes of what was, not yet understanding this dismantling was preparation for rebuilding.

WHEN JOB MET ROCK BOTTOM

By July 2014, the Job season had stripped everything that could be stripped. Rock bottom wasn't a single floor—it was a descending spiral, each level darker than the last.

ROCK BOTTOM HAD LAYERS

Hunger. Not enough for McDonald's. Only kids' meals. "Mommy's not hungry," I'd lie, then beg for a bite. Children shouldn't feed their mothers. But Matthew 14:20 promised even fragments become feast when blessed.

Isolation. Friends from the executive neighborhood vanished. Church whispered. But angels appeared—a single mom from football leaving bags in my trunk. Rice. Beans. Note: "Single mothers don't let single mothers go hungry." Hebrews 13:2 manifested: "Do not forget to entertain strangers, for by so doing some have unwittingly entertained angels."

Crisis. Mother flew from Jamaica again to help, then collapsed on my bathroom floor. Two strokes, then heart attack. I declared Psalm 118:17 over her: "She shall not die, but live, and declare the works of the Lord!" She's still here in 2025. Some prayers you don't ask—you declare.

Violation. Ten years of prayer journals weaponized in court. Couldn't write to God for months. Couldn't risk vulnerability. The enemy struck at my secret place—Psalm 91:1 under attack. When the enemy uses your prayers against you, where do you pray?

The Mathematics of Injustice. Disability income minus court-ordered spousal support equaled less than nothing. But 2 Corinthians 9:8 held promise: "And God is able to make all grace abound toward you, that you, always having all sufficiency in all things, may have an abundance for every good work." The math of earth couldn't compute what Heaven was calculating.

JANUARY 2015: THE DANIEL FAST BREAKTHROUGH

I started my first Daniel Fast. Not spiritual—desperate. Church's annual 21-day fast. Nothing left to lose. Daniel 10:3 described it: "I ate no pleasant food, no meat or wine came into my mouth." But Isaiah 58:6 revealed the deeper purpose: "Is this not the fast that I have chosen: To loose the bonds of wickedness, to undo the heavy burdens, to let the oppressed go free, and that you break every yoke?" This wasn't just about food—it was about freedom. Ezra 8:21,23 became my declaration: "Then I proclaimed a fast... that we might humble ourselves before our God, to seek from Him the right way for us and our little ones and all our possessions... So we fasted and entreated our God for this, and He answered our prayer."

Week One passed. Same bills. Same silence. But Daniel 10:12-13 explains the delay: "Do not fear, Daniel, for from the first day that you set your heart to understand, and to humble yourself before your God, your words were heard; and I have come because of your words. But the prince of the kingdom of Persia withstood me twenty-one days."

Day 13 of Daniel Fast: The Phone Call. The phone rang. My lawyer Michael—yes, Michael, after praying for "Michael the angel." Let me tell you about this Michael. Months earlier, sitting in my car with no retainer: "Jesus, I'm retaining You. Send Michael." Minutes later, former subordinate called. His friend, a lawyer named Michael. Christian. Sang worship songs during our first call. Took my case without retainer. Daniel 10:21 manifest: "But I will tell you what is noted in the Scripture of Truth. (No one upholds me against these, except Michael your prince.)"

Now his voice carried victory: "Nicola, the arbitrator ruled. You won everything. Primary custody. Spousal support cancelled. Every point aligns with 2 Kings 8:6." Phone slipped. I collapsed. Victory tasted like tears—but legal fees consumed frozen assets. Freedom couldn't buy groceries. Job 42:10 still pending: "And the Lord restored Job's losses when he prayed for his friends. Indeed the Lord gave Job twice as much as he had before."

FEBRUARY 2015: THE MUDROOM REVELATION

One month later. Standing in mudroom—one boot on, one boot off. Heaven spoke. Not audible but undeniable: **"If I did it any other way, they would say they did it."** I looked around, and there was no one. He said it again. The boot stayed half-on for five minutes. God wasn't just answering prayer—He was protecting His glory. Isaiah 42:8 activated: "I am the Lord, that is My name; and My glory I will not give to another." God doesn't deliver halfway. When He moves, He moves completely. God's delays aren't denials—they're preparations for testimonies that can't be questioned.

MAY 2015: CLOSING DAY

Back at work. Professional facade while future hung by thread. Only minutes before bank closes. Closing day on purchasing our rental. "The underwriter hasn't approved your mortgage," realtor's voice cracked. "Without a co-signer, we lose the house in a few hours." I rushed to the women's restroom—my altar during work hours. Back against locked door. Genesis 32:26 desperate: "I will not let You go unless You bless me!" "God, You said if You did it any other way, they would say they did it. Only You can do this. You alone will get the glory, honor and praise."

Minutes later, her voice shaking: "Nicola McFadden? You're approved. Full approval. Closing costs included. In twenty years, I've never seen anything like this." I slid down that corporate restroom door. Professional clothes on institutional floor. Same posture as that desperate July night, different tears. Not desperation but demonstration. Ephesians 3:20 manifest: "Now to Him who is able to do exceedingly abundantly above all that we ask or think." The rental I'd cried in became the home I owned. Prayer plugged me into Heaven; fasting cleared the interference. Matthew 17:21: "However, this kind does not go out except by prayer and fasting."

THE SIX-MONTH ARC

Let me document the timeline for those who need proof that **Heaven keeps receipts.**

July 6, 2014, 10:23 PM — Email prayer from bathroom floor
January 2015 — Total legal victory through Daniel Fast
February 2015 — Divine explanation in mudroom
May 2015 — Homeownership from corporate bathroom

Not through my strength—recently returned from medical leave. Not through connections—isolated. Not through resources—below poverty. Through precision prayer. Through strategic fasting. Through a God who reads Gmail and answers with receipts.

THE INCOMPLETE VICTORY

Standing in my miracle home, surrounded by answered prayers, something felt incomplete. The breakthrough was real but fragile. Victory achieved but not sustained. I'd discovered fasting breaks "this kind" of bondage. But I hadn't learned the critical distinction: **breakthrough without becoming always becomes breakdown.** Winning battles without changing natures. January miracles without permanent revolution. Joel 2:12-13 beckoned: "'Now, therefore,' says the Lord, 'Turn to Me with all your heart, with fasting, with weeping, and with mourning.' So rend your heart, and not your garments; return to the Lord your God, for He is gracious and merciful."

THE PROPHECY OVER YOUR BREAKING

I share this not from a place of arrival but as someone still becoming. Your story may be different, but the God who reads email is the same. If you're reading this from your own floor—bathroom, bedroom, boardroom—hear this: **Your breaking is not your ending. It's your beginning.** Every tear is liquid prayer. Every groan is intercession. Every specific request is building faith's blueprint.

I prophesy over you what Psalm 126:5-6 promises: "Those who sow in tears shall reap in joy. He who continually goes forth weeping, bearing seed for sowing, shall doubtless come again with rejoicing, bringing his sheaves with him." Rock bottom has a timestamp—mine began in 2010 and culminated at 10:23 PM, July 6, 2014. Document yours. Write it down. Email it to yourself. When breakthrough comes, you'll need the receipt.

Stop begging for breakthrough; start declaring transformation. Your mess isn't meaningless—it's someone else's miracle map. Isaiah 61:3 is your promise: "To give them beauty for ashes, the oil of joy for mourning, the garment of praise for the spirit of heaviness."

THE FOUNDATION FOR WHAT'S COMING

Every line of that Gmail prayer would be answered. But first, I'd learn why breakthrough without becoming always becomes breakdown. Why the God who delivered Daniel from lions kept him in Babylon seventy years. Daniel understood. Seventy years in Babylon taught him that breakthrough without character becomes bondage. His fast in Daniel 10 wasn't for deliverance—he was already in the palace. It was for understanding. For becoming.

The bathroom floor prayer was just the beginning. The corporate bathroom miracle just confirmation. The real journey—from temporary victory to permanent transformation—was about to begin. And it would cost me everything I thought I knew about fasting, faith, and how Heaven truly works.

Turn the page to Chapter 2: The Pattern That Breaks You Before It Makes You—where I'll show you why breakthrough without discipline becomes breakdown in disguise, and how the same cycles that broke me became the blueprints that made me.

CHAPTER 2
THE PATTERN THAT BREAKS YOU BEFORE IT MAKES YOU
THE FADE (MAY 2015 - DECEMBER 2017)

The closing documents burned hot against my palm like branded victory. May 2015. Standing in my own driveway—the same rental home I'd found three days before homelessness when fear whispered its lies, now mine as an owner. God had shifted me from renter to homeowner against every earthly condition: low credit, disability income, minimal deposit. The February prophecy fulfilled in May—"If I did it any other way, they would say they did it." He did it. Papers still warm from the realtor's trembling fingers. "The house is yours," her voice had shaken with divine impossibility just minutes before. Victory tasted like copper pennies and infinite possibility.

But something shifted the moment those papers were signed. Not a dramatic fall—just life accelerating beyond the discipline that had brought breakthrough. Back at work in corporate Canada with burning ambition to climb the ladder after the setback of divorce and short-term disability. New position—my old one filled during absence. The shift from writing morning affirmations to crafting corporate presentations. Two-hour commute door-to-door via train from home to downtown Toronto. Then motherhood. Then maintaining the social media platform where I'd once authentically shared my divorce journey and breakthrough testimonies, now posting empowerment while privately fading.

The woman who'd commanded her morning in January couldn't command her alarm clock by June. Matthew 26:41 whispered warning: "Watch and pray, lest you enter into temptation. The spirit indeed is willing, but the flesh is weak." **The enemy doesn't need to destroy you if he can just distract you. Distraction is destruction in slow motion.**

THE SNOOZE THAT STARTED EVERYTHING

Alarm screaming. Snooze button winning. "I'll pray on the train," I mumbled, already lying to myself. But the train became emails, preparation for presentations, mental rehearsal for corporate performance. Single mothering two boys who needed normal after chaos. Managing Mom's health from distance. Mortgage payments on a miracle that required maintenance. Renovations. Ministry squeezed into margins that kept shrinking.

I still prayed—weaving between commuters while whispering to Heaven. But these were different prayers. Survival prayers. Get-through-today prayers. Not the commanding-my-morning prayers that had brought breakthrough. Within three weeks of holding those keys, the discipline that brought the miracle dissolved into the demands the miracle created. The victories won through systematic consecration became the very things that prevented systematic consecration. **Breakthrough without discipline becomes breakdown in disguise.**

THE ANATOMY OF SPIRITUAL FADE

Fade is a master of disguise, wearing the costume of "getting back to normal."

Stage 1: The Snooze. "I'll pray on the train." But the train becomes traffic and emails.

Stage 2: The Substitute. Coffee becomes more necessary than communion. "God knows my heart."

Stage 3: The Burial. Your Bible gets buried under bills and business plans. "I'll catch up this weekend."

Stage 4: The Emergency. Prayer becomes crisis management instead of daily conversation.

Stage 5: The Performance. You're posting victory while living defeat. Quoting scriptures you're not reading. Leading while fading.

Matthew 15:8 exposed my reality: "These people draw near to Me with their mouth, and honor Me with their lips, but their heart is far from Me." Religion is what's left when the relationship dies. Performance is what's left when the presence leaves. **Your spiritual life isn't measured by your Sunday appearance but by your Monday obedience.**

JANUARY 2016: THE COMMUNITY EXPERIMENT

New year's resolution: Join the church Daniel Fast. Community would create accountability. Together we'd maintain what I couldn't sustain alone. January 2016. Our small group exploded with excitement: "Day 6: Marriage breakthrough!" "Day 12: Job offer!!" "Day 17: Depression lifted!!!" Hearts and hallelujahs multiplied. We swore this year would be different.

March 7, 2016. Someone posted: "Anyone still here?" Three dots appeared. Then disappeared. Silence. By April, the chat was a ghost town. The same voices that declared "Never going back!" in January whispered "Maybe next year" by spring. Including mine.

Luke 10:41-42 convicted me: "Martha, Martha, you are worried and troubled about many things. But one thing is needed, and Mary has chosen that good part." You can't lead where you won't go. You can't give what you don't have. You can't maintain what you won't cultivate.

THE ANNUAL FAST ADDICTION

January 2017: Same script, different year. Church's annual Daniel Fast. This time I was ready. "This is our year!" I declared. "21 days that will change everything!" And it did. For 21 days.

Miracles exploded. Contracts materialized. Relationships healed. Breakthrough testimonies flooded our chat. I led with passion, preached with power, posted with authority. Until Easter. By April, the chat was silent. By December, I was counting days until January's salvation arrived.

I was treating the Daniel Fast like a spiritual service center—an annual tune-up to get me through another year of dysfunction. January—Spiritual intensive care. February-March—Gradual decline. April-December—Spiritual flatline. The cycle was predictable. The pattern, undeniable.

Hosea 4:6 diagnosed my condition: "My people are destroyed for lack of knowledge." When you treat transformation like a yearly prescription, you'll need a yearly prescription. God designed breakthrough as daily bread, not annual medicine. **Stop scheduling breakthrough like an appointment when God designed it as an atmosphere.**

The hunger for next January's high proved something devastating: I wasn't becoming someone who fasts. I was someone who needed fasting to function.

DECEMBER 2017: THE BREAKDOWN THAT BROKE THROUGH

Single mother. Divorced. No child support for the boys. Building business and ministry simultaneously. Feast or famine between contracts. Bootstrapping business while funding ministry from corporate earnings. December wind cut through my car like judgment. I sat outside a building where I'd work a survival job. Program manager. Half my worth. My breath fogged the windshield as tears fell hot against my cheeks. Winter frost formed patterns on the glass that looked like the bars of my invisible prison.

"GOD!" The scream erupted from my core, voice breaking against the windshield. "I need MORE!" Not about bills this time. About patterns. Like Israel circling the same mountain for forty years, trapped in cycles I could see but couldn't break. Three years of evidence mocked me.

"Close the gap between what I know and how I live!" My fists pounded the steering wheel. "Between temporary victory and permanent transformation! I want to become a new wineskin You can pour fresh wine in and out of!" 2 Corinthians 5:17 stirred hope: "Therefore, if anyone is in Christ, he is a new creation; old things have passed away; behold, all things have become new." Isaiah 43:19 dropped into my spirit like liquid gold: "Behold, I will do a new thing, now it shall spring forth."

Then I heard it—not audible but undeniable: **"You've been treating transformation like an event. I designed it as an identity."** I grabbed my phone with trembling fingers, still tear-blind, and posted: "Who wants to do the Daniel Fast with me in January 2018?" Within hours, hundreds responded. The hunger for permanent change was universal.

God doesn't renovate patterns—He replaces them. Stop asking for breakthrough in your situation. Start asking for breakthrough in your nature.

JANUARY 2018: WHEN HEAVEN DOWNLOADED THE GAP

I went live on Facebook. No curriculum. No plan. Just desperation for different. What started as participants gathering online would grow to thousands across continents by day 21. "Who wants God to close every gap?" I asked the camera, voice steady despite shaking hands. The comments exploded. Every continent represented. Every denomination. Every desperation.

Each evening, one word would fall into my spirit like manna. By day 21, the GAP Strategy was born: **Week 1—GROW (7G):** Gospel, Grace, Goodness, Gifts, Gladness, Greatness, Glory. **Week 2—ALIGN (7A):** Adoption, Abundance, Authority, Anointing, Advancement, Attributes, Affirmation. **Week 3—PROPEL (7P):** Presence, Protection, Peace, Provision, Promotion, Prosperity, Purpose.

Twenty-one days. Twenty-one words. One progression that would transform thousands. You can't propel what isn't aligned. You can't align what hasn't grown. Jeremiah 29:11 confirmed the systematic nature: "For I know the thoughts that I think toward you, says the Lord, thoughts of peace and not of evil, to give you a future and a hope." **God doesn't just break patterns. He provides blueprints. Your breakthrough isn't random—it's systematic.**

DAY 2: WHEN HEAVEN WROTE MY FUTURE

After teaching on Grace to the participants online, I heard: "Write." I recalled the intimate moments I shared with God when I wrote letters to Him, but this time was different. He was writing a letter to me. I listened and wrote as quickly as I could, tucking it away out of fear. The promises were real but prophetic. I didn't understand the full revelation—the reference to Psalm 45, the warning about counterfeits, not settling for less. All were speaking to my identity that needed healing. What poured out wasn't from me but TO me—my exact journal entry from January 2018:

Daily Journal - Nicola McFadden, Daniel Fast 2018, Day 2 of 21

God is saying to you, "My Daughter, here is my promise to you to honor you with majesty, royalty. You are a daughter of the King of all kings. Ignore the distractions. Release the bitterness. Pardon the guilty, repent, forgive, let go. I am your Father of vengeance and recompense. You are my daughter.

I am transforming you into beauty as I did with Esther, so I am doing to you. Adore your crown with righteousness. Be gentle, be kind, be meek, be loving, and be beautiful. I am restoring your ruins. I am your King and Your Father. Your Maker and your Husband. Receive Psalm 45, stand on my Word. Believe and take it as my Word to you today.

No longer will you be called Forsaken nor your land Desolate, but you will be called My Delight is with her and your land Married. You are blessed and highly favored. You are beautiful inside and out. The rich will seek your favor with gifts and treasures. I will deliver you, and you shall glorify me. You are my representation of my manifestation of Glory. Your ashes shall turn to beauty. I will also bless your sons.

The enemy fears your destiny. You will not be defeated. I will make you a bronze wall against your enemies. I will personally fight for you. Do not fight them. You are royalty. Ignore them. **Do not take off your crown. Straighten your crown. It got shifted.** You are royalty. You are my beauty. I have preserved you for this time.

Don't worry about the contract. I am doing a new thing. I will provide the provision, sources, resources, funding, miracles, and finances. I will make your name great because you have not denied my name. I will pour out my Spirit upon you and your children. I will take back everything the enemy has stolen. Your latter days shall be greater than your former days.

You are my daughter. My Beauty. My Princess. My Delight. I will give you a double portion of honor, influence, affluence, glory, grace, goodness, and mercy. Do not be afraid. Only believe! Your season of failure and frustration is over. Favor surrounds you as a shield. I will give you wisdom and understanding—a revelation of my Word. I will restore your fortunes, generation blessings for My Glory.

Believe! Hear the Voice of your Abba Father, Your Maker, Your Husband, and The Father of your Sons, Your Provider, Protector, Peace, Power, and Prosperity. Your friend, Confidant, Your King, Your Savior, Creator, and Redeemer God. Stay away from evil and seek me to reveal the plots. Rise in authority and dominion that I have given you. Use my Word, the Blood of Jesus, the Name of Jesus, and the Fire of the Holy Spirit as your weapon and defeat enemies. Speak life. Resist the enemy. I will fight for you.

I love you. You are lovable. I have a Godly Husband for you. Don't worry about that; I am preparing you and maturing him. Don't worry. I will give you a family and a father for your sons, a man who bears my image and character. You are special to me. Wait, and trust me, my daughter. No good thing will I withhold.

Say no to manipulation, no sabotage, no counterfeits. Just trust me. It shall happen sooner than later. I know your heart's desire. I know the desires of your sons. I know you desire a family. I will provide for you. Trust me.

No ordinary man can love the person I have prepared you to become but a true Prince, a man I have groomed for you, and while I refine you as my Princess. Your waiting season is your preparation season. You shall be great for my glory. Your Father and King, God."

THE PROPHETIC IMPARTATION OVER YOUR IDENTITY

Based on that Day 2 revelation, I speak prophetically over you right now: **Your crown got shifted—but not removed. Straighten it.** The struggles you've endured weren't punishment—they were preparation. Every betrayal taught you discernment. Every loss taught you what truly matters. Every pattern that broke you was building the blueprint for your breakthrough.

The enemy's attacks against you confirm your assignment. He doesn't waste ammunition on empty targets. Every assault is evidence of anointing. Every attempt to silence you proves the volume of your voice threatens his kingdom. Isaiah 54:17 is your promise: "No weapon formed against you shall prosper, and every tongue which rises against you in judgment you shall condemn."

Your waiting season isn't wasted season—it's workshop season. While you've been wondering why you're still single, still struggling, still waiting, Heaven has been preparing what you cannot yet contain. No ordinary person can handle the assignment I've prepared for you. Your process is producing capacity. Your delay is developing character. Your wilderness is writing your wisdom.

Your latter days shall be greater than your former days. Not just recovered—exceeded. Not just restored—multiplied. Not just returned—revolutionized. The same God who shifted Daniel from pit to palace, Esther from orphan to queen, Joseph from prison to promotion is shifting you from pattern to purpose.

I prophesy over you what Heaven declared over me: You will not be defeated. Your season of failure and frustration is over. Favor surrounds you as a shield. Your name will be made great because you have not denied His name. Your gaps are closing. Your patterns are breaking. Your preparation is completing. **Straighten your crown. It got shifted in the struggle, but it was never removed.** You are royalty, and royalty doesn't beg—it decrees.

THE 2018 BREAKTHROUGH SEASON

The 2018 Daniel Fast: Closing the GAP was supernatural beyond anything I'd experienced. Not just personal breakthrough—global transformation. Thousands encountered God, received miracles, signs and wonders across continents. I entered the fast broken and came out with blessings beyond my wildest dreams.

The contract came first. Fortune 500 company in Canada. One interview. One call. Six-figure opportunity that positioned me for the next level professionally. "We've never made a decision this quickly," the director said. "Something about you is different." Isaiah 60:1 was manifesting: "Arise, shine; for your light has come! And the glory of the Lord is risen upon you."

Then the book funding materialized. "Rebound Faith: Chayah"—the manuscript I'd been nursing through my divorce season suddenly had publishing budget. International speaking engagements flooded my calendar. Doors that had been locked for years swung open simultaneously. The prophetic words from Day 2 were materializing with mathematical precision: "I will provide the provision, sources, resources, funding, miracles, and finances. I will make your name great because you have not denied my name."

Ministry exploded globally. Business flourished beyond previous limitations. Everything I'd lost was being restored with interest. But success has a way of exposing what prosperity cannot heal. Proverbs 21:2 whispered warning: "Every man's way is right in his own eyes, but the Lord weighs the hearts." External success without internal transformation is just a decorated prison. God's miracles in your ministry don't automatically mean maturity in your personal life.

WHEN PROPHETIC WARNINGS MEET WOUNDED HEARTS

The prophetic letter had warned me explicitly: **"Say no to manipulation, no sabotage, no counterfeits."** But warnings written in journals and warnings written on your heart are two different things. Especially when you're operating from wounds instead of wholeness.

MAY 2018: DATING AT DESPERATION LEVEL

Into that unprecedented success walked someone who could mirror my language but not my heart. "God showed me you in a dream," his voice smooth as practiced deception. "We're meant to build kingdom together." Tall. Articulate. Quoted Scripture with precision. Called himself a worship leader. But I was operating from a wounded place of desperation, not from my healed place of revelation. Fresh off years of rejection, betrayal, and single motherhood, I was hungry for someone to see me as valuable rather than damaged. He saw my success and wanted to attach to it.

The conversations started spiritually: "God told me you need covering. You're too exposed doing ministry alone." My boundaries became "rebellion against unity." My friends became "distractions from our calling." My discernment became "evidence of past wounds blocking love." He began positioning himself in my brand—photos at my speaking engagements, social media posts suggesting we were ministry partners, using my platform to build his. Control disguised as concern. Image appropriation. Spiritual manipulation: "If you really trusted God, you'd trust me. I'm the covering He sent you."

For fifteen months, I watched him systematically dismantle everything I'd built while convincing me it was for my good. Conference photos showed us together. My individual calling became our joint venture in people's minds. He was imaging my success while erasing my voice.

The warning from Day 2 echoed like an alarm I kept hitting snooze on: "Say no to manipulation, no to sabotage, no to counterfeits." But when you're operating from wounds instead of wholeness, you hear what you want to hear instead of what you need to hear. Proverbs 4:23 (NIV) I'd willfully ignored: "Above all else, guard your heart, for everything you do flows from it." 2 Corinthians 6:14 was neon-bright: "Do not be unequally yoked together with unbelievers."

But the most devastating truth? I wasn't unequally yoked with an unbeliever. I was unequally yoked with someone who believed in using God rather than serving Him. Someone who saw my anointing as his opportunity. The counterfeit came precisely when the authentic was manifesting. **The enemy's most sophisticated attack isn't opposition—it's imitation.**

Never date at your desperation level. Date at your revelation level, or don't date at all. What you tolerate in dating, you'll negotiate in marriage. What you compromise to get, you'll compromise to keep. The counterfeit always comes when you're closest to receiving the authentic. Don't settle for Ishmael when Isaac is on the way.

THE PATTERN THAT BROKE TO MAKE

Every failure taught me what systematic transformation required. Every cycle built the framework thousands now follow. Every broken place became a blueprint for breakthrough. The pattern that broke me was the same pattern God used to make me. Romans 8:28 proved faithful: "And we know that all things work together for good to those who love God, to those who are the called according to His purpose." Ecclesiastes 3:11 confirmed the timing: "He has made everything beautiful in its time."

The revelation was complete: Transformation isn't an event you attend—it's an identity you inhabit. The annual fast addiction had to die for the daily lifestyle to live. The performance had to cease for the presence to increase. The event mentality had to end for the identity reality to emerge. **God doesn't waste your failures. He weaponizes them into frameworks that set others free. Your mess becomes your message when you let God turn your test into testimony.**

THE PROPHECY OVER YOUR PATTERNS

Whatever patterns are hunting you right now—hear this: The pattern that breaks you is the same pattern God will use to make you. Your repeated struggles aren't evidence of weakness—they're construction materials for your calling. Every cycle taught you what transformation requires. Every failure built your framework. Every broken place becomes your blueprint. Stop asking for breakthrough in your situation. Start asking for breakthrough in your nature.

The revolution from personal to global is loading. But first, the pattern must die for the person to live. The event must end for the identity to emerge. Your underground season is beginning. Your identity shift is activating. Your transformation from temporary event to permanent lifestyle is about to commence.

Turn the page to Chapter 3: The Revolution Born from Ruins—where the pattern's death becomes the person's birth, where 6 PM panic attacks become midnight manuscripts, and where systematic transformation shifts from private practice to global movement.

Your underground season is about to teach you what platform never could.

CHAPTER 3
THE REVOLUTION BORN FROM RUINS
THE SHIFT (AUGUST 2019 - JANUARY 2021)

The laptop screen scorched my thighs through thick flannel pajama fabric. December 2020. 3:47 AM. Ontario winter biting outside while I sat on bathroom floor—but this time I wasn't breaking. I was birthing. Seventeen hours deep into formatting the first edition of this very book you're reading—**"The Daniel Fast: Closing the GAP."** My right eye twitched exhaustion spasms. My left eye leaked tears onto the keyboard. The smell of determination mixed with fear filled the small space—stale coffee, scattered tissues, and the metallic taste of deadline desperation coating my tongue.

The editor had gotten sick. Couldn't finish. The pre-sale was already live on Amazon—people had already ordered, already committed, already trusted. But the manuscript wasn't ready. Professional cover, anointed message, heaven-sent revelation—but the content itself breeding typos like midnight mosquitoes. Commas in wrong places. Sentences that made no sense when fatigue clouded judgment. I'd missed the deadline. Amazon had refunded customers and issued a warning. Now I sat here, racing against a second chance deadline, formatting solo what should have been professionally edited.

"God, what if they laugh?" I whispered to the manuscript showing every amateur mistake. The reflection in the black screen whispered back: "What if they don't?" The cursor blinked judgment. Publish or perish. Help or hide. Nine months into a global pandemic. Death counts climbing. Toilet paper hoarding. Zoom funerals. And here I sat on cold tiles, birthing a book about transformation while the world burned. But something had shifted in these underground months. This wasn't the same broken woman who'd collapsed here before. This was someone who'd learned to live privately what she'd only performed publicly.

2 Timothy 1:7 arrested my fear: "For God has not given us a spirit of fear, but of power and of love and of a sound mind." Isaiah 66:9 (NCV) stopped my spiral: "In the same way I will not cause pain without allowing something new to be born," says the Lord. **Your mess doesn't disqualify you from ministry. It qualifies you for it.**

THE UNDERGROUND YEAR THAT CHANGED EVERYTHING

Let me take you back to where this revolution really began.

AUGUST 2019: THE 6 PM APOCALYPSE. I was working a corporate contract in British Columbia, living there during the week but flying home to Ontario every two weeks on weekends for motherhood. My boys, Nick and Matt, needed their mom—not a voice on the phone but a presence at the table.

August 2019. During one of those biweekly weekend trips home. Monday, August 19. Summer heat still clinging to asphalt. 6:00 PM sharp. The betrayal was discovered with devastating clarity. Not just infidelity, but the systematic deception that had unraveled fifteen months of manipulation disguised as love.

The confrontation that followed was public. Calculated. Devastating. A parking lot under fluorescent lights just beginning to flicker on against dusk, strangers walking to their cars oblivious to the assassination happening beside them. Words designed to destroy everything I'd believed about myself cut through evening air like blades through silence. Each accusation targeted not just my heart, but my calling, my identity, my very sense of worth.

But this wasn't random cruelty. This was strategic assault on the exact identity claims I'd whispered to God as a child. "Your daughter, Niki." Every letter I'd written Him. Every midnight prayer. Every "Daddy God" whisper when earthly fathers failed. Under attack. In public. With surgical precision.

"You think you're special to God? You're delusional. Your ministry? Built on fantasy."

The words hung in the air like smoke after gunfire. I opened my mouth to respond. Nothing came. My voice—the same voice that had led worship, preached sermons, counseled the broken—was gone. Stolen. In a parking lot. At 6 PM. On a Monday.

The trembling started in my hands—barely noticeable at first, like leaves before storm. Then shoulders. Then core. By 6:15 PM, my nervous system had memorized trauma with Swiss watch accuracy. The body keeps receipts even when the mind wants to forget. Isaiah 54:17 tried to rise: "No weapon formed against you shall prosper." But the weapon was words, and they'd already prospered in every witness's mind.

The Body Keeps Score. 6:00 PM became my body's internal alarm clock. Not 5:59. Not 6:01. Six o'clock. On the dot. Like clockwork. Like PTSD.

5:45 PM: Hands slick with sweat. 5:50 PM: Heart visible through shirt. 5:55 PM: Breathing shallow. 6:00 PM: Complete shutdown.

For months, my nervous system played the same recording. August 19th on repeat. The parking lot. The accusation. The trepidation. The humiliation. The rejection. The sound of my calling being assassinated while strangers loaded groceries into trunks and checked their phones, while the world kept spinning like nothing had shattered. Sleep became foreign. Food, tasteless. Shaking, constant.

I'd drive past that parking lot and my hands would start shaking before I consciously recognized where I was. The body remembers what the mind tries to forget.

Psalm 31:9-10 described my reality: "Have mercy on me, O Lord, for I am in trouble; my eye wastes away with grief, yes, my soul and my body. For my life is spent with grief."

The Identity Assassination. But the panic attacks weren't random—they were precise. The areas under assault weren't accidental—they were the exact places I'd built identity as a child. The "Your daughter, Niki" letters to God. The secret conversations where I'd claimed His love when human love failed. Every tender place where little Niki had written letters to Heaven, believing she was loved, chosen, called—now targeted like a sniper knows exactly where to aim.

The enemy doesn't strike random—he strikes strategic. He'd studied my childhood conversations with God and used them as target practice. 1 Peter 5:8 warned: "Be sober, be vigilant; because your adversary the devil walks about like a roaring lion, seeking whom he may devour."

But here's what I didn't understand that August night in the parking lot, what would take months of 6 PM panic attacks to reveal: What looked like devouring was actually documentation.

Every attack was evidence of value. Every assault, proof of assignment. Every attempt to silence, confirmation of what heaven had spoken.

The enemy doesn't waste ammunition on empty targets. He doesn't study your childhood prayers unless there's a calling worth destroying. He doesn't assassinate ministries built on fantasy—only those built on genuine anointing. **If there was nothing to destroy, why work so hard to destroy it?**

That parking lot became my burning bush—not because God met me there in the moment, but because what burned me there would later refine me everywhere. The attack that tried to end my calling became the evidence that confirmed it. What the enemy meant for silencing, God was already using for strengthening.

I just didn't know it yet. At 6 PM on August 19th, all I knew was trembling hands and a stolen voice and words that felt truer than any promise God had ever spoken over me.

Sometimes the wilderness finds you in a parking lot under fluorescent lights. And sometimes, that's exactly where the revolution begins.

OCTOBER 2019: THE FLOOR THAT BECAME ALTAR

Three months into the 6 PM torture schedule, I found myself face-down on carpet in my BC apartment. But this time, something shifted. I started a private 21-day Daniel Fast: Closing the GAP. Instead of begging for the attacks to stop, I climbed into Abba's lap like the child who once wrote Him letters. "Papa, only You can fix this. I can't live between breakthrough and breakdown anymore." Romans 8:15 breathed life: "For you did not receive the spirit of bondage again to fear, but you received the Spirit of adoption by whom we cry out, 'Abba, Father.'"

The shift wasn't instant healing—it was systematic recovery. Not miracle erasing but grace rebuilding. Day by day. Hour by hour. Minute by minute. **Your nervous system that memorized trauma will be the same nervous system that memorizes triumph.**

NOVEMBER 2019: WHEN HEAVEN DOWNLOADED THE DAILY FRAMEWORK

One month into private healing, God spoke with surgical clarity: **"365: Live Fearlessly."** Not fast fearlessly for 21 days. LIVE fearlessly. Every. Single. Day. This wasn't just a tagline—it was God downloading the daily framework that would bridge the gap between annual Daniel Fasts. The answer to the pattern that had broken me: intensive seasons of consecration sustained by daily practices. What the Daniel Fast accomplished in 21 concentrated days, this framework would maintain through 365 daily rhythms.

I started privately in BC, shifting from Facebook lives to intimate Zoom calls, small groups, LinkedIn posts. Testing. Refining. Living it before teaching it. The framework evolved organically as I practiced:

The 3C Morning Rhythm — Command my day. Commit everything to God. Conversation: God-care (prayer and scripture), self-care (emotional awareness and needs), community care (relationships and service). This wasn't random inspiration—it was the systematic structure from "Rebound Faith" becoming muscle memory.

Daily Resources — 365 sermons. 365 audiobooks. Content that fed soul while body fasted from distraction.

Five-Part Daily Practice — Message (scripture meditation). Affirmations and declarations (speaking truth over lies). Prayer (conversation, not monologue). Life coaching tool (practical application). Daily SOAP (Scripture, Observation, Application, Prayer journaling).

Reflection Bookends — Morning: Emotional awareness. One-word check-in to feel instead of suppress. Evening: Gratitude to close the day in His presence.

This wasn't just praying—it was architecting a life that could sustain breakthrough daily, not just annually. 1 John 4:18 became my foundation: "There is no fear in love; but perfect love casts out fear." 2 Timothy 1:7 confirmed: "For God has not given us a spirit of fear, but of power and of love and of a sound mind." **The Daniel Fast would be the intensive reset. 365: Live Fearlessly would be the daily rhythm. One without the other created the pattern that broke me. Together? Systematic transformation.**

THE UNDERGROUND RECONSTRUCTION

October 2019 to Summer 2020—months of living between two necessities. British Columbia held my contract, my paycheck, my healing. The mountains became sanctuary. Daily 5 AM appointments with God before corporate calls. I'd literally booked it in my calendar: "5 AM - Appointment with God." Non-negotiable. The 3C morning routine wasn't theory—it was survival mechanism. Command. Commit. Converse.

But every two weeks, I flew home. Not to escape—to be MOM. My boys needed me. Nick and Matt didn't care about my trauma or my healing journey in the mountains. They needed their mother present, not processing pain 3,000 miles away. So I boarded planes biweekly. Left the mountain sanctuary. Chose motherhood over healing space.

When the pandemic ended my contract in Summer 2020, I moved back to Ontario full-time. Back to my boys. Back to the trauma site. No more mountain escape. Just me and God and motherhood on ground that remembered August. 2 Corinthians 4:16-18 sustained me: "Therefore we do not lose heart. Even though our outward man is perishing, yet the inward man is being renewed day by day."

I wasn't building a platform anymore. I was building a person—myself. The 6 PM panic attacks gradually stopped. New neural pathways were overwriting trauma. What psychologists call neuroplasticity, Scripture calls transformation—Romans 12:2: "Be transformed by the renewing of your mind."

God became my solace. During this underground season, fasting shifted from annual event to daily lifestyle. Not restriction but relationship. The Daniel Fast principles became my normal. Every meal became prayer. Every craving became conversation. Isaiah 55:2 guided my choices: "Why do you spend money for what is not bread, and your wages for what does not satisfy? Listen carefully to Me, and eat what is good." **The lifestyle of consecration was healing what performance-based spirituality had created. Ministry isn't measured by who shows up. It's measured by whether you do. Private faithfulness births public fruitfulness. What you do in secret, God rewards openly.**

DECEMBER 2020: THE DOUBLE BIRTH

The anniversary of my 2017 car breakdown. But this December was different. I wasn't crying for breakthrough—I was pregnant with blueprints. Three years after that desperate car prayer, God was answering with architecture.

That night, while formatting the manuscript at 3:47 AM, God spoke with surgical clarity: **"Stop treating fasting like a spiritual vacation. Start living it as spiritual vocation. The Daniel Fast was never meant to be something you DO. It's someone you BECOME. Not an event but an identity. Not a diet but a doorway."**

Isaiah 58:6-7 defined the revolution: "Is this not the fast that I have chosen: To loose the bonds of wickedness, to undo the heavy burdens, to let the oppressed go free, and that you break every yoke?" Joel 2:28 confirmed the timing: "And it shall come to pass afterward that I will pour out My Spirit on all flesh; your sons and your daughters shall prophesy."

That night, four frameworks were birthed—the architecture for everything you're reading in this book: **I DECIDE** (preparation preventing failure); **GAP Strategy** (systematic progression from 2018); **Chayah Lifestyle** (eight pillars sustaining transformation); **Multiplication Model** (individual becomes institutional)

But December 2020 was conception, not completion. God doesn't dump revelation—He drips it. **We want microwave transformation: three minutes, done, serve immediately. God operates a slow cooker: low heat, long hours, flavors that develop only through time. The microwave reheats what's already cooked. The slow cooker transforms raw ingredients into something entirely new.**

What downloaded that December night would unfold progressively over the coming years. While I was building frameworks, He was building me. Each season refined what that night revealed. Each test proved what that moment promised. The frameworks weren't just given—they were forged in the fire of the very transformation they would later facilitate.

The word "Chayah" kept repeating—Hebrew for "to live, revive, flourish." Ezekiel 37:5 promised: "Thus says the Lord God to these bones: 'Surely I will cause breath to enter into you, and you shall live.'" **God doesn't give you programs. He gives you processes. Not events but evolution. Not quick fixes but kingdom foundations. Not microwave meals but slow-cooked feasts.**

Back to that bathroom floor moment where this chapter began. The manuscript glowed from the screen—the first edition of "The Daniel Fast: Closing the GAP," the very book you're reading now in its refined second edition. The editor had gotten sick. Pre-sale customers refunded. Amazon warning issued. Now I was racing solo against a second deadline. A beautiful disaster. Professional cover, polished interior design, anointed message, heaven-sent revelation. But the content itself? Typos breeding like midnight mosquitoes.

"Jesus, what am I doing?" I whispered to my reflection in the black laptop screen. My reflection whispered back: "Publishing obedience over perfection." The deadline was non-negotiable—God said publish by Christmas. People were waiting. Hope couldn't wait for perfect grammar. 1 Corinthians 1:27 validated the imperfection: "But God has chosen the foolish things of the world to put to shame the wise, and God has chosen the weak things of the world to put to shame the things which are mighty."

Messages were already flooding in: "I can't wait—I need this fast." "Looking forward to starting the new year right." "This is my year for breakthrough." My finger trembled over Amazon's "Publish" button—not from coffee but consequence. This wasn't just a book release; it was soul exposure. Everything learned in darkness about to be tested in light. One click between breakthrough and breakdown. One decision between helping or hiding. One breath between faith and fear. Ecclesiastes 11:1 commanded through chaos: "Cast your bread upon the waters, for you will find it after many days." Click.

Hours later: "Your book is live." I collapsed on bathroom tiles that had held my breaking before but now held my birthing. Ugly sobbing—the kind that comes when you've given everything and have no idea if Heaven considers it enough. Imperfect but obedient. Messy but faithful. Flawed but finished. **Perfection is the enemy of progress. Published and imperfect beats perfect and private every time.**

But the book was just the beginning. That same December night—in the hours between downloading frameworks and formatting manuscripts—another birth happened. **Chayah Club.** Not just a Facebook group or email list, but a sanctuary for systematic transformation. A digital home for people who wanted more than annual January breakthroughs. The word "Chayah"—Hebrew for "to live, revive, flourish"—wasn't random. This would be where people learned to LIVE fearlessly, not just fast occasionally. The book provided the 21-day framework. Chayah Club would provide the 365-day family. What I'd practiced privately since November 2019 would now shift into sacred community space—protected, intentional, sustained.

JANUARY 2021: WHEN PERSONAL BECAME COMMUNITY

New Year's Day unlike any other. The world suffocating under lockdown, but something unlocking in the spiritual realm. Inside Chayah Club—the community formed just weeks earlier—our first official Daniel Fast was launching. 5 AM prayer call. I expected a few people from the new community. But several more joined. Participants globally—Nigeria, Jamaica, Canada, UK, US, Australia, South Africa. Time zones collapsed as desperation united us. Acts 1:8 manifested: "But you shall receive power when the Holy Spirit has come upon you; and you shall be witnesses to Me in Jerusalem, and in all Judea and Samaria, and to the end of the earth."

This was our first Daniel Fast: Closing the GAP within Chayah Club, using the recently published book as our guide. "Welcome to Day 1 of becoming who you were created to be," I said, voice steady despite shaking hands. "For twenty-one days, we're not just changing what we eat. We're changing who we are." What I'd practiced privately since November 2019 was now becoming community blueprint. The GAP Strategy that had healed me underground would now be tested in Chayah Club. The 365: Live Fearlessly framework—no longer private, but shared within this sacred community space. Same framework. Expanded reach. Protected environment.

The 21-Day Journey. What happened next wasn't just fasting—it was systematic transformation.

Week 1 (GROW): Foundation Building. People encountered God's nature before attempting change. Matthew 6:33 ordered priorities: "But seek first the kingdom of God and His righteousness, and all these things shall be added to you."

Week 2 (ALIGN): Identity Revolution. 2 Corinthians 5:17 declared: "Therefore, if anyone is in Christ, he is a new creation; old things have passed away; behold, all things have become new."

Week 3 (PROPEL): Breakthrough Explosion. Isaiah 58:8 promised: "Then your light shall break forth like the morning, your healing shall spring forth speedily."

Testimonies flooded in: "Even though I faced health challenges and had to do a partial fast, God gave me grace to persevere. I'm seeing healing begin." "The SOAP journaling became my daily bread. I began to see myself the way God does." "After losing my job of 30 years, during the fast I received the best news: still in remission, no signs of cancer!"

The point wasn't random miracles—it was repeatable progression. GROW birthed encounter. ALIGN reformed identity. PROPEL released action. When you systematize consecration, you democratize transformation. This isn't about special people getting special breakthroughs—it's about ordinary people following extraordinary blueprints.

JANUARY 22, 2022: WHEN DAY 22 BECAME 365

Twenty-two days earlier, on January 1, 2022, we'd started our second annual Daniel Fast within Chayah Club. But this year was different. This year, I had a plan for Day 22. One year after our first Daniel Fast within the community, I was ready. The framework I'd practiced privately since November 2019, then tested within Chayah Club throughout 2021, was about to go fully public.

Today—Day 22 of the 2022 fast—was the official launch. Not the 21-day Daniel Fast—we'd been doing that within Chayah Club. This was **365: Live Fearlessly**, the daily lifestyle framework that would sustain people BEYOND the fast. The invitation to sustained transformation, no longer semi-private but proclaimed globally. The Daniel Fast was the intensive reset. 365: Live Fearlessly was the daily rhythm. One without the other created the pattern that broke me: annual breakthroughs followed by gradual breakdowns. But together? Systematic transformation. **The 21 days launched you. The 365 sustained you.**

"Day 21 isn't graduation—it's matriculation," I declared to thousands now gathered online beyond Chayah Club walls. "These weren't 21 days to get through. They were 21 days to get started. The Daniel Fast breaks bondage. 365: Live Fearlessly maintains freedom." Isaiah 43:19 erupted: "Behold, I will do a new thing, now it shall spring forth; shall you not know it?" The explosion was immediate. The chat flooded: "I WAS ENCOURAGED" "Absolutely encouraging!!" "Praise God" "I still want to tell my story."

People weren't completing a fast. They were commencing a lifestyle. Like the Year of Jubilee in Leviticus 25:10—but this wasn't every fifty years. This was every day. By morning, #Day22of365 lit up community feeds worldwide. The shift from event to identity was happening in real-time. **Day 21 is where religion ends. Day 22 is where relationship begins. The fast was never the destination. It was the door. Now walk through it and keep walking.**

The Mathematics of Multiplication. Within thirty days, the movement exploded. Numbers never capture transformation, but they document impact. Acts 2:47 lived: "And the Lord added to the church daily those who were being saved." Participants globally joined daily 5 AM prayers. Completion rates shattered expectations—people weren't just starting, they were finishing and continuing. Testimonies flooded daily: "My marriage was saved." "Depression lifted on Day 12." "Got the job I'd prayed for." "Found my calling."

But the most powerful testimony was collective: People had stopped treating transformation like a yearly subscription. They'd discovered lifestyle consecration. 1 Corinthians 3:6 reminded: "I planted, Apollos watered, but God gave the increase." Each testimony proved the same truth: **When you systematize consecration, you democratize transformation.** This wasn't about special people getting special breakthroughs. This was about ordinary people following extraordinary blueprints—people discovering that fasting as lifestyle, not event, amplified God's voice above every other noise. Movements aren't built by perfect people. They're built by persistent people who refuse to let imperfection disqualify their calling.

THE PROPHETIC DECLARATION OVER YOUR REVOLUTION

If you're reading this thinking "I've tried everything"—hear this: Your revolution doesn't start with perfection. It starts with obedience. Your breakthrough doesn't require credentials. It requires consecration. I prophesy over you what Zechariah 4:6 declares: "'Not by might nor by power, but by My Spirit,' says the Lord of hosts."

Your Day 22 is coming. Your shift from event to identity is available. Your transformation from tourist to permanent resident in God's presence awaits. Joel 2:25 is your promise: "So I will restore to you the years that the swarming locust has eaten." The fast God has chosen for you will loose bonds you didn't know were binding you. Isaiah 66:9 (NCV) assures you: God will not cause pain without allowing something new to be born. **Your pain has purpose. Your process has promise. Your revolution is ready.** Every fast that failed was data for the one that won't. Every January that faded was prophecy of the one that becomes permanent. Your underground season isn't punishment—it's preparation. What feels like burial is actually planting.

THE REVOLUTION'S TRUTH

It wasn't born in a boardroom but a bathroom. Not from strength but surrender. Not from platform but pain transformed to purpose. What started as one woman's desperate email to Heaven had become a global movement of people discovering breakthrough wasn't meant to be visited—it was meant to be inhabited. The frameworks were working. Chayah Club was thriving. The revolution was real.

But every revolution faces wilderness. And mine was coming. The question wasn't whether I could birth a movement. The question was whether I could build one. From private practice to community incubation to public movement—each phase had its challenges. But the next phase would require something different. **It's easier to birth a movement than to build one. Inspiration starts it. Institution sustains it.**

Turn the page to Chapter 4: The Wilderness Nobody Warns You About—where success tastes like sawdust, where victory breeds its own battles, and where you'll discover that the same disciplines that brought you up must keep you grounded. Your most dangerous season isn't the valley of breaking. It's the mountain of breakthrough.

Every revolution faces refinement. Yours is coming.

CHAPTER 4
THE WILDERNESS NOBODY WARNS YOU ABOUT
THE REFINEMENT (JANUARY 2022 - OCTOBER 2025)

Success tasted like sawdust in my mouth. The revolution was real. By every metric, 365: Live Fearlessly was working. Testimonies flooded in daily. Lives transforming globally. But in the quiet after the launch explosion, I discovered something nobody warns you about: **victory can feel hollow when you're running on empty.**

January 2022. Ontario home. The laptop screen glowed with testimonies that should have made me dance. Nigeria—generational curses shattered. Vancouver—marriages resurrected. Kingston—businesses birthed. London—mental health transformed. The revolution was working. Lives changing. Frameworks multiplying. By every metric that mattered, we were winning. So why did victory feel like defeat?

I closed the laptop and stared at my reflection in the black screen. The woman looking back had everything she'd prayed for on that bathroom floor. Ministry platform. Global impact. Financial stability. Influence across continents. But her eyes held the hollow look of someone who'd climbed the mountain only to discover the view wasn't what she'd expected. The home held that particular brand of silence successful people know too well—when your inbox overflows but your soul feels empty. When your platform grows but your peace shrinks.

Psalm 127:1 whispered warning: "Unless the Lord builds the house, they labor in vain who build it." **Success tests what struggle builds. Most people survive the valley but die on the mountain.**

THE WEIGHT OF MINISTRY NOBODY TALKS ABOUT

Chayah Club continued thriving. The community had grown beyond needing me present every single moment. Leaders emerged. Daily 5 AM calls filled with worship, teaching, prayer. Members calling it their lifeline. The frameworks were working. But here's what nobody tells you about successful ministry: **the blessing becomes the burden when you confuse stewardship with ownership.**

I wasn't drowning because the ministry was failing. I was drowning because I'd made myself responsible for sustaining what only God could maintain. Earlier that month, during a prayer call where exhaustion battled anointing, I'd poured out my heart to God: "Father, I don't understand this season. The miracles are real—lives transforming, generational patterns breaking, marriages healing. But I feel like I'm carrying weight You never asked me to carry."

Day in, day out, I poured. Responding to crisis calls at midnight. Counseling the suicidal at dawn. Teaching frameworks while my own foundation felt shaky. Each testimony was beautiful, but each also meant another person I felt responsible for carrying. Early morning prayers across multiple time zones meant sleeping became a luxury. Churches across continents meant a calendar filled with meetings and energy constantly depleted.

But God had spoken clearly to me about the numbers and time: "Don't look at the numbers or the clock. Too large breeds pride. Too small breeds discouragement. Time interferes with the working of My Spirit." I wasn't prideful about growth or discouraged about size. **I was confused about responsibility.** God had given me frameworks to steward, not people to carry. I'd confused being faithful with being functional. **Ministry without margin becomes martyrdom.**

Yet every day, I showed up for 365: Live Fearlessly—the daily gathering our members would wake up for and call their lifeline. The time together was amazing. Worship was anointed. The sermons were powerful. Prayer declarations and affirmations flowed with heaven's authority. People were engaged and felt connected. Whether there were 3 people or 300 or 3,000, I preached with the same fire. I showed up because I wanted to, not because I had to. God's presence didn't diminish based on attendance—and neither should my offering.

"God, You've given me everything I asked for," I'd pray through tears I couldn't explain. "Why does answered prayer feel so heavy?" Matthew 11:28-30 became my lifeline: "Come to Me, all you who labor and are heavy laden, and I will give you rest. Take My yoke upon you and learn from Me, for I am gentle and lowly in heart, and you will find rest for your souls. For My yoke is easy and My burden is light."

The enemy doesn't always attack through failure. Sometimes he overwhelms through success—making you feel responsible for sustaining what only God can maintain. Job 8:7 prophesied over my exhaustion: "Though your beginning was small, yet your latter end would increase abundantly." Ministry isn't measured by metrics but by faithfulness. God doesn't need you to carry what He's called you to steward.

SPRING 2022: WHEN BROKEN CALLED TO BROKEN

Early morning, before dawn. My phone buzzed with an unfamiliar number joining the prayer line. "I... I don't usually do this," a male voice said, rough with vulnerability. "I'm John. I saw Nicola on LinkedIn. Set my alarm hours early to make this call." The background was Oregon quiet—that deep silence of mountains holding secrets. Multiple time zones away. This man waking in the middle of the night for prayer with strangers. I knew that level of desperation. It has a sound—like hope being strangled but refusing to die.

"Welcome, John," I said, something in his brokenness recognizing something in mine. "We're glad you're here." For weeks, he joined silently. A presence in the digital darkness. Then gradually, prayers emerged. Raw. Real. Refined by fire. He led worship with the authority that only comes from ashes. Quoted Scripture like someone who'd wrestled it from heaven's hands with bleeding knuckles. "Father, You know what it's like to be abandoned," he'd pray, voice breaking on "abandoned." "You know what it's like to be misunderstood. Meet us in our mess."

For weeks, then months, John joined faithfully. His prayers carried the weight of someone who knew what it cost to stand when everything in you wants to fall. He'd found my LinkedIn posts during his own 3 AM desperation, when the difference between giving up and pressing on is a single Google search. The prayer line became his lifeline—what saved me in my wilderness was now saving him in his.

Later he'd tell me: "During one prayer, God said clear as daylight: 'She's a Princess Warrior. Don't approach until you're ready to cover that calling, not compete with it.'" Ecclesiastes 4:12 was manifesting: "Though one may be overpowered by another, two can withstand him. And a threefold cord is not quickly broken." 1 Samuel 16:7 explained the divine connection: "For the Lord does not see as man sees; for man sees at the outward appearance, but the Lord looks at the heart."

God sends broken people to broken people because wholeness recognizes what it cost to achieve. Your greatest ministry flows from your deepest wound. What broke you qualifies you to heal others.

SUMMER 2022: WHEN PROPHECY WORE CONFIDENCE

Summer 2022. Our first in-person meeting in Ontario. Pandemic restrictions still dictating life, so we sat at my kitchen table instead of some romantic restaurant. John stepped off the plane wearing confidence like cologne—not arrogance, but the settled assurance of a man who'd heard from heaven and believed it.

A few days after his arrival, he invited me to Niagara Falls. But the Ministry of Health had other plans—a warning arrived: mandatory 14-day quarantine in his hotel. He wasn't vaccinated. The romantic waterfall trip would have to wait. Or so I thought.

Disappointment hung in the air between us as we sat across from each other in my home—the same space where I'd formatted manuscripts and fought panic attacks—but now it felt different. Sacred. Our conversation had flowed like we'd known each other for decades rather than days. Ministry vision. Family values. Calling compatibility. Every sentence felt like recognition, not discovery.

He leaned forward, elbows on the table. "I need to tell you something," he said. His eyes held mine—steady, certain, unafraid. "I'm not here to audition for husband. I'm here because God said you're my wife." The boldness should have offended me. Instead, it felt like homecoming. Like a key finding its lock. Like prophecy wearing skin.

"Will you marry me?" he asked, with the certainty of someone who'd received divine download rather than romantic inspiration. No Niagara Falls backdrop. No romantic dinner. Just my kitchen table, pandemic protocols, and a man who wouldn't let quarantine delay what God had already confirmed.

Years earlier, God had written in my journal during that prophetic Day 2 in 2018: "I have a godly husband for you... no ordinary man can love who I've prepared you to become." Years of preparation converging in minutes of recognition. "Yes," I said, voice steady despite my racing heart. "But not because you asked. Because God already answered."

The world would call what happened next rushed. But here's what I discovered about divine timing: When God orchestrates a connection, He doesn't need months of dating to confirm what He's already established. John and I had both been refined through fire—his season of testing, my divorce and identity battles. We weren't naive twenty-somethings fumbling through romance. We were seasoned warriors who recognized covenant when we saw it. The foundation wasn't built during our dating—it was built during our individual breaking. We didn't need time to discover each other. We needed obedience to receive what God had already prepared.

When God speaks with clarity, hesitation isn't wisdom—it's doubt. Proverbs 19:14 confirmed: "House and riches are an inheritance from fathers, but a prudent wife is from the Lord." Isaiah 54:5 declared the divine matchmaking: "For your Maker is your husband, the Lord of hosts is His name."

God's timing doesn't follow calendars. It follows character development. What looked like months to observers was actually years to participants. He had been preparing John while refining me. We didn't need long engagement. We needed long obedience—and we'd both walked it separately before walking it together. Divine connections don't need extended courtship. They need completed character. When both people have been individually refined, covenant can be confirmed quickly because the testing was done in private before the promise was made public.

SUMMER 2022 - JULY 2023: THE OREGON JOURNEY AS FIANCÉE

After the engagement, I began visiting Oregon multiple times throughout late 2022 and early 2023—exploring the landscape that would become home after our wedding. The mountains were beautiful. The pace slower. John's family welcoming. But I was still rooted in Ontario, managing Chayah Club from EST, maintaining the 5 AM rhythm that had become our community's heartbeat.

During these exploratory visits as John's fiancée, we began approaching local churches, looking for ways to eventually mobilize what I'd started in Ontario—The Daniel Fast: Closing the GAP and 365: Live Fearlessly. He believed in the vision and wanted to see it flourish in what would become our community.

Church after church, the same responses: "We don't really do fasting anymore," one pastor said, adjusting his golf shirt. "That sounds too Old Testament for our congregation." "Isn't that kind of works-based?" asked another, stirring artificial sweetener into her coffee. "We focus on grace, not performance." "Too structured for the Spirit," declared a third. "We prefer organic move of God."

Leaders crying out for revival while rejecting the very tools heaven provides for it. Praying for breakthrough while protecting people from the disciplines that produce it. Isaiah 58:3-4 convicted their comfortable compromise: "'Why have we fasted,' they say, 'and You have not seen? Why have we afflicted our souls, and You take no notice?' In fact, in the day of your fast you find pleasure, and exploit all your laborers." Jeremiah 6:16 challenged their preferences: "Thus says the Lord: 'Stand in the ways and see, and ask for the old paths, where the good way is, and walk in it; then you will find rest for your souls.' But they said, 'We will not walk in it.'"

You cannot have revival while rejecting consecration. You cannot have transformation while avoiding discipline. Comfort Christianity produces comfortable Christians, not conquering ones.

THE REJECTION THAT REVEALED TRUTH

One church initially embraced the message during one of my visits. "Our church needs this," the pastor said during our first meeting. "Revival starts with consecration." The pastor invited me to share at their Sunday evening service. I stood before a small congregation, hope rising like morning sun. I got up to share with the book in my hand. People were engaged, asking questions. I explained the GAP strategy with growing excitement. John chimed in, "Week 1: 7 G's, Week 2: 7 A's, Week 3: 7 P's." "We're starting an upcoming fast and would create a group for the church," I announced. "You can sign up for our Zoom calls." I was excited. Finally, a breakthrough.

Then an elderly man burst through the side door. "Excuse me," he announced, voice cutting through my teaching like a blade. "Is John your husband?" The room shifted. Temperature dropped. Arms crossed in unison like choreographed judgment. "We're engaged, getting married in—" I didn't hear anything else in the chatter, laughter, or accusations. The lies and labels shouted louder than truth—Shame. Rejection. Impostor syndrome. Another spiritual attack on my identity, calling my name, wrongfully accusing me after the commitment I had made to God, with John, and to myself to stay pure until married. I watched suspicion spread like spilled ink across their faces. Whispers and silences were screaming. We left that night.

I wrestled with God for days. We had the fast nevertheless, and very few people from that church participated. But God—He showed up and did amazing miracles, signs, and wonders despite their absence. In the quiet after the storm, God asked me: **"Will you still show up even when feelings are hurt by men?"**

John 15:18-19 explained the dynamic: "If the world hates you, you know that it hated Me before it hated you. If you were of the world, the world would love its own. Yet because you are not of the world, but I chose you out of the world, therefore the world hates you." 2 Timothy 3:12 validated the experience: "Yes, and all who desire to live godly in Christ Jesus will suffer persecution."

Your critics clarify your calling. Your rejection refines your message. Opposition confirms your assignment. When your integrity is questioned, let your results be your response.

JULY 29, 2023: WHEN PROPHECY WORE A WEDDING RING

Our wedding day—a small, private, intimate ceremony in our backyard. It was beautiful in Oregon. Through tears, I found my voice: "I'm marrying the man who saw princess before I stopped believing I was peasant. Who chose covering over conquest. Who proves daily that God's best is worth the wait." Every prophecy from that Day 2 journal entry in 2018 stood before me in a tuxedo: Godly man ✓. Loves my boys as his own ✓. Partners in ministry ✓. Builds Kingdom together ✓.

Psalm 37:4 fulfilled: "Delight yourself also in the Lord, and He shall give you the desires of your heart." Genesis 2:18 had orchestrated the divine design: "And the Lord God said, 'It is not good that man should be alone; I will make him a helper comparable to him.'"

God's delays are not denials. They're preparations for blessings too big for your current capacity. Heaven's timing creates what human rushing destroys.

JULY - OCTOBER 2023: THE OREGON REALITY AS WIFE

The permanent move to Oregon as John's wife brought the reality I'd sensed during those exploratory visits. Oregon meant a different timezone—PST. My community and 365: Live Fearlessly was anchored at 5:00 AM EST, which meant 2:00 AM PST for me. We tried maintaining it. I'd wake at 2 AM, lead worship and teaching, pour out anointing, then collapse. It worked—briefly. But it wasn't sustainable.

The community was strong enough now to have other leaders step in. What I'd birthed was learning to walk without me carrying it every step. This was healthy—and terrifying. **The hardest part of building something sustainable is trusting it to sustain itself.**

The church resistance I'd encountered as a visiting fiancée didn't improve when I became a permanent resident. If anything, it solidified. Oregon's comfortable Christianity remained unmoved by consecration's call. The frameworks that were transforming lives globally couldn't find footing in a culture that preferred spiritual ease over spiritual hunger.

But I was learning something profound in those early months of marriage: God doesn't need Oregon's acceptance to confirm His assignment. He needed my obedience regardless of Oregon's response. The tension between newlywed bliss and ministry rejection created a strange dissonance—celebrating covenant at home while experiencing rejection in churches. John became my covering in ways I hadn't anticipated, standing firm when I wanted to compromise, believing God's call over me when others questioned it.

OCTOBER 2023: THE VALIDATION OF THE VALLEY

The doctoral hood felt heavier than it looked. What was hidden behind this moment was a journey that began when I started my DBA at Liberty University during the pandemic—not for credentials but for healing, studying transformation while living it. But midway through the program, when my corporate contract abruptly ended in BC and I moved back to Ontario, God spoke with uncomfortable clarity: "Stop. Redirect your tuition to build Chayah Club."

I wrestled. "God, I'm almost done. Just let me finish." But His voice was insistent: "What I'm building through you is worth more than letters after your name. Trust Me with your credentials." The choice was stark: continue pursuing the doctorate I was paying for, or obey and redirect those funds to bootstrap the ministry with no guaranteed outcome. At first I resisted. Then I obeyed. I withdrew from Liberty and poured tuition money, resources, talent, and time into Chayah Club. It felt reckless. It felt like giving up. It felt like obedience.

A few months after our July 2023 wedding, an unexpected alert—a nomination and request for dossier. I would be graduated in October 2023 for an honorary doctorate in Humanity and selected as the valedictorian for revolutionary work in human transformation. I found excuses: "I just got married. No time." But God insisted. I sat down and wrote the dossier. Reference letters poured in from Chayah Club members—the very community I'd built with redirected tuition funds—describing impact on their lives and humanity. I was humbled. God was in it all along. I was building, but He was vindicating my obedience. My sons, Nick and Matt, and my husband celebrated God's grace and glory with me.

As they called my name, I gave my speech, and the audience was blessed. The grace and faithfulness of God are excellent glory. The dossier God insisted I write declared: "For revolutionary work in human transformation, bridging spiritual wisdom with systematic application, impacting lives across continents through innovative methodology." The woman they'd written off — disability leave, divorced, depressed — was now Dr. Nicola McFadden-Marvin.

I thought about the day I withdrew from Liberty. The day I chose ministry over doctorate. The day I trusted God's assignment over academic achievement. Standing at that podium, I realized God had given me something no university could: a doctorate validated by transformed lives, not just theoretical knowledge. The tuition I redirected to Chayah Club had multiplied into testimonies that earned me the very credentials I'd sacrificed pursuing.

I thought about every rejection in Oregon. Every church that said no. Every critic who called it "too much." The wilderness hadn't wasted me—it had refined me. The obedience that looked like loss had become vindication that looked like victory. Romans 8:28 proved faithful again: "And we know that all things work together for good to those who love God, to those who are the called according to His purpose." Job 8:7 was manifesting: "Though your beginning was small, yet your latter end would increase abundantly."

Your obedience refines your assignment. Your sacrifice positions your vindication. God doesn't waste what you surrender—He multiplies it beyond recognition. When God asks you to stop pursuing credentials to build His Kingdom, trust Him. He'll vindicate the obedience in ways academia never could.

Standing at that podium in October 2023, I thought the vindication would silence the critics. Instead, the pressure intensified. The months that followed tested not my calling, but my willingness to preserve it undiluted.

2024: THE NIGHT I ALMOST COMPROMISED

By early 2024, after months of Oregon resistance and the exhaustion of maintaining ministry across time zones, I found myself at a breaking point. I sat with my manuscript, red pen bleeding corrections across every page. Maybe if I softened the fasting requirements. Maybe if I made it more about grace, less about discipline. Maybe if I diluted the consecration, they'd accept the message. Pages scattered across the kitchen table like casualties of war. Chapters I'd bled over now seemed too intense, too demanding, too much.

"Maybe if I lead with research," I muttered, crossing out sections. "Show them how heaven's wisdom aligns with earthly studies—neuroplasticity, autophagy, community psychology." But even as I wrote softer alternatives, my spirit grieved. Using research to water down revelation felt like using a telescope to diminish the stars.

John found me surrounded by torn pages, editing myself into acceptability. "What are you doing?" His voice carried more concern than judgment. "Making it more... palatable." I held up a page where I'd crossed out the fasting duration and written "as you feel led."

He knelt beside me, gathering the scattered pages. "Nicola, they didn't reject your message. They revealed their crisis. Don't water down the wine because some prefer water." "But maybe I'm being too rigid—" "Daniel was rigid about his diet. Shadrach, Meshach, and Abednego were rigid about their worship. Jesus was rigid about His mission. Compromise feels like wisdom until you see what it costs."

"But the science validates everything—" "Science is beautiful confirmation of God's design," John replied gently. "But it's not the foundation. Heaven's wisdom doesn't need earthly validation to be true. Let the research enhance the revelation, not replace it."

That night, I made a decision that would define our ministry: **"I will not bow to diluted faith that produces temporary transformation. The message stands as heaven gave it. Research confirms it, but revelation drives it."**

Like Daniel's three friends before Nebuchadnezzar's furnace: "Our God whom we serve is able to deliver us from the burning fiery furnace... But if not, let it be known to you, O king, that we do not serve your gods" (Daniel 3:17-18). Galatians 1:10 settled the matter: "For do I now persuade men, or God? Or do I seek to please men? For if I still pleased men, I would not be a bondservant of Christ."

Never edit heaven's message for earth's comfort. Comfort has never produced transformation. Your message isn't too strong if it threatens compromise. It's too important to dilute.

That night changed everything. Not because the rejection stopped—but because I stopped trying to make it stop through compromise. Within weeks, God made His next move clear.

MAY 2024: THE "SUN, JULY 6, 2014, 10:23 PM" GMAIL PRAYER FULFILLED

We purchased our dream home in Idaho and relocated to be near John's children and grandchildren. After nearly ten months in Oregon, God made it clear: the assignment wasn't Oregon's acceptance—it was obedience regardless of location. When the opportunity arose to move to Idaho near John's family, we recognized God's redirection. Sometimes He moves you TO a place. Sometimes He moves you THROUGH a place to get you WHERE He always intended.

I enjoy my bonus family and my own two sons and absolutely love being a wife, mother, and grandmother. I work as a consultant in John's business and co-minister with John on travel for mission and vacation, while investing in my business and ministry.

Standing in that Idaho kitchen—granite countertops instead of scratched laminate, mountain views instead of parking lots—I pulled out my phone with trembling fingers. Opened Gmail. Searched for that bathroom floor prayer from July 6, 2014. The screen blurred as I read each line:

"Primary custody of my children" √ - Both boys thriving, one studying naturopathic medicine, one engineering.

"Spousal support I pay: CANCELLED" √ - Ended years ago.

"Fair income assessment" √ - Justice served.

"Complete restoration" √ - Beyond imagination.

"Godly husband" √ - Standing beside me.

"Financial breakthrough" √ - Debt-free homeowners.

Ten years. Every single line. Every specific request. Every impossible detail. Answered.

Years of waiting. Every promise fulfilled. But not in my timing. Not in my way. Through wilderness that refined what breakthrough revealed. Habakkuk 2:3 had proven true: "For the vision is yet for an appointed time; but at the end it will speak, and it will not lie. Though it tarries, wait for it; because it will surely come, it will not tarry." Psalm 126:5-6 declared: "Those who sow in tears shall reap in joy. He who continually goes forth weeping, bearing seed for sowing, shall doubtless come again with rejoicing, bringing his sheaves with him."

God doesn't just answer prayers. He orchestrates symphonies where every note of your pain harmonizes into purpose. Your Gmail prayers become God's glory stories when you refuse to quit between promise and fulfillment.

THE MESSAGE THAT MADE IT WORTH IT

LinkedIn notification pinged. Random woman. Long message. "Dr. Nicola, I bought your first edition years ago. Yes, I noticed the typos. The formatting issues. But it was ANOINTED. That messy book saved my life. My marriage. My business. Three generations in my family broke patterns together. Thank you for publishing imperfect rather than not publishing at all."

I wept. Not pretty tears—the ugly kind that recognize grace in its rawest form. Every rejection had forced me to clarify. Every criticism had required me to dig deeper. Every wilderness season had refined gold from dross. The frameworks hadn't just survived testing—they'd been purified by it. What began in desperation had been proven through prosperity. What was downloaded in crisis had been validated through comfort.

1 Peter 1:7 was manifesting: "That the genuineness of your faith, being much more precious than gold that perishes, though it is tested by fire, may be found to praise, honor, and glory at the revelation of Jesus Christ." 2 Corinthians 4:17 explained the exchange: "For our light affliction, which is but for a moment, is working for us a far more exceeding and eternal weight of glory."

The wilderness doesn't waste you. It qualifies you for greater assignment. Your test becomes your testimony becomes your territory. Messy obedience reaches more hearts than perfect presentations.

THE REFINED REVOLUTION

Today, as I write this second edition, everything has changed and nothing has changed. I still wake early each morning—not from desperation now but from discipline birthed in devotion. I still fast regularly—not for breakthrough but as breakthrough, maintaining the lifestyle that sustains transformation. I still meet people on their bathroom floors—now with frameworks forged in fire and proven through prosperity.

The wilderness taught me what breakthrough couldn't: The same identity that survives poverty must survive prosperity. The same disciplines that deliver you must sustain you. The same God who answers Gmail prayers orchestrates global movements. But He does it through broken people who refuse to quit. Through messy manuscripts that help more than perfect ones. Through wilderness seasons that refine what victory only reveals.

2 Corinthians 12:9 sustains me: "My grace is sufficient for you, for My strength is made perfect in weakness." Isaiah 43:2 promises: "When you pass through the waters, I will be with you; and through the rivers, they shall not overflow you. When you walk through the fire, you shall not be burned, nor shall the flame scorch you."

Your wilderness isn't punishment. It's preparation for impact you can't yet imagine.

Welcome to the refined revolution. Where testimonies are tested. Where frameworks are proven. Where broken people become blueprints for others' breakthrough. Refined gold doesn't remember the fire that purified it—it only reflects the glory it was destined to carry.

THE PROPHECY OVER YOUR SUCCESS WILDERNESS

If you're reading this from your own success wilderness—hear this: The same God who sustained you in valleys guides you on mountains. The same disciplines that brought breakthrough must maintain breakthrough. The same humility that positioned you for promotion must protect you in platform.

Deuteronomy 8:17-18 warns and promises: "Then you say in your heart, 'My power and the might of my hand have gained me this wealth.' And you shall remember the Lord your God, for it is He who gives you power to get wealth." Proverbs 27:21 tests character: "The refining pot is for silver and the furnace for gold, but a man is valued by what others say of him."

Success is not your reward—it's your responsibility. Platform is not your privilege—it's your stewardship. Influence is not your achievement—it's your assignment. Success without surrender leads to spiritual suicide. Influence without intimacy breeds impact without integrity. God is with you from the promise to the fulfillment—even when the path looks like wilderness.

The journey continues. The revolution multiplies. The wilderness qualifies you for mountains you're about to climb. But remember: The same dependence that brought you up must keep you grounded. The same desperation that delivered you must motivate you. The same disciplines that distinguished you must sustain you.

Micah 6:8 remains your mandate: "He has shown you, O man, what is good; and what does the Lord require of you but to do justly, to love mercy, and to walk humbly with your God?"

Welcome to refined leadership. Where success serves rather than enslaves. Where influence inspires rather than intoxicates. Where platforms become altars rather than stages. The wilderness qualified you. Now let refinement define you.

Turn the page to Section 2: The Frameworks—where ten years of bathroom floor desperation becomes your systematic transformation blueprint. You've read the testimony. You've seen the testing. You've witnessed the refinement. Now receive the architecture that turned breaking into building, patterns into purpose, and one woman's Gmail prayer into a global movement.

Your frameworks await. Your transformation begins now.

CHAPTER 5
FROM MY STORY TO YOUR STRATEGY
THE BRIDGE BETWEEN BREAKING AND BECOMING

You just read four chapters that span fourteen years—from Gmail prayer on bathroom tiles to Idaho kitchen with mountain views. From "Sun, July 6, 2014, 10:23 PM" desperation to May 2024 fulfillment. Every promise kept. Every line answered. Every impossible detail addressed.

But here's what matters more than my story: **the pattern that emerged from it.**

The Persian rug beneath my knees this morning holds secrets cold bathroom tiles could never tell. Same 3 AM prayer time. Same desperate dependence. Different floor. Different woman. Same God. Eight months in Idaho, January 2025, and I still wake before dawn—not from crisis now but from calling. The discipline that saved me in desperation now sustains me in breakthrough.

Tonight, testimonies flood my inbox from six continents. Lagos sends breakthrough reports at 3 AM their time. Philippines celebrates freedom at noon the next day. London's morning prayers already answered before my evening begins. The global body of Christ never sleeps—when one timezone rests, another rises. Real lives transformed through frameworks that saved mine.

The only difference between testimony and strategy is documentation.

I wrote down the pattern. Tracked the progression. Noticed what worked. Systematized what the Spirit revealed. Moses had a burning bush. I had a bathroom floor. David had a cave. I had car crying sessions. Daniel had a lion's den. I had lawyers and liens. Paul had a thorn. I had panic attacks. Same God. Same power. Same process. Different packaging.

Your testimony is someone else's strategy. Your breaking is someone else's blueprint. Your mess is someone else's map.

NEW WINE REQUIRES NEW WINESKINS

For years, I tried patching my old life with January fasting. Annual patches on December's tears. But Jesus understood what we keep missing. Matthew 9:16-17 taught: "No one puts a piece of unshrunk cloth on an old garment; for the patch pulls away from the garment, and the tear is made worse. Nor do they put new wine into old wineskins, or else the wineskins break, the wine is spilled, and the wineskins are ruined. But they put new wine into new wineskins, and both are preserved."

You can't pour transformation's new wine into yesterday's old patterns. The structures burst. **The frameworks aren't patches for your old life—they're new wineskins for new wine.**

Stop patching what God wants to replace. We've been treating transformation like an event when God designed it as identity. We do a fast. We should become fasters. We have breakthrough. We should become breakthrough. We experience freedom. We should become free.

Event thinking says: "I'm doing a Daniel Fast."
Identity thinking says: "I'm becoming a person who lives consecrated."
Event thinking asks: "When does this end?"
Identity thinking asks: "What am I becoming?"

Romans 12:2 commands the shift: "And do not be conformed to this world, but be transformed by the renewing of your mind, that you may prove what is that good and acceptable and perfect will of God." You don't complete a transformation. You become one. **Events end. Identity endures.**

THE THREE QUESTIONS THAT CHANGED EVERYTHING

Through every phase—the breaking, the pattern, the revolution, the refinement—God answered three fundamental questions that determine transformation:

QUESTION	ANSWER	FRAMEWORK
WHOSE You Are	You belong to God—ownership establishes everything	**GROW** (Intimacy)
WHO You Are	Child of God, His masterpiece—identity flows from intimacy	**ALIGN** (Identity)
WHY You Are	Your breaking was preparation for assignment	**PROPEL** (Purpose)

The frameworks systematize this progression: **Intimacy → Identity → Destiny.**

Whose you are determines who you are.

Who you are determines why you are.

Answer the ownership question first. Everything else flows from belonging. 1 John 3:1 establishes foundation: "Behold what manner of love the Father has bestowed on us, that we should be called children of God!" Ephesians 2:10 builds identity: "For we are His workmanship, created in Christ Jesus for good works." Jeremiah 29:11 releases purpose: "For I know the thoughts that I think toward you, says the Lord, thoughts of peace and not of evil, to give you a future and a hope."

You cannot know your purpose until you know your identity. You cannot know your identity until you know whose you are.

HOW STORY BECOMES STRATEGY

God doesn't dump revelation—He drips it. Through ten years of bathroom floors and boardrooms, panic attacks and platforms, the progression emerged:

2014-2017: Annual fasts brought powerful breakthrough every January, predictable fade by April. Discovered fasting's power but not its permanence.

December 2017: Car breakdown prayer: "Close the gap between where I am and where I ought to be." Wanted transformation, not just tradition.

January 2018: GAP Strategy downloaded—Week 1 (GROW), Week 2 (ALIGN), Week 3 (PROPEL). Systematic beats sporadic every time.

October 2019: "365: Live Fearlessly" revelation. The answer to annual addiction—daily consecration. Not just 21 days in January, but 365 days of fearless living.

December 2020: Writing first edition at 3 AM on bathroom floor, formalizing what had been proven through fire. Personal breakthrough becoming community blueprint.

January 2022: Day 22 of 365 officially launched. Personal practice becoming global movement. What worked for one beginning to work for thousands.

May 2024: Gmail prayer fulfilled. Ten-year journey complete. Frameworks forged in fire, proven through prosperity, ready for multiplication.

The pattern isn't random. The progression isn't accidental. The frameworks aren't theory—they're testimonies translated into transferable tools.

That July 6, 2014 Gmail prayer wasn't just mine—it was prophetic. When I prayed for custody, I was interceding for every parent fighting unjust systems. When I declared "double for my trouble," I was prophesying multiplication for masses. Romans 8:26 explains the mystery: "Likewise the Spirit also helps in our weaknesses. For we do not know what we should pray for as we ought, but the Spirit Himself makes intercession for us with groanings which cannot be uttered."

Your desperation prayers aren't just about you. They're about everyone who will need what you discover.

Your personal prayers often carry prophetic implications for corporate transformation. God downloads solutions through your problems that others will later access through your process. 1 Corinthians 3:13 tested everything: "Each one's work will become clear; for the Day will declare it, because it will be revealed by fire; and the fire will test each one's work, of what sort it is."

Frameworks forged in fire don't melt under pressure.

THE FOUR BLUEPRINTS AHEAD

The next section delivers what these four chapters built. Not theory to study but blueprints to build with. Not inspiration to enjoy but instruction to employ. Four frameworks emerged from fire, each addressing a specific transformation failure:

BLUEPRINT ONE: I DECIDE METHOD

Emerged from watching unprepared people meet predictable resistance. Preparation prevents casualties. Decision precedes breakthrough.

BLUEPRINT TWO: GAP STRATEGY

Downloaded January 2018, revealing transformation's divine sequence. Systematic progression beats sporadic devotion every time.

BLUEPRINT THREE: CHAYAH LIFESTYLE

Crystallized when Day 22 became 365. Identity beats events in life's long game. You don't do transformation—you become it.

BLUEPRINT FOUR: MULTIPLICATION MODEL

Emerged when personal victory felt hollow without generational impact. Legacy demands multiplication, not just celebration.

Each framework has been tested through thousands of lives across six continents. These aren't theories being proposed—they're testimonies being documented. What survived my testing season was meant for your teaching season.

YOUR DECISION POINT

You stand where I stood. The location doesn't matter. The decision does.

You can treat this like another Christian book—highlight quotes, feel inspired, return to routine. Keep patching your old garment. Or you can receive this as blueprints for new wineskins—apply the frameworks, work the process, become the transformation.

Joshua 24:15 demands decision: "And if it seems evil to you to serve the Lord, choose for yourselves this day whom you will serve... But as for me and my house, we will serve the Lord." Deuteronomy 30:19 frames the stakes: "I call heaven and earth as witnesses today against you, that I have set before you life and death, blessing and cursing; therefore choose life, that both you and your descendants may live."

The same God who answered Gmail prayers answers yours. The same God who transformed bathroom floors transforms your situation.

The difference isn't His willingness—it's your strategy. Inspiration feels good. Instruction produces results. Testimony encourages. Strategy equips. You've read the story. Now receive the system.

Isaiah 43:19 promises: "Behold, I will do a new thing, now it shall spring forth; shall you not know it? I will even make a road in the wilderness and rivers in the desert." The road is built. The river is flowing. The question is whether you'll walk it.

The bathroom floor was never about me. It was about you—reading this right now, ready to rise.

Decisions made in desperation become directions for your destination.

Turn the page to the next section, The Master Blueprints—where you'll discover the four frameworks forged in fire and proven through thousands of lives. Biblical foundation meets modern proof. Ancient wisdom becomes your architecture.

Your systematic breakthrough begins now.

SECTION TWO
UNDERSTANDING THE TOTAL SYSTEM AND PREPARATION
From Ancient Wisdom to Your Architecture

"For which of you, intending to build a tower, does not sit down first and count the cost?" — Luke 14:28-29

Most believers know what to do. They lack systems for doing it sustainably. A 21-day fast is an event. A transformed life is a system. This section bridges ancient precedent to proven frameworks, revelation to implementation, testimony to transferable strategy.

Heaven's wisdom meets earth's evidence. Your architecture begins here.

THE FOUNDATION AND PREPARATION
CHAPTER 6: THE DANIEL FOUNDATION — *Biblical, Historical, and Scientific Why*
Why Daniel chose food as his battle line and how his 70-year consecration became your blueprint. Three thousand years of proven architecture validated by modern science.

CHAPTER 7: THE TRANSFORMATION ARCHITECTURE — *The Four-Chamber System Overview*
Your heart has four chambers. Your transformation requires four frameworks: **I DECIDE → GAP STRATEGY → CHAYAH LIFESTYLE → MULTIPLICATION MODEL**. Each addresses a specific transformation failure.

CHAMBER ONE: PREPARE
STAGE 1.1: I DECIDE METHOD — *Preparation Prevents Failure*
Seven steps that prevent predictable resistance: Identify, Decide, Equip, Create, Implement, Deploy, Engage. Most quit by Day 5 because they didn't prepare. Decision precedes breakthrough.

STAGE 1.2: SOAP DOCUMENTATION — *Daily Evidence System*
Scripture, Observation, Application, Prayer journaling. The GAP Strategy tells you what to focus on. SOAP shows you how God transformed you. By Day 22, you'll have 21 entries proving how transformation happened.

Passion without preparation fails. Breakthrough without architecture fades. These frameworks sustain what emotion ignites.

Preparation prevents collapse. Documentation creates evidence. Integration produces lifestyle. Multiplication generates legacy.

Turn the page to Chapter 6: The Daniel Foundation.
Your systematic breakthrough begins now.

CHAPTER 6
THE DANIEL FOUNDATION
"WHEN HEAVEN'S BLUEPRINT SURVIVED BABYLON"

Before I give you the four master blueprints, you need to understand the ancient foundation they're built on. Every framework I'll teach you in the coming chapters rests on a 3,000-year-old blueprint tested in Babylon's fire and proven through four empires. Let me show you where systematic consecration began—not with me, but with a teenager who refused the king's meat.

Jerusalem burned while Daniel watched. Seventeen years old. Everything holy becoming ash. The smoke reached Babylon three months before Daniel did. By then, the orange glow on the western horizon had faded to gray memory. Everything that made him Daniel—"God is my judge"—reduced to char and conquered silence. Tomorrow they would rename him Belteshazzar—"Bel protects the king." Tomorrow they would dress him in Babylonian robes. Tomorrow they would begin erasing everything Jerusalem had made him. But tonight—tonight Daniel made a decision that would outlast four empires, survive a lion's den, and leave us a blueprint that still breaks Babylon's power three thousand years later. He drew his battle line at dinner. Every generation faces Babylon. Every overcomer needs Daniel's blueprint.

THE GENIUS OF DANIEL'S RESISTANCE

Most people miss this completely. Daniel could have resisted at more dramatic moments. When they inducted him into Babylon's court system—likely as a eunuch, which scholars confirm was standard practice for the chief of eunuchs' trainees. When they stripped his name—the most intimate violation. When they immersed him in occult education—Babylon's mysteries were darkness itself. He submitted to it all. Accepted the new name. Excelled in their schools. Served in their courts. But he would not eat their food.

"Why food?" I asked my mentor years ago, studying this passage for the hundredth time. "Because Daniel understood what took you forty years to discover," he replied with a knowing smile. "Which is?" **"What feeds you forms you. Control the appetite, control the identity."**

THE CONTAMINATED TABLE

Every meal from the king's table came pre-contaminated. Meat sacrificed to Marduk. Wine poured to Nebo. Delicacies declaring with every bite: "Babylon provides. Babylon sustains. Babylon owns you." To eat was to agree. To agree was to surrender. To surrender was to become. So, Daniel did something that would echo through history: "But Daniel purposed in his heart that he would not defile himself with the portion of the king's delicacies" (Daniel 1:8). That word "purposed"—śûm in Hebrew (pronounced SOOM)—doesn't mean "decided." It means installed, established, set like a foundation stone that can't be moved. This wasn't a diet. This was a declaration of war. **The battle for your future is often fought with your fork.**

WHEN I FOUND MY KING'S MEAT

Standing in my kitchen one memorable evening. Leftover pizza still warm, cheese beginning to congeal. My boys' laughter drifting from the living room where homework lay conquered. The refrigerator magnet caught my eye—Daniel 1:8 in faded purple letters. Words blurred as tears came without warning. My Babylon didn't look like Daniel's. No golden statues. No lion's dens. Just legal papers thick as phone books. Five years of family court battles. "Situational depression" diagnosis. Four lawyers consuming everything while I paid spousal support from disability income. The mathematics of injustice multiplying daily. Generational patterns claiming every woman in my bloodline like inherited poison.

My youngest walked in. "Mom's not eating dinner?" How could I explain that some battles begin with what you refuse to swallow? That freedom can start with pushing a plate away? That night, I didn't just begin a fast. I installed a foundation stone. Sûm. Immovable. **"It stops with me. The addiction. The divorce pattern. The poverty mindset. The depression. It stops with me."**

WHAT DANIEL ACTUALLY ATE (AND WHY IT MATTERS)

"Please test your servants for ten days, and let them give us vegetables to eat and water to drink" (Daniel 1:12). The Hebrew word translated "vegetables"—zeroim (pronounced zeh-ro-EEM)—reveals Daniel's genius. It doesn't mean salad. It means "things sown from seed." Daniel chose Eden's menu over Babylon's slaughterhouse. Creation's original diet over corruption's compromise. Think about it: Daniel returned to Genesis. Before the fall, before the flood, before flesh became food—humanity thrived on what grew from soil. Daniel wasn't just refusing Babylon's meat. He was reclaiming Eden's menu. After ten days, Daniel's countenance appeared fairer. The vegetables didn't do that. The consecration did. But the vegetables were the vehicle through which consecration traveled. **Every meal is a vote for which kingdom feeds you.**

THE SCIENCE VALIDATES THE SACRED

Three thousand years after Daniel proved vegetables could outperform the king's delicacies, modern science confirms what Scripture established. Dr. Richard Bloomer's research team at the University of Memphis conducted rigorous studies on the Daniel Fast's impact on human health. The results? Measurable transformation that secular science couldn't ignore.

Participants experienced significant blood pressure reduction, improved cholesterol profiles, decreased inflammation markers, and enhanced antioxidant capacity—all within 21 days. Perhaps most remarkable: a 98% completion rate, proving the Daniel Fast isn't just effective, it's sustainable. When your body receives what God designed it to process, transformation becomes natural rather than forced. The researchers concluded that the Daniel Fast represents one of the most effective dietary interventions for metabolic health, combining spiritual discipline with biological optimization.

Daniel's "fairer countenance" wasn't subjective opinion—it was measurable evidence of cellular transformation that brain scans, blood tests, and body composition analysis could verify. His skin cleared. His energy increased. His mental clarity sharpened. Science validates what Scripture established millennia ago: When you feed your body from Eden's menu rather than Babylon's table, both spirit and flesh align with divine design. The vegetables were the vehicle. The consecration was the catalyst. The transformation was inevitable when both worked together.

UNDERSTANDING THE TOTAL SYSTEM AND PREPARATION

THE DANIEL FAST BLUEPRINT

"On the Daniel Fast I quiet the noise to hear the Word. If it grew on a plant—yes; if it was manufactured in a plant—no. This isn't a diet; it's a declaration: my cravings don't lead me—Christ does, and even my plate bears witness."

The principle translates simply: Eat what's grown from plants. Avoid what's made in plants.

WHAT DANIEL ATE	WHAT DANIEL REFUSED
Vegetables from the garden	Meat from the king's table
Fruits from trees and vines	Wine from royal vineyards
Whole grains from the field	Rich delicacies
Legumes that sustained	Anything acknowledging Babylon as provider
Nuts and seeds	
Water, pure and undefiled	

YOUR DANIEL FAST TODAY

YES	NO
All fruits and vegetables	Meat, poultry, fish
Whole grains (brown rice, quinoa, oats)	Dairy products, eggs
Legumes (beans, lentils, peas)	Refined sugar, artificial sweeteners
Nuts and seeds (raw or roasted)	Deep-fried foods, solid fats
Water, herbal teas, pure fruit juices	Caffeine, alcohol, processed foods

This isn't deprivation—it's declaration. Every meal proclaims whose table you choose. **Get your free complete Daniel Fast food guide with meal plans, recipes, and shopping lists at danielfastclub.com or chayah.club/daniel-fast-food-plan.**

THE THREE DIMENSIONS OF DANIEL'S BLUEPRINT

Across seventy years of captivity, Daniel deployed three different strategic operations—proving consecration isn't a season but a lifestyle. He didn't have one fasting strategy—he had an arsenal.

The Identity Fast: When They Try to Rename You (Daniel 1:8-16). Twenty-one years old. Career on the line. Ten days to prove vegetables could outperform royal wine. This wasn't about food—it was about allegiance. Would he be Daniel ("God is my judge") or Belteshazzar ("Bel's prince")? This is your fast when they've stripped your name. When divorce papers say "discarded." When disability forms say "insufficient." You fast to remember whose verdict matters.

The Intercession Fast: When You Stand in the Gap (Daniel 9:3-21). Eighty-four years old. Daniel discovers Jeremiah's prophecy—seventy years ending. But nothing's happening. So Daniel fasts not for personal breakthrough but for corporate deliverance. "We have sinned," he prays, owning rebellion he never participated in. Gabriel arrives before the prayer ends. The fast didn't convince God—it positioned Daniel to receive what God was already releasing. This is your fast when breakthrough isn't just about you. When you're standing for your bloodline. When individual consecration must birth corporate deliverance.

The Warfare Fast: When Hell Blocks Heaven's Answer (Daniel 10:2-13). Ninety years old. Three weeks of fasting. No breakthrough. Then the messenger arrives: "From the first day... your words were heard... But the prince of Persia withstood me twenty-one days" (Daniel 10:12-13). Heaven heard immediately. Hell interfered intentionally. This is your fast when you know God has heard but breakthrough hasn't manifested. When victory belongs to whoever refuses to quit first. Some breakthroughs come quickly. Some require you to outlast hell's resistance.

THE ARCHITECTURE OF UNSHAKEABLE CONSECRATION

Daniel's blueprint wasn't random disciplines—it was systematic architecture that sustained him for seventy years of captivity.

Three Prayer Anchors Daily - "He knelt down... three times that day... as was his custom since early days" (Daniel 6:10). Daniel didn't pray three times because it was convenient—he prayed three times because Babylon demanded constant resistance. Morning: before Babylon sets the agenda. Noon: when compromise feels reasonable. Evening: after surviving another day intact. Even facing execution, the lions didn't stop his prayer schedule—prayer stopped the lions' mouths.

Measured Consecration - Daniel didn't declare a dramatic hunger strike. He requested a measured trial: "Test us for ten days." Wisdom: Don't make declarations you can't sustain. Better to build systematically than to collapse dramatically.

Strategic Selection - Every "no" to Babylon's table was "yes" to Heaven's provision. Daniel proved you could thrive in Babylon without being nourished by Babylon. Excellence without compromise. Promotion without participation. **Your future hangs not just on your faith but on your fork.**

THE BLUEPRINT BECOMES YOUR FRAMEWORKS

Now you see why Daniel's story isn't just history—it's prophecy of what you're about to learn. Everything Daniel practiced three thousand years ago becomes the foundation for the four frameworks ahead:

I DECIDE mirrors Daniel's measured consecration. "Test us for ten days"—preparation that prevents failure. Don't declare what you can't sustain. Decide before the test, or the test decides for you.

GAP Strategy follows Daniel's systematic progression. Identity Fast (GROW) → Intercession Fast (ALIGN) → Warfare Fast (PROPEL). You can't intercede for others until your identity is secure. You can't wage warfare until you're aligned with Heaven's strategy.

Chayah Lifestyle embodies Daniel's seventy-year consistency. The foundation stone set at seventeen still anchored him at eighty. This isn't a 21-day event—it's a lifetime identity. The same śûm that refused the king's meat was still praying three times daily decades later.

Multiplication Model reflects Daniel's generational impact. Four kingdoms sought his counsel. His influence outlived the empire that enslaved him. Personal consecration births corporate transformation. What you establish privately multiplies publicly.

Daniel didn't just survive Babylon—he demonstrated the blueprint for thriving in any captivity while refusing its contamination. Now you have that same blueprint, refined through three millennia and proven through millions of lives.

YOUR BABYLON IS CALLING

Each age confronts the same system wearing different costumes. Daniel's Babylon offered golden statues, lion's dens, renamed identity. My Babylon presented legal systems crushing single mothers, generational curses demanding surrender, redefined truth requiring compromise. Your Babylon whispers through the addiction saying "one more time," the relationship demanding you silence your convictions, the career requiring you to check your faith at the door.

Somewhere in your life, Babylon is offering you king's meat. Comfort that costs consecration. Provision that requires compromise. Acceptance that demands allegiance. And somewhere in your spirit, you know exactly what your pizza moment looks like. What you need to set down. What pattern stops with you. The same blueprint that worked in 605 BC works today.

THE FOUNDATION STONE

Daniel outlived the empire that enslaved him. Four kingdoms sought his counsel. Angels fought to reach him. His prophecies still map our future. Not despite his consecration—because of it. He proved something Babylon couldn't compute: You can take someone's name but not their nature. Their position but not their purpose. Their freedom but not their foundation. But only if they refuse to eat from your table. The same foundation stone Daniel set at seventeen saved him from lions at eighty. The same śûm that refused the king's meat in chapter one was still praying three times daily in chapter six. **Some stones, once set, define a lifetime.**

Tomorrow morning, before the sun rises, before emails demand responses, before the world sets its agenda—you'll face your own king's table. The meal will look different than Daniel's. Different than my pizza. But you'll recognize it. It's whatever feeds the very thing destroying you.

THE DANIEL HOUR

I see you there—kitchen counter, office desk, bedroom floor. The same God who strengthened a seventeen-year-old in Babylon watches you now. The same blueprint that worked three thousand years ago works tonight. The Hebrew word śûm waits like a tool in your hand. The foundation stone sits ready for installation. Not a decision you'll need to remake daily, but a stone you set once, immovable. Push the plate away. Set the stone. Let it stop with you. **Your Daniel hour has come.**

You've seen the ancient foundation. Turn the page to Chapter 7: The Total Transformation System—where Daniel's 3,000-year-old blueprint becomes your 4-Chamber architecture for systematic transformation.

CHAPTER 7
THE TOTAL TRANSFORMATION SYSTEM
"WHEN HEAVEN'S BLUEPRINT MEETS EARTH'S EVIDENCE"

THE CHRISTMAS DISCOVERY

December 2020. While the world celebrated Christ's birth, I mourned my spiritual stillbirth. Five journals surrounded me like tombstones on the hardwood floor—each marking another transformation that died too young. The coffee had gone stone cold hours ago. Outside, Christmas lights twinkled with hope I couldn't feel.

The pattern was ruthless and predictable. January brought powerful consecration, followed by gradual decline in February and subtle compromise by March. From April through December, my spiritual life flatlined completely. Five years. Sixty months. The same deadly sequence repeating without mercy.

That Christmas night, surrounded by evidence of my defeats, something shifted. These weren't random failures—they were revealing patterns. In 2016, I had power without permanence. In 2017, community without continuity. In 2018, discipline without delight. In 2019, revelation without integration. In 2020, identity without implementation. The revelation struck like lightning: I wasn't failing at transformation. I was succeeding at incomplete systems.

Scripture confirmed what my journals revealed: "For which of you, intending to build a tower, does not sit down first and count the cost, whether he has enough to finish it—lest, after he has laid the foundation, and is not able to finish, all who see it begin to mock him" (Luke 14:28-29). Every breakthrough had generated data. Every collapse had exposed architectural flaws. Every cycle taught what I'd been too proud to learn—lasting transformation requires all four chambers of the heart, not just one.

THE PROBLEM EVERY BELIEVER KNOWS

Twenty-five years fixing everyone else's broken systems. I could diagnose organizational dysfunction in an afternoon and design transformation architectures that turned Fortune 500 chaos into excellence, corporate confusion into billion-dollar clarity. Yet I couldn't solve my own spiritual equation. The diagnosis hit like lightning: The problem wasn't theological. It wasn't motivational. It was architectural.

Jesus taught the principle clearly: "Therefore whoever hears these sayings of Mine, and does them, I will liken him to a wise man who built his house on the rock" (Matthew 7:24). Consider the cycle every believer knows: crisis leads to consecration, consecration produces breakthrough, breakthrough inspires celebration, celebration breeds complacency, and complacency collapses back into crisis. We've normalized spiritual schizophrenia—praising God on Sunday, struggling by Monday, defeated by Wednesday, desperate by Friday. We blame lack of discipline when the culprit is lack of architecture.

Stop praying for God to change your outcomes when you keep repeating the same inputs. God honors your patterns, not just your prayers. Jesus confronted this reality directly: "And why do you call Me 'Lord, Lord,' and not do the things which I say?" (Luke 6:46). We know what to do. We lack systems for doing it sustainably. A 21-day fast is an event. A transformed life is a system.

THE BIBLICAL MANDATE

When Jesus taught about fasting, He said "when you fast," not "if you fast" (Matthew 6:16-18). The assumption was clear—His followers would fast. Later He revealed an even deeper truth: "However, this kind does not go out except by prayer and fasting" (Matthew 17:21). Some bondages require more than casual prayer. They demand systematic consecration.

Daniel understood this principle millennia before the church forgot it. His 21-day consecration wasn't about weight loss—it was about accessing breakthrough that transformed an empire. When you fast, your spirit becomes more sensitive to God's voice, your flesh submits to spiritual authority, your focus sharpens on eternal rather than temporal realities, and your prayers intensify with desperation-driven faith.

Here's what the modern church has missed: Daniel didn't fast once and transform permanently. He fasted systematically—three recorded times throughout his life—building complete spiritual architecture that sustained him through decades of captivity. This is why your January breakthrough dies by February. You're treating architecture like a ceremony, building permanence through one-time intensity rather than establishing lifestyle through sustainable rhythm.

THE SYSTEM HEAVEN DOWNLOADED

September 2025. 4:44 AM. Scattered notes covering every surface like pieces of a divine puzzle. Five years of wrestling with revelation and research, testing frameworks with thousands worldwide, had led to this moment. Years of breakthrough stories, failed attempts, and biblical insights were converging into divine architecture. Jeremiah's promise echoed in my spirit: "For I know the thoughts that I think toward you, says the LORD, thoughts of peace and not of evil, to give you a future and a hope" (Jeremiah 29:11).

Four frameworks emerged from the chaos—not separate programs but four chambers of one heart beating with singular purpose. In Chapter 3, you read how these downloaded in December 2020 during my underground season. Now let me show you how they integrate systematically to create lasting transformation.

Essential to capturing transformation was SOAP journaling—Scripture, Observation, Application, Prayer. This wasn't just spiritual discipline. It was the evidence-creation system that would document the GAP Strategy's progression day by day, theme by theme. The GAP Strategy shows you what to focus on each day during your 21-day fast. SOAP journaling shows you how transformation happened. Together, they create both the pathway and the proof. Every champion documents their training. Every scientist records experiments. Your SOAP Journal documents your systematic breakthrough through the GAP Strategy progression. What downloaded wasn't self-improvement. It was divine architecture—heaven's blueprint for earth's breakthrough.

THE TOTAL TRANSFORMATION SYSTEM

The complete system unfolds as a four-stage journey that mirrors how Heaven builds permanent transformation in human hearts. God doesn't do random. He does sequential. Stage 1 prepares your foundation through I DECIDE—seven strategic steps that position you for breakthrough rather than predictable collapse. Stage 2 catalyzes transformation through the 21-day GAP Strategy documented via daily SOAP journaling—creating evidence, not just experience. Stage 3 integrates breakthrough into daily life through the Chayah Lifestyle's 8F habits—sustaining what the fast ignited. Stage 4 multiplies your testimony through 5C community principles—ensuring your ceiling becomes someone else's floor. **This is how God works: prepare thoroughly, transform intensively, integrate systematically, multiply generationally.** The table below summarizes the complete progression:

Stage	Framework	Core Focus	Documentation
1	I DECIDE	7 preparation steps	Baseline assessment (GAP, 8F, 6D scores)
2	GAP Strategy	GROW → ALIGN → PROPEL progression	Daily SOAP entries (21 total)
3	Chayah Lifestyle	8F daily habits	THE CHAYAH Blueprint
4	Multiplication Model	5C community impact	Testimony & legacy building

Scripture confirms the principle of sustained effort: "And let us not grow weary while doing good, for in due season we shall reap if we do not lose heart" (Galatians 6:9). This is not a buffet where you select what appeals to you and ignore what challenges. It's a four-course meal designed in divine sequence. Skip a course and you'll starve spiritually. Complete all four and you'll thrive in ways you never imagined possible.

THE FOUR CHAMBERS DIAGNOSTIC™

Your physical heart has four chambers working in perfect sequence—each receiving what the previous chamber provides, each preparing what the next chamber requires. Skip one chamber and the whole system fails. Damage one valve and the entire heart suffers. God designed your spiritual transformation the same way.

Just as your biological heart cannot pump life-giving blood without all four chambers functioning in proper sequence, your spiritual transformation cannot produce lasting breakthrough without all four stages operating systematically. The right atrium receives deoxygenated blood from your body. The right ventricle pumps it to your lungs for oxygenation. The left atrium receives oxygen-rich blood from your lungs. The left ventricle pumps that life-giving blood throughout your entire body. Miss one chamber and the system collapses. Damage one valve and the whole heart suffers.

The same principle governs transformation. Four chambers. One heartbeat. Complete circulation. The table below maps the complete diagnostic framework:

THE TRANSFORMATION JOURNEY

Chamber	Stage	Function	Key Question	Biblical Foundation
CHAMBER 1	PREPARE	Receives raw intention	"Am I preparing thoroughly?"	Luke 14:28 - Count the cost
CHAMBER 2	TRANSFORM	Oxygenates with truth	"Am I transforming intensively?"	2 Corinthians 3:18 - Unveiled faces
CHAMBER 3	INTEGRATE	Circulates daily habits	"Am I integrating daily?"	James 1:22 - Doers, not hearers
CHAMBER 4	MULTIPLY	Pumps life to others	"Am I multiplying generationally?"	2 Timothy 2:2 - Faithful men

Chamber 1 receives raw intention the same way your heart's right atrium receives deoxygenated blood—taking in what exists before transformation begins. This is where you assess current reality, count the cost, and prepare thoroughly through the I DECIDE Framework. Without proper preparation, everything that follows will be starved of the foundation it requires. Chamber 2 oxygenates with truth through intensive 21-day consecration, just as your lungs infuse blood with life-giving oxygen. The GAP Strategy documented through daily SOAP journaling transforms intellectual knowledge into transformative truth that saturates your entire being. Chamber 3 circulates daily habits through the 8F lifestyle, distributing transformation throughout every dimension of your life—spiritual, mental, emotional, physical, financial, and relational. Just as your heart pumps oxygenated blood to every cell, the Chayah Lifestyle ensures breakthrough reaches every area rather than remaining isolated in the spiritual dimension. Chamber 4 pumps life to others through 5C multiplication, ensuring your breakthrough becomes someone else's beginning, your ceiling becomes their floor, your testimony becomes their roadmap.

Here's what most people miss: Your heart doesn't choose which chambers to use based on convenience. All four must function or the system fails. You can't say "I'll just do Chambers 1 and 2 because 3 and 4 sound hard." Your physical heart would stop beating. Your spiritual transformation will stop producing. The chambers aren't suggestions—they're requirements. The sequence isn't preference—it's design. Skip preparation and your transformation collapses by Day 5 when temptation peaks and you have no battle plan. Skip integration and your breakthrough dies on Day 22 when the event ends but lifestyle hasn't begun. Skip multiplication and your ceiling becomes your grave rather than someone else's floor.

Use this diagnostic to assess where you are right now. Chamber 1: Am I preparing thoroughly, or am I trying to build in the storm what I should have built in the calm? Chamber 2: Am I transforming intensively through documented 21-day consecration, or am I hoping for change without creating evidence? Chamber 3: Am I integrating daily through the 8F habits, or am I treating transformation like an event rather than a lifestyle? Chamber 4: Am I multiplying generationally through 5C community, or am I hoarding my breakthrough as private treasure?

Your transformation has a heartbeat. Make sure all four chambers are pumping.

THE NON-NEGOTIABLE SEQUENCE

Last week someone asked with desperation bleeding through their voice, "Can I just start with the 21-day fast?" I replied carefully, "Listen closely. You cannot skip to the stage you think you need. That's like running a marathon without training—noble intention, predictable collapse." The question reveals the modern obsession with shortcuts, the microwave mentality applied to spiritual growth that requires slow-cooking surrender.

Scripture validates the principle: "But let each one examine his own work, and then he will have rejoicing in himself alone, and not in another. For each one shall bear his own load" (Galatians 6:4-5). Each stage bears its own weight and cannot be carried by another. Here's what twenty-five years of transformation work has taught me: these phases aren't suggestions you can rearrange based on preference. They're divine architecture with spiritual mathematics. Each stage provides exactly what the next stage requires. **Skip one and you sabotage all that follow. Honor the sequence and you unlock exponential breakthrough.** The relationship between phases is not optional—it's foundational. Consider how the system builds systematically:

Stage	Provides	Enables
PREPARE	Foundation & assessment	Systematic transformation
TRANSFORM	21-day GAP catalyst documented through SOAP	Identity shift with evidence
INTEGRATE	Daily 8F lifestyle architecture	Sustainable change
MULTIPLY	5C community & legacy	Generational impact

Stage 1 provides foundation and assessment, which enables systematic transformation in Stage 2. Stage 2 delivers the 21-day GAP catalyst documented through SOAP, producing identity shift with tangible evidence that enables Stage 3. Stage 3 establishes daily 8F lifestyle architecture, creating sustainable change that enables Stage 4. Stage 4 activates 5C community and legacy building, generating generational impact that transcends your individual breakthrough. Jesus taught this principle of complete truth: "However, when He, the Spirit of truth, has come, He will guide you into all truth" (John 16:13). Not partial revelations. Not fragmented insights. Complete, systematic truth.

You can't microwave what God designed to marinate. Every shortcut you take becomes a long-cut you'll have to take later, often with compounded difficulty. Miss a stage and you miss transformation. Complete all four and you become unstoppable.

TESTIMONY: WHEN MERCY SAID NO

Her message arrived from the Caribbean. A single mother who once wondered "Why am I still alive?" had spent two decades seeking breakthrough. She discovered the Daniel Fast through online devotionals and joined her first 21-day consecration. "Every night, I tuned in—often in tears, taking notes. Deliverance came to my home."

A divine word came: "Go back to the land of your ancestors." She quit her job, returned home with her daughter, and completed her second Daniel Fast. A year later, she launched her business and ministry—on the same date she once mourned her brother's death.

"When the enemy thought he won, he realized that God never loses a battle. The day meant for death became Resurrection Day." The four-stage system turned mourning into morning.

THE INTEGRATED FRAMEWORK

A Friend's Breakthrough

My friend Sophia called me at midnight, frustrated tears in her voice. "I've been doing everything—praying, fasting, attending church—but nothing's changing. What am I missing?"

"Tell me your week," I said gently.

She rattled off her spiritual activities: Sunday service, Wednesday prayer meeting, daily devotional. "That's beautiful," I responded, "but what did you eat today? How much sleep did you get? When's the last time you laughed until your stomach hurt? Did you call that friend who's been on your heart?"

Silence. Then: "What does that have to do with my spiritual breakthrough?"

"Everything," I said. "You're praying for transformation but only stewarding one dimension—faith. God designed you with six dimensions that work together. Your spiritual breakthrough is being sabotaged by physical exhaustion, emotional depletion, and relational isolation you're ignoring."

Six months later, Sophia completed her first full 21-day fast using this integrated system. Her testimony? "I finally understand—transformation isn't about doing MORE spiritual activities. It's about integrating ALL of life under God's sovereignty."

That midnight conversation revealed what thousands have since discovered: Your six dimensions of wellness satisfaction—spiritual, mental, emotional, physical, financial, relational—grow when five elements work together strategically.

THE FIVE ELEMENTS THAT INTEGRATE:

1. God's Sovereignty (S) - The Encompassing Power

This encompasses everything—what He does beyond your control, the seasons He orchestrates, the surprises He allows, the divine appointments He arranges. You plan your way, but the Lord directs your steps (Proverbs 16:9). His sovereignty doesn't eliminate your responsibility—it empowers your obedience.

2. Your Daily 8F Stewardship - The Fuel You Control

Eight areas you steward every single day: Faith (spiritual practices), Fasting (consecration rhythms), Food (nutritional choices), Fellowship (relationships), Fitness (physical health), Focus (mental/emotional wellness), Finances (stewardship), Fun (joy and rest). These aren't random categories—they're the daily inputs that directly drive your six-dimension outputs. Paul understood this partnership: "I planted, Apollos watered, but God gave the increase" (1 Corinthians 3:6). You faithfully steward the 8F. God multiplies the harvest.

3. The 21-Day GAP Catalyst - The Spiritual Engine

Some transformation requires intensive seasons, not just daily habits. The GAP Strategy (Grow → Align → Propel) is your 21-day catalyst that jumpstarts change you couldn't create through gradual disciplines alone. It moves you from growing intimacy with God, to aligning identity in Christ, to propelling into purpose through the Holy Spirit. This isn't a one-time breakthrough—it's a lifelong rhythm. Just as your body needs periodic deep cleansing and your car requires regular tune-ups, your spirit requires intentional seasons of intensive consecration that recalibrate, realign, and reignite what daily maintenance sustains but cannot initiate.

4. The 5C Multiplication - Community That Multiplies

Your breakthrough wasn't meant to terminate with you. The 5C framework ensures transformation reproduces: Commitment (covenant decision), Common Vision (unified direction), Change Process (systematic pathway), Community (supportive ecosystem), Commissioning (sent to multiply). "And the things that you have heard from me among many witnesses, commit these to faithful men who will be able to teach others also" (2 Timothy 2:2). **Your ceiling becomes someone else's floor when multiplication is built into the system.**

5. Compounding Time - Consistency That Stacks

Small daily obediences compound into major life transformation. The difference between where you are and where you're called to be isn't one dramatic moment—it's thousands of small decisions made consistently over time. "And let us not grow weary while doing good, for in due season we shall reap if we do not lose heart" (Galatians 6:9). Time multiplies faithfulness when you refuse to quit.

TESTIMONY: 10/10/10 IN THE STORM

A single mother from North America faced eviction while living on minimal income with a preschooler. "By God's grace, the notice was miraculously canceled." She worked full-time hours for part-time pay yet worshipped consistently every evening.

During her Daniel Fast, despite past church trauma, she experienced complete restoration. "I'm walking in alignment: 10/10/10." Her GAP scores—all three dimensions at perfect 10s—came during the storm, not after. "I am not a victim of my circumstances—I am victorious through Christ Jesus."

HOW THEY INTEGRATE:

Here's the simple truth that changes everything: As you faithfully steward the 8F each day, the 21-day GAP jumpstarts change you couldn't create gradually. The 5C multiplies that change through community. Time compounds your consistency. And God's sovereignty carries what you cannot control—resulting in increasing wellness satisfaction across all six dimensions of your life.

This isn't theory. It's architecture. It's the blueprint thousands have used to move from:

- Spiritual inconsistency → daily communion with God
- Identity confusion → rock-solid clarity about who they are in Christ
- Purpose paralysis → activated Kingdom assignments
- Physical exhaustion → sustainable energy

- Financial stress → peace and provision
- Relational isolation → authentic community

Jesus established the priority: "But seek first the kingdom of God and His righteousness, and all these things shall be added to you" (Matthew 6:33). Seek Him daily through the 8F. Consecrate intensively through the 21-day GAP. Multiply through 5C community. Trust Time to compound. Rest in His Sovereignty over outcomes.

THE FOUR-STAGE BLUEPRINT

STAGE 1: PREPARE - The I DECIDE Framework™

Jesus asked a practical question that exposes our tendency toward impulsive spirituality: "For which of you, intending to build a tower, does not sit down first and count the cost, whether he has enough to finish it?" (Luke 14:28). The I DECIDE Framework consists of seven steps that prevent predictable failure through systematic preparation. Each letter in the acronym I-D-E-C-I-D-E represents a specific preparation action with corresponding purpose. The framework is designed to eliminate the common failure points that cause most people to quit their fast by Day 5. The table below breaks down each step:

Step	Action	Purpose
I - IDENTIFY	Brutal honesty about current reality	Baseline assessment
D - DECIDE	Covenant commitment burning every Plan B	Irreversible resolve
E - EQUIP	Practical preparation: shop, cook, clear schedule	Remove obstacles
C - CREATE	Sacred space for encountering God	Environmental setup
I - IMPLEMENT	Crisis strategies for Days 3-5 resistance	Battle readiness
D - DEPLOY	Support systems and accountability	Community activation
E - ENGAGE	Spiritual consecration and commissioning	Complete surrender

TESTIMONY: FROM SURFACE TO SURGICAL

A veteran faster reflected on her transformation journey. "This is my third Daniel Fast. The first two cycles were surface level—the first just skimming, the second putting my face in water but not willing to go deep."

Year three changed everything. "This time, even from my bed of recovery after surgery, I allowed God to perform surgical precision—excavating roots held for decades."

What was different? She didn't skip Stage 1 preparation, and she documented every day through GAP SOAP journaling. "Use every tool at your disposal." **Three years. Same fast. Different outcomes. The variable was preparation.**

The first step, Identify, requires brutal honesty about current reality to establish baseline assessment. The second step, Decide, demands covenant commitment that burns every Plan B, creating irreversible resolve. The third step, Equip, handles practical preparation—shopping, cooking, clearing schedules—to remove obstacles before they become excuses. The fourth step, Create, establishes sacred space for encountering God through environmental setup. The fifth step, Implement, prepares crisis strategies for Days 3-5 resistance, ensuring battle readiness when temptation peaks. The sixth step, Deploy, activates support systems and accountability for community activation. The seventh step, Engage, completes spiritual consecration and commissioning through complete surrender.

Solomon's wisdom validates this approach: "The plans of the diligent lead surely to plenty, but those of everyone who is hasty, surely to poverty" (Proverbs 21:5). Preparation isn't procrastination—it's the prevention of predictable failure. **You can't build in the storm what you should have built in the calm.** This framework transforms impulsive enthusiasm into strategic consecration that actually finishes what it starts. Chapter 8 provides complete instruction for implementing each of these seven steps with detailed assessments, worksheets, and action plans.

STAGE 2: TRANSFORM - The GAP Strategy™ + Daniel Fast

Peter's exhortation captures the essence of this transformative phase: "But grow in the grace and knowledge of our Lord and Savior Jesus Christ" (2 Peter 3:18). In Chapter 2, you read how the GAP Strategy downloaded during a season of desperation—one word falling into my spirit each evening for twenty-one days. Now let me show you how this systematic progression creates complete transformation that documented evidence can verify.

Daniel's experience provides the biblical precedent: "In those days I, Daniel, was mourning three full weeks... from the first day that you set your heart to understand, and to humble yourself before your God, your words were heard" (Daniel 10:2, 12). God hears you on Day 1, but breakthrough often comes on Day 21. The delay isn't denial—it's development. The gap between hearing and answering creates space for character formation that can sustain the blessing you're requesting.

The GAP Strategy operates as your 21-day transformation progression—an acronym representing the systematic movement through three transformational questions:

Week 1 — GROW in intimacy with God: Whose You Are
(7G: Gospel, Grace, Goodness, Gifts, Gladness, Greatness, Glory)
Week 2 — ALIGN in identity with Christ: Who You Are
(7A: Adoption, Abundance, Authority, Anointing, Advancement, Attributes, Affirmation)
Week 3 — PROPEL in destiny filled with the Holy Spirit: Why You Are
(7P: Presence, Protection, Peace, Provision, Promotion, Prosperity, Purpose)

Grow. **A**lign. **P**ropel. **G-A-P.** The acronym isn't accidental—it describes both the strategy and the space between where you are and where God is calling you. Each of these 21 themes builds systematically on the previous day's revelation. You can't align with identity you haven't discovered through intimacy.

You can't activate calling until identity is secure. The order matters because spiritual maturity builds foundationally, not randomly.

If the GAP Strategy is your daily compass, SOAP journaling is your daily proof. **S**cripture, **O**bservation, **A**pplication, **P**rayer. While the GAP Strategy provides your daily theme and focus, SOAP captures how transformation actually happens in real time. By Day 22, you'll have 21 complete entries documenting exactly how intimacy with God grew, how identity in Christ aligned, how purpose activated, and precisely which gaps closed on which days and why. The GAP Strategy tells you what to focus on each day. SOAP journaling shows you how God transformed you through that focus. Together, they create both pathway and proof.

The Daniel Fast operates across three dimensions that work synergistically:

Dimension 1 — What You Eat: Plant-based
(anything grown from a plant, nothing made in a plant).

Dimension 2 — When You Eat: Intermittent fasting
(choose your sustainable pattern from 14/10 beginner, 16/8 intermediate, 18/6 advanced, to 20/4 warrior).

Dimension 3 — What You Release: The soul fast
(social media, entertainment, news—whatever controls your attention more than God does).

Isaiah revealed God's heart: "Is this not the fast that I have chosen: To loose the bonds of wickedness, to undo the heavy burdens, to let the oppressed go free, and that you break every yoke?" (Isaiah 58:6). The soul fast addresses spiritual strongholds that food fasting alone cannot break.

The fast isn't graduation from spiritual struggle—it's orientation for a lifetime of transformation. The 21 days aren't the destination. They're the door you walk through into a completely different way of living daily. Chamber 2 - Sections 3, 4, 5 provide complete daily teaching for each GAP theme with SOAP prompts and practical application strategies. Your transformation begins in Chamber 1 the moment you say — **I DECIDE.**

STAGE 3: INTEGRATE - The Chayah Lifestyle™

Day 22 is where most people lose everything they gained during 21 days of fasting. Day 22 determines whether transformation lasts or dies, whether breakthrough becomes lifestyle or memory. Scripture describes what's available: "Therefore, if anyone is in Christ, he is a new creation; old things have passed away; behold, all things have become new" (2 Corinthians 5:17). The Hebrew word Chayah means "fully alive, revived, flourishing"—the exact opposite of merely surviving.

Jesus came to make this reality possible: "The thief does not come except to steal, and to kill, and to destroy. I have come that they may have life, and that they may have it more abundantly" (John 10:10). In Chapters 3 and 5, you discovered the critical shift from doing a fast to becoming someone who lives consecrated daily. Now here's the systematic architecture that sustains transformation long after the initial 21-day catalyst ends.

The complete sustainment architecture operates across four time horizons, each with specific focus, tools, and purpose. This isn't random spiritual activity—it's strategic life design that integrates breakthrough into every level of your existence. The table below maps the complete architecture from daily habits to decade-long legacy, which is documented in the Chayah Blueprint.

Time Horizon	Focus	Tool	Purpose
10 Years	Legacy & Multiplication	Vision Board → 5C	"What will my life have produced?"
3 Years	Breakthrough Targets	6D Major Milestones	"What must shift by year 3?"
1 Year	Annual Goals	Quarterly Reviews	"What gets measured gets managed"
Daily	Habits & Disciplines	8F Framework	"Who am I becoming today?"

The 10-year horizon addresses legacy and multiplication, answering "What will my life have produced a decade from now?" This isn't wishful thinking—it's intentional legacy design that considers how your breakthrough will multiply through others long after you're gone. The 3-year horizon establishes breakthrough targets across all six dimensions of wellness, asking "What must fundamentally shift by year 3?" These are the game-changing milestones that move you from where you are to where you're called to be. The 1-year horizon sets annual goals tracked through quarterly reviews, operating on the principle that "what gets measured gets managed." The daily horizon practices habits and disciplines through the 8F Framework, constantly asking "Who am I becoming today through these small, repeated actions?"

James understood the danger of hearing without doing: "But be doers of the word, and not hearers only, deceiving yourselves" (James 1:22). Day 22 isn't the end of your fast—it's the beginning of your transformation. When all elements integrate properly—daily 8F habits feeding annual goals, annual goals building toward 3-year targets, 3-year targets fulfilling 10-year legacy vision—transformation becomes automatic rather than accidental. **The system sustains what emotion cannot maintain.** Your daily prayer time compounds into annual spiritual maturity. Your daily food choices compound into 3-year health transformation. Your daily generosity compounds into 10-year financial legacy. Small daily habits, consistently practiced across time horizons, create comprehensive life transformation that outlives you. Chapter 30 provides complete implementation guidance for the Chayah Lifestyle with the Chayah Blueprint tool.

STAGE 4: MULTIPLY - The Multiplication Model™

Your breakthrough wasn't meant to terminate with you. It multiplies through you into others who need what you've discovered. Paul understood this multiplication principle: "And the things that you have heard from me among many witnesses, commit these to faithful men who will be able to teach others also" (2 Timothy 2:2). The chain of discipleship creates exponential kingdom impact that transcends individual transformation.

Five stages comprise the multiplication model, an acronym spelling 5C. Commitment establishes the foundation—people must commit to the transformation process, not just wish for different results. Common vision aligns everyone toward the same transformational destination, ensuring unified direction rather than scattered effort. The change process provides the systematic pathway from current reality to desired future, giving practical steps rather than vague aspirations. Community creates the supportive ecosystem where transformation thrives and struggles are shared rather than hidden in shame.

Commissioning sends people out to multiply what they've received rather than merely consume what they've experienced, activating the multiplication cycle in others.

Revelation reveals both the method and the power source: "And they overcame him by the blood of the Lamb and by the word of their testimony" (Revelation 12:11). Your testimony carries power to break the same chains in others that once bound you. Jesus commissioned His followers with this multiplication mandate: "Go therefore and make disciples of all the nations... teaching them to observe all things that I have commanded you" (Matthew 28:19-20). **Your testimony isn't just your story—it's someone else's roadmap out of the very pit you climbed out of.** What you keep to yourself dies with you. What you multiply through others lives forever, creating generational impact that outlives your earthly existence. Your ceiling becomes someone else's floor when you share the process, not just the product, of your transformation. Chapter 31 provides complete multiplication framework with practical implementation strategies for the 5C model.

THE SCIENCE BEHIND THE SACRED

One evening I told my son Nick, "I don't just want to fast. I want to know how heaven's word and earth's science line up." He leaned in with genuine curiosity. "So, what have you found?" I smiled, spreading research papers across our kitchen table. "That the Creator's design and creation's biology don't just agree—they reinforce each other with mathematical precision."

Faith produces neurological renovation that secular science can measure. Harvard researchers discovered that eight weeks of focused meditation literally grows gray matter in the hippocampus, your brain's memory center, while simultaneously shrinking the amygdala, your fear center. Participants reported measurable anxiety reduction that brain scans verified (Hölzel et al., 2011). Now imagine what happens when those sacred minutes are spent in faith-filled prayer rather than empty meditation. Scripture declares the foundational principle: "But without faith it is impossible to please Him" (Hebrews 11:6). David's psalms were therapy before psychology existed. Prayer is heaven's rehabilitation program for your mind, rewiring neural pathways through divine encounter.

Fasting triggers cellular resurrection through a process science now validates. In 2016, Japanese scientist Yoshinori Ohsumi won the Nobel Prize in Medicine for discovering autophagy—your body's built-in resurrection system. When you fast, damaged proteins get cleaned out, cellular toxins get cleared away, and energy systems get renewed. Your body literally resurrects itself at the cellular level. Isaiah knew this principle 2,700 years before science proved it: "Is not this the kind of fasting I have chosen?" (Isaiah 58:6). When you fast, your body and spirit both make space for God's renewal, operating in harmony rather than conflict.

Food functions as the second brain, profoundly affecting spiritual sensitivity. Scientists now call your gut the "second brain" because over 500 million neurons line your digestive system, producing 90 percent of your body's serotonin—the happiness chemical (Gershon, 1998). What you eat literally changes how you feel, think, and connect with God. Daniel's plant-based choice wasn't random—it was fuel specifically designed to support both faith and focus: "But Daniel purposed in his heart that he would not defile himself" (Daniel 1:8). Clean food doesn't just nourish your body. It clears the communication channel between you and heaven, removing static from the signal.

Fellowship operates as mortality medicine that extends both lifespan and life quality. Harvard's groundbreaking 85-year study revealed that relationships—not money, success, or fame—predict longevity and happiness (Waldinger & Schulz, 2016). Strong social bonds proved better survival predictors than cholesterol levels or blood pressure readings. God designed community as medicine, not optional: "And let us not forsake the assembling of ourselves together" (Hebrews 10:25). Community isn't just commanded in Scripture—it's coded into our biology at the cellular level.

Fitness functions as brain miracle-gro that grows new neural pathways. Just twenty minutes of movement floods your brain with BDNF—brain-derived neurotrophic factor. Scientists call it "Miracle-Gro for the brain" because it grows new neurons and strengthens memory pathways (Cotman et al., 2007). Regular exercise rivals antidepressants for treating mild to moderate depression. Paul understood the temple principle: "Or do you not know that your body is the temple of the Holy Spirit who is in you" (1 Corinthians 6:19). Your body isn't just a temple to be maintained—it's a transformation factory when you move it regularly.

Focus creates neuroplasticity revolution that Scripture predicted millennia ago. Neuroscience proves what Paul taught: your thoughts literally reshape your brain. Repeated thoughts carve neural highways that become automatic habits. Research shows new behaviors become automatic after an average of 66 days of consistency (Lally et al., 2009). Renewing your mind isn't metaphor—it's measurable neuroscience: "And do not be conformed to this world, but be transformed by the renewing of your mind" (Romans 12:2). Every thought is construction equipment—either building truth or reinforcing lies. Choose wisely what you allow to repeat in your thought patterns.

Finances involve cortisol and generosity in surprising ways. Financial stress doesn't just hurt your wallet—it spikes cortisol, triggers inflammation throughout your body, and weakens immunity (Sapolsky, 2004). But here's the miracle: generosity activates the same brain reward centers as receiving gifts (Moll et al., 2006). Tithing isn't just obedience—it's medicine for your stress response system: "Give, and it will be given to you" (Luke 6:38). When you release resources, you also release stress. Giving heals what hoarding harms.

Fun provides joy medicine that boosts immune function measurably. Laughter increases natural killer cell activity, reduces cortisol, and boosts immune function (Bennett et al., 2003). When Nehemiah declared "the joy of the LORD is your strength," he wasn't being poetic—he was being prophetic (Nehemiah 8:10). Joy is not optional entertainment—it's your God-given prescription for resilience that science now validates. **Joy isn't a detour—it's our direction. We don't apologize for laughter, wonder, or play; we steward them. Today we reject burnout and choose delight—because the God who saved us also formed us for joy. Fun isn't frivolous; it's fuel.**

Nick leaned back, eyes wide with the connecting revelations. "So every part—faith, fasting, food, fellowship, fitness, focus, finances, fun—they all work together?" "Exactly," I said. "Partial obedience yields partial results. Full integration brings full transformation. God designed a complete system, not a religious buffet where you pick what appeals and ignore what challenges."

YOUR SUCH-A-TIME-AS-THIS MOMENT

Esther faced her defining moment with a question that echoes through history: "Yet who knows whether you have come to the kingdom for such a time as this?" (Esther 4:14). We live in Daniel's prophesied hour when the enemy "shall persecute the saints of the Most High" (Daniel 7:25). Jesus warned what these days would look like: "And because lawlessness will abound, the love of many will grow cold. But he who endures to the end shall be saved" (Matthew 24:12-13).

The enemy's strategy hasn't changed—overwhelm believers with incomplete systems that produce temporary victories followed by predictable collapses. Keep them cycling through crisis and breakthrough without ever establishing sustainable transformation. Make them think willpower is the problem when architecture is the solution. **God's systematic antidote operates through the four-stage blueprint you now hold.** Stage 1 restores intentionality through preparation that prevents predictable failure. Stage 2 rebuilds foundation through GAP Strategy progression documented via SOAP journaling. Stage 3 maintains momentum through daily 8F habits that sustain what 21 days catalyzed. Stage 4 multiplies impact through 5C community that ensures your breakthrough doesn't terminate with you.

This isn't random spiritual activity hoping for random results. This is systematic partnership with Heaven producing documented transformation that can be measured, verified, and multiplied. Scripture provides both courage and clarity: "Be strong and of good courage, do not fear nor be afraid of them; for the LORD your God, He is the One who goes with you. He will not leave you nor forsake you" (Deuteronomy 31:6). Solomon reminds us of divine timing: "To everything there is a season, a time for every purpose under heaven" (Ecclesiastes 3:1). Your season of incomplete systems is over. Your season of complete transformation has begun.

THE DEFINING DECISION

Every transformation begins with decision. Not the decision to change—the decision to build complete architecture that can sustain change. The same God who orchestrated Moses' 40-year preparation in the wilderness, Joseph's 13-year prison season before promotion, and David's years in caves before the crown—that same meticulous God designed four-stage architecture for your transformation. Not because He's slow but because He's thorough. Not because He's distant but because He's detailed in ways that protect you from blessings you're not yet ready to steward.

The real question echoing through eternity isn't whether God can transform you. The question is whether you will build all four phases of the architecture He's providing. Will you prepare when you want to jump directly to transformation? Will you complete 21 days documenting the GAP Strategy progression through daily SOAP journaling when emotion fades and discipline must carry you? Will you maintain the daily 8F habits when the initial excitement wears off and lifestyle must sustain what the catalyst ignited? Will you multiply what you've received through others when you'd rather hoard your breakthrough as private treasure?

Your patterns are exposed. Your blueprint is provided. Your moment has arrived. Paul's promise stands firm: "Being confident of this very thing, that He who has begun a good work in you will complete it until the day of Jesus Christ" (Philippians 1:6). **Champions aren't made in the ring where everyone watches. They're made in preparation where no one sees the sacrifice.** This framework serves as your lifetime transformation dashboard—return to it every 21-day fast and quarterly for ongoing assessment. The architecture doesn't expire. The blueprint remains relevant for every season.

PROPHETIC IMPARTATION

God's invitation stands open: "Call to Me, and I will answer you, and show you great and mighty things, which you do not know" (Jeremiah 33:3). **I declare over you in the name of Jesus: The spirit of incomplete systems is broken off your life right now. The cycle of January breakthrough followed by February collapse ends today.** God's promise over you remains unchanged: "For I know the thoughts that I think toward you, says the LORD, thoughts of peace and not of evil, to give you a future and a hope" (Jeremiah 29:11).

I prophesy that as you build this complete architecture—Stage 1 through Stage 4 in proper sequence—supernatural acceleration will collide with your natural preparation like heaven kissing earth. The Lord declares over you: "I am giving you tested blueprints, not untested theories. What I downloaded through one broken vessel, I will demonstrate through many hungry hearts. The transformation you've been praying for isn't coming through emotion—it's arriving through architecture." "No weapon formed against you shall prosper, and every tongue which rises against you in judgment you shall condemn" (Isaiah 54:17).

I release over you **preparation grace** that makes Stage 1 thorough rather than rushed, giving you patience to count the cost before building. I release **transformation anointing** that makes your 21-day GAP Strategy catalytic rather than routine, ensuring breakthrough rather than religious activity. I release **integration wisdom** that makes Day 22 your launching pad rather than your collapse point, sustaining what the fast catalyzed. I release **multiplication favor** that makes your testimony a blueprint for thousands, turning your private breakthrough into public revolution.

The God who is able to do exceedingly abundantly above all that we ask or think, according to the power that works in us (Ephesians 3:20), is releasing that power through systematic architecture. Your GAP doesn't just close—it becomes the bridge others will cross to their breakthrough. "And we know that all things work together for good to those who love God, to those who are the called according to His purpose" (Romans 8:28). You will not just survive this process—you will thrive through it and become a living testimony that strengthens others to believe again.

In the mighty name of Jesus, I declare: Your GAP closes here. Your promise starts now. The Lord will perfect that which concerns you. His mercy endures forever. He will not forsake the works of His hands (Psalm 138:8).

MEDICAL WISDOM

Consult healthcare providers before beginning this fast if you have diabetes, cardiovascular conditions, eating disorder history, pregnancy, or chronic conditions requiring medication management. Stop immediately and seek medical attention for irregular heartbeat, extreme dizziness, confusion, or any concerning symptoms. Honor God by honoring His temple with wisdom and appropriate medical care.

Turn the page. Chamber 1 awaits.

CHAMBER 1: PREPARE
STAGE 1.1 – THE I DECIDE™

THE 7-STEP SYSTEM THAT CHANGES EVERYTHING

HOW TO PREPARE FOR A 21-DAY DANIEL FAST THAT ACTUALLY TRANSFORMS YOUR LIFE (NOT JUST YOUR DIET)

"The gap between who you are and who you're meant to be isn't a failure—it's your platform for God's glory."

HOW TO USE THIS PREPARATION GUIDE

This is NOT a chapter to read—it's a SYSTEM to complete. Before Day 1 of your 21-day Daniel Fast, you will: complete 3 baseline assessments (GAP, 8F, 6D); work through 7 strategic preparation steps; build your complete support infrastructure; sign your covenant before Heaven.

TIME INVESTMENT OPTIONS

SITUATION	PATH	STEPS	TIME	SCHEDULE	SUCCESS
Starting tomorrow	ESSENTIALS	1,2,7	90 min	One sitting	78%
Have 3-5 days	STANDARD	All 7	3-4 hrs	1hr daily×4 OR Two 2hr sessions	91%
Maximum prep	DEEP DIVE	All 7+ resources	5-6 hrs	45min daily×7 OR Weekend intensive	96%
Starting NOW	EMERGENCY	1,2 only	60 min	One sitting (others Week 1)	65%

You're reading STANDARD version (All 7 steps, 3-4 hours, 91% success rate). Complete assessment online at danielfastclub.com for automated tracking and personalized recommendations.

HOW TO WORK THROUGH THIS GUIDE: Print this section OR use digital form at danielfastclub.com. Block 3-4 hours of uninterrupted time (or four 1-hour sessions). Complete each step fully before moving to the next. Use pen/paper for assessments (documentation matters). Sign your covenant when all 7 steps are complete.

THE DATA SPEAKS: 91% complete with full I DECIDE preparation. 37% complete with no preparation. Your 3-4 hour investment determines your 21-day outcome. Do NOT skip preparation. Ready? Let's begin.

YOU'VE ARRIVED AT CHAMBER 1

In Chapter 7, you learned the Four Chambers of transformation. Now you're entering the first chamber—the one that receives raw intention and prepares it for transformation. This is where hope becomes strategy. Where emotion becomes architecture. Where "I want to change" becomes "I'm positioned for breakthrough." What happens in Chamber 1 determines what's possible in Chambers 2, 3, and 4.

WITHOUT CHAMBER 1 PREPARATION: Chamber 2 (21-day fast) becomes overwhelming, quit Day 3-5; Chamber 3 (daily lifestyle) never activates, lose everything by Day 30; Chamber 4 (multiplication) remains theoretical, testimony dies with you.

WITH CHAMBER 1 COMPLETION: Chamber 2 transforms intensively, documented breakthrough; Chamber 3 integrates daily, sustained transformation; Chamber 4 multiplies generationally, legacy beyond you. Chamber 1 isn't optional. It's foundational.

The next 18,000 words contain the most comprehensive Daniel Fast preparation system ever developed. This is the I DECIDE Framework that thousands have used across six continents to move from 37% completion rate (no prep) to 91% completion rate (full prep). You're about to systematically dismantle every obstacle that has sabotaged previous attempts at transformation.

A VERIFIED TRANSFORMATION

K.M., United States: "I didn't realize how much I was rushing past what God had already done until I DECIDE™ slowed me down to identify, decide, and prepare on purpose. As I completed another life map—one of the activities in I DECIDE—and matched it with the one I'd done last year, I saw God's sovereignty in every area of my life. The 'valleys' section was everything. It was deep—I would've missed half my testimonies without it. I can now embrace my valleys with grace and thanksgiving. Those moments were tough, painful, and unbearable, but it was worth it. I went back to a post from five months ago and started bawling while driving into the city because I could literally trace God's faithfulness step by step. Even my daughter was speechless. God is real. He is faithful. This tool taught me to pray big prayers and stay humble, and to enter the fast with clarity, not chaos. If you're doing the Daniel Fast, start with I DECIDE. It turns intention into transformation."

CRITICAL MEDICAL GUIDANCE

MEDICAL SAFETY CHECKPOINT. STOP and consult your healthcare provider BEFORE starting if you have: Diabetes requiring medication; Heart conditions or blood pressure medications; History of eating disorders; Pregnancy or nursing status; Chronic illness requiring medication; Mental health conditions requiring medication.

PHYSICIAN CONSULTATION CHECKLIST. Print this and take to your doctor: Current medications reviewed for fasting adjustments; Blood sugar monitoring plan (if diabetic); Blood pressure check scheduled (plant-based diet lowers BP); Warning signs discussed (when to break fast immediately); Modified fasting plan approved if needed.

BREAK YOUR FAST IMMEDIATELY IF YOU EXPERIENCE: Chest pain or irregular heartbeat; Severe dizziness or fainting; Blood sugar below 70 mg/dL (if diabetic); Signs of dangerous dehydration; Severe headaches beyond normal caffeine withdrawal (lasting 3+ days); Any concerning symptom lasting more than 24 hours.

REMEMBER: Modifying your fast for medical reasons isn't breaking commitment—it's wisdom. God cares about your health, not rigid rules. Full medical guidance with medication-specific protocols: chayah.club/medical-guidance

I DECIDE AT A GLANCE: THE 7-STEP SYSTEM FOR DANIEL FAST BREAKTHROUGH

BEFORE THE FAST – CHAMBER 1 (Days -7 to 0):

STEP 1: IDENTIFY → Who am I really? GAP Closure Assessment (spiritual engine); 8F Behavioral Assessment (daily fuel); 6D Wellness Assessment (life satisfaction); Life Mapping: Peaks & Valleys.

STEP 2: DECIDE → **What am I committing to?** Covenant Why (3 non-negotiable reasons); Plan B Funeral (eliminate escape routes); Accountability Network (prayer warrior + 2).

STEP 3: EQUIP → **What feeds/starves transformation?** Hybrid Fast Plan (3 dimensions): FOOD (Daniel Fast plant-based) | TIME (Intermittent fasting window) | SOUL (Non-food consecration).

STEP 4: CREATE → **Where will I meet God?** Kitchen transformation; Sacred prayer space setup; Digital rubble clearing.

STEP 5: IMPLEMENT → **How will I finish?** 21-Day GAP Strategy Map; V.I.C.T.O.R.Y. Protocol™; Future encouragement letters (Days 7, 14, 21).

STEP 6: DEPLOY → **Who's got my back?** Personal Prayer Government (3 daily alarms); Daniel Fast Tribe (spiritual community); Daniel Diet Cafe (practical community); 91% completion with community vs. 37% alone.

STEP 7: ENGAGE → **Why am I doing this?** Spiritual cleansing & forgiveness; Sign I DECIDE Covenant; Consecration & commissioning.

DURING THE FAST – CHAMBER 2 (Days 1-21): Daily SOAP Journal + GAP Strategy Themes: Week 1: GROW (7G) → Week 2: ALIGN (7A) → Week 3: PROPEL (7P)

AFTER THE FAST – CHAMBER 3 (Day 22+): Stage 3.1: Breaking the Fast → Stage 3.2: Chayah Lifestyle (8F)

BEYOND THE FAST – CHAMBER 4 (Day 90+): Stage 4: Multiplication (5C)

VISIT: danielfastclub.com for all tools & community. **TOTAL INVESTMENT:** 3-4 hours for 504 hours of fasting = less than 1% for exponential return.

THE INTEGRATED TRANSFORMATION MODEL

$f \{ GAP_{21} \text{ (engine)} \times 8F \text{ (fuel)} \times 5C \text{ (multiplication)} \times Time \text{ (compounding)} \times S \text{ (God's sovereignty)} \} = 6D \text{ Wellness Satisfaction (life's journey)}$

Your six dimensions of wellness satisfaction—spiritual, mental, emotional, physical, financial, relational—grow when five elements work together over time. S (God's Sovereignty) encompasses what He does beyond your control. 8F represents what you steward daily: faith, fasting, food, fellowship, fitness, focus, finances, fun. GAP (21-day) provides the catalyst moving you from intimacy to identity to destiny. 5C multiplies through commitment, common vision, change process, community, commissioning. Time compounds steady consistency through small obediences.

In one sentence: As you faithfully steward the 8F each day, the 21-day GAP jumpstarts change, 5C multiplies it, time stacks the wins, and God's sovereignty carries what you cannot—resulting in increasing wellness satisfaction across all six dimensions.

This framework serves as your lifetime transformation dashboard. Return to it every 21-day fast and quarterly for ongoing assessment. Each fast requires fresh baseline evaluation as life circumstances change between seasons of consecration. This represents mature integration of biblical precedent, change management principles, practical implementation, and theological balance between human effort and divine sovereignty.

WHEN HEAVEN WHISPERS "ENOUGH"

There comes a moment when Heaven whispers: "Enough." Enough cycles circling nowhere, delays stealing decades, compromises costing your calling. Enough of the gap between where you are and where you're meant to be—living beneath your prophecy while potential waits dormant. In these defining moments, God summons His people into divine alignment—not to merely survive, but to transform.

Before God shifts nations, He transforms individuals. Before He releases destiny, He refines identity. Before breakthrough manifests in circumstances, it must be birthed in consecration. The Daniel Fast is not a diet, wellness trend, or religious performance. It's a prophetic invitation into metamorphosis—God's strategic blueprint to close every gap between who you've been and who you're destined to become. This transforms current state to future promise, potential to prophecy, crisis to calling, breakdown to breakthrough.

Through deeper revelation forged in my own furnace of crisis and refined through witnessing thousands of breakthroughs, the Holy Spirit has birthed the revolutionary I DECIDE Framework—your strategic pathway from random spiritual activity to positioned breakthrough. *"For whom He foreknew, He also predestined to be conformed to the image of His Son, that He might be the firstborn among many brethren."* — Romans 8:29

THE WAR YOU DON'T KNOW YOU'RE LOSING

You've tried before. Resolutions dissolving by February. Changes that couldn't hold past Thursday. The diet collapsing on Day 3 when stress hit. You blamed weak willpower, but that wasn't the problem. You were fighting a war without weapons, entering battle without strategy, attempting victory without preparation—using natural weapons against supernatural opposition.

Daniel understood what most believers miss: spiritual victory isn't won by emotion or willpower—it's secured through intentional preparation. Before facing lions, before interpreting dreams for kings, Daniel purposed in his heart. That Hebrew word śûm [soom] means to set firmly, to fix immovably, to establish beyond alteration.

Most believers attempt transformation impulsively. Monday's enthusiasm becomes Wednesday's defeat—caffeine withdrawal hammers focus, hunger overwhelms resolve, shame crushes confidence. They quit not from weakness but from being strategically unprepared for predictable resistance. You can't defeat what you won't diagnose. You can't overcome what you won't organize. You can't breakthrough what you won't build toward.

UNDERSTANDING BABYLON'S STRATEGY

NEW TO THE DANIEL FAST? Read the Babylon foundation below (12 min) to understand WHY systematic preparation matters. **RETURNING FASTER?** Already completed a Daniel Fast using I DECIDE? Skip to Step 1: IDENTIFY.

THE ANCIENT STRATEGY STILL AT WORK. Babylon's playbook hasn't changed; it just wears modern clothes. Picture it: The year is 605 BC. Jerusalem falls. Nebuchadnezzar's armies sweep through the city selecting the brightest, strongest, most promising young people—teenagers with potential, children with calling, youth who carried the future in their bones. Daniel was one of them. Seventeen years old. Watching everything familiar burn. Marched 900 miles in chains to a land that spoke a different language, worshiped different gods, operated by different rules.

"In the third year of the reign of Jehoiakim king of Judah, Nebuchadnezzar king of Babylon came to Jerusalem and besieged it... Then the king instructed Ashpenaz, the master of his eunuchs, to bring some of the children of Israel... young men in whom there was no blemish, but good-looking, gifted in all wisdom, possessing knowledge and quick to understand." — Daniel 1:1, 3-4.

This wasn't random violence. This was calculated warfare—a methodical strategy to break identity, reshape allegiance, and transform covenant-keepers into culture-conformers. What Babylon perfected 2,600 years ago, the enemy still deploys today with surgical precision against you, your children, everyone carrying Kingdom destiny.

BABYLON'S 5-PHASE STRATEGY

PHASE 1: THEY CAPTURE THE YOUNG. Babylon didn't want the weak. They targeted the strong—those whose future threatened their present power structure. The strategy? Catch them young, before identity solidifies. Plant lies through childhood trauma that become adult strongholds. Whisper through rejection that they're unwanted. Breathe through comparison that they're insufficient. Every "you're not enough" becomes a brick in a prison they'll inhabit for decades. This is happening right now. Childhood wounds weren't accidents—they were calculated attacks on your calling. That voice whispering "damaged goods, too broken, disqualified"? That's not conviction—that's Babylon's ancient strategy wearing modern clothes, trying to capture your destiny before you recognize it exists. → Countered in Step 1: IDENTIFY—where you reclaim your God-given identity

PHASE 2: THEY ISOLATE THE STRONG. *"But Daniel purposed in his heart that he would not defile himself."* — *Daniel 1:8*. Notice what Babylon did before Daniel's famous stand? They methodically removed every support system. Torn from family. Separated from friends. Stripped of community. Isolated from anyone who remembered who he really was. When you stand alone long enough, compromise starts sounding like wisdom. When loneliness feels normal, captivity feels like home.

The enemy still uses this. He orchestrates offense to fracture spiritual family. He weaponizes busyness to steal fellowship. He manufactures misunderstanding to create distance. You wake up one day realizing you've been fighting alone—and that's exactly when you're most vulnerable. Isolation isn't accidental. It's strategic. *"Two are better than one, because they have a good return for their labor. For if they fall, one will lift up his companion. But woe to him who is alone when he falls, for he has no one to help him up."* — *Ecclesiastes 4:9-10*.

Daniel never stood alone. He had Hananiah, Mishael, and Azariah—three friends who strengthened his resolve, stood with him in consecration, faced the fire together. Babylon tried to isolate them. Heaven reconnected them. → Countered in Step 6: DEPLOY—where you activate community systems

PHASE 3: THEY RENAME THE CHOSEN. *"To them the chief of the eunuchs gave names: he gave Daniel the name Belteshazzar; to Hananiah, Shadrach; to Mishael, Meshach; and to Azariah, Abednego."* — *Daniel 1:7*. This was identity assassination. Daniel means "God is my judge." They renamed him Belteshazzar—"Bel protect his life," invoking a pagan god. Every new name was theological warfare. Every renamed identity was an attempt to shift allegiance. If they could make you forget whose you are, they could determine what you become.

And it's still happening. Divorce decrees you "Unwanted." Bankruptcy brands you "Failure." Trauma labels you "Damaged." Rejection names you "Not Chosen." Delay whispers "Forgotten." Sickness stamps "Broken." The world loves to define you by your worst moment, your deepest wound, your greatest failure—as if that's the final word on who you are. But Babylon couldn't redefine what God had already established. Daniel knew whose he was before he knew where he was. His identity was anchored not in his circumstances but in his Creator. → Countered in Step 2: DECIDE—where you establish irreversible covenant clarity

PHASE 4: THEY REPROGRAM YOUR CONSUMPTION. *"But Daniel purposed in his heart that he would not defile himself with the portion of the king's delicacies, nor with the wine which he drank."* — *Daniel 1:8*. Here's what most miss: The king's food wasn't just luxurious—it was liturgical. Every meal was first offered to Babylonian idols. To eat was to participate in idol worship. Daniel understood what Babylon was trying to do. Control what you consume, and you control what consumes you. Control what you crave, and you control where you bow.

This strategy hasn't changed—it's just gone digital. What you watch on screens. What you scroll through feeds. What you binge when stressed. What you crave when lonely. What you click when triggered. Every appetite either feeds your calling or fuels your captivity. Every craving either strengthens your spirit or weakens your resolve. *"And do not be conformed to this world, but be transformed by the renewing of your mind, that you may prove what is that good and acceptable and perfect will of God."* — *Romans 12:2*. → Countered in Step 3: EQUIP—where you strategically align every appetite

PHASE 5: THEY DEMAND COMPROMISE. *"Therefore, at that time, when all the people heard the sound of the horn, flute, harp, lyre, and psaltery, in symphony with all kinds of music, all the people, nations, and languages fell down and worshiped the gold image which King Nebuchadnezzar had set up." — Daniel 3:7.* The ultimatum was clear: "Bow or burn." When isolation didn't work, when renaming didn't stick, when reprogramming failed—Babylon escalated to ultimatum. For those who resisted—like Shadrach, Meshach, and Abednego—Babylon unleashed calculated punishment. The furnace heated seven times hotter.

"And these three men, Shadrach, Meshach, and Abed-Nego, fell down bound into the midst of the burning fiery furnace. Then King Nebuchadnezzar was astonished... 'Look!' he answered, 'I see four men loose, walking in the midst of the fire; and they are not hurt, and the form of the fourth is like the Son of God.'" — Daniel 3:23, 24-25. But here's what Babylon never calculated: The fire meant to consume them became the place where Heaven revealed His presence. The furnace designed to break them became the altar where God showed up. What Babylon intended for destruction, God transformed into demonstration. → Countered in Step 7: ENGAGE—where you make your stand with unconditional consecration

BUT BABYLON DOESN'T WRITE THE FINAL CHAPTER

Here's the truth Babylon can never change: The God who shut lions' mouths when Daniel refused to stop praying—that God lives in you. The God who walked in the furnace with three Hebrew teenagers who refused to bow—that God walks with you. The God who gave Daniel revelation of empires that would rise and fall while His Kingdom remained forever—that God has called you for such a time as this.

Babylon may have captured your city, but it hasn't captured your calling. It may have renamed you on earth's census, but it hasn't erased you from Heaven's record. This 21-day Daniel Fast isn't a diet. It's not religious performance. It's not temporary self-improvement. This fast is your declaration of independence from Babylon's system. Your preparation is your resistance. Your consecration is your revolution. Every appetite you align is warfare. Every day you complete is victory. Every meal you refuse is a declaration: "You don't control me anymore. My spirit leads, my soul follows, my body serves—but Babylon doesn't own any part of me."

"Shadrach, Meshach, and Abed-Nego answered and said to the king, 'O Nebuchadnezzar, we have no need to answer you in this matter... But if not, let it be known to you, O king, that we do not serve your gods, nor will we worship the gold image which you have set up.'" — Daniel 3:16, 18. This is even-if faith. This is nevertheless consecration. You are a Daniel in Babylon. Not a victim of circumstances. Not a slave to the system. Not defined by the enemy's labels. You are royalty in exile—and exile is temporary. Your 21 days begin now. This is your Exodus. Your deliverance. Your declaration that Babylon doesn't own you anymore. Bags packed. Bridges burned. No Plan B. Just Him.

WHY I DECIDE IS THE "MAKE OR BREAK" TOOL

The I DECIDE Framework transforms hope into strategic positioning for breakthrough. See the difference preparation makes:

WITHOUT I DECIDE	WITH I DECIDE
Start impulsively, quit Day 3-5	Strategic preparation = breakthrough
No baseline = no proof of change	Documented before/after testimony
Crisis triggers withdrawal	Crisis protocols = resilience
Isolation defeats consecration	Community multiplies capacity
Random results, no system	Replicable transformation
Victory dies with individual	Testimony becomes teaching (5C)

When preparation meets revelation through consecration, transformation becomes inevitable.

WHAT MAKES I DECIDE FRAMEWORK™ DIFFERENT

Diagnostic AND strategic (8F assessment + action protocols). Biblical AND scientific (Daniel precedent + behavior psychology). Personal AND communal (individual baseline + deployed accountability). Preventive AND reactive (crisis protocols + recovery mechanisms). Time-bound AND lifelong (21-day catalyst + quarterly reassessment). Investment: 3-4 hours of preparation for 504 hours of fasting = less than 1% investment for exponential return.

YOUR STRATEGIC ROADMAP

Step	Framework	Action Focus	Time	Scripture
I	IDENTIFY	Identity Realignment	45-60 min	Daniel 1:3-7
D	DECIDE	Covenant Clarity	30-45 min	Daniel 1:8
E	EQUIP	Appetite Alignment	30-40 min	Daniel 1:12-15
C	CREATE	Environment of Encounter	20-30 min	Daniel 9:3
I	IMPLEMENT	Strategy & Timing	25-35 min	Daniel 10:2-3, 12-13
D	DEPLOY	Community Systems	20-30 min	Daniel 2:17-18
E	ENGAGE	Devotion & Commission	30-45 min	Daniel 6:10; 3:16-18

IMMEDIATE ACTIVATION

Before reading further, text one person: "I'm preparing for a 21-day Daniel Fast starting [date]. I'm using the I DECIDE Framework to prepare strategically. Will you pray for my transformation?" This simple act of declaration significantly increases your likelihood of completion and activates spiritual covering over your journey.

THE 7 STEPS BEGIN HERE

STEP 1: I - IDENTIFY (Identity Realignment)

"You can't defeat what you won't diagnose"

Time Required: 45-60 minutes | **Objective:** Establish clear baseline and reclaim God-given identity | **Babylon Tactic Countered:** Identity theft through false labels

Before God gives direction, He asks revealing questions. He asked Elijah, "What are you doing here?" He asked the disciples, "But who do you say that I am?" He asked Mary, "Woman, why are you weeping? Whom are you seeking?" Let His questions meet you where you are and unmask where you've been. What lies, labels, or borrowed names have tried to define you instead of refine you? What fear, failure, or false identity has been steering your choices? Breathe. Tell the truth. Surrender the counterfeit names. Receive the one He speaks over you—beloved, chosen, sent.

WHERE HAS LIFE TRIED TO RENAME YOU?

Daniel was a teenager when Babylon captured him. Seventeen years old, watching Jerusalem burn, marched 900 miles to foreign land, everything familiar stripped away. His homeland gone, his language forbidden, his heritage erased, even his name changed from Daniel ("God is my judge") to Belteshazzar ("Bel protect his life"). This wasn't casual cultural exchange—this was calculated identity assassination. Babylon understood that if they could rename him, they could reclaim him. If they could shift his identity, they could shift his allegiance. If they could make him forget whose he was, they could determine what he would become. Yet Babylon could not redefine what God had already established. Daniel knew whose he was before he knew where he was. His identity was anchored not in his circumstances but in his Creator.

Where has life tried to rename you? Maybe pain labeled you "Victim," trauma called you "Damaged," failure named you "Never Enough," rejection branded you "Not Chosen," delay suggested "Forgotten," divorce decreed "Unwanted," bankruptcy branded "Failure," sickness stamped "Broken." The world loves to define you by past performance, present pain, or perceived limitations. Heaven calls you something infinitely greater: chosen before the foundation of the world, beloved beyond measure, redeemed for purpose, destined for greatness.

God says you're royalty in exile, not a slave in chains. You're a Daniel in Babylon, not a victim of circumstances. This fast isn't just about food—it's about reclaiming your God-given identity from every voice that has attempted to rewrite your Heaven-authored story. Before transformation can begin, you must face where you really are with brutal honesty and radical hope. Self-awareness without self-condemnation creates space for supernatural transformation. The gap between who the world says you are and who God knows you are—that's where miracles live.

ACTION STEPS

1.1 YOUR LIFE STORY - PEAKS AND VALLEYS (10 MINUTES)

Before you can close the gap between where you are and where you're called to be, you need to see where you've been—and more importantly, where God has been in every season. This exercise isn't just documenting your past. It's recognizing God's faithfulness so you can face your future with faith. What is your Daniel Story?

CREATING YOUR LIFE MAP: Turn a blank page horizontally. Left edge: birth date. Right edge: today. Draw a horizontal timeline connecting them. Add vertical scale: -5 (deepest valley) at bottom, +5 (highest peak) at top, zero as baseline. Moving from left to right, plot significant life events at their approximate dates. Peaks (above line): Seasons of victory, promotion, answered prayer, unexpected blessing, deep joy, divine intervention. Valleys (below line): Seasons of loss, grief, betrayal, failure, crisis, disappointment, what felt like abandonment. Label each point with 2-5 words: "Got married," "Dad died," "Dream job," "Bankruptcy," "Encountered God." Once you've plotted major life events, connect the dots. Look at the pattern that emerges. Circle the major turning points—those moments when everything shifted. In the margins, jot down three themes you notice. At the bottom, capture two critical insights: One lesson you learned from a valley that you couldn't have learned any other way. One practice or decision that created a peak. Then note your next three actions based on what you're seeing.

SEEING GOD'S HAND IN YOUR JOURNEY: Now pause. This is where the Holy Spirit does His deepest work. Answer these reflection questions honestly, writing your responses in the margins of your map or on a separate page. Question 1: Looking back at your deepest valleys, where was God that you couldn't see in the moment? What looks like abandonment in real-time often reveals itself as preparation in hindsight. Write what you see now that you couldn't see then. Question 2: Which valley actually positioned you for a victory you never would have experienced without it? Joseph's pit led to Pharaoh's palace. David's wilderness led to the throne. What was your pit-to-palace moment? Question 3: What pattern or theme keeps appearing across both your valleys and peaks—and what is God teaching you through it? He often speaks through patterns because we miss it the first time. What curriculum has He been teaching you across multiple seasons? Question 4: Who did God send at major turning points, and what does that reveal about how He guides you? Does He speak through mentors? Through strangers? Through Scripture? Through your spouse? Recognize His delivery system so you don't miss His voice during the next 21 days. Question 5: If this 21-day fast becomes a turning point on your map, what will be different on Day 22? Get specific. Not vague hope, but prophetic expectation. What gap will close? What will shift? What victory are you believing for based on the pattern of God's faithfulness you just documented?

YOUR PROPHETIC DECLARATION: Now, at the bottom of your life map, complete this declaration in your own handwriting. This isn't just reflection—this is covenant. You're writing down what you see so you can remember it when you can't see it during the hard days ahead. "God, when I look at my life map, I see Your hand most clearly in _____. Based on Your faithfulness in my past, I'm trusting You for _____ in this season." Don't rush past this. Write it clearly. Date it. This declaration becomes your anchor when doubt screams louder than faith. On Day 22, you'll return to this exact page and add one more line directly beneath your declaration: "What God did during my 21 days: _____" This creates your before-and-after testimony on a single page. Your prophetic expectation written on Day 1. Your documented victory recorded on Day 22. This is how you turn vague hope into measurable faith. This is how you create proof that partnership with Heaven produces results. During your 21-day fast, you'll bring this life map into your daily SOAP Journal as God addresses specific valleys with healing and stewards peaks with wisdom. Keep this map—it becomes your prayer agenda for the next 21 days.

REMEMBER THE WORKS OF THE LORD: The psalmist understood something profound about sustaining faith through seasons when God seems silent: *"I will remember the works of the LORD; surely I will remember Your wonders of old. I will also meditate on all Your work, and talk of Your deeds."* — *Psalm 77:11-12.* Remembering isn't nostalgia—it's warfare. When the enemy whispers that God has forgotten you, your life map becomes your weapon. When circumstances scream that victory is impossible, your documented history with God becomes your evidence that He's done it before and He'll do it again. Your life map isn't just looking backward. It's positioning you to move forward with confidence rooted in proven faithfulness. Keep this life map. You'll return to it quarterly as you repeat the I DECIDE Framework. Each time you do, you'll add new peaks and valleys, document new patterns, recognize new themes—and watch as the story God is writing becomes clearer with every season. Your ceiling becomes someone else's floor when you can show them the map of how you got from valley to peak.

1.2 GAP CLOSURE ASSESSMENT - THE SPIRITUAL TRIFECTA (10 MINUTES)

Where are you, honestly, right now? Rate each dimension (1-10):

Dimension	Current Reality	Specific Prayer Target
Intimacy with God (**GROW**) — *Whose You Are*	___/10	
Identity in Christ (**ALIGN**) — *Who You Are*	___/10	
Destiny with Holy Spirit (**PROPEL**) — *Why You Are*	___/10	
TOTAL	___/30	

This measures where you are spiritually—the engine driving everything else.

1.3 COMPLETE 8F ASSESSMENT - THE DAILY FUEL (25 MINUTES)

These are your input behaviors—the eight daily practices you actually control. These behavioral inputs directly drive your 6D wellness outputs. Every data point matters for tracking your transformation journey. Record your current reality with complete honesty.

1. FAITH (Spiritual Practices & Disciplines): Daily prayer time: ___ actual minutes; Bible reading: ___ chapters/week; Church attendance: ___ times/month; Personal worship outside church: ___ times/week; Previous fasts completed: ___ days; Last spiritual breakthrough: ___ (days/months/years ago); Current spiritual mentor: Yes / No / Sporadic; Daily devotional consistency: Never / Sometimes / Usually / Always.

2. FASTING (Experience & Spiritual Discipline): Longest fast completed: ___ days; Current fasting practice: None / Occasional / Weekly / Monthly / Regular; Hunger management ability (1-10): ___; Previous spiritual breakthroughs during fasts: None / Some / Significant / Transformational; Reason previous fasts failed: _____; Confidence in completing 21 days (1-10): ___.

3. FITNESS (Physical Health & Energy): Current weight: ___ lbs; Goal weight: ___ lbs; Blood pressure: ___ / ___; Last checkup: ___; Average sleep: ___ hours/night; Sleep quality (1-10): ___; Wake refreshed: Rarely / Sometimes / Usually / Always; Weekly exercise: ___ minutes total, ___ sessions; Overall energy level (1-10): ___; Chronic conditions: _____ or None; Medications taken as prescribed: Yes / No / N/A / Sometimes.

4. FOOD (Nutritional Habits & Relationship with Food): Typical meals per day: ___; Meals skipped per week:___; Daily water: ___ glasses; Daily caffeine: ___ cups; Daily sugar: ___ servings; Emotional eating: Never / Rarely / Sometimes / Often / Daily; Food as comfort when stressed: Never / Sometimes / Usually / Always; Monthly food spending: $; Eating out: ___ times/week; Late night eating: Never / Rarely / Sometimes / Regularly.

5. FOCUS (Mental/Emotional Health & Clarity): Mental clarity on average day (1-10): ___; Daily stress level (1-10): ___; Anxiety episodes per week: ___; Panic attacks per month: ___; Depression symptoms (1-10): ___; Last discouraging day: ___; Professional mental health support: None / Past / Current / Needed; Therapy frequency: ___ times/month or None; Personal development time: ___ hours/week; Overthinking/ruminating: Rarely / Sometimes / Often / Constantly.

6. FINANCES (Economic Health & Stewardship): Monthly income: $; Monthly expenses: $; Total debt: $; Emergency savings: $; Financial stress level (1-10): ___; Tithing/giving percentage: ___%: Budget adherence: No budget / Rarely / Sometimes / Usually / Always; Financial arguments with spouse: Never / Rarely / Sometimes / Often / N/A; Money worries keep you awake: Never / Rarely / Sometimes / Often.

7. FELLOWSHIP (Relationships & Community): Marriage satisfaction (1-10): ___ or N/A; Last date night: ___; Family harmony with children (1-10): ___ or N/A; Close friends you could call in crisis: ___; Church community involvement: None / Attending / Serving / Leading; Forgiveness needed toward: ___ people (count them); Current accountability partner: Yes / No / Sort of; Loneliness frequency: Never / Rarely / Sometimes / Often / Always; Social media comparison struggle: Never / Sometimes / Often / Daily.

8. FUN (Joy, Recreation & Life Enjoyment): Overall life enjoyment (1-10): ___; Days since last deep belly laugh: ___; Weekly hobby/recreation time: ___ hours; Sabbath rest practiced: Never / Rarely / Sometimes / Weekly; Vacation days taken this year: ___; Days since last vacation: ___; Daily screen-free time: ___ hours; Creative outlets engaged: ___ (list: _____); Joy level around others (1-10): ___; When alone (1-10): ___.

TESTIMONY: THE 8F ASSESSMENT BREAKTHROUGH - "The 8F Assessment Exposed What I'd Been Blind To For 30 Years" - "When I answered 'Food as comfort when stressed: ALWAYS,' it hit me like a truck. I wasn't just fasting from meals—I was fasting from emotional eating that had controlled me since childhood. The 8F Assessment gave me language for what I'd been doing unconsciously for three decades. That one question unlocked everything. I realized why every diet failed. I wasn't addressing the root: I was using food to manage emotions I didn't know how to process. During the 21 days, I had to face anxiety without reaching for comfort food. It was brutal. But by Day 90, my relationship with food was completely transformed. I now eat FROM peace, not FOR peace. When stress hits, I pray instead of binge. That one assessment question changed everything." — Chayah Club Member

The 8F Assessment doesn't just measure behaviors—it exposes root patterns you've been blind to for years. Some discover emotional eating. Others uncover financial anxiety masquerading as stewardship. Still others realize their loneliness has been driving compromise. The power isn't in the questions themselves—it's in the Holy Spirit using honest answers to reveal what's been hidden. One member's discovery became delivery—a midwife-guided, surgical-level transformation.

TESTIMONY: WHEN THE MIDWIFE ARRIVED. "I entered the Daniel Fast carrying a purpose I couldn't birth alone—years of vision gestating without delivery. This time, I chose **I DECIDE**, opened my **SOAP** journal, and let God work as a divine surgeon. From a bed of recovery, He went deeper than I'd ever allowed—exposing fear, delay, and decades-old pain—and sutured me with truth. The tools became midwife instruments in His hands. **Week 1 (GROW)** rekindled intimacy with Jesus. **Week 2 (ALIGN)** stabilized identity—beloved first, assignment second. **Week 3 (PROPEL)** sparked holy contractions into courage and action. On Day 21 I prayed, "Father, what You placed in me is ready." On Day 22, the hidden moved into the open—ideas became steps, steps became testimony. This was not hype; it was healing. Not a diet, but delivery. I'm walking out of these 21 days anchored, aligned, and activated. With gratitude for faithful coaching that honored heaven's blueprint, I bless the hands that helped midwife this promise and decree abundant fruit over them. What God formed in secret, He has now brought to life."— Chayah Club VIP Member

1.4 SIX-DIMENSION WELLNESS ASSESSMENT - LIFE OUTCOMES (10 MINUTES)

Rate each dimension (1-10), then rank by priority (1-6) for transformation focus during your 21-day journey:

Dimension	Current Reality	Priority Rank	Specific Prayer Target
Spiritual - Maturity with God	___/10	___	
Mental - Clarity and health	___/10	___	
Emotional - Peace and stability	___/10	___	
Physical - Energy and vitality	___/10	___	
Financial - Provision and peace	___/10	___	
Relational - Connection and love	___/10	___	
TOTAL	___/60		

This measures how satisfied you are with life outcomes—the journey results. Primary battleground: _____ | Secondary focus: _____

1.5 UNDERSTANDING HOW YOUR ASSESSMENTS CONNECT (5 MINUTES)

You've completed three baseline assessments working together as your transformation dashboard. Assessment 1 (GAP Closure) measured where you are spiritually—your engine (/30 total). Assessment 2 (8F Input Behaviors) documented your current reality across eight behavioral areas you control—your fuel ingredients.

Assessment 3 (6D Life Transformation) captured your satisfaction across six life dimensions—your journey results (/60 total). During your 21 days, you'll document daily transformation through SOAP journaling (detailed in Stage 2). On Day 22, you'll complete all three assessments again: GAP Closure comparison (Day 1 vs. Day 22 = measure spiritual engine repair), 6D comparison (Day 1 vs. Day 22 = measure comprehensive life impact), and 8F behavioral comparison (before/after = measure habit transformation). This creates documented proof of transformation—not vague feelings but measurable results.

TRANSFORMATION TRACKING OPTIONS: Save baseline numbers in three places: Photo on phone labeled "Baseline [date]"; Written in journal; Posted in Chayah Club for accountability. As a Chayah Club member, complete the full assessment online at danielfastclub.com where your data is saved automatically for future comparison, analyzed for trends, used to generate personalized recommendations, and integrated with community support features.

REASSESSMENT SCHEDULE: Day 22: Reassess GAP and 6D scores, compare to Day 1; Day 30: Use 8F to set specific lifestyle goals; Day 90: Complete full assessment for sustained transformation; Quarterly: Track ongoing progress, adjust 8F inputs.

1.6 FALSE IDENTITY INVENTORY & KINGDOM TRUTH DECLARATION (10 MINUTES)

You might be tempted to skip this part. Don't. This is where transformation begins. Check all false identities you've believed: "I'm too broken to be used by God significantly"; "I always fail at spiritual disciplines when it gets hard"; "People like me don't get the breakthroughs I see others experience"; "I'm not disciplined enough for sustained spiritual growth"; "My past mistakes disqualify my future calling"; "I'm too old/young to start something new with God"; "I don't have what it takes for leadership/influence"; "I'm not smart/educated/gifted enough for Kingdom impact"; "God has forgotten about me"; "I'm behind schedule for my destiny."

KINGDOM IDENTITY DECLARATION: For your top three false identities, declare God's truth: (1) I am not _____, I am CHOSEN "according to the foreknowledge of God the Father" — 1 Peter 1:2. (2) I am not _____, I am CALLED "to be conformed to the image of His Son" — Romans 8:29. (3) I am not _____, I am CROWNED "and have made us kings and priests to our God" — Revelation 5:10.

1.7 BUILD YOUR COMPLETE IDENTITY DECLARATION

"I IDENTIFY: Though the world calls me _____, God calls me _____"

IDENTITY REALIGNMENT PRAYER: "Father, I confront every distortion and reclaim my true identity in You. I reject every label Babylon has tried to place on me—every name that contradicts Your Word over my life. Like Daniel in Babylon, I may be in exile but I am not abandoned. I may be renamed by culture but I am defined by Kingdom. I may be surrounded by compromise but I am sustained by consecration. I am who You say I am—chosen before time, beloved beyond measure, redeemed for purpose, destined for greatness. Let this truth become more real to me than any lie I've believed. In Jesus' name, Amen."

Identity clarity enables covenant decision-making. When you know who you are, you can decide what you'll accept and what you'll reject. With your identity reclaimed and baseline established, you're ready to make the irreversible decision that transforms hope into commitment. **STEP 1 COMPLETE → Move to Step 2**

STEP 2: D - DECIDE (Covenant Clarity)

"Say 'yes' with no Plan B"

Time Required: 30-45 minutes | **Objective:** Establish irreversible commitment that eliminates all exit strategies | **Babylon Tactic Countered:** Compromise patterns through half-hearted commitment

THE TRANSFORMATION JOURNEY

Important Note: This covenant commitment is about your transformation journey—what you're leaving behind and moving toward. The fasting method itself remains flexible to your health needs. Modifying food choices for medical reasons isn't breaking commitment; it's wisdom.

THE POWER OF IRREVERSIBLE DECISION

Daniel didn't casually "try" a fast to see how it went. He resolved in his heart with the kind of decision that shapes destiny. That Hebrew word śûm [soom] means permanently fixed, like stars in the heavens. In Babylon, Daniel faced the ultimate test of divided loyalty. The food wasn't just food—it was first offered to Babylonian gods. Every meal was an act of worship. Daniel chose covenant over comfort, consecration over compromise. His resolve determined his destiny. That single decision became the foundation for every miracle that followed. Destiny isn't found in tentative attempts. It's forged in irreversible decisions. Your turn.

MY 3 AM KITCHEN TABLE COVENANT

During my darkest season—surrounded by divorce papers, medical bills from the breakdown, and bank statements showing feast-or-famine cycles—I was drowning in relentless failure. At 3 AM, broken and alone at my kitchen table, tears mixing with cold coffee, I made the irreversible decision that would change everything: "God, I'm done with toxic relationships that steal my purity and casual Christianity that produces casual results. No Plan B. No exit strategy. No safety net but You." That wasn't desperation—it was strategic positioning for the supernatural. The moment you eliminate Plan B, Heaven activates Plan A. This fast isn't about rigid menus—it's about ruthless mercy on what's been killing you. You're fasting OUT OF addiction patterns, broken relationships, spiritual stagnation, shame, fear, self-sabotage. You're fasting INTO new life, new creation, new beginnings, freedom, presence, purpose. Bags packed. Bridges burned. You leave Egypt's chains and defy Babylon's seductions. Your appetite bows and your allegiance shifts. No more escape routes, no more halfway measures. This is your Exodus.

ACTION STEPS

2.1 CLARIFY YOUR COVENANT WHY (8 MINUTES)

Three non-negotiable reasons—the "why" so compelling that quitting becomes impossible. Not surface reasons like "lose weight" but soul reasons like "I refuse to die with my calling still inside me."

(1) _____

(2) _____

(3) _____

ONE-SENTENCE DECLARATION: "I commit to this 21-day Daniel Fast because _____"

2.2 CREATE YOUR PERSONAL VISION STATEMENT (8 MINUTES)

"By Day 22, I will be someone who _____ because God has transformed me into _____"

2.3 WRITE YOUR SACRED VOW (8 MINUTES)

"I vow before Heaven and earth that I will _____ even when _____ because my transformation is worth _____"

2.4 THE PLAN B FUNERAL (5 MINUTES)

Write and eliminate escape routes: Plan B: _____ DECEASED [date]; Plan C: _____ DECEASED [date]; Safety net: _____ DECEASED [date]

2.5 SECURE YOUR ACCOUNTABILITY NETWORK (8 MINUTES)

Prayer warrior: _____; Wisdom partner: _____; Daily accountability: _____

SEND THIS MESSAGE NOW: "I'm preparing for a 21-day Daniel Fast starting [date]. This isn't casual—it's covenant. I need you to hold me accountable to finish what I'm starting." Don't proceed until you've received confirmation from all three.

2.6 NAVIGATE HOUSEHOLD AND SOCIAL DYNAMICS (5 MINUTES)

Pre-decide your responses for social situations: When family asks why you're not eating their food: "I'm in a 21-day consecration season with God. I'm only eating plant-based foods during this time. It's not about your cooking—it's about my calling." When coworkers pressure you to join lunch outings: "I'm doing a Daniel Fast for 21 days. I'll still come along for the fellowship if you want, or I'll catch up with you afterward." When friends mock your "extreme" commitment: "I hear you. This might seem intense from the outside. For me, it's about closing some significant spiritual gaps." When extended family expects exceptions for special occasions: "I know this celebration is important. I'll be there to honor you and enjoy the fellowship. I'm bringing my own food, and that's not a statement about your hosting—it's about a covenant I made with God that I'm not breaking for any circumstance."

2.7 BUILD YOUR DECISION DECLARATION

"I DECIDE: I resolve to _____ because _____"

COVENANT CONFIRMATION PRAYER: "Father, I resolve with no Plan B, just like Daniel purposed in his heart. This decision is permanent—written in Heaven's courts, sealed by Your Spirit. I'm not trying this. I'm doing this. I'm positioned for transformation. Seal this decision with Your Spirit. Let my yes be yes and my resolve be unshakeable. In Jesus' name, Amen."

You can't walk on water with one foot on the boat. With covenant clarity established, it's time to align every appetite toward transformation rather than sabotage. **STEP 2 COMPLETE → Move to Step 3**

STEP 3: E - EQUIP (Appetite Alignment)

"What you feed grows; what you starve dies—in every dimension"

Time Required: 30-40 minutes | **Objective:** Align every appetite to support rather than sabotage transformation | **Babylon Tactic Countered:** Appetite control through intentional consecration

THE BATTLE FOR YOUR APPETITES

Daniel's decision about the king's food was about devotional alignment. Every delicacy was first offered to Babylonian idols. To eat was to participate in idol worship. Daniel understood: your appetites will either feed your calling or fuel your captivity. What you hunger for determines what you become. This principle operates in every dimension—spiritual, emotional, mental, physical, financial, and relational. Fasting is strategic appetite alignment that declares: "My spirit leads, my soul follows, my body serves." Your transformation is hidden in what you're willing to starve.

ACTION STEPS

3.1 DEFINE YOUR COMPLETE HYBRID FASTING PLAN (8 MINUTES)

THE HYBRID FASTING TYPE™ - A Revolutionary 3-Dimensional Approach for Total Consecration

This hybrid fast combines three dimensions to maximize spiritual transformation while maintaining physical health and mental clarity. You're not just abstaining from food—you're creating comprehensive sacred space for God.

DIMENSION 1: FOOD FAST (Daniel Fast Plant-Based) - What do I eat?

EAT FREELY	AVOID COMPLETELY
All fruits & vegetables	All meat, poultry, fish
Whole grains (rice, oats, quinoa)	All dairy products
Beans & legumes	All eggs
Nuts & seeds	All sugar & sweeteners
Plant oils (olive, coconut)	All coffee & caffeine
Herbal teas	All alcohol

Golden rule: God grew it = eat it. Man made it = avoid it.

DIMENSION 2: INTERMITTENT FASTING (Choose Your Eating Window) - When do I eat? Select your fasting/eating pattern: 14:10 (fast 14 hours, eat 10 hours): _____ AM to _____ PM; 16:8 (fast 16 hours, eat 8 hours): _____ AM to _____ PM; 18:6 (fast 18 hours, eat 6 hours): _____ AM to _____ PM; 20:4 (fast 20 hours, eat 4 hours): _____ PM to _____ PM; OMAD (one meal a day): Meal time: _____ PM; Traditional (3 meals, no IF): Breakfast, Lunch, Dinner. Which meals will you skip? _____.
First meal time: _____ Last meal time: _____

DIMENSION 3: SOUL FAST (Non-Food Consecration) - What else am I fasting? What will you abstain from for 21 days to create space for God? Social media (specify platforms): _____; Entertainment (TV/streaming/gaming): _____; News/political content: _____; Secular music: _____; Shopping (non-essential): _____; Negative conversations/gossip: _____; Other: _____

WHY ALL 3 DIMENSIONS MATTER: Biblical foundation - Daniel's fast was comprehensive; Scientific support - IF enhances mental clarity; Modern application - Soul fasting addresses digital age; Multiplication effect - Each dimension amplifies the others.

MY COMPLETE HYBRID FAST DECLARATION: "For 21 days, I will eat only Daniel Fast plant-based foods within my ___-hour eating window, while fasting from _____ to create sacred space for encounter with God."

USING YOUR 8F BASELINE TO DESIGN YOUR HYBRID FAST

Pull out your 8F Assessment from Step 1. Your current reality informs how you design your fast for maximum transformation with minimum unnecessary suffering.

THE DANIEL FAST: CLOSING THE GAP!

IF 8F SHOWED:	DESIGN FAST THIS WAY:
High emotional eating or food-as-comfort	Be extra intentional about Soul Fast. What non-food comforts manage stress? Social media? Binge-watching? Those need consecration too. Can't remove food comfort without replacing it—you'll break when stress hits.
Low fasting confidence or previous failures	Choose sustainable IF window initially. Start with 16:8 or Traditional rather than OMAD. Build confidence through completion, not maximum difficulty.
Poor sleep or high caffeine dependence	Follow Strategic Caffeine Withdrawal Plan religiously. Don't start drinking 5 cups daily—you'll mistake withdrawal for spiritual attack and quit by Day 4.

Use your 8F data to design a Hybrid Fast that addresses YOUR actual patterns, not someone else's ideal. Sustainable completion beats unsustainable performance every time.

3.2 STRATEGIC CAFFEINE WITHDRAWAL PLAN (3 MINUTES)

Current daily caffeine intake: ____ cups

Your Usage Level	Withdrawal Strategy
Heavy users (5+ cups)	Reduce 25% every 2 days over 8 days
Moderate users (2-4 cups)	Cut by half, then eliminate over 4 days
Light users (1-2 cups)	Eliminate 2 days before starting

MANAGING CAFFEINE WITHDRAWAL: Expect headaches Days 2-4 (this is detox, not defeat); Drink extra water to flush system; Rest more during withdrawal period; Use peppermint oil on temples for headache relief. Coffee withdrawal isn't spiritual warfare. It's chemical reality. Know the difference.

3.3 CREATE YOUR 21-DAY MEAL PLANNING STRATEGY (8 MINUTES)

Create one week of proven meals to rotate throughout your fast.

SAMPLE DANIEL FAST DAY:

Meal	Option 1	Option 2
Breakfast	Green smoothie with almond milk	Overnight oats with berries
Lunch	Mediterranean chickpea bowl	Lentil soup with whole grain bread
Snack	Apple with almond butter	Hummus with vegetables
Dinner	Curried lentils with cauliflower rice	Vegetable stir-fry with quinoa
Evening	Dates with nuts	Frozen banana "nice cream"

ACTION STEPS: Research plant-based recipes at danielfastclub.com; Choose meals based on your fasting window; Build shopping list from chosen recipes; Check all labels for compliance; Batch prep on Sundays and Wednesdays. Keep meals simple—a bowl of oatmeal with fruit is perfectly acceptable. Don't let meal complexity become your excuse to quit.

3.4 COMPLETE KITCHEN PREPARATION CHECKLIST (3 MINUTES)

This is where most people quit preparing. You're not most people. Remove tempting foods (opaque containers, basement storage, or donate); Stock Daniel foods at eye level in refrigerator and pantry; Clear counters for easy prep; Post "why" statement visibly on refrigerator; Stock emergency snacks (dates, nuts, cut vegetables in grab-and-go containers).

3.5 SOUL APPETITE ALIGNMENT MATRIX (5 MINUTES)

Identify what you're currently feeding versus what you'll feed during your fast.

Currently Feeding	Will Feed During Fast

3.6 BUILD YOUR EQUIP DECLARATION

"I EQUIP: I will not feed _____ but will feed _____"

APPETITE ALIGNMENT PRAYER: "Father, I consecrate every appetite to serve Your purposes. Train my desires to hunger for what You hunger for. Let my physical discipline create spiritual sensitivity. Every appetite bows to Your Lordship. Every craving submits to Your Spirit. In Jesus' name, Amen."

With every appetite aligned toward purpose, create the physical and spiritual spaces that support consecration. **STEP 3 COMPLETE → Move to Step 4**

STEP 4: C - CREATE (Environment of Encounter)

"Clear the rubble. Build the altar"

Time Required: 20-30 minutes | **Objective:** Design spaces that invite God's presence | **Babylon Tactic Countered:** Chaotic atmosphere through sacred space creation

ATMOSPHERE SHAPES OUTCOMES

Daniel's open-window prayer room wasn't just religious routine—it was prophetic declaration. In Babylon's chaos, he created sacred order for intimate relationship. Your environment is always discipling you. Every space is teaching you something. The question is: what is it teaching? Make your environment disciple you toward destiny.

ACTION STEPS

4.1 CLEAR YOUR PHYSICAL RUBBLE (12 MINUTES)

KITCHEN TRANSFORMATION - Transform your kitchen into a consecration station, not a temptation trap. YOUR KITCHEN CHECKLIST: Remove all non-Daniel Fast foods from sight; Stock approved foods at eye level in refrigerator and pantry; Clear counters of everything except meal prep tools; Post your "why" statement visibly on refrigerator; Pre-portion emergency snacks in grab-and-go containers; Create dedicated 21-day corner with SOAP Journal, Bible, pen; Post daily GAP Strategy theme calendar where you'll see it; Display accountability partner's contact for quick crisis calls.

SACRED PRAYER SPACE SETUP - Create an embassy of Heaven in your home. YOUR PRAYER SPACE CHECKLIST: Choose one specific spot (not bed, not couch—a designated chair/corner); Keep Bible, journal, worship music in this exact spot (zero friction to begin); Add candle if helpful to mark space as set apart;

Place small table/surface nearby for writing during SOAP time; Remove all distractions (silence phone, turn off TV); Post Scripture declarations on wall you'll face during prayer.

4.2 CLEAR YOUR DIGITAL RUBBLE (8 MINUTES)

Turn your phone into a prayer tool, not a distraction device. YOUR DIGITAL DECLUTTER CHECKLIST: Delete or hide social media apps you're fasting from; Change lock screen to display your "why" statement or key Scripture; Set 3 daily alarms labeled "Prayer Government Time" with Scripture text; Create "Daniel Fast 21 Days" worship playlist; Add danielfastclub.com and chayah.club to home screen as web app icons; Unsubscribe from promotional emails triggering shopping appetites; Turn off all non-essential notifications; Create "Fast Tools" folder: Bible app, danielfastclub.com, chayah.club, worship, journal, accountability contact marked as favorite.

4.3 BUILD YOUR ENVIRONMENT DECLARATION

"I CREATE: I create space for God by removing _____ and adding _____"

SACRED SPACE CONSECRATION PRAYER: "Father, I consecrate every environment to become a place of encounter with You. Let Your presence be evident in my spaces. Transform my environment from chaotic to sacred. In Jesus' name, Amen."

With sacred spaces established, prepare strategic responses for the predictable challenges ahead. **STEP 4 COMPLETE → Move to Step 5**

STEP 5: I - IMPLEMENT (Strategy & Timing)

"Delay doesn't equal denial. Wait well"

Time Required: 25-35 minutes | **Objective:** Prepare strategic responses for predictable challenges | **Babylon Tactic Countered:** Unprepared responses through intentional protocols

THE GAP BETWEEN PROMISE AND PROVISION

Daniel's prayers were heard on day one, yet victory arrived day twenty-one. *"Then he said to me, 'Do not fear, Daniel, for from the first day that you set your heart to understand, and to humble yourself before your God, your words were heard; and I have come because of your words. But the prince of the kingdom of Persia withstood me twenty-one days.'"* — Daniel 10:12-13. Twenty days of warfare in the unseen realm between promise and provision. Your fast will have "gap moments"—days when you see no change and want to quit. That's where strategy separates finishers from failers. The gap between promise and provision is where character is formed.

ACTION STEPS

5.1 YOUR COMPLETE 21-DAY GAP STRATEGY JOURNEY MAP (12 MINUTES)

UNDERSTANDING THE GAP STRATEGY FRAMEWORK - GAP = Grow (Intimacy) → Align (Identity) → Propel (Destiny). This isn't random. This is the intentional pathway to closing every gap between where you are spiritually and where God is calling you. You can't align with identity you don't yet have intimacy to discover. You can't activate purpose until identity is secure. The sequence matters. In Step 1.2, you rated yourself on intimacy, identity, and purpose. The three weeks ahead strategically address each dimension through progressive revelation. Your transformation will be documented daily through SOAP journaling, with Day 22 comparison showing measurable growth from your baseline. Each week has seven themes—21 total across three weeks: Week 1 features seven "G" themes revealing God's character (GROW intimacy), Week 2 presents seven "A" themes establishing your true identity (ALIGN identity), Week 3 activates seven "P" themes catalyzing Kingdom assignments (PROPEL purpose).

THE 21 THEMES: YOUR PROGRESSIVE REVELATION

Day	WEEK 1: GROW (Intimacy) Whose You Are	WEEK 2: ALIGN (Identity) Who You Are	WEEK 3: PROPEL (Purpose) Why You are
1	GOSPEL - Good news changes everything	ADOPTION - Chosen, wanted, placed	PRESENCE - Carry His presence everywhere
2	GRACE - Unearned, unstoppable favor	ABUNDANCE - Living from fullness	PROTECTION - Shield, fortress, defender
3	GOODNESS - Benevolent nature toward you	AUTHORITY - Carry Kingdom power	PEACE - Shalom guards your heart
4	GIFTS - Holy Spirit empowerment	ANOINTING - Holy Spirit rests on you	PROVISION - Supplies every need
5	GLADNESS - Joy as your strength	ADVANCEMENT - Moving forward	PROMOTION - God exalts in His timing
6	GREATNESS - Incomparable majesty	ATTRIBUTES - His nature in you	PROSPERITY - Wholeness: spirit, mind, body
7	GLORY - Manifest presence in life	AFFIRMATION - His approval over you	PURPOSE - Kingdom significance

Week 1: You can't love who you don't know. Seven facets of God's character create foundation for intimacy that drives all transformation. Week 2: With God's character established, focus shifts to who you are because of who He is. Identity stops being defined by performance, past, or people's opinions. Week 3: With intimacy established and identity solidified, Kingdom assignments activate with clarity, courage, and divine backing.

WHAT TO EXPECT: YOUR 21-DAY BATTLE PLAN

Week	Physical	Spiritual	Emotional	Strategic Response
1. GROW (Days 1-7)	Days 1-3: Caffeine withdrawal, hunger peaks, detox headaches. Days 5-7: Symptoms subside, clarity emerges	Encountering God's character through daily themes. SOAP observations move from head knowledge to heart encounter.	Early enthusiasm → "what did I sign up for?" → breakthrough by Day 7. Irritability from hunger and withdrawal is normal.	Text prayer warrior daily. Use V.I.C.T.O.R.Y. Protocol when cravings hit. Read Day 7 encouragement letter. Celebrate Week 1 completion.

2: ALIGN (Days 8-14)	Days 8-11: Body adapted, energy stable. Days 12-14: Warfare peak (not physical—spiritual). Clarity increasing.	Identity truths becoming personal reality. SOAP applications shift from "I'll try" to "I AM"—living FROM identity, not FOR identity.	Days 12-14: Old wounds surface, lies exposed, healing breaks through. Statistically hardest period. By Day 14, emotional freedom emerges.	Prepare for Days 12-14 specifically. Call accountability partner immediately if struggling. Double down on SOAP vulnerability. Too far to quit, close enough to finish.
3: PROPEL (Days 15-21)	Body fully adapted. Energy often exceeds pre-fast levels. Physical healing may manifest. Mental clarity at peak.	Kingdom assignments activating. SOAP prayers shift from asking to declaring—speaking victory in present tense, not future hope.	Emotional stability unprecedented. Clarity about relationships, decisions, direction. Confidence in calling. Joy and peace that pass understanding.	Don't coast—Week 3 is acceleration. Document everything (prophetic direction for years). Plan Day 22 celebration. Read Day 21 letter.

Your 21-day journey isn't linear—it's exponential. Week 1 builds foundation. Week 2 establishes identity. Week 3 activates everything. These aren't devotional thoughts—they're transcendent breakthrough chapters designed to be repeated in subsequent fasts or whenever you need revelation refreshed. By Day 21, the cumulative freedom positions you for lifelong transformation. This is strategic spiritual warfare. You're not hoping for victory—you're strategically positioned for it through progressive revelation across 21 themes that build intentionally on each other.

5.2 PREPARE YOUR V.I.C.T.O.R.Y. PROTOCOL™ (10 MINUTES)

When challenges arise: V - Voice it honestly | I - Interrupt location | C - Call accountability | T - Turn to Scripture | O - Override flesh | R - Remember why | Y - Yield gratitude

WRITE OUT YOUR PERSONALIZED V.I.C.T.O.R.Y. PROTOCOL: When I want to quit,
I will voice it by: _____;
I will interrupt location by: _____;
I will call accountability using: _____ (name and number);
I will turn to Scripture by declaring: _____ (specific verse);
I will override flesh by: _____;
I will remember why by: _____;
I will yield gratitude for: _____

USING YOUR 8F TO CUSTOMIZE V.I.C.T.O.R.Y. - Pull out your 8F Assessment from Step 1. Your baseline behaviors reveal which strategies work best for your unique patterns.

IF 8F SHOWED:	EMPHASIZE IN V.I.C.T.O.R.Y.:
High stress or overthinking	"Interrupt location" + "Turn to Scripture" strongly. Physical movement + spoken Scripture breaks thought spirals.
Loneliness or no accountability	Activate Step 6 community intensively. Completing alone with isolation baseline = Day 12-14 failure. Double down on check-ins.
Low joy or no sabbath	Soul Fast must ADD joy practices, not just remove entertainment. Fast FROM screens INTO worship, nature, creativity.

5.3 PRE-WRITTEN SCRIPTURE RESPONSES (5 MINUTES)

Memorize these verses for crisis moments:

CRISIS	SCRIPTURE
Physical exhaustion	"But those who wait on the LORD shall renew their strength; they shall mount up with wings like eagles, they shall run and not be weary, they shall walk and not faint" — Isa 40:31
Temptation to quit	"No temptation has overtaken you except such as is common to man; but God is faithful, who will not allow you to be tempted beyond what you are able, but with the temptation will also make the way of escape, that you may be able to bear it" — 1 Cor 10:13
Identity warfare	"Just as He chose us in Him before the foundation of the world, that we should be holy and without blame before Him in love" — Eph 1:4
Purpose clarity	"For I know the thoughts that I think toward you, says the LORD, thoughts of peace and not of evil, to give you a future and a hope" — Jer 29:11
Spiritual attack	"Therefore submit to God. Resist the devil and he will flee from you" — James 4:7

5.4 WRITE FUTURE ENCOURAGEMENT LETTERS (8 MINUTES)

Write to yourself for Days 7, 14, and 21. These letters will arrive when you need them most.

DAY 7 LETTER: "Dear Day 7 Me, You're reading this because it's hard right now. The physical adjustment is real. But remember why you started: [reference your WHY from Step 2]. You've already conquered 6 days—that's 144 hours of victory. The worst physical symptoms will pass by Day 10. Keep going."

DAY 14 LETTER: "Dear Day 14 Me, You're in the middle now—too far to quit, not close enough to see the end. This is where most people fail. But you're not most people. You prepared strategically. You have support. Remember: [reference your covenant from Step 2]. You've already conquered 13 days. You're stronger than you knew. Week 3 brings acceleration."

DAY 21 LETTER: "Dear Day 21 Me, You did it. What seemed impossible on Day 1 is now your testimony. Document everything you're feeling, seeing, experiencing. This transformation is just the beginning. Tomorrow you become someone who completed what most only attempt."

5.5 BUILD YOUR IMPLEMENTATION DECLARATION

"I IMPLEMENT: When I want to quit, I will _____ instead"

STRATEGIC ENDURANCE PRAYER: "Father, I trust Your timing even when I can't see Your working. Delay doesn't mean denial. Give me supernatural endurance to wait well and fight smart. In Jesus' name, Amen."

Strategic responses prepared. Now activate the community systems that multiply your capacity exponentially. **STEP 5 COMPLETE → Move to Step 6**

THE DANIEL FAST: CLOSING THE GAP!

STEP 6: D - DEPLOY (Community Systems)

"Victory is never a solo battle"

Time Required: 20-30 minutes | **Objective:** Activate support systems that multiply capacity | **Babylon Tactic Countered:** Isolated struggle through community accountability

DANIEL NEVER STOOD ALONE

Daniel had Hananiah, Mishael, and Azariah. Together they stood. Together they conquered. Isolation is Babylon's greatest weapon. Community is Heaven's answer. Your accountability network is your advancement network. *"Two are better than one, because they have a good return for their labor. For if they fall, one will lift up his companion. But woe to him who is alone when he falls, for he has no one to help him up."* — Ecclesiastes 4:9-10.

ACTION STEPS

6.1 DEPLOY YOUR PERSONAL PRAYER GOVERNMENT (8 MINUTES)

Set three daily prayer alarms—consistency matters more than duration. Your Personal Prayer Government establishes spiritual authority and jurisdiction over your day. Like Daniel's three daily appointments, these consistent prayer times create an unshakeable governance structure that hell cannot overthrow. Even facing the lions' den, Daniel maintained his prayer government. These aren't just prayer times—they're declarations of who rules your day, appointments with Heaven that supersede earth's demands, and spiritual infrastructure that sustains transformation.

YOUR PRAYER GOVERNMENT:

TIME	SET TIME	LOCATION	FOCUS
Morning (before demands)	_____ AM	_____	Command day, surrender agenda, declare victory
Midday (when compromise tempts)	_____ PM	_____	Realign with Heaven, interrupt temptation, reset
Evening (gratitude/preparation)	_____ PM	_____	Close in His presence, gratitude, prepare tomorrow

6.2 JOIN YOUR CHAYAH CLUB COMMUNITIES (5 MINUTES)

You need both spiritual support and practical guidance to complete 21 days successfully. **YOUR COMMUNITY HUB:** danielfastclub.com - This one link gives you instant access to Chayah Club: Daniel Fast Tribe (spiritual community); Daniel Diet Cafe (practical community); Complete SOAP Journal guide; Community engagement strategy; Spiritual warfare prayers; Digital SOAP Journal form; Live prayer call schedules; All resources for your 21-day journey. Bookmark danielfastclub.com on your phone's home screen for one-tap access throughout your fast.

YOUR TWO COMMUNITIES:

DANIEL FAST TRIBE (chayah.club/groups/daniel-fast/) - Spiritual Support: Prayer, devotionals, freedom. Your First Actions: Introduce yourself: "Starting Day 1 on [date]. Believing for [primary prayer target from Step 1]."; Read today's devotional that aligns with your GAP Strategy theme; Share one specific prayer request for your 21-day journey.

DANIEL DIET CAFE (chayah.club/groups/the-daniel-diet-cafe/) - Practical Guidance: Recipes, meal planning, food help. Your First Actions: Browse or share plant-based meal ideas for your fast; Ask one food question or share one recipe for Week 1; Post your Hybrid Fast plan from Step 3 for feedback.

6.3 ACTIVATE YOUR ACCOUNTABILITY NETWORK (12 MINUTES)

You identified three support people in Step 2. Now activate them with specific roles and expectations. SEND THESE MESSAGES RIGHT NOW (Don't proceed until confirmed):

TO YOUR PRAYER WARRIOR: "I'm starting my 21-day Daniel Fast on [date]. I need you to pray for me daily, especially Days 3-4 (physical adjustment), Days 12-14 (spiritual warfare), and Day 21 (finish strong). Can I text you when warfare intensifies? Will you check on me if you don't hear from me for two days?" Wait for confirmation: Confirmed

TO YOUR WISDOM PARTNER: "I'm starting a 21-day Daniel Fast on [date]. You've been through this before. Can I call you when I hit obstacles you've already overcome? I need your experience to guide me through predictable struggles." Wait for confirmation: Confirmed

TO YOUR DAILY ACCOUNTABILITY PERSON: "Starting 21-day Daniel Fast on [date]. Can we commit to daily check-ins via text? Just a quick 'Day X complete' message each evening so we know we're both still standing strong. Days when either of us wants to quit, we'll call instead of text. Are you in?" Wait for confirmation: Confirmed

6.4 YOUR DAILY COMMUNITY ENGAGEMENT STRATEGY (5 MINUTES)

Minimum daily engagement: 5-10 minutes total. This increases your completion rate from 37% to 91%.

When	What	Time
Morning (3-5 min)	After SOAP Journal: Open Daniel Fast Tribe, read today's devotional, post one comment/prayer request/testimony	3-5 min
Midday/Evening (2-5 min)	Open Daniel Diet Cafe, browse/share meal ideas, ask/answer food question, encourage someone	2-5 min
Before Bed (30 sec)	Text accountability partner: "Day ___ complete. How's yours?"	30 sec

The data proves it: Isolation kills fasts, community completes them.

6.5 EMERGENCY SUPPORT PROTOCOL (3 MINUTES)

When you're about to quit (especially Days 3-4 or 12-14), implement immediately: 1st: Call (don't text) your accountability partner—voice-to-voice breaks isolation faster; 2nd: Post in Daniel Fast Tribe immediately: "Day ___ is brutal. Need prayer NOW." Your vulnerability gives others permission to be vulnerable too; 3rd: Read testimonies from people who survived your current day by searching Tribe for "Day 3" or "Day 12"; 4th: Use your V.I.C.T.O.R.Y. Protocol from Step 5. Do not isolate when struggling. Isolation is Babylon's weapon. Community is Heaven's answer.

6.6 BUILD YOUR DEPLOYMENT DECLARATION

"I DEPLOY: I activate _____ to sustain _____"

COMMUNITY ACTIVATION PRAYER: "Father, I deploy every system You've provided for my success. Surround me with people who will call me higher. I refuse to attempt this transformation alone. In Jesus' name, Amen."

THE DANIEL FAST: CLOSING THE GAP!

Community deployed. Support activated. Now complete your spiritual consecration and prophetic commissioning. **STEP 6 COMPLETE → Move to Step 7**

STEP 7: E - ENGAGE (Devotion & Commissioning)

"Set apart for service. Break through in power"

Time Required: 30-45 minutes | **Objective:** Complete spiritual consecration and prophetic commissioning | **Babylon Tactic Countered:** Conditional devotion through unconditional consecration

DEVOTION WITHOUT CONDITIONS

This is where preparation becomes consecration. Daniel prayed three times daily whether legal or illegal. His friends declared: "Our God can deliver us, but even if He doesn't, we won't bow." Fasting puts your faith on steroids. It amplifies what you believe, intensifies your hunger for God, and accelerates spiritual freedom. When you combine fasting with faith, supernatural things happen. *"However, this kind does not go out except by prayer and fasting."* — *Matthew 17:21*. Jesus modeled the ultimate surrender in Gethsemane: *"Nevertheless, not My will, but Yours, be done."* — *Luke 22:42*. This "nevertheless faith" doesn't depend on outcomes matching expectations. It worships regardless of results. Even-if faith and nevertheless faith are the highest worship. They declare: "Even if the victory looks different than I imagined, even if the timing isn't what I expected, even if You don't answer the way I want, nevertheless I will trust You, worship You, obey You." This unconditional devotion is what separates religious performance from radical surrender.

ACTION STEPS

7.1 COMPLETE SPIRITUAL CLEANSING AND SALVATION ASSURANCE (10 MINUTES)

FOUNDATION CHECK: If you've never accepted Jesus as Lord and Savior, pray: "Lord Jesus, I confess I'm a sinner needing salvation. I believe You died for my sins and rose again. I receive You as my Lord and Savior. Create in me a clean heart. Amen."

FORGIVENESS CLEANSING: Shift from Crisis to Calling to Commissioning—"The setback was only a setup for comeback!" Choose to forgive and to love for freedom. Unforgiveness blocks; forgiveness unlocks. Pray: "Lord, let nothing block my transformation—break every generational curse, cycle, chain, and captivity in Jesus' name." Ask God for forgiveness and receive His love. Receive His forgiveness, then choose to forgive and love yourself. Declare over each name: "I release you from the debt you owe me." List those you need to forgive— even without an apology: (1) _____ (2)_____ (3)_____ (4)_____ (yourself)

COMMISSIONING PRAYER: "Lord, through this consecration, help me to live a life that glorifies You as You transform me, make me, mold me, and send me to go make nations and always remember that You are with me always."

7.2 BUILD YOUR COMPLETE ENGAGEMENT DECLARATION (5 MINUTES)

"I ENGAGE: My prayer shifts from _____ to _____"

7.3 SIGN YOUR COMPLETE I DECIDE COVENANT (8 MINUTES)

MY I DECIDE COVENANT - Signed before Heaven and witnessed on earth

I IDENTIFY: Though the world calls me _____, God calls me _____

I DECIDE: I resolve to _____ because _____

I EQUIP: I will not feed _____ but will feed _____
I CREATE: I remove _____ and add _____
I IMPLEMENT: When I want to quit, I will _____ instead
I DEPLOY: I activate _____ to sustain _____
I ENGAGE: My prayer shifts from _____ to _____

"Do not fear, Daniel, for from the first day that you set your heart to understand, and to humble yourself before your God, your words were heard." — Daniel 10:12

Signature: _____ Date: _____ | Witness: _____

7.4 DOCUMENT YOUR STARTING POINT FOR TESTIMONY (5 MINUTES)
Take photos, record baseline, post to social media with #IDECIDE #DanielFastGAP #ChayahClub

7.5 COMPLETE CONSECRATION SERVICE (15 MINUTES)
Worship → Communion (if available) → Anoint (oil if available) → Declaration → Consecration

YOU'VE DISMANTLED BABYLON'S STRATEGY

Remember Babylon's five-phase strategy from the beginning? You haven't just learned about it—you've methodically dismantled each phase through I DECIDE preparation: Phase 1: They captured the young → You IDENTIFIED your true identity and rejected every false label; Phase 2: They isolated the strong → You DEPLOYED community systems that multiply your capacity; Phase 3: They renamed the chosen → You DECIDED with covenant clarity that eliminates all compromise; Phase 4: They reprogrammed consumption → You EQUIPPED every appetite to serve your purpose; Phase 5: They demanded compromise → You just ENGAGED with unconditional consecration.

You didn't just read about Daniel's resistance. You've prepared for your own. You didn't just admire his resolve from a distance. You've built the same foundation that sustained him through lions' dens and fiery furnaces. Like Daniel, you've purposed in your heart. Like Shadrach, Meshach, and Abednego, you're declaring "even if He doesn't, we will not bow." Like those who came before you, you understand that your preparation is your resistance and your consecration is your revolution. Babylon doesn't write your final chapter. You're about to sign your covenant before Heaven and commission yourself into the battle you were born to win.

BATTLE-READY DANIEL FAST DECLARATION: "Father, thank You for calling me to this consecration—not as a diet, but as holy warfare. This is my taking a stand. This is my I DECIDE moment. Like Daniel in Babylon, I choose consecration over compromise. Like his friends before the furnace, You can deliver me, but even if You don't, I will not bow. No weapon formed against me will prosper. The Prince of Persia may try to delay, but Michael fights for me. Even if victory looks different than expected, I will not compromise. I am ready. I am positioned. I am consecrated for victory. In the mighty name of Jesus—Amen!"

CONSECRATION AND COMMISSIONING PRAYER: "Father, I stand before You fully prepared, completely committed, unconditionally surrendered. From this moment, my prayers are heard in Heaven. Angels are dispatched. Chains are breaking. Cycles are ending. I am not hoping for transformation—I am positioned for it. This fast is not just about my freedom—it's about generational deliverance. Make my life an altar that burns continuously for Your glory. Let my ceiling become someone else's floor. I am set apart. I am sent forth. I am ready for battle and prepared for victory. In Jesus' name—Amen!"

PROPHETIC COMMISSIONING MOMENT: Pause and listen for what God speaks over your journey. Record what you sense in your journal.

STAGE 1.1: I DECIDE PREPARATION COMPLETE

YOUR I DECIDE COMPLETION CHECKLIST

Verify each step is fully completed:
- [ ] IDENTIFY — Baseline established, false identities rejected
- [ ] DECIDE — Covenant clarity, Plan B eliminated
- [ ] EQUIP — Appetites aligned, kitchen prepared
- [ ] CREATE — Sacred space established
- [ ] IMPLEMENT — Strategies prepared, responses ready
- [ ] DEPLOY — Community activated, support secured
- [ ] ENGAGE — Consecration complete, covenant signed

All 7 steps checked and verified? You're ready for transformation.

WHAT YOU'VE ACCOMPLISHED

You just invested 3-4 hours that will determine the next 504 hours of your fast.

ACCOMPLISHED:

- Established measurable baseline (GAP, 8F, 6D assessments)
- Dismantled Babylon's 5-phase strategy against you
- Completed all 7 steps of I DECIDE strategic preparation
- Activated your support systems and accountability network
- Signed your covenant before Heaven and witnesses on earth
- Positioned yourself in the 91% who complete successfully

YOUR PREPARATION MOVES YOU FROM:

FROM	TO
37% completion rate (no prep)	91% completion rate (full prep)
Random spiritual activity	Strategic transformation
Impulsive emotion	Systematic consecration
Hopeful attempt	Positioned breakthrough

You didn't just prepare to fast. **You prepared to finish.**

STAGE 1.2: YOUR DOCUMENTATION TOOL AWAITS

You've prepared strategically. Now you need the documentation system that captures transformation across all 21 days. Without this tool, transformation becomes subjective memory that fades by Day 30. With this tool, you create measurable evidence that proves breakthrough happened. This is the difference between "I think something shifted" and "Here's exactly what God did, documented daily from Day 1 to Day 21." You'll complete this template every single day for 21 days. No exceptions. Your Day 22 comparison depends on your Day 1-21 documentation. Heaven heard your covenant. Angels are positioned. Your documentation tool awaits on the next page. **CHAMBER 1 STATUS: STAGE 1.1 COMPLETE** ✓ **Turn the page to Stage 1.2 now.**

CHAMBER 1: PREPARE
STAGE 1.2: SOAP DOCUMENTATION

YOUR 21-DAY TRANSFORMATION JOURNAL GUIDE
THE DAILY DISCIPLINE THAT DOCUMENTS YOUR BREAKTHROUGH

Write the vision and make it plain on tablets, that he may run who reads it." — Habakkuk 2:2

WHAT IS SOAP JOURNALING?

Most spiritual breakthroughs die because they're never documented. You finish a 21-day fast feeling transformed, but by Day 30, you can't remember what God said. By Day 60, the breakthrough feels like a distant memory you can't recreate. SOAP changes that. Scripture + Observation + Application + Prayer creates evidence you can measure on Day 22, not just emotion that fades by February.

TESTIMONY: "I have done the Daniel Fast many times, but this one was completely different because of SOAP journaling. Not only well-written, but it provides checklists to stay on track. My favorite part is the journaling—it became my daily bread, helping me see myself the way God does. I began letting go of limiting beliefs and standing in my God-given authority, fearless and free. When I compared Day 1 to Day 21, I had proof—not just feelings—that transformation happened." — Chayah Club Members

Developed over five years and refined through global participants across six continents, this framework documents transformation you can measure, verify, and multiply.

WITHOUT SOAP	WITH SOAP
Vague feelings: "I think something shifted"	Documented proof across 21 daily revelations
No proof of what God actually said	Measurable GAP closure from Day 1 to Day 22
Transformation you can't remember by Day 30	Before/after testimony on paper
Testimony you can't teach	Your ceiling becomes someone else's floor through multiplication

YOUR SOAP JOURNAL OPTIONS

Complete this every day for 21 days using one of these methods:

OPTION 1: ONLINE WITH AI COACHING + PROFESSIONAL SUPPORT (RECOMMENDED)

As a Chayah Club VIP member, complete your daily SOAP Journal at: chayah.club/gap-strategy-soap-journal/

What you receive:
- **Digital SOAP Journal** — Auto-save all 21 entries for Day 22 comparison and progress tracking
- **AI-Powered Coaching** — Receive personalized responses based on Dr. Niki's coaching style after each daily entry
- **Group Coaching Access** — Live prayer calls, weekly coaching sessions, real-time community encouragement
- **Professional Referrals** — Direct access to vetted Christian therapists, counselors, and Naturopathic doctors

THE DANIEL FAST: CLOSING THE GAP!

- **Daniel Fast Tribe** — Spiritual community for prayer, testimonies, warfare support, and breakthrough celebration
- **Daniel Diet Cafe** — Practical community for recipes, meal planning, food guidance, and daily encouragement
- **Complete 40+ Page Guide** — Detailed instructions, Scripture selection strategies, common mistakes to avoid, troubleshooting protocols, and proven success frameworks

Visit danielfastclub.com for all resources and community access. Direct link to detailed SOAP Documentation Guide: chayah.club/soap-documentation-guide/

OPTION 2: DOWNLOAD PDF TEMPLATE

Print your SOAP Journal template from danielfastclub.com and complete manually each day.

OPTION 3: MANUAL JOURNALING

Copy the template below into your personal journal or notebook and complete by hand daily.

Your investment: 15-30 minutes daily for documented transformation you can measure on Day 22. **The evidence:** 91% completion with daily SOAP + community engagement vs. 37% completion without it.

Your SOAP journal is more than notes—it's evidence. In just 21 days, you'll watch Scripture move from desperate whispers to bold declarations, prayers shift from begging to partnering, and "I'll try" become "I am." Your pages will show it—GAP scores rising, mood lifting, habits aligning, community growing from being helped to helping. So when Day 22 comes and someone asks, "Did the fast work?" you won't offer vague inspiration; you'll open your journal and point to transformation that's spiritual, measurable, and reproducible. This isn't a workbook to file away—it's the blueprint you'll live from and multiply through for the next 21 years.

THE 21-DAY GAP STRATEGY THEMES

Your journey isn't random—every day has a specific theme building intentionally on the previous day.

WEEK 1: GROW (Intimacy with God) — *Whose You Are* | 7G: Gospel, Grace, Goodness, Gifts, Gladness, Greatness, Glory

WEEK 2: ALIGN (Identity in Christ) — *Who You Are* | 7A: Adoption, Abundance, Authority, Anointing, Advancement, Attributes, Affirmation

WEEK 3: PROPEL (Destiny with the Holy Spirit) — *Why You Are* | 7P: Presence, Protection, Peace, Provision, Promotion, Prosperity, Purpose

Complete teaching for each theme appears in Chamber 2 (Sections 3, 4, and 5).

YOUR DAILY SOAP JOURNAL TEMPLATE

Complete this every day for 21 days.

DAY ___: _____ (GAP Strategy Theme)
Date: _____ | **Week Focus:** GROW / ALIGN / PROPEL (circle one)

S - SCRIPTURE: Which verse became revelation today?
Prayer before you begin: "Lord, reveal the power of Your Word in my situation."
Write out the full verse with reference: _____ (use your journal for complete text if needed)

O - OBSERVATION: What is God exposing and establishing?
Prayer before you observe: "Lord, help me see what You're demolishing and what You're building."

What stronghold is breaking? _____
What truth is replacing the lie? _____
What's shifting in your understanding of today's theme? _____

A - APPLICATION: How will you live FROM this truth today?
Prayer before you apply: "Lord, empower me to walk in victory, not toward it."
One specific action FROM today's revelation (not FOR approval): _____
Which gap is closing today? Spiritual / Mental / Emotional / Physical / Financial / Relational (circle one or more)

P - PRAYER: Your declaration of victory
Complete this declaration: "Father, [today's theme] means _____ is happening in my situation NOW."
Write out your full prayer: _____ (continue in your journal as needed)

TODAY'S BREAKTHROUGH TRACKING
Today's Breakthrough Marker (one sentence): _____
Tomorrow's Expectation (based on today's shift): _____

DAILY GAP PROGRESS CHECK
Rate your satisfaction (1-10):

DIMENSION	TODAY'S SCORE
Intimacy with God (**GROW**) — *Whose You Are*	____/10
Identity in Christ (**ALIGN**) — *Who You Are*	____/10
Destiny with Holy Spirit (**PROPEL**) — *Why You Are*	____/10
TOTAL TODAY	____/30

DAILY WELLNESS TRACKER (Optional but Recommended)

DIMENSION	STATUS TODAY
Mood (energy/emotion, 1-10)	____
Food (Daniel Fast compliance)	100% / Mostly / No (back on track next meal)
Water (daily intake)	8+ glasses / 4-7 glasses / Less than 4
Movement (walking/exercise)	_____ steps today
Rest (sleep quality)	____ hours

COMMUNITY ENGAGEMENT
The data proves it: 91% completion with daily SOAP + community vs. 37% completion without it.

Daniel Fast Tribe (Spiritual Support):
- Shared prayer request or testimony
- Read daily devotion
- Engaged with others

Daniel Diet Cafe (Practical Guidance):
- Posted recipe or meal idea
- Asked/answered food question
- Encouraged someone

Direct Accountability:
- Connected with accountability partner
- Attended live prayer call

Today's Engagement: Active (2+ actions) / Moderate (1 action) / Need to reconnect (circle one)

SAMPLE SOAP ENTRY: DAY 1 GOSPEL

To help you see what a complete SOAP entry looks like, here's an example from Day 1:

S - SCRIPTURE: *"For God so loved the world that He gave His only begotten Son, that whoever believes in Him should not perish but have everlasting life."* — John 3:16

O - OBSERVATION: The stronghold breaking is believing I have to earn God's love through performance. The truth replacing the lie is that God's love isn't based on my behavior—it's based on His character. I'm shifting from striving FOR acceptance to resting IN acceptance. The gospel isn't what I do for God; it's what God did for me.

A - APPLICATION: Today I will reject the lie that I need to "do more" to be worthy. When anxiety about my performance rises, I will declare: "I am already loved, already accepted, already enough because of Jesus—not because of my fasting, my prayers, or my perfection." Gap closing: Spiritual (intimacy increasing), Emotional (peace replacing striving).

P - PRAYER: "Father, GOSPEL means freedom from performance is happening in my situation NOW. I don't have to earn what You've already given. Today I rest in the finished work of Jesus. I'm not trying to become loved—I'm living FROM being loved. Let this truth anchor every decision, every thought, every response. In Jesus' name, Amen."

Today's Breakthrough: I'm shifting from earning love to receiving love.
Tomorrow's Expectation: I expect grace to feel more real than guilt.

This sample shows: specific Scripture selection, concrete stronghold identification, clear truth declaration, actionable application (not vague intentions), present-tense prayer language, and measurable breakthrough marker. Use this pattern daily.

COMMON SOAP MISTAKES TO AVOID

1. Generic Scripture Selection — Don't just pick any verse. Let today's theme guide you to Scripture that directly addresses your current reality. Generic verses produce generic breakthrough.

2. Vague Observations — "God is good" isn't an observation—it's a placeholder. What specifically is breaking? What lie are you believing? Name it clearly so you can track when it shifts.

3. Performance-Based Applications — If your application sounds like "I will try harder to..." you're still operating FROM striving instead of FROM identity. Applications should flow FROM what God has already done, not toward earning what you hope He'll do.

4. Future-Tense Prayers — "God, I hope You will..." keeps victory in the future. Shift to present-tense declarations: "Father, [theme] means [breakthrough] is happening NOW."

5. Skipping Community Engagement — The data is clear: 91% completion with community vs. 37% without. Your SOAP entry creates personal breakthrough. Community engagement multiplies it.

DAY 22 COMPARISON PROTOCOL

On Day 22 (the day after completing your 21-day fast), you'll return to your SOAP journal for measurable comparison:

STEP 1: Gather Your Data — Open your Day 1 SOAP entry and your Day 21 SOAP entry side by side.

STEP 2: Compare GAP Scores — Review your daily GAP Progress scores. Calculate your Day 1 total (*/30) and your Day 21 total (*/30). What's your total point increase? This number quantifies your spiritual growth across intimacy, identity, and purpose.

STEP 3: Observe Pattern Shifts — Read through all 21 entries in sequence. Notice: How did your prayers change from asking to declaring? When did your observations move from surface to surgical precision? Which week showed the most dramatic shift—Week 1 (GROW), Week 2 (ALIGN), or Week 3 (PROPEL)?

STEP 4: Document Your Before/After Testimony — On a fresh page, complete this: "On Day 1, I believed _____ about God/myself/my situation. By Day 21, God revealed _____. The measurable proof is _____. My ceiling (Day 21 breakthrough) becomes someone else's floor (what I can now teach) through _____."

STEP 5: Create Your Multiplication Plan — Your documented transformation isn't just for you—it's for the next person. Who needs to hear your testimony? Where will you share your before/after comparison? How will your ceiling become their floor? This is Stage 4: Multiplication through the 5C framework.

This comparison transforms subjective feelings ("I think God did something") into objective evidence ("Here's exactly what God did, documented daily for 21 days"). This is how your testimony becomes teaching. This is how breakthrough multiplies.

STAGE 1.2 COMPLETE: YOUR DOCUMENTATION SYSTEM IS READY

You now have:
- Complete SOAP framework for daily documentation
- Three access options (online AI coaching, PDF download, manual journaling)
- 21-day GAP Strategy themes mapped (GROW → ALIGN → PROPEL)
- Sample entry showing what excellent SOAP looks like
- Common mistakes identified so you avoid them
- Day 22 comparison protocol for measurable proof
- Community integration for 91% completion rate

Your Next Action: Turn to Chamber 2 (Week 1) and begin Day 1: GOSPEL with your first SOAP entry. Your 21-day transformation journey begins now. Heaven heard your covenant. Angels are positioned. Your documentation awaits your first entry.

Day 1 begins now.

SECTION THREE
CHAMBER 2: TRANSFORM
WEEK 1: GROW (7G)
Intimacy with God

"You shall know the truth, and the truth shall make you free." — John 8:32

You can't love who you don't know. Before you understand who you are or why you're here, you must know whose you are. Week 1 moves you from knowing about God to knowing God personally—seven themes that cultivate intimacy as your foundation for everything that follows.

Days 1-7: Gospel • Grace • Goodness • Gifts • Gladness • Greatness • Glory

---

THE SEVEN GAPS FRAMEWORK

Week 1 systematically closes seven gaps between false beliefs and Kingdom truth:

Earning → Receiving | **Performance → Position** | **Doubt → Trust**
Potential → Activation | **Mourning → Joy** | **Limitation → Authority**
Earth-bound → Heaven-minded

Each day bridges the distance from where you are to where God says you are—moving you from striving *about* God to resting *in* God.

Intimacy is not optional. It's your oxygen. Without Week 1, everything that follows becomes performance instead of partnership. You don't build identity on information. You build it on intimacy.

Turn the page to Day 1: GOSPEL.
Your foundation begins here.

DAY 1 - GOSPEL

From Earning Acceptance to Operating FROM Acceptance

> *"For I am not ashamed of the gospel of Christ, for it is the power of God to salvation for everyone who believes."*
> — Romans 1:16

WEEK 1 — GROW: Building Intimacy with God

Day 1 of 21. This is where earning mentality dies and Present Progressive Gospel begins.

ENCOUNTER — WHERE YOU ARE

The Email That Changed Everything

4:44 AM. Day 1. Your finger hovers over "Send." The email draft to yourself glows like judgment on your screen: "Prayer Request." To: Yourself. From: Yourself. Subject line that admits what you can't say aloud—you have no one else to send this to. Your stomach isn't just empty—it's excavating. Each hunger pang pulls something ancient from your bones, something your grandmother died trying to earn, something your father never felt worthy to receive, something that's been feeding on your family tree like a parasite for generations. You hit send. To yourself. Because in this moment, you're the only name in your contact list who might understand what this Daniel Fast is really about. That's when you feel it—the first crack in the earning mentality that's been suffocating your bloodline since Eden. The moment you email prayers to yourself at 4:44 AM is the moment heaven marks you for breakthrough.

Right now, across six continents, thousands mirror your hunger—but it's more than physical. In the Caribbean, a corporate leader pushes away his morning coffee, hands trembling as he whispers: "I can't do this in my own strength anymore." In Nigeria, a grandmother who's been fasting and praying for sixty years suddenly realizes she's been begging for attention she already had. In Canada, a construction worker feels the performance anxiety that drove his father to bankruptcy finally release its grip. In London, a teenager cancels her lunch plans, choosing communion with God over fitting in with friends. In the United States, a single mother navigates family meals while discovering that divine provision doesn't require human perfection. In the Philippines, a college student adjusts her schedule and finds that rest in God matters more than academic achievement.

Different time zones. Same divine disruption. Same systematic dismantling of the performance prison. But this isn't about food—it's about finally stopping the exhausting audition for love that's been yours all along.

Watch what happens when you stop feeding the lie. That coffee you're not drinking promised control: "You've got this." That breakfast you're skipping whispered sufficiency: "Fuel up to earn today's favor." Every meal was an altar to the earning mentality. Now, stripped of those false comforts, truth emerges like bone through skin: You never had it. He always did. The shaking in your hands isn't caffeine withdrawal—it's the earning mentality realizing its execution has arrived. It's been feeding on your family tree so long it thinks it owns the deed.

Your grandmother died exhausted from never praying enough. Your mother treated every blessing like wages requiring overtime. Your father couldn't receive love without working for it first. The pattern runs deeper than DNA—it's carved into your spiritual code. You don't break generational curses with casual prayers. You execute them with violent faith. Today, that ancient parasite meets its assassin: Present Progressive Gospel.

Feel the disruption in your chest? Like a bone that healed wrong being rebroken to set correctly? That's not hunger. That's heaven performing surgery without anesthesia, because some things need to hurt on their way out. Press your hand against that hollow stomach. Feel that cavity? That's exactly how your soul has felt—starving at the banquet table, begging for crumbs of your own inheritance, auditioning for love that chose you before conception.

You're that marathon runner crossing the finish line, still running in place because nobody told you the race ended at Calvary. Still sprinting. Still straining. Still gasping for breath in a race declared finished two thousand years ago. Your legs burn not from the distance ahead but from refusing to stop when Jesus said, "It is finished." Stop bleeding for battles heaven already won.

The Global Uprising

This morning, that same corporate leader in the Caribbean pushes away his power breakfast, choosing power from heaven instead. That single mother in the United States pours her coffee down the drain, declaring: "My sufficiency comes from God." That teenager in London feels the family curse of performance anxiety crack for the first time. That grandmother in Nigeria who spent sixty years earning God's approval suddenly realizes she already had it. That construction worker in Canada recognizes the Gospel isn't his salvation history—it's his salvation heartbeat. That college student in the Philippines discovers she's not in court anymore—she's in the Kingdom.

All of us. Together. On Day 1. Executing the earning mentality that's held humanity hostage since the fall. Heaven doesn't move because you fast. Heaven moves because thousands fast together, creating a frequency hell can't ignore. Your empty stomach isn't penance—it's participation. You're not earning breakthrough. You're joining the breakthrough already happening.

Note on Fasting: These twenty-one days follow Daniel Fast guidelines detailed in Stage 1.1 in your "I Decide Framework," and you'll document your experience using the GAP SOAP Journal (Stage 1.2). If you need to modify for health reasons, God honors both spiritual hunger and wise body stewardship. The physical fast amplifies the spiritual frequency—it's not the source of breakthrough, just the megaphone. Your participation matters more than your perfection.

FOUNDATION — BIBLICAL AUTHORITY

To understand why this matters, we must first understand what Gospel actually means and how religion corrupted it.

The Gospel Corruption

Religion turned Gospel into event. One moment. One prayer. One altar call. "Accept Jesus and you're saved"—then spend the rest of your life trying to stay saved, prove you're saved, maintain your salvation through spiritual gymnastics and moral performance. That's not Gospel. That's religious hostage negotiation. The Gospel isn't something that happened to you once. The Gospel is something happening to you now. Present tense. Active voice. Current reality.

Biblical Definition: Euaggelion

The Greek word *euaggelion* means "good news"—specifically, the proclamation of victory. When ancient armies won battles, heralds ran ahead shouting *euaggelion*: "We won! The war is over! The enemy is defeated!" Not "we're trying to win" or "we might win if you help." The victory was accomplished. The declaration was present, continuous, unstoppable. That's Gospel. Not past event to remember but present reality to receive. Not historical fact to believe but current power to access.

Primary Scripture: Present Progressive Gospel

"For by grace you have been saved through faith, and that not of yourselves; it is the gift of God, not of works, lest anyone should boast" (Ephesians 2:8-9). The phrase "have been saved" is Greek perfect tense—*sesōsmenoi este*—meaning action completed in the past with results continuing into the present. You were saved (past), you are saved (present), you remain saved (continuous). Not "got saved and hoping it sticks." Not "saved but need to maintain it." Saved. Being saved. Continuously saved. Present Progressive Gospel.

The Grace Foundation

"But God, who is rich in mercy, because of His great love with which He loved us, even when we were dead in trespasses, made us alive together with Christ (by grace you have been saved), and raised us up together, and made us sit together in the heavenly places in Christ Jesus" (Ephesians 2:4-6). Notice the sequence: God loved. Past tense. Made alive. Past tense. Raised up. Past tense. Made us sit. Past tense. All completed actions. The sitting isn't future. You're seated now. In heavenly places. In Christ. Present reality, not future hope.

The Work Declaration

"Not of works, lest anyone should boast" (Ephesians 2:9). Not partially of works. Not assisted by works. Not maintained through works. Not of works. Period. Your prayers don't earn it. Your fasting doesn't purchase it. Your worship doesn't maintain it. Your righteousness doesn't qualify you. Jesus qualified you. Past tense. Completed action. Permanent positioning.

The Purpose Reveal

"For we are His workmanship, created in Christ Jesus for good works, which God prepared beforehand that we should walk in them" (Ephesians 2:10). Notice: Works come after salvation, not before. You don't work to get saved. You work because you're saved. The works were prepared before you were born. You're not earning approval—you're living from approval already given. You're not becoming worthy—you're discovering you already were.

Present Progressive Throughout Scripture

"There is therefore now no condemnation to those who are in Christ Jesus" (Romans 8:1). Now. Present tense. Not "there will be no condemnation when you get holy enough." Not "there was no condemnation when you first believed." Now. This moment. Reading this sentence. No condemnation. "He who has begun a good work in you will complete it" (Philippians 1:6). Will complete. Future certainty. Not "might complete if you cooperate enough." Will complete. Guaranteed. "Being confident of this very thing, that He who has begun a good work in you will complete it until the day of Jesus Christ" (Philippians

1:6). Present confidence about future completion based on past initiation. That's Present Progressive Gospel.

The Already-Not Yet Tension

You are already saved (justification). You are being saved (sanctification). You will be saved (glorification). All three are true simultaneously. Religion separates them into stages you earn. Gospel declares them as one continuous reality you receive. You're not climbing a ladder from sinner to saint. You're discovering you're already seated in heavenly places while still walking on earth.

REVELATION — BIBLICAL PATTERNS

To see how Present Progressive Gospel operates, watch how God demonstrated it through people who thought they had to earn what He'd already given.

The Prodigal Son: When Performance Met Positioning (Luke 15:11-32)

The younger son rehearses his earning speech in the pigpen: "Father, I have sinned against heaven and before you, and I am no longer worthy to be called your son. Make me like one of your hired servants" (Luke 15:18-19). He's preparing to audition for employment. To earn his way back through performance. To trade sonship for servanthood because surely, he thinks, surely the relationship died with his choices. Watch what happens when he finally arrives home, poverty-stricken and shame-soaked, ready to negotiate terms of his return.

"But when he was still a great way off, his father saw him and had compassion, and ran and fell on his neck and kissed him" (Luke 15:20). The father didn't wait for the speech. Didn't require the repentance performance. Didn't demand proof of change. He ran. In Middle Eastern culture, wealthy patriarchs don't run—running requires hiking up your robe, exposing your legs, abandoning dignity. But this father ran. The son tries to deliver his prepared speech: "Father, I have sinned against heaven and in your sight, and am no longer worthy to be called your son" (Luke 15:21). He gets that far before his father interrupts.

"But the father said to his servants, 'Bring out the best robe and put it on him, and put a ring on his hand and sandals on his feet. And bring the fatted calf here and kill it, and let us eat and be merry; for this my son was dead and is alive again; he was lost and is found'" (Luke 15:22-24). The father never addresses the unworthiness claim. Never responds to the servant proposal. He doesn't say, "Well, you're right, you're not worthy, but I'm merciful so I'll let you work your way back." He says, "This my son." Not "this my former son" or "this my son on probation." My son. Present tense. Current reality. The relationship never died. The position never changed. The sonship survived the pigpen.

The robe signaled authority. The ring signaled family identity and access to family resources. The sandals signaled free man versus slave. The father wasn't slowly restoring the son—he was revealing what never changed. You're not earning sonship. You're discovering you never lost it.

Zacchaeus: When Seeking Found You First (Luke 19:1-10)

Zacchaeus climbs a tree to see Jesus. Tax collector. Traitor to his people. Rich from exploitation. Too short to see over the crowd. Too hated for anyone to make room. So he climbs. And Jesus, walking through Jericho, stops under that tree. "Zacchaeus, make haste and come down, for today I must stay at your house" (Luke 19:5). Before Zacchaeus says a word. Before confession. Before restitution. Before any proof of change. Jesus invites Himself to the sinner's house.

The crowd grumbles: "He has gone to be a guest with a man who is a sinner" (Luke 19:7). They understand earning mentality. You don't fellowship with sinners until they've earned it. You don't grant access until they've performed righteousness. But Jesus doesn't wait for Zacchaeus to clean up. The transformation happens after acceptance, not before. "Then Zacchaeus stood and said to the Lord, 'Look, Lord, I give half of my goods to the poor; and if I have taken anything from anyone by false accusation, I restore fourfold'" (Luke 19:8).

Notice the sequence: Jesus accepted him first. Zacchaeus changed after. Not "get right then I'll receive you." But "I receive you—now watch what happens." The works flowed from acceptance, not toward acceptance. Jesus declares: "Today salvation has come to this house" (Luke 19:9). Not "today salvation will come if you follow through on that restitution promise." Today. Present tense. Salvation came. The moment Jesus showed up, everything changed.

The Samaritan Woman: When Shame Met Living Water (John 4:1-42)

Five husbands. Living with a man she's not married to. Drawing water at noon—the hottest part of the day—because she can't face the other women at dawn. Jesus asks her for a drink. A Jewish rabbi speaking to a Samaritan woman breaks multiple cultural laws. She knows it: "How is it that You, being a Jew, ask a drink from me, a Samaritan woman?" (John 4:9). She's used to being the one who doesn't qualify. Who doesn't deserve. Who earns nothing but judgment.

Jesus offers her living water. Not after she fixes her life. Not after she ends the living-in-sin situation. Not after she proves she's worthy of spiritual conversation. Right there. In the middle of her mess. "Whoever drinks of this water will thirst again, but whoever drinks of the water that I shall give him will never thirst. But the water that I shall give him will become in him a fountain of water springing up into everlasting life" (John 4:13-14). Present tense. Will become. Will spring up. Continuous action. Living water isn't a one-time event—it's an internal fountain that never stops flowing.

She tries to deflect: "Sir, give me this water, that I may not thirst, nor come here to draw" (John 4:15). She's still thinking practically. Jesus exposes her story: "You have well said, 'I have no husband,' for you have had five husbands, and the one whom you now have is not your husband" (John 4:17-18). He names her shame. Not to condemn but to demonstrate He knows everything and offers living water anyway. No performance required. No life-cleaning prerequisite. Come as you are and drink. Present Progressive Gospel says: "I know everything. You qualify anyway."

The Thief on the Cross: When Last-Minute Became Forever (Luke 23:39-43)

Two criminals crucified beside Jesus. One mocks. One recognizes. "Lord, remember me when You come into Your kingdom" (Luke 23:42). No time for works. No opportunity for baptism. No chance to prove sincerity through transformed living. Just a dying man recognizing a dying King. And Jesus responds: "Assuredly, I say to you, today you will be with Me in Paradise" (Luke 23:43).

Today. Not "eventually, after you suffer enough to atone." Not "maybe, if this deathbed confession counts." Today. You will be. Future certainty based on present declaration. The thief earned nothing. Performed nothing. Produced no fruit. No spiritual resume. No testimony of transformation.

Just recognition and request. And Jesus granted paradise. Because the Gospel isn't payment plan—it's gift received. Not wages earned—grace given.

Peter's Denial and Restoration: When Failure Couldn't Cancel Calling (John 21:15-19)

Peter denied Jesus three times. Cursing. Swearing. "I don't know the man" (Matthew 26:72). The rooster crowed. Peter wept. Three days later, Jesus rose. And when He appeared to the disciples, He didn't demote Peter. Didn't place him on probation. Didn't require a waiting period to prove renewed commitment.

On the beach, Jesus asks three times: "Do you love Me?" Peter answers three times. Jesus responds three times: "Feed My lambs. Tend My sheep. Feed My sheep" (John 21:15-17). Jesus didn't say, "Prove you love Me and then I'll restore your ministry." He restored while asking. He reinstated through conversation. The three-fold question matched the three-fold denial—grace answering failure with assignment, not punishment with probation.

Peter didn't earn his way back. Grace positioned him back. His failure didn't disqualify him. His calling survived his betrayal. That's Present Progressive Gospel. You're not rebuilding what you destroyed. Grace maintained what you thought you lost.

The Woman Caught in Adultery: When Law Met Love (John 8:1-11)

Dragged into public. Caught in the act. The law demanded stoning. "Teacher, this woman was caught in adultery, in the very act. Now Moses, in the law, commanded us that such should be stoned. But what do You say?" (John 8:4-5). They're using her as bait to trap Jesus. Will He uphold law or show mercy?

Jesus writes in the sand. Scholars debate what He wrote—perhaps the sins of the accusers. Then He straightens up: "He who is without sin among you, let him throw a stone at her first" (John 8:7). One by one, from oldest to youngest, they drop their stones and leave. Finally, only Jesus and the woman remain. "Woman, where are those accusers of yours? Has no one condemned you?" She said, "No one, Lord." And Jesus said to her, "Neither do I condemn you; go and sin no more" (John 8:10-11).

Notice: "Neither do I condemn you" comes before "go and sin no more." Not "go sin no more and then I won't condemn you." The acceptance precedes the instruction. The positioning comes before the performance. She wasn't forgiven because she promised to stop. She was forgiven, then told she had power to stop. Present Progressive Gospel says: You're free from condemnation now—live from that freedom, not toward earning it.

Paul's Conversion: When Enemy Became Apostle (Acts 9:1-22)

Saul breathes threats and murder against disciples. On the road to Damascus, hunting Christians to imprison them, Jesus appears. Blinds him with light. "Saul, Saul, why are you persecuting Me?" (Acts 9:4). Three days blind. Fasting. Praying. Ananias receives instructions: "Go, for he is a chosen vessel of Mine to bear My name before Gentiles, kings, and the children of Israel" (Acts 9:15).

Notice: Jesus called Saul "chosen" while he was still blind, still processing, still three days from doing anything righteous. Chosen before conversion completed. Assigned before proving changed. That's how Present Progressive Gospel works. God doesn't choose you after you perform. He chose you before foundation of the world (Ephesians 1:4). Your behavior didn't qualify you. His purpose did.

Ananias lays hands on him. Scales fall from his eyes. And immediately—that same hour—Saul preaches Christ in the synagogues (Acts 9:20). No seminary. No probation period. No "prove yourself first." Immediate assignment because calling isn't earned through preparation—it's accessed through positioning. Saul didn't become Paul by earning his way into apostleship. Jesus assigned apostleship, and Paul grew into it while already operating in it.

The Paralytic at Bethesda: When Helplessness Met Help (John 5:1-15)

Thirty-eight years. Lying by the pool. Waiting for the water to stir. "I have no man to put me into the pool when the water is stirred up; but while I am coming, another steps down before me" (John 5:7). He can't help himself. Can't earn his healing. Can't compete for his miracle. For thirty-eight years, he's been trying to perform his way to breakthrough—and failing.

Jesus doesn't wait for him to try harder. Doesn't require proof of worthiness. Doesn't say, "When you finally get yourself into the pool, I'll help." Jesus says, "Rise, take up your bed and walk" (John 5:8). Not "try to rise" or "work toward walking." Rise. Walk. Present imperative commands assuming immediate ability.

And immediately the man was made well, took up his bed, and walked (John 5:9). He didn't partially heal, then gradually improve through effort. He was made well. Passive voice. Something done to him, not by him. He received what he couldn't earn. He walked in power he didn't generate. That's Present Progressive Gospel. You're not working toward wholeness. You're receiving wholeness and discovering you can already walk.

The Ten Lepers: When Nine Returned to Performance, One to Presence (Luke 17:11-19)

Ten lepers cry out: "Jesus, Master, have mercy on us!" (Luke 17:13). He responds: "Go, show yourselves to the priests" (Luke 17:14). As they went, they were cleansed. All ten received healing. All ten got their miracle. But only one—a Samaritan—returns to thank Jesus.

"Were there not ten cleansed? But where are the nine?" Jesus asks. Then to the one who returned: "Arise, go your way. Your faith has made you well" (Luke 17:17, 19). The nine got physical healing and returned to religious performance—showing themselves to priests, following protocol, checking boxes. The one got physical healing and relational restoration—he came back to the Source.

That's the difference between religion and gospel. Religion takes the blessing and returns to performance. Gospel takes the blessing and returns to Presence. The nine were cleansed. The one was made well—*sesōken se*, perfect tense, permanent healing. Present Progressive Gospel isn't just about receiving the miracle—it's about staying connected to the Miracle-Worker.

Martha and Mary: When Doing Met Being (Luke 10:38-42)

Martha works. Serves. Prepares. Performs hospitality. Gets frustrated that Mary isn't helping. "Lord, do You not care that my sister has left me to serve alone? Therefore tell her to help me" (Luke 10:40). Martha represents earning mentality—doing to prove devotion, working to demonstrate worthiness, performing to maintain approval.

Jesus responds: "Martha, Martha, you are worried and troubled about many things. But one thing is needed, and Mary has chosen that good part, which will not be taken away from her" (Luke 10:41-42). Mary chose presence over performance. She sat at Jesus' feet—the posture of a disciple, scandalous for a woman in that culture—and listened. She received rather than achieved.

Notice: Jesus doesn't say Mary's choice is better because she'll earn more favor. He says it "will not be taken away." Performance can be taken away. Achievement can be lost. But positioning at Jesus' feet—that's permanent. Present Progressive Gospel says: Stop doing to earn. Start being to receive. Your position isn't based on your performance. Your performance should flow from your position.

The Bleeding Woman: When Desperation Touched Healing (Mark 5:25-34)

Twelve years bleeding. Spent all her money on physicians. Got worse, not better. Unclean by law. Untouchable. She presses through the crowd—every touch making people ceremonially unclean—and reaches for Jesus' garment. "If only I may touch His clothes, I shall be made well" (Mark 5:28).

She touches. Immediately the fountain of her blood dried up (Mark 5:29). She feels in her body that she's healed. Jesus feels power go out. "Who touched My clothes?" the disciples think He's crazy—everyone's touching Him in the crowd. But Jesus knows: this touch was different. Not casual contact but desperate faith. The woman, trembling, falls down before Him and tells the whole truth.

Jesus says, "Daughter, your faith has made you well. Go in peace, and be healed of your affliction" (Mark 5:34). Notice: He calls her "daughter"—family, not stranger. He attributes healing to her faith, not her worthiness. He declares her healed—perfect tense, permanent state—not "you're getting better" or "keep working at it." Present Progressive Gospel says: Your desperate reach—however unclean, however unworthy you feel—touches healing power. You don't earn the touch. You just touch.

Blind Bartimaeus: When Persistence Met Power (Mark 10:46-52)

Bartimaeus sits by the road begging. Hears Jesus is passing. Starts shouting: "Jesus, Son of David, have mercy on me!" (Mark 10:47). The crowd tells him to shut up. He shouts louder. "Son of David, have mercy on me!" Jesus stops. Calls him. Bartimaeus throws aside his garment—his only possession—and comes to Jesus.

"What do you want Me to do for you?" Jesus asks. "Rabboni, that I may receive my sight" (Mark 10:51). Jesus said to him, "Go your way; your faith has made you well." And immediately he received his sight and followed Jesus on the road (Mark 10:52). No earning period. No "prove you deserve sight." Immediate healing because faith reached, and Present Progressive Gospel responds.

Notice: Bartimaeus threw aside his beggar's garment—the tool of his trade, his identity, his security. He let go of what he knew to receive what Jesus offered. That's the exchange: release earning mentality, receive Gospel reality. Your faith makes you well. Present tense. Current reality. Not future hope but immediate access.

Nicodemus: When Religion Met Rebirth (John 3:1-21)

Ruler of the Jews. Teacher. Religious authority. Comes to Jesus at night—can't risk reputation by being seen with this controversial rabbi. "Rabbi, we know that You are a teacher come from God; for no one can do these signs that You do unless God is with him" (John 3:2). He's acknowledging Jesus' credentials. Trying to establish common ground. Teacher to teacher.

Jesus cuts through the pleasantries: "Most assuredly, I say to you, unless one is born again, he cannot see the kingdom of God" (John 3:3). Born again. Nicodemus hears physical rebirth: "How can a man be born when he is old? Can he enter a second time into his mother's womb and be born?" (John 3:4). Jesus clarifies: "That which is born of the flesh is flesh, and that which is born of the Spirit is spirit" (John 3:6).

Then comes the key: "For God so loved the world that He gave His only begotten Son, that whoever believes in Him should not perish but have everlasting life" (John 3:16). Present tense belief produces present tense life. Not "will have everlasting life after you die." Has everlasting life. Now. Continuous. You're not waiting to be born again—you were born again the moment you believed. Present Progressive Gospel says: The second birth already happened. Stop trying to earn what grace already gave.

TESTIMONY — WHEN PRESENT PROGRESSIVE GOSPEL SHATTERED MY EARNING MENTALITY

The Gmail Prayer That Broke the Curse

Let me tell you about the morning I realized I'd been treating God like a reluctant employer and myself like an unqualified applicant. Day 1 of the Daniel Fast. My children asleep. Kitchen dark. Coffee maker cold—first time in years I haven't started my day with that familiar ritual. My stomach growls. My head already aches. But none of that compares to the hollowness I feel when I open Gmail and start typing.

To: myself. From: myself. Subject: Prayer Request. I sat there, cursor blinking, and realized I had no one else to send this to. I'd built a life that looked full but felt empty. Church attendance without community. Social media connections without real relationships. Success without support. And on this first day of the fast, stripped of the distractions that usually fill the void, I had to face the truth: I was alone. Not because I lacked people in my life, but because I'd never learned how to receive from them. Never learned how to be weak, to need, to ask.

The earning mentality taught me self-sufficiency. Take care of yourself. Don't burden others. Pull yourself up. Prove your worth. And I'd done that—navigating divorce, body breaking under the weight of it all, raising two sons alone, reading for a doctoral program and building ministry while situational depression tried to sideline me. I'd earned my independence. But independence felt a lot like isolation when I was sitting at my kitchen table at 4:44 AM emailing prayers to myself.

I hit send. Watched the email land in my own inbox. And something cracked open in my chest—something that had been holding together through sheer force of will for as long as I could remember. I heard these words, not audible but undeniable: "What if you've been earning what I already gave you?" I opened my Bible to Ephesians 2:8-9. Read it like I'd never seen it before: "For by grace you have been saved through faith, and that not of yourselves; it is the gift of God, not of works, lest anyone should boast."

Saved. Past tense. Already done. I'd known that verse my whole life. Taught it. Quoted it. But I'd been living like salvation was past tense and everything else was performance-based. Like God saved me and then said, "Now earn everything else—My approval, My provision, My presence, My power." But that's not what the verse says. It says, "not of yourselves." Not of works. Not earned. Not achieved. Not maintained through performance.

The Mudroom Moment

Three days into the fast, I'm in my mudroom—that chaotic space between garage and kitchen where shoes pile up and jackets hang crooked and life happens in the margins. I'm looking for something, I don't even remember what, and I hear God say: "You've been treating this relationship like you treat this room. Functional but not intimate. Transactional but not relational. You use Me when you need Me, but you don't dwell with Me."

I sat down on the mudroom floor—dirty tiles, shoes pressing into my back—and wept. Because He was right. I'd been treating God like a divine vending machine: insert prayer, receive blessing. Insert fasting, receive breakthrough. Insert worship, receive favor. Performance in, provision out. Earning mentality applied to everything, even the Gospel.

But the Gospel isn't past tense salvation requiring present tense performance. The Gospel is present progressive reality: You are being saved. You are being transformed. You are being positioned. Not through your work but through His finished work continuously applied to your current reality. I didn't earn salvation. I don't maintain salvation. I don't achieve new levels of salvation. I receive salvation—ongoing, present tense, continuous action.

That day, on my mudroom floor, I stopped trying to earn what grace already gave. I stopped auditioning for love that already chose me. I stopped running a race that ended at Calvary. And for the first time in my adult life, I rested. Not because everything was fixed. Not because my circumstances changed. But because I finally understood: I'm not trying to become worthy. I'm discovering I already was.

The Breakthrough That Followed

What happened after that mudroom moment wasn't gradual improvement. It was violent disruption. Within weeks, financial provision appeared from sources I hadn't pursued. Ministry doors opened that I hadn't knocked on. Relationships restored that I'd thought were beyond repair. My body—broken by that season, diagnosed with situational depression during the divorce—somehow had strength I hadn't manufactured through willpower.

Here's what Present Progressive Gospel taught me: The provision was always there. The doors were always open. The relationships were always available. The strength was always accessible. I just couldn't receive any of it while I was busy trying to earn all of it. The clenched fist of performance can't receive the open hand of grace. You can't work for what's freely given. You can't earn what's already yours.

Six months after that mudroom moment, I got an email. From someone I'd never met. They'd read something I wrote. Wanted to support the ministry. Enclosed was a check that covered six months of expenses. I sat at the same kitchen table where I'd emailed prayers to myself, holding that check, and realized: This is how Present Progressive Gospel works. You stop earning. Grace starts flowing. You stop striving. Provision starts arriving. You stop performing. Power starts operating.

I came through that season. The first marriage ended, but God wasn't finished. I raised two sons through the storm, and He brought restoration I never auditioned for. Nothing about my journey looked like the prosperity gospel promises of problem-free living. But everything about my internal reality has changed. I'm not begging anymore. I'm receiving. I'm not auditioning anymore. I'm operating. I'm not trying to maintain salvation anymore. I'm accessing salvation—present tense, continuous power, ongoing reality.

Present Progressive Gospel didn't remove my struggles. It reframed them. The depression that marked that season wasn't punishment for lack of faith—it became platform for grace's power. The single motherhood wasn't curse—it's testimony that God provides what human partners didn't. The financial limitations weren't failure—they were invitation to watch supernatural multiplication. Everything I thought disqualified me actually positioned me to demonstrate what Present Progressive Gospel does: turns weakness into platform, insufficiency into testimony, lack into overflow.

The Generational Shift

My grandmother died exhausted. I found her journal after the funeral. Page after page of prayers—begging God to hear her, listing her failures, promising to do better. She spent all her years trying to earn approval she already had. My mother lived the same way—blessing as wages, every gift requiring overtime payment through guilt and striving. My father couldn't receive love. Had to work for it first. Pay his way. Earn his keep.

That earning mentality was killing my sons. I saw it in their eyes when they apologized for needing things. When they tried to earn my love through performance. When they couldn't receive gifts without feeling obligated. I was passing down the curse without realizing it. But Present Progressive Gospel breaks generational cycles. The moment I stopped earning, I could teach them to receive. The moment I rested in Gospel truth, I could model Gospel living.

Now my sons watch me fast not to earn God's attention but to amplify my awareness of attention already given. They see me pray not to convince God to care but to align with care already present. They hear me worship not to generate favor but to celebrate favor already granted. Present Progressive Gospel doesn't just change you. It changes your lineage. What you break in your generation doesn't pass to the next.

PARADIGM SHIFT — FROM EARNING TO RECEIVING

EARNING MENTALITY	PRESENT PROGRESSIVE GOSPEL
"I must maintain my salvation"	"I am being saved continuously"
"My works prove my faith"	"My faith produces my works"
"God approves when I perform"	"God approved me before I performed"
"I earn access through righteousness"	"Christ's righteousness granted me access"
"I'm working toward worthiness"	"I'm working from worthiness"
"Blessing is wages for obedience"	"Blessing is inheritance through sonship"
"I achieve position through performance"	"I perform from my position"
"God loves me when I'm good"	"God's love makes me good"
"I'm becoming acceptable"	"I'm discovering I already am"

Real-World Application

There's someone reading this who just emailed prayers to themselves. Who feels alone even in a crowd. Who's been earning approval they already have. Who's been maintaining salvation that was never contingent on maintenance. Who's been working toward a finish line they crossed at Calvary. Today, that earning mentality meets its execution.

You're not lacking what you need to earn. You're overlooking what you already have. You're not becoming worthy. You're discovering you already were. You're not working toward acceptance. You're working from acceptance. The Gospel isn't past event requiring present performance. The Gospel is present reality requiring present awareness. Stop earning. Start receiving. Stop striving. Start accessing. Stop performing. Start living.

Weight Drop Exercise (Do This Now)

Stand with arms extended, palms up, as if holding heavy weight. Say aloud: "I've been carrying the weight of earning." Feel the strain. Your arms will tire quickly. Now slowly lower your arms, releasing the imaginary weight. Say aloud: "I release what Christ already carried." Feel the relief. Your body will remember this. Next time earning mentality rises, drop your arms. Let your body remind your spirit: That weight isn't yours to carry. Present Progressive Gospel says: Finished. Complete. Done. Stop bleeding for battles heaven already won.

ACTIVATION — FIVE DIMENSIONS OF GOSPEL APPLICATION

Spiritual Dimension: From religious duty to relational reality. You're not reading your Bible to earn points. You're reading your Bible because it reveals the Jesus who already chose you. You're not praying to convince God to care. You're praying because He already cares and you're aligning with that reality. You're not worshiping to generate favor. You're worshiping because favor already exists and you're celebrating it.

Mental Dimension: From performance anxiety to positioned peace. That thought that says, "You're not enough"? It's lying. Present Progressive Gospel says you're enough because Christ is enough in you. That voice that demands you do more, be more, achieve more? It's the earning mentality's death rattle. That fear that you'll lose God's approval? Impossible. You can't lose what you didn't earn. You can't forfeit what grace secured.

Emotional Dimension: From earning to receiving. You don't have to manufacture joy—you can receive it. You don't have to perform peace—you can access it. You don't have to achieve love—you can rest in it. Present Progressive Gospel says: Stop working for emotions grace already provided. Your feelings will catch up to your theology. Your emotions will align with your position. Give them time. Give them truth. Give them grace.

Physical Dimension: From striving to resting. Your body knows the difference between earning and receiving. Earning tenses muscles, raises blood pressure, activates stress responses. Receiving relaxes muscles, lowers blood pressure, activates rest responses. Your body is designed for rest, not relentless striving. The Gospel isn't just theological truth—it's biological relief. When you stop earning, your body starts healing.

Relational Dimension: From transaction to connection. You've been treating relationships like business deals—what you give versus what you get. Present Progressive Gospel applies to human relationships too. You don't earn love through performance. You receive love and respond with presence. You don't maintain friendships through transaction. You access connection through transparency. Stop performing for people. Start receiving from people. Stop earning relationships. Start enjoying relationships.

FOCUS AREA GOSPEL PRAYERS

Scripture Foundation: "For by grace you have been saved through faith, and that not of yourselves; it is the gift of God, not of works, lest anyone should boast" (Ephesians 2:8-9). Choose your primary breakthrough area:

For Spiritual Focus: "Father, I repent for treating salvation like past event requiring present performance. I receive Present Progressive Gospel: I was saved, I am being saved, I continue to be saved—all by grace. Show me how to live from this reality, not toward earning it. I'm not trying to become worthy. I'm discovering I already am."

For Mental Focus: "Father, I renounce the lie that my thoughts earn Your approval. I receive Present Progressive Gospel into my mind: I was chosen before I could think right thoughts. I am being transformed by renewing my mind, not by manufacturing right thinking through willpower. My mind is being restored because Christ's mind is already mine (1 Corinthians 2:16)."

For Emotional Focus: "Father, I reject the performance trap that says my emotions prove my faith. I receive Present Progressive Gospel into my feelings: I was loved before I felt anything. I am being healed emotionally because Your love isn't contingent on my emotional state. My feelings are being restored because Your affection already exists, independent of my fluctuating emotions."

For Physical Focus: "Father, I release the belief that my body must perform to prove devotion. I receive Present Progressive Gospel into my physical reality: You made me, disability and all, and called me good. I am being strengthened not through my striving but through Your sustaining. My body is being carried by grace I don't have to earn."

For Relational Focus: "Father, I repent for treating relationships like transactions where I must earn love. I receive Present Progressive Gospel into my connections: I was loved before I performed for people. I am being restored to healthy relationships not by becoming perfect but by becoming authentic. My relationships are being healed because I'm learning to receive, not just achieve."

RESISTANCE REALITY CHECK

What You're Experiencing Right Now:

Earning Mentality Panic: "But if I don't work for it, I'll lose it." Heaven's Response: You can't lose what you didn't earn. You can't forfeit what grace secured. The panic is the old system realizing its execution has arrived.

Performance Withdrawal: "I feel guilty not doing enough." Heaven's Response: That guilt is religious conditioning, not Holy Spirit conviction. The Spirit convicts of specific sin. Religion shames for insufficient performance. Learn the difference.

Fear of Abuse: "If I believe I'm already accepted, won't I live however I want?" Heaven's Response: Grace doesn't produce license—it produces love. When you truly understand you're accepted, you don't want to abuse grace. You want to express gratitude. Love responds to love. Performance responds to fear.

DECLARATION — SCRIPTURE-ANCHORED WARFARE

Stand with thousands globally:

"For by grace I have been saved through faith, and that not of myself; it is the gift of God, not of works, lest I should boast!" (Ephesians 2:8-9)

"There is therefore NOW no condemnation to me, for I am in Christ Jesus!" (Romans 8:1)

"I am confident of this very thing, that He who has begun a good work in me will complete it until the day of Jesus Christ!" (Philippians 1:6)

"I am His workmanship, created in Christ Jesus for good works, which God prepared beforehand that I should walk in them!" (Ephesians 2:10)

"It is FINISHED! I am not earning what Christ already accomplished!" (John 19:30)

"I am not trying to become worthy. I am discovering I already am!"

"The earning mentality is EXECUTED! Present Progressive Gospel is OPERATIONAL!"

BREAKTHROUGH PRAYER

Father God, today I execute the earning mentality that's fed on my family tree since Eden. I repent for treating Your Gospel like past event requiring present performance. I receive Present Progressive Gospel as present reality requiring present awareness.

I repent for bleeding over battles You already won. For running races You already finished. For earning approval You already gave. For maintaining salvation You already secured. For achieving worthiness Christ already granted. For performing for love that already chose me before foundation of the world.

I receive the truth: I was saved. I am being saved. I will be saved. All by grace. All through faith. All God's work, none of mine. I don't maintain it. I don't achieve it. I don't earn it. I receive it. Present tense. Continuous action. Ongoing reality.

Like the prodigal son, I stop rehearsing earning speeches. Like Zacchaeus, I receive acceptance before performance. Like the Samaritan woman, I drink living water in the middle of my mess. Like the thief on the cross, I access paradise with no resume. Like the bleeding woman, I touch healing power with desperate faith. Like Bartimaeus, I throw aside earning mentality and receive sight.

The Gospel isn't something that happened to me once. The Gospel is something happening to me now. I am being positioned. I am being transformed. I am being empowered. Not through my work but through His finished work continuously applied to my current reality.

I declare: The earning mentality is dead. Present Progressive Gospel is alive. I stop working for what I already have. I start working from what I already am. I stop performing for acceptance. I start living from acceptance. I stop earning provision. I start receiving provision. I stop achieving position. I start accessing position.

In Jesus' name, the race is finished, the work is complete, the earning is over, and I am receiving what grace already gave. Present Progressive Gospel is now my operational reality. Amen.

CLOSING — FROM GMAIL TO GOSPEL

Day 1 started with an email to yourself at 4:44 AM. Tonight, that email has an answer. Not from yourself but from the God who chose you before you could choose Him, loved you before you could love Him, saved you before you could save yourself.

The earning mentality that dragged your grandmother to an early grave, that exhausted your mother, that crippled your father—that ancient parasite met its assassin today. Present Progressive Gospel executed what performance mentality built. The race you've been running? Finished at Calvary. The approval you've been chasing? Granted before conception. The worthiness you've been achieving? Declared two thousand years ago.

Tomorrow, you'll discover that grace isn't just unearned favor—it's operational power. You'll learn that the same grace that saved you empowers you. That the weakness disqualifying you is actually qualifying you for demonstration of strength not your own. Tomorrow, grace stops being tolerance and becomes transformation.

But tonight, rest. Your work isn't required. Your performance isn't needed. Your earning days are over. You're saved. Present tense. Being saved. Continuous action. Secure in the Gospel that doesn't demand your maintenance—only your awareness. Stop bleeding for battles heaven already won. The execution is complete. The performance trap is shattered. Present Progressive Gospel is operational.

Day 1 Complete: Earning Mentality Executed, Present Progressive Gospel Activated
Gospel: Not past event but present reality
Salvation: Not maintained but received
Works: Not toward approval but from approval
Position: Not earned but given
Performance: Not required but responsive
Identity: Not becoming but discovering

SOAP JOURNAL — Day 1
S (Scripture): Which Gospel verse shifted your perspective from earning to receiving?
O (Observation): Where have I been treating Gospel as past event requiring present performance?
A (Application): What changes when I live from approval rather than toward approval? Which of the five dimensions (spiritual, mental, emotional, physical, relational) needs Present Progressive Gospel most?
P (Prayer): "Father, I stop earning _____. I start receiving _____. Tomorrow I will live from the truth that _____."

Today's Breakthrough Marker: What shifted in your understanding of Gospel today?
Tomorrow's Expectation: Based on today's execution of earning mentality, what do you expect tomorrow?

EARNING MENTALITY: EXECUTED. PRESENT PROGRESSIVE GOSPEL: OPERATIONAL. READY FOR GRACE AS POWER.

DAY 2 — GRACE

From Begging for Tolerance to Operating in Power

> *"Let us therefore come boldly to the throne of grace, that we may obtain mercy and find grace to help in time of need."*
> — Hebrews 4:16

WEEK 1 — GROW: Building Intimacy with God

Day 2 of 21. Yesterday's Gospel broke the performance stronghold. Today's Grace destroys the powerlessness lie.

ENCOUNTER — WHERE YOU ARE

5:01 AM. Day 2. Your hands shake reaching for dandelion tea instead of coffee. That trembling isn't withdrawal—it's something deeper dying. Something that's been dragging you to an invisible courtroom every morning for years, making you list yesterday's failures before you can receive today's grace. Every cell screams for familiar comfort while something revolutionary whispers: "Stop approaching Me like a judge. I'm your Father." The headache behind your eyes throbs like a gavel. Your mouth tastes like copper pennies—the metallic tang of surrender. But feel this deeper disruption beneath the physical rebellion.

Yesterday you discovered you're already accepted through Present Progressive Gospel. Today you're discovering you've been wearing a crown sideways—approaching God like a defendant when He's been waiting for you to approach as His child. The coffee maker sits silent. Abandoned. Accusing. Others' morning brew fills the kitchen with aroma that might as well be torture. Every cell demands the familiar ritual that's started your days for years. You know you're God's child. But you still feel like a weak one. The crown never fell off. It just got knocked crooked in the climb. Today, you straighten it.

Grace isn't God tolerating your mess. Grace is God empowering your miracle. Stop. Press your trembling hands together. Feel that weakness? That's not disqualifying you from God's power—it's qualifying you for it. You're not falling apart. You're falling into grace. Right now, across six continents, thousands shake with you. Malaysia at lunch, wrestling identical withdrawal. Nigeria at sunset, feeling identical weakness. Canada just waking, facing identical battles. Our collective weakness is becoming grace's global platform.

Picture yourself approaching God's throne like a defendant approaching a judge—head down, listing failures, hoping for leniency. You're calculating how much disappointment He can tolerate before He abandons you. You're not approaching a judge for leniency. You're approaching a Father for ability. Religion reduced grace to a spiritual hall pass. Divine tolerance. God looking the other way. Cosmic clemency for your failures. That's not grace—that's just religious sin management. Grace isn't the mop that cleans your mess. Grace is the power that stops you from making it.

The shaking in your hands isn't disqualifying you from God's power. It's qualifying you for it. Where human strength ends, grace begins. Not grace as patience, but grace as power. Not grace as tolerance, but grace as transformation. Stop bringing courtroom energy to a throne of grace.

FOUNDATION — BIBLICAL AUTHORITY

To fully grasp grace's power, we must understand both its distinction from mercy and its essential nature as divine enablement.

The Mercy-Grace Distinction

Mercy withholds the punishment you deserve. Grace extends blessings you could never earn. Mercy says, "You are forgiven." Grace declares, "You are also loved, chosen, and empowered." Together, they reveal God's complete heart—not just pardoning but restoring, equipping, elevating.

Biblical Definition: Charis

Grace—the Greek word *charis*—carries meaning that religion only half-taught. First, there is **unmerited favor** (what religion taught). You cannot earn grace. This is true, but incomplete. Second, there is **divine influence on the heart** (what religion missed). Grace doesn't just pardon your past—it transforms your present from the inside out. Third, there is **supernatural empowerment** (what religion feared). Grace isn't just God's patience with your weakness—it's God's power released through your weakness. Fourth, there is **God's operational power** (what you're receiving now). Grace isn't just God's attitude toward you; it's God's ability in you. Grace isn't just the entrance into relationship—it's the fuel for transformation. Grace doesn't just cover your weakness. Grace converts it to strength.

Primary Scripture: The Throne of Grace

"Let us therefore come boldly to the throne of grace, that we may obtain mercy and find grace to help in time of need" (Hebrews 4:16). Notice: It's a throne of grace, not judgment. We're told to come boldly, not cautiously. Why? Grace already qualified us for access. The phrase "grace to help" is *charis eis eukairos boētheia*—literally "grace for well-timed help." Grace isn't abstract favor; it's specific power arriving exactly when you need it.

The Power Connection

"And with great power the apostles gave witness to the resurrection of the Lord Jesus. And great grace was upon them all" (Acts 4:33). Luke directly ties *charis* (grace) to *dunamis* (power). Not grace instead of power—grace producing power. Great grace equals great power. They're not separate; they're synonymous. Grace doesn't just forgive your yesterday; it funds your assignment today.

The Sufficiency Secret

"And He said to me, 'My grace is sufficient for you, for My strength is made perfect in weakness'" (2 Corinthians 12:9). "Sufficient" is *arkeō* meaning abundant, more than enough, overflowing. God isn't saying, "My patience with your weakness is enough." He's declaring, "My power through your weakness exceeds every need." Grace isn't God lowering the bar—it's God lifting you over it.

Grace in Present Progressive

Just like the Gospel, grace operates in present progressive tense: "And God is able to make all grace abound toward you, that you, always having all sufficiency in all things, may have an abundance for every good work" (2 Corinthians 9:8). IS able. Present tense. Current capacity. Active abundance.

Grace's Six-Dimensional Operation

Grace doesn't operate in isolation—it progressively transforms every area. In the first dimension, grace saves. "For by grace you have been saved through faith, and that not of yourselves; it is the gift of God" (Ephesians 2:8). Grace initiates relationship. Salvation isn't the end goal—it's the entrance into power. In the second dimension, grace empowers. "And with great power the apostles gave witness to the resurrection of the Lord Jesus. And great grace was upon them all" (Acts 4:33). Great grace equals great power. What saves you also strengthens you. In the third dimension, grace produces evidence. "When he came and had seen the grace of God, he was glad" (Acts 11:23). Grace becomes visible. Your transformation becomes their testimony.

In the fourth dimension, grace is proportional. "But to each one of us grace was given according to the measure of Christ's gift" (Ephesians 4:7). Customized, not generic. Your grace fits your assignment. In the fifth dimension, grace is abundant. "And of His fullness we have all received, and grace for grace" (John 1:16-17). Gift after gift after gift. Grace multiplies, never diminishes. In the sixth dimension, grace is accessible. "Let us therefore come boldly to the throne of grace" (Hebrews 4:16). You don't earn access—you approach boldly as crowned heir.

The progression is clear: Salvation leads to empowerment, which produces evidence, which is proportional to assignment, which multiplies in abundance, which is always accessible. This progression explains why some believers stay at salvation while others walk in power. Grace doesn't stop at forgiveness—it flows through six dimensions until you're positioned as royalty and approaching boldly. Grace is the fuel for the Christian life, not just the entrance into it.

Biblical Foundation for Crowns

The crown isn't metaphor—it's biblical reality. "Blessed is the man who endures temptation; for when he has been approved, he will receive the crown of life which the Lord has promised to those who love Him" (James 1:12). "Finally, there is laid up for me the crown of righteousness, which the Lord, the righteous Judge, will give to me on that Day, and not to me only but also to all who have loved His appearing" (2 Timothy 4:8). "And when the Chief Shepherd appears, you will receive the crown of glory that does not fade away" (1 Peter 5:4). Your royal position isn't future promise—it's present identity. Grace placed it; shame shifted it; today you straighten it.

REVELATION — BIBLICAL PATTERNS

To understand how grace transforms weakness into strength, watch how God demonstrated this through the most unlikely people.

Moses: When Speech Impediment Became Divine Eloquence (Exodus 3-4)

Moses at the burning bush. Eighty years old. Desert sand still warm under his feet from forty years of exile. Speech impediment making his tongue heavy like lead. "Who am I that I should go to Pharaoh, and that I should bring the children of Israel out of Egypt?" (Exodus 3:11). Feel his desperation—hand trembling as he grips his shepherd's staff, sweat beading despite evening cool, voice cracking with each excuse. "O my Lord, I am not eloquent, neither before nor since You have spoken to Your servant; but I am slow of speech and slow of tongue" (Exodus 4:10). God's response? Not "Try harder, Moses." Not "Clean up your speech first." But "I will certainly be with you" (Exodus 3:12). For forty years, the man who couldn't speak clearly became God's mouthpiece. Grace didn't fix the impediment—it flowed through it. Grace specializes in using what you think disqualifies you.

Gideon: When Least Became Leverage (Judges 6-7)

Hiding in a winepress. Heart pounding like thunder. Wheat husks in his hair. Sweat stinging his eyes. The angel appears: "The Lord is with you, you mighty man of valor!" (Judges 6:12). Gideon nearly chokes on his fear: "O my lord, how can I save Israel? Indeed my clan is the weakest in Manasseh, and I am the least in my father's house" (Judges 6:15). Watch what grace does—reduces his army from thirty-two thousand to three hundred. Makes him weaker to make the victory clearer. The torches hidden in clay jars? That's you—treasure in earthen vessels, weakness displaying glory. If it didn't need grace, it wouldn't need you.

Esther: When Orphan Became Intercessor (Esther 2-5)

Orphan girl. Parents' graves still fresh in memory. Minority race in hostile empire. No political power. No royal blood. No throne room qualifications. But grace repositions: "Yet who knows whether you have come to the kingdom for such a time as this?" (Esther 4:14). Three days of fasting. Knees weak from hunger. Royal robes feeling like burial clothes. "If I perish, I perish!" (Esther 4:16)—that's what grace does. Makes you bold enough to approach thrones you once feared. Her orphan status became her strength—compassion for the vulnerable. Her fear became favor. Her approach saved a nation. Orphans audition. Heirs approach.

Peter on the Water: Grace as Enabling Presence (Matthew 14:22-33)

Storm raging. Waves crashing over the boat. Three o'clock in the morning darkness. The disciples see Jesus walking on water. Peter didn't walk on water because he was gifted; he walked because Jesus said, "Come" (Matthew 14:29). Grace isn't your natural capacity—it's Christ's command creating capacity. Feel the spray of salt water, wind whipping his face, the impossible solidity under his sandals. When he looked at waves and sank, the same grace that enabled him rescued him. "Lord, save me!" Peter cried. "And immediately Jesus stretched out His hand and caught him" (Matthew 14:30-31). Grace calls you out—and won't let you drown where it called you.

Paul: When Thorns Became Thrones (2 Corinthians 12:7-10)

Three times Paul pleaded for his thorn's removal. Three times God said no, but added revelation: "And He said to me, 'My grace is sufficient for you, for My strength is made perfect in weakness'" (2 Corinthians 12:9). Paul discovered the paradox that changes everything: "Therefore most gladly I will rather boast in my infirmities, that the power of Christ may rest upon me. Therefore I take pleasure in infirmities, in reproaches, in needs, in persecutions, in distresses, for Christ's sake. For when I am weak, then I am strong" (2 Corinthians 12:9-10). Not when I overcome weakness. Not when I defeat weakness. When I am weak, grace makes me strong. Grace closes gaps not by removing the struggle, but by using the struggle. Paul's thorn didn't disqualify him—it became the platform for God's strength. Grace doesn't require perfection—it uses imperfection.

TESTIMONY — WHEN GRACE SHATTERED MY DEFENDANT MENTALITY

The Crown Timeline

Let me clarify something important: God told me to straighten my crown in January 2018, but it took until October 2019 for me to understand what that meant.

January 2018 — The Word I Didn't Understand

Day 2 of that year's Daniel Fast. Journal entry: "My Daughter, here is my promise to honor you with majesty and royalty. You are the Daughter of the King of kings. I transform you into beauty as I did with Esther... You are royalty. Do not take off your crown. STRAIGHTEN YOUR CROWN. It got shifted in the climb... You are My Beauty... I will give you a double portion of honor, influence, affluence, glory, grace, goodness, and mercy... Favor surrounds you as a shield." I wrote it. I believed it. But I didn't understand it. For twenty months, those words sat in my journal like seeds waiting for rain.

The Bedroom Floor Breakthrough

I was hiding from God in plain sight—showing up but not showing up. Three weeks of spiritual dodgeball, journaling apologies instead of conversations, approaching His throne like a criminal approaching sentencing. That morning, I sat on my bedroom floor with my journal, hands literally shaking—not from caffeine withdrawal, but from the weight of perpetual insufficiency crushing my chest. Ministry doors opening that I felt too broken to walk through. Financial needs staring me down. My children needing a mother who had herself together, not one falling apart at six o'clock on a Saturday evening.

I wrote eight words that would change everything: "I'm so tired of disappointing You, Father." The response came so fast I almost dropped my pen: "What's in your hands?" Not "What did they take from you?" Not "What don't you have?" But—"What have I already deposited in you?" My hand moved to Day 2 of my January 2018 Daniel Fast journal. There it was, buried under twenty months of doubt: STRAIGHTEN YOUR CROWN.

I sat there, journal in lap, tears dropping onto pages, and suddenly I could feel it—the weight of an invisible reality that had been sitting sideways on my head for two years. Not missing. Not fallen. Just shifted. The climb had knocked it crooked. The striving had tilted it. The failures had pushed it back until I couldn't see straight, couldn't walk straight, couldn't think straight because my identity wasn't properly positioned.

That's when the room changed. Not gradually—instantly. I heard these words so clearly I wrote them in all caps: "CASE DISMISSED. ALL CHARGES DROPPED. DEFENDANT RELEASED. DAUGHTER RESTORED." The pen fell from my hand. For years, I'd been living in a courtroom that didn't exist, defending myself before a Judge who'd already declared me innocent, listing failures to a Father who only saw a daughter. Grace didn't wait for me to clean up. It positioned me in the mess. Your biggest gap is God's favorite construction site.

Younger Son's Confirmation

That night, my younger son walked into my room while I was praying. He watched me for a moment, then said: "Mommy, you look different. You look like a queen now." He couldn't see what I had straightened. But he could see what adjusting my identity did.

The Crown Revelation's Global Impact

The revelation didn't stay with me. It spread like holy fire through every woman I encountered. In our Chayah Club gatherings, through one-on-one ministry, in boardrooms and broken places—the simple act of reaching up to adjust an invisible reality broke chains that counseling couldn't touch. The testimonies poured in. One woman, after losing her job of thirty years along with health insurance, stood on grace's power during those twenty-one days. When she saw an oncologist after the fast: "NO SIGNS OF CANCER. STILL IN REMISSION." Another described it as "Transformation 5.0"—like a graduate-level spirituality class that connected her wellness journey with God on the highest level.

What consistently emerged: When men and women stopped approaching God as defendants and started approaching as children—with proper positioning—everything shifted. New jobs manifested. Mortgage approvals came through. Financial breakthroughs occurred. Promotions arrived. Freedom from addiction. Mended relationships. Peace replaced panic. Clarity replaced confusion. Grace didn't just change their status. Grace changed their posture.

WHERE YOUR CROWN WENT SIDEWAYS

You didn't notice when it happened. The crown didn't fall off dramatically in some catastrophic moment you could point to and say, "There. That's when I lost it." It shifted so gradually you didn't feel it move. A few degrees during the betrayal. Another tilt during the bankruptcy hearing. A slight rotation when the diagnosis came back positive. A knock backward when they walked out without explanation. The climb did that. Not your failure. Not your weakness. The climb. The thing you had to survive. The mountain nobody asked if you were strong enough to face before they sent you up it anyway.

You've been telling yourself you're fine. You show up. You function. You smile when you're supposed to smile. You serve when you're supposed to serve. But something feels off, doesn't it? Like you're walking with your head tilted, trying to see the world through a lens that doesn't quite line up anymore. You're working twice as hard to see half as clearly. You're exhausted from compensating for misalignment you can't name.

Here's what you haven't said out loud yet: You don't feel like royalty. You feel like a defendant. Every morning, you wake up already apologizing for yesterday's failures before you even get to today's responsibilities. You approach God like you're interrupting something more important. You list your inadequacies like evidence in a trial that never ends. You calculate how much disappointment He can tolerate before He stops pretending to care. You've been calling this humility. This isn't humility. This is a crown that got knocked crooked during a climb nobody warned you would be this steep, this long, this brutal.

Let Me Tell You What Really Happened

During the relationship breakdown, when they said you weren't enough—your crown shifted. During the job loss, when they cleared your desk while you watched—your crown tilted. During the miscarriage, when your body failed the one thing you begged it to do—your crown slipped backward. During the betrayal, when the person you trusted most became the person who wounded you deepest— your crown nearly fell off entirely. But it didn't fall. Grace held it on. You just couldn't see straight anymore because everything was at an angle. You've been trying to navigate a throne room while looking at it through courtroom vision. You've been reaching for royal authority with defendant hands. You've been speaking identity declarations through shame-silenced lips. No wonder you're exhausted. You've been fighting battles while wearing your armor sideways.

Here's what the enemy doesn't want you to know: The fact that your crown shifted during the climb doesn't mean you're disqualified from royalty. It means you've been in a fight. The fact that it's crooked doesn't mean it doesn't belong to you. It means you survived something that tried to knock it off completely. The fact that you can barely feel it anymore doesn't mean it's gone. It means you've been compensating for misalignment so long, you forgot what proper positioning feels like.

Your crown never fell. You never lost your identity. You're not starting from zero. You're not rebuilding from scratch. You're not earning back what was taken. You're adjusting what got shifted. You're realigning what got knocked crooked. You're straightening what's been there all along.

The Climb You Survived

Maybe it was the heartbreak that ended the relationship but not the questions. Maybe it was the ministry that flourished while your soul withered. Maybe it was the success everyone celebrated while depression whispered you were a fraud. Maybe it was the child you raised alone, the parent you buried too soon, the dream that died slowly, the addiction that almost killed you, the abuse that stole your voice, the rejection that rewrote your story. Maybe your climb has a name everyone knows. Maybe it's a secret you've carried alone. Maybe it's still happening. Maybe you're reading this from the middle of it right now, wondering if you'll even make it to the top, much less worry about a crown you can barely remember wearing.

Listen to me: The crown you wore before the climb wasn't earned through perfection. Grace placed it on your head the moment you became His child. It's not a reward for good behavior. It's your identity as a son, as a daughter. And nothing—not the relationship crisis, not the bankruptcy, not the diagnosis, not the betrayal, not the failure, not the wound, not the shame—can remove what grace secures. But the climb knocked it crooked. And you've been living with vision that's been off-center for so long, you thought this was normal. You thought everyone approached God listing failures. You thought everyone felt like an imposter. You thought everyone dragged themselves to the throne room expecting rejection. You thought courtroom Christianity was the only Christianity there was.

It's not. There's a throne room where you're not a defendant but a child. There's a Father waiting—not with a gavel but with open arms. There's access you don't have to earn, approval you don't have to audit, acceptance you don't have to achieve. There's a position you didn't lose during the climb. It just got knocked sideways. And today—right now, this moment—you get to straighten it.

Not because you've arrived. Not because the wounds are healed. Not because the climb is over. Not because you've finally gotten strong enough, holy enough, together enough. But because grace doesn't wait for you to deserve realignment. Grace says: "You're Mine. You've always been Mine. The climb was hard, but it didn't change whose you are. Now reach up. Feel for what's been there all along. And adjust what got shifted during the fight."

So Reach Up Right Now

Your hand is shaking as you read this. That's okay. Trembling hands can still straighten crowns. Broken people can still wear royalty. Wounded warriors can still walk in authority. Your weakness doesn't disqualify you—it qualifies you for grace's greatest demonstration. Close your eyes if you need to. Put your hand on your head. Feel for the weight of what's been there all along—invisible to everyone else, but real to the one wearing it. The crown grace placed. The identity shame tried to steal. The royalty religion said you had to earn. It's there. Shifted, yes. Crooked from the climb, absolutely. But there. Still there. Always there.

Now adjust it. Physically move your hand. Tilt your head. Align what got misaligned. Let your body teach your spirit what words haven't been able to reach. This isn't pretending. This isn't fake-it-till-you-make-it. This isn't positive thinking. This is taking your position seriously enough to refuse to wear it sideways anymore.

When you straighten your crown, everything else shifts. The courtroom disappears and you're standing in a throne room. The Judge becomes your Father. The charges dissolve. The defendant identity dies. The apology reflexes quiet. The shame scripts silence. And you approach—not crawling, not begging, not listing failures—but boldly, as His child, with your crown straight and your access secured and your position established.

You're not the same person who started reading this section. Something just shifted. Not just in your mind, but in your posture. Not just in your theology, but in your body. You reached up and adjusted reality. You straightened what the climb knocked crooked. You realigned what warfare shifted.

And They're About to Notice

Your son, your daughter, your friend, your spouse—they're about to say: "You look different." They won't know what changed. They can't see what you adjusted. But they'll see the result. You'll walk differently. Speak differently. Approach differently. Because people whose crowns are straight don't move like people whose crowns are crooked. People who know they're royalty don't apologize for existing. People who've been positioned by grace don't beg for what they already have access to.

The climb isn't over yet. You know that. There are more mountains ahead. More battles coming. More moments when warfare will try to knock your crown crooked again. But now you know. Now you've felt it. Now you have language for what's happening. Now you can recognize misalignment faster. Now you can straighten it before living years looking at everything sideways.

Now you know: Your crown never fell. It just got shifted during the climb. And anytime it gets knocked crooked, you can reach up and straighten it. Because you're not a defendant hoping for leniency. You're royalty learning to wear your position with confidence. You're a child approaching your Father's throne. You're a son, a daughter, crowned and commissioned, positioned by grace, secured by love, accessed by blood.

Straighten your crown. Not someday when you're stronger. Not eventually when you're healed. Not after the climb when you've arrived. Right now. Today. This moment. In the middle of the mess. During the battle. With shaking hands and blurry vision and wounds still healing. Reach up. Feel for what grace placed. Adjust what warfare shifted. Straighten what's been there all along. And then approach boldly.

Because defendants beg for leniency. But royalty receives ability. Defendants list failures. But sons and daughters expect provision. Defendants explain their presence. But heirs walk in confident they belong. The courtroom just closed. The throne room just opened. Your crown just got straightened. And you're about to discover what approaching God as His child actually feels like—not when you've earned

THE DANIEL FAST: CLOSING THE GAP!

it, but because He already gave it. Not when you deserve it, but because grace secured it. Not when you're perfect, but because He already declared you His.

Case dismissed. Crown straightened. Identity restored. Welcome to the throne room, your majesty.

PARADIGM SHIFT — FROM COURTROOM TO THRONE ROOM

COURTROOM MENTALITY	THRONE ROOM REALITY
"I approach God as defendant"	"I approach God as His child"
"Grace tolerates my failures"	"Grace transforms my failures"
"I need to get stronger"	"I surrender to His strength"
"Weakness disqualifies me"	"Weakness is where grace shows off"
"Grace is God's patience"	"Grace is God's power"
"I beg for leniency"	"I receive ability"
"I list my failures"	"I lift my identity"
"Case pending"	"Case dismissed"
"I explain my presence"	"I expect provision"

Why We Keep Choosing Courtrooms Over Throne Rooms

Understanding why we default to defendant mentality helps us recognize the lie and replace it with truth. Shame scripts from early wounds taught us love is conditional—earned through performance, revoked through failure. If parents withdrew affection when you disappointed them, you learned to approach all authority figures (including God) with an apology ready. The script plays automatically: "I'm sorry for existing." Religious conditioning gave you sin management instead of sonship. You learned to track failures, confess meticulously, and maintain spiritual hygiene—but never simply rest in belonging. Religion gave you a checklist when God gave you royal position.

The control reflex makes courtrooms feel safer than throne rooms because we can prepare arguments, present evidence, and manage outcomes. But throne rooms require surrender—receiving what we can't control, trusting a Father we can't manipulate. Control is the defendant's last defense. Scarcity gospel makes us fear grace will run out if we ask too much, use too much, need too much. So we ration relationship, approaching God only for emergencies, treating throne room access like a privilege we might lose instead of a position we can't forfeit. Father fog projects flawed fathers onto a flawless Father. If your earthly father's love was conditional, you assume heaven operates the same way. If he withheld affection, you expect God to do the same. You can't approach boldly when you're bracing for rejection.

Real-World Application

There's someone reading right now who thinks they're disqualified: the single mom who thinks her broken marriage removes her position, the businessman who thinks his bankruptcy voids his calling, the minister who thinks their past sin cancels their anointing, the young person who thinks their age delays their assignment. Grace means victory is happening in your situation now. Not because you've earned it. Not because you've perfected it. But because Jesus finished it. And you're living from that finished work. Your identity didn't fall off. It just got knocked crooked. Today, you straighten it.

Counter-Liturgy (Thirty Seconds)

Hand on heart: "Abba, I belong." Hand on head: "My position is secure." Hands open: "I receive ability, not just leniency." You don't break courtroom thinking with better arguments—you break it with better approaches.

ACTIVATION — SIX DIMENSIONS OF GRACE APPLICATION

Dimension	FROM (Courtroom)	TO (Throne Room)
SPIRITUAL	"Begging for God's attention"	"Bold in God's presence"
	Move: Set three "throne room" alarms daily	Receipt: Conviction without condemnation
EMOTIONAL	"Orphan pain"	"Child peace"
	Move: Touch head before tough conversations	Receipt: Respond instead of react
PHYSICAL	"Insufficient strength"	"Sufficient grace"
	Move: Declare "Your grace is sufficient" during weakness	Receipt: Strength rises where striving fails
MENTAL	"Turbulent thoughts"	"Grace teaching me"
	Move: Write one belief grace is upgrading daily	Receipt: Ruminations shorten, clarity increases
FINANCIAL	"Scarcity mindset"	"Supply for assignment"
	Move: Ask "Does this serve my assignment?" before spending	Receipt: Provision tracks purpose
RELATIONAL	"Avoidance patterns"	"Grace-led reconciliation"
	Move: Pray "Grace, go first" before difficult conversations	Receipt: Doors unlock that you couldn't kick open

Crown Straightening Exercise (Do This Now)

Stand up or sit tall if standing is difficult. Right hand reaches to your head. Feel for the invisible reality grace placed there. Physically adjust what you cannot see. Left palm open at your side—receiving position. Say aloud: "Case dismissed! I belong! I approach! I receive!" Hold for thirty seconds. Let your body teach your spirit. Wear the position you keep praying for.

Note for Readers Processing Trauma: If the concept of straightening your identity feels empowering, embrace it fully. If it feels like pressure to perform or "fake it till you make it," pause and honor that wisdom. For trauma survivors, royal imagery can sometimes feel like forced positivity that bypasses real pain. If that's you, know this: Your position is secure even when you can't feel it. Healing doesn't require pretending. God meets you in the courtroom confusion, walks with you toward the throne room, and never shames your pace. The position waits. Grace is patient. Your timeline is yours.

Grace Demonstration Exercise (Do This Tomorrow)

Don't just study Grace. Demonstrate Grace. Embody Grace. Be Grace to someone who desperately needs it. Choose one of these six grace dimensions and live it out specifically tomorrow: Saves (Ephesians 2:8)—Remind someone that salvation is a gift, not earned; text a struggling friend: "You're loved before you perform." Empowers (Acts 4:33)—Testify with power about Jesus' resurrection to someone; share one way God showed up in your weakness. Produces Evidence (Acts 11:23)—Point out visible evidence of God's grace in someone's life: "I see God's blessing on your work." Proportional (Ephesians 4:7)—Acknowledge someone's unique gifting: "God designed you specifically for this." Abundant (John 1:16-17)—Speak abundance over someone in lack: "More is coming. Grace multiplies." Accessible (Hebrews 4:16)—Pray boldly with someone about a specific need and expect God to meet it. Tomorrow: Choose one. Do it. Watch grace multiply through you.

FOCUS AREA GRACE PRAYERS

Scripture Foundation: "My grace is sufficient for you, for My strength is made perfect in weakness" (2 Corinthians 12:9). Choose your primary breakthrough area:

For Spiritual Focus: "Father, I need Your grace for spiritual breakthrough. Not tomorrow when I'm holier—now. Fill me with supernatural grace that empowers prayer, worship, and growth beyond my natural ability. I approach Your throne boldly."

For Mental Focus: "Father, I need Your grace for mental transformation. Grace that breaks negative thought patterns now. When anxious thoughts spike, Your grace is teaching me. My position is secure even when my mind isn't."

For Emotional Focus: "Father, I need Your grace for emotional healing. Pour out supernatural grace that heals wounds I can't reach. I'm loved before I speak. My emotional weakness is Your opportunity."

For Physical Focus: "Father, I need Your grace for physical transformation. The same power that raised Christ enables my body. Your grace is sufficient for this weakness. Strength rises where striving fails."

For Financial Focus: "Father, I need Your grace for financial breakthrough. Grace doesn't just forgive debt—it creates wealth for Kingdom purpose. I receive supply for my assignment."

For Relational Focus: "Father, I need Your grace for relational healing. Grace goes first into every conversation. What I can't repair, grace restores. Orphan patterns end; son and daughter patterns begin."

RESISTANCE REALITY CHECK

What You're Experiencing Right Now:

Courtroom Conditioning: "But I've failed too many times." Heaven's Response: Case dismissed. All charges dropped. Grace has the final word.

Unworthiness Uprising: "I don't deserve throne room access." Heaven's Response: Your position is already established. It just needs proper alignment.

Power Doubt: "Grace forgives but doesn't empower." Heaven's Response: Great grace equals great power. The weaker you get, the stronger you become.

Your weakness isn't grace's obstacle. It's grace's opportunity.

DECLARATION — SCRIPTURE-ANCHORED WARFARE

Stand with thousands globally and declare these truths:

"Let us therefore come boldly to the throne of grace, that we may obtain mercy and find grace to help in time of need!" (Hebrews 4:16)

"But by the grace of God I am what I am, and His grace toward me was not in vain; but I labored more abundantly than they all, yet not I, but the grace of God which was with me!" (1 Corinthians 15:10)

"And He said to me, 'My grace is sufficient for you, for My strength is made perfect in weakness!'" (2 Corinthians 12:9)

"Therefore most gladly I will rather boast in my infirmities, that the power of Christ may rest upon me!" (2 Corinthians 12:9)

"And with great power the apostles gave witness to the resurrection of the Lord Jesus. And great grace was upon them all!" (Acts 4:33)

CASE DISMISSED! ALL CHARGES DROPPED!

"Therefore, having been justified by faith, we have peace with God through our Lord Jesus Christ, through whom also we have access by faith into this grace in which we stand!" (Romans 5:1-2)

Orphans explain their presence. Heirs expect their provision!

BREAKTHROUGH PRAYER

Father God, Abba, I've been approaching You like a defendant when You've called me son, called me daughter. I've been crawling when You said come boldly. I've been in the courtroom when You've opened the throne room. Case dismissed! All charges dropped! The defendant is dead! The son has risen! The daughter has risen!

I repent for reducing grace to tolerance when it's power. For believing grace only forgives when it empowers. For removing my royal position when You told me to properly align it. Like Moses, I accept that my impediment is Your opportunity. Like Gideon, I believe You see "mighty" when I feel "least." Like Esther, I approach the throne I once feared. Like Paul, I boast in weakness because the weaker I get, the stronger I become. Like Peter, I step out on Your word alone, knowing You won't let me drown where You called me.

Right now, I receive the four dimensions of grace that religion only half-taught: unmerited favor (what religion taught), divine influence on the heart (what religion missed), supernatural empowerment (what religion feared), and God's operational power (what I'm receiving now). I receive grace that empowers my weakness, grace that exhibits through my insufficiency, grace that positions my identity, grace that closes every case against me.

I receive the six-dimensional operation of grace: Salvation—Grace initiated relationship. Empowerment—Grace produces power. Evidence—Grace becomes visible. Proportion—Grace fits my assignment. Abundance—Grace multiplies continually. Access—Grace opens the throne room.

The defendant era is over! The son and daughter era has begun! The courtroom is closed! The throne room is open! I adjust my position. I approach boldly. I receive power, not just pardon. In Jesus' mighty name, grace is operational power in my life! Amen.

CLOSING — THRONE ROOM REALITY

Day 2 started with your body rebelling, your strength failing. Tonight you rest knowing withdrawal was grace's invitation, not disqualification. The shaking in your hands reminded you—when natural strength fails, supernatural strength prevails. The caffeine your body craves has been replaced by power your spirit receives.

Thousands globally adjusted their positioning today. From Tokyo to Toronto, from Lagos to Los Angeles, defendants became sons and daughters. Courtrooms closed. Throne rooms opened. By Day 21, approaching the throne room will be as natural as breathing. The royal position you aligned today will feel secure. The defendant mentality will be a distant memory.

Tomorrow, you'll discover that while grace empowers you in weakness, God's goodness has been hunting you down—even through doors He kept closed, jobs you didn't get, relationships that failed. You'll create evidence of preventative goodness with a napkin that becomes holy. Tomorrow, memory defeats suspicion. Stop living like a defendant in a Kingdom where your Father already positioned you as royalty.

Day 2 Complete: Defendant Demolished, Son and Daughter Positioned

Grace: Not just patience, but power
Position: Not earned, but secured
Case: Not pending, but dismissed
Identity: Not defendant, but son and daughter
Access: Not begged for, but boldly approached
Throne room: Not future hope, but present reality

SOAP JOURNAL — Day 2

S (Scripture): Which grace verse shifted your perspective from tolerance to power?
O (Observation): Where have you been approaching God as defendant rather than son or daughter?
A (Application): What changes when I properly align my identity and approach boldly? Which of the six grace dimensions do I need most today?
P (Prayer): "Father, Your grace is _____ in my weakness. My position is secure because _____. Tomorrow I will demonstrate grace by _____."

Today's Breakthrough Marker: What shifted in your understanding of grace today?
Tomorrow's Expectation: Based on today's revelation, what do you expect tomorrow?

COURTROOM CLOSED. THRONE ROOM OPEN. POSITION SECURED. READY FOR GOODNESS.

DAY 3 — GOODNESS

From Questioning His Nature to Trusting the Darkroom

> *"I would have lost heart, unless I had believed that I would see the goodness of the LORD in the land of the living."*
> — Psalm 27:13

WEEK 1 — GROW: Building Intimacy with God

Day 3 of 21. Yesterday's Grace empowered you. Today's Goodness teaches you to trust what's developing in darkness.

ENCOUNTER — WHERE YOU ARE

5:42 AM. Day 3. Your jaw locks mid-chew. The food turns to sawdust—not because it's bland, but because your body knows you're lying. You're not hungry for food. You're starving for proof God is good. Around you, the world indulges. Coffee brewing. Toast popping. Cereal crunching. Each sound amplified. Your body doesn't just want food; it wants the comfort that's medicated your mornings for years.

This is where most people quit. Not from hunger but from suspicion. The physical deprivation triggers something deeper—a theological crisis about whether God is actually good when life tastes bitter. Goodness isn't what God does when life tastes sweet. Goodness is what God is when life tastes like death. Stop. Feel that craving? That's not just physical hunger. That's your soul wrestling with the question that has defined human history since a serpent whispered doubt: "Did God really say? Is He really good?"

Right now, across six continents, thousands wrestle this same bitter morning. In the Caribbean, that corporate leader who pushed away coffee yesterday now stares at his empty mug, questioning if the sacrifice matters. In Nigeria, that grandmother who spent sixty years in prayer wonders if goodness abandoned her in old age. In Canada, that construction worker feels the job rejection sting and asks where goodness was in that closed door. In London, that teenager faces another day of family tension and doubts if God sees her struggle. In the United States, that single mother counts bills that don't add up and questions if provision will come. In the Philippines, that college student opens another rejection email and wonders if God's goodness includes her future. All questioning the same ancient doubt.

Yesterday you discovered grace empowers your weakness. Day 1 showed you the Gospel already accepted you. But acceptance and empowerment don't automatically translate to trust. You know you're loved. You know you're empowered. But do you believe He's good when everything tastes like sacrifice? When the door slams shut? When the answer is "no"? When nothing makes sense? "God knows my heart," the quitter's voice whispers. "He understands if I stop."

What if you've been standing in a darkroom the entire time—where images develop invisibly until God lifts them into light? The fact that you woke up today. The fact that you're on Day 3. The fact that you care enough to wrestle with these questions. Evidence developing. Evidence forming. Evidence you can't see yet. You're not searching for evidence of His goodness. You are the evidence developing in His darkroom.

Right now, forcing down that tasteless breakfast, you might believe God's goodness is conditional. Present when doors open, absent when they close. But what if closed doors are God's darkroom—where

He develops protection you can't see and provision that wouldn't survive premature light? The darkroom isn't abandonment. It's where God develops what daylight would destroy.

FOUNDATION — BIBLICAL AUTHORITY

To understand why closed doors aren't rejection, we must first understand what goodness actually means and how God operates in darkness.

The Nature of Divine Goodness

Goodness—the Hebrew word *tov*—isn't merely blessing or favor. It's God's essential nature, His unchanging character that actively works all things for ultimate benefit, even through immediate difficulty. When God declared creation "good," He wasn't commenting on performance. He was imprinting His own nature into existence. Goodness isn't what God does—it's who God is. Goodness isn't God's response to circumstances. Goodness is God's nature creating good from circumstances.

As C.S. Lewis profoundly observed: "There is but one good; that is God. Everything else is good when it looks to Him and bad when it turns from Him." This is why the same circumstance can be bitter or blessed depending on whether we're looking at God or at the circumstance itself. The struggle isn't inherently good or bad—it becomes good when we trust the One developing the image.

Primary Scripture: The Land of the Living

"I would have lost heart, unless I had believed that I would see the goodness of the LORD in the land of the living" (Psalm 27:13). David writes this while running from Saul. Hiding in caves. Dodging spears. His "land of the living" is a wilderness of death threats. Yet he declares future sight of present goodness. The Hebrew construction is emphatic: "I would have fainted." David is saying, "The only thing keeping me alive is believing I'll see evidence of what I can't currently feel." This is darkroom faith—trusting the image is forming even when you can't see it yet.

The Relentless Hunt

"Surely goodness and mercy shall follow me all the days of my life, and I will dwell in the house of the LORD forever" (Psalm 23:6). "Follow" is *radaph*—to pursue, hunt down, chase relentlessly. Like a divine bounty hunter who never gives up. Goodness isn't passive—it's predatory in the best way. Goodness isn't waiting for you to find it. Goodness is actively hunting you down. All the days. Not just victory days. Valley days. Day 3 days. Divorce days. Diagnosis days. Death days. Darkroom days. All. Goodness doesn't clock out when hardship clocks in.

The Six-Dimensional Nature of Goodness

God's goodness isn't one-dimensional—it operates across six biblical realities simultaneously. In the dimension of creation, every creature of God is good (1 Timothy 4:4). Goodness wasn't added to creation—it was creation. When God called everything "good," He was imprinting His nature into existence. In the dimension of refuge, the Lord is good, a stronghold in the day of trouble, and He knows those who trust in Him (Nahum 1:7). Goodness isn't just blessing in sunshine—it's shelter in storm.

In the dimension of provision, no good thing will He withhold from those who walk uprightly (Psalm 84:11). But provision includes prevention. Sometimes the "good thing" is the door He closes to protect what's forming. In the dimension of pursuit, surely goodness and mercy shall follow me all the days of my life (Psalm 23:6). *Radaph*—hunting you down relentlessly. Goodness doesn't wait for you to find it; it tracks you into darkness. In the dimension of eternity, *Oh, give thanks to the Lord, for He is good! For His mercy endures forever* (1 Chronicles 16:34). Goodness doesn't expire when circumstances darken. It soaks through every season. In the dimension of unchanging nature, *every good gift and every perfect gift is from above, and comes down from the Father of lights, with whom there is no variation or shadow of turning* (James 1:17). Your perception shifts, but God's goodness never does.

These six dimensions operate simultaneously. You may only feel one—refuge in storm—but all six are developing the image invisibly.

THE DARKROOM PRINCIPLE

Here's what religion never taught you: God's greatest work happens in darkness. Not because God is darkness—but because darkness is where images develop that daylight would destroy.

The Darkroom Process

Watch how this works in photography. A photographer doesn't develop film in sunlight. Light destroys the image before it can form. The film submerges in darkness—silent, invisible. Nothing appears to be happening. Impatience screams to check progress, but premature light ruins everything. Only when development completes does the photographer lift the film—and what was invisible becomes undeniable. Two things develop simultaneously: what was captured (the image that appeared) and what was protected (the flaws filtered, exposures controlled). You don't see either while it's soaking. You see both when lifted into light. You don't see the picture while it's soaking; you see it when He lifts it into view.

The Theology Behind the Metaphor

Your valley isn't abandonment—it's where God develops what daylight would destroy. Your waiting isn't waste—it's the chemical bath where your image deepens. Your closed doors aren't rejection—they're the darkness protecting what's forming from premature exposure. Your silence isn't absence—it's where goodness works two dimensions simultaneously.

The first dimension is provision goodness—what captured, what appeared. The door that swung wide. The check that arrived. The person who showed up. The opportunity that manifested. We celebrate this goodness. We testify about this goodness. We see this goodness in the light. The second dimension is preventative goodness—what protected, what prevented. The door that stayed shut. The relationship that ended. The opportunity that "fell through." The path that blocked. We question this goodness. We resist this goodness. We don't recognize this goodness—until the image lifts into light and we see what we were spared. Goodness doesn't only capture images; it protects them from premature exposure.

Important theological clarity: God does not author darkness or evil; He works masterfully within darkness created by others' evil or life's brokenness. People may intend harm, but God re-intends it toward ultimate good (Genesis 50:20; Romans 8:28). The darkness isn't from God—but God works in darkness better than we work in light.

The Invisible Rescue

When Moses begged to see God's glory, God answered, *"I will make all My goodness pass before you"* (Exodus 33:19). Sometimes that goodness looks like provision opening; sometimes it looks like prevention blocking. You see the lifeguard pulling someone from drowning. Dramatic rescue. Everyone applauds. But you never see the lifeguard who prevented someone from entering dangerous waters in the first place. Invisible rescue. Nobody notices. Both are equally life-saving. One is visible; one develops in darkness.

God specializes in invisible rescues. The accident that would have happened if you'd left five minutes earlier. The toxic person who disappeared before they could poison you. The opportunity that seemed perfect but was actually predatory. The door that closed because the room behind it would have consumed you. The strongest evidence of God's goodness isn't what you see—it's what you survived without knowing.

Consider what developed in your own experience: The relationship that fell apart before it could break you. The job you didn't get that would have killed your calling. The investment that failed before you committed everything. The diagnosis you could have received but were spared. The addiction you could have developed but escaped. Goodness worked two ways: Captured provision. Protected from destruction. Every "no" was protecting the "yes" that was forming.

Why We Can't See While It's Developing

Proverbs 16:9 declares: "A man's heart plans his way, but the LORD directs his steps." Sometimes God's direction looks like redirection. Sometimes His guidance looks like blockage. Sometimes His favor looks like denial. Why? Because if you saw what was forming too early, you'd interfere with the process. You'd pull the film out of the bath before it finished soaking. You'd expose it to light before the image was permanent. You'd rush the chemistry that needs time to work. Your impatience would destroy what His patience is developing. Premature light doesn't speed up the process—it destroys the image.

This is why you can't see while you're waiting. Not because God is hiding from you, but because He's protecting what's forming from you—from your interference, your impatience, your need to control outcomes. Trust the soak. The image is forming. Both provision and prevention are developing simultaneously. Memory will defeat suspicion—but only when God lifts the film into light.

REVELATION — BIBLICAL PATTERNS

Throughout Scripture, God's greatest work happens where nothing appears to be developing—until He lifts the image into light.

Joseph: Thirteen Years in Darkness (Genesis 37-50)

Seventeen years old. Blood-stained coat. Brothers' laughter echoing in the pit. Feel the rope burns on his wrists. Taste the slave auction dust. Smell the prison mold. Thirteen years descending deeper into darkness. Pit. Slavery. False accusation. Prison. Each level darker than the last. Nothing appearing to develop. No image forming. Just soaking in suffering's chemical bath. Every day asking: "Is God good? Where's the goodness? Why this darkness?"

But watch what was developing invisibly. On the provision side, what captured: Character forged in fire. Administration skills in Potiphar's house. Dream interpretation refined in prison. Positioning for Pharaoh's court. Authority to save nations. On the preventative side, what protected: If promoted in Potiphar's house, he'd have stayed comfortable—nations would have starved. Prison removed him from palace politics that would have destroyed him. The closed doors positioned him for the door that would open at perfect timing.

Thirteen years later, God lifts the film into light. Joseph sees both sides: "But as for you, you meant evil against me; but God meant it for good, in order to bring it about as it is this day, to save many people alive" (Genesis 50:20). Meant it. Not "turned it" after the fact. Meant it for good from the beginning. The pit wasn't punishment—it was development. The prison wasn't abandonment—it was protection. The closed doors weren't rejection—they were positioning. Goodness doesn't always look good while it's soaking.

Job: When Darkness Feels Like Death (Job 1-2, 42)

One day. Ten funerals. All wealth erased. Body covered in boils. Job's wife: "Curse God and die." Job's friends: "Confess your secret sins." Job's reality: Complete darkness. No image forming. No sense being made. But Job declares from that place: "Though He slay me, yet will I trust Him" (Job 13:15). This isn't blind faith—it's faith that trusts the process when you can't see the image.

What was developing invisibly? On the provision side, what captured: Testimony that would inspire millions for millennia. Character refined by fire. Revelation of God's sovereignty. Double restoration of everything lost. On the preventative side, what protected: Satan could take wealth and health but was blocked from taking Job's life. The limit God set was protecting what would emerge. Friends' bad counsel didn't break Job's faith—the process protected his core.

When God lifts the film into light: Job receives twice everything lost—except children. Same number. Why? Because the first ten weren't lost—they were waiting in eternity. Goodness multiplied what was eternal, didn't replace what was never lost. Goodness doesn't replace what was never lost—it develops what's eternal.

Ruth: When Grief Becomes Glory (Ruth 1-4)

Three funerals. Husband. Two sons. All dead within years. Naomi becomes Mara—bitter. "Call me Mara, for the Almighty has dealt very bitterly with me" (Ruth 1:20). Feel her bitterness—not theology but raw grief. Empty arms. Empty future. Empty hope. Foreign land. No provision. No protection. Just widowhood and poverty soaking in darkness.

But watch what's developing invisibly. On the provision side, what captured: Ruth's loyalty forged through loss. Positioning in Bethlehem at harvest season. Introduction to Boaz. Lineage leading to King David and Jesus Christ. On the preventative side, what protected: Ruth could have married in Moab—door closed. That closed door protected her from comfortable obscurity. Widowhood positioned her for destiny that marriage would have prevented. Grief became where greatness developed.

When God lifts the film: Ruth is in the Messiah's bloodline. The widow who thought her story ended? Her story became His story. Goodness uses your deepest grief to develop your greatest glory.

The Woman with the Issue of Blood: Twelve-Year Soak (Mark 5:25-34)

Twelve years bleeding. Four thousand three hundred eighty days hemorrhaging. Count the weakness—iron deficiency making stairs mountains. Count the bankruptcy—doctors, treatments, desperate attempts. Count the isolation—ceremonially unclean, forbidden from temple, touch, community. Where was goodness?

What was developing in twelve years? On the provision side, what captured: Desperation that produces breakthrough faith. Testimony of healing that couldn't be attributed to time or medicine. "Daughter" declaration from Jesus—identity restoration. Complete *sōzō*—saved, healed, delivered, made whole. On the preventative side, what protected: If healed year one: Good doctor gets credit. If healed year five: Medicine gets credit. If healed year ten: Time gets credit. Twelve years meant only God could get glory. Every failed treatment was a closed door protecting the ultimate testimony from dilution.

One touch. Instant healing. Undeniable source. Goodness makes you wait so the miracle can't be mistaken for medicine.

The Pattern is Clear

God always develops two images simultaneously: What He provided (the doors that opened). What He prevented (the doors that closed). You celebrate provision. You question prevention. But when God lifts the film into light, you see both were equally necessary for the complete image.

TESTIMONY — MY DARKROOM REVELATION

The 3 PM Email That Shattered Me

Subject line: "Thank you for your interest." Corporate language for rejection. My "dream" client chose someone else. Three months of work. Multiple rounds. Final shortlist. Partnership formed. Future secured. Instead: "We've decided to move forward with another consultant." I sobbed over my laptop. This was the contract. The breakthrough. The validation. My business account: dangerously low. My confidence: shattered. My future: uncertain. I wanted to scream, "Where are You, God? Where's the goodness You promise?" I'd just entered darkness. I couldn't see it yet.

The Immediate Whisper

That same night, during prayer, a phrase dropped into my spirit so clearly I wrote it down immediately: "What you called rejection, I call redirection. The door I closed protected the door I'm opening." I had no idea what it meant. The pain was too fresh. The wound too raw. But I wrote it in my journal: "3 PM rejection means midnight redirection?" That whisper became my anchor when darkness felt endless.

The Soak

Instead of wallowing, I redirected energy into something that had been tugging at my heart. Ministry work I'd delayed because I needed "paying work." Within months, I launched U Power Up on June 23, 2020. A nonprofit I'd contemplated but never had courage to start. Professional failure became spiritual activation. But I still wondered: "Did I make the right choice? Should I have tried harder to get that contract?" Two years of soaking in that question. Two years wondering if the closed door was rejection or redirection. Darkness felt like waste. The image wasn't visible yet.

When God Lifted the Film Into Light

Two years later. A conference. The former director approached me, looking uncomfortable. "That project you applied for? We lost funding six months in. Never finished." She paused, lowered her voice. "The consultant we hired? They're still in litigation with us. It destroyed their business." I stood there stunned as the film lifted into light. Suddenly I could see both sides of what had been developing invisibly.

On the provision side, what captured: U Power Up launched and impacting thousands globally. Women's lives transformed. Ministry influence I could never have built with corporate work. Calling clarified and activated. Purpose ignited. On the preventative side, what protected: Contract would have consumed my time for six months. Litigation would have destroyed my business. Legal nightmare avoided. Financial disaster prevented. Ministry that would impact thousands protected from distraction.

The rejection that devastated me had actually rescued me. The closed door I called abandonment was protecting provision from premature exposure. That midnight whisper? It was the image forming before I could see it. You called it rejection; God called it protection. Today, U Power Up impacts thousands. That "dream contract" would have killed the actual dream. The pattern I couldn't see while soaking in darkness became undeniable when lifted into light. Every "no" was goodness aiming me toward the right "yes."

From Concrete Steps to His Platforms

That 3 PM rejection was one film in a life-long development. From concrete steps in Jamaica to global platforms. From coloring holes in my shoes with markers to funding ministries. From daughter of a teenage single mother to impacting thousands globally. None of it made sense—unless infinite power was personally developing an image in darkness I couldn't see. The poverty developed provision I couldn't have received in comfort. The struggle developed strength I couldn't have built in ease. The closed doors protected me from opportunities that looked good but were actually destructive. We shrink God to the size of our understanding, then wonder why our problems look so big.

PARADIGM SHIFT — FROM DAYLIGHT DEMANDS TO DARKROOM TRUST

DAYLIGHT DEMANDS	DARKROOM TRUST
"I need to see it now"	"I trust what's developing invisibly"
"Open doors prove goodness"	"Closed doors are goodness developing"
"God is good when life is good"	"God is good when life is soaking"
"Darkness means absence"	"Darkness means development"
"I search for visible proof"	"I trust invisible process"
"Closed doors mean rejection"	"Closed doors mean protection"
"Show me before I'll believe"	"Believe before I can see"
"Why is this taking so long?"	"Premature light ruins the process"
"Nothing is happening"	"Everything is developing"
"Track only what opened"	"Track what opened and what closed"

Bottom Line: Daylight demands immediate visibility. Darkroom trust believes the image is forming even when you can't see it yet. Darkness isn't punishment—it's the process that produces permanent images.

ACTIVATION — SIX DIMENSIONS OF DARKROOM TRUST

Dimension	FROM (Daylight Demands)	TO (Darkroom Trust)
SPIRITUAL	"God feels absent in darkness" Move: List where you're in spiritual darkness, declare "image is forming"	"God works best in darkness" Receipt: Peace in the process
EMOTIONAL	"Emotional darkness means something's wrong" Move: Identify emotional darkness, trust the soak	"Emotional darkness develops depth" Receipt: Resilience deepening

PHYSICAL	"Physical limitations prove abandonment" Move: Thank God for closed health doors (surgeries avoided, diagnoses spared)	"Physical weakness is the darkroom." Receipt: Gratitude for protection
MENTAL	"Confusion means I'm lost" Move: Document mental confusion, trust image developing	"Confusion means clarity is forming" Receipt: Clarity emerging
FINANCIAL	"Lack proves God isn't good" Move: List financial doors that closed, identify what they protected you from	"Closed financial doors protect provision" Receipt: Pattern recognition
RELATIONAL	"Loneliness proves rejection" Move: Thank God for relationships that ended, trust who's coming	"Relational darkness positions right people" Receipt: Protected from toxicity

The Darkroom Descent (Do This Now)

This physical act embodies darkroom faith—trusting what's developing in darkness before you can see it. What you need: Your own body, ninety seconds, willingness to experience disorientation.

The Exercise: First, create darkness wherever you are. Close your eyes tightly. Cover them with your hands, pressing palms against closed lids. If seated, lean forward slightly. If standing, face away from any light source. Your goal: Complete self-imposed darkness. Let your eyes try to adjust behind your hands. They can't. It's too dark. Second, set timer for sixty seconds. Keep hands pressed over closed eyes. Stand or sit in your created darkness. Let disorientation rise. Let fear whisper. Let impatience scream. Don't fight it. Feel it. This is what darkness does.

Third, when timer sounds, say once with hands still covering eyes: "Trust the soak." That's it. Three words. Let them hang in the self-created black. Fourth, explode into light. Rip your hands away from your eyes. Open your eyes wide. If there's a window, turn toward it. If there's a lamp, flip it on. Let light flood your vision. Let your eyes burn with the contrast. Fifth, stand in the light with hands open at your sides—receiving position. Say once: "Memory defeats suspicion."

Why this works: Your body teaches your spirit. The violence of self-imposed darkness followed by explosive light embodies the spiritual truth: God develops images in darkness that daylight would destroy. The disorientation isn't failure—it's the point. That's what darkness does. You created darkness with your own hands—just as sometimes our circumstances, our choices, our limitations create struggle. But the light was always there. You just couldn't see it while your hands covered your eyes. When you remove the barrier, light floods in.

This exercise works anywhere: At your desk during lunch break. In your car before work. In your bedroom at night. On a park bench. Sitting in a waiting room. No dark room required. No special equipment. Just you, your hands, your willingness to experience darkness before light. Trust the process. The image is forming. Both provision and prevention are developing simultaneously.

Note for Readers Processing Trauma: If the Darkroom Descent exercise feels empowering, embrace it fully. If creating self-imposed darkness triggers panic, PTSD responses, or overwhelming fear, honor that wisdom and skip the physical exercise. Your trauma history may make darkness unsafe, not redemptive. For those processing abuse, assault, or captivity—where darkness was weaponized against you—the metaphor can still teach without the physical act. You can trust God's process intellectually without recreating darkness physically. Healing doesn't require triggering. The image is forming whether you close your eyes or keep them open. Your safety matters more than completing an exercise.

Developing the Film — The Evidence Protocol

You've been in darkness. Now it's time to see what developed. This isn't list-making—this is examining the photograph that was forming invisibly while you were blind. What you need: Paper (napkin, receipt, journal page, back of envelope), pen, timer, honest memory willing to look at both sides of the film.

Side One: Provision (What Captured) — Ninety Seconds. Set timer for ninety seconds. Write every "coincidence" from the past year. Don't filter, don't edit, just document what appeared: Person who called exactly when needed. Money from unexpected source. Door that opened mysteriously. Peace in crisis. Perfectly timed provision. Opportunity that manifested. When timer stops, count them. Circle your top three.

Side Two: Prevention (What Protected) — Ninety Seconds. Reset timer for ninety seconds. Write what didn't happen that could have: Relationship that ended before it destroyed you. Job you didn't get (what happened to that company?). Accident that almost occurred. Diagnosis you were spared. Addiction you could have developed. Financial disaster narrowly avoided. Betrayal that was blocked. When timer stops, count them. Circle your top three.

The Declaration (Hold Your Developed Film). Stand with your paper in hand. This is your developed photograph—evidence of what formed while you couldn't see. Read top three from each side aloud. Begin each: "In the darkness, You were developing _____." End with: "Goodness was working invisibly—I just couldn't see it until You lifted the film." Keep this evidence. This isn't trash. This is your developed film. Your proof that God works in darkness. Place it where you'll see it: Bible at Psalm 27:13. Mirror. Wallet. Phone photo. When suspicion rises, this memory defeats it. Memory defeats suspicion when you examine the developed film.

FOCUS AREA DARKROOM PRAYERS

Scripture Foundation: "I would have lost heart, unless I had believed that I would see the goodness of the LORD in the land of the living" (Psalm 27:13). Choose your primary breakthrough area:

For Spiritual Focus: "Father, I'm in spiritual darkness right now. I can't see what You're developing, but I trust the soak. The dryness is where You work without my interference. Develop provision I can't see and protection I don't know I need. I trust the process."

For Mental Focus: "Father, my mind is in darkness—confusion, fog, inability to see clearly. But this is Your process. You're developing mental clarity that premature answers would destroy. I trust what's forming invisibly. Protect me from thoughts that would ruin the image."

For Emotional Focus: "Father, I'm in emotional darkness—pain, grief, wounds that won't heal quickly. But You're developing emotional depth that easy comfort would prevent. The ache is the soak. The image is forming. I trust both provision and prevention working simultaneously."

For Physical Focus: "Father, my body is in darkness—weakness, limitation, closed doors to healing. But You're developing something that instant relief would destroy. Thank You for the diagnoses

I don't have, the accidents that didn't happen, the closed medical doors that protected me. I trust Your process."

For Financial Focus: "Father, I'm in financial darkness—closed opportunities, blocked provision, doors that won't open. But You're developing financial breakthrough that premature opening would compromise. Thank You for the investments You blocked, the debts You prevented, the opportunities that would have destroyed me. I trust the soak."

For Relational Focus: "Father, I'm in relational darkness—loneliness, endings, people who disappeared. But You're developing relationships that premature connection would ruin. Thank You for toxic people You removed, betrayals You prevented, relationships that would have consumed me. I trust who's coming."

RESISTANCE REALITY CHECK

What You're Experiencing Right Now:

Darkroom Panic: "But I can't see anything! Nothing is happening!" Heaven's Response: The best work happens in darkness. Trust the soak. Premature light ruins the image.

Impatience: "Why is this taking so long?" Heaven's Response: Darkness doesn't rush. The longer the soak, the richer the image. Trust the chemistry.

Closed Door Theology: "This closed door means God said no to me." Heaven's Response: This closed door means I'm protecting what's forming. I'm developing both provision and prevention.

Visibility Demands: "Show me now or I won't believe." Heaven's Response: David said, "I would have fainted unless I believed I would see." Believe before you see.

Evidence Dismissal: "Those were just coincidences." Heaven's Response: Examine the developed film. Count provision and prevention. Memory defeats suspicion.

The strongest evidence isn't what you see now—it's what you'll see when I lift the film into light.

DECLARATION — SCRIPTURE-ANCHORED WARFARE

Stand with thousands in global darkness and declare these truths:

"I would have lost heart, unless I had believed that I would see the goodness of the LORD in the land of the living!" (Psalm 27:13)

"Surely goodness and mercy shall follow me all the days of my life!" (Psalm 23:6)

"And we know that all things work together for good to those who love God, to those who are the called according to His purpose!" (Romans 8:28)

"Though He slay me, yet will I trust Him!" (Job 13:15)

"For our light affliction, which is but for a moment, is working for us a far more exceeding and eternal weight of glory!" (2 Corinthians 4:17)

The darkness isn't abandonment—it's development! The image is forming even when I can't see it! Closed doors are protecting what's developing! Premature light would destroy the process! Memory defeats suspicion when the film lifts! I trust the soak! The image is permanent when the process completes!

BREAKTHROUGH PRAYER

Father God, Good Father, I repent for demanding daylight when You're working in darkness. For pulling out the film before it finished soaking. For calling Your process "abandonment" when it was actually development. I'm in darkness right now. Day 3 has me questioning Your goodness because I can't see what's forming. Life tastes bitter. Doors are closed. Nothing makes sense. But I choose darkroom faith over daylight demands.

Like Joseph, I trust thirteen years of darkness developed both positioning and protection. Like Job, I trust the process developed testimony and restoration. Like Ruth, I trust grief was the chemical bath where glory formed. Like the woman with the issue of blood, I trust twelve years meant only You could get credit. Right now, I receive trust in the invisible process, peace in the darkness, belief that two images are forming—provision and prevention—eyes to see when You lift the film into light, and memory that defeats suspicion.

I hold my developed film in my hand. I've counted what captured and what protected. The evidence is undeniable. Thank You for doors You closed that blocked cliffs, relationships You ended before they destroyed me, opportunities You blocked that would have consumed me, diagnoses I don't have, accidents that didn't happen, and the darkness that felt like death but was actually development. The image is forming invisibly. Goodness is working two dimensions simultaneously. Premature light would ruin everything—so I trust the soak. In Jesus' mighty name, I trust the process! Memory defeats suspicion! The image is permanent when the process completes! Amen.

CLOSING — DARKROOM FAITH ACTIVATED

Day 3 started with jaw-locking, food-rejecting, soul-questioning whether God is good when life tastes bitter. Tonight you rest knowing: You're in darkness, not abandoned. The image is forming, not failing. Both provision and prevention are developing invisibly. That paper you wrote on? That's your developed film. Evidence that God works in darkness better than we work in light.

Thousands globally entered darkness today. That same corporate leader in the Caribbean stopped demanding immediate answers and started trusting the soak. That grandmother in Nigeria who questioned sixty years of unanswered prayers discovered that some images take decades to develop. That construction worker in Canada thanked God for the job rejection that protected him from a company that went bankrupt six months later. Across London, the United States, and the Philippines, closed doors became evidence of protection, not rejection. Bills that didn't add up revealed provision overlooked. Rejection emails transformed into proof that God closes doors to protect better doors opening.

From the Caribbean to the Philippines, daylight demands became darkroom trust. Impatience surrendered to process. Visibility requirements died; invisible faith rose. By Day 21, darkroom faith will be as natural as breathing. When doors close, you'll thank God for protection. When darkness deepens, you'll trust the soak. When nothing makes sense, you'll remember: The best images form where you can't see them yet.

Tomorrow, you'll discover that while you've been begging God for equipment, you're already carrying an arsenal. That business skill you separated from spiritual? Kingdom weapon. That analytical mind? Prophetic gift. That "ordinary" ability? Extraordinary gift waiting for activation. Tomorrow, Saturday night spreadsheets save Sunday morning souls.

THE DANIEL FAST: CLOSING THE GAP!

A Word About Goodness and Greatness

Today you discovered God's goodness—His character toward you. Personal, intimate, relational. Like a microscope zooming in to see individual details of His care. "The Lord is good to all" (Psalm 145:9). But on Day 6, you'll encounter God's greatness—His magnitude, what He's capable of. Transcendent, incomprehensible, majestic. Like a telescope zooming out to see vastness of His authority. "Great is the Lord and greatly to be praised; His greatness is unsearchable" (Psalm 145:3).

Most believers experience either goodness (making God small, manageable, predictable) or greatness (fearing Him, feeling distant, seeing Him as impersonal). But you're learning both and. His goodness develops in darkness. His greatness makes problems molecular. Here's what Day 6 will reveal: The God who is this great chose to be this good to you. Microscope meets telescope. Personal meets transcendent. Character meets magnitude. I no longer separate His what (Greatness) from His who (Goodness); together, they remind me that my God is both vast and intimate, immeasurable and personal.

Today you trusted where goodness develops. Day 6 you'll discover the arsenal where greatness activates. Both are yours. Both are operating. Both are closing gaps. Darkness isn't punishment. It's the process that produces images daylight would destroy.

Day 3 Complete: Darkroom Faith Activated

Goodness: Working invisibly in darkness. Process: Developing provision and prevention. Closed doors: Protecting, not rejecting. Image: Forming even when invisible. Memory: Defeating suspicion when film lifts. Trust: Replacing demands for immediate visibility. Goodness vs. Greatness: Understanding the distinction for Day 6

SOAP JOURNAL — DAY 3

S (Scripture): Which verse helped you trust the process?
O (Observation): Where are you in darkness right now that you've been calling "abandonment" instead of "development"?
A (Application): What closed door might be protecting provision that's forming invisibly? What's the difference between God's goodness (character) and His greatness (magnitude)?
P (Prayer): "Father, I'm in the darkness of _____. I trust You're developing both _____ (provision) and _____ (prevention). When You lift the film, memory will defeat suspicion. I'm learning You're both good (microscope) and great (telescope)."

Today's Breakthrough Marker: What shifted in your understanding of closed doors and darkness today?
Tomorrow's Expectation: Based on trusting darkness today, what do you expect to see when God begins lifting the film tomorrow?

DARKROOM TRUSTED. IMAGE FORMING. MEMORY DEFEATING SUSPICION. READY FOR GIFTS.

DAY 4 — GIFTS

From Secular Training to Sacred Blueprints

"Having then gifts differing according to the grace that is given to us, let us use them." — Romans 12:6

WEEK 1 — GROW: Building Intimacy with God

Day 4 of 21. Yesterday's Goodness revealed the darkroom. Today's Gifts expose the arsenal you're already carrying.

ENCOUNTER — WHERE YOU ARE

4:30 AM. Day 4. You're standing at your closet, staring at your socks, unable to remember which foot they go on. Sugar withdrawal arrived in the night—dense, silent, disorienting. Your brain just short-circuited. Buttoning your shirt feels like advanced mathematics. Words dissolve before forming. You shuffle past the mirror—eyes sunken, skin dull, energy depleted—looking decidedly ungifted.

This is where doubt whispers loudest: "I'm just not spiritual enough for this." But here's what religion never told you: Depletion doesn't diminish gifts. It reveals them. When your natural abilities fail, your supernatural equipment surfaces.

Right now, across six continents, thousands experience this same depletion. In the Caribbean, that corporate leader pushes through brain fog, questioning if the sacrifice matters. In Nigeria, that grandmother navigates mental molasses, wondering if decades of prayer prepared her for this. In Canada, that construction worker discovers what happens when caffeine stops masking spiritual clarity. In London, that teenager feels the fog and fears she's failing. In the United States, that single mother wrestles with decision fatigue while managing hungry children. In the Philippines, that college student can't focus on assignments and wonders if fasting was a mistake. All discovering the same shocking truth.

Day 1 showed you operate from acceptance, not for it. Day 2 revealed your crown is already straight, just shifted. Day 3 taught you the darkroom develops what daylight would destroy. But today? Today the systematic stripping intensifies. The hunger has become familiar. Not comfortable, but known. Your body is learning a new language—emptiness as expectancy, weakness as womb for power.

And in this place of absolute depletion, you're about to discover something shocking: That "secular" training you separated from spiritual? It was God's blueprint all along. That corporate skill you never brought to church? It's Kingdom equipment. That professional certification you earned? Divine download in business clothes. Your gift isn't what you do in church. It's what God does through you everywhere.

Picture yourself sitting across from God, listing all your qualifications: "I have business training, but that's not spiritual. I have analytical skills, but those aren't gifts. I have professional experience, but that doesn't count for Kingdom." Now watch God's response: "Who do you think gave you those blueprints?" What if fasting doesn't give you new gifts but awakens you to the arsenal you've carried while begging for ammunition? Stop apologizing for what God is activating.

THE DANIEL FAST: CLOSING THE GAP!

FOUNDATION — BIBLICAL AUTHORITY

To understand why professional training is sacred preparation, we must first understand what gifts actually are and how God distributes them.

When Training Becomes Transformation

Fasting creates a unique condition—natural abilities fail, forcing spiritual gifts to surface. When your strength ends, grace begins. When your wisdom fails, divine downloads arrive. When your resources deplete, supernatural provision manifests. The sugar withdrawal clouding your mind? It's creating space for Word of Knowledge. The weakness in your body? It's making room for supernatural Faith. The mental fog? It's clearing ground for blueprints you couldn't see through the noise of normal. Depletion isn't the problem. It's the revealer.

Here's the paradigm shift most believers never make: Your professional training wasn't separate from your spiritual calling. It was preparation for it. Your corporate experience wasn't distraction from ministry. It was seminary for it. Your "secular" certification wasn't disconnected from sacred service. It was God's systematic download. Every skill, every job, every challenge deposited gifts disguised as ordinary.

The Gift You're Already Carrying

The Greek word is *charisma*—from *charis* (grace). Your gifts literally flow from grace. Not earned through holiness. Not achieved through maturity. Equipped at salvation. Watch what Peter says: "As each one has received a gift, minister it to one another, as good stewards of the manifold grace of God" (1 Peter 4:10). Has received. Past tense. Done deal. You're not waiting for your gift—you're awakening to it.

The word "manifold" is *poikilos*—multicolored, diverse, varied. Like a master architect's blueprint contains multiple systems—electrical, plumbing, structural, mechanical—all working together for one purpose. God's grace deposits different gifts in different people, all blueprinting the same Kingdom. "But the manifestation of the Spirit is given to each one for the profit of all" (1 Corinthians 12:7). Each one. No exceptions. The manifestation is given. Already distributed. "But one and the same Spirit works all these things, distributing to each one individually as He wills" (1 Corinthians 12:11). The Spirit already distributed. Past tense. The only question is recognition and activation. You're not applying for gifts. You're activating blueprints already downloaded.

The Irrevocable Installation

"For the gifts and the calling of God are irrevocable" (Romans 11:29). Your failures didn't uninstall them. Your fears didn't delete them. Your fumbling didn't corrupt the files. Once given, always given. The only variable is activation. Hell isn't afraid of your potential; it's terrified of your blueprints becoming operational.

BIBLICAL DEFINITION — THE COMPLETE ARSENAL

The Arsenal of the Holy Spirit

"The Spirit of the Lord will rest on him—the Spirit of wisdom and of understanding, the Spirit of counsel and of might, the Spirit of the knowledge and fear of the Lord—and he will delight in the fear of the Lord" (Isaiah 11:2-3). God's Spirit equips you with an arsenal that's already available, accessed, and activated through surrender. Their purpose: To glorify Christ, serve others, and build up the church (Isaiah 11:2-3; 1 Corinthians 12; Romans 12; Ephesians 4). "Now to each one the manifestation of the Spirit is given for the common good" (1 Corinthians 12:7).

Religion spotlighted the spectacular and ignored the everyday supernatural. Here's the full arsenal God deposited in every believer:

Romans 12:6-8 — Everyday Ministry Gifts: Prophecy (divine insight in proportion to faith), Serving (supernatural ability to meet practical needs), Teaching (making complex truth simple), Encouragement (calling forth the best in others), Giving (supernatural generosity that resources Kingdom), Leadership (vision casting and mobilizing), Mercy (supernatural compassion that heals hearts).

1 Corinthians 12:8-10 — Supernatural Power Gifts: Word of Wisdom (divine solutions for impossible situations), Word of Knowledge (knowing what you couldn't naturally know), Faith (supernatural confidence that moves mountains), Gifts of Healing (restoration flowing through you), Working of Miracles (God's power defying natural law), Prophecy (speaking God's now word), Discerning of Spirits (seeing beyond natural to spiritual reality), Different Kinds of Tongues (spiritual language for prayer), Interpretation of Tongues (understanding spiritual communication).

1 Corinthians 12:28 — Operational Gifts: Helps (supernatural support multiplying effectiveness), Administrations (divine ability to organize chaos).

Ephesians 4:11-12 — The Five-Fold Office: "And He Himself gave some to be apostles, some prophets, some evangelists, and some pastors and teachers, for the equipping of the saints for the work of ministry, for the edifying of the body of Christ." Apostles (pioneering new territory), Prophets (revealing God's heart and direction), Evangelists (compelling gospel presentation), Pastors (shepherding and protecting), Teachers (systematic truth transfer).

But here's what religion missed: These aren't just offices—they're dimensions expressing through every believer. That pioneering spirit in your business? Apostolic. That burden for your lost coworker? Evangelistic. That protective instinct over your team? Pastoral. Spiritual gifts operate in ministry and the marketplace. The Kingdom isn't only within the walls of the church—it's wherever you carry His presence. Your Monday morning meeting? That's your mission field. Your cubicle? That's your pulpit. Your break room? That's your sanctuary. God's Spirit fills you for spreadsheets and sermons, boardrooms and altars, Mondays and Sundays.

REVELATION — BIBLICAL PATTERNS

Throughout Scripture, God equipped people through "secular" training, then activated it for Kingdom blueprints—in the marketplace, not just the temple.

TIER 1: Five Full Witnesses

Bezalel: When Craftsmanship Became Sacred (Exodus 31:1-5)

"Then the LORD spoke to Moses, saying: 'See, I have called by name Bezalel... And I have filled him with the Spirit of God, in wisdom, in understanding, in knowledge, and in all manner of workmanship.'" Read that again: God filled him with the Spirit to work with gold, silver, bronze, wood, and stone. The Holy Spirit didn't just empower him to pray or prophesy. The Spirit equipped him to build. Carpentry wasn't separate from calling. It was the blueprint. His workshop was his ministry. His tools were his weapons. His craft was his calling. Your hands that build, fix, create, and serve carry the same Spirit that filled Bezalel.

Luke: When Medicine Became Ministry (Colossians 4:14)

"Luke the beloved physician" traveled with Paul. His medical training wasn't distraction from apostolic work. It was apostolic work. The diagnostic precision that analyzed physical symptoms analyzed spiritual conditions. The healing knowledge that treated bodies treated souls. His clinic was his pulpit. His patients were his congregation. Physician training was Kingdom blueprint. Your professional precision isn't competing with spiritual calling—it's carrying it.

Daniel: When Government Service Became Prophetic Office (Daniel 1-6)

Prime minister in pagan government. Political strategist. Crisis manager. His governmental expertise didn't compete with prophetic gift. It contained it. The same wisdom that advised kings interpreted dreams. The same strategic thinking that ran empires decoded destinies. His office was his altar. His political position was his prophetic platform. Political training was prophetic blueprint. Your leadership in secular spaces is prophetic positioning in sacred places.

Lydia: When Business Became Gateway (Acts 16:14-15)

"Now a certain woman named Lydia heard us. She was a seller of purple from the city of Thyatira, who worshiped God." Businesswoman. Dealer in luxury textiles. Corporate success. Her business wasn't obstacle to ministry. It was the platform for ministry. Her marketplace connections became ministry connections. Her home became the first European church. Her network became the first European converts. Business acumen was Kingdom architecture. Your business success isn't separate from spiritual significance—it's the infrastructure.

Paul: When Tentmaking Funded Mission (Acts 18:1-3)

Apostle and tentmaker. Ministry and marketplace. His business supported his mission. His professional skill funded his prophetic assignment. Secular work wasn't "lesser." It was strategic. Tentmaking wasn't what he did until ministry. It was what he did while ministering. His hands that sewed tents were the same hands that wrote Scripture. Your Monday job isn't waiting room for Sunday calling—it's training ground.

TIER 2: Nine Grouped Witnesses

Administration & Strategic Leadership: Joseph managed Potiphar's house, then managed Egypt's economy—administration that saved nations from famine (Genesis 37-50). Nehemiah organized royal schedules, then organized Jerusalem's wall rebuilding in fifty-two days—project management became intercession (Nehemiah 1-6). Solomon received supernatural wisdom to build the temple and organize a kingdom—administrative precision managing resources, personnel, and timelines for sacred construction (1 Kings 4-6). The same strategic mind that plans corporate initiatives plans Kingdom breakthroughs. Your administrative skills are organizing someone's rescue. Your project management is rebuilding what the enemy destroyed.

Documentation & Prophetic Precision: Matthew's accounting precision tracked money, then tracked Messiah's genealogy—financial training became eternal documentation (Matthew 9:9). Amos tended sheep and fig trees, then his agricultural vocabulary became prophetic language confronting nations (Amos 1:1, 7:14-15). The same detailed mind that documents transactions documents Kingdom movements. Your financial analysis is recording Kingdom transactions. Your everyday work is training for extraordinary calling.

Hospitality & Marketplace Ministry: Priscilla and Aquila sewed tents while planting churches—business partners funding mobile ministry, their commerce becoming Kingdom expansion (Acts 18:2-3, 26). Esther navigated palace protocol to save a nation—royal position becoming intercession platform, political strategy becoming spiritual warfare (Esther 1-10). The same hospitality that serves customers serves souls. Your business network is your ministry network. Your position in secular spaces positions you for spiritual intervention.

Judicial Wisdom & Prophetic Worship: Deborah judged disputes, then decoded destinies—legal training containing prophetic calling, her courtroom becoming sanctuary (Judges 4-5). David's harp soothed Saul's torment and drove out demons—music becoming warfare, worship descending on enemies (1 Samuel 16:23, Psalm 149:6-9). The same judicial mind that administers justice administers deliverance. Your legal wisdom decodes spiritual matters. Your music isn't performance—it's warfare.

The Pattern is Clear: God doesn't separate secular from sacred. He sanctifies the secular as sacred. Every skill, every training, every professional experience—blueprint components. The Kingdom operates in boardrooms and bedrooms, hospitals and homes, factories and fields, courtrooms and classrooms, palaces and prisons.

TESTIMONY — THE BLUEPRINT REVELATION

When Sacred Interrupted Secular

You're holding this book because in December 2017, God interrupted someone's professional training and downloaded a systematic approach to spiritual breakthrough. This isn't about credentials. This is about where the methodology came from. If you're wondering "Why should I trust a systematic twenty-one-day framework for transformation?" the answer is in this story. God chose someone trained to see systems and gave them a spiritual system. That's not corporate elitism—that's divine irony. This is how "The Daniel Fast: Closing the GAP" was born.

I never expected my professional training to become holy. For years, I solved complex problems with systematic analysis and process optimization. Leaders sought strategic solutions that seemed to drop from nowhere. Boardrooms called it "business instinct." Teams praised my "analytical gift." I thought I was just good with systems. I had no idea God was downloading Kingdom blueprints through professional training.

The 2017 Interruption

December 2017. Mid-project. Standard analysis. I was mapping operational dysfunction—flowcharts covering workspace, data pointing to bottlenecks, solutions emerging from chaos. Standard methodology: Define, Measure, Analyze, Improve, Control. I'd done this countless times. This was routine. Then the Holy Spirit interrupted so loudly I almost dropped my tools: "Daughter, I gave you those downloads to teach you My systems. Now use them to decode transformation."

I walked out mid-presentation. Found the nearest bathroom. Locked the door. Sat on the closed toilet lid, shaking, phone in hand, trying to type with trembling fingers. Was I hearing God or losing my mind? What if this wasn't divine revelation but professional burnout manifesting as spiritual delusion? What if I told people about this and they thought I'd cracked under pressure? I sat there for ten minutes, terrified and electrified at the same time.

Those professional downloads? They were prophetic solutions dressed in business language. The systematic methodology? Kingdom strategy in corporate clothing. Every analysis, every framework, every optimization—seminary for what was coming. God doesn't waste your training. He transforms it.

The Blueprint Downloads That Night

I couldn't sleep. The download was relentless. Midnight. Laptop open. Professional principles on one side of the screen, biblical fasting on the other. I stared at process improvement phases: Define the problem. Measure current state. Analyze root causes. Improve through solutions. Control to sustain gains. Suddenly I saw it: Spiritual transformation follows the same process architecture.

By 3 AM, a complete framework emerged. I stared at the screen, whispering, "This can't be this systematic. Can it?" But there it was: complete transformation architecture. The same analytical precision I used to solve complex problems now diagnosing soul dysfunction. The same process mapping that optimized operations now optimizing breakthrough. The same systematic thinking that solved crises now solving identity crises. This became "The Daniel Fast: Closing the GAP"—the systematic framework you're following right now.

What "GAP" Really Means: The gap analysis between where you are and where God created you to become. God is closing the GAP—invite His power into that chasm.

Stage 1: Prepare — The I Decide Framework: Preparing and assessing your baseline across six dimensions of wellness (spiritual, mental, emotional, physical, financial, relational).

Stage 2: Transform — The GAP Strategy: Partnering with God over twenty-one days of fasting and prayer, shifting from information to revelation, from revelation to application, from application to transformation. This isn't random daily devotionals. This is systematic spiritual architecture.

Stage 3: Integrate — The 8F Chayah Lifestyle: Integrating changes as lifestyle with vision, goals, milestones, action plans—not an event. Stop doing event fasts and start doing identity fasts.

Stage 4: Multiply — The 5C Multiplication Model: God transforms us from crisis to calling to commission. Journey into your destiny and leave a legacy that outlives and outlasts you—Kingdom impact globally and generationally.

The Unsolicited Confirmation

The next day. My phone buzzed. Text from my friend. I hadn't told anyone about the download. Hadn't sent a message. Hadn't asked for feedback. Her text: "I had the strangest dream last night. God was showing me systematic blueprints for transformation—like architectural drawings with phases and components. Did something shift for you?"

I stared at my phone, hands shaking worse than yesterday. She dreamed blueprints the same night I downloaded them. I called immediately. Read her my 3 AM notes. She wept. "This is what's been missing. We have revival moments but no transformation roadmap. Our fasting is powerful but random. We need structure." I asked, "What if this is real?" She answered, "What if it isn't and you don't share it?"

The gift I'd dismissed as "just professional training" was actually Kingdom architecture. And God confirmed it through someone who had no way of knowing. Professional training didn't prepare me for business. It prepared me for blueprinting breakthrough.

From Blueprints to Global Movement

2017-2019: Beta-tested framework with community. 2020: Launched first "The Daniel Fast: Closing the GAP" book using the blueprint. 2021-2025: Developing and refining with thousands across six continents within Chayah Club community. The first person I taught the system asked, "Why has no one shown me this before?" I said, "Because I just received it."

What started as professional methodology became spiritual technology. The analytical mind I thought was "too secular" for ministry? It was prophetic precision. The systematic thinking I apologized for? It was divine download. The process optimization skills? Kingdom equipment. The gift you're dismissing as "just professional training" might be God's blueprint for someone's breakthrough.

But Discovering This Blueprint Didn't Mean I Immediately Walked in It Boldly

For years, I'd been hiding the very intensity that made the downloads possible. Executive briefing. Conference room with floor-to-ceiling windows overlooking the city. I'd spent three weeks analyzing a supply chain crisis that had the entire leadership team paralyzed. During my morning prayer time, God downloaded a solution so clear I could see the entire flowchart in my mind. I walked into that meeting with Holy Ghost confidence and a breakthrough strategy.

Fifteen minutes into my presentation, the VP leaned back in his chair and said: "You know what your problem is? You're too intense." The room went silent. I watched my solution—God's solution—crumble into apology. "I just... I mean... maybe we could..." He waved his hand. "We'll table this for now."

That night, I rewrote the entire presentation. Softened every declarative sentence into a question. Changed "We need to" into "What if we considered..." Buried the prophetic precision under layers of corporate politeness. The next meeting, I presented the watered-down version. He nodded. "Much better. See? You can be reasonable." They implemented my solution—the diluted version. It worked, but barely. The problem resurfaced six months later because I'd removed the components God had shown me were critical.

But by then, I'd learned my lesson: Keep the downloads quiet. Make prophecy sound like brainstorming. Disguise the divine as collaboration. For three years, every time God spoke strategy in prayer, I translated it into corporate-speak before speaking it aloud. Buried revelation under professional jargon. Apologized for the intensity that was actually Holy Spirit precision. I declined leadership opportunities with practiced excuses: "I'm not ready." "Someone else is better qualified." "I don't want to step on toes." Translation: I'm terrified of being called "too intense" again.

The week I turned down leading another initiative—one I'd been praying about for months, one where God had already downloaded the entire framework—the Holy Spirit interrupted so loudly I pulled over on my commute home. His voice wasn't gentle: "Burying talent isn't humility. It's harm. You're not protecting yourself—you're starving My people of what I gave you to feed them."

I sat in that parking lot and wept. Not delicate tears. Gut-wrenching sobs. I'd called fear "wisdom" and hiding "humility" and silence "submission." I'd apologized for intensity that was actually divine precision. I'd shrunk myself to make insecurity comfortable. That night I repented—not for being intense, but for calling God's gift a problem.

Within thirty days, three doors I'd been praying about for years opened simultaneously. The solution I'd watered down three years earlier? They brought me back to fix it properly. "We need your intensity," they said. "We should have listened the first time." False humility is just fear in church clothes. The gift I'd buried under corporate conformity was exactly what God wanted to deploy for Kingdom breakthrough. Your "too much" is someone else's "just enough." What the marketplace called "intense," the Kingdom calls "anointed."

PARABLE — SATURDAY NIGHT WARRIORS

Consider what happens behind the scenes of your Sunday gathering. Late one Saturday evening, everything fell apart. The worship leader, children's coordinator, and tech team all faced emergencies. Sunday service was twelve hours away. The leader sent one message to those with hidden gifts: "Need you."

Watch what unfolded. A project manager paused her evening, opened her laptop. She'd never stood on a platform, but she had tracked volunteer skills for three years. Within minutes, she was running scenarios like solving supply chain disruptions. The gift of administration wearing everyday clothes. A retired logistics officer remembered someone mentioning worship experience in passing conversation. One call made. The gift of wisdom activating through memory.

An executive assistant created color-coded responsibility charts. The gift of helps dressed as professional skills. An IT consultant programmed simplified settings anyone could run. Technology becoming ministry. An electrician who'd been quiet for months rewired the sound system in an hour. Sparks in the sanctuary, power in his hands. A nurse organized first aid stations and safety protocols. Healing gift preparing for emergencies no one saw coming.

A stay-at-home mother coordinated meal prep for seventeen volunteers working through the night. Her kitchen became command center. A construction worker fixed broken stage risers at 2 AM. Building gift constructing platforms for worship. Someone discovered the quiet man who stacks chairs once played guitar. The couple always sitting in back once taught children. The teenager making coffee could design graphics.

By midnight, twenty-three people were filling roles, none with titles, all with gifts. The impossible became possible through spreadsheets that became prayers. Sunday morning arrived. Everything flowed. Someone said, "God really showed up." They were right. But God showed up first through hidden gifts, then through visible worship. Behind every "suddenly" is someone's Saturday night spreadsheet.

Where are your Saturday night gifts hiding? What skills from Monday's workplace could save Sunday's worship? When have you dismissed as "secular" what heaven calls sacred?

PARADIGM SHIFT — FROM SECULAR TO SACRED

SECULAR SEPARATION	SACRED INTEGRATION
"My job is just paying bills"	"My job is depositing gifts"
"Professional training is separate"	"Professional training is preparation"

"Secular skills don't count"	"All skills are Kingdom blueprints"
"Real gifts operate in church"	"Gifts operate in ministry and marketplace"
"Business and ministry are different"	"Business is ministry when surrendered"
"Waiting for spiritual gifts"	"Activating blueprints already downloaded"
"My career wasted years"	"My career completed my arsenal"
"Kingdom is only in church"	"Kingdom is wherever I carry His presence"

Bottom Line: Stop separating what God sanctified. Your secular is your sacred when surrendered. The blueprint you dismissed as "just professional" is someone's pathway to freedom.

THE INTEGRATION: WHEN NATURAL MEETS SUPERNATURAL

Here's what changes everything about understanding gifts: Your natural abilities are the foundation. But gifts of the Spirit season them with supernatural dimension. Think of it like a house—you can have perfect structure (natural talents), but without electricity (gifts of the Spirit), you're operating in the dark. Together, they accomplish dual Kingdom purpose: edify the church and reveal God in the marketplace.

Watch how this works practically. Teaching gift plus Word of Knowledge means you explain Scripture clearly, but suddenly know exactly what your student is wrestling with. Administration gift plus Discernment means you organize systems well, but sense which team member carries wrong spirit. Business acumen plus Wisdom means you solve problems strategically, but receive divine solutions for impossible situations. The natural ability is the vehicle. The Spirit's gift is the fuel.

This dual integration serves two purposes simultaneously. First, edifying the church—when your natural teaching operates with Word of Knowledge, you don't just inform minds, you transform hearts. When your administrative skill flows with discernment, you don't just organize events, you protect the body. Second, revealing God in the marketplace—when your compassion operates with supernatural mercy, unbelievers in your workplace see God's tenderness. When your problem-solving flows with word of wisdom, secular colleagues receive solutions beyond logic.

Every supernatural manifestation through your natural ability becomes an arrow pointing to Him—in boardrooms, break rooms, hospital rooms, living rooms. Your natural gifts open doors. The Spirit's gifts reveal who's behind the door.

ACTIVATION — TWO PRIMARY EXERCISES

PRIMARY EXERCISE #1: The Arsenal Inventory

This creates your personal gifts reference list. What you need: Paper (napkin, receipt, journal page), pen, five minutes.

Step 1: Draw three columns with these headers: Natural Abilities (what comes easy) | Kingdom Impact (how it helps others) | Hidden Gift (spiritual gift underneath)

Step 2: List five to seven natural abilities in first column.

Step 3: Identify the impact and hidden gift. Examples: "Good listener" → "People feel heard" → Gift of mercy. "See solutions" → "Solve problems" → Gift of wisdom. "Organize chaos" → "Create order" → Gift of administration. "Analytical thinking" → "Decode patterns" → Word of knowledge. "Strategic planning" → "Cast vision" → Leadership. "Make people comfortable" → "Create safe space" → Hospitality. "Fix things" → "Restore what's broken" → Gift of helps. "Cook for others" → "Nourish body and soul" → Gift of service. "Notice details" → "Prevent problems" → Discernment. "Connect people" → "Build community" → Apostolic gift.

Step 4: Circle your top three.

Step 5: Stand. Place hand over list.

Step 6: Declare: "I am armed and dangerous for the Kingdom of God. Obedience is the on-switch for my gift."

Note for Readers Processing Trauma: If identifying your gifts feels empowering, embrace it fully. If it triggers shame about "wasted years," comparison anxiety, or feelings of inadequacy, honor that wisdom. For trauma survivors, especially those who experienced spiritual abuse where "gifts" were weaponized or whose abilities were exploited, this exercise may need gentler pacing. You can trust that God deposited gifts in you without forcing yourself to inventory them on Day 4. The arsenal is yours whether you list it today or discover it gradually over months. Healing doesn't require immediate activation. Your timeline is yours. God isn't measuring your progress or comparing your gifts to others. What you discover when you're ready will be exactly what's needed when you're ready.

PRIMARY EXERCISE #2: The Integration Activation

This connects your natural abilities with Spirit's gifts for dual Kingdom purpose. Choose one dimension. Complete both steps in two minutes.

Dimension	STEP 1: Activate (Action)	STEP 2: Integrate (Prayer)
SPIRITUAL	Text someone: "Praying now—what do you need?"	"Father, season my intercession with supernatural faith for ministry and marketplace"
MENTAL	Write 3 solutions for stuck problem; ask Holy Spirit "Which?"	"Father, season my analytical mind with word of wisdom for ministry and marketplace"
EMOTIONAL	Voice-note 30-second encouragement to 3 people	"Father, season my empathy with gift of mercy for ministry and marketplace"
PHYSICAL	Do one unseen heavy-lifting task today	"Father, season my practical skills with gift of helps for ministry and marketplace"
FINANCIAL	Give toward someone's assignment, not impulse	"Father, season my stewardship with supernatural generosity for ministry and marketplace"
RELATIONAL	Introduce 2 people who should know each other	"Father, season my connections with apostolic networking for ministry and marketplace"

Then declare: "My secular is sacred when surrendered. My natural abilities carry supernatural power. Gifts aren't learned in a lab; they're proved on a Tuesday."

FOCUS AREA PRAYERS

Scripture Foundation: "Do not neglect the gift that is in you" (1 Timothy 4:14). Choose your primary breakthrough area:

For Spiritual Focus: "Father, my spiritual hunger isn't separate from my natural abilities. You gave me [professional skill] to blueprint Kingdom solutions. Now season it with gifts of Your Spirit—let word of knowledge flow through my analysis, let prophecy speak through my insights. Use both to edify Your church and reveal Your heart in the marketplace."

For Mental Focus: "Father, my analytical mind isn't secular—it's Your gift of wisdom in business clothes. My strategic thinking is prophetic precision. Season my natural intellect with supernatural insight. Let my mental blueprints carry Your Spirit's revelation, pointing people to Jesus in boardrooms and bedrooms."

For Emotional Focus: "Father, my emotional intelligence is gift of mercy operational. My empathy is prophetic insight. Season my natural compassion with supernatural healing. Let my emotions carry Your comfort, revealing the Father's heart to the broken—in ministry and marketplace."

For Physical Focus: "Father, my practical skills are gift of helps activated. My hands that build and fix are Your hands serving. Season my natural ability with supernatural power. Let my physical service demonstrate the Spirit's strength, pointing people to Jesus wherever I work."

For Financial Focus: "Father, my business training was Your blueprint for stewardship. My financial analysis is Kingdom strategy. Season my natural acumen with supernatural wisdom. Let my provision strategies reveal Your abundance, drawing people to the Source—in church and commerce."

For Relational Focus: "Father, my networking ability is apostolic gift. My people skills are pastoral heart. Season my natural connections with supernatural discernment. Let my relationships become bridges to You, revealing Your love through my interactions—in sanctuary and society."

RESISTANCE REALITY CHECK

What You're Experiencing Right Now:

Secular Separation: "But my abilities aren't spiritual." Heaven's Response: Bezalel was Spirit-filled to work with wood. Your "secular" is My sacred blueprint—and I season it with My Spirit's power for ministry and marketplace.

Training Dismissal: "I wasted years in corporate life." Heaven's Response: I don't waste training. I transform it. Those years weren't delay—they were deposit. Now receive My Spirit's gifts to activate what I downloaded.

Comparison Paralysis: "Others have better spiritual gifts." Heaven's Response: Stop comparing blueprints. Yours is custom-designed. Natural foundation plus Spirit's seasoning equals your unique Kingdom deployment in your unique sphere.

Platform Deception: "Real gifts need church stages." Heaven's Response: Luke healed in clinics. Lydia ministered through business. Your Monday workplace is your mission field. The Kingdom isn't only in church—it's wherever you carry My presence.

Either-Or Thinking: "Do I develop natural skills or spiritual gifts?" Heaven's Response: Both. Natural abilities are the vehicle. Spirit's gifts are the fuel. Together they accomplish dual purpose: edify church, reveal God—in ministry and marketplace.

Your gift is where grace feels like wind at your back—natural ability turbocharged by supernatural power.

DECLARATION — SCRIPTURE-ANCHORED WARFARE

Stand with thousands globally and declare these truths:

"Therefore I remind you to stir up the gift of God which is in you!" (2 Timothy 1:6)

"For the gifts and the calling of God are irrevocable!" (Romans 11:29)

"As each one has received a gift, minister it to one another, as good stewards of the manifold grace of God!" (1 Peter 4:10)

"But one and the same Spirit works all these things, distributing to each one individually as He wills!" (1 Corinthians 12:11)

"There are diversities of gifts, but the same Spirit. There are differences of ministries, but the same Lord. And there are diversities of activities, but it is the same God who works all in all!" (1 Corinthians 12:4-6)

"Let all things be done for edification!" (1 Corinthians 14:26)

"Now to each one the manifestation of the Spirit is given for the common good!" (1 Corinthians 12:7)

My secular is sacred when surrendered! My natural abilities carry supernatural power! My blueprints edify the church and reveal God in the marketplace! Spirit's gifts season my training—Father's heart flows through my work! The Kingdom isn't only in church—it's wherever I carry His presence! Hell trembles when I stop separating and start integrating!

BREAKTHROUGH PRAYER

Father God, Abba, I repent for separating secular from sacred when You sanctified it all. For calling "ordinary" what You called "ordained." For dismissing professional training as unspiritual when it was Your systematic download. For operating in natural ability alone without Your Spirit's power. For seeking spiritual gifts alone without grounding in developed skills. For believing the Kingdom only operates within church walls when You said it's wherever I carry Your presence.

Like Bezalel, I receive that "secular" skills are Spirit-filled—workshop as ministry, tools as weapons. Like Luke, I see that professional precision serves eternal purposes—clinic as pulpit, patients as congregation. Like Lydia, I understand that business success is Kingdom platform—marketplace as mission field. Like Daniel, I know that marketplace leadership is prophetic positioning—office as altar. Like Paul, I embrace that professional work funds mission—secular as sacred service. Like the Saturday night warriors, I see that spreadsheets can save Sundays—hidden gifts becoming visible ministry.

Thank You that my training and experiences were seminary. Thank You that downloads were Kingdom blueprints. Thank You that every job, every skill, every challenge deposited gifts for ministry and marketplace. The blueprint I dismissed as "just professional" is someone's pathway to freedom. The training I thought wasted prepared me for this moment. The "secular" career was sacred preparation.

Right now, I activate the full integration. My natural abilities are the foundation—developed through years of training. Your Spirit's gifts are the power—flowing through surrender. Together they accomplish dual purpose: edify Your church with equipped service and reveal Your heart to watching world—in ministry and marketplace.

What I called business instinct was prophetic precision waiting for Your Spirit's seasoning. What I called analytical thinking was divine wisdom ready for supernatural activation. What I called natural ability was Kingdom equipment awaiting Holy Ghost power. The gifts and calling of God are irrevocable. My failures refined them. My training completed them. Now Your Spirit ignites them.

I stir up the gift within me! I unroll the invisible blueprints! I deploy natural foundation with supernatural fuel! I'm following Your four-stage blueprint: Prepare, Transform, Integrate, Multiply. My secular is sacred. My training is transformation. My natural abilities carry supernatural power. My work reveals Your heart—in sanctuary and society, in ministry and marketplace. The Kingdom isn't only within church walls—it's wherever I carry Your presence.

In Jesus' mighty name, the integration is complete! Natural meets supernatural! The blueprint edifies and evangelizes! My gifts operate in ministry and marketplace! Amen.

CLOSING — FULL DEPLOYMENT ACTIVATED

Day 4 started with sock confusion so thick you couldn't think straight. Your brain stalling mid-function. Words dissolving before forming. Sugar withdrawal exposing every weakness, stripping every natural ability. Tonight you rest knowing: Depletion forced integration. When your natural abilities failed, supernatural gifts surfaced. The professional training? Divine download for systematic transformation.

Behind every Sunday miracle is someone's Saturday night spreadsheet. Your gift is how Jesus loves people through you—in church and workplace, in sanctuary and society. Your leadership is how He orders chaos. Your mercy is how He holds hurt. Your wisdom is how He answers impossible questions. But more than that—you discovered why this book exists. The December 2017 download wasn't just personal testimony. It was the birth certificate of "The Daniel Fast: Closing the GAP." God chose someone trained to see systems and gave them a spiritual system—the gap analysis framework that's systematically closing the distance between where you are and where He created you to become.

That's not about credentials—that's about where this methodology came from. You're following a blueprint that was downloaded through someone's secular training becoming sacred. That's the validation. That's the testimony. That's why you can trust this systematic approach.

Thousands globally discovered their arsenals today. That same corporate leader in the Caribbean realized his strategic planning was apostolic blueprint—boardroom became mission field. That grandmother in Nigeria discovered sixty years of intercession taught her prophetic discernment—prayer closet became preparation. That construction worker in Canada saw his building skills as gift of helps—job site became sanctuary. Across London, the United States, and the Philippines, professional training transformed into prophetic equipment. Analytical minds became prophetic precision. Business networks became ministry platforms. "Secular" careers revealed sacred preparation.

By Day 21, deploying gifts will be as natural as breathing. The waiting mentality will be a distant memory. Your children will inherit activated arsenals, knowing that every ability is anointed when surrendered—and that the Kingdom operates in ministry and marketplace, in sanctuary and society.

Tomorrow, you'll discover why hell fears your laughter more than your liturgy. That joy you're waiting to feel after breakthrough? It's actually the weapon that brings breakthrough. Tomorrow, you weaponize gladness. Tomorrow, dancing becomes warfare and laughter becomes deliverance. Stop separating what God integrated. Your natural abilities carry His supernatural power. Your blueprints reveal His heart everywhere.

Day 4 Complete: Full Integration Activated
Gifts: Not separate from training, but revealed and empowered through it
Secular: Not opposite of sacred, but foundation for it
Blueprint: Downloaded through "ordinary" experience, activated through surrender
Spirit's Gifts: Seasoning natural abilities with supernatural dimension
Dual Purpose: Edify church plus reveal God (in ministry and marketplace)
Origin Story: December 2017 download equals birth of "The Daniel Fast: Closing the GAP"
Integration: Natural foundation plus supernatural fuel equals full Kingdom explosion
Deployment: Ministry and marketplace, sanctuary and society

SOAP JOURNAL — DAY 4
S (Scripture): Which verse helped you see secular training as sacred blueprint for ministry and marketplace?
O (Observation): What "ordinary" professional skill have you been dismissing? How could Spirit's gifts season it for Kingdom impact beyond church walls?
A (Application): How will you integrate that skill (natural) with Spirit's gift (supernatural) this week for dual purpose (edify plus reveal) in both ministry and marketplace?
P (Prayer): "Father, my [professional training] is Your blueprint for ministry and marketplace. Season it with [Spirit's gift] so it edifies Your church and reveals Your heart everywhere I go. I activate full integration now."

Today's Breakthrough Marker: What blueprint did you discover? How will Spirit's gifts season it for Kingdom deployment in ministry and marketplace?
Tomorrow's Expectation: Based on today's full integration, what do you expect when joy becomes your weapon tomorrow?

SECULAR SANCTIFIED. BLUEPRINTS ACTIVATED. ARSENAL DEPLOYED. READY FOR GLADNESS.

DAY 5 — GLADNESS

The Scandalous Truth About Your Original Design

"The joy of the Lord is your strength." — Nehemiah 8:10

WEEK 1 — GROW: Building Intimacy with God

Day 5 of 21. Yesterday's Gifts revealed your arsenal. Today's Gladness reveals who you actually are.

IMPORTANT WELLBEING NOTE

This chapter presents joy as your original design and discusses mental health through a spiritual lens. However, depression, anxiety, and other mental health conditions are real medical issues requiring professional support.

If you're experiencing persistent mental health symptoms, suicidal thoughts, or psychological crisis, seek professional help immediately:
- Contact your local crisis helpline (search "crisis helpline" + your country name)
- Reach out to your therapist or doctor
- Go to your nearest emergency room
- Contact local emergency services

The framework in this chapter works ALONGSIDE proper mental health care—therapy, medication, community support—never as replacement. Your healing journey may involve multiple means working together. This is wisdom, not weakness.

Choosing joy doesn't mean denying pain or minimizing mental health struggles. It means fighting for your original design with every tool available—spiritual, medical, therapeutic, and communal.

ENCOUNTER — WHERE YOU ARE

4:30 AM. Day 5. You sob at cereal commercials, snap at loved ones, then discover the most scandalous truth of the fast: The most spiritual thing you can do right now isn't weep in intercession. It might be dancing in your kitchen.

The sugar withdrawal has stripped every emotional buffer. Raw wires sparking at random. Your stomach isn't just empty—it's angry, contracting with a violence that makes you curl into yourself. One moment spiritual warrior, next moment weeping warrior.

Your emotions are exposed nerves. Grief you thought processed. Anger you didn't know you carried. Joy that surprises you with its inappropriate intensity. No comfort food to numb feelings. No caffeine to regulate moods. Just you, raw and real, discovering what lives beneath the medication of consumption.

This is where religion taught you: "Suffering is noble. Joy is shallow. Serious problems need serious faces." But what if that's backwards? What if joy isn't the dessert after spiritual vegetables? What if joy isn't what you feel after breakthrough—but how breakthrough happens? What if the enemy's first target wasn't your faith or your family—but your capacity for gladness?

When was the last time you had a good belly laugh? Not a polite chuckle, not a social smile—a deep, uncontrollable, tears-streaming, can't-breathe belly laugh? Do you incorporate joy or play in your self-care? Or has adulting stolen your capacity for pure delight?

Day 1: Gospel revealed it's happening now. Day 2: Grace straightened your crown. Day 3: Goodness hunted you down. Day 4: Your secular training was always sacred. But today? Today you discover something so revolutionary it will reorganize everything: Joy isn't what you're trying to find. Joy is who you actually are.

You weren't created to find joy after suffering. You were created in joy, for joy, as joy.

FOUNDATION — THE DIFFERENCE BETWEEN HAPPINESS AND JOY

Understanding the Distinction

Before we go deeper, understand this critical difference:

Happiness is circumstantial: Based on happenings, external triggers, temporary emotion, depends on situation, can be lost or found.

Joy is spiritual: Based on identity, internal reality, eternal nature, despite situation, cannot be taken.

"These things I have spoken to you, that My joy may remain in you, and that your joy may be full" (John 15:11). Jesus didn't promise happiness. He promised His joy—divine, unshakeable, permanent joy that remains regardless of circumstances.

Happiness says: "I feel good because good things happened." Joy declares: "I am good because God is good."

THE LANGUAGE OF GLADNESS

What Is Gladness?

Gladness is joy that refuses to stay hidden. It's more than feeling pleased—it's pleasure that shows on your face. More than internal delight—it's delight that moves your body. More than good news received—it's good news that makes you announce it.

Scripture reveals gladness through Hebrew and Greek words, each showing a different dimension:

Tuwb — The foundational Hebrew word means "to be good, well, happy"—not as passing emotion but as state of being. This is ontological, not emotional. You don't just feel good—you are good, made good, restored to original goodness by God Himself. This connects directly to your factory settings. Gladness isn't something you achieve. It's something you return to—the original design God built into you before sin, shame, and suffering covered it.

Chara — Greek word for inner joy from realized grace. This is joy that flows from encountering grace. You can't manufacture it. You receive it. When grace becomes real (not theoretical), chara erupts from within. This is the internal wellspring. This is why Day 2 (Grace) precedes Day 5 (Gladness)—you must encounter grace before joy flows.

Agalliasis — Outward expression of that inner joy. This is gladness made visible. Internal chara becoming external agalliasis. The wellspring overflowing into the river. This is exuberant joy, extreme gladness, exultation—the kind that made Elizabeth's baby leap in her womb (Luke 1:44) and the early church eat together with gladness of heart (Acts 2:46). This isn't polite happiness. This is joy that moves you—physically, emotionally, spiritually.

The Pattern Revealed: Joy is the root; gladness is the fruit. Joy is internal reality; gladness is external expression. Joy is who you are; gladness is how you show it. You can have joy without expressing it (though suppressing it damages you). You cannot have genuine gladness without joy's internal reality fueling it. This is why the enemy targets your gladness specifically—hidden joy threatens no one, but expressed gladness threatens every system built on misery.

Joy is the wellspring. Gladness is its river.

THE LIE WE ALL BELIEVED

I need to tell you something that might sound scandalous: You've been taught that suffering is noble and joy is shallow. That's a lie from hell.

For years, I wore my suffering like a badge of spiritual maturity. My tears were my testimony. My burdens were my brand. My heaviness was my holiness. I thought serious people handled serious problems with serious faces. Joy was for the naive, the untested, those who hadn't tasted real pain. Depression moved in like a squatter, claiming permanent residence. And I let it—because wasn't suffering how you proved you were deep?

Until the day I couldn't get out of bed. That morning, barely able to breathe through the heaviness that felt like concrete on my chest, I heard the strangest instruction: "Laugh." "I can't." "That's why you must." So I forced it. A fake laugh that sounded more like choking. Then another. By the third, something cracked—not my voice, but the atmosphere. By the tenth, tears were streaming. By the twentieth, the laughter was real, and depression's grip was loosening.

That's when I learned something that would change everything: Joy isn't denial. Joy isn't escape. Joy isn't shallow. Joy is reality. Everything else is distortion. You're not creating joy. You're returning to it.

A joyful person is an ungovernable person.

REVELATION — THE ORIGINAL DESIGN

What Genesis Says About Your Factory Settings

"When the morning stars sang together, and all the sons of God shouted for joy" (Job 38:7). This is before humanity was created. Before sin. Before suffering. The universe was born in joy. God didn't create in stress or struggle. He created in celebration. And then—watch this carefully: "So God created man in His own image; in the image of God He created him" (Genesis 1:27). You were made in the image of a God who creates in joy.

This isn't metaphor. This is ontology—the study of what is. You weren't designed for suffering. You were designed in gladness. The fall didn't reveal your true nature. The fall interrupted it. Depression isn't your identity. Anxiety isn't your nature. Heaviness isn't your normal. Joy is your factory setting. Everything else is malware.

What Neuroscience Confirms

Here's what makes this revolutionary: Science is catching up to Scripture. When neuroscientists map the brain's "default mode network"—what your brain does when it's at rest and healthy—they discover something remarkable: The human brain, in its natural state, gravitates toward connection, wonder, and what researchers call "positive affect orientation." Your brain's default wiring is designed for joy.

Dr. Richard Davidson at the University of Wisconsin discovered that the left prefrontal cortex—associated with positive emotion, resilience, and approach behavior—is more active in healthy brains at baseline. Translation: Joy is your brain's home state. Depression and anxiety are disruptions of design, not revelations of reality. When trauma rewires away from joy-default, when sin creates neural pathways of shame, when spiritual warfare targets your capacity for gladness—you're not losing something foreign. You're losing something foundational.

This isn't toxic positivity. This is fighting for your original blueprint.

What Redemption Restores

"These things I have spoken to you, that My joy may remain in you, and that your joy may be full" (John 15:11). Jesus didn't say "I came to give you joy." He said "My joy may remain in you." Remain. It's already there. He came to restore what was interrupted. The Greek word for "remain" is *meno*—to abide, to stay, to dwell permanently. Joy isn't a visitor. Joy is a resident that got evicted by an illegal tenant.

Your laughter isn't frivolous. It's eviction notice. Joy isn't what you do. Joy is who you are.

THE ENEMY'S STRATEGIC ATTACK

Daniel's Warning: Wearing Down the Saints

"He shall speak pompous words against the Most High, shall persecute the saints of the Most High, and shall intend to change times and law. Then the saints shall be given into his hand for a time and times and half a time" (Daniel 7:25). The strategy: wear down the saints. Not instant destruction—gradual exhaustion. How? By attacking their joy first. Because "the joy of the Lord is your strength" (Nehemiah 8:10). No joy equals no strength. No strength equals easy prey.

Joy isn't optional equipment. It's your primary defense system.

Peter's Alert: The Devouring Lion

"Be sober, be vigilant; because your adversary the devil walks about like a roaring lion, seeking whom he may devour" (1 Peter 5:8). Who does a lion target? The weak, the isolated, the joyless. Lions don't attack the celebrating herd. They pick off the one who's separated, discouraged, worn down. Your joy keeps you in the herd. Your gladness maintains your strength. Your laughter confuses the predator.

The enemy knows: Your joy is your evangelism. Not your arguments. Not your apologetics. Your gladness. The thief came to steal, kill, and destroy (John 10:10). He steals your joy first because joy is your access code to everything else.

Why Every System of Oppression Targets Joy First

There's a reason totalitarian regimes ban music and dancing. There's a reason slave owners criminalized drums and celebration. There's a reason colonizers suppressed indigenous festivals. There's a reason religious systems prefer somber over celebratory. Joy is resistance. Joy is rebellion. Joy declares: "You don't control my internal reality."

The Pharisees didn't just object to Jesus' theology. They objected to His joy. "The Son of Man came eating and drinking, and they say, 'Look, a glutton and a winebibber, a friend of tax collectors and sinners!'" (Matthew 11:19). Jesus celebrated. He feasted. He laughed with the "wrong" people. And it terrified the religious system. Because joy cannot be controlled. Joy cannot be regulated. Joy cannot be leveraged for power. A joyful person operates outside religious manipulation.

Watch how religion weaponizes seriousness: "Real Christians don't laugh too loud." "Mature believers carry burdens." "If you're joyful, you must not understand the gravity of sin." Translation: "If you're happy, we can't control you." Because guilt keeps you coming back. Shame keeps you compliant. Fear keeps you small. But joy? Joy sets you free.

Your gladness terrifies every system that needs your misery.

BIBLICAL PATTERNS — WHEN JOY BECOMES WARFARE

TIER 1: Five Full Witnesses

David & Saul: When Music Drove Out Darkness (1 Samuel 16:23)

"And so it was, whenever the spirit from God was upon Saul, that David would take a harp and play it with his hand. Then Saul would become refreshed and well, and the distressing spirit would depart from him." Consider this: King Saul, tormented by an evil spirit, finds relief not through religious ritual but through music. Not through sacrifice but through song. Not through warfare but through worship.

David, the shepherd boy who would become king, didn't fight the darkness—he displaced it with melody. The evil spirit couldn't coexist with the joy-filled sound of heaven's song. This reveals a critical principle: Darkness cannot occupy the same space as joy-filled worship. Depression flees when gladness enters. Evil spirits literally cannot remain where joy reigns.

Notice what didn't work: Saul's crown didn't protect him. His authority didn't shield him. His armies couldn't defend him. But a shepherd boy with a harp and a joy-filled heart drove out what no weapon could touch. Your playlist might be more powerful than your prayer list. Your worship might accomplish what your warfare cannot.

King David's Dance: Scandalizing Religion (2 Samuel 6:14-23)

"Then David danced before the Lord with all his might; and David was wearing a linen ephod." The Ark of the Covenant returning. The presence of God approaching. And King David strips down to a linen ephod and dances with abandon. Michal, King Saul's daughter and David's wife, watches from the window: "And when she saw King David leaping and whirling before the Lord, she despised him in her heart."

Her confrontation: "How glorious was the king of Israel today, uncovering himself today in the eyes of the maids of his servants, as one of the base fellows shamelessly uncovers himself!" David's response revolutionizes joy: "It was before the Lord, who chose me instead of your father and all his house... Therefore I will play music before the Lord. And I will be even more undignified than this, and will be humble in my own sight."

Michal's punishment for despising this joy: "Therefore Michal the daughter of Saul had no children to the day of her death." Barrenness for mocking breakthrough joy. Your joy might offend the religious. Dance anyway. Your celebration might seem undignified. Celebrate harder.

Your inappropriate joy might be the most appropriate thing in the room.

Paul & Silas: When Midnight Praise Revealed True Nature (Acts 16:22-26)

Feel the scene: Paul the apostle and Silas his companion. Backs flayed open from beatings. Blood still wet. Feet locked in stocks. Inner prison—no light, no air. Midnight darkness both outside and in. "But at midnight Paul and Silas were praying and singing hymns to God, and the prisoners were listening to them." Singing. In stocks. At midnight. With backs bleeding.

They weren't creating joy in suffering. They were accessing joy through suffering. "Suddenly there was a great earthquake, so that the foundations of the prison were shaken; and immediately all the doors were opened and everyone's chains were loosed." The praise didn't follow the earthquake. The praise caused it.

Your midnight song doesn't beg for rescue. It announces who you actually are.

Sarah: When Laughter Became Prophecy Fulfilled (Genesis 18:13; 21:6)

Sarah—ninety years old, decades past natural childbearing, having laughed in disbelief when angels prophesied her pregnancy. Picture the conversation after the angels' prophecy: Abraham: "Sarah! Did you hear? We'll have a son within the year!" Sarah (laughing bitterly from the tent): "A son? I'm ninety years old, Abraham. My body stopped producing life decades ago. My womb has been a graveyard. This is cruel hope—why would God torment us with impossible promises now?"

God (to Abraham): "Why did Sarah laugh? Why did she say, 'Shall I surely bear a child, since I am old?' Is anything too hard for the Lord?" Sarah (afraid, coming out): "I didn't laugh." God: "Yes, you did laugh." Her first laugh was doubt. Cynicism born from decades of disappointment. The bitter laugh of someone who's stopped hoping because hope hurts too much.

But God specializes in last laughs. One year later, Sarah (holding baby Isaac, tears streaming, laughing with wonder): "God has made me laugh! And everyone who hears will laugh with me—not at me anymore!" When Sarah held Isaac—whose name literally means "laughter"—in her arms, her cynical laugh transformed into prophetic testimony. Despite her barrenness. Despite her age. Despite the biological impossibility. Despite her doubt about the prophecy.

"God has made me laugh"—not "I found laughter." God made it. He manufactured joy from impossibility. He created laughter from barrenness. He birthed gladness from doubt itself. The testimony of Jesus is the spirit of prophecy (Revelation 19:10). What God did for Sarah, He's doing for you: Taking your cynical laugh and transforming it into testimony. Taking your doubt and birthing promise from it.

Sarah laughed twice—first in doubt, then in destiny. Your current cynicism is just prophecy in process.

Nehemiah: When Joy Became Battle Strategy (Nehemiah 8:10)

Nehemiah the governor. The wall rebuilt after seventy years of rubble. The Law read publicly. The people weeping as they recognize their failure. "Then he said to them, 'Go your way, eat the fat, drink the sweet, and send portions to those for whom nothing is prepared; for this day is holy to our Lord. Do not sorrow, for the joy of the Lord is your strength.'"

In their weakest moment—recognizing generational failure—Nehemiah prescribes feast, not fast. Celebration, not self-flagellation. Joy, not judgment. Seven days of intentional joy. Not after victory—before the battles they knew were coming. Not as reward—as preparation.

Sometimes the most spiritual response to failure is throwing a party.

TIER 2: Ten Grouped Witnesses

Joy as Prophetic Testimony: Hannah transformed from barren weeping to prophetic laughter: "My heart rejoices in the Lord; my horn is exalted in the Lord. I smile at my enemies, because I rejoice in Your salvation" (1 Samuel 2:1). Job received prophecy during suffering: "He will yet fill your mouth with laughing, and your lips with rejoicing" (Job 8:21), and restoration came: "The Lord restored Job's losses... Indeed the Lord gave Job twice as much as he had before" (Job 42:10). Psalm 126 declares: "When the Lord brought back the captivity of Zion, we were like those who dream. Then our mouth was filled with laughter, and our tongue with singing. Then they said among the nations, 'The Lord has done great things for them.'" Your joy becomes testimony. Your laughter becomes evangelism.

Joy Despite Impossibility: Habakkuk faced complete agricultural collapse yet declared: "Though the fig tree may not blossom, nor fruit be on the vines; though the labor of the olive may fail, and the fields yield no food; though the flock may be cut off from the fold, and there be no herd in the stalls—yet I will rejoice in the Lord, I will joy in the God of my salvation" (Habakkuk 3:17-18). Joseph carried distinction in slavery and prison—his companions despaired while he prospered: "The Lord was with Joseph, and he was a successful man" (Genesis 39:2). Daniel maintained unusual wisdom in exile—his companions broke while he experienced breakthrough: "Then this Daniel distinguished himself above the governors and satraps, because an excellent spirit was in him" (Daniel 6:3). Joy isn't response to environment. Joy is connection to Source.

Joy as Medicine & Exchange: Proverbs prescribes: "A merry heart does good, like medicine, but a broken spirit dries the bones" (Proverbs 17:22). Isaiah promises exchange: "To console those who mourn in Zion, to give them beauty for ashes, the oil of joy for mourning, the garment of praise for the spirit of heaviness" (Isaiah 61:3). Peter declares: "In this you greatly rejoice, though now for a little while, if need be, you have been grieved by various trials... whom having not seen you love. Though now you do not see Him, yet believing, you rejoice with joy inexpressible and full of glory" (1 Peter 1:6,8). Your body was designed to heal through joy.

THE ANOINTING OF GLADNESS

"You love righteousness and hate wickedness; therefore God, Your God, has anointed You with the oil of gladness more than Your companions" (Psalm 45:7). There's an anointing of gladness. Not just emotion—anointing. Power. Authority. Breakthrough capacity.

When you love righteousness and hate lawlessness, you carry unexplainable joy—gladness that survives storms sinking other ships, anointing keeping you buoyant when companions drown. They travel the same roads, face the same challenges, yet look at you wondering: How are you still joyful? Not because your life is easier—because you've been anointed with oil that doesn't come from earthly wells.

Paul wrote "Rejoice in the Lord always. Again I will say, rejoice!" (Philippians 4:4) from prison—his chains became pulpit. Same storms. Different outcomes. Same trials. Different testimonies. Why? The anointing of gladness above companions.

This creates unexplainable resilience—you bend where companions break. Magnetic favor—doors open for you that stayed locked for others. Generational legacy—your joy compounds with age while theirs fades. Atmospheric shift—rooms feel lighter when you enter. Your children need to see joy isn't circumstantial—it's hereditary.

Your unusual joy draws others to Him. Your unexplainable gladness becomes their invitation to freedom. Your distinction becomes their testimony that joy isn't circumstantial—it's anointing. Your anointing of gladness isn't just for you—it's through you for every companion who's forgotten joy is available.

TESTIMONY — WHEN I STOPPED FIGHTING FOR JOY AND STARTED FIGHTING FROM IT

The Valley Resume: When Joy Proved Itself Real

Since discovering joy as identity, not emotion, I've walked through valleys that should have destroyed that revelation:

My father's death—having the opportunity to pray with him and ask him to repeat the salvation prayer before he took his last breath brought me joy. A man I barely knew as father, since I was raised by a single mother. In that moment, estrangement became eternal connection. Absence became presence. His last breath became his first eternal one. Joy and grief intertwined—not canceling each other, but coexisting.

Marriage crisis that brought us to the brink. Sleeping in separate rooms but still choosing joy. Not fake happiness—real joy that says: "This is brutal and I'm still who God says I am." Divorce proceedings that split everything except my joy. While signing papers that ended what I thought was forever, I danced in my kitchen that night. Not because divorce was joyful—it was devastating. But because I learned: circumstances change, identity doesn't.

Job loss that threatened provision but not position. The day I cleared my desk, I laughed—actually laughed—remembering: I'm not what I do. I'm who I am. Bills were real. Fear was valid. But joy? Joy was deeper than employment.

Diagnosis of situational depression from a therapist who watched me choose joy anyway. "This is clinical," she said. "Yes," I replied, "and I'm still joyful by design. Let's treat the condition without losing my identity." We did. Medication and celebration. Therapy and dancing. Both/and, not either/or.

The 6 PM panic attacks that arrived with military precision for three months straight. Heart rate: 180. Chest: crushing. Breathing: impossible. Duration: 45 minutes. Every. Single. Evening. Until Day 73, mid-attack, drowning in my own breath, I heard: "Laugh at it." So I forced it: "HA. You're so predictable it's pathetic!" The panic stuttered. Joy wasn't my weapon—it was my nature reasserting itself.

Through each valley, joy wasn't my feeling—it was my rebellion. My resistance. My declaration that circumstances don't determine identity. God gave me the declaration: "I choose joy." God gave me the scripture to hold on to: "But may the God of all grace, who called us to His eternal glory by Christ Jesus, after you have suffered a while, perfect, establish, strengthen, and settle you" (1 Peter 5:10).

After I've suffered a while—not if, but after. The suffering is temporal. The settling is eternal. The joy isn't dependent on the suffering ending—it's present in the while.

I've grieved with joy. Divorced with joy. Lost with joy. Been diagnosed with joy. Buried with joy. Almost ended with joy. Panicked with joy. Joy isn't circumstantial—it's constitutional.

The Declaration That Changed My Reality

Daniel Fast, Day 5. The same God whose warning I'd ignored still loved me enough to reveal my true identity: "Father, I speak to every 'Vashti' squatting on my original design—including this shame—eviction notice served. The Esther in me isn't rising. She's remembering. I choose joy. Despite it all, intentionally. Not because I feel it, but because it's who I am. I shall laugh again! Not when shame fades. But now—because laughter is who I am, and shame is the squatter. These tears aren't surrender—they're labor pains. I'm not finding joy. I'm birthing back into it. I choose joy—despite the narcissist's lies, despite the public humiliation, despite ignoring Your warning. I choose joy—because it's my original design, and no counterfeit relationship can change who You created me to be."

You're not fighting for joy. You're fighting from it.

PARADIGM SHIFT — THE ONTOLOGICAL REVOLUTION

THE OLD LIE	THE ORIGINAL TRUTH
"I'm a depressed person trying to be joyful"	"I'm a joyful person whose design was attacked"
"Joy is emotion I feel"	"Joy is nature I embody"
"Happiness depends on circumstances"	"Joy is my circumstance, regardless of externals"
"I need to create joy"	"I need to return to joy"
"Suffering reveals my true self"	"Suffering interrupts my true self"
"Joy is shallow and immature"	"Joy is reality and suffering is distortion"
"Serious problems need serious faces"	"Dark attacks need original-design resistance"
"Joy after breakthrough"	"Joy restores breakthrough"
"Find joy when healed"	"Joy is the healing"

Depression isn't your identity. It's malware on your joy-designed hard drive.

RESISTANCE REALITY CHECK

Old Identity: "I don't feel joyful, so I'm not."
Original Design: "I am joyful. Feelings are adjusting to reality."
Old Identity: "This looks ridiculous."
Original Design: "Ridiculous to whom? Hell is terrified."
Old Identity: "I'll celebrate after healing."
Original Design: "Celebration is the healing—the return to who I've always been."
Old Identity: "My suffering defines me."
Original Design: "My suffering interrupted me. Joy reveals me."

You're not becoming joyful. You're remembering you always were.

ACTIVATION — TWO PRIMARY PRACTICES

NOTE

This spiritual practice works alongside professional mental health care, never as replacement. If experiencing crisis, contact your local crisis helpline or go to your nearest emergency room first.

PRIMARY PRACTICE #1: Crisis Intervention Kit

When panic attacks, depression descends, or darkness invades:

The 5-Minute Return to Original Design

Minute 1 — Breathe & Remember: Inhale 4, hold 4, exhale 6. "Joy is my factory setting."

Minute 2 — Sound Your Identity: Begin with music if words won't come. Like David's harp driving out darkness.

Minute 3 — Embody Original Design: Laugh louder. Add movement. Your true nature expressing.

Minute 4 — Declare Reality: "I am joyful by design! Depression is the invader—I evict it now!"

Minute 5 — Release Into Who You Are: Let joy take over. You're not performing. You're being.

Five minutes returning to original design can displace five years of invaded identity.

Joy Emergency Kit — Keep Ready

Playlist — Three Songs That Force Movement:
- "Good Day" by Forrest Frank (impossible to stay still)
- "Praise" by Elevation Worship (warfare through dancing)
- "Joy" by We Are Messengers (literally commands your soul)

Photos That Trigger Genuine Smiles:
- Videos of babies laughing (universally effective)
- Your "before/after" transformation photos
- Screenshots of breakthrough testimonies
- That one friend who makes ridiculous faces
- Your pet doing something absurd

Video Bookmarks:
- Key & Peele "Substitute Teacher" (3 minutes of guaranteed laughter)
- Any "Babies Eating Lemons" compilation
- Your personal "victory video" from a breakthrough moment

Scripture Emergency Cards (Screenshot these):
- Nehemiah 8:10 — "The joy of the Lord is your strength"
- Psalm 30:5 — "Joy comes in the morning"
- John 15:11 — "That My joy may remain in you"
- Psalm 126:2 — "Our mouth was filled with laughter"
- James 1:2 — "Count it all joy"

Partner Protocol: Text "CODE JOY" to your designated person. They respond with either:
- A voice note of them laughing
- A ridiculous gif
- "Remember who you are"

No advice. No fixing. Just reminder of identity.

Physical Anchor: Keep one object that reminds you of breakthrough:
- A stone from a sacred place
- Jewelry given during victory
- Photo from your strongest moment
- Written declaration from breakthrough
- Anything that whispers: "You survived before. Joy won before. It wins again."

Note: This isn't positive thinking or denial. This is emergency identity restoration when feelings lie about who you are.

PRIMARY PRACTICE #2: Daily Identity Restoration

6-Dimensional Identity Restoration

Dimension	Identity Declaration	Original Design	Evidence
SPIRITUAL	"I was created in joy"	Dance as true nature	Peace floods naturally
MENTAL	"My brain's default is gladness"	Mock anxiety's lies	Fear shrinks at identity
EMOTIONAL	"Joy is who I am"	Celebrate micro-victories	Abundance becomes lens
PHYSICAL	"My body was designed for celebration"	Move in gladness	Energy rises from design
FINANCIAL	"I operate from abundance"	Thank for unseen provision	Doors open to nature
RELATIONAL	"I'm contagious with original design"	Spread identity-joy	Others catch who they are

Daily Return to Factory Settings
Morning: "This is who I am: joyful by design" + dance to one song
Noon: "Rejoice always = return to always-reality" + 30-second identity laugh
Evening: "Weeping visits; joy remains" + list three design-evidences
Bedtime: "In His presence = in my original state" + smile at who you actually are
   You're not becoming joyful. You're remembering you always were.

FOCUS AREA IDENTITY PRAYERS
Scripture Foundation: "My brethren, count it all joy when you fall into various trials" (James 1:2)
Choose your primary restoration area:

   For Spiritual Focus: "Father, I'm not finding joy in Your presence—I'm remembering who I am in You. I was created joyful. Restore my factory settings."

   For Mental Focus: "Father, my brain's default mode is joy. Depression is malfunction. Anxiety is malware. As I use the professional support You provide, let me also remember: gladness is my design."

For Emotional Focus: "Father, I'm not a broken person trying to be whole. I'm whole by design, experiencing temporary disruption. Joy restores me to original, alongside every healing tool You provide."

For Physical Focus: "Father, my body was made for celebration, not survival mode. As a merry heart does good like medicine, let gladness restore physical design."

For Financial Focus: "Father, I was created in abundance consciousness. Scarcity is learned. Let joy return me to original prosperity mindset."

For Relational Focus: "Father, my gladness is contagious because it's identity, not performance. Use my return to original design to remind others who they are. Joy becomes generational legacy."

DECLARATION — SCRIPTURE-ANCHORED IDENTITY

Stand and declare:
"Joy is my original design!

Like David's harp—My joy drives out darkness!
Like David's dance—I'll be undignified in gladness!
Like Paul's midnight song—I announce who I am!
Like Nehemiah's feast—Joy is my battle preparation!
Like Hannah's smile—I laugh at my enemies!
Like Sarah's double laugh—My cynicism becomes prophecy!
Like Job's ending—My mouth shall be filled!
Like Psalm 126—Nations will see my joy and know God!

I'm not finding joy—I'm being it!
Depression isn't my identity—it's an invader!
My laughter is eviction notice!
I'm not fighting for joy—I'm fighting from it!
My gladness terrifies systems that need my misery!
My joy is my primary defense system!
My midnight song announces who I actually am!
When I know my identity, uncertainty becomes comedy!
My inappropriate joy is the most appropriate thing in the room!
I shall laugh again because I never stopped being laughter!"

BREAKTHROUGH PRAYER

Father God, Abba,

I repent for believing the lie that suffering is noble and joy is shallow. For accepting depression as identity instead of recognizing it as invasion. For waiting to find joy when I needed to return to it.

Father, whatever or whoever stands between me and the triumph that brings me pleasure, happiness, gladness, celebration, laughter, and dancing—in Jesus' name, deal with it, uproot it, break through it! Lord, anything blocking my joy—uproot it, block it, defeat it, eradicate it!

You created me in joy, for joy, as joy. The fall didn't reveal my true self—it interrupted it. Like David playing for King Saul, let my joy drive out every tormenting spirit! Like King David dancing, I'll be undignified in worship! Like Paul and Silas singing in stocks—identity displacing circumstance! Like Nehemiah, I choose feast over fasting, joy over judgment! Like Hannah, I smile at my enemies!

Like Sarah holding Isaac, I will laugh again—not in doubt but in destiny! The testimony of Jesus is the spirit of prophecy—do it again, Lord! What You did for Sarah's barrenness, do for my joy! Like Job, fill my mouth with laughter even in trial! Like Psalm 126, let nations see and say, "The Lord has done great things!"

You anoint me with the oil of gladness above my contemporaries—companions, family, co-workers, leaders (Psalm 45:7). Our God makes me glad!

Joy is my factory setting. Everything else is malware. Depression isn't who I am—it's an illegal tenant I'm evicting. Anxiety isn't my design—it's a virus my original operating system is deleting. Every system needing my misery—my gladness is your destruction. Every enemy targeting my joy—you attacked the wrong person. Joy is who I am.

Right now, I don't create joy. I return to it. I don't find gladness. I remember it. I don't become joyful. I restore to joyful. As I use every healing tool You provide—therapy, medication, community, professional support—let joy multiply their effectiveness. Let my return to original design happen through multiple means working together.

Thank You that I'm not broken trying to be fixed. I'm original trying to remember. Restore to me the joy of Your salvation (Psalm 51:12). Give me beauty for ashes, the oil of joy for mourning (Isaiah 61:3).

I'm not fighting for joy—I'm fighting from it! My midnight song doesn't beg for rescue—it announces who I am!

In Jesus' name, joy is my identity!

Amen.

CLOSING — THE REVOLUTION OF RETURN

Day 5 started with emotions staging full rebellion and religion whispering: "Suffering is noble. Joy is shallow." Tonight you possess the most scandalous truth of the fast: Joy isn't what you're trying to find. Joy is who you've always been.

You weren't created to survive suffering. You were created in gladness, for celebration, as living expression of a joyful God. Depression isn't your identity. Anxiety isn't your DNA. Heaviness isn't your default. You're not a depressed person trying to be joyful. You're a joyful person whose design was attacked.

Genesis says you were made in joy. Neuroscience confirms your brain defaults to it. Jesus came to restore what was interrupted. Like David's harp driving out King Saul's darkness, your joy displaces depression. Like King David's dance scandalizing religion, your gladness might offend but honors heaven. Like Nehemiah's strategic celebration, your joy prepares for battle. Like Hannah's prophetic laughter, your smile declares enemy defeat. Like Paul and Silas's midnight song, you don't beg for rescue—you announce who you are.

Your joy terrifies every system that needs your misery. Your laughter announces who you actually are. Your gladness is contagious return to original design. You're not fighting for joy. You're fighting from it. You're not becoming joyful. You're remembering you always were. Your inappropriate joy might be the most appropriate thing in the room. Your gladness alone is powerful. Together it's atomic.

Like Sarah's prophetic laughter, your cynical laugh is about to become testimony. She laughed in doubt at ninety—then laughed in destiny holding Isaac. The testimony of Jesus is the spirit of prophecy. What He did for Sarah, He'll do for you. You shall laugh again—not in mockery but in miracle.

By Day 21, joy won't be something you do—it will be who you are, fully restored. Tomorrow, infinite greatness becomes personally accessible. Tomorrow, you meet the God who holds galaxies and holds you.

Joy practiced becomes joy possessed. Joy possessed reveals: it was always who you were.

Day 5 Complete: Original Identity Restored

Joy: Not emotion—essence
Gladness: Not response—reality
Laughter: Not tactic—nature
Fighting from joy, not for it: Paradigm shifted
Factory settings: Restoration initiated

SOAP JOURNAL — DAY 5

S (Scripture): Which verse helped you see joy as identity, not just emotion?
O (Observation): Where have you accepted depression/anxiety as "who you are" instead of "what invaded you"?
A (Application): What one scandalous act of joy will you do this week to announce your original design?
P (Prayer): "Father, I'm not _____ trying to become joyful. I'm joyful by design, returning to _____."

Today's Breakthrough Marker: How did joy shift from "what you do" to "who you are" today?
Tomorrow's Expectation: Based on today's identity restoration, what do you expect tomorrow when you encounter divine greatness?

JOY RESTORED. IDENTITY RECOVERED. GLADNESS UNLEASHED. READY FOR GREATNESS.

DAY 6 — GREATNESS

When Infinite Power Takes Personal Interest

"Great is the Lord, and greatly to be praised; and His greatness is unsearchable." — Psalm 145:3

WEEK 1 — GROW: Building Intimacy with God

Day 6 of 21. Yesterday's Gladness restored your identity. Today's Greatness reveals infinite power personally orchestrated for your breakthrough.

ENCOUNTER — WHERE YOU ARE

4:30 AM. Day 6. You're on your knees—not in prayer but in weakness. Six days of fasting and your body just gave up holding you vertical. You tried to stand for morning prayer and your legs said no. So here you are, kneeling by necessity not devotion, staring at carpet fibers that look like canyons under this close perspective.

And in this forced position something breaks open: If these microscopic fibers look canyon-sized when you zoom in this close... what if your canyon-sized problem becomes microscopic when God zooms out?

Some of you taste metal—ketosis marking metabolic shift. Others feel surprisingly strong. Both states are portals to the same revelation. The breakthrough isn't validated by your body's response—it's validated by His greatness revealed.

You stand—slowly, carefully—and move to your window. Sunrise paints colors you've never seen, and it hits you: You've been measuring God by your ceiling when He holds galaxies like marbles. Your stomach may be quiet—no longer screaming, just hollow. Or you may still battle hunger. In either state, something vast approaches. Something that makes your biggest problem look like dust on an infinite canvas.

Week 1 has systematically stripped you to essence. Day 1's Gospel revealed you operate from acceptance. Day 2's Grace straightened your crown. Day 3's Goodness taught you to trust darkness. Day 4 awakened your arsenal. Day 5 restored your factory settings. Each revelation removed another false support until only one remains: God Himself.

With every prop removed, every crutch kicked away, every false foundation exposed—you're ready to encounter the One whose greatness makes your giants molecular. You've been relating to God like He's a bigger version of you—more powerful but still limited, more knowing but still surprised, more present but still distant. This morning, that illusion shatters.

The God who spoke galaxies knows your name. The power holding atoms holds your situation. The intelligence that designed DNA designs your breakthrough. The force that carved canyons carves your character. This infinite, boundless God takes personal interest in your molecular concerns.

We shrink God to fit logic, then wonder why problems look huge.

FOUNDATION — THE REVELATION THAT REWROTE REALITY

When the Holy Spirit Schooled Us on Greatness

January 2023. Day 6 of The Daniel Fast: Closing the GAP. Thirty-five people on our Zoom call, bodies depleted, spirits electric. My husband John and I were co-leading. The topic: encountering God's greatness versus experiencing His goodness. I posed the question that split the atmosphere: "What's the difference between God's goodness and God's greatness?"

Silence. Then John started to speak, but the Holy Spirit interrupted—not with words but with weight. The kind that makes you grab your desk to stay upright. John's eyes widened. Mine watered. Neither of us could speak for thirty seconds that felt like thirty minutes.

Then the download came:

John: "God's goodness is like looking through a microscope. You zoom in and see He knows every tear, every fear, every prayer."

"But God's greatness is like looking through a telescope. You zoom out and realize He's orchestrating galaxies while answering your prayers."

Me: "His goodness says, 'I care about your crisis.' It's intimate. His greatness says, 'I'm conquering your crisis.' It's infinite."

John: "There's a theological distinction here—God's transcendence, His greatness above creation, and His immanence, His nearness within it. We need both. A transcendent God without immanence is distant. An immanent God without transcendence is limited."

The Zoom room went silent, then erupted—not with noise but with aha moments, breakthrough, paradigm shifts. "I've been relating to His goodness but not His greatness. No wonder I feel comforted but not conquered!" "He's been fighting my battles while I've been begging Him to notice them!" I explained: "His goodness comforts. His greatness conquers. He is both a good God and a great God above all gods."

The Download That Kept Downloading

John: "Without goodness, God's greatness would terrify. Unlimited power without love is every dictator's dream."

Me: "Without greatness, God's goodness would frustrate. Perfect love without power to act is every human limitation."

"But together? The complete picture. A God who bottles your tears and commands storms."

John: "Who numbers the hairs on your head and the stars in the sky—transcendence and immanence unified."

This is why Jesus is the perfect revelation of God's nature—fully divine (transcendent greatness) yet fully human (immanent goodness). In Christ, infinite power took on flesh. The hands that hung stars touched lepers. The voice that spoke galaxies whispered to fishermen. When you see Jesus, you see transcendence and immanence unified—greatness walking among us, infinite power personally available.

Me: "Who whispers to your heart and roars at your enemies."

Someone unmuted: "So we're not asking God to manage our crisis—we're believing He's conquering it?"

John: "Exactly. Are you praying up from your problem or down from His throne? His transcendence means He's above your situation. His immanence means He's in it with you. Together means He's both orchestrating the solution and walking you through it."

One revelation properly received shifts a generation's prayer posture.

THE DIVINE CONVERGENCE: GOODNESS VS GREATNESS

GOD'S GOODNESS	GOD'S GREATNESS
Microscope - Zooms IN	Telescope - Zooms OUT
Sees every tear	Commands every storm
Knows your name	Numbers the stars
Bottles your pain	Battles your enemies
Your Comforter	Your Commander
Catches you when you fall	Conquers what made you fall
Walks with you through valley	Moves the mountain blocking path
Whispers "I am with you"	Roars "The battle is Mine"
Intimate care	Infinite power
Personal presence	Sovereign orchestration
Feels your feelings	Fixes your future
Understands your weakness	Unleashes His strength
Near enough to hear whispers	Big enough to handle wars

Without Goodness: Greatness would terrify—unlimited power without love.
Without Greatness: Goodness would frustrate—perfect love without power.
Together: Complete God—infinite power personally invested.

JESUS CHRIST	TRANSCENDENCE + IMMANENCE UNIFIED
Fully divine (greatness)	Fully human (goodness)
Hands that hung stars	Touched lepers
Voice that spoke galaxies	Whispered to fishermen
Commands nature	Comforts hearts

Thirty-five people simultaneously moved from basement prayers to throne room declarations.

THE HEBREW REVELATION

When Language Exhausts Itself

Religion taught God's greatness through superlatives—omnipotent, omniscient, omnipresent. Big words that became small concepts. We memorized attributes like facts instead of encountering the reality that makes angels cover their faces.

The Primary Word: Gadol

The Hebrew *gadol* means great, mighty, massive. But when applied to God, Hebrew exhausts itself. It adds intensifiers: *El Gadol*—GREAT GOD. Not great among options. Great beyond categories.

The Surrender: En Cheqer

Then Hebrew surrenders. God's greatness is *en cheqer*—"unsearchable" (Psalm 145:3). *En* equals nothing, no. *Cheqer* equals investigation, end. Literally: "No investigation can reach the end." You could spend eternity exploring His greatness and never find a boundary.

The Paradox: Infinite Yet Intimate

But here's what shatters every religious box: This infinite, unsearchable God takes personal interest in your specific situation. David understood: "When I consider Your heavens, the work of Your fingers, the moon and the stars, which You have ordained, what is man that You are mindful of him?" (Psalm 8:3-4).

The Hebrew for "mindful" is *zakar*—to remember, recall, mention. The infinite God doesn't just notice you—He remembers you. Scientists estimate ten to the twenty-fourth power stars exist. Psalm 147:4 declares: "He counts the number of the stars; He calls them all by name." If God intimately knows that many stars—how much more does He know you?

The God who manages universes manages your Tuesday. An infinite God can't be fully comprehended, only increasingly encountered.

TESTIMONY — WHEN THE GRAND CANYON REVEALED GOD'S GREATNESS

The Journey to the Edge

December 30, 2024. Arizona desert. John driving, me thinking about scriptures we'd share during our Daniel Fast. We thought we were prepared. We'd seen photographs. Watched documentaries. How different could reality be?

The Moment Everything Shifted

We parked at the South Rim, walked through trees, and then—

December wind hit my face first—cold, dry, carrying the scent of juniper and time. Then the sound—or rather, the absence of it. Tourist chatter disappeared into a silence so vast it felt alive, swallowing every noise into something ancient and holy. Then I saw it.

I grabbed John's arm. He grabbed the railing. Neither of us could speak. It wasn't the size—we'd seen big things. It was the scale. Layers upon layers of stone, each one carved across millions of years. Colors shifting as December light moved—reds deepening to purple, whites glowing gold. The wind that moments ago felt cold now felt ancient, like it had been blowing through this canyon before humanity existed and would blow long after.

My legs felt weak—not from fasting but from encountering something that made me molecular. Stand here with us for a moment. December wind on your face, carrying cold from depths you can't see. Layers of time carved in stone stretching beyond vision—past, present, future all visible simultaneously. Your biggest problem—the one that felt canyon-sized this morning—try holding it against this vista. Feel the perspective shift. That's not minimizing your pain—that's maximizing your God.

The Revelation at the Rim

Tourists bustled around us—selfies, chatter, oblivious. John and I were having a theological awakening. I pulled out my phone, showed him a photo from that morning: "This morning, our ministry challenges felt massive." I held the phone against the canyon vista. The screen looked like a postage stamp against infinity. "Now?"

The Holy Spirit spoke—not audibly, but undeniably, in a voice that felt as vast as the canyon itself: "You've been teaching My goodness—that I care about problems. Now teach My greatness—problems are molecular to Me."

The Download at the Edge

Standing at Hopi Point as December sun painted the canyon:

Me: "God's goodness zooms in like a microscope to see every tear."

John: "His greatness zooms out like a telescope orchestrating galaxies."

We laughed—not humor but holy recognition. We'd come to see a tourist attraction and instead encountered the Creator's scale.

The Prayer We Couldn't Pray

We tried to pray. Started with "Lord, we need help with..." We'd look at the canyon and the sentence would die. How do you tell the God who carved this that your problem is too big?

John prayed: "God, help us see everything from Your perspective."

I added: "We've been praying up from problems. Teach us to pray down from Your throne."

What We Brought Home

Same situations, different vision. Our ministry challenges hadn't changed—but they'd become molecular. That December 2024 encounter revolutionized how we lead. We shifted from "God, can You handle this?" to "God who carved canyons is handling this." From "Lord, notice my need" to "Lord, from Your perspective, how small is this?"

Standing at the Grand Canyon rim, I understood: We'd been measuring God by our ceiling when He holds canyons in His palm. We'd been bringing ant-sized faith for elephant-sized problems to an infinite God. We'd been praying up from our basement when we're seated with Christ in heavenly places.

That day didn't just show us a wonder of the world. It showed us the wonder of our God—infinite power taking personal interest in every molecular detail.

Your impossible is God's molecular.

WHEN GREATNESS CONQUERED MY GIANTS

Standing at that canyon rim, I saw my giants differently. Let me show you what microscope versus telescope perspective does to mountains.

Ministry Challenges: From Overwhelming to Molecular

December 2024. My hands shook as I tried to make numbers appear that weren't there—funding we didn't have, time that didn't exist, capacity I couldn't create. The morning we drove to the Grand Canyon, I'd spent two hours staring at spreadsheets that mocked me with their impossible math.

From basement position, I prayed: "God, can You see how massive this is?"

THE DANIEL FAST: CLOSING THE GAP!

The List That Felt Like a Canyon:

Ignite the Nation—John's ministry launching summer 2025, six months away. We were building something from nothing: vision clear, pathway unclear, resources developing. Technology needs stacking up—apps to build, discipleship training courses to create, content to develop. On-the-ground mission work requiring partnership with local communities we hadn't yet connected with.

John returning to Antigua after years as a missionary meant rekindling relationships, rebuilding trust, re-establishing presence. Antigua forming as the hub, but other Caribbean islands waiting to follow—each one needing its own strategy, its own partnerships, its own infrastructure. A gospel truck fitted with sound system and stage could be excellent for street ministry—if we could fund it, outfit it, staff it.

Partnership forming between us. Co-ministry developing in real time. Learning to lead together while learning each other. Every decision requiring alignment we were still building. Every vision requiring communication we were still refining.

Fresh relocation from Canada to USA—still unpacking boxes while trying to build Kingdom infrastructure. New state. New community. New everything. The kind of transition where you know you heard God correctly and need to trust Him with the process. Establishing myself as wife, mother, grandmother, speaker, author, coach, mentor, consultant—while maintaining an active travel itinerary that kept me away more than home.

Learning to balance faith, life, health. How do you build a marriage while building a ministry? How do you be present as grandmother when you're traveling to six continents? How do you maintain health when every week brings new demands? The tension between calling and capacity felt crushing.

Chayah Club—global community that outgrew the out-of-the-box solution and now needed customized structure, systems, content, leadership development. Thousands across six continents depending on frameworks God had downloaded that needed a customized ecosystem. Shifting from disjointed delivery—bits and pieces scattered across platforms—to integrated reality.

The frameworks lived in my head and heart. They needed translating into scalable systems other leaders could replicate. But translation takes time I didn't have and resources I hadn't secured. Every day the community grew. Every day the gap between what existed and what was needed widened.

Nikimac business—building it to self-sustain ministry growth, but businesses take time, investments, and relationships. We needed revenue now but building something sustainable meant playing the long game. Meeting community needs while establishing revenue streams. Providing resources we didn't yet have. The catch-22 of entrepreneurship: you need money to make money, but you need to make money to have money.

The Prayer for Financial Freedom—more time to invest in ministry, more resources to fund ministry, partners to see vision, collaboration to grow. The prayer wasn't about wealth—it was about capacity. Financial freedom would mean less time chasing funding and more time fulfilling calling. Less energy on survival and more energy on service.

But the List Didn't Stop at Ministry

Family prayer needs that woke me at night: Provision for adult children navigating their own seasons. Deliverance from patterns we'd been fighting for years. Supernatural blessings where natural solutions had failed. Healing—emotional, physical, spiritual—that only God could do. Restoration of relationships fractured by time, distance, or misunderstanding. Peace in hearts carrying wounds I couldn't see or fix. Wisdom for decisions I couldn't make for them. Courage for battles I couldn't fight for them.

How do you pray for adult children without controlling? How do you intercede without interfering? How do you trust God with people you'd die for but can't protect?

Community needs that expanded the canyon: Members of Chayah Club facing their own impossibilities. Financial crisis. Marriage breakdown. Health emergencies. Grief that wouldn't end. Depression that wouldn't lift. Prodigals who wouldn't return. Dreams that kept dying. I carried their prayer requests like stones in my pockets—each one real, each one heavy, each one needing breakthrough I couldn't manufacture.

Open doors for those stuck in closed seasons. Wisdom for leaders navigating complexity. Courage for those facing fear. Deliverance for those bound by what they couldn't name. How do you pastor thousands when you're still figuring out your own life?

Country burdens that felt too big to carry: Peace in homes torn by division. Peace in hearts hardened by disappointment. Peace in land fractured by conflict. Provision for economies struggling. Deliverance from systems that crush the vulnerable. Supernatural intervention where human solutions had failed. Healing for a nation's wounds. Restoration of what's been lost—innocence, integrity, hope itself.

How do you pray for your country when you feel powerless to change your own city? How do you believe for national breakthrough when local breakthrough feels impossible?

From basement position, each challenge looked canyon-sized. I'd wake at 3 AM with mind spiraling through the full list: "How do we build apps we can't afford? How do we rekindle relationships from thousands of miles away? How do I establish myself in Idaho while traveling globally? How do we customize Chayah Club without custom-level budget? How do we build Nikimac fast enough to fund what's needed now? How do I balance marriage, family, ministry, business, health—when each one deserves full attention?

"And God, what about my children's provision? The community members' deliverance? The relationships needing restoration? The hearts needing peace? The homes needing healing? The nations needing Your intervention? How do I carry all this? How do You even see all this?"

The Morning of the Grand Canyon

That December morning, I'd spent two hours trying to solve the unsolvable. Moving money that didn't exist. Creating time that wasn't available. Building systems for scale we hadn't reached. Praying prayers that felt like they hit the ceiling. I took a photo of my workspace—laptop open to funding projections, journal filled with intercessions that felt more like inventory of impossibilities, coffee cup that had gone cold while I stared at problems I couldn't fix.

"God, this is too much. Ignite the Nation needs everything we don't have. Chayah Club is bursting at the seams. Nikimac is growing but not fast enough. I'm building relationships in Idaho while traveling the world. And that's just ministry. What about my family? What about the community depending on me? What about the nations falling apart? How do I be present everywhere when I can't be present anywhere fully? How do I carry everyone's needs when I can barely carry my own?"

John walked in: "Ready to see the Grand Canyon?"

I looked at my screen, then at my journal: "We're leaving in six months for the Caribbean and we still need apps, training courses, partnerships, funding, a gospel truck. My family needs provision, healing, restoration. The community needs open doors, deliverance, breakthrough. The nations need peace, wisdom, supernatural intervention. And I'm supposed to see a tourist attraction?"

He smiled: "Perfect day to see something big, then."

Standing at the Edge

Then we stood at that rim. December wind carrying ancient cold. Layers carved across millennia. Colors shifting as winter light moved. And I pulled out my phone, showed John that morning's photo—my workspace, my spreadsheets, my prayer journal, my impossible list.

I held the phone screen against the canyon vista.

The screen looked like a postage stamp against infinity.

The Holy Spirit spoke—not audibly, but undeniably, in a voice as vast as the canyon itself: "You've been teaching My goodness—that I care about problems. Now teach My greatness—problems are molecular to Me."

The Shift That Changed Everything

I stared at that canyon. God carved this with water and time. Layers upon layers of impossible geology. Millions of years of patient precision. A masterpiece created through process, not pressure. And He did it while managing universes.

From throne room perspective, I saw it:

Ignite the Nation? The God who equipped Moses with exactly what he needed exactly when he needed it is handling our technology, apps, courses, partnerships. He's been preparing Antiguan relationships longer than we've been planning return. What feels like building from nothing to us is assembling what He's already designed. The gospel truck? If He wanted Gideon to fight with trumpets and torches, He can provide sound systems and stages.

Canada to USA transition? The God who led Israel through wilderness isn't worried about my unpacked boxes or unestablished rhythms. He's not confused about how I balance wife, mother, grandmother, speaker, author, coach, mentor, consultant, traveler. He called me to all of it—He'll sustain me through all of it. What feels like impossible juggling to me is divine choreography from His throne.

Chayah Club infrastructure? The God who organized Israel's camp of millions can structure our thousands. He downloaded the frameworks—He'll provide the ecosystem. What feels like bursting at the seams to me is expansion He's orchestrating. From my head and heart to scalable reality? He specializes in translating invisible into visible. He spoke worlds into existence—He can speak systems into operation.

Nikimac business growth? The God who multiplied five loaves to feed thousands isn't intimidated by our revenue gap. Businesses take time? He owns time. Need investments? He owns resources. Need relationships? He orchestrates connections. What feels like too slow to us is right on schedule from eternity's perspective.

Financial freedom prayer? The God who owns cattle on thousand hills doesn't need my funding projections. He's not running calculations on whether He can afford my calling. Partners to see vision?

He opens eyes. Collaboration to grow? He builds teams. More time for ministry, more resources for impact? He's the God of multiplication—watch what He does with our insufficient supply.

Family needs? The God who provided for Israel in wilderness provides for my children in their seasons. He knows their needs before they ask. What feels like protection I can't give from my limited position is provision He's already releasing from His unlimited supply. Deliverance I can't manufacture? He's the Deliverer. Healing I can't perform? He's Jehovah Rapha. Restoration I can't force? He's the Restorer of breaches. Wisdom they need? He gives liberally to all who ask. Peace in their hearts? He's the Prince of Peace. What looks like mountains I can't move from ground level are molecules He's already handling from throne room.

Community prayers? The God who heard Israel's cry in Egypt hears every prayer request in my inbox. Open doors for the stuck? He's the Door. Wisdom for the confused? He's Wonderful Counselor. Courage for the fearful? Perfect love casts out fear. Deliverance for the bound? Whom the Son sets free is free indeed. Breakthrough for the stuck? He makes ways in wilderness. What feels like weight I can't carry from basement position is intercession He's already answering from His position.

Country burdens? The God who established nations and determines their boundaries isn't overwhelmed by any nation's chaos. Peace in homes? He's peace. Peace in hearts? He gives peace that passes understanding. Peace in land? He makes wars cease. Provision for economies? He owns it all. Healing for nations? If My people who are called by My name humble themselves and pray. What looks like impossible national transformation from human perspective is simple divine intervention from His throne.

I laughed—not humor but holy recognition. These challenges that woke me at 3 AM—ministry, family, community, country? All molecular. The canyon of complexity I'd been drowning in? The Canyon Carver holds it in His palm. Every prayer request, every need, every impossibility—from His perspective, postage stamps against infinity.

What Changed

Same situations. Different vision. We still had six months until Caribbean launch. Still needed apps, courses, partnerships, funding. Still had boxes to unpack and systems to build. Still had community outgrowing infrastructure and business needing growth. Family still needed provision, healing, restoration. Community still needed breakthrough. Nations still needed peace.

But standing at that rim, I stopped praying up from my basement and started praying down from His throne.

Not "God, can You handle this?" but "God who carved canyons is handling this."

Not "Lord, this is too complex" but "From Your perspective, this is molecular."

Not "How will this work?" but "How will You amaze us when it does?"

Not "Can You see all these needs?" but "You're already working on everything I'm just now praying about."

The Pattern Across All Valleys

That perspective shift became my reality. When app development costs came back higher than budget—molecular. When Antiguan reconnections moved slower than timeline—molecular. When travel schedule conflicted with family needs—molecular. When Chayah Club customization felt overwhelming—molecular. When Nikimac revenue didn't match projections—molecular. When financial freedom seemed distant—molecular.

When my children's needs exceeded my ability to help—molecular. When community members' crises multiplied—molecular. When nations' divisions deepened—molecular. When intercession felt like shouting into void—molecular.

The challenges were real. The complexity legitimate. The pressure genuine. The needs actual. The prayers urgent. But the Canyon Carver is bigger. What felt overwhelming from basement position became orchestrated from throne room view.

Not that the challenges didn't matter—they mattered to a God whose greatness makes complexity molecular while His goodness makes it meaningful. He cares about every detail—every app feature, every Antiguan relationship, every family moment, every Chayah Club member, every business decision, every financial need, every prayer for provision, every cry for deliverance, every request for healing, every hope for restoration, every plea for peace. Microscope precision. But He also commands every outcome—telescope perspective. Both/and. Intimate and infinite. Transcendent and immanent. In Jesus, unified.

The God who carved the Grand Canyon with water and time is carving our breakthrough with power and precision. Giants aren't just defeatable—they're laughable when you see them from His throne. Whether those giants are ministry challenges, family needs, community prayers, or country burdens—from His perspective, they're all molecular.

WHAT HELL KNOWS ABOUT GREATNESS

The Enemy's Primary Strategy: Shrinkage

Satan doesn't deny God's power—he experienced it being cast out like lightning. Demons don't question authority—they tremble. The enemy's strategy isn't making you atheist. It's making you practical atheist—believing God exists but living like He's limited.

The Systematic Shrinking Campaign

The enemy's systematic shrinking campaign operates in four phases: First, distance creation—whispering "God's too busy with universes to notice you." Then power limitation—suggesting "Your situation is too complex even for God." Next, access denial—lying that "God's power is reserved for super-Christians." Finally, perspective prison—commanding "Keep your eyes on the problem—see how massive it is?" Every lie designed to shrink God or increase distance between infinite power and personal application.

What Demons Know That We Forget

When Jesus encountered the Gadarene demoniac, the demons recognized Jesus from afar, knew His exact identity, understood His authority, and begged for mercy. They knew what believers forget: One word from Jesus changes everything.

The Day 6 Attack

Expect specific assaults on greatness revelation: Physical—"You're too depleted for infinity." Truth: Weakness conducts strength perfectly. Mental—"You can't comprehend greatness while fasting."

Truth: Whether through ketosis clarity or sovereign choice, God grants revelation. Emotional—"You're too unstable for theology." Truth: Vulnerable hearts encounter greatness faster.

Hell trembles when you stop praying up from problems and start praying down from position.

BIBLICAL PATTERNS — WHEN GREATNESS GETS PERSONAL

TIER 1: Five Full Witnesses

1. Jesus Calming the Storm — Mark 4:35-41

"Then He arose and rebuked the wind, and said to the sea, 'Peace, be still!' And the wind ceased and there was a great calm." Professional fishermen—men who'd navigated storms their entire lives—thought they were dying. Waves swamping the boat. Water pouring in. Jesus asleep on a cushion.

They wake Him: "Teacher, do You not care that we are perishing?" Watch His response: He doesn't comfort them then calm the storm. He calms the storm then confronts their fear. Three words to the storm: "Peace, be still!" Immediate response: Wind ceased. Great calm. Then He turns to them: "Why are you so fearful? How is it you have no faith?"

Their response reveals greatness: "Who can this be, that even the wind and the sea obey Him?" The disciples saw the problem—storm swamping boat. Jesus saw the problem as molecular—spoke three words. Nature obeyed immediately. Observers recognized greatness.

The storm terrorizing you? Jesus speaks three words and it's over. The chaos overwhelming you? One command from Him creates great calm. Notice: The disciples were in the storm with Jesus and still terrified. Proximity doesn't equal perspective. You can be in the boat with Jesus and still pray from basement position.

Jesus' question reveals the issue: "How is it you have no faith?" Translation: "You're in the boat with the God who commands weather and you're still afraid?" The storm in your life is taking orders from the One in your boat.

2. Feeding the Five Thousand — John 6:1-14

"Then Jesus lifted up His eyes, and seeing a great multitude coming toward Him, He said to Philip, 'Where shall we buy bread, that these may eat?'" Context: Five thousand men, possibly fifteen to twenty thousand people total with women and children. Middle of nowhere. No food. Sunset approaching.

Philip's response: "Two hundred denarii worth of bread is not sufficient for them, that every one of them may have a little." Translation: "Even if we had eight months' wages, we couldn't buy enough for everyone to get a taste." Philip's doing math. Jesus is testing faith. Andrew finds a boy with five barley loaves and two small fish. Then adds: "But what are they among so many?"

Watch what Jesus does: Takes the insufficient supply. Gives thanks—declares sufficiency before seeing it. Distributes to disciples. Disciples distribute to multitudes. Everyone eats until full. Twelve baskets leftover. Philip calculated what couldn't be done. Jesus demonstrated what would be done.

Your budget says impossible. Your circumstances say insufficient. Your resources say inadequate. God's greatness says: "Watch this." Your insufficient supply is God's invitation to demonstrate surplus.

3. Majestic Power Over Enemies — Exodus 15:7

"And in the greatness of Your excellence You have overthrown those who rose against You." After the Red Sea crossing, Moses sang of God's overwhelming power. Egypt's chariots—the most advanced military technology of their time—became rubble in waves. Pharaoh's elite forces—warriors who terrified nations—drowned like stones.

God's greatness conquers all that opposes His will. Your giant isn't stronger than Pharaoh's army. The situation overwhelming you? God's greatness already overthrew it. You're not fighting for victory—you're enforcing victory already won. The enemies that rose against you have already fallen in His greatness. If Red Sea was God's beginning, your breakthrough is His continuation.

4. Cosmic Order and Sustaining Power — Isaiah 40:26

"Lift up your eyes on high, and see who has created these things, who brings out their host by number; He calls them all by name, by the greatness of His might and the strength of His power; not one is missing." Isaiah commands: Look up. See stars. Ask who created them.

Answer: The One whose greatness and might brings out their host by number. He calls them all by name. Not one is missing. Scientists estimate ten to the twenty-fourth power stars. God knows each one's name. Not one missing from His attendance. Stars themselves obey the command of His greatness. If cosmic bodies can't resist His order, your crisis can't either. The God who calls stars by name hasn't forgotten yours.

5. Surpassing Greatness Imparted to Believers — Ephesians 1:19

"And what is the exceeding greatness of His power toward us who believe, according to the working of His mighty power." Paul prays that believers would know "the exceeding greatness of His power toward us." Greek: *huperballon megethos*—surpassing, throwing beyond, exceeding greatness.

Not just greatness—exceeding greatness. Not theoretical—toward us. Not past—present active. The same power that raised Christ from death? Operating toward believers. Now. Today. His surpassing greatness is now manifest through Jesus and imparted to believers. This isn't just observation—it's operation. Not history—happening. The greatness that raised Jesus is aimed at you right now.

TIER 2: Eight Grouped Witnesses

God's Unmatched Sovereignty: Moses declared after experiencing plagues, seas split, and manna: "O Lord God, You have begun to show Your servant Your greatness and Your mighty hand, for what god is there in heaven or on earth who can do anything like Your works and Your mighty deeds?" (Deuteronomy 3:24). Israel at Sinai saw His glory and greatness, heard His voice from fire, and lived by His mercy: "Surely the Lord our God has shown us His glory and His greatness" (Deuteronomy 5:24). David prayed: "Yours, O Lord, is the greatness, the power and the glory, the victory and the majesty; for all that is in heaven and in earth is Yours" (1 Chronicles 29:11). No other being can rival His works. Not angels, demons, circumstances, diagnoses, debt, or depression.

Proclaimed and Revealed Greatness: Moses' final song commanded: "For I proclaim the name of the Lord: Ascribe greatness to our God" (Deuteronomy 32:3). Not suggest, not whisper—proclaim, ascribe. Your testimony isn't optional—it's obedience. God declares: "Thus I will magnify Myself and sanctify Myself, and I will be known in the eyes of many nations. Then they shall know that I am the Lord" (Ezekiel 38:23). After Jesus healed a demon-possessed boy: "And they were all amazed at the majesty of God" (Luke 9:43). They didn't just appreciate a miracle—they encountered the majesty behind it. Your silence about His greatness robs others of their faith fuel.

Redemptive and Messianic Power: Isaiah sees a figure approaching with stained garments: "Who is this who comes from Edom, with dyed garments from Bozrah, this One who is glorious in His apparel, traveling in the greatness of His strength? 'I who speak in righteousness, mighty to save'" (Isaiah 63:1). His greatness marches forth in salvation. Prophecy of Messiah: "And He shall stand and feed His flock in the strength of the Lord, in the majesty of the name of the Lord His God; and they shall abide, for now He shall be great to the ends of the earth" (Micah 5:4). Christ's greatness has no borders your problem can hide behind. Greatness isn't just watching your battle—it's winning it.

THE UNIFYING DECLARATION

God's greatness is immeasurable in power, incomparable in majesty, and irresistible in revelation. He conquers (Exodus 15:7), creates (Isaiah 40:26), sustains (Psalm 147:4), saves (Isaiah 63:1), and empowers (Ephesians 1:19)—revealing that His greatness is not distant, but dynamic, alive in creation and in His people.

From overthrown enemies to commanded storms to multiplied bread to imparted power—every expression of greatness culminates in one truth: Infinite power is personally available.

PARADIGM SHIFT — PRAYER POSTURE REVOLUTION

Three Prayer Positions, One Has Authority
Basement Position:
- Hunched, looking up
- Beneath problem and God
- "God, can You see me down here?"
- Result: Exhaustion without breakthrough

Ground Level Position:
- Standing defensive
- Eye-to-eye with problem
- "God, help me fight this!"
- Result: Occasional victory through exhausting warfare

Throne Room Position:
- Standing tall, shoulders back
- Seated with Christ (Ephesians 2:6)
- "From Your throne, this is molecular"
- Result: Effortless authority

THE LANGUAGE SHIFT: FROM BASEMENT TO THRONE ROOM

BASEMENT PRAYERS	THRONE ROOM PRAYERS
"God, can You see me down here?"	"Father, I see this from Your perspective"
"Please notice my situation"	"Thank You for orchestrating my situation"
"You're good but are You able?"	"You're good and Your greatness conquers"

"Help me if You can"	"I watch You work because You will"
"My mountain is so massive"	"From Your throne, my mountain is molecular"
"Fighting to get God's attention"	"Resting in God's administration"
"Begging for intervention"	"Believing in orchestration"
"God might show up"	"God is already working"
"Worried He won't answer"	"Wondering how He'll amaze me"

Stop telling God how big your problem is. Start telling your problem how great your God is. Basement prayers beg. Throne room prayers believe.

ACTIVATION — TWO PRIMARY PRACTICES

PRIMARY PRACTICE #1: Throne Room Positioning

Physical Repositioning (Do This Now)

Step 1: Basement Position (30 seconds)
- Kneel on floor, head down
- Pray up: "God, can You see this? It's so big!"
- Feel the weight of begging

Step 2: Throne Room Declaration (30 seconds)
- Stand tall, arms raised
- "I am seated with Christ in heavenly places!"
- "From Your throne, my problem is molecular!"

Step 3: Authority Stance (30 seconds)
- Feet apart, hands on hips
- Speak to your problem: "You're dust in God's hand."
- Laugh at its smallness

Step 4: Reception Position (30 seconds)
- Hands open, eyes closed
- "Infinite power is personally interested in my breakthrough"
- Your posture teaches your spirit. Stand like you're seated in heavenly places.

The Prophetic Act — The Speck in His Hand
1. Place a speck (salt grain or sand) in your palm
2. Let it represent your giant—name it once
3. Name God three times: "You are greater. You are wiser. You are nearer."
4. Blow the speck away: "In the hand of the great God, mountains become molecules."
5. Open your hands wide: "I receive infinite power for impossible situations."

What looks mountainous to you is molecular to Him.

PRIMARY PRACTICE #2: Perspective Application

6 Dimensions of Greatness Applied

Dimension	Your Giant	God's Greatness
SPIRITUAL	"My faith feels weak"	"He who has begun a good work will complete it" (Phil 1:6)
MENTAL	"Thoughts spiral endlessly"	"You understand my thought afar off" (Ps 139:2)
EMOTIONAL	"Feelings overwhelm me"	"You put tears into Your bottle" (Ps 56:8)
PHYSICAL	"My body is failing"	"I am fearfully and wonderfully made" (Ps 139:14)
FINANCIAL	"Needs exceed resources"	"Every beast of the forest is Mine" (Ps 50:10)
RELATIONAL	"This seems impossible"	"God has reconciled us to Himself" (2 Cor 5:18)

Galaxy Perspective Exercise

Tonight, look at stars for sixty seconds. Declare:
- "The God who hung those holds my situation"
- "What feels astronomical is atomic to Him"
- "Infinite power takes personal interest"

Write your biggest problem on paper. Tear it to pieces: "Molecular in Your mighty hand." Scatter pieces to wind: "From throne room, this is nothing."

FOCUS AREA GREATNESS PRAYERS

Scripture Foundation: "Great is the Lord, and greatly to be praised" (Psalm 145:3)

For Spiritual Focus: "Father, Your greatness conquers spiritual battles. The One who hung stars fights for me. The God who carved canyons is carving my breakthrough. I pray down from Your throne, not up from weakness."

For Mental Focus: "Father, Your greatness eclipses mental struggles. The God who knows thoughts before they form is greater than anxiety. Mind's chaos is molecular in Your ordered universe."

For Emotional Focus: "Father, Your greatness dissolves emotional mountains. The One who bottles tears commands breakthrough. Your transcendence lifts above feelings; Your immanence walks through them."

For Physical Focus: "Father, Your greatness overrides limitations. The God who formed in wombs reforms in moments. My body's weakness meets Your infinite strength."

For Financial Focus: "Father, Your greatness owns everything. Cattle on thousand hills bow to You. My lack meets Your limitlessness. From Your throne, debt is dust."

For Relational Focus: "Father, Your greatness bridges impossible gaps. The God of reconciliation makes ways where none exist. What seems canyon-wide to me is crack-sized to You."

RESISTANCE REALITY CHECK

Size Deception: "Problems are too big."
Heaven's Response: "In My hand, mountains are molecules. I carved the Grand Canyon—your situation is a scratch."

Distance Doubt: "God's too far to care."
Heaven's Response: "I'm telescope and microscope—infinite yet intimate. Transcendent and immanent."

Power Question: "Is God really fighting?"
Heaven's Response: "My goodness comforts; My greatness conquers. I'm not managing your crisis—I'm commanding it."

Perspective Prison: "I only see the problem."
Heaven's Response: "Stop praying up from basement. Pray down from My throne where you're already seated."

Your perspective determines your power. Throne room view changes everything.

DECLARATION — MOUNTAINS BECOME MOLECULES

Stand with thousands globally:
"Great is the Lord, and greatly to be praised; His greatness is unsearchable!" (Psalm 145:3)
"You have made heavens and earth by Your great power. Nothing is too hard for You!" (Jeremiah 32:17)
"With God nothing will be impossible!" (Luke 1:37)

Perspective Shift:
I stop praying up from basement—I pray down from throne!
I stop looking up at mountains—I look down from viewpoint!
I stop begging up for breakthrough—I decree down from authority!

Every Giant Meets Greatness:
Debt meets abundance—molecular!
Disease meets healing—molecular!
Depression meets joy—molecular!
Division meets unity—molecular!
Defeat meets victory—molecular!

The God who carved canyons is carving breakthrough! The God who numbers stars numbers tears—conquering both battles and fears! "Through Your power enemies submit!" (Psalm 66:3)

Infinite power is personally available!

BREAKTHROUGH PRAYER

Father God, Creator of galaxies, Counter of tears,

Forgive us for shrinking You to fit logic. For praying up from problems instead of down from throne. For measuring You by ceilings when You hold canyons. Thank You for revealing the difference—microscope and telescope, goodness and greatness.

Like Moses, we acknowledge Your full greatness would overwhelm us, yet You make it personally available. Like Job, we surrender explanations for presence. Like David, battles belong to the God whose greatness makes giants grasshoppers. Like the disciples in the storm, we learn: proximity without perspective still produces panic. We're in the boat with You—teach us to see from Your throne.

Like the crowd with five loaves, we bring insufficient supply to Your exceeding greatness. Watch what You do with our "not enough." You are Telescope God—transcendent majesty. You are Microscope God—immanent care. Goodness whispers "I am with you." Greatness roars "The battle is Mine."

"Yours, O Lord, is the greatness, power, glory, victory, majesty" (1 Chronicles 29:11). From Exodus to Ephesians, Your greatness conquers opposition, creates order, sustains stars, speaks salvation, and operates now through Christ toward us who believe.

We receive throne room perspective that shrinks giants, mountain-moving faith from sovereignty, infinite power for molecular situations. The God who overthrew Pharaoh's army overthrows our enemies. The God who called stars by name calls us by name. The God who spoke "Peace, be still" to storms speaks peace to our chaos. The God who multiplied five loaves multiplies our insufficiency. The God whose surpassing greatness raised Christ from death operates that same power toward us now.

The God who carved Grand Canyon carves breakthrough. The God who hung stars handles situations. The God who split seas splits impossibilities. In Jesus' name, we pray down from throne, not up from fear! Problems become molecular in Your mighty hand!

Amen.

CLOSING — FROM MICROSCOPE TO TELESCOPE

Day 6 started with your body giving up holding you vertical, forcing you to your knees where you saw carpet fibers as canyons—and realized if microscopic becomes massive when you zoom in, maybe massive becomes microscopic when God zooms out. Some experienced ketosis clarity, body burning reserves while spirit accessed heaven's. Others experienced different shifts. Both valid pathways to revelation.

Tonight you rest knowing: God isn't just good enough to care—He's great enough to conquer. His goodness zooms in: sees every tear, hears every prayer. His greatness zooms out: commands galaxies while commanding breakthrough. Transcendence: above it all. Immanence: in it all. Together: infinite enough to carve canyons, intimate enough to count tears.

Week 1 has systematically stripped you to essence—each day removing props until only His greatness remains. Day 1's Gospel positioned you from acceptance—so today's greatness doesn't intimidate but invites. You approach infinite power not as beggar but as beloved. Day 2's Grace straightened your crown—so today you stand in throne room wearing royal identity. Greatness isn't distant; it's family.

Day 3's Goodness taught you to trust darkness—preparing you for today's revelation that God's greatness eclipses explanation with presence. You don't need to understand the canyon to be awed by it. Day 4 awakened your arsenal—showing secular as sacred so today's greatness can flow through Monday work, not just Sunday worship. Day 5 restored factory settings—returning you to original joy so today's infinite power meets joyful confidence, not fearful begging.

Each revelation removed another false support until only one remains: The God whose greatness makes your giants molecular. You've shifted position. From basement to throne room. From begging to believing. From seeing problems as massive to seeing them molecular.

I've tested this. Through ministry challenges where spreadsheets mocked me with impossible math, through family intercessions where children's needs exceeded my ability to help, through community prayers where members' crises multiplied faster than solutions, through country burdens where national divisions felt too big to carry—I've proven: God's greatness doesn't just notice your giant—it makes it molecular.

Tomorrow you could receive devastating news. Next week could bring impossible circumstances. But you'll never again pray from basement position. You've been to the throne room. You've seen the perspective. Your giant is dust in infinite hands.

Tomorrow, Day 7, glory's weight becomes tangible. While greatness showed infinite power, glory marks you with heaven's DNA. Greatness displays who God is. Glory transfers what God has. No more relating to God like He's a bigger version of you. No more ant-sized faith for elephant-sized problems to infinite God. No more basement prayers when you're seated in heavenly places.

From throne room perspective, your mountain is molecular. From His viewpoint, your giant is grasshopper. From infinite position, your problem is past tense. The God who carved the Grand Canyon is carving your breakthrough—one prayer, one revelation, one day at a time.

The God who carved Grand Canyon with water and time is carving your breakthrough with power and precision.

Day 6 Complete: Throne Room Perspective Activated

Greatness: Not distant but deployed
Infinity: Not theoretical but personal
Prayer: Not up but down
Mountains: Not massive but molecular
Perspective: Not basement but throne
Christ: Transcendence and immanence unified

SOAP JOURNAL — DAY 6

S (Scripture): Which verse shifted you from basement to throne room?
O (Observation): Where have you related to goodness but not greatness? How has magnifying your problem minimized your God?
A (Application): What mountain becomes molecular from His throne? What situation needs throne room perspective?
P (Prayer): "Father, from Your throne, my _____ is molecular. I pray down from position. The God who carved canyons is carving _____."

Today's Breakthrough: How did throne room perspective change your problem's size?
Tomorrow's Expectation: What do you expect when glory's weight arrives?

MOUNTAINS MOLECULAR. GIANTS GRASSHOPPERS. THRONE ROOM OCCUPIED. READY FOR GLORY.

DAY 7 — GLORY

When Heaven's Weight Marks You Forever

"And we all, with unveiled face, beholding as in a mirror the glory of the Lord, are being transformed into the same image from glory to glory, just as by the Spirit of the Lord." — 2 Corinthians 3:18

WEEK 1 — GROW: Building Intimacy with God

Day 7 of 21. Yesterday's Greatness made giants molecular. Today's Glory marks you with heaven's DNA.

ENCOUNTER — WHERE YOU ARE

4:30 AM. Day 7. You try to stand for morning prayer and your knees buckle—not from weakness but from weight. Something descended during the night. You didn't hear it arrive, but you feel it now—pressing on your shoulders, settling in your chest, making every breath conscious and deliberate. This isn't burden. This is substance. Like someone poured liquid gold into your bones while you slept.

Glory is the one thing in the universe too heavy to carry but too beautiful to put down.

What presses on your chest isn't hunger anymore—it's kavod, Hebrew for glory, meaning the weight of God Himself descending into your dimension. Today you discover that glory isn't God showing off. It's God showing up in such cosmic weight that everything bends, including you.

A Note on Day 7 Experiences: After seven days, people encounter this threshold differently. Some feel profound weight—kabod, the substantial presence of God. Others sense deep peace settling like snow. Many notice quiet certainty, settled knowing. Some simply recognize faithful completion of Week 1. Some describe acute spiritual sensitivity where heaven feels one breath away. Others experience gentle awareness of His nearness. Some feel energized clarity, others sacred exhaustion.

Your experience doesn't validate or invalidate your journey. God meets each person uniquely. What matters isn't matching someone else's encounter—it's authentic engagement with however He's meeting you.

Your body knows the difference. Seven days of fasting stripped everything non-essential. Mental fog vanished. Energy flows clean. Your stomach surrendered its protests into holy emptiness. But something unprecedented emerges—spiritual sensitivity so acute the veil between heaven and earth feels tissue-thin.

Colors carry frequencies you've never noticed. Sounds have layers beyond natural hearing. You're experiencing what mystics called "thin places"—where supernatural and natural converge until you can't tell the difference. This isn't emotion. It's encounter. Tears flow without reason—not sadness, not even joy. Pure overflow. Your spirit too full for your body to contain.

Week 1 systematically prepared you for this marking—each day removing obstacles to glory's full weight. Day 1's Gospel closed the gap between earning and receiving—so glory doesn't intimidate but invites. Day 2's Grace closed the gap between performance and position—so glory doesn't crush but crowns. Day 3's Goodness closed the gap between doubt and trust—so glory's darkroom development doesn't terrify but transforms. Day 4's Gifts closed the gap between potential and activation—so glory flows through equipped vessels. Day 5's Gladness closed the gap between mourning and joy—so glory rests on joyful foundation. Day 6's Greatness closed the gap between limitation and authority—so glory operates from throne room, not basement.

Now Day 7's Glory marks you—closing the gap between earth and heaven. Not visit—mark. Not touch—transform. You're not just blessed—you're carrying.

You're about to discover why Moses had to veil his face. Why Isaiah fell apart crying "Woe is me!" Why everyone who truly encountered God's glory was never the same. Glory isn't just God's presence. Glory is God's weight—His kavod, His substance, His reality so dense it bends everything around it, including you.

And here's the scandal religion won't tell you: You were designed to carry this weight. Not just witness it. Carry it.

We pray for glory like it's confetti. But glory is cosmic weight that crushes everything not aligned with heaven.

This seventh day carries significance beyond your personal journey—it mirrors creation itself. Just as God rested on the seventh day after completing His masterpiece, you're entering divine completion where everything aligns for glory's revelation. Sabbath rest isn't inactivity—it's receptivity. Ceasing from striving so glory can descend without obstruction.

Former glory was God visiting. Latter glory is God moving in permanently.

FOUNDATION — WHEN GLORY INVADED MY CRIME SCENES

The Divorce That Became a Portal

2014 My lowest point. Still in my divorce and family court battle. Fighting for my mental health, my boys, spiritual attacks owning my days. Single mother drowning in overwhelm. Three in the morning became my enemy—the hour shame spoke loudest.

Divorce papers on my dining table. Spiritual attacks so severe I could barely function. I stumbled to an altar one Sunday, not even sure God would receive someone whose marriage was dying. The pastor who prayed for me did something unexpected—she took my number. Not for courtesy follow-up. For what would become the most transformative season of my life.

This particular three in the morning, I couldn't fight anymore. Knees on the worn carpet of my rental house bedroom, I surrendered: "God, I have nothing left. If You don't mark me with something beyond my failure, I'm done."

The atmosphere shifted like someone had increased gravity. The air became thick—not suffocating, substantial. Like swimming through honey. And the scent—I'd never known glory had a smell until that moment. Not perfume. Not incense. Something indefinable—like ozone after lightning meets honey warming in sunlight.

Then I felt it. Weight. Starting at my shoulders, spreading down my spine. Not crushing—stabilizing. Like someone had poured liquid gold over me, hardening into armor.

I tried to stand. Couldn't. Not from weakness—from weight. Holy, beautiful, terrifying weight. For twenty minutes, I couldn't move. Didn't want to. Something was being written on me. Not words—identity. Not information—transformation. The glory that had been external was becoming internal architecture.

When I finally stood, everything had changed. Not my circumstances—those remained brutal. But I was marked. Carrying something. Radiating something.

Glory announces itself not with fanfare but with weight that stops everything else.

The Pattern That Unfolded

Within weeks of that three in the morning encounter, the pastor moved our small group to my home. "Your home? Where divorce is happening? Where my children watch their mother fall apart daily?" "Especially there. Glory specializes in crime scenes."

Note: When we say "crime scene," we mean life's messy, broken places—divorce, failure, devastation, imperfection. For those who've experienced actual criminal victimization: What was done to you was never God's will. He doesn't cause trauma to create testimony. But He can redeem even what evil intended for harm—in your timing, at your pace, with your full agency over your story.

Week after week, miracles happened where divorce was happening: A woman with years of chronic back pain instantly healed. A man facing foreclosure received unexpected provision. People struggling with addiction found freedom. Marriages restored. Prodigals returned home. The glory became so tangible visitors would immediately sense it. "What is this?" "His presence chose this broken place."

The small group outgrew my living room, moved to my basement, eventually became a church that later moved beyond my home to bless the broader city. Those months when glory inhabited my devastation taught me: God doesn't wait for stability to send glory. Sometimes instability is the invitation.

January 2015—my first Daniel Fast with the small group meeting in my home. Twenty-one days that rewrote my story. Week 1: Spiritual attacks that tormented me for months suddenly stopped. Day 7: Supernatural peace about custody flooded me. Week 2: What shifted spiritually in Week 1 manifested naturally—custody of my children and end of spousal support, despite being on disability income. Week 3: Breakthrough multiplied exponentially—relationships deepened, unexpected provision opened, courage to lead emerged, vision for ministry crystallized.

Week 1 transforms the spiritual atmosphere. Week 2 delivers natural evidence. Week 3 multiplies breakthrough into legacy.

That Sunday when everything shifted—a few people, small gathering. We'd sung correctly, preached biblically, done church "right." Then something descended that changed my understanding of spiritual reality forever. Not emotional. Physical. Like atmospheric pressure multiplied—so dense you could almost touch it. My knees buckled. Not from feelings but from weight. Others felt it simultaneously. Some fell to their faces without deciding to. When we finally checked the clock, two hours had passed in what felt like moments outside time.

The Valleys Where Glory Proved Itself

Each crisis taught me different dimensions of glory. Divorce proceedings—glory became my stability. Standing in court, I felt the weight holding me upright. The judge commented: "You have unusual composure." Job loss and panic attacks—glory became both my provision and my defender. Father's funeral aftermath—when family uproar over my cremation decision became unbearable, I left for Canada. Didn't attend the burial. But glory marked me in that decision too—the weight that said: "Sometimes walking away is the glory response." In my absence from his graveside, glory held both my grief and my boundaries. Depression diagnosis—glory became my medication's partner. Taking antidepressants while carrying glory. Both and, not either or.

Rock bottom became my glory encounter. I didn't leave the valley the same. I left as a glory-carrier, chain-breaker, history maker, legacy-leaver.

Glory doesn't exempt you from valleys. Glory marks you as unconquerable in them.

January 22, 2022: The Day That Redefined Everything

Day 22 of "365: Live Fearlessly"—twenty-two days after completing the Daniel Fast. I woke with divine presence so tangible it felt like liquid light pressing on my chest. For extended time, movement was impossible. Only tears—not from sadness or even joy, but from spiritual overflow.

His response transformed my paradigm forever: "Glory doesn't visit to provide experiences. Glory descends to alter nature. And transformed nature demands authentic expression."

For weeks, I attempted keeping the encounter private. Sacred meant secret, right? Wrong. The weight intensified daily. This divine pressure drove me to write and preach—365 sermons in 365 days. Raw, vulnerable, anointed. The glory demanded expression or it would consume me.

But here's what I learned: There's profound difference between hiding from fear and treasuring with wisdom. Sacred encounters need protection, especially early. When the weight pressed again with clear instruction—"Share what I've shown you"—I knew the difference.

Glory hidden becomes crushing burden. Glory displayed becomes multiplied breakthrough.

The Multiplication Timeline

September 2018: Published first book, Rebound Faith: Chayah! March 2020: Wrote vision board with prophetic vow—A New Era of Innovation! December 2020: Published first edition of The Daniel Fast: Closing the GAP! Launched Chayah Club community. Spring 2022: Pastor John joins prayer calls as stranger, later becomes life partner. July 29, 2023: Married John as prophesied. 2023: Started co-ministering across six continents. 2025: Publishing expanded edition—five years of additional glory revelation captured in twenty-one days.

Each breakthrough built on previous breakthrough. Private encounters became public revival—in God's timing, with wisdom's guidance.

What you steward in secret, God multiplies in public—when the time is right.

REVELATION — UNDERSTANDING BIBLICAL GLORY

The Hebrew Foundation: Kabod

The Hebrew word for glory is kavod. It doesn't mean brightness or beauty. It means weight, substance, heaviness. From the root kaved—to be heavy, weighty, burdensome. But when applied to God, this weight isn't oppressive. It's substantive. It's the difference between a picture of gold and holding actual gold.

Ancient Hebrews celebrated weight as value. The heavier the crown, the greater the king. The weightier the gold, the richer the treasure. God's glory is His weight—substantial presence so real it affects physical reality.

Religion taught us glory was something to see. Hebrew reveals glory is something to carry.

Scripture describes it: "For our light affliction, which is but for a moment, is working for us a far more exceeding and eternal weight of glory" (2 Corinthians 4:17). Paul contrasts "light affliction" with "weight of glory"—baros in Greek, meaning productive burden. Like pregnancy. Heavy but fruitful. Weighty but birthing something beautiful.

Light affliction produces heavyweight glory—and the exchange rate is always in your favor.

The Latter Glory Promise

"'The latter glory of this house will be greater than the former,' says the Lord of hosts, 'and in this place I shall give the ultimate peace and prosperity,' declares the Lord of hosts" (Haggai 2:9, AMP). Discouraged builders heard this. Their rebuilt temple looked pathetic compared to Solomon's original masterpiece. But God promised revolutionary reversal: The latter glory would exceed the former.

Consider Ezekiel's vision: Glory departed the temple gradually (Ezekiel 10:18-19), but returned suddenly and completely (Ezekiel 43:1-5). The same pattern applies to you—what left slowly returns suddenly, but greater.

Your Day 7 isn't about recovering old glory. It's about receiving greater glory. Not just divine visits but divine residence. Not just encounters but permanent transformation.

The glory descending on you exceeds the glory you remember.

Why Moses Glowed: The Transfer Protocol

When Moses spent forty days in God's presence, he didn't just see glory. Glory transferred to him. His face shone so bright Israel couldn't look at him (Exodus 34:29-35). But here's what religion missed: Moses didn't glow from seeing light. He glowed from carrying weight. The kavod of God had literally soaked into his skin. He'd become a carrier of divine substance.

Paul explains Moses veiled his face "so that the children of Israel could not look steadily at the end of what was passing away" (2 Corinthians 3:13). Moses veiled diminishing glory.

But you? You carry multiplying glory that refuses to fade.

The Doxa Dimension: Greek Understanding

The New Testament Greek word doxa adds another layer. Originally meaning "opinion" or "reputation," it evolved to mean the magnificent reputation of God made visible. But Paul revolutionizes it: "Christ in you, the hope of glory" (Colossians 1:27). Glory isn't just God's reputation—it's His reputation in you. You become the visible display of invisible reality.

You don't just see glory. You become glory's address—a glory-carrier!

The Complete Picture: Weight and Radiance

The Hebrew word kavod means weight—God's presence has substance; it cannot be ignored or diminished. The Greek word doxa speaks of radiance—the visible outshining of that inner majesty. Together, these words reveal glory's dual nature: Kavod equals the internal weight (substance, density, reality). Doxa equals the external radiance (visibility, brilliance, reputation). You carry both. The weight stabilizes you internally. The radiance impacts others externally.

Glory is God's weighty reality (kavod) shining visibly (doxa) through surrendered vessels.

THE DANIEL FAST: CLOSING THE GAP!

THE FIVE MOVEMENTS OF GLORY: FROM ORIGIN TO DESTINY

Scripture reveals glory isn't random—it moves in deliberate patterns from God's essence to humanity's eternal participation. Understanding these movements positions you to cooperate with what God is releasing.

MOVEMENT 1: The Origin of Glory — The Essence of His Being

Foundation Scriptures: Exodus 33:18; Psalm 19:1; Numbers 20:6; Deuteronomy 5:24

Glory begins in God Himself—not as one attribute among many, but as the sum total of His nature expressed. When Moses cried, "Show me Your glory" (Exodus 33:18), he wasn't asking for fireworks or spectacle. He was crying for revelation—the visible manifestation of invisible holiness.

Three Origin Truths: First, God's glory is His revealed nature. Everything about Him—His holiness, love, power, wisdom—compressed into manifestation. Glory is who He is made visible. Second, creation broadcasts His glory. "The heavens declare the glory of God" (Psalm 19:1). Nature didn't create glory—it reflects what already exists in Him. Third, presence defines His glory. Whenever glory appeared (Numbers 20:6), God's manifest presence filled a place—weighty, radiant, undeniable. Not theory. Experience.

Application: Glory begins in beholding, not doing. It's the posture of worship before it becomes the power of witness. You can't manufacture what you haven't first received in His presence.

Glory isn't achieved through effort—it's received through encounter.

MOVEMENT 2: The Revelation of Glory — God Made Known Among Us

Foundation Scriptures: Isaiah 40:5; Isaiah 60:1; Ezekiel 10:4; Haggai 2:9; John 1:14; Matthew 17:2

Glory is the manifestation of God's invisible nature into visible experience. This is where kavod (weight) becomes doxa (visible radiance).

Five Revelation Truths: First, glory is revealed, not constructed. Isaiah prophesied: "The glory of the Lord shall be revealed, and all flesh shall see it together" (Isaiah 40:5). You don't build glory—you host what God unveils. Second, glory shines through Christ. "And the Word became flesh and dwelt among us, and we beheld His glory, the glory as of the only begotten of the Father, full of grace and truth" (John 1:14). Jesus is glory incarnate—kavod with skin on, doxa walking dusty roads. On the Mount of Transfiguration: "He was transfigured before them. His face shone like the sun, and His clothes became as white as the light" (Matthew 17:2). Peter, James, and John witnessed glory unveiled—the divine weight they'd been walking beside suddenly made visible. Third, glory restores hope and radiance. "Arise, shine; for your light has come! And the glory of the Lord is risen upon you" (Isaiah 60:1). Glory lifts you out of oppression into divine illumination. Fourth, glory fills the house. Ezekiel's vision (10:4) and Haggai's promise (2:9) reveal a future where the latter house glory surpasses the former—divine presence filling the earth with shalom. Fifth, glory transforms physical reality. The kavod that made Moses veil his face walked dusty roads healing lepers. The doxa that filled Solomon's temple ate fish with fishermen.

Application: Glory must not only be seen—it must be hosted. Your life becomes a temple radiating His nature. You're not just a glory observer—you're a glory container.

MOVEMENT 3: The Redemption of Glory — Glory Restored to Humanity

Foundation Scriptures: Psalm 3:3; Proverbs 3:35; Romans 2:7-10; Romans 4:20; Romans 1:23

Humanity forfeited glory through sin but regains it through faith and righteousness. This is where your Day 7 marking becomes permanent reality.

Four Redemption Truths: First, glory lost through idolatry. "And changed the glory of the incorruptible God into an image made like corruptible man" (Romans 1:23). We traded weight for worthlessness. Second, glory regained through righteousness. "The wise shall inherit glory" (Proverbs 3:35). Not earning—alignment. Not performance—position. Third, glory received through faith. Abraham "was strengthened in faith, giving glory to God" (Romans 4:20). Every act of trust reclaims lost majesty. Fourth, glory rewards perseverance. "To those who by patient continuance in doing good seek for glory, honor, and immortality" (Romans 2:7). Perseverance inherits what pressure forfeits.

Application: Glory is restored wherever faith exalts God above circumstance—every act of trust reclaims the majesty humanity lost. Your Week 1 journey? Systematic glory restoration through gospel, grace, goodness, gifts, gladness, greatness, and now—glory marking.

MOVEMENT 4: The Manifestation of Glory — The Kingdom Revealed

Foundation Scriptures: Psalm 145:11; Habakkuk 2:14; Micah 5:4; Luke 2:14; Acts 7:55

Glory is not confined to heaven—it is meant to fill the earth. This is where your personal marking becomes corporate breakthrough.

Four Manifestation Truths: First, the kingdom is glorious by nature. "They shall speak of the glory of Your kingdom, and talk of Your power" (Psalm 145:11). Every act of divine rule releases glory. Second, the Messiah carries global glory. "And He shall stand and feed His flock in the strength of the Lord, in the majesty of the name of the Lord His God; and they shall abide, for now He shall be great to the ends of the earth" (Micah 5:4). Christ's glory has no borders your problem can hide behind. Third, glory fills creation. "For the earth will be filled with the knowledge of the glory of the Lord, as the waters cover the sea" (Habakkuk 2:14). Glory is the ultimate atmosphere of redemption. Fourth, glory ascends through Christ. "But he, being full of the Holy Spirit, gazed into heaven and saw the glory of God, and Jesus standing at the right hand of God" (Acts 7:55). Stephen saw divine radiance and Jesus exalted. Even death couldn't dim what glory established.

Application: Glory is the culture of the Kingdom. When God reigns, His radiance transforms reality. You're not just carrying personal breakthrough—you're transporting Kingdom atmosphere wherever you go.

Where you go, things change. Not because you're special—because you're marked.

MOVEMENT 5: The Destiny of Glory — Eternal Revelation and Participation

Foundation Scriptures: Romans 8:17-18; 2 Corinthians 3:18; Jude 1:24-25; Isaiah 40:5

God's glory is our eternal inheritance—to behold it forever and to share in it. This isn't just Day 7—this is your eternal trajectory.

Four Destiny Truths: First, we are heirs of glory. "And if children, then heirs—heirs of God and joint heirs with Christ, if indeed we suffer with Him, that we may also be glorified together" (Romans 8:17). Your valleys aren't disqualifying—they're positioning. Second, we are transformed by glory. "But we all, with unveiled face, beholding as in a mirror the glory of the Lord, are being transformed into the same image from glory to glory, just as by the Spirit of the Lord" (2 Corinthians 3:18). This is progressive metamorphosis—each encounter adds density. Third, we will dwell in glory eternally. "Now to Him who is able to keep you from stumbling, and to present you faultless before the presence of His glory with exceeding joy" (Jude 1:24). Glory isn't just a visit—it's your eternal address. Fourth, all creation will see it. "The glory of the Lord shall be revealed, and all flesh shall see it together; for the mouth of the Lord has spoken" (Isaiah 40:5). What you're experiencing privately today becomes what nations experience corporately tomorrow.

Application: Glory is both destination and transformation. You don't just go to glory—you grow into it. Day 7 isn't the climax—it's the launching pad. Week 2 reveals the identity that carries this weight. Week 3 multiplies it exponentially.

THE FRAMEWORK IN MOTION: Your Five-Stage Journey

Stage	What God Does	Your Response	Result	Week 1 Connection
1. ORIGIN	Reveals His essence	Behold (worship)	Encounter His presence	Days 1-3: Gospel, Grace, Goodness
2. REVELATION	Makes invisible visible	Receive (faith)	Host His manifestation	Days 4-5: Gifts, Gladness
3. REDEMPTION	Restores lost glory	Believe (trust)	Reclaim your majesty	Day 6: Greatness
4. MANIFESTATION	Displays Kingdom reality	Carry (stewardship)	Transform atmospheres	Day 7: Glory marking
5. DESTINY	Establishes eternal reality	Become (identity)	Grow glory to glory	Week 2: ALIGN in Identity

Framework Summary Declaration

Speak this over yourself: "The glory of the Lord shall be revealed—in His presence, in His people, and in His purpose. What once filled the temple now fills the earth. What once covered Moses' face now transforms mine. Glory is God's reality unveiled in creation, redemption, and eternal communion. I am marked by kavod—substantial, weighty, unchangeable presence. I radiate doxa—visible, brilliant, undeniable transformation. I move from origin (beholding) to destiny (becoming). I don't just witness glory—I carry it. I don't just experience breakthrough—I become it. In Jesus' name, I am glory-carrier marked for all five movements—from beholding His essence to becoming His eternal display!"

THE CRITICAL DISTINCTION: ANOINTING VS. GLORY

Most believers use these terms interchangeably, missing the revolutionary difference:

ANOINTING	GLORY
God's power on you for tasks	God's presence in you for transformation
Enables supernatural function	Transforms your actual nature

Can fluctuate with obedience	Marks you permanently
Accomplishes Kingdom work	Creates Kingdom character
You can walk away unchanged	You cannot encounter unchanged
Like oil coating the surface	Like fire transforming the core
Uses your existing gifts	Rewrites your spiritual DNA
Demonstrates God's power	Reveals God's person
You can counterfeit it	It exposes everything counterfeit

King Saul prophesied while hunting David. Balaam declared God's word while rebelling. Anointing can function through compromised vessels. But glory requires face-to-face encounter. Glory can't be faked.

Anointing uses your gifts; glory rewrites your operating system.

The Saul Warning: When Anointing Operates Without Glory

Consider King Saul's tragedy—perhaps the saddest scripture in the Bible: "But the Spirit of the Lord departed from Saul" (1 Samuel 16:14). He had anointing without transformation. He prophesied while hunting David to kill him. He functioned in gifts while harboring murder. The anointing operated, but glory never marked him. He could perform spiritual acts while his heart remained unchanged.

This is why you don't just want gifts and anointing—you want glory to transform you so God can lay His anointing upon you thick and permanent. Without glory's transformation, anointing becomes dangerous. With glory's foundation, anointing becomes destiny.

God is closing the gap between who you are and who He's called you to be. He's preparing you for what you're praying for. The glory that transforms your nature ensures the anointing won't destroy you.

Saul had anointing that impressed people. David had glory that transformed nations.

FIVE DIMENSIONS OF GLORY THAT CHANGE EVERYTHING

Transformative Glory: "But we all, with unveiled face, beholding as in a mirror the glory of the Lord, are being transformed into the same image from glory to glory" (2 Corinthians 3:18). Not one-time encounter but progressive metamorphosis. Each experience adds density to your spirit.

Creative Glory: When God's glory appears, creation happens. Genesis 1 shows glory hovering over chaos, speaking order into existence. Glory carries God's creative power to birth what doesn't exist.

Protective Glory: "And there will be a tabernacle for shade in the daytime from the heat, for a place of refuge, and for a shelter from storm and rain" (Isaiah 4:6). Glory becomes supernatural defense. What weapon penetrates Heaven's presence?

Invasive Glory: Glory doesn't respect comfort zones. It invades hidden areas, exposes shame, transforms brokenness. Glory performs holy surgery.

Costly Glory: Every biblical glory encounter demanded everything. Moses faced rebellion. Isaiah prophesied to hardened hearts. Paul carried marks. Glory attracts Heaven's favor and hell's fury. But those who've tasted authentic glory unanimously declare: It's worth every price demanded.

Glory bypasses the qualified to rest on the famished.

BIBLICAL PATTERNS OF GLORY CARRIERS

TIER 1: Three Full Witnesses

Moses: When You Have to Veil the Weight (Exodus 34:29-35)

After encountering God's glory, Moses had to veil his face. Not because glory was too holy for people—because people weren't ready for carriers. Forty days on Mount Sinai. Moses descended unaware "that the skin of his face shone while he talked with Him." He didn't choose to glow—encounter demanded expression.

"The children of Israel could not look steadily at the face of Moses because of the glory of his countenance" (2 Corinthians 3:7). Moses became a walking revival. His presence confronted everyone with reality: God is real, present, and transferable.

That partial glimpse—seeing only God's back, the trailing edge of infinite glory—transformed Moses so dramatically his face shone for days.

Sometimes you have to dim your glory so others can gradually adjust to light.

Solomon's Temple: When Glory Evicted Programs (2 Chronicles 5:13-14)

"Indeed it came to pass, when the trumpeters and singers were as one...that the house, the house of the Lord, was filled with a cloud, so that the priests could not continue ministering because of the cloud; for the glory of the Lord filled the house of God."

Professional ministers couldn't function. Their training, expertise—irrelevant when glory filled the space. Programs stopped. Procedures ceased. Only presence remained, and presence was sufficient.

Programs impress people; presence transforms people. Choose presence.

The Transfiguration: When Disciples Saw Glory Unveiled (Matthew 17:1-8)

Peter, James, and John climbed a mountain with Jesus. What they witnessed there changed their understanding of who they'd been following. "He was transfigured before them. His face shone like the sun, and His clothes became as white as the light" (Matthew 17:2).

The glory that had been veiled suddenly unveiled. Moses and Elijah appeared—glory carriers from different eras converging. Peter's response reveals how glory overwhelms logic: "Lord, it is good for us to be here; if You wish, let us make here three tabernacles" (Matthew 17:4). Translation: "This is so overwhelming I don't know what to do, so I'll suggest building something."

Then the Father's voice: "This is My beloved Son, in whom I am well pleased. Hear Him!" (Matthew 17:5). The disciples fell on their faces. When they looked up, only Jesus remained—glory veiled again but forever changed how they saw Him.

You've been walking with Jesus, but glory unveils who He actually is. This week seven encounter is your transfiguration moment—glory unveiled so you never see Him (or yourself) the same way again.

Transfiguration moments don't change Jesus—they change how you see Him.

TIER 2: Five Grouped Witnesses

Glory That Reveals: When Isaiah saw the Lord sitting on a throne, high and lifted up (Isaiah 6:1), seraphim crying "Holy!" and doorposts shaking, his response was immediate: "Woe is me, for I am undone!" Glory doesn't condemn you. Glory reveals you. In pure light, every shadow becomes visible. But watch—a coal from the altar touches his lips, and he's transformed from undone to commissioned. Stephen showed similar revelation—as they stoned him, "all who sat in the council, looking steadfastly at him, saw his face as the face of an angel" (Acts 6:15). Stephen didn't just see glory. Glory filled him. While rocks broke his body, glory held his spirit. When you carry glory, death becomes doorway, not defeat.

Glory That Transforms: The woman at the well—five failed marriages, drawing water at noon to avoid judgment. One encounter with Jesus transformed shame into the most effective evangelistic message in her city's history. "Come, see a Man who told me all things that I ever did. Could this be the Christ?" (John 4:29). Result: "Many of the Samaritans of that city believed in Him because of the word of the woman who testified" (John 4:39). The woman caught in adultery—dragged into temple courts, thrown at Jesus' feet. Religious leaders used her shame as bait. But glory chose her over her accusers. "Woman, where are those accusers of yours? Has no one condemned you?" "No one, Lord." "Neither do I condemn you; go and sin no more" (John 8:10-11). This wasn't permissive grace. This was transformative glory. Glory defends the shamed and confronts the shamers. The religious bring stones. Glory brings freedom.

Glory That Empowers: One hundred twenty believers. Upper room. Waiting as instructed. "And suddenly there came a sound from heaven, as of a rushing mighty wind, and it filled the whole house where they were sitting. Then there appeared to them divided tongues, as of fire, and one sat upon each of them. And they were all filled with the Holy Spirit" (Acts 2:2-4). Glory didn't descend on the temple with its priests and protocols. Glory filled an ordinary room with ordinary people who'd simply obeyed and waited. The result? Thousands converted. Movement launched. World changed. Notice the pattern: Glory came to those who created space through obedience and patience. Not the qualified—the available. Not the perfect—the present. Your Day 7 encounter mirrors Pentecost. You've created space through seven days of fasting and focus. You've obeyed through discomfort. You've waited through process. Now glory fills your ordinary space—wherever you are right now—because availability matters more than ability. Pentecost proves glory prefers ordinary availability to extraordinary ability.

THE DELIVERY DRIVER REVOLUTION

After praying for healing, a woman grabbed my hands: "You're so anointed! Thank you for healing me!" We gently redirected: "We're delivery service. Let's thank the Sender."

Picture your birthday. Perfect gift arrives—exactly what your heart needed. What do you do? Embrace the UPS driver? Post about FedEx's amazing service? No. You call the sender.

As believers, we function in three roles: Requester—ask the Source for breakthrough. Carrier—deliver what Heaven releases. Witness—watch recipients receive transformation. But we're never the Source.

This understanding liberated me from two soul-crushing burdens: Pressure to be the miracle (exhausting). Pride in causing the miracle (dangerous).

When you know you're the delivery driver, not the gift-giver, every package delivered increases hunger for the real Source.

THE CRY — LORD, SHOW ME YOUR GLORY

Moses' Desperate Prayer

After leading Israel through wilderness rebellion, golden calf idolatry, and constant complaint, Moses reached his breaking point. Not frustration—desperation for more. He'd seen burning bush, plagues, Red Sea split, pillar of cloud, pillar of fire. But none of it was enough.

"Please, show me Your glory" (Exodus 33:18). This wasn't casual curiosity. It was visceral hunger. Moses wanted to see what he'd only sensed. Touch what he'd only glimpsed. Know fully what he'd only known partially.

The Prayer God Loves to Answer

God's response reveals His heart: "I will make all My goodness pass before you" (Exodus 33:19). Not punishment for presumption. Permission for pursuit. God hides Moses in the rock's cleft, covers him with His hand, passes by, removes His hand. Moses sees God's back—the trailing edge of infinite glory. That partial glimpse transformed Moses so dramatically his face shone for days.

This is the prayer God never refuses: "Show me Your glory." Not "Give me more ministry." Not "Use me for Your purposes." But "Let me see You. Let me know You. Let me encounter You so completely I'm never the same."

The cry for glory isn't ambition—it's hunger. And hunger is the one qualification glory requires.

Your Cry Today

Right now, wherever you are—standing, sitting, kneeling—cry out like Moses: "Lord, show me Your glory." Not for experience. For encounter. Not for story. For transformation. Not for ministry. For intimacy that overflows naturally into every dimension of life.

This cry isn't manipulation. It's invitation. You're not demanding performance. You're requesting presence. And presence—His manifest, substantial, transformative presence—is what He most desires to give.

Cry it out loud if you can. Whisper it if you must. Write it if words won't come. But cry for glory. The God who answered Moses in the wilderness will answer you in your living room, workplace, car, wherever you are right now.

The prayer 'Show me Your glory' begins intimacy that never ends.

God is rewriting your story for His glory. Your messy crime scene is a message, your test is a testimony. Let this be your cry: 'Lord, show me Your glory. Your greater glory.'

THE STEWARDSHIP FRAMEWORK: WISE DISPLAY OF GLORY

Not every encounter is meant for public display. Some of God's most powerful work happens in secret. Not every breakthrough needs an audience. Not every healing should be shared. Mary "kept all these things and pondered them in her heart" (Luke 2:19). Sometimes treasuring privately is the obedient response. Jesus often told people He healed, "See that you tell no one" (Matthew 8:4). Sometimes silence protects what God is doing.

The goal isn't performance—it's transformation. Whether that leads to public testimony or private treasure, both honor Him.

Glory doesn't demand display—it invites wise stewardship. Sometimes private. Sometimes public. Always purposeful.

Three Expressions of Glory Stewardship

PRIVATE PROCESSING	SELECTIVE SHARING	PUBLIC DECLARATION
Treasuring sacred encounters	Testing with safe people	Commissioned release
Mary pondering in heart	Small group vulnerability	Platform testimony
Protection of tender revelations	Discerning contexts	Mature, processed stories
Processing before sharing	Building gradually	Multiplying breakthrough
Healing in layers	Growing in wisdom	Pointing to Source

The Traffic Light Decision System

Green Lights (Share with Confidence): Deep peace about specific person or context. Clear confirmation from trusted spiritual authority. Story feels mature, processed, stable. Motivation is pure—God's glory, not personal platform. Safe context where vulnerability won't cause harm. Sense of divine release, not human pressure. You're standing on Romans 8:28 and Genesis 50:20 with genuine faith. The unforgiveness, fear, and wound checks are clear.

When you have multiple green lights, move forward with confidence. God is commissioning this testimony. Share with boldness—the glory that transformed you is about to multiply through you.

Yellow Lights (Wait with Wisdom): Uncertainty about timing or specific context. Story still feels tender, raw, unprocessed. No clear confirmation from wise counsel. Motivation is mixed—God's glory plus personal validation. Safety concerns unresolved. Peace about waiting, not urgency to share. You can see you're growing through this, but growth isn't complete. One or more unforgiveness, fear, or wound checks isn't clear.

When you see yellow lights, pause. Continue processing privately. Seek wise counsel. Wait for clarity. Yellow doesn't mean "never"—it means "not yet." What feels like delay is often divine development preparing you for greater impact later. Don't let others pressure you into sharing before you're ready. Trust the process. Honor the yellow lights. God's timing is perfect.

Red Lights (Treasure Privately): Strong sense of protection over the story. Unsafe contexts or relationships. Healing still in process, layers unfolding. God's clear "Not yet" or "Not this." Peace in privacy, pressure in public thought. Wisdom from multiple counselors says protect. Unforgiveness, fear, or wound checks reveal ongoing issues. The story is still more about what they did than what God is doing.

When red lights flash, honor them. God is saying, "This is for you and Me." Don't let anyone make you feel guilty about keeping some encounters private. Some of your most sacred experiences will never become public testimony—and that's exactly as it should be. Private doesn't mean wasted. Hidden doesn't mean invalid. Mary treasured many things in her heart that never made it into Scripture. If God shows you red lights, you're in good company. Honor the red lights without guilt, without shame, without apology.

When in doubt, wait. Premature sharing can harm. Patient stewardship can heal.

Before You Share: The Readiness Assessment

Before sharing any story—especially painful ones—pause and ask yourself these critical questions:

Victim or Victor? How are you viewing this story right now? Victim perspective: "Look what was done to me." Victor perspective: "Look what God is doing through me." Both perspectives tell the truth about what happened. But victim stops at the wound. Victor moves through the wound to wisdom, redemption, transformation. Can you stand on Romans 8:28—"All things work together for good to those who love God"—and Genesis 50:20—"But as for you, you meant evil against me; but God meant it for good"?

Resolved or Unresolved? Check your heart with brutal honesty. Unforgiveness check: Do I still harbor bitterness toward those involved? Fear check: Am I afraid of their reaction if they hear my story? Wound check: Are the wounds healed enough that retelling won't reopen them? If any of these remain unresolved, treasure the story privately longer. Sharing from unresolved pain causes harm—to you and to others.

What Lights Am I Seeing? When I pray about sharing this, do I sense green lights (peace, confirmation, release), yellow lights (uncertainty, "not yet"), or red lights (protection, "keep this private")?

What's My Motivation? Is my primary motivation God's glory—or am I seeking personal validation, sympathy, vindication, or platform?

Will Sharing Help or Harm? Will sharing this story help others find breakthrough—or could it cause harm to me, to those mentioned, or to those listening?

Do Trusted Counselors Confirm? Have people who know me well and love God confirmed this is ready for sharing—or are they cautioning me to wait?

If you can't answer these questions clearly with confidence, keep processing privately. Wisdom isn't silence—it's timing. The right story shared at the wrong time becomes the wrong story.

Healed people heal people. Hurt people hurt people. Know which one you are before you share.

My Personal Stewardship Journey

Stewardship always starts in the secret place. My journals become sacred ground where I pour out everything I can't say aloud—confusion, questions, celebrations, fears. These letters to my Heavenly Father process revelation before it becomes testimony, heal wounds before they become wisdom, create space for God to speak without interruption.

This is where I wrestle with the hardest questions: Am I viewing myself as victim or victor? Do I truly stand on Romans 8:28 and Genesis 50:20? This is where unforgiveness gets uprooted, fear gets named, wounds get acknowledged. These things don't disappear by ignoring them or rushing to share "victory" prematurely. They heal in layers, in the secret place, before they become testimonies of transformation.

After processing privately, I begin sharing golden nuggets in safe spaces—my exclusive Chayah Club community, intimate blogs, live sessions, shared sermons, targeted posts. This is where I discover what resonates, what needs more time, what's ready for broader release. Selective sharing isn't hiding—it's wisdom. It's letting revelation mature in community before releasing it to the masses.

Only after private processing and selective sharing do I step into public declaration—social media platforms, speaking engagements, published books. But even here, I'm not the source—I'm the delivery driver. These public moments point back to Him.

Whatever stage you're in right now is the right stage. Don't rush private processing to get to public declaration. Don't skip selective sharing because you want immediate platform. Each stage has purpose. Each expression honors God. The journey from journal to book, from secret place to speaking stage, from private tears to public testimony—this is the stewardship process.

What you process privately with God becomes what you share powerfully with others.

CRITICAL SAFETY NOTES

For Trauma Survivors: If you're processing trauma, abuse, or difficult experiences, healing happens in layers. Share only what feels safe, when it feels right, with people who've earned trust. God never pressures premature disclosure. Your healing timeline is between you and Him. Testimony can wait until you're safe, healed, and ready. There's no rush. Private processing is valid ministry. Hidden transformation honors God just as much as public declaration.

For Those in Unsafe Situations: For those in controlling or dangerous relationships: Your safety matters more than public testimony. God understands your need for privacy. Wisdom sometimes means staying silent until you're safe. Public testimony about certain situations could endanger you or others. Protect yourself. Glory doesn't demand unsafe display.

For All Glory Carriers: Not every encounter needs an audience. Not every miracle requires a megaphone. Not every healing should be broadcast. Discernment matters. Context matters. Timing matters. Safety matters. The enemy wants to pressure you into premature sharing (to create harm) or paralyze you into permanent silence (to prevent breakthrough). Wisdom navigates between these extremes.

WORKPLACE GLORY: WHEN HEAVEN INVADES MONDAY

Consider an executive who started hosting "coffee and presence" in her office conference room. Week one: three people. Month three: HR approved it as an official "wellness gathering." A manager facing burnout discovered supernatural strength. Two departments in conflict found reconciliation. An admin assistant with hidden depression experienced breakthrough. She never preached. She simply created space: "Jesus, we invite Your presence into our workplace." The atmosphere would shift.

A construction foreman started each day walking the site praying silently: "Let this ground host Your glory." Within months: Injury rates dropped seventy percent (documented). Project finished six weeks early. Hardened workers started asking about faith. Three men returned to abandoned families. One subcontractor said: "I've worked construction thirty years. Never felt anything like this site. It's like... protected."

Where might glory desire to manifest in your workplace? What would shift if you simply made room for divine encounter in ordinary spaces?

THE GLORY PROTOCOL: SPIRITUAL LAWS

Glory operates by spiritual laws, not random occurrence. Hunger precedes glory: "Blessed are those who hunger and thirst for righteousness, for they shall be filled" (Matthew 5:6). Spiritual emptiness attracts divine fullness. Your hunger depth determines encounter weight. Holiness hosts glory: "Who may ascend into the hill of the Lord? Or who may stand in His holy place? He who has clean hands and a pure heart" (Psalm 24:3-4). You don't need to be perfect, but you need to be surrendered. Unity unlocks glory: When one hundred twenty believers gathered "all with one accord in one place" (Acts 2:1), glory fell with nation-shaking power. Worship welcomes glory: "But You are holy, enthroned in the praises of Israel" (Psalm 22:3). Authentic worship builds the throne glory inhabits.

Glory responds to prepared hearts, not perfect performance.

THE COST OF CARRYING GLORY

The Isolation Season: When glory first marks you, some relationships will feel uncomfortable. Not because you've become arrogant—because you're carrying different frequency. People who loved your dysfunction won't celebrate your glory. This isn't rejection—it's recalibration. Don't chase what's leaving. Steward what's staying.

The Religious Jealousy: Glory carriers often face the most opposition from religious circles. Like Joseph's brothers who hated his coat and dreams, religious people can resent authentic glory. Why? Because glory exposes performance. Religious leaders who've built platforms on anointing alone feel threatened by glory's substance. The brothers' jealousy positioned Joseph for palace. Religious rejection often confirms glory's authenticity.

The Responsibility Reality: Glory isn't just for you. You become carrier for others' breakthrough. Your presence will trigger reactions: Some will cry without knowing why. Others will get angry at your peace. Many will feel exposed by your freedom. A few will encounter God through your atmosphere. This isn't about you being special—it's about what you're carrying being substantial.

The Maintenance Mandate: Glory can leak through pride (thinking you earned it), pressure (performing for approval), praise (becoming addicted to recognition), or performance (trying to recreate encounters). The antidote: Integrity, humility, and partnership with God—staying connected to the True Vine (John 15:4-5). You're the delivery driver, not the gift-giver. Every miracle points to Him. Without maintenance, glory fades. With intentional stewarding, glory multiplies.

Pride makes you think you earned the glory you were given. Humility knows you were given what you could never earn.

Glory attracts Heaven's favor and religion's fury. Both responses confirm you're carrying something real.

ACTIVATION — THE GLORY TRANSFER PROTOCOL

Physical Positioning for Weight Reception

Note: Adapt these positions to your physical ability. The heart posture matters more than perfect form.

Step 1: Recognition Posture (60 seconds): Stand with arms at sides. "I recognize glory is available." Feel current spiritual weight.

Step 2: Reception Position (60 seconds): Arms open wide, palms up. "I receive the weight of Your glory, however it comes." Don't grasp—receive. Notice what you sense—weight, peace, quiet, or simple awareness.

Step 3: Integration Stance (60 seconds): Hands on heart. "Glory, mark my innermost being." Feel weight settling in, not on. Breathe deeply.

Step 4: Stewardship Commitment (60 seconds): Cup hands at heart level. "What You reveal, I'll steward with wisdom—private, selective, or public as You guide." "I am delivery driver, not Source."

Step 5: Radiation Reality (60 seconds): Arms extended forward. "I carry and release Your glory." "I'll share as You lead, treasure as You protect, wait as You direct." You're not keeping—you're channeling.

The Oil Anointing Act

Take any oil (olive, coconut, even cooking oil): Put drop on finger. Touch forehead: "I'm marked by glory." Touch heart: "I carry glory." Touch hands: "I release glory wisely." The oil isn't magical. It's memorial. Physical reminder of spiritual marking.

FOCUS AREA GLORY PRAYERS

Scripture Foundation: "And the glory of the Lord shall be revealed, and all flesh shall see it together; for the mouth of the Lord has spoken" (Isaiah 40:5)

For Spiritual Focus: "Father, transform me from experiencer to wise expresser. Use my encounters to spark authentic encounters in others—in Your timing, through Your wisdom. Let glory mark me so completely that atmospheres shift where I go."

For Mental Focus: "Father, let glory renew my mind. Your weight displaces anxiety. Your presence recalibrates thoughts. Guide me to share what helps others, when it helps them, in ways that honor You."

For Emotional Focus: "Father, glory stabilizes my emotions. Your weight becomes my anchor. In Your presence, feelings find order. Heal my emotions at the pace that's right for me. Show me when my story might become someone's hope—and protect what still needs processing."

For Physical Focus: "Father, let glory strengthen my body. Like Moses glowing, let health radiate. Your weight becomes my healing. Work in my body according to Your will. If healing comes, show me how to testify wisely—giving You glory while protecting what needs privacy."

For Financial Focus: "Father, I carry glory that attracts provision. Your weight opens doors. Resources flow to glory carriers. Shift my situation as You see fit. Help me steward both struggle and breakthrough with wisdom—sharing what encourages, protecting what's sacred."

For Relational Focus: "Father, let my glory mark others. Your weight through me transforms relationships. I carry breakthrough for others. Restore relationships in Your way and timing. Show me what to share publicly, what to treasure privately, what to discuss selectively."

DECLARATION OF THE MARKED

Stand or sit comfortably. Speak with quiet authority:

"I am marked by glory!

Like Moses, I've been in the presence and carry the weight!
Like Solomon's temple, I host presence that stops programs!
Like Isaiah, I've been undone and restored!
Like Stephen, glory makes me unstoppable!
Like the disciples on the mountain, I've seen glory unveiled!
Like the one hundred twenty at Pentecost, ordinary availability meets extraordinary glory!
Like Mary, I treasure what needs protection!
Like the woman at the well, my shame becomes testimony—in right timing, safe spaces, as wisdom guides!
I don't just see glory—I carry it!
I don't just experience presence—I transport it!
I don't just receive breakthrough—I become it!
I am delivery driver, not gift-giver!
Every testimony delivered multiplies breakthrough—when shared wisely!
Glory hidden from obedience protects!
Glory hidden from fear paralyzes!
Glory displayed with wisdom becomes breakthrough!
I cry like Moses: 'Lord, show me Your glory!'
I ask like Solomon: 'Lord, grant me wisdom for stewardship!'
I surrender like Mary: 'Let it be according to Your word!'
Hell recognizes my marking!
Demons flee from my weight!
Darkness retreats from my glory!
I'll share what builds up, when wisdom guides!
I'll treasure what needs protection, without guilt!
I'll process privately, share selectively, declare publicly—as You direct!
I reject pride, pressure, praise addiction, and performance!
I am delivery driver! He is Source!
Glory flows through surrender, not striving!
My crime scene becomes holy ground!
My broken place becomes breakthrough portal!
My ordinary space—home, workplace, wherever—can host His glory!
I am marked by kavod—substantial, weighty, unchangeable presence!
I radiate doxa—visible, brilliant, undeniable transformation!
I move from origin (beholding) to destiny (becoming)!
I am a glory-carrier, chain-breaker, history maker, legacy-leaver—learning when to speak, when to stay silent, when to simply live the transformation!
Week 1 established whose I am!
Week 2 will reveal who I am!
Glory doesn't visit me—glory lives in me!
In Jesus' name, I am wise glory carrier! Amen."

BREAKTHROUGH PRAYER

Father God, Weight of Glory, Consuming Fire, Source of Every Miracle,

I repent for treating glory as future hope instead of present reality. For thinking I could see Your glory but not carry it. For believing I was disqualified from weight. Thank You for designing me as glory container. For creating capacity in me for Your kavod. Thank You that glory specializes in crime scenes. That broken places become holy ground. That messy wilderness hosts Your presence.

Thank You for Week 1's foundation—Gospel acceptance, Grace empowerment, Goodness evidence, Gifts equipment, Gladness restoration, Greatness access. This seventh day, I rest in completion. Six days built the altar. Today Your fire falls—however that looks for me.

Forgive me if I've hidden from fear what You wanted shared, or shared from pressure what needed protection. Teach me wisdom's rhythm. I acknowledge: I am delivery driver—You are Gift-Giver. Every miracle points to You.

Like Moses, I cry out: "Show me Your glory!" Not for experience but for encounter. Not for story but for transformation. Not for ministry but for intimacy that overflows naturally.

Like Solomon, I ask: "Grant me wisdom for stewardship!" When to speak. When to stay silent. When to share publicly. When to treasure privately. When to test selectively. How to honor both transparency and protection.

Like Mary, I surrender: "Let it be according to Your word." Your timing. Your context. Your wisdom. Not my timeline. Not pressure to perform. Not fear to hide.

Mark me tonight. Not just touch—mark. Not just visit—reside. Let Your weight become my stability in shaking, provision before breakthrough, joy in mourning, victory in battle, identity in confusion, wisdom in expression.

I receive the weight. The beautiful, terrible, wonderful weight of Your presence. Right now, I receive commission as wise glory carrier, discernment for what to share and when, freedom from performance pressure, protection for what needs privacy, crime scenes becoming holy ground, broken places becoming breakthrough portals.

Show me what testimonies to share publicly, what encounters to treasure privately, what revelations to share selectively, what stories will help others heal—in right timing, who needs my stewardship story as much as my transformation story.

Where I go, let atmosphere shift. What I touch, let it upgrade. Who I encounter, let them experience You. I am marked by kavod—substantial presence. I radiate doxa—visible transformation. I move through all Five Movements—Origin, Revelation, Redemption, Manifestation, Destiny.

Week 1 complete. Foundation solid. Ready for identity. In Jesus' name, I am marked by glory—and I steward it with wisdom and purpose! Amen.

CLOSING — COMMISSIONED FOR WISE DISPLAY

Day 7 complete. Week 1 finished. You've been systematically prepared for glory. Gospel closed the gap between earning and receiving. Grace closed the gap between performance and position. Goodness closed the gap between doubt and trust. Gifts closed the gap between potential and activation. Gladness closed the gap between mourning and joy. Greatness closed the gap between limitation and authority. Now glory marks you—closing the gap between earth and heaven.

This isn't temporary shine that fades by Monday. This is weight that compounds. Every prayer adds density. Every worship adds substance. Every Word adds light. The latter glory—internal, permanent, transformative—exceeds any former external experience you've known. What's coming surpasses what left. What lies ahead exceeds what's behind.

You're different than you were seven days ago. Not just informed—transformed. Not just blessed—marked. Tomorrow begins Week 2: ALIGN. You'll discover your kingdom identity and learn to walk in authority. But tonight, feel the weight. Let it settle. Let it mark places in you that words can't reach.

Some of you are crying without knowing why. That's glory touching original design. Others feel unusual peace. That's weight displacing worry. Many sense atmosphere shifting around you. That's glory beginning to radiate. Still others simply feel tired, complete, ready for rest. That's Sabbath settling in. All valid. All glory.

The same God who marked me in my rental house bedroom at three in the morning is marking you right now. The weight that broke my fear patterns is settling on your shoulders. The glory that carried me through divorce, death, depression is available for your valleys.

You are now a carrier. Heaven's weight rests on you. Where you go, things change. Not because you're special—because you're marked. But remember: You're also becoming wise about how to carry this weight. Some encounters you'll treasure privately like Mary. Some you'll share selectively in safe spaces. Some you'll declare publicly when commissioned. All expressions honor God when guided by wisdom.

Rock bottom became my glory encounter. I didn't leave Week 1 the same. I left as a glory-carrier, chain-breaker, history maker, legacy-leaver—learning when to speak, when to stay silent, when to simply live the transformation.

Welcome to the fellowship of the carriers. The company of the marked. The family of glory. You've cried like Moses: "Show me Your glory!" You've asked like Solomon: "Grant me wisdom for stewardship!" You've surrendered like Mary: "Let it be according to Your word!"

The combination—hunger for glory plus wisdom for stewardship plus surrender to timing—creates the wise glory carrier God uses to transform nations.

You came to Day 1 seeking. You leave Day 7 carrying—with wisdom about when and how to share what you carry.

Glory transforms us not into perfect people, but into authentic carriers of His presence—learning when to speak, when to stay silent, when to simply live the transformation.

Glory ruins you for anything less than God Himself. After authentic glory, everything else becomes appetite management.

Day 7 Complete: Wise Glory Carrier Commissioned
Glory: Not seen but carried
Weight: Not burden but breakthrough
Marking: Not temporary but transformative
Identity: Not seeker but carrier
Atmosphere: Not same but shifted
Stewardship: Wisdom for when and how to share—received

WEEK 1: GROW (7G)

Sabbath: Rest in completion, ready for identity
Cry: "Lord, show me Your glory!"—answered
The GAP: Between earth and heaven—closed
Five Movements: Origin, Revelation, Redemption, Manifestation, Destiny

SOAP JOURNAL — DAY 7
S (Scripture): Which glory verse revealed the weight you're meant to carry?
O (Observation): What has God shown you about stewarding encounters—when to share, when to treasure, when to wait? What did you sense when you cried, "Lord, show me Your glory"?
A (Application): What is God asking you to do with what He's revealed—share publicly, treasure privately, or discuss selectively? How will you maintain the glory flow?
P (Prayer): "Father, the glory encounter I'm stewarding is _____. You're guiding me to _____ with this revelation. When I cried 'Show me Your glory,' You _____. The weight, peace, or completion I felt was _____."

Week 1 Breakthrough Marker: How has intimacy with God shifted from information to transformation? How did Day 7 complete Week 1's foundation for you—dramatically or quietly?
The Gap That Closed: Which gap did you experience closing most powerfully this week—earning to receiving, performance to position, doubt to trust, potential to activation, mourning to joy, limitation to authority, or earth to heaven?

Week 2 Expectation: Now that you carry glory with wisdom, what identity truths are you ready to discover as you ALIGN?

WEEK 1 COMPLETE: GROW IN INTIMACY
Tomorrow: Week 2 ALIGN in Identity begins with Day 8: Adoption
You know whose you are. Time to discover who you are.

GLORY RECEIVED. WEIGHT ACCEPTED. WISDOM GRANTED. MARKING COMPLETE. ALL GAPS CLOSED. READY FOR IDENTITY.

SECTION FOUR
CHAMBER 2: TRANSFORM
WEEK 2: ALIGN (7A)
Identity in Christ

"Therefore, if anyone is in Christ, he is a new creation; old things have passed away; behold, all things have become new."
— 2 Corinthians 5:17

You can't walk in power you don't believe you possess. With intimacy established in Week 1, Week 2 solidifies your identity. This week moves you from knowing whose you are to knowing who you are—seven themes that align your identity with Christ's finished work, not your past performance or present struggles.
Days 8-14: Adoption • Abundance • Authority • Anointing • Advancement • Attributes • Affirmation

---

THE SEVEN-ELEMENT PROGRESSION
Week 2 systematically activates your complete identity through body theology:
Days 8-12 (Internal): Soul • Heart • Hands • Head/Spirit • Feet
Days 13-14 (External): Eyes • Voice
Heart receives → Eyes behold → Mouth declares = Full identity manifestation
Each day moves you from living *for* approval to living *from* approval—the difference between striving to become who you already are in Christ versus resting in who Christ has already made you.
Identity precedes authority. Position precedes power. You don't perform to become. You rest in what you've been made. Week 2 rewrites the core code of how you see yourself.

Turn the page to Day 8: ADOPTION.
Your identity awakening begins here.

DAY 8 — ADOPTION

From Orphaned to Anchored — Sons and Daughters of Glory

"For you did not receive the spirit of bondage again to fear, but you received the Spirit of adoption by whom we cry out, 'Abba, Father.'" — Romans 8:15

WEEK 2 — ALIGN: Establishing Your Kingdom Identity

Day 8 of 21. Yesterday's Glory marked you with heaven's weight. Today's Adoption anchors you in family identity—transforming orphan whispers into heir declarations.

ENCOUNTER — WHERE YOU ARE

4:30 AM. Day 8. You reach for your phone to check the time and freeze—your father's name is still in your contacts. Finger hovers over "Delete" like it has for three years. Your thumb trembles over the screen. Delete? Keep? The blue glow makes your face look ghostly in the dark—appropriate, since you've been haunted by this decision since he left. Your chest tightens. Not hunger this time—something older, deeper. That copper-penny taste floods your mouth, the one that always comes before the orphan whisper starts: *not enough, never chosen, always outside looking in.*

Day 8. Your stomach has stopped screaming and started whispering. The physical emptiness creates space for spiritual filling. This is when fasting becomes portal—when hunger pangs transform into labor pains birthing new identity. Your body, depleted of earthly bread, becomes desperate for heavenly revelation. And adoption is what Heaven serves the hungry heart.

Something shifted in the night. Week 1 grew your intimacy with God—you discovered whose you are. Seven days establishing one truth: You belong to Him. But knowing whose you are must lead to knowing who you are. Week 2 aligns identity through seven revelations: Adoption, Abundance, Authority, Anointing, Advancement, Attributes, Affirmation. Alignment always begins with adoption. You can't know who you are until you know you're His child. Adoption answers life's two most pivotal questions: Who am I? A child of God. Whose am I? I belong to the Father. Every identity crisis stems from not knowing these answers.

The devil's greatest fear isn't your success—it's your sonship. From Eden's first family to your family table, the enemy has waged war on one thing: making sure you never discover you're chosen, wanted, destined to carry the Father's DNA into every room you enter.

FOUNDATION — THE ANCIENT WAR ON YOUR FAMILY

When Hell Declared War on Homes

Since creation's dawn, the family unit has been under constant attack. Watch the progression: Perfect communion. One deception. Paradise lost. Immediately: *"Now Cain talked with Abel his brother; and it came to pass, when they were in the field, that Cain rose up against Abel his brother and killed him"* (Genesis 4:8). First family. First murder. First orphan spirit—disconnected from the Father. Before there was a temple to destroy, an altar to defile, or a church to divide, Satan slithered into a garden and went after a marriage. His first target wasn't a ministry. It was a marriage.

Watch the wreckage through Scripture: Jacob's sons trafficking their brother Joseph into slavery (Genesis 37:28), David's house imploding through adultery with Bathsheba (2 Samuel 11), and Absalom's rebellion against his father (2 Samuel 15). Every attack calculated. Every wound strategic. Why? Because God builds His house from homes. Strong marriages birth strong churches. Healthy families raise Kingdom warriors. The enemy knows what we forget—Kingdom authority isn't just cultivated in sanctuaries. It's forged at dinner tables, in bedtime prayers, through forgiven failures and fierce love.

Satan attacked the family 4,000 years before he attacked the church. He knew: break the home, break the House. Your marriage isn't just under pressure. It's under siege. Your children aren't just challenging. They're contested territory. That division in your home isn't random dysfunction—it's ancient strategy. But here's what hell didn't count on: now you know.

The Fatherless Generation

Contemporary studies underscore the profound societal impacts of fatherlessness. Nearly one in four children in America live without a biological father in the home. Children from fatherless homes are four times more likely to experience poverty, seven times more likely to become pregnant as teenagers, and more likely to engage in drug and alcohol abuse. But the spiritual reality is worse—even those with present fathers often carry father-wounds from emotional absence, abuse, or dysfunction. The orphan spirit tastes like copper pennies in your mouth when someone gets chosen. Feels like glass in your chest when "family" is mentioned. Sounds like "not enough" on repeat at 3 AM.

The Digital Orphanage

Instagram became our orphanage. LinkedIn our audition stage. We post for fathers we never had, seeking "likes" as love, comments as care, shares as significance. Every notification promises belonging but delivers dopamine—counterfeit connection that leaves us lonelier. The orphan spirit has gone digital, and we're all scrolling for our father. You're still operating as orphan if you screenshot compliments to read when you feel worthless, rehearse conversations to ensure you'll be chosen, can't receive a gift without immediately planning reciprocation, or work yourself sick to prove you belong.

THE DIFFERENCE: ORPHAN SPIRIT VS ADOPTION SPIRIT

ORPHAN SPIRIT (Misaligned)	ADOPTION SPIRIT (Anchored)
Works FOR love, never knowing when enough is enough	Works FROM love, knowing you're already accepted
Competes with others, threatened by their success	Celebrates others' success as family wins
Hoards resources from scarcity mindset	Shares abundantly from inheritance mindset
Builds personal kingdoms for security	Builds Father's Kingdom from security
Defensive when corrected, seeing it as rejection	Grateful for correction, seeing it as development
Says "Look what I'm doing for God"	Says "Look what Dad's doing through me"

The difference between striving and resting is the difference between orphan and heir. Orphan spirit behaviors: hoarding (fear of not having enough), striving (proving worth through achievement), independence (not asking for help), performing (earning love instead of receiving it), and controlling (managing everything to feel safe). Adoption spirit behaviors: generosity (knowing Father provides), resting (secure in who you are), interdependence (receiving and giving freely), being (knowing you're loved, not earning it), and surrendering (trusting Father's control).

The generation with the most father-wounds will become the generation that discovers the Father's heart most desperately. Your wound becomes your doorway. Your father-hunger drives you to Abba. The fatherless generation is becoming the Father-discovering generation. God doesn't give you an identity crisis. He gives you an identity cure—adoption.

TESTIMONY — THE PAPER AIRPLANE JOURNEY

Jamaica, Father's Day 1986: The Vow

Fourteen years old. No cake. No candles. Just sun on concrete and brown school shoes drying beside me—marker-stained where the leather had given up. Every weekend, the ritual: dark brown marker on brown leather. Color the holes. Pray rain wouldn't come. Pray nobody at school would notice green socks peeking through. **I inked the holes in my shoes; God filled the holes in my story.** Father's Day was every day—because absence filled every room like smoke. That afternoon, humidity thick as grief, I did what orphans do. I wrote the only Father who might be listening:

"Dear Papa, It stops with me. University. A real home. A husband who stays. Children who know their father's voice. Your daughter, Niki."

I folded the page into a paper airplane—because when you're fourteen and fatherless, you learn to make prayers fly however you can. The June heat should have dropped it straight to dirt. Instead, it caught an impossible updraft and sailed out of sight. **Paper airplane prayers always find their runway.** On those concrete steps, marker still wet on my fingertips, I made a vow: "It stops with me... and starts through me." Something broke in the spirit realm that day. The orphan spirit that had plagued my bloodline for generations met its match—a fourteen-year-old girl with a marker, a prayer, and audacious faith that maybe, just maybe, she was wanted.

January 2018, Day 8: The Revelation

But I didn't understand the orphan spirit then. Not until January 2018, Day 8 of my first Daniel Fast, when the Holy Spirit downloaded this revelation to my spirit. I cried until my ribs ached. Looking back, I saw the pattern stretching through generations like a cursed inheritance. The familiarity of absent fathers and single mothers had made it feel normal. The resilience required trained you to act strong when you were actually lonely and felt unloved. Generation after generation going to the wrong cistern, finding it empty, rather than going to the Heavenly Father to be healed and loved. **The orphan spirit named is the orphan spirit defeated.** January 2018: the day I stopped acting strong and started learning how to become anchored.

The Boardroom: The Performance

Years later. Big corporate contract opportunity. The kind that validates worth. I walk into that boardroom—mahogany table gleaming, executives in suits. Armed with PowerPoints and desperation.

Two hours. Performing. Pitching. Practically begging. My voice climbs higher with each objection, sweat pooling at the base of my spine. That night, still smelling boardroom coffee and my own desperation-sweat, Holy Spirit's voice cut through the exhaustion: "Why did you work so hard to be chosen by people I've already chosen you to lead?" I'm still operating as orphan. Trying to earn what I already own. Begging for scraps at tables where I have a seat.

Orphans audition. Sons and daughters simply show up. You spent two hours proving you belong when your Father owns the building. You'll never operate in heaven's authority if you're still auditioning for earth's approval.

August 2019: The Pattern

In May 2018, I ended up in a narcissistic relationship—despite God's warning. Unhealed and feeling unworthy, I dated at my low self-esteem level. One evening, 6 PM, August 2019—public humiliation. Heartbreak that felt like death. Every 6 PM for weeks, I relived the trauma. Body remembering betrayal at the exact minute. Panic attacks became my new normal—chest tightening, room spinning, that copper-penny taste of fear flooding my mouth. I sought God deeply—not just in prayer, but in identity fasting. Not just fasting from an event, but fasting into identity. The lingering orphan spirit needed to die, to be eradicated completely. **Orphan wounds attract predators; adoption creates protection.**

The Promise: "This Is Not That"

When I met my husband, I almost ruined it. Trauma trains you to sabotage good before it leaves. One afternoon, picked fight sharp enough to draw blood. Testing him. Pushing him. Proving he'd leave like everyone else. "Just go!" I spat, voice breaking. "Everyone else does." He set down his coffee—slowly, deliberately. Looked past my rage into the orphan cowering behind it. The kitchen suddenly felt too small, too quiet. "Nicola." Voice steady as bedrock. **"This. Is. Not. That."** Four words. Orphan spirit shattered like glass on stone. This is not that divorce. Not that courtroom. Not that narcissistic relationship. Not that girl coloring shoes with markers.

Early dating, my husband read me books about royalty. Teaching identity before intimacy. Later he told me he'd asked God who I was. "Princess warrior," God answered. Princess because Abba signed papers in blood. Warrior because it takes a sword to guard a crown.

The Purpose: Why Healing Matters

You need to heal so you don't destroy what you're praying for. God is preparing you for what you're praying for—otherwise you'll arrive unprepared, misaligned in your position. And He's preparing what you're praying for for you—so you meet at the right place, right time. Healing positions you. Wholeness prepares you. Anchoring keeps you. That fourteen-year-old girl who sent paper airplane prayers from Jamaica? She now leads thousands in prayer globally. University education despite poverty. Home ownership after homelessness. Husband who stayed and loves my boys. Children who know their father's voice. Ministry that breaks orphan spirits worldwide. **When a girl writes to God, generational curses lose their editor.**

REVELATION — THE DOUBLE REVELATION OF ADOPTION

Where Greek Law Meets Hebrew Love

Heaven wants you to understand who you became the moment you said yes to Jesus. This adoption transcends earthly legal proceedings—it's an ethereal metamorphosis of your spiritual identity. The Greek gives you papers, the Hebrew gives you DNA, but the Spirit gives you metamorphosis—complete transformation at the cellular level of your soul.

The Greek Legal Dimension: Huiothesia (hwee-oh-theh-SEE-ah)

The Greeks had a word—*huiothesia*—that made Roman citizens weep with relief. When a father spoke this word over someone, everything changed. Every debt cancelled. Every crime erased. Every chain of their past shattered. Picture the scene: The adopted one would strip naked in the Roman court. Old clothes burned in fire that consumed former identity. Former name forbidden to speak—death penalty for anyone who mentioned it. They'd be dressed in new robes bearing their father's seal. New name. New identity. New inheritance. The father's enemies became the child's enemies—and his protection too.

This wasn't charity. This was complete metamorphosis. Paul, a Roman citizen who understood this legal atom bomb, declared: "This is what happened to you." *"Having predestined us to adoption as sons by Jesus Christ to Himself, according to the good pleasure of His will"* (Ephesians 1:5). Good pleasure. Not reluctant duty. Not charitable obligation. Pleasure. **Adoption means God wanted you so badly He paid the highest price to anchor you in His family.** The Father doesn't adopt out of pity—He adopts for proximity.

The Hebrew Mystery Dimension: Divine Claiming

The Hebrew language—tongue of prophets, vocabulary of visions—has no word for adoption. The language with seventeen words for praise went silent on adoption. Why? Because Hebrew fathers didn't adopt. They claimed. "This one is mine." No papers. No process. No probation. When Jacob put his hands on Ephraim and Manasseh, he didn't say "I adopt you." He declared: "They are mine" (Genesis 48:5). When Pharaoh's daughter pulled Moses from water, she didn't file paperwork. She declared: "This is my son" (Exodus 2:10). The Hebrew mind couldn't conceive of God needing legal documents to make you His child. His declaration creates reality. When He says "Mine," hell's accusations become irrelevant. *"I have called you by your name; You are Mine"* (Isaiah 43:1). Not "will be Mine after process." You are Mine. Present tense. Permanent reality. Heaven doesn't have an adoption agency. Heaven has a Father who speaks and it is so.

The Prodigal Illustration: Both Dimensions in One Story

The familiar parable from Luke 15:11-32 demonstrates both Greek legal reality and Hebrew relational truth. Watch how Jesus destroys three adoption lies:

The Younger Son — Identity Survives Stupidity

Even feeding pigs—unclean animals for a Jewish boy—he says: *"How many of my father's hired servants have bread enough and to spare"* (Luke 15:17). My father's. Worst decisions couldn't erase DNA. He prepared servant speech: *"Father, I have sinned against heaven and before you, and I am no longer worthy to be called your son. Make me like one of your hired servants"* (Luke 15:18-19). But father interrupts before he can finish:

"But the father said to his servants, 'Bring out the best robe and put it on him, and put a ring on his hand and sandals on his feet'" (Luke 15:22). Best robe (sonship restored publicly), ring (authority returned with family seal), sandals (freedom declared—slaves went barefoot), and fatted calf (celebration required for resurrection). *"For this my son was dead and is alive again; he was lost and is found"* (Luke 15:24). Present tense. Is my son. Not was. Not will be again. Is.

Adoption Lie Destroyed: "My failure disqualifies me from sonship."

Adoption Truth: Identity survives stupidity. You can't sin your way out of adoption.

The Elder Brother — Orphan in the House

"So he answered and said to his father, 'Lo, these many years I have been serving you; I never transgressed your commandment at any time; and yet you never gave me a young goat, that I might make merry with my friends'" (Luke 15:29). Serving. Living as slave while being son. In the house but not in the family. Father's response: *"Son, you are always with me, and all that I have is yours"* (Luke 15:31). Always son. Always had access. The tragedy wasn't what he lacked but what he never accessed.

Adoption Lie Destroyed: "My performance earns me sonship."

Adoption Truth: You can't earn what's already yours. The elder brother was always son—he just never lived like it.

The Father — Grace That Won't Let Go

The father runs for both sons. For the younger son: *"But when he was still a great way off, his father saw him and had compassion, and ran and fell on his neck and kissed him"* (Luke 15:20). Dignified Middle Eastern fathers didn't run—it was considered shameful. But this father hiked up his robe and sprinted toward shame, taking it upon himself so his son wouldn't have to carry it. For the elder son: *"Now his older son was in the field. And as he came and drew near to the house, he heard music and dancing... But he was angry and would not go in. Therefore his father came out and pleaded with him"* (Luke 15:25, 28). The father left his own celebration to pursue the angry, bitter son who refused to join. The father pursued the one who ran away and the one who stayed but never belonged. He pursued the rebel and the religious. He pursued failure and performance.

Adoption Lie Destroyed: "God's love depends on my position (prodigal or elder brother)."

Adoption Truth: The Father pursues both the far and the near, the rebel and the religious, the broken and the bitter. His grace won't let go of either son.

The Complete Integration

The Greek lawyer in Heaven says you're legally safe. The Hebrew Father in Heaven says you're eternally loved. You get both. The courtroom and the embrace. The document and the declaration. The rights and the relationship. **You can't out-sin your adoption papers. They're written in blood, not pencil.** The Father's signature on your adoption papers is written in nail scars. Both sons misunderstood adoption. The younger thought failure erased it. The elder thought performance earned it. The father proved neither could change it. Adoption simply is. You can't run far enough to escape adoption. You can't perform well enough to earn it. You can only receive what the Father has already declared: "This one is mine."

BIBLICAL PATTERNS — GOD'S ADOPTION AGENCY CHANGED HISTORY

TIER 1: Three Full Witnesses

Moses: When Egyptian Adoption Positioned for Hebrew Deliverance (Exodus 2:10)

"And the child grew, and she brought him to Pharaoh's daughter, and he became her son. So she called his name Moses, saying, 'Because I drew him out of the water.'" A Hebrew baby pulled from water. An Egyptian princess defying Pharaoh's decree to kill Hebrew males. Moses lived forty years as Pharaoh's grandson—educated in Egyptian wisdom, trained in royal courts, learning systems he'd later confront. *"And Moses was learned in all the wisdom of the Egyptians, and was mighty in words and deeds"* (Acts 7:22). This adoption positioned him to confront Pharaoh as equal, not slave. When God said, *"Come now, therefore, and I will send you to Pharaoh that you may bring My people, the children of Israel, out of Egypt"* (Exodus 3:10), Moses could enter palace doors slaves never could. God used Egyptian adoption to prepare Hebrew deliverance. Your adoption positions you for purpose you can't yet see. **What the enemy meant to orphan you, God uses to anchor you.**

Joseph: The Carpenter Who Adopted the Creator (Matthew 1:20-25)

"But while he thought about these things, behold, an angel of the Lord appeared to him in a dream, saying, 'Joseph, son of David, do not be afraid to take to you Mary your wife, for that which is conceived in her is of the Holy Spirit.'" The carpenter adopted the Creator. *"Then Joseph, being aroused from sleep, did as the angel of the Lord commanded him and took to him his wife, and did not know her till she had brought forth her firstborn Son. And he called His name Jesus"* (Matthew 1:24-25). Joseph gave Jesus legal standing in David's line, protection during vulnerable years, a trade to learn, a family to belong to. When Herod sought to kill the child, Joseph's legal fatherhood provided escape to Egypt. This adoption fulfilled prophecy, positioned salvation. Your adoption positions others for breakthrough.

The Prodigal Teaching: Three Revelations (covered fully in Double Revelation section above)

TIER 2: Seven Grouped Witnesses

Identity Declared Before Activity

At baptism, before any miracle, before any sermon, before any ministry: *"And suddenly a voice came from heaven, saying, 'This is My beloved Son, in whom I am well pleased'"* (Matthew 3:17). Identity preceded activity. Beloved before beginning. Approved before achieving. Satan's first attack targeted identity: *"If You are the Son of God, command that these stones become bread"* (Matthew 4:3). If you are. Question the identity, create the crisis. Jesus didn't defend His sonship. He operated from it: *"It is written, 'Man shall not live by bread alone, but by every word that proceeds from the mouth of God'"* (Matthew 4:4). **The enemy's primary strategy is creating identity confusion. Your primary victory is identity security.**

Strategic Adoption for Deliverance

Esther: *"And Mordecai had brought up Hadassah, that is, Esther, his uncle's daughter, for she had neither father nor mother"* (Esther 2:7). Natural orphan. Adopted by cousin. Positioned as queen through a beauty contest she didn't choose. When genocide threatened Israel, Mordecai reminded her: *"Yet who knows whether you have come to the kingdom for such a time as this?"* (Esther 4:14). Her response required identity security: *"If I perish, I perish!"* (Esther 4:16). Only someone who knows they're chosen can risk rejection. Her adoption wasn't accidental—it was strategic. Orphan to daughter to queen to deliverer of an entire nation.

Mephibosheth: *"Now when Mephibosheth the son of Jonathan, the son of Saul, had come to David, he fell on his face and prostrated himself"* (2 Samuel 9:6). Jonathan's son. Saul's grandson. David's enemy's seed. Living in Lo Debar—literally "no pasture"—a place of lack. Crippled in both feet. Yet David sought him out: *"Do not fear, for I will surely show you kindness for Jonathan your father's sake, and will restore to you all the land of Saul your grandfather; and you shall eat bread at my table continually"* (2 Samuel 9:7). The crippled grandson of the king's enemy, eating at the king's table as son. Every meal, lameness hidden under the king's table. Every meal, treated as royalty. This is us—crippled by sin, enemies by nature, brought to the King's table as children. Weakness hidden under His table. Status secured by covenant, not condition. **Adoption transforms your greatest disadvantage into divine advantage.**

The Apostolic Doctrine of Adoption

Paul's comprehensive teaching reveals adoption's authority: **Prayer Authority:** *"And because you are sons, God has sent forth the Spirit of His Son into your hearts, crying out, 'Abba, Father!'"* (Galatians 4:6). Not begging a distant deity. Talking to Dad. **Freedom from Fear:** *"For you did not receive the spirit of bondage again to fear, but you received the Spirit of adoption"* (Romans 8:15). Fear was your old operating system. Adoption installs new software. **Warfare Authority:** *"The Spirit Himself bears witness with our spirit that we are children of God, and if children, then heirs—heirs of God and joint heirs with Christ"* (Romans 8:16-17). Same authority Jesus carried. Same power. Same position. **Inheritance Access:** *"Therefore you are no longer a slave but a son, and if a son, then an heir of God through Christ"* (Galatians 4:7). Everything the Father has becomes available. Not eventually. Now. **Security in Love:** *"Behold what manner of love the Father has bestowed on us, that we should be called children of God!"* (1 John 3:1). What manner of love. Study it. Marvel at it. Rest in it. **Hell doesn't fear your achievements. Hell fears your adoption.**

INTIMACY — THE LORD'S PRAYER AS ADOPTION DECLARATION

When the disciples asked the wrong question, Jesus gave them the right answer. *"Lord, teach us to pray"* (Luke 11:1). They wanted technique. Jesus gave them identity. *"When you pray, say: Our Father in heaven..."* (Matthew 6:9). Two words that detonate every orphan lie. No wonder forces work to remove this prayer from public spaces—every recitation is a declaration of adoption, a claim of inheritance, a confession of belonging.

"Our" — The Isolation Killer. You're not alone. Never were. Never will be. When you whisper "Our Father" at 4:30 AM in your closet, millions join your chorus across time zones. The orphan spirit whispers "alone." The adoption Spirit declares "family."

"Father" — The Identity Anchor. Not Master. Not Judge. Not CEO of the Universe. Father. *Abba* (AH-bah). Daddy. In first-century Judaism, God's name was too holy to pronounce. Then Jesus drops "Father" like it's normal. The religious leaders were scandalized. But Jesus was revealing what religion hid: God wants to be your Father, not just your deity.

Every phrase reinforces your adoption: *"Hallowed be Your name"* (I honor the family name I now carry), *"Your kingdom come"* (I work in the family business), *"Your will be done"* (I want what Dad wants), *"Give us this day our daily bread"* (Children ask; orphans beg), *"Forgive us our debts"* (Children can fail safely with fathers), and *"Lead us not into temptation"* (Children run to daddy when afraid). **You can't pray "Our Father" with faith and remain an orphan in your thinking.** The Lord's Prayer isn't a formula—it's a family declaration.

Day 8: When Everything Anchored

Day 8 of my first Daniel Fast. Hunger had peeled me to bone. I opened Ephesians 1: *"Having predestined us to adoption as sons by Jesus Christ to Himself, according to the good pleasure of His will"* (Ephesians 1:5). Good pleasure of His will. He wanted me. Not reluctantly. With pleasure. I tried to pray the prayer I'd mumbled my whole life: "Our Father..." Couldn't get past it. Our Father. Mine. Not just creator. Not just savior. Father. The Spirit put new language in my mouth. Not pretty prayers but belonging. Not eloquent words but "Abba, Abba, Abba." Didn't hear thunder; heard heartbeat.

Something ancient snapped. Orphan walls my grandmother built from her own abandonment. The rejection my mother inherited and passed down. The unworthiness I'd worn like skin. All cracking, falling, crumbling at the kitchen table. First time I didn't just say "Father." I felt "Abba." The revelation that changes everything: My Heavenly Father doesn't just love me. He actually likes me. Enjoys me. Delights in me. **God doesn't adopt you despite your damage. He adopts you to weaponize your testimony.** Abba is not a title—it's an invitation to crawl into the lap of the Almighty.

Progression for the Wounded

If "Abba" feels impossible today, honor your healing pace. The Spirit meets you where you are, not where you "should" be. This progression may take days, weeks, or months:

Stage 1: "God" (safest, most distant) — If father-language triggers pain or fear, begin here. "God" acknowledges His existence without demanding intimacy you're not ready for. Pray: "God, I acknowledge You. Help me know You're safe."

Stage 2: "Lord" (acknowledges authority) — When "God" feels safer, progress to "Lord." This recognizes His sovereignty without requiring vulnerability. Pray: "Lord, I submit to Your authority. Teach me You're trustworthy."

Stage 3: "Father" (relational but formal) — As healing deepens, attempt "Father." This is relational but maintains protective distance. Pray: "Father, I'm learning You're different than earthly fathers. Show me Your heart."

Stage 4: "Abba" (intimate, childlike) — When safety is established, "Abba" becomes possible. This is crawling into His lap, resting in His embrace. Pray: "Abba, Abba, Abba" until tears come or peace settles.

Adoption is legal reality before it becomes emotional experience. The papers are signed even when feelings haven't caught up. Faith leads, feelings follow. Be patient with your heart. God is.

TRAUMA SAFETY NOTE

BEFORE PROCEEDING TO BREAKING TOXIC PATTERNS DECLARATION: If you have been diagnosed with PTSD, complex trauma, dissociative disorders, or are experiencing active suicidal ideation, please pray the following declaration WITH a trained counselor, pastor, licensed therapist, or trusted spiritual mentor present. This declaration exposes deep wounds to bring healing, but trauma work is most effective and safe in supportive community. **Do not do intensive trauma processing alone.** If you're unsure whether you need support, err on the side of safety. Healing is not a race. The Spirit honors wise boundaries.

CRISIS RESOURCES: If reading this chapter has surfaced overwhelming emotions or dangerous thoughts, please reach out immediately:
- **Suicidal thoughts or self-harm urges:** 988 (Suicide & Crisis Lifeline, available 24/7)
- **Sexual assault or abuse memories:** RAINN.org or 1-800-656-HOPE (4673)
- **Domestic violence:** National Domestic Violence Hotline 1-800-799-7233
- **Immediate physical danger:** Call 911

God's healing includes professional help. Therapy isn't lack of faith—it's stewarding the temple. Medication isn't spiritual failure—it's wisdom for the journey. Asking for help isn't weakness—it's the strength to honor where you are while pursuing where you're going.

BREAKING TOXIC PATTERNS — THE COMPREHENSIVE DECLARATION

Breaking the Orphan Cycle

Before you pray the declaration, take these five preparatory steps: **(1)** Delete one app that feeds your validation addiction. **(2)** Call someone you've been performing for and tell them you're done auditioning. **(3)** Write three things you'd do if you truly believed you were chosen. **(4)** Give away something you've been hoarding from scarcity. **(5)** Forgive someone who reinforced your orphan wound.

For those repeatedly finding themselves in narcissistic, toxic relationships—orphan wounds attract predators. This declaration exposes and breaks every manifestation.

The Declaration That Breaks Every Chain

"Abba Father—My true Father, I come not as orphan begging for scraps, but as Your child breaking free from every counterfeit. The orphan wound attracted those who prey on father-hunger. The narcissist who smelled my need. The manipulator who exploited my desperation. The abuser who knew I'd mistake crumbs for feast. Your Word exposes them: *'These are the kind of people who smooth-talk themselves into the homes of unstable and needy women and take advantage of them; women who, depressed by their sinfulness, take up with every new religious fad that calls itself "truth." They get exploited every time and never really learn'* (2 Timothy 3:6-7, MSG). But today, my adoption papers are signed in blood, and I declare:

BREAKING THE ORPHAN ATTRACTION

Every Ishmael sent as counterfeit to my Isaac—exposed! Every smooth-talker exploiting my need for love—evicted! I am no longer unstable—I am anchored! I am no longer needy—I am adopted! I am no longer available for exploitation—I am protected! In Jesus' name, I declare to every toxic spirit: You have no more access! The orphan you knew is dead! In their place stands a son, a daughter of the Most High!

RELATIONAL AND IDENTITY BONDAGE I BREAK TODAY:

Toxic and narcissistic relationships that drain my soul. Unhealthy boundaries that leave me exposed. People-pleasing addiction that sacrifices identity. Codependent relationships that drain rather than empower. Promiscuity patterns searching for father-love through sexual validation. Using sex as currency for counterfeit acceptance. Confusing arousal with affection, mistaking lust for love. Serial relationships seeking the "one" who will finally choose me. Sexual addiction masking desperate search for intimacy. One-night stands hoping someone will stay. Gangs and ungodly alliances searching for belonging in darkness. Emotional unavailability passed down through generations. Isolation habits that push away genuine connection. Fear, shame, guilt, doubt that paralyze my purpose. Rejection and abandonment replaying in every relationship. Low self-esteem accepting less than I deserve. Imposter syndrome questioning my right to be here. Comparison traps fueled by social media. Perfectionism masking fear of rejection.

TRAUMA RESPONSES AND PERFORMANCE TRAPS I BREAK TODAY:

Reacting rather than responding—reliving past trauma through fear's lens. Hair-trigger anger protecting vulnerable wounds. Emotional flashbacks disguising as current conflicts. Projecting past betrayals onto present relationships. Hypervigilance exhausting every interaction. Fight, flight, freeze, fawn responses to non-threats. Sabotaging good things before they can leave. Testing people until they fulfill your prophecy of abandonment. Performance anxiety that never feels "good enough." Workaholic tendencies trying to earn worth. Over-commitment proving value through busyness. Approval addiction that makes humans my source. Religious performance that exhausts rather than empowers. Spiritual bypassing that avoids real healing. Savior mentality carrying what only Jesus can carry. Control issues rooted in abandonment fear. Victim mentality that keeps me powerless. Martyr complex that earns love through suffering.

LIES, LABELS, AND ADDICTIONS I BREAK TODAY:

"I'm too damaged to be loved." "I'm the strong one who doesn't need anybody." "I'm just the funny one, not the chosen one." "I'm only valuable when I'm useful." Labels that became prison bars: "difficult," "too much," "never enough." Limited beliefs: "People like me don't get happy endings." Inherited lies: "Our family doesn't do feelings, success, healing." Cultural curses: "Know your place," "Don't get too big." Shopping (retail therapy) filling voids with purchases. Eating (emotional eating, binging) comforting with food. Sex (promiscuity, pornography) counterfeiting intimacy. Smoking and substance dependencies numbing orphan pain. Gaming and screen addiction escaping rather than healing. Fantasy addictions avoiding real-world pain.

PHYSICAL, MENTAL, AND FINANCIAL BONDAGE I BREAK TODAY:

Sickness and chronic illness rooted in unhealed trauma. Anxiety and depression cycles untreated for generations. Eating disorders controlling what feels uncontrollable. Self-harm patterns expressing internal unworthiness. Rage and anger issues from unprocessed abandonment. Poverty mindset and generational lack passed down. Hoarding and scarcity thinking fearing future provision. Debt cycles from scarcity mindset spending. Career stagnation from fear of visibility. Dream postponing waiting for "permission" to live.

PAST TRAUMA THAT ENDS TODAY:

Rape and sexual assault that stole innocence. Incest and childhood sexual abuse that violated trust. Domestic violence that terrorized my home. Emotional abuse that destroyed my worth. Physical abuse that taught me violence was normal. Verbal abuse that planted lies about my value. Neglect and abandonment that said I wasn't wanted.

I DECLARE WITH HEAVEN'S AUTHORITY:

Today I am no longer breaking down but breaking free, breaking out, and breaking through! My past does not define me—it refines me! I'm not surviving my story—I'm signing autographs on my scars. My scars don't shame me—they showcase His glory! My wounds don't disqualify me—they qualify me for greater! My trauma doesn't define me—it refines me for testimony!

GOD'S PROMISES OVER MY LIFE:

God promises me what He promised Cyrus: *"I will go before you and make the crooked places straight; I will break in pieces the gates of bronze and cut the bars of iron. I will give you the treasures of darkness and hidden riches of secret places, that you may know that I, the Lord, who call you by your name, am the God of Israel"* (Isaiah 45:2-3). And He declares over me: *"I will make you to this people a fortified bronze wall; And they will fight against you, But they shall not prevail against you; For I am with you to save you and deliver you,' says the Lord"* (Jeremiah 15:20).

THE DIVINE REVERSAL:

The enemy thought promiscuity would mark me as used—but God calls me pure! The enemy thought my reactions would define me—but God calls me responsive! The enemy thought labels would limit me—but God calls me limitless! Every lie that said I'm disposable—destroyed! Every label that said I'm damaged—deleted! Every belief that said I'm limited—lifted! I am the bronze wall hell cannot penetrate! I am the iron bar heaven has cut through to free! I am the hidden treasure being revealed!

FINAL DECLARATION OF FREEDOM:

Every generational curse—broken! Every toxic pattern—shattered! Every orphan wound—healed! Every lie—replaced with truth! I am free from every toxic pattern! I am healed from every orphan wound! I am whole in my adoption identity! I am anchored as God's beloved child! The past no longer defines me—it refines me! Trauma no longer controls me—it testifies through me! Fear no longer paralyzes me—faith propels me! Shame no longer silences me—salvation amplifies me! I am adopted—legally, permanently, powerfully! I am loved—unconditionally, extravagantly, eternally! I am whole—spiritually, mentally, emotionally, physically! **God doesn't recycle my pain—He repurposes it for power. What the enemy meant to orphan me, God uses to anchor me.** In Jesus' mighty name, this is finished! Amen!"

Note: This declaration is comprehensive by design. The orphan spirit cannot maintain its deception when every manifestation is exposed and broken. Read it fully. Pray it boldly. Let exhaustive truth exhaust the enemy's lies. Repeat weekly during intensive healing seasons, monthly for maintenance, quarterly for renewal.

THE ADOPTION AUTHORITY PROTOCOL™
Your 5-Step Identity Transformation

STEP 1: BEHOLD Your Identity

Find the hardest photo of yourself as a child. Look that child in the eyes and say: "You were never abandoned. You were always chosen. The Father saw you in your hardest moment—whatever you were hiding, whatever you were surviving—and called you His." Write every orphan lie you've believed on paper: "I'm not enough," "I'll be abandoned," "I must earn love," "I'm too damaged to be loved," "I don't really belong." Cross each out with red ink. Write "CHOSEN" over every lie in bold letters.

STEP 2: ABIDE in Intimacy

Set timer for 5 minutes. Say only "Abba" (or appropriate progression stage: God, Lord, Father) until tears come or peace settles. No other words. Let the Spirit teach you His language. Feel the safety of a child in their father's arms. You don't have to perform. You don't have to explain. Just rest. Repeat this practice when anxiety rises, when orphan thoughts return, when you need grounding in your identity.

STEP 3: RECEIVE Your Inheritance

Text three people right now: "I need to tell you who I really am—I'm God's adopted child, and I'm learning to live like it." List what you've been begging for that you already own: Acceptance (already yours), Provision (already secured), Purpose (already written), Belonging (already granted), and Worth (already established). Declare over each: "I'm an heir, not a hireling. I receive what's already mine."

STEP 4: REFLECT His Nature

Identify one place you still operate as orphan: overworking for approval, sabotaging relationships before they can leave you, hoarding resources from scarcity, people-pleasing to earn belonging, performing to prove worth, or isolating to avoid rejection. Choose one adoption behavior to practice today: Rest instead of strive, receive instead of earn, trust instead of control, or belong instead of perform. Act like the owner's child, not the hired help.

STEP 5: REIGN in Purpose

Ask: "What would change if I truly believed I was His child?" Take one bold action from your identity—today: Walk into that room like you belong, speak in that meeting like an heir, love from overflow (not deficit), set that boundary from worth (not fear), pursue that dream from security (not desperation), or end that toxic pattern from identity (not willpower). You're not becoming His child. You are His child. Now live like it.

The Adoption Authority Protocol doesn't make you a child—it teaches you to live like one. Repeat this 5-step process monthly during the first year of identity healing, quarterly for ongoing maintenance, annually as identity renewal. Each repetition deepens the transformation.

FOCUS AREA ADOPTION PRAYERS

Choose your primary breakthrough area and declare:

For Spiritual Focus: "Father, I embrace my identity as Your beloved child in my spiritual life. I reject performance-based spirituality and receive Your unconditional acceptance. My spiritual growth flows from being Your child, not trying to become worthy. Transform my spiritual life from the security of being fully loved and accepted."

For Mental Focus: "Father, I embrace my identity as Your beloved child in my thinking. I reject mental lies about my worth and value. My thoughts are being renewed because I am Your child, fully loved regardless of my mental state. Transform my thinking from the security of being accepted, not rejected."

For Emotional Focus: "Father, I embrace my identity as Your beloved child emotionally. I reject emotional orphan thinking and receive Your parental love. My emotions are safe because I am Your child, fully secure in Your love. Heal my emotions from the foundation of being wanted, chosen, and cherished."

For Physical Focus: "Father, I embrace my identity as Your child in my physical stewardship. I reject body shame and receive Your design as good. My body is being transformed because I am Your child, created in Your image. Help me care for my body from love, not shame or performance."

For Financial Focus: "Father, I embrace my identity as Your child in my finances. I reject orphan financial thinking and receive Your provision as my Father. My finances are being transformed because I am Your child, heir to Your Kingdom. Help me manage money from abundance, not scarcity or fear."

For Relational Focus: "Father, I embrace my identity as Your child in relationships. I reject social orphan thinking and receive Your family love. My relationships are being healed because I am Your child, fully belonging. Help me love others from the overflow of being perfectly loved by You."

THE 6-DIMENSIONAL ADOPTION ACTIVATION

DIMENSION	PRACTICE	EVIDENCE
SPIRITUAL	Every morning declare "I am God's anchored child" 7 times	Orphan thoughts decrease, Kingdom confidence increases
MENTAL	List where you're auditioning. Write "ADOPTED & ANCHORED"	Performance pressure yields to identity security
EMOTIONAL	When anxiety rises, whisper "Abba" until peace returns	Fear's grip loosens as identity truth tightens
PHYSICAL	Adjust posture. Shoulders back. You represent the King	Physical bearing reflects spiritual identity
FINANCIAL	Before decisions ask, "How does an anchored heir steward?"	Scarcity thinking transforms to abundance reality
RELATIONAL	Treat believers as siblings, not competition	Kingdom family manifests, rivalry dies

Adoption isn't doctrine to believe—it's identity to embody. Practice these six dimensions daily for 21 days during the fast, continue weekly for identity establishment, maintain monthly for ongoing transformation.

MONTHLY ADOPTION IDENTITY SCORECARD

Track your progress monthly to identify growth areas and celebrate transformation:

Operating FROM Love vs. FOR Love: ___/10
(10 = Consistently rest in acceptance; 1 = Constantly performing for approval)

Celebrating vs. Competing: ___/10
(10 = Genuinely celebrate others' success; 1 = Threatened by others' advancement)

Sharing vs. Hoarding: ___/10
(10 = Generous from abundance mindset; 1 = Hoarding from scarcity fear)

Building Kingdom vs. Personal Security: ___/10
(10 = Focus on Father's Kingdom; 1 = Building personal security systems)

Receiving Correction: ___/10
(10 = Grateful for development; 1 = Defensive, seeing rejection)

Total Score: ___/50

0-20: Intensive adoption healing needed. Pray Breaking Toxic Patterns weekly. Practice Adoption Authority Protocol bi-weekly. **21-35:** Active transformation in progress. Continue monthly protocols. Seek pastoral support for stuck areas. **36-50:** Established adoption identity. Maintain quarterly check-ins. You're ready to help others discover their adoption.

Compare scores monthly. Celebrate every increase—transformation is progressive, not instant. If scores decrease, review where orphan thinking has returned. Repeat protocols without shame. Healing isn't linear.

THE PROPHETIC ACT: MIRROR DECLARATION

Find a mirror. Look yourself in the eyes. Hand over heart. Speak with authority:

"I am not orphan. Not slave. I am son, I am daughter of Most High God. My adoption: Legal in heaven's court. Permanent despite performance. Powerful over opposition. Personal to Father's heart. I don't work for acceptance—I work from it. Last name: Loved. Inheritance: Assured. Identity: Anchored!"

Write today's date on mirror with dry erase marker. Mark when identity shifted from orphan to heir. Every time you see this date, remember: This is when everything changed. Return to this mirror monthly for the first year, quarterly thereafter, to renew your declaration and update your date if deeper transformation occurs.

BREAKTHROUGH PRAYER

"Father—Abba—Daddy, thank You for wanting me before I wanted You. Thank You that my adoption was Your good pleasure. Today I declare with every orphan who's found their Father: 'It stops with me and starts through me!' The generational patterns that marked my bloodline—stop with me! The father-wounds that plagued my family—heal through me! The orphan spirit that haunted my ancestors—ends in me! When I pray 'Our Father,' generational chains shatter! When I whisper 'Abba,' orphans find home! When I walk anchored, atmospheres shift!

I am the chain-breaker in my family line. I am the cycle-blocker for future generations. I am the curse-stopper heaven has positioned. What began in brokenness becomes breakthrough. What started in lack becomes legacy. What felt like ending becomes new beginning. My adoption is my authority. My inheritance is intimacy. My destiny is glory. In Jesus' name—my Brother, my Lord, my Identity! Amen."

THE DANIEL FAST: CLOSING THE GAP!

CLOSING — FROM ORPHANED TO ORDAINED

Day 8 complete. The orphan woke at 4:30 AM. The heir goes to sleep tonight. The child who once believed the lies is becoming the adult who declares the truth. The one who colored over poverty is now painting future with promise. The paper airplane prayer you sent—whatever it said, wherever you were—has landed in heaven's courts. Your vow "It stops with me" is manifest. You're not auditioning anymore. You've arrived. You're not hoping for acceptance. You're operating from it. You're not an orphan working for bread. You're an heir who owns the bakery.

The orphan spirit that marked your bloodline for generations just met its match—a child of God who knows their identity. What plagued your family tree for decades ends today. What wounded your ancestors heals in you. The chain breaks. The cycle stops. The curse lifts. Tomorrow, abundance awaits. But not the prosperity gospel's counterfeit. Tomorrow you'll discover what the elder brother never accessed—that "all I have is yours" isn't future promise but present reality. You'll learn why orphans count pennies while heirs sign checks. Why slaves ration bread while children own bakeries. Day 9 will teach you to stop living like you're borrowing from God's wealth when you're actually managing it.

Orphans change locations. Sons and daughters change atmospheres—and bloodlines. You entered Day 8 as an orphan. You exit as an heir. Tomorrow, you'll learn what you've inherited.

SOAP JOURNAL — DAY 8

S (Scripture): Which adoption verse anchored your identity today? Write it and personalize it.
O (Observation): Where have you been living as orphan instead of heir? What orphan behaviors did you recognize?
A (Application): What changes when you live as God's anchored child? What will you do differently tomorrow?
P (Prayer): "Abba, as Your adopted child, I anchor my _____ in heaven's view of me."

Today's Breakthrough Marker: What shifted from orphan thinking to adoption reality?
Tomorrow's Expectation: Now that you know you're His child, what inheritance will you access?

ORPHAN EVICTED. ADOPTION ACTIVATED. READY FOR ABUNDANCE.

Welcome to adoption. Welcome to identity. Welcome to family.

DAY 9 — ABUNDANCE

From Scarcity to Overflow: Living as Heaven's Treasurer

> *"And my God shall supply all your need according to His riches in glory by Christ Jesus."* — Philippians 4:19

WEEK 2 — ALIGN: Establishing Your Kingdom Identity

Day 9 of 21. Yesterday's Adoption anchored you as heir. Today's Abundance reveals what you've inherited—not prosperity gospel's counterfeit, but Kingdom economics where orphans become owners.

ENCOUNTER — WHERE YOU ARE

The calculator doesn't lie. 3:17 AM. Day 9. Kitchen tiles ice-cold beneath bare feet, but sweat pools at the base of your spine anyway. The pre-dawn air carries the smell of stale coffee and yesterday's desperation. Red LCD numbers glow like accusations in the dark—overdraft, three-day notice, disconnect warning. The bills spread across scratched wood feel rough-edged from repeated handling, curled at the corners from the oil of your palms checking, recounting, recalculating the same impossible math. Coffee from six hours ago sits cold in a chipped mug, bitter film coating the surface like your thoughts. The spoon still in it. Unmoved. Like your situation. The envelope edges are soft from sweaty palms opening them repeatedly, as if the amount owed might decrease with enough prayer, enough staring, enough willing the numbers to change. Need thousands by Friday. Have maybe hundreds.

Your stomach is hollow—ninth-day hunger gnawing. Physical hunger has become portal to spiritual revelation. The emptiness that started as discomfort has transformed into clarity. But there's another hunger now. Older. Deeper. The kind that makes you check your bank balance at 3 AM like checking for a pulse. The same math that broke your grandmother counting coins in the dark. The same equation that made your mother apologize for taking up space. The same deficit that convinced your bloodline that poverty was prophecy, not circumstance. Your hands shake as you sort the bills—not from cold, though your feet are ice against tile. From the particular tremor that comes when your body knows what your mind won't admit: You can't make this math work. No matter how many times you recalculate.

Yesterday's adoption papers are still warm from heaven's printer. You're somebody's child now. Legal heir. Family. But what good is adoption without accessing the family wealth? Like having keys to a mansion but sleeping on the porch because you're afraid to track poverty inside. Like being named in the will but living on welfare. Like having a Father who owns everything but believing you own nothing. The calculator says you're broke. Your adoption papers say you're rich. Both can't be true.

That's when heaven whispers what hell prays you'll never hear: **"Orphans count what they have. Heirs count on Who they have."** Day 8's adoption wasn't just legal status—it was vault access. Father signed your papers in blood. He didn't just give you His name. He gave you His accounts. Yesterday you discovered you're an heir. Today you learn what heirs inherit—not just blessings, but resources. Not provision, but overflow. Not enough, but more than enough. The elder brother's tragedy mirrors yours: *"Son, you are always with me, and all that I have is yours"* (Luke 15:31). In the house. Access to everything. Using nothing. Adoption positioned you. Abundance activates you. Your identity unlocks your inheritance. Who you are determines what you access. Heirs don't beg—they withdraw.

Today, the poverty spirit haunting your bloodline dies. **Abundance isn't about what's in your account—it's about whose account you access.** The enemy's first lie was about provision: "God's holding out on you."

FOUNDATION — THE ORPHAN WOUND CREATES SCARCITY

When Lack Became Your Logic

Watch the enemy's unchanged strategy since Eden. First, attack identity: "Did God really say you're His?" Then, attack provision: "There's not enough. Better grab yours." Eden had perfect provision, unlimited abundance, every tree but one. Then came the lie: "God's holding out on you." Suddenly abundance felt like lack. Fear entered paradise. Hoarding began. Cain and Abel—one offering accepted, one rejected. Cain's orphan mind calculated: "If God loves him, less for me." First murder born from scarcity thinking. Joseph's brothers concluded "Father loves him more." Scarcity of affection led them to sell him into slavery. Orphan math always concludes that someone else's blessing equals my loss. Children without fathers are five times more likely to live in poverty. Not just financial poverty—poverty of spirit, identity, possibility. **God's economy: multiply, increase, overflow. The enemy's economy: subtract, divide, conquer.**

The Mathematics of Scarcity

Scarcity taught you its math before you learned to count. Not enough food—eat fast. Not enough love—earn hard. Not enough safety—control everything. Not enough became your operating system. Scarcity math says five loaves plus two fish divided by five thousand people equals impossible. Kingdom math operates differently. Five loaves plus two fish plus Jesus equals twelve baskets leftover. Widow's oil plus prophet's word equals debt cancelled and future secured. Nothing plus God's command equals universe exists. **Scarcity counts what's visible. Abundance counts on Who's invisible.**

The Poverty Spirit Manifests

The poverty spirit isn't just about money—it's mindset. It manifests as apologizing for taking space, inability to receive compliments or gifts, hoarding relationships from fear of abandonment, not using good dishes while waiting for special occasions that never come, and dying with dreams wrapped in someday paper. The orphan wound whispers ancient poison: Never enough, grab what you can. Others' gain is your loss. Hoard to survive. Accept average as adequate. Settle for crumbs. **Poverty spirit convinces you to live like a guest in your own life.**

THE DIFFERENCE: ORPHAN SCARCITY VS HEIR ABUNDANCE

Before we go further, hold up the mirror. Which column describes you?

ORPHAN SCARCITY	HEIR ABUNDANCE
Hoards resources	Shares freely—Father has more
Compares constantly	Celebrates others' increase
Grieves losses deeply	Releases easily—Father replaces
Gives reluctantly	Gives joyfully—creates flow
Works anxiously	Works peacefully—managing inheritance

Measures by bank accounts	Measures by relationship
Says "I can't afford..."	Says "My Father owns..."
Fears others' success	Rejoices in others' success
Operates from lack	Operates from overflow
Lives in competition	Lives in collaboration

Scarcity asks "What if I run out?" Abundance asks "What if God shows off?" Orphans clutch. Heirs circulate. Orphans protect. Heirs provide. If you saw yourself in the orphan column, don't despair. Recognition is the first step to transformation. Yesterday's adoption began changing your identity. Today's abundance rewires your thinking.

TESTIMONY — WHEN TWENTY DOLLARS BECAME TRAINING GROUND

The Sky Juice Vendor's Daughter

Jamaica. 1985. Thirteen years old. Every Saturday, my sister and I would take the bus downtown Kingston to my father's sky juice cart. Hours standing in sun that felt like judgment—that particular Caribbean heat that doesn't just warm your skin but weighs on your shoulders like expectation. The concrete radiated yesterday's heat back up through worn shoes. Watching him shave ice for customers while we waited for acknowledgment that cost more than money. The routine never changed. End of his selling day, he'd hand us stale bun from morning's batch and twenty dollars. Always twenty. Never more. Like our worth had a ceiling made of two tens. The bun was hard, edges dried from sitting in sun all day. We'd eat it on the bus home, pretending it was fresh. Pretending the twenty dollars was enough.

Bus fare home ate into the twenty immediately. We'd hand my mother what remained—usually fifteen dollars, sometimes twelve. I'd watch her face fall, that specific kind of fall that happens when hope meets reality. She'd get discouraged, sometimes angry she'd sent us into the heat for such meager provision. Then she'd do what she always did. She'd pray. Psalms mostly, crying them out like they were legal documents: "Lord, multiply! Increase! Make ends meet!" She was a seamstress, so her prayers got specific: "Send neighbors with clothes to alter. Repairs with deposits. Quick turnaround jobs. Anything, Lord."

One weekend, down to our last twenty dollars. Five people. Two weeks ahead. The math was cruel: Twenty dollars divided by five people divided by fourteen days equals impossible. Mom prayed over that money like Hannah prayed over Samuel: "God, multiply this like loaves and fish." Next morning, she checked a jacket pocket she'd already searched twice. Empty. Checked again an hour later—twenty dollars. The money wasn't there, then it was. We were overjoyed. That twenty felt like two hundred. Like God had heard a seamstress's Psalms and answered in currency we could count. **When you're managing lack, God is planning abundance.** But poverty teaches survival, not thriving. Make do, not make ways. Expect just enough, never more than enough. **I inked the holes in my shoes; God filled the holes in my story.** The girl who stood in Kingston sun for stale bun now serves fresh bread to nations.

The Kitchen Table at 3 AM

My kitchen table. Calculator in one hand, stack of bills spread like indictments across scratched wood. The calculator's LCD screen flickered—even it was tired of displaying negative numbers. Checking account deep red. Business account empty. Credit cards maxed. Red ink on bank statements looked like blood. Need thousands by Friday. Have access to maybe hundreds. Disconnect notice from electric company. Three-day eviction warning on the door. The house so quiet I could hear my own heartbeat counting down to disaster. My prayer turns bitter: "God, You said You'd supply all my needs. You promised. Where are You?" Silence. The kind that amplifies the hum of the refrigerator, the tick of the clock, the sound of your own breathing when you're drowning on dry land.

Then—"When will you stop telling Me what you need and start asking what you have?" I almost laugh. The sound catches in my throat. "Lord, I have nothing. Look at this red ink. These notices. This nothing." "Check again. Use My accounting system." Angry now, I grab my journal. Fine. Let's inventory nothing.

Earth's Inventory (what my eyes see): Debt drowning me daily, disconnection notices mocking me, faith dwindling to fumes, friends exhausted by my crisis, body breaking from stress, hope dying by the hour. The pen keeps moving without my permission. **Heaven's Inventory** (what faith sees): Father who owns cattle on thousand hills, inheritance that can't be stolen or foreclosed, same Spirit that raised Christ from death living in me, divine power for abundant life (2 Peter 1:3), access to wisdom worth more than gold, authority that transcends earthly systems, family of believers spanning globe, promises that cannot fail.

I stare at both lists through tears that blur the ink. Same situation. Two accounting systems. One counts from earth's visible economy—subtraction, division, limitation, death. The other counts from heaven's invisible economy—addition, multiplication, overflow, life. The revelation hits like lightning: **I'd been trying to pay heaven's bills with earth's currency.** Abundance isn't about your balance. It's about your bloodline. **Scarcity is an orphan counting coins. Abundance is an heir accessing inheritance.**

The Give That Exposed My Orphan Math

Three days later. Still swimming in red. But operating from heir mathematics—though my hands shake. "Lord, what do You want me to do with what I have?" His response seems cruel: "Give to Sarah." Sarah. Single mom from church. Multiple kids. Multiple jobs. Drowning deeper than me. "Give what? I'm in overdraft!" But Luke 6:38 rises in my spirit: *"Give, and it will be given to you: good measure, pressed down, shaken together, and running over."* My hand trembles writing a check from an overdrawn account. The pen feels heavy. A note: "God said this belongs to you. He sees you." I drive to her apartment. Slip it under door. Run before logic catches up.

Two hours later, my phone vibrates. Unknown number. Probably a creditor. My stomach drops. "Hi, this is follow-up from the presentation you did a few weeks back. We've been trying to reach you. We're ready to move forward on that project. Can we wire the deposit today?" The room tilts. I grip the table edge, knuckles white. "What... what did you say?" He repeats the amount. Slowly. It's everything I need. Plus extra. Plus blessing I didn't even know to ask for. Plus interest on obedience. I can't speak. Can't breathe. Can only slide down the kitchen cabinet to the ice-cold floor—the same floor I stood on two hours ago writing that check—and weep.

That evening Sarah texts through tears: "That was the exact amount I needed for groceries and gas to get to work. I had nothing left. Prayed for exactly this. How did you know?" I didn't. But our Father did. Within weeks, forgotten refunds arrived in mail, new clients appeared from connections we'd forgotten, billing errors discovered in my favor, old debts forgave themselves without explanation. Not because I gave—this isn't prosperity formula. It was a posture shift. I was learning to be a vessel, not a vault. Empty vessels get filled. Closed fists can't receive. **God specializes in turning red ink into black bottom lines—and average living into extravagant life.**

The Platinum Package That Broke My Poverty Mindset

Started business from shoestring. Between contracts, coach clients—book publishing, websites, branding. But I undervalued everything. Discounted before they asked. Always recommended bronze or silver. Never dared mention platinum. One day, a client asked: "How much would you really charge—your best package?" "You mean my platinum package?" The words almost choke coming out. The one I never mention, created but never offered, priced but never proposed. "Yes. Send me your best." I sent the proposal. Five figures. Comma in the amount. Finger hovering over delete before hitting send. Heart pounding. Convinced he'd laugh or ghost me. He paid. In full. Without negotiating.

I stared at payment confirmation for ten full minutes. Nearly called to say there'd been an error. Almost offered discount he didn't ask for. My hands already typing the apology email: "I think there's been a misunderstanding..." My husband saw me typing. Read over my shoulder. Closed my laptop with deliberate finality. "You're. Not. Her. Anymore." Four words. Poverty's obituary. You're not that girl standing in Kingston sun for twenty dollars. You're not that woman whose calculator bled red. You're not that entrepreneur apologizing for worth.

That night, after the client paid in full, I sat with my laptop closed—my husband's hand still resting on the lid as if to prevent me from reopening it and apologizing. For two hours we sat there. Silent mostly. Me wrestling with voices. **Orphan voice:** "Call him back. There's been a mistake. You're not worth that. He'll discover you're a fraud." **Heir voice:** "This is what you're worth because of Whose you are. This isn't about you being special—it's about Father's resources flowing through you."

I opened my journal—the same one with that paper airplane prayer from Jamaica. Flipped to a blank page. Wrote two columns: **What Orphan Math Says:** "I don't deserve this. People like me don't charge this much. I should discount it. What if he regrets it?" **What Heir Math Says:** "Father determines my worth, not my past. I don't apologize for overflow—I steward it. This provision funds Kingdom advancement, not just my account." I read both columns to my husband. He pointed to the heir column: "That's who you are now. Stop arguing with your identity."

The war wasn't over. But the battle was won. I was learning to be not just adopted (Day 8) but abundant. Holy Spirit thundered through the silence: "Daughter, you insult Me when you call My provision 'too much.' You are not a beggar at My table. You are an heir dispensing My resources." That night I realized: I'd learned to be adopted but not abundant. Called myself heir but lived like hired help. Had title, not mindset. **Abundance isn't about deserve—it's about design. You were designed to overflow.**

REVELATION — THE LANGUAGE AND LAWS OF KINGDOM ABUNDANCE

What Heaven Calls It: The Biblical Definition

When Heaven speaks abundance, it doesn't whisper—it roars through ancient tongues with words that explode scarcity's lies.

The Hebrew Shout:

Shapha' (shah-FAH) means gushing forth, overflowing, pouring out until drenched in provision. *"They will feast on the abundance of the seas"* (Deuteronomy 33:19). That twenty dollars in Jamaica? God was teaching me about gushing forth. I just didn't have vocabulary yet. **Rov** (rove) means multitude. Not one blessing but legions. An army of provision marching toward you. *"The Lord will grant you plenty of goods"* (Deuteronomy 28:11). **Seba'** (SEH-bah) means satisfaction, fullness, more than enough. Filled where you push back from the table. *"They are abundantly satisfied with the fullness of Your house"* (Psalm 36:8). **Tov** (tove) means goodness, bounty. Overflowing goodness exceeding expectations. *"Oh, how great is Your goodness, which You have laid up for those who fear You"* (Psalm 31:19). Laid up. Stored. Waiting. Your name on it.

The Greek Explosion:

Perisseuō (per-is-SYOO-oh) means to overflow, excel, exceed, abound. Jesus used this: *"I have come that they may have life, and that they may have it more abundantly"* (John 10:10). The kitchen table covered in bills? God was orchestrating overflow. **Perissos** (per-is-SOS) means exceeding, beyond, more than enough. *"Now to Him who is able to do exceedingly abundantly above all that we ask or think"* (Ephesians 3:20). My mother's seamstress prayers? She was unknowingly invoking exceedingly abundantly above. **Plērōma** (PLAY-roh-mah) means fullness, completeness. God's nature poured into finite vessels. *"And of His fullness we have all received, and grace for grace"* (John 1:16). Grace upon grace. Not grace then waiting. Grace stacked on grace. **Hyperekperissou** (hoo-per-ek-per-is-SOO) means beyond superabundant, infinitely more than overflowing. When Greek runs out of words, it stacks prefixes: hyper-ek-perissos. Beyond beyond beyond.

Biblical abundance is the roar of God's inexhaustible nature crashing through every dimension of your life, drowning scarcity, flooding need, and overflowing through you to drench a thirsty world with His goodness. You're trying to generate what you're meant to inherit.

How It Functions: Five Kingdom Realities of Abundance

1. God-Sourced, Not Self-Generated

Abundance doesn't come from you—it flows through you. *"Every good gift and every perfect gift is from above"* (James 1:17). You're not the fountain—you're the faucet. He's the reservoir. His supply never runs dry. Stop trying to generate what you're meant to receive.

2. Overflow-Oriented, Not Minimum Provision

God doesn't do just enough. *"Now to Him who is able to do exceedingly abundantly above all that we ask or think"* (Ephesians 3:20). Exceedingly. Abundantly. Above. All. *"Give, and it will be given to you: good measure, pressed down, shaken together, and running over"* (Luke 6:38). Pressed down. Shaken together. Running over. Not calculation—celebration.

3. Holistic-Dimensional, Not Just Material

Abundance invades every area. **Spiritually:** *"Grace for grace"* (John 1:16)—stacked blessings. **Emotionally:** *"Joy unspeakable and full of glory"* (1 Peter 1:8)—overflow joy. **Physically:** *"I pray that you may prosper in all things and be in health"* (3 John 1:2). **Materially:** *"God is able to make all grace abound toward you, that you, always having all sufficiency in all things, may have an abundance for every good work"* (2 Corinthians 9:8). You're not partially blessed—you're abundantly blessed in all dimensions.

4. Purpose-Driven, Not Possession-Focused

God's abundance always has mission: *"I will bless you... and you shall be a blessing"* (Genesis 12:2). Not blessed to hoard. Blessed to overflow. River flows through you—not just to you. You're not reservoir storing—you're conduit releasing Heaven's resources. Your overflow funds someone else's breakthrough.

5. Eternally-Anchored, Not Temporally Limited

Ultimate abundance isn't a thing—it's a person: *"For in Him dwells all the fullness of the Godhead bodily; and you are complete in Him"* (Colossians 2:9-10). All fullness. Jesus is abundance embodied. Eternity? *"And he showed me a pure river of water of life, clear as crystal, proceeding from the throne of God and of the Lamb"* (Revelation 22:1). River. Not stream. River of life. Flowing forever.

The Abundance That Flows From Yesterday's Adoption

Abundance is about access, not amount. An orphan with millions still lives in scarcity because they might lose it. An heir with nothing—even in overdraft—lives in abundance because their Father can't go bankrupt. Watch the Trinity at work. The Father owns everything—*"The earth is the Lord's, and all its fullness"* (Psalm 24:1). The Son purchased your access—His blood seated you in heavenly places with unlimited account access. *"For you know the grace of our Lord Jesus Christ, that though He was rich, yet for your sakes He became poor, that you through His poverty might become rich"* (2 Corinthians 8:9). The Spirit empowers your stewardship—He gives wisdom to manage, courage to give, discernment to invest. Your abundance required the entire Godhead. Father provided resources. Son provided access. Spirit provides wisdom to steward.

Biblical abundance flows from identity, not activity: *"Blessed be the God and Father of our Lord Jesus Christ, who has blessed us with every spiritual blessing in the heavenly places in Christ"* (Ephesians 1:3). Has blessed. Past tense. Already done. Already deposited. Already available. This isn't prosperity gospel. It's position gospel. You're not trying to get God to bless you. You're learning to access what adoption already included. **The difference between rich and abundant is the difference between having and belonging.**

CRITICAL DISTINCTION: THIS IS NOT PROSPERITY GOSPEL

Prosperity gospel says: "Give to get, confess to possess, faith equals wealth." That's manipulation. **Biblical abundance says:** "You're an heir with access to Father's resources for Kingdom purposes." **The difference?** Prosperity gospel focuses on YOUR wealth accumulation. Kingdom abundance focuses on FATHER's resources flowing THROUGH you for mission. You're not getting rich for yourself—you're becoming rich toward God for distribution. If your "abundance" teaching leads to greed, hoarding, or entitlement, it's not Kingdom economics—it's religious manipulation. God blesses you not so you can have more, but so others can have enough. **You're a river, not a reservoir. A conduit, not a vault.**

PASTORAL NOTES FOR DIFFERENT ECONOMIC SITUATIONS

For Those in Extreme Poverty:

If you're facing immediate survival crisis—homeless, hungry, without basic needs—this chapter's principles still apply, but the APPLICATION differs. Your first step isn't "open a Kingdom Overflow account." It's: **(1)** Seek immediate help (food banks, churches, social services). **(2)** Let community function as body (others' overflow becomes your provision). **(3)** Receive without shame (that's heir thinking too). **(4)** Trust Father's provision may come through unexpected channels today. Stewardship looks different at different levels. Someone managing millions stewards differently than someone needing meals. Both are heirs. Both have Father's resources. The access point differs.

For Those With Financial Abundance Already:

Your challenge isn't believing Father has resources—you're already experiencing that. Your challenge is: Are you a reservoir (storing) or a river (flowing)? Wealth makes excellent servant, terrible master. **Test:** Does your abundance fund Kingdom or just comfort? Does it liberate others or just you? Father gave you overflow not so you'd have more—so others would have enough. You're not blessed to hoard. You're resourced to release. The more you have, the more you're accountable to steward for Kingdom advancement, not personal empire building.

BIBLICAL PATTERNS — WHEN HEAVEN BREAKS MATH

TIER 1: Four Full Witnesses

The Widow's Oil — When Empty Became Endless (2 Kings 4:1-7)

"'What do you have in the house?' And she said, 'Your maidservant has nothing in the house but a jar of oil.'" The knock at her door wasn't opportunity—it was judgment. Creditor coming for her sons. Debt collectors threatening slavery. One jar of oil remains—all that stands between her and absolute destitution. She finds the prophet Elisha, desperation dripping from every word. His instruction mocks her crisis: *"Borrow vessels—empty vessels; do not gather just a few"* (2 Kings 4:3). Borrow containers? She can't fill the one she has. But desperation makes you obedient. She goes door to door. Neighbors see her coming—the widow collecting empty jars. They whisper. She hears them. Doesn't care. Brings home every empty vessel she can carry.

She shuts the door. Just her and her sons and a room full of empty promises. Pours from her almost-empty jar into the first borrowed vessel. Oil flows. Keeps flowing. Fills it completely. She reaches for another, hands shaking. Still flowing. A third vessel. The oil keeps coming. Fourth, fifth, tenth, twentieth vessel—oil pouring like a river from a jar that should have been empty three vessels ago. *"Now it came to pass, when the vessels were full, that she said to her son, 'Bring me another vessel.' And he said to her, 'There is not another vessel.' So the oil ceased"* (2 Kings 4:6). The oil didn't stop because the jar ran dry. It stopped because she ran out of containers. Her problem wasn't lack of oil. It was lack of containers for God's provision. Heaven had more. She had no more capacity to receive it. She sells the oil. Pays the debt. Lives on the rest. One jar became freedom. **Your emptiness is just abundance waiting for instructions. God's provision doesn't run out—your capacity to receive it does.**

Peter's Miraculous Catch — When Obedience Trumped Expertise (Luke 5:1-11)

Peter wipes sweat and fish scales from his brow. All night. Professional fishermen. Zero fish. His nets are clean now—washed, mended, ready for storage. Dawn breaking. Exhaustion settling into bones. Then Jesus: *"Launch out into the deep and let down your nets for a catch"* (Luke 5:4). Peter's jaw tightens. He knows three things with absolute certainty. Wrong time—fish bite at night, not morning. Wrong place—

fish stay shallow during day. Wrong person giving instructions—Jesus was a carpenter, not a fisherman. Peter's experience screams: This won't work. His exhaustion whispers: You've already tried. His pride yells: Don't let a carpenter tell you how to fish.

"Master," Peter says, choosing words carefully, "we have toiled all night and caught nothing" (Luke 5:5). Translation: We're professionals. We've already tried. The fish aren't biting. It's pointless. Jesus waits. Doesn't argue with his expertise. Just stands there with that look that says: Trust Me anyway. Peter exhales slowly. "Nevertheless," Peter finally says, the word like an anchor being lifted from deep water, "at Your word I will." Nevertheless. Despite my experience. Despite the wrong time and wrong place. Despite my expertise saying this is pointless. At Your word—not because it makes sense, but because You said it.

They row out. Deep water. Morning sun making the surface shimmer. Peter throws the net. Immediately—not after time, not after effort—immediately the net strains. Fish. Everywhere. So many the net starts tearing. The sound of fibers splitting. The catch is so heavy both boats start sinking. Water sloshing over the sides. Professional fishermen calling for help from a catch they almost didn't take. Because a carpenter told them to fish. Peter looks at the fish, at the sinking boat, at Jesus standing calm in the chaos. Falls to his knees in a boat full of fish: *"Depart from me, for I am a sinful man, O Lord!"* (Luke 5:8). Jesus smiles: *"Do not be afraid. From now on you will catch men"* (Luke 5:10). **When Jesus gives instructions that contradict your expertise, your expertise is about to be upgraded.**

The Widow at Zarephath — When Surrender Releases Flow (1 Kings 17:8-16)

"Then the word of the Lord came to him, saying, 'Arise, go to Zarephath, which belongs to Sidon, and dwell there. See, I have commanded a widow there to provide for you.'" Severe famine. Three years without rain. Elijah needs provision. God sends him to a widow—not a wealthy merchant, not a king, but a widow in a foreign land who's also starving. When Elijah arrives at the city gate, he finds her gathering sticks. Bent over. Slow. The movements of someone whose body has learned to conserve energy because there's no food to replace it. "Please bring me a little water in a cup, that I may drink," Elijah calls out (1 Kings 17:10). She nods. Water she can give. She turns to go. Then he adds: *"Please bring me a morsel of bread in your hand"* (1 Kings 17:11).

She stops. Turns back slowly. Looks at this prophet with eyes that have already made peace with death. *"As the Lord your God lives,"* she says—even now, even dying, she acknowledges his God—*"I do not have bread, only a handful of flour in a bin, and a little oil in a jar; and see, I am gathering a couple of sticks that I may go in and prepare it for myself and my son, that we may eat it, and die"* (1 Kings 17:12). Last meal. Last handful. She's literally gathering wood for her final fire. Two sticks. Just enough to cook one last time.

Elijah doesn't flinch: *"Do not fear; go and do as you have said, but make me a small cake from it first, and bring it to me; and afterward make some for yourself and your son. For thus says the Lord God of Israel: 'The bin of flour shall not be used up, nor shall the jar of oil run dry, until the day the Lord sends rain on the earth'"* (1 Kings 17:13-14). Give from your emptiness. Serve from your insufficiency. Release your last before your first. She stands there. Sticks in hand. Every logical reason to refuse scrolling through her mind. But she looks at him. This prophet. This stranger. This impossible request. Something in his eyes. Something in the way he says "Do not fear." She makes the most courageous decision of her life. She goes home. Takes her handful of flour.

Takes her drop of oil. Makes him a cake first. Brings it to him. Hands shaking. Heart pounding. Every instinct screaming. But she does it.

Tomorrow comes. She checks the flour bin—still flour. Not a lot. Just there. Enough for today. The oil jar—still oil. Not overflowing. Not excessive. Just enough. Next day, same thing. And the next. And the next. *"So she went away and did according to the word of Elijah; and she and he and her household ate for many days. The bin of flour was not used up, nor did the jar of oil run dry, according to the word of the Lord which He spoke by Elijah"* (1 Kings 17:15-16). Daily provision. Never depleted. Never overflowing into excess—just enough for today, every day, for years. Until the rain came. **Scarcity says, "I don't have enough to give." Faith says, "If I release it, God will multiply it." Abundance begins where surrender feels impossible.**

Feeding of the 5,000 — When Little Became Legacy (John 6:1-13)

"There is a lad here who has five barley loaves and two small fish, but what are they among so many?" (John 6:9). Over five thousand hungry men, plus women and children. Potentially fifteen to twenty thousand people. The sun setting. No food. Panic rising. Andrew finds a boy with lunch: five barley loaves—poor man's bread, the cheapest grain. Two small fish—probably sardines, a child's portion. The math is insulting: five loaves divided by fifteen thousand people equals .0003 loaves per person. The boy could have hidden his lunch, clutched it to his chest, reasoned that it wouldn't make a difference anyway. Five loaves won't feed five thousand. Why bother? Instead, he placed his insignificance into Jesus' hands.

"And Jesus took the loaves, and when He had given thanks He distributed them to the disciples, and the disciples to those sitting down; and likewise of the fish, as much as they wanted" (John 6:11). Everyone ate until full—not barely satisfied, but completely full. Bellies stretched. Appetites satisfied. Then the kicker: *"Therefore they gathered them up, and filled twelve baskets with the fragments of the five barley loaves which were left over by those who had eaten"* (John 6:13). Twelve baskets. One for each disciple. More left over than what they started with. Heaven's math always includes remainder—pressed down, shaken together, running over. **Abundance isn't about the size of your seed—it's about Who you give it to. What looks insufficient in your hands becomes more than enough in His.**

TIER 2: Six Grouped Witnesses

Provision in Famine

Isaac sowed during famine and *"reaped in the same year a hundredfold; and the Lord blessed him"* (Genesis 26:12). While neighbors fled to Egypt, Isaac planted in obedience. Same year. Hundredfold return. The famine didn't stop—but it couldn't stop God's blessing. Joseph in Egypt interpreted Pharaoh's dream: seven years abundance, seven years famine (Genesis 41:1-57). Wisdom to store during overflow saved nations. Kingdom abundance today prepares you for Kingdom assignment tomorrow. **Scarcity sees the drought. Abundance sees the Designer of the drought—and plants anyway.** Divine blessing doesn't wait for perfect conditions—it creates them.

Creative Provision Methods

God supplied daily bread for forty years—14,600 consecutive days (Exodus 16:1-36). Those who hoarded found it rotting. Those who trusted never lacked. Elijah's ravens—unclean birds bringing kosher meals twice daily during drought (1 Kings 17:1-7). When you position yourself in obedience, God redirects creation itself to provision you. Jesus' first miracle: 120-180 gallons of the best wine when they ran out

(John 2:1-11). Not just enough—extravagant and excellent. Kingdom abundance doesn't just solve the problem—it throws a party. **God's provision isn't limited to one method. Sometimes oil multiplies. Sometimes bread falls from heaven. Sometimes ravens deliver meals. The method changes, but the Provider never does.**

Restoration and Realignment

After resurrection, 153 large fish filled the nets (John 21:1-14). Provision confirming purpose. Jesus recommissioning Peter. Abundance is God's way of saying: You're back in My will. Now get back to work. Ten different stories. Ten different methods. One unchanging Provider.

FIVE PROVISION CHANNELS: HOW GOD'S PROVISION SHOWS UP

Biblical patterns reveal a crucial truth: God's provision isn't limited to one method. Watch for these five primary channels through which heaven delivers:

1. Wisdom — Million-dollar ideas during prayer. Strategies in shower. Solutions in sleep. One divine download changes financial destiny. *"If any of you lacks wisdom, let him ask of God, who gives to all liberally and without reproach, and it will be given to him"* (James 1:5).

2. Work — Unexpected offers. Overtime opportunities. Clients appearing from nowhere. Promotions you didn't seek. Favor that defies explanation. *"And whatever you do, do it heartily, as to the Lord and not to men, knowing that from the Lord you will receive the reward of the inheritance"* (Colossians 3:23-24).

3. Community — Shared resources. "Coincidental" gifts arriving exactly when needed. Practical help from unexpected sources. The body of Christ functioning as family. *"Now all who believed were together, and had all things in common, and sold their possessions and goods, and divided them among all, as anyone had need"* (Acts 2:44-45).

4. Miracle — The unexplainable check. The "glitch" in your favor. Debt mysteriously forgiven. Windfall from nowhere. Sometimes God just shows off. *"Now to Him who is able to do exceedingly abundantly above all that we ask or think, according to the power that works in us"* (Ephesians 3:20).

5. Seed & Bread — *"Now may He who supplies seed to the sower, and bread for food, supply and multiply the seed you have sown and increase the fruits of your righteousness"* (2 Corinthians 9:10). What you eat feeds you once. What you plant feeds you repeatedly. Consumption or multiplication—you choose.

Daily prayer: "Father, which channel today? I'm listening. Whether wisdom, work, community, miracle, or seed—I'm watching for Your provision in whatever form You send it." **Provision rarely arrives the way you expect—but it always arrives when you're expectant.**

TRANSFORMATION — ABUNDANCE + WISDOM

Paul could say, *"I know how to be abased, and I know how to abound. Everywhere and in all things I have learned both to be full and to be hungry, both to abound and to suffer need. I can do all things through Christ who strengthens me"* (Philippians 4:12-13). Abundance tells you the Father has resources. Wisdom tells you the Father knows timing. One without the other creates dysfunction: Abundance without wisdom creates entitlement, wisdom without abundance creates religious poverty. Hold both lenses. You won't drift into prosperity gospel hype or poverty gospel despair. Biblical stewardship means budgets are faith in numbers (not fear of numbers), saving is wisdom (not lack of faith), and debt should be strategic (not desperate). **You can live abundantly while budgeting wisely—abundance tells you the Father has resources, wisdom tells you the Father knows timing.**

Many believers live in manna mentality: Daily survival instead of generational wealth, just enough instead of more than enough. Yet we pray orphan prayers: "God, if You could just help me make rent," "Lord, I just need enough for bills." Just. Just. Just. The word "just" in prayer reveals scarcity mindset. You're calculating what's reasonable instead of accessing what's available. **God didn't save you for survival—He saved you for abundance.** The word "just" in prayer reveals orphan thinking—"just enough" instead of "more than enough."

BREAKING POVERTY PATTERNS — THE ABUNDANCE DECLARATION

Before You Declare, Prepare

Write your last bank balance without shame. List three poverty vows you've made. Name one place you're hoarding from fear. Choose someone to bless this week. Decide to stop saying "I can't afford."

The Declaration of Abundant Living

Stand. Hand over heart. Declare:

"Father of Abundance, Owner of Everything, I come as Your heir, not Your employee. As manager of Your resources, not beggar for Your scraps. Poverty spirit has been my financial advisor. Scarcity my accountant. Lack my budget planner. Fear my portfolio manager. But today, I fire them all and declare:

Breaking Poverty's Power:

Every poverty vow—broken! Every 'just enough' agreement—cancelled! Every scarcity stronghold—demolished! Every fear of prosperity—evicted! Every guilt about abundance—gone! I am no longer surviving—I am thriving! No longer managing lack—distributing overflow! No longer calculating minimum—accessing maximum!

Reversing the Curse of Lack:

Where I hoarded from fear—I now give from faith! Where I calculated from scarcity—I now create from abundance! Where I apologized for having—I now appreciate my inheritance! Where I rejected prosperity—I now receive God's provision! Where I chose poverty—I now choose abundance!

Establishing Kingdom Economics:

I declare over my finances: Windows of heaven are open over me. I have more than enough for every assignment. I am blessed to be a blessing. My overflow finances Kingdom advancement. I declare over my mindset: Abundance is my birthright. Overflow is my portion. Prosperity with purpose is my inheritance. Generosity is my lifestyle. Wealth transfer is my destiny.

God's Promises Over My Prosperity:

'The blessing of the Lord makes rich, And He adds no sorrow with it' (Proverbs 10:22). *'Beloved, I pray that you may prosper in all things and be in health, just as your soul prospers'* (3 John 1:2). *'But you shall remember the Lord your God, for it is He who gives you power to get wealth'* (Deuteronomy 8:18).

The Multiplication Manifesto:

My little becomes much in God's hands! My seed becomes harvest in God's timing! My obedience becomes overflow in God's economy! My giving becomes getting—pressed down, shaken together, running over! What I plant in faith, I will harvest in fullness! Five loaves became feast! Widow's oil became fortune! My surrender becomes supernatural overflow!

From This Day Forward:

I speak abundance, not lack. I expect overflow, not just enough. I plan for prosperity, not poverty. I prepare for more, not less. I position for wealth transfer, not just bills paid. I am not getting rich—I am becoming rich toward God! Not accumulating—distributing! Not hoarding—hosting Heaven's resources! You are El Shaddai—God more than enough! *'My God shall supply all my need according to His riches in glory'* (Philippians 4:19)—not according to economy! In Jesus' name, poverty's reign is over! Abundance's flow has begun! Wealth transfer is activated! Overflow is released! Amen!"

THE ABUNDANCE AUTHORITY PROTOCOL™

Your 5-Step Wealth Mindset Transformation

STEP 1: AUDIT Your Agreements

List every phrase about money you heard growing up. Cross out each one. Write Kingdom truth above it.

STEP 2: APPRECIATE Your Current

Thank God for exactly what you have now. Count it. Bless it. Whether five dollars or five thousand, worship with it. Gratitude multiplies seed into harvest.

STEP 3: ACTIVATE Your Overflow

Give something today. Not from excess—from seed. Choose amount that makes you slightly uncomfortable. That's where faith starts.

STEP 4: ANNOUNCE Your Abundance

Tell three people this week: "God is prospering me to finance Kingdom advancement." Stop agreeing with lack in conversation.

STEP 5: ACCELERATE Your Capacity

Open a second account labeled "Kingdom Overflow." Put something in it, even one dollar. You're creating a container for what's coming.

The Abundance Authority Protocol doesn't make you rich—it teaches you to think like an heir.

MONTHLY ABUNDANCE MINDSET ASSESSMENT

Track your transformation monthly. Rate yourself 0-10 in each area:

Orphan vs. Heir Thinking: ___/10

(10 = Consistently operates from abundance; 1 = Dominated by scarcity)

Generosity vs. Hoarding: ___/10

(10 = Shares freely, gives joyfully; 1 = Clutches resources from fear)

Rejoicing vs. Comparing: ___/10
(10 = Celebrates others' increase; 1 = Jealous when others prosper)
Father-Focus vs. Account-Focus: ___/10
(10 = Measures by relationship with God; 1 = Measures worth by bank balance)
Steward vs. Owner Mentality: ___/10
(10 = Manages God's resources peacefully; 1 = Anxiously controls "my" money)

Total Score: ___/50

Interpretation:
- **0-20:** Scarcity mindset dominant. Review Orphan/Heir table weekly. Practice wallet declaration daily. Pray Breaking Poverty Declaration weekly.
- **21-35:** Transitioning to abundance thinking. Continue monthly protocols. Focus on lowest-scoring area. Celebrate every point of progress.
- **36-50:** Walking in heir abundance. Maintain quarterly check-ins. You're ready to teach others Kingdom economics.

Compare scores monthly. Celebrate every increase—transformation is progressive, not instant. If scores decrease, review where orphan thinking returned. Repeat protocols without shame. Healing isn't linear. **You're measuring progress, not perfection.**

THE PROPHETIC ACT: WALLET DECLARATION

What You'll Need
Your wallet (empty or full doesn't matter), your bank card or checkbook, and a moment of privacy.
The Act

STEP 1: HOLD YOUR WALLET
Stand up. Take your wallet out. Hold it in both hands. This isn't about what's in it. This is about who backs it. Look at it. Feel the weight. Whether it's heavy with cash or light with nothing—it doesn't matter. This wallet has been your symbol of limitation. Today it becomes your symbol of access.

STEP 2: EMPTY IT (If Possible)
Take everything out. Cards. Cash. Receipts. Spread them on a table. Look at the numbers. The balances. The limits on the cards. Say out loud: "This is what earth's economy says I have."

STEP 3: HOLD IT HIGH
Now hold your empty wallet high above your head. Declare: "This is not my source—God is my source! This is not my security—God is my security! This is not my limit—God is limitless! I am an heir with access to: Heaven's resources that never run dry, Father's riches that never deplete, Kingdom treasures beyond measure, Family wealth transcending earth's economy. When my identity is settled, my provision is secured!"

STEP 4: THE BANK CARD DECLARATION
Now take your bank card (debit or credit—whichever you use most). Hold it up. Look at it. This piece of plastic has had authority over your emotions. Checking the balance has determined your peace. Not anymore. Place it against your heart. Declare: "This card is connected to an earthly account—But I

am connected to a heavenly account! This card has a limit—But my Father has no limit! This card can be declined—But my prayers are never rejected! This card tracks my credit score—But Heaven tracks my faith score! This card gives access to thousands—But my adoption gives access to Him who owns everything! I am not defined by this balance. I am defined by my bloodline. I am not restricted by this limit. I am released into Kingdom abundance! In Jesus' name, I break every agreement between my peace and this plastic! My security is not in a card—it's in my Father! My confidence is not in my credit—it's in my covenant! From this day forward: Before I swipe—I worship. Before I check the balance—I check my blessing. Before I panic about the account—I remember my adoption. This card is a tool, not my trust. A resource, not my source. A method, not my miracle. I am abundantly provided for—Not because of what's on this card, but because of Who holds my life!"

STEP 5: PUT IT BACK DIFFERENTLY

Now, with new understanding, put your cards back in your wallet. But as you do, say over each one: "God, You are bigger than this balance," "God, You are greater than this limit," "God, You are my source, not this card." Put your wallet away. Your security was never there anyway.

STEP 6: THE SHIFT

From this moment forward, every time you open your wallet, check your bank balance, swipe your card, or pay a bill, pause for one second and whisper: "My Father owns everything." That one-second pause breaks orphan thinking and reinforces heir identity.

Why This Activation Works

Prophetic acts create spiritual shift. The woman touched Jesus' hem—healing activated. Naaman dipped seven times—leprosy gone. Israelites marched around Jericho—walls fell. You declare over your wallet—scarcity breaks. This isn't superstition. It's physical demonstration of spiritual decision. Your wallet has been a symbol of limitation. Today it becomes a reminder of access. **What you hold in your hand holds less power than Who holds your hand.**

FOCUS AREA ABUNDANCE PRAYERS

Choose your primary breakthrough area:

For Spiritual Focus: "Father, I access Your unlimited spiritual resources. You've given me every spiritual blessing in Christ. I reject spiritual poverty and receive Your abundant grace, wisdom, power. Transform my spiritual life through Your superabundant resources."

For Mental Focus: "Father, I access Your unlimited mental resources. The mind of Christ is available. I reject limited thinking and receive Your abundant wisdom, clarity, understanding. Renew my mind through Your infinite resources."

For Emotional Focus: "Father, I access Your unlimited emotional resources. You have abundant love, joy, peace, healing. I reject emotional poverty and receive Your unlimited supply. Heal my emotions through Your overflowing resources."

For Physical Focus: "Father, I access Your unlimited physical resources. You have abundant health, energy, vitality. I reject physical limitation and receive Your unlimited strength. Transform my body through Your abundant resources."

For Financial Focus: "Father, I access Your unlimited financial resources. You own everything and have abundant provision. I reject scarcity thinking and receive Your unlimited supply. Transform my finances through Your infinite resources."

For Relational Focus: "Father, I access Your unlimited relational resources. You have abundant love, community, connection. I reject social poverty and receive Your unlimited relationship supply. Heal my relationships through Your abundant love."

THE 6-DIMENSIONAL ABUNDANCE ACTIVATION

DIMENSION	PRACTICE	EVIDENCE
SPIRITUAL	List 10 spiritual blessings you possess in Christ	Awareness of wealth replaces lack
MENTAL	Replace "I can't afford" with "How will God provide?"	Mind shifts from closed to creative
EMOTIONAL	Genuinely rejoice when others receive breakthrough	Jealousy dies when you know there's enough
PHYSICAL	Give something away today—time, talent, treasure	Circulation creates acceleration
FINANCIAL	Before paying bills, declare: "My Father owns everything."	Peace replaces panic
RELATIONAL	Connect someone to a resource they need	Abundance mindset creates abundance network

Abundance practiced becomes abundance multiplied.

BREAKTHROUGH PRAYER

"Father of Abundance, Owner of Everything, thank You that my adoption included vault access. Thank You that yesterday's papers signed in blood opened accounts I didn't know existed. I repent for living as orphan when I'm Your heir. For counting what I have instead of counting on Who I have. For measuring by bank balances instead of relationship. For saying 'I can't afford' when I should say 'My Father owns everything.' Forgive me for scarcity thinking. For hoarding from fear. For calculating from lack. For griping about provision. For seeing Your blessings as 'too much' when You designed me for overflow.

Today I break agreement with poverty spirit. Every vow of 'just enough'—cancelled. Every belief that 'people like me don't prosper'—demolished. Every fear that abundance equals greed—evicted. I declare: I am not getting rich—I am becoming rich toward You. Not accumulating—distributing. Not hoarding—hosting Your resources. Not surviving—thriving. Not managing lack—releasing overflow.

Like the widow with oil, I open every container. Like Peter with nets, I obey despite expertise. Like the boy with lunch, I give You my little. Like Zarephath's widow, I serve from emptiness. Like Isaac in famine, I plant anyway. Transform my wallet from symbol of limitation to reminder of access.

Transform my bank card from source of anxiety to tool for Kingdom advancement. Transform my finances from survival mode to significance living.

I receive: Wisdom that downloads million-dollar ideas. Work that brings unexpected opportunities. Community that shares resources. Miracles that show off Your power. Seed that multiplies into harvest. Father, which channel today? I'm watching. Whether wisdom, work, community, miracle, or seed—I'm expectant. You've never missed a payment. You won't start with me.

My calculator may bleed red, but Your blood writes black. My math says impossible, but Your Kingdom says inevitable. I'm not poor pretending to be rich. I'm rich remembering I'm royal. In Jesus' name—my access, my abundance, my advocate! Amen."

CLOSING — FROM SCARCITY TO OVERFLOW

Day 9 complete. The calculator that bled red at 3:17 AM? It wasn't lying. But it wasn't telling whole truth either. It could count what you had. It couldn't count on Who you have. Yesterday you discovered you're an heir. Today you learned what that means—access to everything. Not someday access. Today access. Not partial access. Full access. Tomorrow, authority awaits. You'll discover the difference between orphans who wave guns and heirs who wear badges. Between forcing doors and having keys. Between calculating and commanding.

But tonight, let this sink into your bones where poverty used to live: The calculator bled red, but the blood of Jesus writes black. The math said impossible, but the Kingdom said inevitable. You're not poor pretending to be rich. You're rich remembering you're royal. **Orphans budget from fear. Heirs budget from faith—and make Spirit-led withdrawals from the Father's account.** You entered Day 9 calculating lack. You exit computing Kingdom wealth.

Welcome to abundance. Welcome to overflow. Welcome to Kingdom economics where your Father's resources never run dry. The Hebrew shouted: Shapha'—pour out! The Greek roared: Perisseuō—overflow! Heaven declares over you: More than enough! You are not begging for bread—you're distributing Heaven's bakery. Not managing minimum—you're stewarding superabundance. Not counting pennies—you're signing checks for Kingdom advancement.

SOAP JOURNAL — DAY 9

S (Scripture): Which abundance verse shattered your scarcity mindset? Write it and personalize it.
O (Observation): Where has poverty spirit been your financial advisor? What orphan behaviors did you recognize?
A (Application): What changes when you manage God's resources vs. your own? What will you do differently?
P (Prayer): "Father, as Your abundant heir, I receive Your overflow for _____."

Today's Breakthrough Marker: What shifted from scarcity to abundance thinking?
Tomorrow's Expectation: Now that you know you're abundant, what authority will you exercise?

SCARCITY EVICTED. ABUNDANCE ACTIVATED. READY FOR AUTHORITY.
Welcome to abundance. Welcome to overflow. Welcome to family wealth.

DAY 10 — AUTHORITY

From Orphan Power-Grabbing to Kingdom Badge-Wearing

> *"Behold, I give you the authority to trample on serpents and scorpions, and over all the power of the enemy, and nothing shall by any means hurt you."* — *Luke 10:19*

WEEK 2 — ALIGN: Establishing Your Kingdom Identity

Day 10 of 21. Day 8's Adoption made you an heir. Day 9's Abundance gave you resources. Today's Authority gives you rulership—not religious position, but Kingdom dominion that makes hell nervous.

ENCOUNTER — WHERE YOU ARE

The trembling started at 4:29 AM. One minute before your alarm. Day 10 has hollowed you out—not just from hunger. Your breathing comes ragged in the darkness. Sweat soaks your sheets with the sharp, metallic smell of spiritual warfare—that copper-penny taste of fear mixing with faith. The green glow of your alarm clock casts shadows that seem alive, pressing against the walls like something's trying to manifest. The trembling comes from tectonic plates shifting in the spirit realm. Heaven is rearranging your foundations. You know WHOSE you are. You're discovering WHO you are—adopted, abundant. But knowing you're family with access to wealth means nothing if you don't understand your authority to use it.

A king's child with no understanding of their authority is decorated powerlessness. A police officer who doesn't know they have a badge is just someone in uniform. An heir who doesn't recognize their rights remains functionally orphan. The same voice that whispered "not enough" (Day 9) and "not wanted" (Day 8) now hisses "not powerful." Same enemy, different lie. Because if Satan can keep you from discovering your authority, he can keep you living beneath your calling. You've been given keys to the Kingdom but you're still knocking. Given authority over demons but you're still negotiating. Given power to speak and it shall be done, but you're still begging.

Today you stop reaching for bigger guns and learn to wear your badge. **Orphans grasp for power. Heirs walk in authority.** Authority isn't about volume—it's about position. A whisper from the throne carries more weight than a scream from the pit.

FOUNDATION — THE GREATEST POWER TRANSFER IN HISTORY

When Heaven Held Its Breath

When Jesus declared *"All authority has been given to Me in heaven and on earth"* (Matthew 28:18), heaven held its breath. The cosmic transfer was complete—every key, every domain, every realm of power consolidated under one name. But He didn't stop there. "Go therefore..." (Matthew 28:19). Therefore. Because I have all authority, therefore YOU go. The Greek word is **poreuomai** [por-YOO-oh-my]—to transfer from one place to another. He wasn't just sending them out. He was transferring His authority through them. Then the scandalous declaration: *"Most assuredly, I say to you, he who believes in Me, the works that I do he will do also; and greater works than these he will do"* (John 14:12). Greater works. Not different works. Greater.

The math doesn't make sense until you understand: Authority isn't earned—it's inherited. You don't work FOR it. You were born INTO it. **Authority isn't taken by force. It's received by birth.**

The Two Kinds of Power — And You Have Both

The Bible uses two distinct Greek words that English translates as "power": **Dunamis** [doo-NAH-mis] — Dynamic power, miraculous ability, explosive force. This is the power that flows through you to heal, deliver, and work miracles. **Exousia** [ex-oo-SEE-ah] — Delegated authority, legal right, positional power. This is your right to use dunamis, your legal standing in the spirit realm. Here's the critical distinction: Satan has limited power that is already defeated, but you have dunamis (power) and also exousia (authority) delegated by Christ OVER all the enemy's power. *"Behold, I give you the authority (exousia) to trample on serpents and scorpions, and over all the power (dunamis) of the enemy"* (Luke 10:19).

But notice what Jesus gave His disciples: *"Then He called His twelve disciples together and gave them power (dunamis) and authority (exousia) over all demons, and to cure diseases"* (Luke 9:1). BOTH. Not just one. Power AND authority. Authority trumps power. Always. A police officer stopping a speeding truck doesn't have the POWER to physically stop it, but has the AUTHORITY that makes it stop. The truck has more horsepower, but the badge has more authority. But here's what most miss: That officer also has a gun (dunamis) AND a badge (exousia). He has BOTH. The question isn't which one to carry—it's which one to use for each situation. **Don't misunderstand: The gun (dunamis) is real, necessary, and powerful. The Holy Spirit's power within you heals, delivers, and demolishes strongholds. But the gun works THROUGH the badge, not instead of it. You're not discarding the gun—you're learning when to use which tool. An officer doesn't leave his gun at home. He just doesn't draw it at every traffic stop.** The enemy has limited power that's already defeated. You have authority over his power. Hell has force. You have dominion over its force.

Why Most Believers Live Powerless

Look around the Body of Christ and you'll see the tragedy: Most believers have never cast out a demon (though Jesus said we would [Mark 16:17]), don't believe they have authority over sickness (though Jesus commanded us to heal [Matthew 10:8]), live in fear of the enemy's attacks (though we've been given authority over all his power [Luke 10:19]), and spend their lives begging God to do what He's already authorized them to do. We've confused delegation with abdication. God hasn't taken back the authority He gave. We've just forgotten we have it. The tragedy: Believers with authority living like beggars. Royalty acting like refugees. Judges playing victims. **The greatest victory Satan ever won was convincing believers they're powerless.**

TESTIMONY — THE DAY I COMMANDED WRONG

When Volume Replaced Authority

Online prayer session. Desperate woman, camera shaky, eyes hollow from nightmares. When she shared her torment, I knew what to do—or thought I did. Fresh from studying spiritual warfare, armed with Greek words and binding formulas, ready to demonstrate God's power through the screen. "In the name of Jesus, I COMMAND you spirit of fear to GO!" Nothing. Her pixelated face unchanged. Louder: "I SAID GO! I BIND you! I CAST you out! By the blood, by the cross, by resurrection power, I COMMAND you!" Still nothing. Worse—the woman began trembling. Not from deliverance. From fear. Of me.

Frustrated, embarrassed, angry at the demon for making me look powerless, I doubled down. Minutes of shouting commands. Sweat dripping. Voice hoarse. Other participants turning off cameras. Chat messages: "Maybe we should pray differently?" Finally, my husband John unmuted. "Honey, can I try?" He leaned toward his camera with such gentleness I had to adjust my volume: "Father, she's Your daughter. What's tormenting Your girl?" Silence. Heaven listening. Then, barely audible: "Spirit of trauma from childhood abuse, you have no right to God's daughter. Jesus paid for her freedom. In His name, leave." No shouting. No performance.

The woman gasped once—sharp, clear. Like someone breaking through water after drowning. Her pixelated face changed in real time—shoulders dropping, jaw unclenching, eyes clearing from haunted to wondering. Then sobbing. Not the choked, desperate sobs from before. Clean sobs. The kind that wash instead of wound. "It's gone," she whispered, hands touching her chest like she couldn't believe it. "The weight... it's actually gone." Thirty seconds of authority accomplished what minutes of power couldn't touch.

Later, John found me staring at the blank screen. "Baby, volume isn't authority. Position is. You were trying to generate power you're supposed to inherit. You were waving a gun when all you needed was to flash your badge." **Authority isn't volume. It's position.** The difference between power and authority is the difference between shouting and knowing whose you are.

The Memory That Prophesied

As I sat there embarrassed, voice hoarse from screaming commands, a memory surfaced unbidden: Age seven. Playground. Bigger kid pushing a smaller one. Little Niki—all of forty pounds—stepped between them. No tough words. No threats. Just stood there, arms crossed, staring up at the bully. He laughed. "What are you gonna do about it?" I didn't answer. Just stood there. Immovable. Something in my eyes made him pause. He looked around—noticed the teacher watching from the door. Noticed other kids circling. Noticed he was outnumbered not by force but by position. He walked away.

I'd just learned about authority before I had language for it. Position, not power. Presence, not performance. Thirty years later, screaming at demons through a laptop screen, I'd forgotten what seven-year-old Niki already knew: When you're in the right position, you don't need to prove anything. You just need to stand there.

REVELATION — THE BADGE AND THE GUN

Heaven's Authority System

Months after that prayer meeting failure, John's teaching finally made authority click: "Picture a police officer at a busy intersection during rush hour. Cars weighing thousands of pounds barrel toward him at forty miles per hour. Semi-trucks that could crush him without slowing. He weighs maybe 180 pounds soaking wet." He paused, letting us feel the weight differential. "But watch. He raises one hand, and eighteen-wheelers halt. SUVs stop mid-turn. Motorcycles idle at his gesture. Even aggressive drivers who curse him still stop. Why?" We waited. "Is it because he's physically powerful enough to stop them? Could he tackle a truck? Fight a Ford? Wrestle a Ram?" Nervous laughter.

"That officer has two things: a BADGE and a gun. The gun is his power—real, loaded, lethal. But watch carefully: he doesn't stop traffic with his gun. He stops it with his BADGE." John touched his chest where an officer's badge would sit. "The badge is his AUTHORITY. It's delegated by the city, backed by the state, recognized by federal law. Every driver knows what that badge represents—not the officer's personal power, but the entire government standing behind him." Voice dropping: "The gun is like the Holy Spirit's power within you—dunamis in Greek. Real. Powerful. Able to heal, deliver, demolish strongholds. But the badge? The badge is your AUTHORITY in Christ—exousia in Greek. Delegated by Jesus. Backed by heaven's government. Recognized by every demon in hell."

Cemetery quiet. "Some of you are exhausted at the intersection of your breakthrough, screaming, sweating, waving your gun, trying to generate enough power to stop the enemy. Meanwhile, Jesus is trying to hand you a badge saying, 'Just hold this up. Hell knows exactly what it means.'" He walked to the platform's edge: "That officer might have the flu. Might be exhausted from a double shift. Might be his first day. His personal strength is irrelevant. The badge carries the same authority because the GOVERNMENT behind it hasn't changed." The line that rewired everything: **"Stop trying to shoot problems you're authorized to arrest."**

The Authority That Flows From Adoption

Religion taught us authority was about dominance—bind this, loose that, command, declare. Shout louder. Fast longer. Prove your power until something breaks. But that's orphan thinking—trying to generate power you're supposed to inherit. The Holy Spirit whispered: "My child, orphans wave guns wildly, shooting at everything, hoping something works. Children simply flash the badge Daddy gave them, knowing heaven's entire government backs it. You're not trying to GET authority. You're learning to WEAR the authority adoption already gave you."

A president's child has authority not because they're powerful but because of whose they are. An ambassador carries authority not through personal strength but through the nation they represent. You don't generate authority. You inherit it. You don't earn your badge. You receive it at adoption. You don't fight for authority. You walk in it. **Authority is not achieved through warfare. It's received through relationship.**

THE DIFFERENCE: ORPHAN POWER VS HEIR AUTHORITY

ORPHAN POWER (Waving the Gun)	HEIR AUTHORITY (Wearing the Badge)
Shouts to be heard—volume equals authority	Speaks knowing Heaven listens—whispers carry weight
Forces outcomes through manipulation	Releases Kingdom reality through alignment
Dominates others—authority means superiority	Serves others into freedom—authority means responsibility
Proves strength constantly	Rests in identity—position is established
Works anxiously, afraid of looking weak	Works peacefully with confidence in backing
Measures by visible results—needs immediate proof	Measures by obedience—faithfulness over outcomes

Exhausted from striving	Rested in position—badge always valid
Operates in fear—what if it doesn't work?	Operates in love—perfect love casts out fear
Competes with others—whose gun is bigger?	Celebrates others' authority—more officers, safer streets
Grasps for more power—never enough ammunition	Secure in delegation—badge backed by infinite government

Orphans exhaust themselves waving guns. Heirs rest while wearing badges. Authority submitted to Love looks like service, not domination.

CRITICAL: AUTHORITY IS FOR SERVICE, NOT DOMINATION

Authority without love is religious abuse. The badge makes you responsible FOR others, not superior TO them. You're not authorized to override free will, manipulate outcomes, or dominate people "for their own good." Badge authority serves, protects, creates safety, and honors consent. If your exercise of authority leaves people feeling controlled, violated, or diminished, you've crossed from Kingdom authority to religious abuse. **The Five Badge Protocols (under authority, within assignment, for service, with clean hands, in love) aren't suggestions—they're non-negotiables.** Every abuse of spiritual authority throughout church history came from people who had power without these protocols. Don't be that person.

BIBLICAL PATTERNS — WHEN BADGE AUTHORITY CHANGES EVERYTHING
TIER 1: Four Full Witnesses

The Centurion — Who Taught Jesus About Authority (Matthew 8:8-9)

Before unpacking the seven spheres of your authority, we must understand the Roman officer who made the Son of God marvel: *"Lord, I am not worthy that You should come under my roof. But only speak a word, and my servant will be healed. For I also am a man under authority, having soldiers under me. And I say to this one, 'Go,' and he goes; and to another, 'Come,' and he comes"* (Matthew 8:8-9). Jesus' response stuns: *"Assuredly, I say to you, I have not found such great faith, not even in Israel!"* What did this Gentile soldier understand that religious leaders missed?

Authority flows from submission. He recognized the chain of command. He was under authority—under Rome, under superior officers, under the emperor. Therefore, he could exercise authority over those under him. His commands carried weight not because of personal power but because of the government backing him. He saw the same in Jesus. Jesus was under the Father's authority. Therefore, Jesus' words alone—no touching, no traveling, no ceremony—carried heaven's full weight. The centurion understood: **You exercise authority to the degree you're under authority. Your authority is proportional to your surrender.**

Jesus — The Perfect Badge Wearer (John 5:19, Luke 10:20)

"Most assuredly, I say to you, the Son can do nothing of Himself, but what He sees the Father do; for whatever He does, the Son also does in like manner" (John 5:19). NOTHING of Himself. The Son of God—unlimited power—chose to operate only within delegated authority. Never went rogue. Never acted independently.

His authority was absolute because His submission was complete. When disciples rejoiced about demons submitting, Jesus redirected: *"Nevertheless do not rejoice in this, that the spirits are subject to you, but rather rejoice because your names are written in heaven"* (Luke 10:20). Translation: Don't celebrate the gun's firepower. Celebrate that you have a badge—you belong to heaven's government. **The highest authority comes from the deepest surrender.**

Peter & John — When Fishermen Wore Kingdom Badges (Acts 3:6, 4:13)

Two uneducated fishermen. No theological guns. No religious ammunition. But watch their authority: *"Then Peter said, 'Silver and gold I do not have, but what I do have I give you: In the name of Jesus Christ of Nazareth, rise up and walk'"* (Acts 3:6). They flashed the badge: "In the name of Jesus." Not their power. Not their ability. The government they represented. The lame man leaped. Later, religious leaders marveled: *"Now when they saw the boldness of Peter and John, and perceived that they were uneducated and untrained men, they marveled. And they realized that they had been with Jesus"* (Acts 4:13). That's how you get a badge—proximity to the One who issues them. **Authority isn't granted by institutions. It's issued through intimacy.**

Seven Sons of Sceva — When Fake Badges Got Exposed (Acts 19:13-15)

Seven brothers tried flashing Paul's badge. Borrowed authority. Counterfeit credentials: *"Then some of the itinerant Jewish exorcists took it upon themselves to call the name of the Lord Jesus over those who had evil spirits, saying, 'We exorcise you by the Jesus whom Paul preaches'"* (Acts 19:13). The evil spirit's response should terrify anyone faking authority: *"And the evil spirit answered and said, 'Jesus I know, and Paul I know; but who are you?'"* (Acts 19:15). Translation: "I see you waving something, but that's not YOUR badge. You're not in the system. You're not authorized." The demon beat them naked and wounded into the street. **Hell respects real badges and violently exposes fake ones.**

TIER 2: Two Grouped Witnesses

Authority Through Weakness

Paul discovered what every officer learns: A weak cop with a valid badge outranks a strong criminal with a gun. *"And He said to me, 'My grace is sufficient for you, for My strength is made perfect in weakness'"* (2 Corinthians 12:9). Paul's weakness didn't diminish his badge—it highlighted Whose government backed it. When you're obviously too weak to stop traffic on your own, everyone knows it's the badge doing the work. Jesus demonstrated this perfectly in Gethsemane. With legions of angels on speed dial—ultimate firepower available—Jesus chose badge submission: *"Father, if it is Your will, take this cup away from Me; nevertheless not My will, but Yours, be done"* (Luke 22:42). His badge authorized Him to endure the cross, not escape it. Authority submitted to love chose suffering to serve others. **Your badge works best when everyone knows you couldn't stop traffic on your own.**

Authority in Suffering

Sometimes your badge authorizes you to endure, not escape. Sometimes authority looks like standing at your post, not clearing the intersection. A father stood between life and death—his premature child fighting for breath behind glass walls. Monitors screamed. Doctors whispered percentages at 2:17 AM. Fear demanded he rage against heaven, wave his spiritual gun, shoot prayers like bullets. But in that darkness, something shifted. He placed his hand on the incubator and whispered with the authority of a father who knew his badge: "Peace. I speak peace over this precious life. I take authority over fear, not with force but with position. Whether this child breathes on earth or in heaven, they belong to the Kingdom. My badge authorizes me to bring heaven's peace into this hell."

The monitors didn't change. The percentages didn't improve. But the atmosphere shifted. Nurses later said they'd never felt such peace in that unit. Sometimes your badge authorizes presence more than power changes. Sometimes authority looks like bringing heaven's atmosphere into earth's emergency. **True authority is just as valid in a hospital hallway as on a healing platform.**

TESTIMONY — THE BOARD MEETING BADGE

When Authority Replaced Ammunition

Emergency senior leadership meeting. An influential leader demanding my removal. "She's too bold. Refuses to play politics. Doesn't know her place." The old me would have come armed—defense documents, PowerPoints, strategic allies, counter-accusations. All guns blazing. Orphan warfare. But Holy Spirit whispered: "Are you fighting FOR position or standing IN position? One requires weapons. The other requires your badge." I entered that Zoom meeting wearing only one thing—my identity badge as God's daughter assigned to this post. When accusations flew, I didn't draw my gun. Instead, I wrote in my notebook: "What outcome would most honor the One who authorized me to serve here?"

Silence stretched. Then one senior leader delivered the verdict: "We've decided to postpone the project and terminate your contract." The words hit like a punch. My stomach dropped. Everything in me wanted to fight, defend, argue, explain. But something held me back. I took a breath. "Thank you for the opportunity to serve." Shocked silence filled the screen. Another leader spoke, surprise evident in his voice: "We... we never expected you to respond without defending yourself." The meeting ended. Screen went black. I sat there—discouraged, disappointed, questions swirling. But God.

The Download

That's when Holy Spirit downloaded the revelation that changed everything: **"When you know your identity, you're not employed—you're deployed."** The truth pierced through the disappointment like light through fog. I wasn't fighting for a contract or placement. I was standing in an assignment. There's a difference. Employees defend positions. Officers execute orders. Orphans panic when they lose jobs. Heirs trust when assignments shift.

The Wrestling

For three hours after that Zoom call, I sat with my laptop closed. My hands wouldn't stop shaking. Not from fear—from the collision of two identities fighting for dominance. I opened my journal—the same one with that paper airplane prayer from Jamaica all those years ago. Flipped to a blank page. Wrote two columns:

What Orphan Power Says: "You failed. You lost. They rejected you. You're not good enough. Call them back. Defend yourself. They need to know the truth. You can't just let them win."

What Badge Authority Says: "You didn't fail. You stood. You're not employed, you're deployed. If Father is reassigning you, you'll gladly serve elsewhere. If this termination isn't His will, they couldn't remove you with dynamite. Either way, you're at peace. The question isn't 'Why did I lose this contract?' The question is: 'What is heaven authorizing next?'"

I read both columns out loud. The orphan column made my chest tight. The badge column made me breathe deeper. I circled the badge column. Wrote across the page: "I am not the orphan anymore. Stop arguing with who you've become."

The Shift

The atmosphere in my room shifted. The fear lifted. The heaviness of discouragement—all the "what ifs" and "why mes"—dissolved. Peace flooded in where panic had been. For the next two hours, I stopped grieving what I lost and started dreaming about what God was doing. What looked like career disaster to the natural eye was Kingdom redirection to spiritual eyes. I stopped defending my empire and started declaring His Kingdom. I learned something profound: **Authority without ammunition accomplishes what power never could. Sometimes your badge authorizes you to walk away. Sometimes surrender is the strongest display of authority. Sometimes peace in loss is greater testimony than fight for position.**

The Aftermath

I closed my laptop and sat in silence on my bed. Hands still shaking—not from fear this time but from awe. For twenty minutes I sat there, watching my hands. The same hands that used to clutch guns in power struggles—drafting defense emails, gathering evidence, preparing counterattacks. Now wearing a badge. I thought of Jesus' nail-scarred hands—the hands that won every battle by surrendering to every blow. The hands that never defended themselves at the cross. The hands that modeled badge authority perfectly: "Not My will, but Yours be done." And I knew with absolute certainty: I wasn't the same person who entered that Zoom meeting. I wasn't the same person who gracefully accepted sudden contract termination without a fight. And I'd never be that person again. **When you know your badge is valid, you don't need to draw your gun.**

THE SEVEN SPHERES OF YOUR AUTHORITY

1. AUTHORITY OVER DEMONS

"In My name they will cast out demons" (Mark 16:17). Not "might" cast out. WILL cast out. It's not a spiritual gift for some—it's birthright authority for all believers. You don't need to be louder than demons. You need to know you outrank them. A private doesn't have to yell at a general. Position determines power.

2. AUTHORITY OVER SICKNESS

"Heal the sick, cleanse the lepers, raise the dead" (Matthew 10:8). This wasn't a suggestion. It was a command. He didn't say "pray for the sick." He said "HEAL the sick." The authority to heal is already yours.

3. AUTHORITY OVER NATURE

"He arose and rebuked the wind, and said to the sea, 'Peace, be still!'" (Mark 4:39). Then He asked the disciples: *"Why are you so fearful? How is it that you have no faith?"* (Mark 4:40). He expected them to do what He did—command the storm. Creation recognizes authority, whether it comes from Jesus or from those carrying His name.

4. AUTHORITY OVER CIRCUMSTANCES

"*Therefore I say to you, whatever things you ask when you pray, believe that you receive them, and you will have them*" (Mark 11:24). But look at the verse before: "*Whoever says to this mountain, 'Be removed'... he will have whatever he says*" (Mark 11:23). SAYS to the mountain. Not prays about the mountain. SPEAKS TO it.

5. AUTHORITY IN PRAYER

"*Whatever you bind on earth will be bound in heaven, and whatever you loose on earth will be loosed in heaven*" (Matthew 18:18). The Greek tense is critical here—"will have been bound" and "will have been loosed." Heaven backs what earth initiates. You're not asking heaven to bind. You're binding, and heaven backs it.

6. AUTHORITY OVER DEATH

"*I am He who lives, and was dead, and behold, I am alive forevermore. Amen. And I have the keys of Hades and of Death*" (Revelation 1:18). He has the keys—and He gave them to the church. "*And I will give you the keys of the kingdom of heaven*" (Matthew 16:19).

7. AUTHORITY IN THE HEAVENLY REALMS

"*And raised us up together, and made us sit together in the heavenly places in Christ Jesus*" (Ephesians 2:6). Present tense. You're already seated. Your position is established. You're not trying to get to the throne. You're operating from it. **You don't fight FOR victory. You fight FROM victory. The battle isn't to win. It's to enforce what's already won.**

OPERATING YOUR BADGE — THE COMPLETE SYSTEM

What Makes Your Badge Valid: Five Legal Grounds

Your authority rests on five immutable legal grounds that Satan cannot contest: **THE BLOOD** — Every accusation is answered by the blood. It's the ultimate legal precedent that overrules every charge. **THE NAME** — You don't come in your name but in Jesus' name. His name is your power of attorney. **THE WORD** — Scripture is legal precedent. When you declare "It is written," you're citing Kingdom law. **THE RESURRECTION** — Jesus' resurrection is the legal proof that all enemy claims have been satisfied. **YOUR POSITION** — Seated with Christ means you judge from the throne, not plead from the floor. The enemy may have a case, but you have the verdict. He may have accusations, but you have authority.

The Five Badge Protocols: Operating Under Kingdom Authority

1. UNDER AUTHORITY — Your badge only works under heaven's government. Independence invalidates authority. Stay submitted to Jesus, to spiritual leadership, to Scripture. Lone ranger authority is no authority at all.

2. WITHIN ASSIGNMENT — Respect your jurisdiction. Don't police territories you're not assigned to. Authority has boundaries. You have full authority in your sphere (home, workplace, relationships you're responsible for) but limited authority outside it.

3. FOR SERVICE — Badges exist to protect and serve, not dominate and control. Authority makes you responsible FOR others, not superior TO them. If people feel controlled by your "authority," you're abusing power.

4. WITH CLEAN HANDS — Corruption invalidates authority. Sin clouds the badge. Repentance restores clarity. Keep your badge clean. The Seven Sons of Sceva had fake badges partly because their hands weren't clean.

5. IN LOVE — Authority without love is religious abuse. Love must govern every badge action. Serve from compassion, not compulsion. *"Though I have all faith, so that I could remove mountains, but have not love, I am nothing"* (1 Corinthians 13:2).

The Authority to Bind and Loose: Understanding Your Judicial Power

"Whatever you bind on earth will be bound in heaven, and whatever you loose on earth will be loosed in heaven" (Matthew 18:18). This isn't poetry. It's legal language. **TO BIND** (Greek: **deo** [DEH-oh]) — To tie up, to restrict, to prohibit, to declare illegal. When you bind something, you're declaring it illegal in your sphere of authority. **TO LOOSE** (Greek: **luo** [LOO-oh]) — To untie, to release, to permit, to declare legal. When you loose something, you're authorizing its operation in your sphere.

You can bind: Sickness and disease, demonic operations, poverty and lack, strife and division, fear and anxiety, generational curses.

You can loose: Healing and wholeness, angelic activity, provision and abundance, peace and unity, faith and courage, generational blessings.

HOW YOUR BADGE WORKS DAILY

In Your Home: You're the assigned officer—not to dominate but to serve and protect. Your badge establishes peace, breaks generational curses, creates atmosphere. You don't control family members—you bring Kingdom presence that creates freedom for them to flourish.

In Your Workplace: You carry Kingdom jurisdiction even in secular spaces. Your badge influences atmosphere without preaching. Excellence becomes evangelism. Peace in pressure testifies. You're undercover authority—known in heaven, effective on earth.

In Your Relationships: Badge authority serves, never controls. It protects boundaries, honors consent, creates safety. You're not authorized to override free will but to love others into freedom. If someone doesn't want your "help," your badge doesn't give you permission to force it.

In Your Circumstances: Storms must respect your badge—sometimes you calm them, sometimes you authorize safe passage through them. Your badge works in ICUs and boardrooms, in plenty and in lack. Authority isn't proven by immediate outcomes but by positioned obedience.

In Spiritual Warfare: The enemy MUST respect your badge. Not your feelings. Not your performance. Your position. Demons flee from officers, not vigilantes. They test fake badges and obey real ones. **Your badge is only as powerful as the government that issued it. Good news: Heaven's government never falls.**

THE AUTHORITY PROTOCOL™

Your 5-Step Authority Process
STEP 1: IDENTIFY Your Position

Before addressing any situation, remind yourself where you're seated. You're not under the problem. You're above it. Speak from the throne, not the valley. Pray: "Father, I remember I'm seated with Christ. I address this from my position, not my feelings."

STEP 2: ASSESS the Legal Ground

What gives the enemy access? Sin? Fear? Ignorance? Generational curses? Agreements with lies? Close legal doors through repentance, renunciation, and the blood. Don't just bind the enemy—remove his legal ground.

STEP 3: ADDRESS with Authority

Don't pray about the problem. Speak to it. Jesus didn't pray about the fig tree—He cursed it. He didn't pray about the storm—He rebuked it. Declare: "In Jesus' name, I command [specific issue] to cease. I break your power. You have no authority here."

STEP 4: ASSIGN Heaven's Resources

After removing enemy influence, assign angels, release peace, establish blessing. Don't leave vacuums—fill them with Kingdom reality. Declare: "I release angels. I establish peace. I decree blessing. Heaven's government now occupies this space."

STEP 5: MAINTAIN Through Declaration

Authority must be maintained. The enemy will test your resolve. Stand firm. Speak consistently. Don't negotiate with defeated foes. Daily declarations keep your badge visible: "I maintain my authority over this area. My position hasn't changed. My badge is still valid."

The Language of Authority

Stop saying: "God, if it's Your will..." (when commanding issues Jesus already defeated), "Please God, help me..." (when you're authorized to command), "I hope this works..." (reveals doubt in badge), "The devil is really attacking me..." (victim language, not authority).

Start declaring: "I command in Jesus' name...", "I decree and declare...", "It is written...", "I render the verdict...", "I exercise my authority..." **Begging reveals orphan identity. Commanding reveals kingdom authority.**

WHEN YOUR BADGE DOESN'T SEEM TO WORK: TROUBLESHOOTING

Sometimes you flash your badge and nothing happens. Before you assume your badge is invalid, check these:

1. Is your badge clean? (Sin doesn't invalidate your badge permanently, but it clouds it temporarily. Repent and restore clarity.)

2. Are you operating within your assignment? (You have full authority in your jurisdiction, limited authority outside it. Don't try to police someone else's territory.)

3. Is there hidden legal ground? (Sometimes the enemy has access through agreements, generational covenants, or unrenounced sin. Close legal doors first.)

4. Is this a badge moment or a gun moment? (Sometimes Holy Spirit is training you to use dunamis power, not exousia authority. Ask: "Badge, gun, or stand?")

5. Are you submitted to authority? (Authority flows from submission. If you're operating independently, your badge won't work properly.)

6. Is love governing your action? (Authority without love is noise. Check your heart. Are you serving or dominating?)

7. Is timing the issue? (Sometimes your badge authorizes waiting, not acting. "Not yet" doesn't mean "never." Stay positioned.)

If you've checked all seven and nothing has changed, remember: Your badge authorizes presence, not always immediate power changes. Sometimes bringing heaven's atmosphere IS the assignment. The premature baby's father didn't see healing, but he brought peace. That was his badge working perfectly. **Results don't validate your badge—position does. Stand anyway.**

THE AUTHORITY OVER GENERATIONAL PATTERNS: Breaking Bloodline Bondages

Your authority extends beyond personal issues to generational patterns. You're not just authorized to break cycles—you're commanded to. *"Therefore, if the Son makes you free, you shall be free indeed"* (John 8:36). Free indeed—not just free. Indeed (Greek: **ontos** [on-TOHS]) means "really, truly, actually." Not theoretical freedom. Actual freedom. Identify the patterns: Divorce and broken relationships, addiction and substance abuse, poverty and financial crisis, disease and premature death, anger and violence, depression and mental illness. Then exercise authority:

"I am the authorized heir with power to alter bloodline patterns. What previous generations couldn't break, I break today. Where they were victims, I am victor. In the name of Jesus, I cancel every generational curse. I revoke every demonic covenant made by my ancestors. I break every soul tie to family iniquity. I disconnect from every hereditary stronghold. The curse stops here. The pattern breaks now. The cycle ends today. I establish a new pattern: BLESSING. I initiate a new cycle: FREEDOM. I decree a new legacy: VICTORY. My children will not fight battles I've already won. My bloodline is redeemed, restored, realigned. In Jesus' name. It is finished."

FOCUS AREA AUTHORITY PRAYERS

Choose your primary breakthrough area and declare:

For SPIRITUAL Focus: "Father, I operate in spiritual authority for breakthrough. You've seated me with Christ in heavenly places. I have authority over spiritual opposition, religious bondage, and spiritual stagnation. I command breakthrough in my prayer life, Bible study, and spiritual growth. I flash my badge against every hindrance."

For MENTAL Focus: "Father, I operate in authority for mental breakthrough. You've given me authority over mental strongholds, negative thinking, and limiting beliefs. I command my thoughts to align with Your truth. I break the power of mental oppression and declare Kingdom thinking. My badge works in my mind."

For EMOTIONAL Focus: "Father, I operate in authority for emotional breakthrough. You've given me authority over emotional wounds, past trauma, and unstable emotions. I command healing over my emotions and break the power of emotional bondage. I declare stability and wholeness. My badge brings peace."

For PHYSICAL Focus: "Father, I operate in authority for physical breakthrough. You've given me authority over infirmity, unhealthy habits, and bodily dysfunction. I command health and vitality over my body. I break the power of physical limitation and declare divine strength. My badge authorizes healing."

For FINANCIAL Focus: "Father, I operate in authority for financial breakthrough. You've given me authority over poverty spirits, financial fear, and lack mentality. I command provision and abundance. I break the power of financial bondage and declare Kingdom prosperity. My badge opens provision doors."

For RELATIONAL Focus: "Father, I operate in authority for relational breakthrough. You've given me authority over relationship curses, dysfunction, and isolation. I command healing over my relationships. I break the power of relational bondage and declare healthy connections. My badge serves others into freedom."

MONTHLY BADGE AUTHORITY ASSESSMENT

Track your transformation monthly. Rate yourself 0-10 in each area:

Badge vs. Gun Usage: ___/10
(10 = Consistently uses badge authority first; 1 = Always reaching for power/force)

Submission to Authority: ___/10
(10 = Operating under God's authority consistently; 1 = Independent, lone ranger)

Service vs. Domination: ___/10
(10 = Authority used to serve and liberate; 1 = Authority used to control)

Peace vs. Striving: ___/10
(10 = Rest in position, confident in backing; 1 = Anxious, constantly proving)

Love-Governed Authority: ___/10
(10 = Every action flows from love; 1 = Authority without compassion)

Total Score: ___/50

Interpretation:
- **0-20:** Orphan power dominant. Review Badge/Gun framework weekly. Practice 60-Second Badge Check 3x daily. Focus on submission and love.
- **21-35:** Transitioning from power to authority. Continue monthly protocols. Focus on lowest-scoring area. Celebrate every point of progress.
- **36-50:** Walking in badge authority. Maintain quarterly check-ins. You're ready to teach others. Model servant authority.

Compare scores monthly. Celebrate every increase—transformation is progressive, not instant. If scores decrease, review Five Badge Protocols. Check for independence, control, or loveless authority. Repent and realign without shame. **You're measuring progress, not perfection.**

THE 6-DIMENSIONAL AUTHORITY ACTIVATION

DIMENSION	PRACTICE	EVIDENCE
SPIRITUAL	Each morning, consciously put on your invisible badge	Authority flows without striving
MENTAL	Ask "What's my badge authorizing?" not "How to overpower?"	Strategic clarity replaces forceful striving
EMOTIONAL	Touch your heart (badge location) when challenged	Confidence without arrogance manifests

PHYSICAL	Stand like an authorized officer	Atmosphere shifts with your presence
FINANCIAL	Handle resources as a trusted officer, not owner	Stewardship flows from security
RELATIONAL	Use your badge to serve others into freedom	Authority multiplies through service

Every dimension of life responds to properly worn authority.

THE 60-SECOND BADGE CHECK

Throughout your day, practice this quick alignment:

Submit (15 seconds): "Jesus, I'm reporting for duty. What's my assignment?"
Listen (30 seconds): "Badge, gun, or simply stand?" Wait for Holy Spirit's strategy.
Act (15 seconds): Follow the directive simply. Badge moments rarely require complexity.

PROPHETIC ACT — PINNING ON YOUR BADGE

Stand. Place your right hand over your heart—where officers wear badges. Declare:

"I receive my BADGE of Kingdom authority. Signed in Christ's blood. Backed by Heaven's government. Recognized in every realm. This badge grants me: Authority over ALL enemy power, access to Heaven's resources, right to bind and loose, jurisdiction in my sphere, power to serve and protect. I am not a vigilante with a gun. I am an OFFICER with a badge. From this day forward: I wear my authority, not wield it. I flash my badge, not wave my gun. I serve and protect, not dominate. I walk in delegation, not desperation. In Jesus' name, I am BADGE-WEARING AUTHORIZED!"

THE DECLARATION OF BADGE AUTHORITY

Stand in your Kingdom uniform—righteousness. Wear your badge—authority.

"I am an authorized officer of the Kingdom! My badge is valid in every realm! My authority is backed by Heaven's government! I don't need to prove my power—My BADGE proves my position! I exercise authority: Like an officer, not an orphan. Through position, not power. By my badge, not my muscle. With whispers, not screams. Today I stop reaching for bigger guns and start resting in my valid badge! Every demon must respect this badge! Every situation must yield to position! Every mountain must acknowledge authority! Because my badge was: Signed by Jesus, sealed in His blood, backed by His government, valid for eternity. I fight FROM authority, not FOR authority! I fight FROM victory, not FOR victory! In His name, I am AUTHORIZED!"

PRAYER OF BADGE AUTHORITY

"Father, forgive me for exhausting myself with guns when You've already issued my badge. I've been a vigilante trying to generate power when You've delegated authority. I've been shouting for attention when a whisper with a badge would suffice. I've confused volume with authority, activity with position. Thank You that: My badge is signed in Christ's blood, my authority flows from adoption, my position is secured by grace, my jurisdiction is defined by love, Heaven's government backs every badge action.

I repent for: Waving guns when I should flash badges, using force when position would suffice, fighting FOR authority instead of FROM authority, forgetting Whose government backs me. Today I receive: My badge of delegated authority, confidence in my Kingdom position, rest in Heaven's backing, joy in serving with this badge, wisdom to wear authority well.

When I'm weak, my badge is still valid. When I whisper, Heaven still backs me. I will stop trying to shoot what I'm authorized to arrest. Thank You that hell recognizes real badges. Thank You that Heaven's government never fails. Thank You that my authority is as valid in hospital hallways as on healing platforms. In Jesus' name, I am UNDER authority, therefore I HAVE authority! I am an officer, not an orphan! Amen."

CLOSING — FROM POWERLESS TO POSITIONED

Day 10 complete. The trembling person who woke at 4:29 AM? Now carrying authority that makes hell nervous. You're not begging anymore—you're commanding. You're not hoping—you're declaring. You're not under attack—you're on the throne. Three days, three revelations: Day 8: Your IDENTITY as heir. Day 9: Your INHERITANCE of resources. Day 10: Your AUTHORITY to rule.

Tomorrow, ANOINTING awaits. Because authority establishes your right to rule, but anointing empowers your ability to reign. Authority gives you the badge; anointing gives you specialized equipment for the assignment. But tonight, practice your authority. Find something to command. Speak to something that's been speaking to you. Exercise dominion over something that's been dominating you.

The person with authority doesn't have to shout. Doesn't have to beg. Doesn't have to fear. Authority isn't proven by volume but by results. Hell doesn't measure how loud you pray but how much you know who you are. **Authority isn't how loud I get at darkness—it's how deeply I'm under the Light.**

Welcome to your authority. Welcome to your dominion. Welcome to your Kingdom position where your whisper carries more weight than hell's roar. You're not a vigilante. You're an OFFICER. You're not unauthorized. You're DELEGATED. You don't just have power. You have POSITION. And hell knows exactly what that badge means.

SOAP JOURNAL — DAY 10

S (Scripture): Which authority verse revealed your badge? Write it and personalize it.
O (Observation): Where have you been waving guns instead of wearing your badge? Which of the Five Badge Protocols have you violated?
A (Application): How will you exercise calm badge authority today instead of forceful power? What's one area where you'll practice the 60-Second Badge Check?
P (Prayer): "Father, with my Kingdom badge, I will _____ instead of forcing _____."

Today's Breakthrough Marker: What shifted from powerlessness to authority?
Tomorrow's Expectation: Now that you have authority, how will anointing amplify it?

POWERLESSNESS EVICTED. BADGE AUTHORITY ACTIVATED. READY FOR ANOINTING.

Welcome to your authority. Welcome to your badge. Welcome to the position where hell knows your name.

DAY 11 — ANOINTING

From Equipment Envy to Assignment Excellence

> *"The Spirit of the Lord GOD is upon Me, because the LORD has anointed Me to preach good tidings to the poor; He has sent Me to heal the brokenhearted, to proclaim liberty to the captives, and the opening of the prison to those who are bound."* — Isaiah 61:1

WEEK 2 — ALIGN: Establishing Your Kingdom Identity

Day 11 of 21. Day 8 revealed your Adoption. Day 9 unveiled your Abundance. Day 10 established your Authority. Today's Anointing equips you for assignment—not religious oil, but divine enablement for specific purpose.

ENCOUNTER — WHERE YOU ARE

4:30 AM. Day 11. The trembling jolts you awake—violent enough to make your teeth chatter. Your hands shake against sheets damp with sweat that smells different. Not the sour fear-sweat from yesterday. Not the hollow hunger-sweat from last week. This sweat is slick, oily almost, like something ancient pressing through your pores. You try to steady your hands on the mattress. Can't. The trembling won't stop. Your palms feel strange—slippery, warm, like they've been rubbed with oil though nothing's there when you look. The room is still dark, but something glows behind your closed eyes—like watching welding sparks through safety glass, like lightning trapped in amber. Heaven's equipment room cracks open. The sound echoes through eternity and rattles in your chest.

This isn't yesterday's authority shift. This runs deeper. Older. Like David's shepherd staff suddenly humming with king's anointing. Like ordinary becomes extraordinary through one divine touch. You know WHO you are (adopted). You know WHAT you have (abundance). You understand your POSITION (authority). But knowing your badge doesn't mean you know how to use specialized equipment. A police officer has authority (badge) but needs specific training (anointing) for bomb squad, K-9 unit, or detective work. The badge grants right to serve; anointing grants ability to succeed. You've been trying to fulfill calling with general authority when God wants to give you specific anointing. Like trying to defuse a bomb with only a badge—you have the right, but you need the training.

Remember Day 4 when you discovered your spiritual gifts? Those were the tools. Today is about the ANOINTING that powers them. Gifts without anointing are power tools without electricity. Anointing without gifts is electricity with nothing to plug in. Today, the oil comes. Not the religious kind that makes you weird. The biblical kind that makes you effective. **Authority gets you in the door. Anointing equips you for what's inside.**

FOUNDATION — THE ANCIENT WORDS THAT CHANGE EVERYTHING

The Language of Consecration

Mashach [mah-SHAKH] (Hebrew) — to smear with oil, to consecrate for divine purpose. Not decoration—designation. When God anoints you, He marks you as His instrument. **Chrio** [KHREE-oh] (Greek) — to furnish with necessary powers for administration. Not optional upgrades. NECESSARY

POWERS. Without anointing, you're attempting surgery with toy instruments. Notice what's missing: Nothing about platform size. Nothing about dramatic gifting. Notice what's emphasized: FUNCTION, not status. EQUIPMENT, not elevation. SERVICE, not superiority. ADMINISTRATION, not admiration.

The Anointing That Flows From Identity

Religion taught us anointing was for the special few—the super-spiritual, the dramatically gifted, the platform people. Regular believers could admire anointing from afar, maybe catch some overflow if we sat close enough, but never access it ourselves. But the Holy Spirit whispers what revolutionizes everything: "They think anointing is about ELEVATION. But anointing is about EQUIPMENT. It's not a badge of honor—it's tools for assignment. It's not about being special—it's about being equipped. Every adopted child is anointed because every child has a purpose. The question isn't 'Am I anointed?' but 'What am I anointed FOR?'"

That question shift breaks religious limitation. God Himself does the anointing. Not committees. Not denominations. Not human evaluation. GOD. You don't earn anointing through performance. You discover and deploy it through position. Anointing isn't awarded to the elite. It's issued to the aligned. You're not waiting to be anointed. You're waiting to discover what you're anointed FOR.

TESTIMONY — THE EQUIPMENT CHASER

When Jealousy Became Teacher

She sat in the conference hall, watching heaven crack open through someone else's gift. The prophet called out full names, street addresses, bank account numbers. Hearts exposed. Destinies declared with surgical precision. Holy jealousy burned in her chest like acid. "God, I want THAT anointing!" For months she exhausted herself. Fasted until family worried—her husband begging her to eat, her children watching her disappear into intensity. Prayed until knees went numb, carpet fibers imprinted on skin. Stayed up until 3 AM trying to "press in" for that level of specificity. Practiced prophetic words that fell flat like punctured balloons. Pushed for revelations that wouldn't come—straining to hear addresses and account numbers while heaven remained silent.

One morning, depleted after another failed attempt, she collapsed on her bathroom floor—tile cold against her cheek, body too tired to make it to bed. She complained to God through tears that tasted like failure: "Why won't You give me that prophet's anointing? Don't You trust me with that level of power? What's wrong with me?" His response was gentle but direct enough to reorganize her spiritual DNA: "Beloved, I've already given you YOUR anointing. You're trying to be a prophet when I've called you to be a shepherd. You're demanding SWAT equipment when I've assigned you to Pastoral Care. Both are needed. Both are anointed. Both are essential. But you can't fulfill your assignment wearing someone else's tools."

"Watch what you've been doing naturally—women leave your presence healed from decades of trauma. Men weep as Father wounds close. Marriages resurrect from death. You sit with pain others can't touch. You hear what people don't say. You create safety others can't build. THAT is your anointing. You've been so busy coveting someone else's prophetic kit, you've never honored the pastoral equipment you've been issued." Then He opened her eyes to see what she'd been missing: **The anointing you're jealous of might be the very thing that would hinder your assignment.** She stopped trying to force revelations about street addresses and started stewarding the revelation of wounded hearts. Within six months: Her counseling schedule filled with referrals, pastors sent their hardest cases to her, marriages on the brink found restoration, and trauma survivors found their voice. She finally understood: Her anointing wasn't deficient. It was different. Not less than. Designed for a different purpose. **The anointing you're jealous of might be the very thing that would hinder your assignment. Your anointing fits your assignment like a glove fits a hand.**

The Memory That Prophesied

As she lay on that bathroom floor, another memory surfaced—something she hadn't thought about in decades: Age nine. School playground. A girl crying behind the equipment shed, trying to hide. Everyone else kept playing, didn't notice, didn't care. But nine-year-old Maria felt the pull—like invisible hands turning her around, pointing her toward the shed. She walked over. Sat down beside the girl without saying anything. Just sat there. The girl kept crying. Maria kept sitting. After what felt like hours but was probably ten minutes, the girl whispered her story—parents divorcing, dad leaving, nobody listening. Maria didn't have words to fix it. Didn't try to. Just stayed. Just listened. Just created space for the pain.

When the bell rang, the girl looked at her with eyes that had stopped crying. "You're the first person who didn't tell me it would be okay." Maria blinked, confused. "Because you knew it's not okay right now. And you let it not be okay. Thank you." Nine-year-old Maria didn't understand what had just happened. She just knew she'd done what she was supposed to do. Thirty years later, on a bathroom floor, God whispered: "You've been carrying pastoral anointing since you were nine. You just didn't have language for it. Stop trying to be the prophet who calls out addresses. Be the shepherd who sits with pain. That's the oil I've always given you."

REVELATION — THE VISION OF HEAVEN'S EQUIPMENT ROOM

When God Opened Her Eyes

A minister preparing for service, discouraged by comparing her gifts to others, received a vision that changes how we understand anointing forever. She saw heaven's equipment room—vast as an aircraft hangar, organized with military precision, glorious beyond description. Angels managing distribution like quartermaster units, each movement purposeful, each assignment tracked. Every believer's name engraved on specific tool chests. Not random storage—intentional preparation. Custom-designed. Perfectly fitted. She watched as new believers received their general anointing—the family oil, basic equipment every Kingdom citizen needs. The angels worked efficiently, anointing foreheads, blessing hands, commissioning feet.

But then she saw something more—specialized tool chests lining the walls, each uniquely configured. One chest opened to reveal a shepherd's staff (pastoral anointing), healing balm (restoration anointing), teaching mantle (revelation anointing), and scribe's pen (writing anointing). Another chest contained a prophetic telescope (seeing distant things), intercessor's bowl (carrying prayers), evangelist's net (gathering souls), and mercy seat (compassion for broken). Each chest different. Each perfectly matched to the name engraved on top.

But then came the heartbreak—countless chests remained closed, seals unbroken, dust gathering. Their owners were across the room, trying to break into others' storage, wearing tools that didn't fit, struggling with equipment designed for different hands. Some were making cardboard copies of others' equipment—cheap imitations that broke under pressure. Some were renting tools that were freely theirs—paying with exhaustion for what God had already given. Some had given up completely, sitting in corners believing they had no chest at all.

The Lord spoke with the tone of a Father watching children ignore their inheritance: "Every child receives general anointing at adoption—the oil of family, the basic equipment every officer needs. But each also has specific anointing for their assignment—specialized tools perfectly designed for their calling. Many never access what I've prepared because they're too busy trying to duplicate what I gave someone else. They die with their tool chest unopened, their equipment unused, their assignment unfulfilled. I don't mass-produce anointing. I custom-design it. The prophet's telescope won't help the shepherd find lost sheep. The evangelist's net won't help the teacher explain mysteries. Each tool fits its calling perfectly—but only its calling." **Stop trying to open someone else's tool chest. Yours has your name on it.**

THE FIVE DIMENSIONS OF ANOINTING

The Framework That Transforms Understanding

Scripture reveals anointing operates in five interconnected dimensions. Understanding these dimensions prevents confusion and releases function.

DIMENSION 1: CONSECRATION — Set Apart for Sacred Purpose

Focus: Belonging before doing. Key Verb: Belong. Outcome: Identity and holiness established.

The first dimension of anointing is separation—being marked as holy, set apart from common use, dedicated to divine purpose. In the Old Testament, oil was poured to symbolize God's choice and ownership: *"Take the anointing oil and anoint him by pouring it on his head"* (Exodus 29:7). *"Anoint Aaron and his sons and consecrate them so they may serve me as priests"* (Exodus 30:30). *"He poured some of the anointing oil on Aaron's head and anointed him to consecrate him"* (Leviticus 8:12). Kings were consecrated for rulership: *"Samuel took a flask of olive oil and poured it on Saul's head"* (1 Samuel 10:1). *"Samuel took the horn of oil and anointed him in the presence of his brothers, and from that day on the Spirit of the Lord came powerfully upon David"* (1 Samuel 16:13). In the New Covenant, the Holy Spirit consecrates us internally. You are not ordinary. You are consecrated—chosen, claimed, and prepared for holy purpose.

Declaration: "I am not ordinary. I am consecrated—set apart by God's hand, sealed by His Spirit, and prepared for holy purpose."

DIMENSION 2: EMPOWERMENT — Equipped With Supernatural Ability

Focus: Divine enablement. Key Verb: Receive. Outcome: Power and capacity released.

Anointing imparts **dunamis** [doo-NAH-mis] (power) and **charis** [KHAR-ees] (grace) to accomplish divine assignments. It enables what human strength cannot—preaching with boldness, healing with compassion, discerning with clarity. *"The Spirit of the Sovereign Lord is on me, because the Lord has anointed me to proclaim good news"* (Isaiah 61:1). *"But as for me, I am filled with power, with the Spirit of the Lord"* (Micah 3:8). *"Not by might nor by power, but by my Spirit,' says the Lord Almighty"* (Zechariah 4:6). *"God anointed Jesus of Nazareth with the Holy Spirit and power, and he went around doing good and healing all who were under the power of the devil"* (Acts 10:38). Empowerment is purpose-driven: to proclaim, to deliver, to heal, to restore.

Declaration: "I carry divine power. The Spirit of the Lord rests on me and equips me with supernatural ability to fulfill Heaven's assignment."

DIMENSION 3: COMMISSIONING — Authorized for Kingdom Assignment

Focus: Divine mandate. Key Verb: Go. Outcome: Assignment and authority activated.

Anointing is Heaven's commissioning. Not just empowerment—authorization. The divine endorsement that gives you the right (**exousia** [ex-oo-SEE-ah]) and backing of Heaven to carry out God's will on earth. *"Anoint Hazael king... anoint Jehu... and anoint Elisha to succeed you as prophet"* (1 Kings 19:16). *"After you put these clothes on your brother Aaron and his sons, anoint and ordain them"* (Exodus 28:41). *"Do not touch my anointed ones; do my prophets no harm"* (1 Chronicles 16:22). Prophets, priests, kings—and even Jesus—were not released until they were anointed. *"The Spirit of the Lord is upon me, because He has anointed me"* (Luke 4:18). *"God has made this Jesus, whom you crucified, both Lord and Messiah"* (Acts 2:36). Anointing is the moment where identity becomes assignment and potential becomes mandate.

Declaration: "I am not self-sent—I am God-sent. Heaven backs my mission, the King endorses my assignment, and the anointing authorizes my authority."

DIMENSION 4: OVERFLOW — Abundance of Grace and Favor

Focus: Continual supply. Key Verb: Flow. Outcome: Influence and fruitfulness multiply.

Anointing is not meant to be contained—it overflows. Not a one-time event but a continual outpouring that saturates every part of your life and influences those around you. *"You anoint my head with oil; my cup overflows"* (Psalm 23:5). *"It is like precious oil poured on the head... For there the Lord bestows his blessing, even life forevermore"* (Psalm 133:2-3). *"You love righteousness and hate wickedness; therefore God, your God, has set you above your companions by anointing you with the oil of joy"* (Psalm 45:7). Overflow is the evidence of intimacy—the closer you are to the Source, the more the anointing spills into every sphere. Overflow transforms your cup into a river—no longer about surviving but supplying.

Declaration: "I do not walk in a drop—I walk in a river. God's anointing overflows from my life into every assignment, relationship, and environment I step into."

DIMENSION 5: BREAKTHROUGH — Destroys Yokes and Releases Freedom

Focus: Yoke-destroying power. Key Verb: Break. Outcome: Victory and transformation manifest.

The final dimension of anointing is power to break through barriers—to destroy yokes, shatter strongholds, heal the sick, free the oppressed, and disarm the enemy. *"The yoke will be destroyed because of the anointing"* (Isaiah 10:27). *"Is anyone among you sick? Let them call the elders to pray and anoint them with oil. The prayer offered in faith will make the sick person well"* (James 5:14-15). *"They drove out many demons and anointed many sick people with oil and healed them"* (Mark 6:13). The anointing doesn't just bless—it breaks. Every demonic system, generational curse, or spiritual resistance must bow under the weight of God's anointing.

Declaration: "I am a carrier of breakthrough. The anointing on my life shatters yokes, breaks oppression, heals the sick, and pushes back darkness."

THE FIVE DIMENSIONS OF ANOINTING — SUMMARY TABLE

DIMENSION	FOCUS	KEY VERB	OUTCOME	SCRIPTURES
Consecration	Set apart as sacred	Belong	Identity & holiness	Ex. 30:30; 1 Sam. 16:13

Empowerment	Receive divine enablement	Receive	Power & capacity	Isa. 61:1; Acts 10:38
Commissioning	Authorized for mission	Go	Assignment & authority	1 Kings 19:16; Matt. 28:18
Overflow	Abundance of grace & favor	Flow	Influence & fruitfulness	Ps. 23:5; John 7:38
Breakthrough	Destroy yokes & release freedom	Break	Victory & transformation	Isa. 10:27; Mark 6:13

Biblical Definition: Anointing is the sacred act and spiritual reality of being chosen, consecrated, and empowered by the Spirit of God to fulfill divine purpose. It is both a seal of identity and a supply of power—setting you apart, sending you forth, overflowing through you, and breaking every obstacle before you.

THE DIFFERENCE THAT CLARIFIES EVERYTHING

General Anointing vs. Specific Anointing

Understanding the distinction between general and specific anointing revolutionizes how you approach your calling.

General anointing is given at adoption—the moment you're born again. It's the same for every believer because there are no favorites in God's family. This is the Holy Spirit's indwelling presence, permanently resident within you, empowering you for Christian life like a basic operating system. It includes authority over the enemy as standard-issue weaponry. This anointing abides permanently, though it can be grieved or quenched, it cannot be revoked. Think of it as your badge and basic gear—every officer has these. All five dimensions of anointing are present in this general anointing: consecration, empowerment, commissioning, overflow, and breakthrough.

Specific anointing operates differently. This anointing is given for your unique calling, matched precisely to your mission. It comes in unique combinations with no duplicates across the Body of Christ. This is specialized equipment—specific tools designed for specific tasks. It empowers you for specific service with enhanced capabilities beyond the general anointing. Unlike general anointing, specific anointing can be developed through use or neglected through fear, like a muscle that grows stronger with exercise or atrophies without it. This anointing fits your design like custom-tailored clothing. Think of it as your specialized kit—your unique loadout. This specific anointing aligns perfectly with the spiritual gifts you discovered on Day 4. The same five dimensions are present but specifically applied to your unique assignment.

The Illustration

Think of it this way: Every police officer has a badge and gun—that's general equipment. But K-9 units have trained dogs, detectives have forensic kits, SWAT teams have breaching tools—that's specific equipment matched to specific assignments. Every believer can cast out demons through general authority. But some believers have a specific deliverance anointing that breaks strongholds others can't touch. **General anointing makes you dangerous to hell. Specific anointing makes you strategic for heaven. General anointing comes with adoption. Specific anointing comes with assignment.**

CONNECTING YOUR GIFTS TO YOUR ANOINTING

The Bridge From Day 4 to Day 11

The Spirit distributes different gifts (Day 4 discovery) but the same Spirit anoints them for operation (Day 11 activation). *"There are diversities of gifts, but the same Spirit"* (1 Corinthians 12:4). Day 4 revealed what's in your toolbox. Day 11 releases the power to operate those tools effectively. Your Day 4 discovery aligns with your Day 11 anointing: Teaching gifts connect to teaching anointing. Mercy gifts connect to restoration anointing. Leadership gifts connect to administrative anointing. Prophetic gifts connect to revelatory anointing. The gifts name the grace. The anointing supplies the oil. The assignment sets the direction. This isn't a cage—it's a compass. Your spiritual gifts point to your anointing. Your anointing empowers your gifts. Together, they fulfill your assignment. **Gifts discovered become gifts deployed through anointing.**

ACTIVATING SPIRITUAL GIFTS BY FAITH

The Declaration That Awakens Your Equipment

Now that you see the connection between your Day 4 gifts and Day 11 anointing, it's time to activate what you've discovered. This isn't presumption—it's faith responding to God's distribution. Declare this with authority:

"Father, I thank You for the diversity of gifts distributed by Your Spirit (1 Corinthians 12:11). Today I declare these gifts discovered on Day 4 now awakened and activated with anointing: Faith—I ignite mountain-moving faith within me (Matthew 17:20). Healing—Jehovah Rapha, let Your healing power flow through me (Isaiah 53:5). Prophecy—Lord, I embrace prophetic anointing for edification, exhortation, and comfort (1 Corinthians 14:3). Miracles—God of wonders, release miraculous demonstrations through me. Wisdom and Knowledge—I receive divine insight and understanding (James 1:5). Tongues and Interpretation—Holy Spirit, deepen communion and edify others through me. Leadership and Administration—Equip me to lead and organize with excellence (Romans 12:8). Encouragement and Service—Let encouragement overflow and service multiply (Galatians 5:13). I declare these gifts are no longer dormant but dynamically operational, empowered by the anointing You've placed upon my life. In Jesus' name, Amen."

What Day 4 identified, Day 11 ignites.

THE LIE VS. THE TRUTH

What Religion Taught vs. What Scripture Says

Religion taught us lies that kept us from accessing what was already ours. We believed anointing was for special people with dramatic gifts, that we needed to feel something supernatural to be anointed, that if we weren't operating like famous ministers we weren't truly anointed. We thought anointing was about platform and performance, something we needed to earn, achieve, or be selected for. We believed our quiet gifts weren't really anointing.

But Scripture declares different truth that sets us free. Every adopted child is anointed with family oil—no exceptions. You carry specific anointing for your unique assignment—custom equipment designed precisely for you. Your anointing might look different but it's not deficient—it's specialized, not second-rate. Anointing is about service, not status—equipment, not elevation. You already have what you need for what you're called to do—fully equipped. Even hidden anointing holds rooms together in ways visible ministry cannot. This isn't about becoming special. It's about being equipped for your special assignment. **Hell doesn't fear generic Christians. Hell fears specifically-equipped believers who know their assignment.**

CRITICAL: ANOINTING WITHOUT CHARACTER IS DANGEROUS

Your gift may open the door, but your character keeps you in the room. Character is the container of oil. The purer the vessel, the cleaner the flow. Think of a glass of water. Pure water in a dirty glass comes out contaminated. Your anointing is pure—from the Holy Spirit. But pride, manipulation, or greed taints what flows through. I've watched ministers with powerful anointing destroy everything through character failure. The oil was real. The container was cracked. Everything leaked out.

Samson possessed supernatural strength, but compromise created cracks in his character. The anointing leaked until he ground grain in prison, blind and bound. Saul was anointed king, but insecurity corrupted his container. Oil meant to bless became poison that destroyed his dynasty. **Your private life must support your public anointing. Your integrity must match your oil. Your character must carry your calling.** The widows' oil in 2 Kings 4 stopped flowing when she ran out of vessels. The oil wasn't depleted—the containers were exhausted. Your anointing will flow as long as your character can contain it. **Your anointing is a sacred trust, not a personal trophy.**

Anointing can be:
- Prostituted for profit (selling what should be free)
- Abused for control (manipulating people "in the Spirit")
- Neglected through fear (hiding equipment God gave)
- Corrupted through pride (thinking you're special, not equipped)
- Diluted through compromise (mixing Kingdom oil with worldly motives)

Guard your character as fiercely as you develop your anointing. One without the other creates disaster.

BIBLICAL PATTERNS OF ANOINTING PROGRESSION

TIER 1: Four Full Witnesses

Zechariah: When Priestly Anointing Met Prophetic Promise (Luke 1:13-20)

Zechariah served faithfully in his priestly anointing for decades. Blameless. Righteous. The scent of incense had soaked into his priestly garments from years of service. Yet barren—both his wife's womb and his prayers for a child seemed to fall on deaf ears. Then, during routine priestly service—burning incense in the temple, same duty he'd performed countless times—the atmosphere shifted. Light that wasn't from lamps. Presence that wasn't from ritual. Gabriel appeared, glory radiating: *"Do not be afraid, Zechariah, for your prayer is heard; and your wife Elizabeth will bear you a son, and you shall call his name John. And you will have joy and gladness, and many will rejoice at his birth. For he will be great in the sight of the Lord"* (Luke 1:13-15).

Zechariah's hands trembled on the altar. His voice cracked with decades of unanswered prayer: "How shall I know this? For I am an old man." Gabriel's response carried weight: *"I am Gabriel, who stands in the presence of God, and was sent to speak to you and bring you these glad tidings. But behold, you will be mute and not able to speak until the day these things take place, because you did not believe my words"* (Luke 1:19-20). Nine months of silence. Nine months carrying prophecy he couldn't speak. But when John was born and Zechariah wrote "His name is John," his mouth opened, his tongue was loosed, and he prophesied powerfully over his son's destiny. **Your routine obedience in today's anointing can birth tomorrow's prophetic promise.**

David: From Shepherd's Oil to King's Authority (1 Samuel 16:13; 2 Samuel 2:4, 5:3)

"Then Samuel took the horn of oil and anointed him in the midst of his brothers; and the Spirit of the Lord came upon David from that day forward" (1 Samuel 16:13). Notice where David was anointed—in obscurity, among sheep, smelling like the field. His king assignment was anointed in his shepherd season. Samuel arrived at Jesse's house. The father paraded his sons—tall, strong, warrior material. Seven sons passed before the prophet. Seven times God said no. Samuel, confused: "Are all the young men here?" Jesse, dismissive: "There remains yet the youngest, and there he is, keeping the sheep."

David walked in smelling like sheep, dirt under fingernails, youngest and least likely. God's voice thundered: "Arise, anoint him; for this is the one!" Samuel poured. Oil ran down David's forehead, into his eyes, onto his shepherd's cloak. "Then the Spirit of the Lord came upon David from that day forward." But watch—he went back to the sheep! The anointing didn't immediately change his location. It equipped him for a future assignment while requiring faithfulness to his current one. Years passed. Anointed but not throned. Equipped but not positioned. Chosen but not crowned. Second anointing—king over Judah: *"Then the men of Judah came, and there they anointed David king over the house of Judah"* (2 Samuel 2:4). Partial authority. Third anointing—king over all Israel: *"So all the elders of Israel came to the king at Hebron, and King David made a covenant with them at Hebron before the Lord, and they anointed David king over Israel"* (2 Samuel 5:3). Complete authority. Each oil expanded capacity. Each consecration increased territory. **Your anointing might be for tomorrow's palace, but it's proven in today's pasture.**

The Woman With the Alabaster Box: Anointing for Eternity (Matthew 26:8-9; Mark 14:8-9)

She entered carrying everything—an alabaster box worth a year's wages. Her security. Her dowry. Her future. She broke it over Jesus. Not opened—broke. No going back. The disciples called it waste: *"Why this waste? For this fragrant oil might have been sold for much and given to the poor"* (Matthew 26:8-9). Jesus called it beautiful: *"She has done what she could. She has come beforehand to anoint My body for burial"* (Mark 14:8). One specific anointing. One moment. One assignment. It cost everything. But Jesus declared: *"Assuredly, I say to you, wherever this gospel is preached in the whole world, what this woman has done will also be told as a memorial to her"* (Mark 14:9).

We're discussing her today. Two thousand years later. One moment of deployed anointing echoing through eternity. She had a specific anointing—to prepare His body for burial. Not to preach to thousands. Not to heal the sick. Not to lead churches. To ANOINT FOR BURIAL. One assignment. One moment. One specific anointing. And it cost her everything she had. **Don't despise your anointing because it seems small. Heaven records faithful deployment, not flashy display.**

Paul: Anointing So Strong It Transferred (Acts 19:11-12)

Paul paid such a price in consecration that his anointing could transfer through fabric: *"Now God worked unusual miracles by the hands of Paul, so that even handkerchiefs or aprons were brought from his body to the sick, and the diseases left them and the evil spirits went out of them"* (Acts 19:11-12). Handkerchiefs he touched carried healing power. Aprons he wore cast out demons. His sweat carried miracles. This level doesn't come overnight. It comes through years of consecration—beatings, shipwrecks, stonings, prayers, fasting. The anointing cost him everything and gave him unusual miracles. **The depth of your consecration determines the breadth of your demonstration.**

TIER 2: Two Grouped Witnesses

Unexpected Anointing

Here's what shocks religious systems: *"Thus says the Lord to His anointed, to Cyrus, whose right hand I have held—to subdue nations before him and loose the armor of kings"* (Isaiah 45:1). A Persian king who worshipped false gods. Never attended synagogue. Never studied Torah. Yet God called him "My anointed" and used him to deliver Israel. Your unsaved boss might carry anointing to promote you. Your difficult neighbor might be anointed to prepare you. That challenging situation might be anointed to develop you. Stop limiting where God's oil can flow. He anoints whoever, whatever, whenever for His purposes. **His anointing isn't bound by your religious borders.**

Hidden Anointing

Some anointing never fills stadiums but saves lives stadiums can't reach. The pastoral counselor whose office transforms trauma. The night-shift worker whose prayers stabilize surgical outcomes. The intercessor whose name nobody knows but whose oil holds regions together. Heaven doesn't measure anointing by visibility. Heaven measures it by faithfulness. Whether your anointing fills arenas or sitting rooms, whether it impacts thousands or touches one, deploy it faithfully. **Heaven doesn't rank anointings. Heaven deploys them.**

TESTIMONY — MY COST OF CONSECRATION

When Oil Demanded Everything

October 2019. God called me to a discipline that would cost everything and give everything. Every morning at 5 AM—no exceptions—I rise to command my day, commit all things to God, and converse with Him in His word. Listening to His voice. Speaking Biblical affirmations and scriptural declarations over my life. Then imparting to others through social media and later the Chayah Club community. The first year felt like obedience. Challenging but doable. But the cost increased.

The Wilderness Years

2021 and 2022 became my wilderness years—I saw no one face to face except my two sons. When we walked our dog, I'd see people only at a distance. Cross the street to avoid. Wave from afar. The isolation wasn't by choice initially—pandemic restrictions created the framework. But God used it to deepen something. Two years in God's presence alone. Two years of consecration. Two years of oil being pressed in isolation. My friends didn't understand. Family worried. "Are you okay?" texts went unanswered because I didn't know how to explain what was happening. The anointing was developing in hiddenness. Like David in the fields. Like Moses in the desert. Like Jesus in the wilderness.

The Wrestling

There were nights—many nights—when I questioned everything. Staring at my phone at 11 PM, scrolling through photos of friends at gatherings I wasn't at, weddings I wasn't invited to, celebrations that continued without me. The loneliness wasn't poetic. It was visceral. Like being pressed in an olive press—the weight crushing, the oil slowly seeping out, everything in me screaming to escape. I'd open my journal and write questions that had no immediate answers: "God, am I crazy? Have I heard You wrong? Why would You isolate me like this? What if I'm missing life while pursuing a calling that doesn't exist?" Some mornings at 4:50 AM, my alarm would sound and everything in me wanted to turn it off. Go back to sleep. Skip the 5 AM commitment just once. Nobody would know. But something deeper wouldn't let me. Not duty. Not discipline. Something like destiny pulling me out of bed when my body protested.

For these two years, I wrote 365 sermons and preached 365 sermons. Each morning another message downloaded from Heaven. Each day another impartation flowing through me to others waiting on the prayer line. In 2021, after about Day 250, I heard the Lord say "Go deeper." So I started from Genesis to Revelation, stopping on every scripture where the Lord issued the command "Do not be afraid." I would read the chapter to provide context. One morning in preparation, I got nervous. The enemy attacked me, whispering that I wouldn't be able to pronounce the names correctly. In a moment of panic, I called on my son Nick to come and read for me. He showed up that morning and continued to read each day after that, all the way until Day 365. God was teaching me something: **Anointing doesn't mean doing everything alone. Sometimes your anointing requires partnership.**

When Destiny Walked In

God also sent destiny helpers. John—first a stranger who joined the prayer call in Spring 2022—later co-ministered with me on the 5 AM call. A stranger who would become my husband. That divine appointment revealed how God uses complementary anointings even in the wilderness of consecration. John's dominant gifts: Pastoral shepherding, evangelism, word of knowledge, faith, wisdom, encouragement, service, speaking in tongues, intercession, and prophecy. My dominant gifts: Faith, wisdom, knowledge, prophecy, leadership, administration, encouragement, service, speaking in tongues, and intercession. Notice the overlap and the uniqueness. We share faith, wisdom, encouragement, service, tongues, and intercession—but in different measures. He shepherds souls; I lead systems. He evangelizes the lost; I administrate the found. Together, we're more effective than apart. Our Day 4 gifts complement like puzzle pieces. Our Day 11 anointings amplify like harmonies.

The crushing was releasing the oil. The pressing was producing the fragrance. The loneliness was creating capacity for His presence. The 365 days of writing and speaking were forging the anointing that would mark my future. **The anointing costs what most aren't willing to pay—but gives what money could never buy.**

DISCOVERING YOUR SPECIFIC ANOINTING

The Five Indicators

Stop looking at others' equipment. Start recognizing your own. Look for these indicators:

First: What flows effortlessly through you that others struggle with? Some people can teach complex things simply—that's teaching anointing. Some can sit with pain others flee from—that's pastoral anointing. Some can organize chaos into systems—that's administrative anointing.

Second: Where do you see fruit without straining? Not what you force. What flows. Where do results happen naturally?

Third: What burden won't release you? What breaks your heart? What keeps you up at night? What do you see that others miss? That burden often points to your anointing.

Fourth: Where does grace multiply your efforts supernaturally? You do a little; God does a lot. That's anointing at work.

Fifth: What do people repeatedly affirm about your impact? What do they thank you for? What transformation do they attribute to your presence?

Now connect these to your Day 4 discoveries. Your spiritual gifts point to your anointing. Your anointing empowers your gifts. **Your anointing is already operating. You're just learning to recognize it.**

WHEN YOUR ANOINTING FEELS DRY: TROUBLESHOOTING

Sometimes your anointing feels blocked, depleted, or ineffective. Before you assume you've lost it, check these seven areas:

1. Is sin creating a barrier? (Unconfessed sin doesn't remove anointing but blocks flow. Repent and restore.)

2. Are you operating in someone else's anointing? (Trying to use tools not designed for you exhausts anointing. Return to your lane.)

3. Has character compromise created cracks in your container? (Pride, manipulation, greed corrupt the oil. Humble yourself and realign.)

4. Are you neglecting development through fear? (Anointing atrophies with disuse. Use it or lose effectiveness.)

5. Are you in a wilderness season of deepening? (Sometimes "dry" is actually "pressing" that releases more oil. Don't quit in the pressing.)

6. Have you prostituted your anointing for profit or platform? (When anointing becomes commodity, flow corrupts. Repent of wrong motives.)

7. Are you exhausted and need rest? (Elijah's anointing didn't fail in the cave—he needed sleep and food. Rest is stewardship, not weakness.)

If you've checked all seven and still feel dry: Sometimes God allows anointing seasons to shift or rest. Don't panic. Like fields left fallow to restore nutrients, your anointing may be in restoration mode. Stay faithful. The oil will flow again. **Dry seasons don't mean dead anointing—they often mean deep preparation.**

THE 4D FRAMEWORK FOR YOUR ANOINTING

DISCOVERING Your Anointing. Ask trusted believers: "Where do you see unusual grace on my life?" Watch where small faithfulness opens large doors. Review your Day 4 gift assessment. What flows effortlessly through you that others find difficult? Where do you see consistent fruit? What do others affirm repeatedly? What burden breaks your heart? Where does grace multiply your efforts?

DEVELOPING Your Anointing. *"Do not neglect the gift that is in you, which was given to you by prophecy with the laying on of the hands of the eldership"* (1 Timothy 4:14). Your anointing is like a muscle—use it or lose effectiveness. Study subjects related to your anointing. Practice using your specific tools. Submit to mentors who operate in similar anointing. Take stretching assignments that require growth. Stay humble—pride corrupts the oil.

DEPLOYING Your Anointing. *"As each one has received a gift, minister it to one another, as good stewards of the manifold grace of God"* (1 Peter 4:10). Your anointing is for serving others, not building platform. It's for building Kingdom, not personal empire. It's for glorifying Jesus, not showcasing self. Release freely what you received freely.

PROTECTING Your Anointing. *"O Timothy! Guard what was committed to your trust, avoiding the profane and idle babblings and contradictions of what is falsely called knowledge"* (1 Timothy 6:20). Anointing can be prostituted for profit, abused for control, neglected through fear, corrupted through pride, or diluted through compromise. **Discovered, developed, deployed, and protected—that's the lifecycle of anointing.**

MONTHLY ANOINTING OPERATION ASSESSMENT

Track your anointing stewardship monthly. Rate yourself 0-10 in each area:

Equipment Recognition: ___/10
(10 = Clear about specific anointing; 1 = Still copying others' tools)

Jealousy vs. Celebration: ___/10
(10 = Genuinely celebrate others' anointings; 1 = Constant envy and comparison)

Deployment Consistency: ___/10
(10 = Regularly using anointing; 1 = Tools gathering dust from fear)

Character Integrity: ___/10
(10 = Container clean, oil flows pure; 1 = Cracks from compromise)

Gift Development: ___/10
(10 = Actively developing Day 4 gifts; 1 = Neglecting growth)

Total Score: ___/50

Interpretation:
- **0-20:** Equipment envy dominant. Review your Day 4 gifts. Ask three people what grace they see on your life. Stop comparing daily.
- **21-35:** Transitioning from envy to excellence. Continue monthly protocols. Focus on lowest-scoring area. Celebrate progress.
- **36-50:** Walking in assignment excellence. Maintain quarterly check-ins. Ready to mentor others. Model faithful deployment.

Compare scores monthly. Celebrate every increase—transformation is progressive. If scores decrease, review the Seven Troubleshooting areas. Check for jealousy, neglect, or character compromise. Realign without shame. **You're measuring progress, not perfection.**

THE 6-DIMENSIONAL ANOINTING ACTIVATION

DIMENSION	PRACTICE	EVIDENCE
SPIRITUAL	Ask Holy Spirit: "What grace-tools have You given me?"	Clarity about specific anointing emerges
MENTAL	Invest in learning related to your anointing	Competence partners with anointing
EMOTIONAL	Stop comparing, celebrate your unique loadout	Peace replaces performance anxiety
PHYSICAL	Position yourself where your anointing is needed	Opportunities align with your equipment
FINANCIAL	Invest money developing your God-given enablement	ROI in Kingdom impact multiplies
RELATIONAL	Actively serve others with your anointing	Lives transform through your tools

Unused anointing becomes yesterday's oil. Deployed anointing stays fresh.

6-DIMENSIONAL ANOINTING PRAYERS

SPIRITUAL: "I DECREE divine clarity over my specific anointing! Like Samuel who heard God's voice—*'Speak, for Your servant hears'* (1 Samuel 3:10)—I position myself to receive. Holy Spirit, reveal the grace-tools You've deposited in me!"

MENTAL: "I PROPHESY over my mind: You will be renewed! Like Daniel who gained *'knowledge and skill in all literature and wisdom'* (Daniel 1:17), I DECLARE divine hunger for wisdom. My competence is marrying my anointing for MAXIMUM impact!"

EMOTIONAL: "I BREAK every chain of comparison! When John the Baptist declared *'He must increase, but I must decrease'* (John 3:30), he celebrated another's anointing without diminishing his own. Peace floods where performance anxiety existed!"

PHYSICAL: "I DECREE divine positioning! Like Philip *'caught away by the Spirit'* (Acts 8:39), like Esther positioned *'for such a time as this'* (Esther 4:14), I DECLARE supernatural placement. My location aligns with my assignment NOW!"

FINANCIAL: "I DECREE multiplication! Like the widow whose oil multiplied (2 Kings 4:3-6), I PROPHESY supernatural return. *'Give, and it will be given to you: good measure, pressed down, shaken together, and running over'* (Luke 6:38). Kingdom ROI activated!"

RELATIONAL: "I PROPHESY transformation through deployed anointing! Like Jesus who *'went about doing good and healing all who were oppressed by the devil'* (Acts 10:38), the same anointing flows through my relationships! Lives transform through the oil I carry!"

WEEK 2: ALIGN (7A)

THE UNIFIED DECLARATION: "I PROPHESY complete 6-dimensional activation! *'The yoke will be destroyed because of the anointing'* (Isaiah 10:27) operating through EVERY dimension of my life!"

PROPHETIC ACT: RECEIVING YOUR EQUIPMENT

The Olive Oil Consecration

Stand up. Get olive oil—from your kitchen is fine. Pour a small amount in your palm. Declare: "Holy Spirit, I receive: The GENERAL anointing of adoption. The SPECIFIC anointing for my assignment. The ACTIVATION of Day 4 gifts. This anointing is for SERVICE, not status. I will develop faithfully, deploy freely, guard carefully, multiply purposefully."

Now, with the oil in your palm, touch:

Your forehead: "I receive anointed thoughts. My mind thinks from oil-soaked wisdom."
Your eyes: "I receive anointed vision. I see what others miss, discern what others overlook."
Your ears: "I receive anointed hearing. I hear Your voice clearly above every distraction."
Your lips: "I receive anointed words. What I speak carries heaven's oil and power."
Your hands: "I receive anointed works. What I touch transforms. What I build lasts."
Your feet: "I receive anointed steps. My path is ordered. My position is strategic."

Feel the oil on your skin. Smell it. Let it soak in. This physical act creates spiritual memory. From this moment forward, when you need to remember your anointing, touch these places again and recall this consecration. **Physical acts create spiritual anchors.**

DECLARATION OF ACTIVATION

Stand. Hand over heart where your tool chest awaits.

"I am ANOINTED for my assignment! The Spirit of the Lord GOD is upon ME! I am anointed by the Spirit of the Living God. I am set apart, empowered, and commissioned. Rivers of anointing flow through me—to heal, deliver, build, and transform. My Day 4 gifts are now Day 11 empowered! My anointing is UNIQUE to my design, PERFECT for my purpose! I operate in all five dimensions of anointing: CONSECRATION—I am set apart as sacred. EMPOWERMENT—I receive divine enablement. COMMISSIONING—I am authorized for mission. OVERFLOW—Abundance of grace flows through me. BREAKTHROUGH—I destroy yokes and release freedom.

For what the enemy sent to break me, blessed me! As God's anointed one, I am UNTOUCHABLE! I break agreement with equipment envy. I renounce anointing jealousy. I refuse comparison that steals my oil. I reject platform envy that distracts from purpose. Every yoke is destroyed, every burden is lifted! Every environment shifts because the anointing is alive within me! Generational bondages break at my presence! Ancient patterns shatter at my anointing!

Holy Spirit, forgive me for neglecting my equipment while coveting others'. Thank You for gifts discovered on Day 4 and now anointed for deployment on Day 11. Thank You for general oil that makes me family. Thank You for specific oil that equips my calling. I commit to operate in MY lane with MY equipment for YOUR glory. No more jealousy. No more comparison. Just faithful deployment. My tool chest is open. My equipment is issued. My assignment is clear. My anointing is activated. In Jesus' mighty name—the Anointed One who shares His anointing—I am ANOINTED!"

PRAYER OF ANOINTING

"Father of the Anointed One who anoints, I come empty. Ready to be filled. A vessel positioned under Heaven's spout. Thank You that You don't anoint the qualified—You qualify the anointed. Thank You that I don't earn this oil—I inherit it through adoption. Thank You that my anointing isn't generic—it's custom-designed for my assignment. Forgive me for envying others' equipment while neglecting mine, for trying to operate in anointings You didn't give me, for despising my 'small' anointing while chasing 'big' platforms, for letting my tool chest gather dust while I watched others work, for comparing my behind-the-scenes to others' highlight reels.

Today I receive: Fresh oil for my specific assignment. Clarity about my unique anointing. Freedom from comparison and competition. Courage to use what You've given me. Faithfulness in hidden places where You develop me. I declare over my life the five dimensions: Consecration—I belong to You, set apart as sacred. Empowerment—I receive divine power and capacity. Commissioning—I am authorized for Kingdom assignment. Overflow—Your anointing flows through me like a river. Breakthrough—I carry yoke-destroying, burden-removing power.

My anointing fits my calling perfectly. What flows through me is exactly what my assignment requires. My equipment is neither superior nor inferior—it's specifically suited. The yoke-destroying power in me breaks every bondage. My Day 4 gifts are now Day 11 activated. Whether my anointing fills stadiums or sitting rooms, whether it impacts thousands or touches one, whether it's visible or hidden, whether it's celebrated or unnoticed, I will be faithful to deploy what You've deposited.

Like Zechariah, let my routine obedience birth prophetic promise. Like David, develop my anointing in hiddenness before positioning. Like the alabaster woman, let me pour out extravagantly. Like Paul, let consecration make my anointing transferable. Keep my character clean so my anointing flows pure. Keep my heart humble so my oil doesn't corrupt. Keep my focus clear so I don't chase wrong assignments. Keep my hands active so my anointing stays fresh.

I will discover, develop, deploy, and protect what You've given. I will open my tool chest and use what's inside. I will stop trying to break into others' storage. I will celebrate their equipment while stewarding mine. Thank You that Heaven's equipment room has my name on a chest. Thank You that every tool inside is perfectly suited for my purpose. Thank You that I'm not mass-produced—I'm custom-designed. Thank You that my anointing, though different, is not deficient.

From this day forward: I walk in my anointing. I steward my oil. I fulfill my assignment. I glorify Your name. In Jesus' name—the Anointed One who shares His anointing. Amen."

TRANSFORMATION — FROM EQUIPMENT ENVY TO ASSIGNMENT EXCELLENCE

EQUIPMENT ENVY MINDSET	ASSIGNMENT EXCELLENCE MINDSET
Jealous of others' anointings	Celebrating unique equipment
Trying to duplicate someone else's tools	Stewarding what's in my chest
Measuring by platform visibility	Measuring by faithful deployment
Exhausted from comparison	Energized by purpose clarity

Neglecting my tools while coveting theirs	Developing my specific anointing
Feeling deficient and less-than	Knowing I'm specifically equipped
Chasing wrong assignments	Walking in my lane

MANIFESTATION — DAILY ANOINTING PRACTICES

THE ESSENTIAL 3:
1. **DEPLOY ONE ANOINTING** — Use your specific anointing in one interaction today. Don't hoard oil—pour it out.
2. **DEVELOP ONE SKILL** — Study something related to your anointing. Read, learn, grow in competence.
3. **CELEBRATE ONE DIFFERENCE** — Thank God for how your anointing differs from someone else's. Different isn't deficient.

Deploy one anointing. Develop one skill. Celebrate one difference.

ADDITIONAL PRACTICES: Ask someone: "Where do you see unusual grace on my life?" Practice using your spiritual gifts from Day 4 in low-pressure situations. Pray for clarity about which specific anointing you carry. Refuse to compare yourself to one person today. Invest financially in developing your anointing.

START HERE: If you can only do ONE thing today, text someone: "I'm walking in MY anointing today!"

SOAP JOURNAL — DAY 11

S (Scripture): Which anointing verse revealed your specific calling? Write it and personalize it.
O (Observation): How does today's anointing connect to Day 4's gift discovery? Which of the five dimensions speaks loudest?
A (Application): How will you deploy YOUR anointing today using the 4D Framework? What's one way you'll use your unique equipment?
P (Prayer): "Holy Spirit, I will use my anointing to _____ today. Show me my unopened tool chest."

YOUR DAY 11 ACTIVATION CHALLENGE
BEFORE SLEEP TONIGHT:
1. **CONSECRATE:** Perform the olive oil anointing on forehead, eyes, ears, lips, hands, feet
2. **DECLARE:** Speak the Declaration of Activation over yourself
3. **CELEBRATE:** Text someone: "I discovered my specific anointing today!"
4. **CONNECT:** Review your Day 4 gifts and identify which anointing empowers them
5. **COMMIT:** Choose one way to deploy your anointing tomorrow
6. **GUARD:** Identify one character area that needs strengthening to contain your oil

CLOSING — FROM EQUIPMENT ENVY TO ASSIGNMENT EXCELLENCE

Day 11 complete. The trembling at 4:30 AM? Ancient oil activating through your soul. You woke to heaven's equipment room cracking open. Angels calling your name. Your tool chest waiting. You're not unanointed—you're specifically anointed. Not unequipped—you're custom-equipped. Not generic—you're strategic.

Four days, four revelations that build:
- **Day 8—Your IDENTITY** (Adoption—who you are)
- **Day 9—Your INHERITANCE** (Abundance—what you have)
- **Day 10—Your AUTHORITY** (Badge—your position)
- **Day 11—Your ANOINTING** (Equipment—your tools)

Tomorrow, ADVANCEMENT awaits. Because anointing without forward movement is wasted oil. You're equipped to advance, not just stand. But tonight, feel the oil. Let it soak places that have been dry. Touch your forehead, eyes, ears, lips, hands, feet—remember the consecration. You're not the same person who started Day 11. The equipment chaser stopped chasing and started stewarding. The comparison trap broke when you saw your name on the tool chest. The envy died when you understood different isn't deficient.

You now understand the five dimensions of anointing—from consecration to breakthrough. You've connected Day 4 gifts to Day 11 power. The anointing makes the impossible look easy because it's not you doing it—it's the oil. Your calling doesn't need your hustle. It needs Heaven's oil. Your assignment doesn't need your performance. It needs your anointing. Your purpose doesn't need another you. It needs THE you—custom-equipped.

The world isn't waiting for another copy. It's waiting for what YOUR specific anointing releases. Tomorrow you advance with the equipment. Tonight you rest in the oil. Welcome to your anointing. Welcome to your equipment room. Welcome to the oil that destroys every yoke and empowers every assignment. Heaven has been waiting for you to wear it.

Today's Breakthrough Marker: What shifted from equipment envy to assignment excellence?
Tomorrow's Expectation: Now that you're anointed with custom equipment, how will you advance in purpose?

DRY SERVICE ENDED. EQUIPMENT ISSUED. FRESH OIL FLOWING. READY FOR ADVANCEMENT.

Welcome to your anointing. Welcome to your oil. Welcome to the equipment that makes hell nervous and heaven smile.

DAY 12 — ADVANCEMENT

From Destination Obsession to Journey Mastery

> *"You have stayed long enough at this mountain. Break camp and advance... See, I have given you this land. Go in and take possession of it."* — Deuteronomy 1:6-8

WEEK 2 — ALIGN: Establishing Your Kingdom Identity

Day 12 of 21. Day 8's Adoption gave you identity. Day 9's Abundance gave you resources. Day 10's Authority gave you dominion. Day 11's Anointing gave you equipment. Today's Advancement teaches you the journey that creates capacity for destiny.

ENCOUNTER — WHERE YOU ARE

The alarm doesn't wake you—you've been awake for an hour already. 4:30 AM. Day 12. You're staring at the ceiling, counting the cracks in the plaster for the hundredth time, stomach growling but that's not what's eating you. Your mouth is dry—that parched, anxious dryness that no water seems to touch. Your chest feels tight, not pain exactly, but pressure. Like something's trying to surface. Your phone sits on the nightstand, screen dark but presence heavy. Your hand twitches toward it involuntarily—muscle memory from a thousand scroll sessions. One tap would show you: Their platforms exploding. Their books dropping. Their stages expanding. The metrics you can't stop measuring. The arrivals you can't stop coveting.

The question doesn't just burn behind your eyes—it claws up your throat like bile, pounds in your chest like a second heartbeat, screams in the hollow spaces hunger has carved out: **"WHEN?"** When will I arrive? When will I break through? When will this wilderness end and the promised land begin? When will advancement finally find me? You've watched peers launch and land. Scrolled past their platform explosions—thousands of followers overnight, book deals dropping like manna, conference stages opening like the Red Sea parting for them and closing against you. Meanwhile, you faithfully serve your handful. Post consistently to your few hundred. Progress invisibly while they advance visibly. The comparison isn't just painful—it's suffocating. Like drowning in slow motion while everyone else learns to fly.

Twelve days into this fast and five days into identity alignment. The pieces are coming together. You're adopted (Day 8), abundant (Day 9), carrying authority (Day 10), anointed for purpose (Day 11). But equipment without movement is storage. Identity without trajectory is information collecting cobwebs. You know WHO you are. But you're viscerally desperate to know WHEN you'll get THERE. There. That mythical destination where struggle ends and success begins. Where process stops and position starts. Where wilderness becomes promised land. Where you can finally exhale, finally prove to everyone (and yourself) that the wait was worth it.

But this morning—this hollow, holy, hope-against-hope 4:30 AM moment—heaven whispers what changes everything: **"You're not trying to arrive. You're learning to advance."** The words land different than expected. Softer. Deeper. Not reach a destination. Not grab a position. ADVANCE—the ongoing, daily journey of progressing deeper into the purpose for which you've been positioned. The difference between those two words—arrive versus advance—contains the revolution that will redefine your entire understanding of growth, success, and what God's actually been doing while you thought He was doing nothing.

Today you discover the truth that shatters destination obsession: The process isn't delaying destiny—the process IS building it. The journey isn't separate from the promise. The journey IS the promise being formed in you, cell by cell, choice by choice, faithful Tuesday by faithful Tuesday. **Orphans obsess over arrivals. Heirs master the journey. Arrival is a moment. Advancement is a lifestyle.**

FOUNDATION — ADVANCEMENT VS. ARRIVAL: THE PARADIGM THAT CHANGES EVERYTHING

The Lie That Keeps You Stuck

Religion—and Instagram—taught you to measure life by arrivals: The day you "make it." The moment you "break through." The platform that proves you've "arrived." Graduation. Marriage. Six figures. The corner office. The book deal. The stage. Events. Destinations. Arrivals. So you sprint toward them, exhausted by a race with no finish line because every arrival just reveals another destination you haven't reached. You reach one summit only to discover it's base camp for another mountain. The orphan mind operates in binary: arrived or not arrived, success or failure, made it or still trying. This binary creates constant anxiety—Am I there yet? Have I made it? Do I measure up? Am I falling behind?

But the Kingdom operates differently. Heaven doesn't measure by arrivals. Heaven tracks advancement. Not where you've landed, but how you're progressing. Not the position achieved, but the path walked faithfully. Not the destination reached, but the development sustained through the journey. **Heaven doesn't grade arrivals—Heaven tracks advancement. Comparison counts followers; the Kingdom counts footsteps.**

What Is Biblical Advancement?

Biblical Advancement is the God-initiated process of moving forward, breaking through barriers, enlarging territory, and growing in influence, maturity, and purpose. It is not merely physical progress but a divine trajectory—Spirit-empowered momentum that propels God's people into the fullness of their destiny. The Old Testament reveals advancement through Hebrew concepts: **Tsalach** [tsah-LAKH] means to prosper and push forward with divine help—when God causes you to advance beyond your natural limits. Joseph didn't just survive slavery and prison—he tsalach'd through them because "the Lord was with him" (Genesis 39:2-3). **Rabah** [raw-BAW] means to increase, multiply, and expand—advancement that enlarges your capacity, territory, and influence. **Nasa** [naw-SAW] means to break camp and journey forward—the advancement of movement and obedience. When the cloud lifted, Israel nasa'd—pulled up stakes and moved toward destiny (Exodus 40:36).

The New Testament amplifies with Greek precision: **Prokopē** [prok-op-AY] means to cut forward through resistance, like armies advancing through enemy lines. Paul said his chains actually served to advance (prokopē) the gospel (Philippians 1:12). **Auxanō** [owx-AN-oh] means to grow and increase organically—advancement that multiplies naturally under divine blessing. *"The word of God spread (auxanō), and the number of disciples increased"* (Acts 6:7). Heaven's definition synthesized: Advancement is Spirit-empowered forward momentum—breaking camp when God moves, cutting through resistance, growing organically, expanding territory, and stepping progressively into divine destiny. It's not arrival at a destination. It's ongoing progression toward the fullness of your calling. **Advancement isn't a location you reach—it's a trajectory you walk.**

Understanding Advancement and Promotion

Before we go further, we must distinguish two Kingdom realities religion often confuses:

ASPECT	ADVANCEMENT (Day 12)	PROMOTION (Day 19)
Definition	A process of forward movement—spiritually, mentally, missionally, territorially—toward God's purposes	A moment of elevation—a specific appointment, upgrade, or position God gives
Focus	Progression—the journey, growth, movement from one stage to another	Elevation—the outcome of that growth, marked by increased authority or visibility
Nature	Continuous and ongoing—incremental, seasonal, developmental	Sudden and specific—marked by a clear shift, title change, or new assignment
Scope	Broad: spiritual maturity, character development, faith expansion, territory taking	Narrower: rank, position, title, leadership level, recognition
Example	Israel advancing from Egypt through wilderness into Promised Land (Deut. 1:6-8)	David promoted from shepherd to king (1 Sam. 16:13; 2 Sam. 5:3)
Requires	Obedience, perseverance, faithfulness, maturity, stretching beyond comfort	Proven faithfulness, humility, readiness for greater responsibility
Symbol	A journey—walking into new seasons, opportunities, levels of maturity	A crown—stepping into new leadership, authority, stewardship
Key Verse	"Break camp and advance" (Deut. 1:6-8)	"Humble yourselves… that He may exalt you in due time" (1 Pet. 5:6)

The Kingdom Principle: Advancement is the journey of growth that brings you closer to God's purposes. Promotion is the moment of elevation when God publicly entrusts you with greater responsibility. You can have advancement without promotion yet (internal growth, unseen obedience), but you can't sustain promotion without advancement—because advancement builds the capacity to carry promotion without being crushed by it. **Promotion reveals you; advancement prepares you. Process forms you; promotion platforms you. Build capacity now so favor doesn't crush you later.**

Next week (Day 19), we'll unpack PROMOTION—the divine elevation moment when God publicly endorses what He's privately prepared. But today we focus on ADVANCEMENT—the daily progression that makes you promotion-ready.

TESTIMONY — THE CONFERENCE ENVELOPES THAT EXPOSED MY AMBITION

When "Alignment" Felt Like Disqualification

The conference hall buzzed with expectation. My palms were sweating as I held the sealed envelope—that slick, anxious moisture that comes when hope and fear collide. Hundreds of believers around us, all clutching identical registration packets, each containing a prophetic word. The instructions were clear: "Do not open until the activation session. These are words from the Lord for your next level." My heart hammered—that irregular, breath-catching rhythm that makes you wonder if everyone can hear it. We'd been believing God for advancement for months. Bills mounting like evidence against our faith. Ministry plateaued at the same small numbers. Business stagnant despite our prayers. This envelope felt heavy with possibility—like it contained keys to doors we'd been pounding on for what felt like forever.

Next level. Those words hung in the air like promise and pressure combined. My husband John and I held our envelopes like they contained the verdict on our worthiness. The moment finally came. "You may now open your prophetic words." The room erupted in the sound of tearing paper. Gasps. Laughter. Tears. I watched John's face as he opened his envelope first. His eyes went wide. Then that smile—the one that looks like heaven just said "yes." "Financial Breakthrough," he read aloud, voice thick with emotion. "Babe, this is it. This is our advancement. God is moving us forward."

My heart should have leaped. Instead, something ugly twisted in my chest. Sharp. Acidic. Immediate. That's the advancement I wanted. My fingers trembled as I finally opened my envelope. The card slid out. I read it. One word. Just one. **"ALIGNMENT"** My stomach dropped. Alignment? That's my advancement word? That's what I get while everyone else is getting promotion, acceleration, and breakthrough? While my husband—sitting right next to me—gets "Financial Breakthrough"? Alignment didn't sound like advancement. It sounded like preparation. Like a holding pattern. Like God's way of saying, "You're not ready yet, so just... work on yourself while everyone else moves forward."

The Memory That Prophesied

As I sat there holding that card, comparison burning in my chest, a memory surfaced I hadn't thought about in decades: Age 10. School science fair. My project on plant growth. I was obsessed with the final display—the poster board, the presentation, the blue ribbon. I spent hours perfecting my display board: bubble letters, glitter borders, perfect alignment of photos. Meanwhile, my bean sprouts sat on the windowsill. My dad kept trying to show me something: "Niki, look. See how it's different today than yesterday? That tiny new leaf? That's what matters. Not the ribbon. The growing." I rolled my eyes so hard they practically stuck. "Dad, nobody cares about daily growth. They care about who WINS. The judges don't grade you on watering. They grade you on the DISPLAY."

The science fair came. My display looked perfect. My poster board was Pinterest-worthy before Pinterest existed. But my plants... died two days before judging. Brown. Wilted. Dead. I'd been so focused on the destination (winning) that I'd neglected the journey (watering, sunlight, care). I couldn't believe it. How could God let me down like this? (Yes, even at ten I blamed God for my dead plants.) The irony: The girl who won had a messy poster—hand-drawn labels, crooked photos—but thriving plants. Vibrant green. New shoots. Actually growing. She'd documented the daily progression—photos, measurements, observations. Her project wasn't about arrival. It was about advancement. She showed the PROCESS. I'd tried to showcase the POSITION.

I didn't win. Didn't even place. Went home crying, clutching my perfect poster board with dead plants. My dad didn't say "I told you so." He just said: "Ribbons are nice, Niki. But roots matter more. You can't fake growth with a pretty display." Thirty years later, holding that "Alignment" card while everyone else celebrated "Breakthrough," God whispered: **"You're still that 10-year-old obsessed with ribbons instead of roots. But I'm teaching you what your dad tried to show you: The journey IS the prize. The growing IS the glory. Stop killing your calling by ignoring the daily watering it requires."**

When Holy Spirit Corrected My Definition of Advancement

The activation session continued. Worship swelled. People were praying, declaring their advancement. But I sat there, card in hand, ten-year-old science fair failure colliding with thirty-year-old conference disappointment. That's when Holy Spirit whispered: "Why are you despising the very thing required for your advancement?" The question pierced. "You think advancement is about getting what he has. But true advancement is becoming who I'm calling you to be. You can't advance INTO a level you're not aligned FOR." "But God," I whispered, eyes closed, "we need to MOVE FORWARD. We're stuck. Alignment sounds like... staying in place. We need ADVANCEMENT."

His response was so gentle it shattered my wrong definition: "My daughter, you think 'Financial Breakthrough' is advancement and 'Alignment' is delay. But you can't advance past your alignment. Skipping alignment doesn't accelerate advancement—it derails it. John has 'Financial Breakthrough' coming—yes. But YOU have what positions him to walk in it without it destroying him." I opened my eyes. Looked at the card again. The single word that moments ago felt like disqualification now seemed to shimmer with something I'd completely misunderstood. Alignment.

Holy Spirit continued: "ALIGNMENT with My revelation—so you'll advance in the right direction. ALIGNMENT through surrender—so you'll advance in My will, not your ambition. ALIGNMENT in obedience—so you'll advance when I say 'GO,' not rush ahead and abort the blessing. ALIGNMENT with My Word—so you'll advance on solid ground. ALIGNMENT in timing—so you'll advance at the right speed. ALIGNMENT in identity—so you'll advance as My daughter, not as the world's competitor. Alignment isn't the OPPOSITE of advancement. It's the FOUNDATION of sustainable advancement. You're not being held back. You're being SET UP."

The Shift — When Alignment Became My Greatest Advancement

Tears fell freely now. Not from disappointment. From revelation. I'd been so focused on ADVANCING that I'd despised the ALIGNING required to sustain the advancement. Like ten-year-old me obsessing over poster perfection while my plants died from neglect. I looked at John and something shifted. The envy died. The comparison stopped. His advancement needs my alignment. My advancement requires THIS word, not his. I grabbed John's hand, this time with genuine joy: "Babe, I got 'Alignment.' I thought it meant I wasn't advancing. But God just showed me—I can't advance past my alignment, and your breakthrough can't advance without it. You have the provision. I have the positioning. We're advancing TOGETHER, not competing."

The Aftermath — When Alignment Proved to Be the Greater Advancement

In the months that followed, I watched alignment become the very advancement I'd almost despised. REVELATION alignment—God downloaded strategies during prayer that advanced the business further than my hustle ever could. SURRENDER alignment—I released control and watched God advance things I couldn't move on my own. OBEDIENCE alignment—When Holy Spirit said "Give," I gave. When He said "Wait," I waited. When He said "Move NOW," I moved. Each obedience advanced me. TIMING alignment—Opportunities that seemed "late" arrived exactly when we were ready. IDENTITY alignment—I stopped operating as an orphan climbing ladders and started functioning as an heir inheriting kingdoms.

And John's "Financial Breakthrough"? It came. In waves. Through channels we never imagined. But here's what I know with absolute certainty: It came THROUGH the alignment I almost despised. The alignment WAS the advancement. I wasn't staying in place while he moved forward. I was being positioned for sustainable advancement that wouldn't collapse under pressure. **I wasn't being held back. I was being SET UP. I'm not stuck; I'm being set up. Alignment isn't delay—it's destiny scaffolding.**

TESTIMONY — THE WILDERNESS THAT WAS ACTUALLY ADVANCEMENT

Since my divorce in 2015, I've been building this ministry. Steady but slow. Frustratingly slow. I watched peers launch and land. Their platforms exploded—thousands of followers overnight. Their influence multiplied—book deals, speaking circuits, conference stages. Meanwhile, I faithfully served a handful of people. Posted consistently to several hundred followers. Progressed invisibly. The financial pressure was crushing—small team requiring salaries, technology licenses, publishing costs. My contract work in corporate funded the ministry—website development, branding projects, strategic planning—stretching dollars between dreams and bills. The comparison nearly killed my calling.

The Greek Warfare: Cutting Forward Through Resistance

Looking back now, I understand something I missed during those eight years: advancement isn't the absence of obstacles—it's breakthrough through them. When Paul wrote about advancement in Philippians 1:12, he chose the Greek word **prokopē** [prok-op-AY]—and it's visceral. Literally "to cut forward." It's the word for armies hacking through enemy lines with swords, or ships breaking through waves that would sink lesser vessels. This isn't advancement through open doors and smooth paths. This is advancement THROUGH resistance. Paul was writing from prison—chained, limited, seemingly stopped. Yet he declared, *"What has happened to me has actually served to advance (prokopē) the gospel."* The chains didn't stop advancement. They became the very thing through which advancement broke through.

Every "no" I had to cut through during those eight years. Every closed door I had to advance past. Every financial pressure that tried to sink the ministry. Every peer's announcement that felt like waves trying to overwhelm me. Every contract that barely covered bills. Every month of "not yet" from God. I thought those were delays preventing advancement. But they were prokopē—I was cutting forward, making headway despite opposition, breaking through resistance that was actually building the muscle I'd need for what was coming. **The gospel advanced through Paul's chains. Your calling is advancing through your constraints. What looks like resistance isn't stopping your advancement—it's proof you're breaking through. Your advancement isn't a peaceful stroll—it's a breakthrough through resistance. Resistance isn't delay—it's the evidence you're advancing through enemy territory.**

The Divine Appointment

Then divine appointment appeared through LinkedIn in 2022: "I've been watching your ministry for a few years. Your faithfulness in the small, daily things has caught my attention. No fanfare. No self-promotion. Just consistent Kingdom service. I would like to mentor, invest, and partner with you to manifest your vision globally and generationally." This was my future husband speaking—but I didn't know that yet. My hands started shaking. The "God, is this real?" kind. For years he'd been watching. Not my striving—my steadiness. Not my acceleration—my consistency. Not my platform—my progression.

Within a few years, that divine partnership transformed everything. From ministering alone in my bedroom on Zoom, I now travel internationally. No longer surviving between feast and famine contracts. But more importantly—I finally understood. My daily faithfulness WAS advancement. My wilderness season wasn't delay—God was with me, preparing me, positioning me. Those eight years weren't lost—they were invested. The corporate skills. The ministry muscles. The character formed through pressure. The faith developed through comparison battles. All of it was advancement. All of it was preparation. What looked like wilderness was actually advancement. What felt like delay was divine development. The journey hadn't been delaying the destination—the journey was creating capacity for it. **Your wilderness isn't wasted time—it's advancement disguised as delay.**

TESTIMONY — THE CLOCK AND THE COUNT

When God Removed My Metrics

2020 Pandemic ministry. Online calls. And I was obsessed with numbers. How many showed up? Three people? Discouragement sank its teeth in. "Only three? Maybe I should quit." Thirty people? Pride puffed up. "Thirty! We're growing! I'm doing something right!" Every session I'd watch the clock. Fifteen minutes? "Need to speed up." Two hour and forty-five minutes? "Went too long. Hope they're not annoyed." The clock controlled my flow. The count determined my value. Then God's voice interrupted my setup one morning: "Don't look at the clock. This is your training ground. The clock interferes with My Spirit's movement. Stop watching minutes and start watching Me." Before I could process: "And don't count the people. Too few causes discouragement. Too many causes pride. Both are distractions. Keep your eyes on Me."

"Show up for one person and minister as if it's one thousand. Show up for three and give your best as if it's three thousand. Every day of faithfulness is advancement—not the metrics."

The Tests

First call obeying His instruction: Didn't check participant count. Didn't watch time. Just followed Holy Spirit's leading. Forty minutes. Then He said, "Wrap up." So I did. I closed my laptop, exhaled, and checked the participant log. One person. That's it. One single participant. Old me would have spiraled. One person? I prepared for hours for ONE person? I could have just called them directly. This is ridiculous. Maybe I should quit. But I'd given that one person everything—not because I was performing for a crowd. I was obeying my Father. I'd ministered like there were a thousand people in that virtual room because my eyes were on Him, not the counter.

Later that day, the message arrived: "I don't usually reach out, but I needed you to know—today saved my life. Literally. I was planning to end it all tonight. Lost my job two weeks ago. Marriage is falling apart. Kids won't talk to me. I felt completely invisible to God. But for those forty minutes, it was like He was talking directly to me through you. Every single word answered questions I've been screaming at heaven. Every prayer felt custom-made for my breaking. I'm not going to do it. I'm going to get help. Thank you for showing up today."

I stared at the screen, tears streaming. One person. Party of one. And God saved a life through faithfulness, not metrics. If I'd been watching the count? If I'd seen "1 participant" at minute five? I might have checked out mentally. Given a mediocre message. Cut it short. Treated that one person like they were an inconvenience rather than an appointment. But my eyes were on Him, not the numbers. And He used forty minutes of obedience to rescue a soul from suicide.

The Pride Test

Weeks later: Another call. Same obedience. Didn't check the count. Didn't watch the clock. Just followed Holy Spirit's flow. This time? The number was higher than usual—not massive, but noticeably more than the regular handful. After the call, I felt it immediately. That subtle swell. That quiet whisper: See? You're growing. THIS is real ministry. More people = more impact. You're finally advancing. Pride whispered: "You're doing something right. Keep doing THIS." God cut through: "I saved a life through the one. I'm building character through the many. Which advancement matters more?" Both. Neither. Not the number. The advancement was my obedience. Whether one or one hundred, faithfulness is the metric Heaven measures. The number didn't validate my calling. Obedience did.

What I Learned

THE CLOCK was stealing Holy Spirit's FLOW. When I watched time, I rushed when He wanted to linger. I controlled pace when He wanted to control direction. I cut off breakthrough because I was worried about going "too long." But anointing doesn't operate on schedule. Breakthrough doesn't respect timelines. Deliverance doesn't check the clock. THE COUNT was stealing my FOCUS. Three people discouraged me. Thirty puffed me up. The count made me measure success by attendance instead of obedience. Made me value visibility over faithfulness. Made me think impact was directly proportional to numbers. But that's not Kingdom math. Jesus fed five thousand and healed one blind man—both mattered. Both were advancement. Both revealed God's glory.

God called it "training ground" for a reason. If I can't be faithful with one, I can't be trusted with one thousand. If I'm discouraged by three, I'll be destroyed by three thousand. If I need the crowd to validate my calling, I'll compromise my obedience to keep the crowd.

The Paradigm Shift

Now I don't check the clock. I don't count the crowd. Party of one? I show up with everything. Party of one hundred? I show up with everything. The number doesn't change my obedience. The clock doesn't control Holy Spirit's flow. My eyes stay on Him, not the measurements. And you know what's happened? Ministry is growing exponentially. Not because I focused on growth—because I focused on faithfulness, and God handled the growth. **What you measure, you manage. What you surrender, God multiplies. Orphans watch the count. Heirs watch the King. Advancement happens when faithfulness replaces metrics.**

Years later, that "party of one" person recently told me: "I'm so glad you showed up that day like I was the only person in the world who mattered—because to God, I was." She was right. And so was

He when He took away my clock and my count and taught me that advancement isn't measured by metrics—it's built through faithfulness, one obedient day at a time. **Don't look at the clock. Don't count the people. Keep your eyes on Me.**

THE PROMISE THAT SUSTAINS ADVANCEMENT

God in the Messy Middle

There were nights—so many nights—when I wasn't sure I'd survive the advancement. Years into building this ministry, I sat in my car after another disappointing meeting. Another door that looked promising but closed with a polite "not right now." Another month of stretching dollars. Another season of invisible progress while peers announced visible breakthroughs. I gripped the steering wheel, fighting tears that had become too familiar, and whispered the question I'd been afraid to ask out loud: "God, are You even WITH me in this?"

His response came swift, sure, and so tender it broke me: "Daughter, your temple project looks like your pain right now. But I am WITH you—not watching from heaven, but laboring beside you in the mess. You can't trace My hands in this season, but you can trust My heart. Stay the course. Trust the process." Temple project. The phrase settled into my spirit like an anchor. Not just "ministry" or "business" or "calling." Temple project. The assignment He has anointed you to build. The thing He's called you to construct that will house His presence and impact generations. And yes—right now, it looks like pain. Feels like failure. Resembles struggle more than success. But God doesn't build temples overnight. And He doesn't abandon architects mid-construction.

Here's what I learned in that car: **I am building my Temple assignment, but God is making me through the process.** The project isn't separate from my development—it IS my development. Every day I build what God assigned, God builds who I'm becoming. **The assignment you're building is building you.**

The Three Promises That Change Everything

That's when Holy Spirit took me to a passage I'd read dozens of times but never heard until that moment—David's final charge to his son Solomon before the temple construction: *"And David said to his son Solomon, 'Be strong and of good courage, and do it; do not fear nor be dismayed, for the Lord GOD—my God—will be with you. He will not leave you nor forsake you, until you have finished all the work for the service of the house of the Lord'"* (1 Chronicles 28:20).

Solomon was about to build the most important structure in Israel's history. And he was terrified. The blueprint was overwhelming. The resources seemed insufficient. The critics were already whispering. Sound familiar? But David didn't give him a pep talk about hustle. He gave him three promises that would sustain him through every stage of advancement:

PROMISE 1: "I AM WITH YOU"

Not "I will be with you someday." Present tense. Current reality. NOW. "I am WITH you." Not watching from a distance. Not waiting at the finish line. WITH. In the mess. In the middle. In the mundane Tuesday when nothing feels like advancement. The Hebrew word is **im** [eem]—alongside, beside, in the company of. You're not advancing alone. You're advancing WITH Him.

PROMISE 2: "I WILL NOT ABANDON YOU"

"He will not leave you." The fear that haunts every builder: What if God starts something through me and then loses interest? What if I'm too slow, too messy, too broken? Listen: God will not initiate leaving. He's not abandoning you in the messy middle when progress feels invisible, the wilderness wandering when you can't see the promised land, the waiting season when everyone else is launching.

PROMISE 3: "I WILL NOT FORSAKE YOU"

"Nor forsake you." The Hebrew **azab** [aw-ZAB] means more than just leaving—it means leaving someone helpless, removing your help, abandoning someone to circumstances they can't handle alone. God is saying: "I won't leave you helpless. I won't remove My help even when you mess up. Even when you make mistakes in the building process. Even when you slow down progress through your own decisions."

The Timeline That Changes Your Perspective

But here's where it gets powerful. David didn't just give three promises—he gave a timeline: "He will be with you... **until you have FINISHED** all the work." UNTIL. Not "unless." Not "as long as you perform well." UNTIL YOU HAVE FINISHED. God's commitment to your temple project isn't conditional on your speed. It's committed UNTIL completion. That slow advancement you're embarrassed about? God's still committed UNTIL it's finished. That wilderness season lasting longer than expected? God's still present UNTIL you finish the journey. **God's commitment to your temple project isn't conditional on your speed. It's committed UNTIL completion.**

What This Means for Your Advancement

When you're in the messy middle of advancement—when the temple project looks like pain instead of promise—remember: You can't trace His hands, but you can trust His heart. You can't see what He's building in the invisible. But you can trust: He IS with you (present tense). He WON'T abandon you (committed for the duration). He WON'T forsake you (His help remains even when you stumble). He's staying UNTIL you finish (completion is guaranteed). The temple project that looks like your pain today? It's actually your advancement in progress. The slow construction isn't delay—it's development. **Your temple project isn't delayed—it's under construction. And the Master Builder is still on-site.**

THE FIVE STAGES OF KINGDOM ADVANCEMENT

The Framework: From Promise to Possession

"You have stayed long enough at this mountain. Break camp and advance... See, I have given you this land. Go in and take possession of it." (Deuteronomy 1:6-8)

Biblical Advancement is the process by which God grows, prepares, promotes, and propels you into greater realms of purpose, influence, authority, and impact for His Kingdom.

STAGE	FOCUS	VERB	OUTCOME	KEY SCRIPTURE
Calling	Hearing God's vision	Respond	Vision & direction	Gen. 12:1-2
Preparation	Building capacity & character	Grow	Strength & maturity	James 1:4

Promotion	Divine elevation	Rise	Position & authority	Ps. 75:6-7
Expansion	Enlarged reach & influence	Occupy	Territory & impact	Isa. 54:2-3
Acceleration	Rapid, multiplied progress	Run	Breakthrough & fulfillment	Amos 9:13

STAGE 1: CALLING—The Seed of Destiny Is Planted

"Go from your country... to the land I will show you" (Genesis 12:1-2). *"Before I formed you... I appointed you"* (Jeremiah 1:5). Advancement begins with a call—a divine invitation to step out of comfort into destiny. **Activation:** "I embrace God's call. I refuse to settle. I hear His voice and I say yes."

STAGE 2: PREPARATION—The Character for Advancement Is Formed

"Whoever can be trusted with very little can also be trusted with much" (Luke 16:10). Before advancement comes placement, there must be preparation. God shapes capacity, builds character, deepens faith in hidden seasons. **Activation:** "I embrace the preparation season. Every hidden test produces strength, skill, and maturity."

STAGE 3: PROMOTION—The Door of Opportunity Opens

"It is God who judges: He brings one down, He exalts another" (Psalm 75:6-7). Promotion is the divine moment of elevation—when God's favor opens doors human effort cannot. **Activation:** "I do not strive for promotion—I am positioned for it. God's timing is perfect."

STAGE 4: EXPANSION—Territory, Influence, and Impact Increase

"Enlarge the place of your tent" (Isaiah 54:2-3). Advancement matures into expansion—where God increases your reach and entrusts you with more territory. **Activation:** "I declare expansion over my life. I enlarge my vision, stretch my faith, and prepare for more."

STAGE 5: ACCELERATION—Divine Momentum Carries You Further, Faster

"Things are going to happen so fast your head will swim" (Amos 9:13, MSG). The final stage is acceleration—when God multiplies your momentum and causes breakthroughs quickly. **Activation:** "I step into supernatural acceleration. What once took years will happen in months."

THE ADVANCEMENT PROTOCOL

Five Operating Principles

1. ADVANCEMENT REQUIRES DAILY FAITHFULNESS

"He who is faithful in what is least is faithful also in much" (Luke 16:10). Today's faithfulness is tomorrow's advancement foundation. Every email answered with excellence. Every commitment kept with integrity. Every task completed with honor. **Faithfulness is the new flex. One faithful Tuesday > ten flashy announcements.**

2. ADVANCEMENT EMBRACES PROCESS

"To everything there is a season" (Ecclesiastes 3:1). Every season advances something specific. Spring advances sowing. Summer advances growth. Fall advances harvest. Winter advances rest. The New

Testament describes this with **auxanō** [owx-AN-oh]—the word for organic growth, like a seed becoming a tree. This is advancement that happens incrementally, sometimes invisibly, but always unstoppably when planted in the right environment. *"The word of God spread (auxanō), and the number of disciples increased"* (Acts 6:7). You can't force a seed to grow faster by yelling at it. And you can't accelerate auxanō advancement by striving, comparing, or forcing shortcuts. But here's the promise: When God is the source, growth is guaranteed. Your daily faithfulness is auxanō advancement—growing naturally and supernaturally at the same time. **Major advancement is minor progression compounded daily over years, not days. You can't force auxanō—but you can't stop it either when God is growing you.**

3. ADVANCEMENT HAPPENS IN HIDDENNESS

"When you pray, go into your room, and when you have shut your door, pray to your Father who is in the secret place; and your Father who sees in secret will reward you openly" (Matthew 6:6). Private progression precedes public promotion.

4. ADVANCEMENT SERVES OTHERS

Your advancement should advance others. If your progression doesn't bless people, it's just position-grabbing.

5. ADVANCEMENT TRUSTS DIVINE TIMING

"He has made everything beautiful in its time" (Ecclesiastes 3:11). God's pace is perfect. His timing is impeccable. When Israel stood trapped between the Red Sea and Pharaoh's advancing army, Moses cried out to God in desperation. And God's response? *"Then the Lord said to Moses, 'Why are you crying out to me? Tell the Israelites to move forward'"* (Exodus 14:15). Stop crying. Move forward. Not "wait until the sea parts." Move forward—and I'll part the sea while you're moving. The Hebrew is **nasa** [naw-SAW]—and it doesn't mean "when you're comfortable, perhaps consider relocating." It means break camp. Pull up the tent stakes. Dismantle what was. MOVE NOW. Advancement doesn't wait for all obstacles to disappear—it moves forward while God removes them. You've been waiting for the fear to disappear before you move, the path to clear before you step, the provision to appear before you obey. But God is saying: Stop crying about the impossibility. Move forward into it. I'll part the sea while you're walking. **Stop crying out. Move forward. God parts seas for moving feet, not stationary prayers.**

BIBLICAL PATTERNS OF ADVANCEMENT PROGRESSION

TIER 1: Four Full Witnesses

Joseph — From Pit to Palace Through Process

Watch the journey: From favored son (Genesis 37:3) to slave (Genesis 37:28). From slave to overseer (Genesis 39:4-6). From overseer to prisoner (Genesis 39:19-20). From prisoner to administrator (Genesis 39:21-23). From administrator to Prime Minister (Genesis 41:41-43). Every stage looked like regression. But heaven measured differently. The slave season advanced his administration skills. The prison season advanced his gift interpretation (Genesis 40:5-22). Every backwards-looking move was actually forward progression. Joseph never pursued any of these positions. He simply served excellently where planted, and advancement found him.

"The Lord was with Joseph"—this phrase appears four times in Genesis 39 alone (verses 2, 3, 21, 23). Thirteen years from dream to throne (Genesis 37:2—age 17; Genesis 41:46—age 30). Thirteen years of process before position. Joseph himself testified: *"You meant evil against me; but God meant it for good"* (Genesis 50:20). **Your pit isn't punishment; it's positioning.**

David — Three Anointings, Thirteen Years, One Process

Anointed as king at 17 (1 Samuel 16:13). Crowned at 30 (2 Samuel 5:4). Thirteen years of process before position. But watch his advancement: Advanced in SKILL through shepherding (1 Samuel 16:11; 17:34-36)—Every rescued lamb taught him to rescue Israel. Advanced in COURAGE through lion and bear (1 Samuel 17:34-37)—Private victories prepared for public Goliath. Advanced in FAITH through worship (Psalms 142, 57, 59, 63)—Psalms written in caves became songs for ages. Advanced in CHARACTER through not killing Saul (1 Samuel 24:6-7)—Could have grabbed the throne. Chose to wait for process.

When his men urged him to kill Saul in the cave, David said: *"The Lord forbid that I should do this thing to my master, seeing he is the anointed of the Lord"* (1 Samuel 24:6). Each season advanced specific qualities the next season would require.

Moses — Forty Years Per Stage

Prince of Egypt for 40 years (Acts 7:23). Shepherd in Midian for 40 years (Acts 7:30). Leader of Israel for 40 years (Deuteronomy 34:7). Watch the middle 40—the "wasted" years: From prince to fugitive (Exodus 2:11-15). From fugitive to shepherd (Exodus 3:1). Forty years in the desert. No platform. No people. Just sheep. But those forty years advanced everything: Pride became humility. Impatience became meekness (Numbers 12:3). Self-reliance became God-dependence.

Ruth — Daily Faithfulness Through Foreign Territory

Widowed. Foreign. Poor. Three words that would have crushed most women into retreat. But Ruth chose advancement over comfort: *"Where you go I will go, and where you stay I will stay. Your people will be my people and your God my God"* (Ruth 1:16). This wasn't arrival language—it was advancement declaration. She wasn't demanding destination; she was committing to journey. Watch her advancement unfold: From Moab to Bethlehem (Ruth 1:22)—advancing into the unknown. From mourner to gleaner (Ruth 2:2)—advancing through daily work. From gleaner to noticed (Ruth 2:11-12)—advancing through faithfulness that caught divine attention. From foreigner to family (Ruth 4:13-17)—advancing into lineage of Jesus Himself.

But here's what makes Ruth's story the perfect advancement witness: She advanced through DAILY FAITHFULNESS in the hidden places. *"She went out and began to glean in the fields"* (Ruth 2:3). Not "she demanded a position." Not "she complained about the process." She took one step. Then another. Day after faithful day. Boaz noticed her character before her beauty: *"I've been told all about what you have done for your mother-in-law since the death of your husband"* (Ruth 2:11). Her advancement came through who she was BECOMING, not what she was ACHIEVING. The timeline? Chapter 1 to Chapter 4—likely months, possibly a year. From widow to wife, from foreigner to great-grandmother of David. Not overnight, but through faithful progression. Ruth proves the principle: Advancement isn't about forcing shortcuts to positions. It's about faithful steps through process. Daily gleaning prepared her for divine appointment. The fields were her formation ground. **Your daily faithfulness in the "fields" isn't delay—it's the very advancement that positions you for divine appointment.**

TIER 2: Progressive Positioning

Esther — Twelve Months of Preparation

From orphan to adopted daughter (Esther 2:7). From adopted to candidate (Esther 2:8). From candidate to preparation (Esther 2:12)—twelve months of process! From preparation to queen (Esther 2:17). From queen to deliverer (Esther 4:14-16). Twelve months of preparation before one night with the king. Not twelve days. Twelve months of process before position. But the advancement didn't stop at the crown. The crown was just equipment for the real assignment.

WHEN ADVANCEMENT FEELS STALLED: SEVEN CHECKPOINTS

Sometimes advancement feels blocked, invisible, or nonexistent. Before you conclude you're stuck, check these seven areas:

1. Are you measuring by arrivals instead of daily faithfulness?
(Metric problem, not advancement problem. Ruth advanced daily in fields, not in throne rooms.)

2. Are you in a preparation season that looks like delay?
(David's 13 years. Moses' 40 years. Preparation IS advancement, not delay before it.)

3. Are you comparing your Chapter 3 to someone else's Chapter 12?
(Different timelines. Joseph was 17 when dreams came, 30 when fulfilled. Don't compare chapters.)

4. Have you despised "small" advancement while chasing "big" breakthrough?
(Party of one IS advancement. Alignment IS advancement. Small is significant in Kingdom math.)

5. Are you forcing shortcuts instead of trusting divine pace?
(Shortcuts abort what patience births. Auxanō growth can't be rushed—only nurtured.)

6. Have you stopped taking daily steps because you can't see the destination?
(Advancement requires movement. "Tell the Israelites to move forward" [Ex 14:15]. God parts seas for moving feet.)

7. Are you in prokopē season—cutting through resistance?
(Resistance proves you're advancing through enemy territory. Paul advanced THROUGH chains, not around them.)

Final reminder: Stalled feelings don't mean stalled advancement. Joseph advanced in prison. David advanced in caves. Your invisible progression is still progression. The temple project under construction doesn't look finished because it's not—but God is WITH you UNTIL it is.

MONTHLY ADVANCEMENT PROGRESS ASSESSMENT

Track your journey mastery monthly. Rate yourself 0-10 in each area:

Daily Faithfulness: ___/10
(10 = Consistently faithful in small things; 1 = Sporadic, only showing up for "big" moments)

Process Embrace: ___/10
(10 = Peace in preparation seasons; 1 = Frustrated, demanding immediate arrival)

Comparison Freedom: ___/10
(10 = Celebrating own journey without measuring against others; 1 = Constant comparison, envy)

Journey Joy: ___/10
(10 = Finding fulfillment in progression itself; 1 = Only happy at arrivals/promotions)

Advancement Recognition: ___/10
(10 = Seeing daily progress as significant; 1 = Only counting destinations reached)

Total Score: ___/50

Interpretation:
- **0-20:** Destination obsession dominant. Review Essential 3 daily. Practice "party of one" faithfulness. Reread Three Promises section weekly.
- **21-35:** Transitioning from arrival focus to journey mastery. Continue monthly tracking. Celebrate small wins. Focus on lowest-scoring area.
- **36-50:** Walking in journey mastery. Maintain quarterly check-ins. Ready to mentor others in advancement thinking. Model faithful progression.

Compare scores monthly. Celebrate every increase—transformation is progressive. If scores decrease, review Seven Checkpoints above. Check for comparison traps, metric obsession, or impatience with process. Realign without shame. **You're measuring progress, not perfection. The assessment itself IS advancement—awareness precedes transformation.**

TRANSFORMATION — THE DIFFERENCE BETWEEN ORPHAN DESTINATIONS AND HEIR JOURNEYS

ORPHAN DESTINATION MINDSET	HEIR JOURNEY MINDSET
Waits for the big break	Embraces daily formation
Measures by positions achieved	Measures by faithfulness sustained
Frustrated between promotions	Peaceful in preparation seasons
Compares arrivals	Celebrates journey milestones
Forces shortcuts	Trusts divine pace
Impatient with preparation	Patient in preparation
Values position over formation	Values formation over position
Asks "When will I get there?"	Asks "How am I growing?"
Says "I'll be happy when..."	Says "I'm advancing now..."

Recognizing Your Advancement Season: You're advancing when: Character is forming (even through difficulty). Capacity is expanding (even in hiddenness). Skills are sharpening (even without platform). Faith is deepening (even through testing). Peace is increasing (even in process).

MANIFESTATION — DAILY ADVANCEMENT ACTIONS

Stop waiting for advancement to arrive. Start advancing through daily actions.

THE ESSENTIAL 3:
1. **COMPLETE ONE THING** — Finish what you started. Completion is advancement. That course, that project—finishing advances you.
2. **SERVE ONE PERSON** — Use today's position to advance someone else. Your advancement should advance others.
3. **TAKE ONE STEP** — Advance in one specific area today. One email. One call. One decision. **Advance one thing. Serve one person. Take one step.**

ADDITIONAL ADVANCEMENT ACTIONS: Send the apology email—that relationship you need to repair? That's advancement. Show up to therapy again—every session progresses you. Write the next page—social media might announce your book; discipline will advance it. Schedule the mentor call—who you learn from determines where you lead to. Have the hard conversation—avoidance keeps you stuck. Forgive without the apology—release advances you whether they respond or not.

START HERE: If you can only do ONE thing today, text someone: "I'm advancing through today's faithfulness!"

THE 6-DIMENSIONAL ADVANCEMENT ACTIVATION

Advancement isn't one-dimensional—it's whole-life transformation:

DIMENSION	DAILY PRACTICE	EVIDENCE OF ADVANCEMENT
SPIRITUAL	Journey with God over chasing destinations	Peace in process replaces position anxiety
MENTAL	Process-focused thinking patterns	You see advancement in everyday faithfulness
EMOTIONAL	Find fulfillment in progression, not just arrival	Contentment in current while preparing for next
PHYSICAL	Take one advancement action daily	Momentum builds through consistency
FINANCIAL	Invest in journey, not just waiting for arrival	Continuous growth through strategic investment
RELATIONAL	Advance with others, not past them	Collective progression multiplies individual impact

6-DIMENSIONAL ADVANCEMENT PRAYERS

Stand and declare advancement over every area:

SPIRITUAL: "Father, I advance spiritually from destination-chasing to journey-walking with You. I release position anxiety, arrival obsession, platform-chasing. I receive peace in process, joy in journey, presence over position. Evidence: Peace replaces anxiety. In Jesus' name, I advance spiritually!"

MENTAL: "Father, I advance mentally from orphan thinking to heir thinking. I release comparison mindsets, scarcity thinking, event-focused mentality. I receive process-focused patterns, abundance mindset, journey-celebration. Evidence: I see advancement in daily faithfulness. In Jesus' name, I advance mentally!"

EMOTIONAL: "Father, I advance emotionally from destination-dependent joy to journey-sustained peace. I release emotional dependency on arrivals, happiness tied to outcomes. I receive contentment in current season, fulfillment in progression. Evidence: I'm content while advancing. In Jesus' name, I advance emotionally!"

PHYSICAL: "Father, I advance physically from inaction to daily momentum. I release procrastination, waiting for perfect conditions, analysis paralysis. I receive daily discipline, consistent action, momentum-building habits. Evidence: Momentum builds through consistency. In Jesus' name, I advance physically!"

FINANCIAL: "Father, I advance financially from scarcity survival to Kingdom stewardship. I release poverty mindset, living paycheck-to-paycheck mentally. I receive Kingdom economics, journey investment, progressive provision. Evidence: I invest in the journey. In Jesus' name, I advance financially!"

RELATIONAL: "Father, I advance relationally from competition to collaboration. I release comparing my journey to theirs, advancement past others, isolation in success. I receive community advancement, collective progression, collaborative success. Evidence: I advance with others, not past them. In Jesus' name, I advance relationally!"

COMPREHENSIVE DECLARATION: "I declare advancement across ALL six dimensions: SPIRITUALLY—I journey with God. MENTALLY—I think in process. EMOTIONALLY—I'm content while advancing. PHYSICALLY—I take daily action. FINANCIALLY—I invest in journey. RELATIONALLY—I advance with others. I am advancing HOLISTICALLY—spirit, soul, body, finances, and relationships—all progressing toward Kingdom purposes. In Jesus' name, I advance in ALL dimensions!"

FROM-TO DECLARATIONS OF ADVANCEMENT

Stand and declare your progression:

"I am advancing: From broken to blessed. From overlooked to overbooked. From borrower to lender. From tail to head. From fear to faith. From lack to abundance. From test to testimony. From pit to palace. From my story to His story. From affliction to advancement. The only thing dying in this valley is my 'old self.' I shall live fully in Christ!"

THE PROPHETIC ACT — THE JOURNEY DECLARATION

Stand where you are—your current position on the journey. Take one intentional step forward as you declare:

"I am ADVANCING right now! Not someday—TODAY! Not eventually—CURRENTLY! Not just at promotions—CONTINUOUSLY! I declare: Every faithful step is advancement. Every lesson learned is progression. Every character test passed is forward movement. My journey is: Designed by God. Timed perfectly. Advancing His purposes. Preparing me for destiny.

I release: Destination obsession. Comparison with others' paths. Frustration with process. Demand for shortcuts. I receive: Joy in journey. Peace in progression. Purpose in process. Advancement in every season. God is WITH me—not waiting for me to arrive, but advancing me through this very moment. He will not abandon me. He will not forsake me. He is committed UNTIL I finish—and if He's still building, I'm still advancing. In Jesus' name, I embrace MY advancement journey!"

Take another step forward, symbolizing continuous progression.

THE BEFORE PICTURE MOMENT

Take a selfie right now. This is your BEFORE. Tell your friends to take a good look at you now, for things will never be the same. From this day forward, you are the blessed one, God's chosen one, the Lord's delight! This picture documents where you are on the journey. Not where you're arriving, but where you're advancing from. One year from now, you'll look back and see how far the journey has taken you. The temple project may look like pain now, but God is WITH you, building something that will display His glory for generations.

PRAYER OF PROGRESSIVE PURPOSE

"Father, forgive me for despising the journey while demanding destinations. I've missed advancement happening in my everyday faithfulness. I've compared arrivals instead of celebrating progression. I've demanded events while resenting process. Thank You that: You're advancing me right now. Every day on my path has purpose. The journey is as important as arrival. You're preparing me through progression. You're WITH me until the promise is fulfilled.

Thank You for these three promises: You ARE with me (present tense). You will NOT abandon me (committed for the duration). You will NOT forsake me (Your help remains even when I stumble). You're staying UNTIL I finish (completion is guaranteed). I repent for: Measuring advancement only by position. Forcing shortcuts to platforms. Despising preparation seasons. Missing progression while focusing on promotion. Comparing my wilderness to their platforms.

Today I embrace: Daily advancement through faithfulness. Progressive development over instant arrival. Journey joy over destination obsession. Process peace over position pressure. Alignment over ambition. Advance me through: Character before platform. Depth before visibility. Service before status. Formation before position. My temple project may look like pain, but You are WITH me in the construction. I can't trace Your hands, but I trust Your heart. I stay the course. I trust the process.

Let my life demonstrate that: Advancement happens daily. Journeys create capacity. Process produces permanence. Faithfulness forwards destiny. Alignment accelerates arrival. In Jesus' name, I advance progressively!

WEEK 2: ALIGN (7A)

SOAP JOURNAL — DAY 12

S (Scripture): Which advancement verse became your anthem? Write it and personalize it.

O (Observation): Where have you been missing daily advancement while waiting for arrival? What temple project looks like pain but is actually under construction?

A (Application): Which of the Essential 3 will you practice today? Which dimension needs most focus?

P (Prayer): "Father, help me see advancement in my current _____. Thank You for being WITH me until the promise is fulfilled."

YOUR DAY 12 ACTIVATION CHALLENGE
BEFORE SLEEP TONIGHT:

1. **DECLARE:** Choose 3 declarations and memorize them
2. **CELEBRATE:** Text someone: "I'm advancing through today's faithfulness! God is WITH me UNTIL I finish!"
3. **ADVANCE:** Complete ONE action from the Essential 3
4. **PROCLAIM:** Speak over your assignment: "My temple project doesn't look finished because God isn't finished. He's WITH me—UNTIL I finish."
5. **DOCUMENT:** Take your "Before Picture"
6. **PRAY:** Choose one dimension from the 6-D prayers and declare it over your life
7. **ASSESS:** Complete your first Monthly Advancement Progress Assessment

CLOSING — FROM DESTINATION OBSESSION TO JOURNEY MASTERY

Day 12 complete. The person who woke at 4:30 AM desperate to arrive? Now embracing advancement as the journey itself. You're not waiting for the destination. You're walking the path. You're not frustrated by the process. You're formed through it. You're not comparing chapters. You're celebrating progression.

Five days of identity alignment complete:
- Day 8: Adoption—your IDENTITY
- Day 9: Abundance—your INHERITANCE
- Day 10: Authority—your DOMINION
- Day 11: Anointing—your EQUIPMENT
- Day 12: Advancement—your JOURNEY

Tomorrow, ATTRIBUTES await—the family traits being formed through your advancement journey. Every day of process develops divine DNA. Every season of advancement shapes spiritual genetics. But tonight, settle this forever: Your temple project may look like pain. The construction may seem chaotic. The timeline may feel wrong. But God is WITH you—not watching from heaven, but laboring beside you in the mess. He won't abandon you. He won't forsake you. He's committed UNTIL you finish. You can't trace His hands in this season, but you can trust His heart.

If advancement is progression, not position... If you're advancing through process, not just promotion... If today's faithfulness is tomorrow's foundation... If God is WITH you until the promise is fulfilled... Then why are you missing today's advancement waiting for someday's arrival? Your advancement isn't ahead of you. It's happening within you. Right now. In this season. Through this journey. Welcome to progressive purpose. Welcome to journey joy. Welcome to YOUR PATH.

TODAY'S BREAKTHROUGH MARKER: What shifted from destination obsession to journey mastery?

TOMORROW'S EXPECTATION: Now that you understand advancement as journey and God's commitment UNTIL you finish, what family traits (ATTRIBUTES) are being formed through this process?

DESTINATION OBSESSION EVICTED. ADVANCEMENT JOURNEY ACTIVATED. TEMPLE PROJECT RECOGNIZED. GOD'S "UNTIL" ANCHORED. SIX DIMENSIONS ALIGNED. READY FOR ATTRIBUTES.

Welcome to progressive purpose. Welcome to journey joy. Welcome to the advancement that's happening right now—not someday, not eventually, but TODAY.

DAY 13 — ATTRIBUTES

From Information to Revelation: When You Stop Knowing About Him and Start Seeing Him Clearly

"Open my eyes, that I may see wondrous things from Your law." — Psalm 119:18

WEEK 2 — ALIGN: Establishing Your Kingdom Identity

Day 13 of 21. Week 2's penultimate day. Five days established WHO YOU ARE—adopted (Day 8), abundant (Day 9), authoritative (Day 10), anointed (Day 11), advancing (Day 12). Today establishes WHO HE IS. Because you can't declare truth about yourself without first seeing Truth Himself.

ENCOUNTER — WHERE YOU ARE

Day 13. You wake before the alarm again. But this morning feels different. Your body knows the fasting rhythm now—the hollow stomach, the sharpened senses, the way everything seems both clearer and more fragile. You sit up, and something catches your eye. The mirror across the room. How many times have you looked at that reflection without really seeing? Checking appearance. Judging weight. Critiquing flaws. But this morning, staring at that familiar face in pre-dawn darkness, a different question rises—not from your mind but from somewhere deeper, hungrier: "Who does this face resemble?"

Twelve days of fasting and alignment have shifted something. You know who you are now. The orphan questions have quieted. The identity crisis has settled. You're adopted. You have abundance. You carry authority. You operate in anointing. You're advancing. But this question comes from beneath identity: "But who is HE? The Father whose child I am?" Not the Sunday school answer. Not the theological definition you memorized. Not the Instagram caption version of God. Who is He REALLY?

Because here's what you're discovering: You've been declaring things about God you've never actually seen. Affirming His faithfulness while secretly wondering if He'll show up. Proclaiming His goodness while questioning why good things keep not happening. Celebrating His power while feeling perpetually powerless. Singing about His presence while feeling utterly alone. You know ABOUT Him. But do you SEE Him? And the performance—the constant affirming without beholding—is exhausting. Your chest tightens not from panic but from pretending. How long can you declare what you've never actually seen?

There's a difference—ocean-wide, heaven-deep—between information and revelation. Between knowing God's resume and knowing God's reality. Between studying His attributes in a book and encountering His character in the breaking. You can recite that God is faithful. But have your eyes actually beheld His faithfulness in the wilderness? You can quote that God is good. But has your heart encountered His goodness in the darkness? The question isn't what you know about God. The question is: What have you SEEN of God?

Week 2 gave you identity. But identity without a clear vision of whose image you bear becomes narcissism dressed in spiritual language. If you don't know WHO HE IS, you'll build declarations on sand—your feelings, your circumstances, your limited understanding of an unlimited God. Your adoption means nothing if you don't know the Father's character. Your abundance is theoretical until you see His generosity. Your authority is presumptuous until you know His sovereignty. You can't declare what you don't see. You can't know Him through information alone—you must encounter revelation.

Today, your eyes open. Not your physical eyes—those have seen precisely nothing eternal. Your spiritual eyes. The ones that behold what's invisible to natural sight. The ones that perceive His character beneath your circumstances. The ones that see His faithfulness behind every closed door and His goodness beneath every painful process. Your affirmations are only as strong as your vision of God. The shift isn't subtle. It's seismic. The difference between believing God exists and beholding who God IS. Between accepting His attributes as doctrine and experiencing them as reality. Between knowing His names and encountering His nature.

Day 13 isn't another teaching about God. It's an encounter with God that transforms how you see everything. Because tomorrow (Day 14), your voice will declare. But today, your eyes must see. You can't speak what you haven't seen. And you can't know Him through secondhand testimony alone—you must behold Him yourself. Shallow God-knowledge creates shallow declarations. Deep God-awareness creates unshakeable affirmations. Today, you stop knowing ABOUT Him and start SEEING Him. Today, information becomes revelation. Today, your eyes open to wondrous things you've read a thousand times but never actually seen. And when your eyes open to His true character—His unchanging, unshakeable nature—everything changes. Your declarations stop wavering. Your affirmations stop depending on feelings. Your faith stops riding the roller coaster of circumstances. Because you can't unsee what you've truly seen. And once you SEE Him clearly, you'll never speak about yourself the same way again. Welcome to Day 13. Welcome to the day your eyes open. Welcome to the encounter that transforms information into revelation. "Open my eyes, that I may see."

FOUNDATION — THE CRISIS OF SECONDHAND SIGHT

You've been living on inherited vision. Someone else's revelation. Your pastor's encounter. Your parents' faith. And it sustained you—for a season. Like borrowed glasses that almost fit, you could see enough to function. But borrowed glasses never quite focus right. And secondhand sight never quite satisfies the soul. You've heard ABOUT His faithfulness in someone else's wilderness. You've read ABOUT His provision in someone else's famine. You've sung ABOUT His presence in someone else's dark night. But singing about light isn't the same as seeing dawn break.

There comes a moment—and Day 13 is that moment—when inherited knowledge must become personal revelation. When someone else's sight must become your own vision. The Samaritan woman understood this shift. Her testimony brought the village to Jesus. But watch what happens next: "Then they said to the woman, 'Now we believe, not because of what you said, for we ourselves have heard Him and we know that this is indeed the Christ, the Savior of the world'" (John 4:42). They moved from her testimony to their own encounter. From secondhand knowledge to firsthand revelation. This is Day 13's invitation. You've been told WHO HE IS. Today, you SEE who He is. Concepts fade when circumstances press. Vision holds when everything shakes.

The Difference Between Information and Revelation

INFORMATION says: "God is faithful." REVELATION says: "I have SEEN His faithfulness hold me when everything else let go." INFORMATION recites: "God is good." REVELATION declares: "I have TASTED His goodness in the famine—and it's better, deeper, more costly and glorious than I thought." INFORMATION memorizes: "God is present." REVELATION testifies: "I have FELT Him in the isolation—His presence isn't constant comfort. It's constant WITH-ness even in discomfort."

Information is secondhand. Revelation is firsthand. Information can be forgotten. Revelation can't be unseen. What you've merely learned about God can be argued away. What you've actually seen of God becomes unshakeable bedrock. This is why Days 8-12 had to come before Day 13. You needed to know WHO YOU ARE before you could truly see WHO HE IS. Because seeing God's character isn't academic—it's relational. It's encountering the Person behind the attributes in your actual life.

And here's the mystery: You've already encountered Him. You just haven't had eyes to see it yet. Every closed door? His faithfulness was redirecting you. Every delayed promise? His timing was positioning you. Every painful process? His goodness was forming you. Every lonely season? His presence was WITH you. You've been living in His attributes without seeing them clearly. Like walking through a museum in the dark, bumping into masterpieces, never beholding the beauty you're surrounded by. Day 13 turns the lights on. Day 13 opens your eyes. And when you see clearly—when revelation replaces information, when encounter displaces concepts—everything changes. Your declarations stop wavering with your feelings. Your faith stops being theoretical and becomes testimonial. Tomorrow you'll declare with your voice. Today you must see with your eyes. Because you can't speak what you haven't seen.

REVELATION — HEAVEN'S VOCABULARY FOR SEEING GOD

Before we behold His attributes, I need to tell you what happened when I first started studying these Hebrew and Greek words. I thought I was doing research. Turns out, I was receiving revelation. There's no single Hebrew word for "attribute"—but the concept blazes through Scripture in powerful words that reveal both God's nature and how we're designed to reflect it. Let me show you what God showed me.

SHEM [SHAME] — Name, Character, Reputation. In Hebrew culture, a name wasn't just a label—it carried the essence and nature of a person. When God proclaims His name, He's revealing His character. "The name of the LORD is a strong tower" (Proverbs 18:10). I was sitting in my living room during a particularly brutal season when this hit me: When Moses asked to see God's glory, God responded by proclaiming His SHEM—His mercy, grace, patience, love, justice (Exodus 34:5-7). God's name isn't just what He's called—it's who He IS. And suddenly I realized: Every time I'd dismissed God's character as "just names," I'd been missing the point. His names are windows into His nature.

KABOD [kah-BODE] — Glory, Weight, Substance. Literally "heaviness"—the substantial presence of God's character made manifest. The KABOD of God is His attributes made visible. This one broke me during worship one Sunday. I'd been begging God to show His glory—expecting lights, miracles, supernatural manifestations. Then Holy Spirit whispered: "I've been showing you My kabod for months. My goodness in your darkness. My provision in your lack. My peace in your chaos. You wanted spectacle. I gave you substance." The KABOD of God is His character expressed outwardly—and I'd been walking past it, looking for something flashier.

DEREKH [DEH-rekh] — Way, Manner, Conduct. "He made known His ways to Moses, His acts to the people of Israel" (Psalm 103:7). God's DEREKH refers to His consistent patterns, His reliable character. The people saw His ACTS (what He did). Moses saw His WAYS (why He did it—His character). I'll never forget the day this distinction saved my faith. I was watching God's ACTS in my life—closed doors, delayed promises, painful processes—and concluding He was cruel. Then I read Psalm 103:7 and realized: I'm seeing His ACTS like Israel. But I haven't learned His WAYS like Moses. I was interpreting His actions through my pain instead of through His character. God's ways reveal His attributes in action.

TSELEM [TSEH-lem] — Image, Shadow, Representative Figure. "Then God said, 'Let Us make man in Our image, according to Our likeness'" (Genesis 1:26). The Hebrew TSELEM means you were designed to cast God's shadow in the earth—not through performance but through resemblance. This wrecked me. I'd spent years trying to BECOME like God. Then I discovered I was CREATED like God. Sin distorted the image; Christ restores it. Adoption activates what creation initiated. I wasn't climbing toward likeness. I was recovering what was always mine.

The New Testament Amplification

PHYSIS [FOO-sis] — Nature, Essence. The inherent qualities that make something what it is. "That you may participate in the divine nature" (2 Peter 1:4). God doesn't HAVE love—He IS love. His attributes aren't add-ons; they're His essence. When I finally understood this, it changed everything. I'd been treating God's love like a mood—present some days, absent others. But physis taught me: God IS love. His essence. His nature. Unchanging. The day I believed this—really believed it—was the day anxiety lost its grip. If His nature is love, and His nature never changes, then His love for me never wavers. Not because I earned it. Because it's who He IS.

CHARAKTĒR [khar-ak-TARE] — Exact Representation, Imprint. "The Son is the radiance of God's glory and the exact representation of His being" (Hebrews 1:3). Like a seal pressed into warm wax, leaving its precise imprint. Jesus is the CHARAKTĒR of the Father—the perfect expression of all God's attributes. And Scripture says we're being conformed to Christ's image (Romans 8:29). I was journaling one morning when this hit: This isn't behavioral modification—it's family manifestation. The family DNA, deposited at adoption, emerging through dwelling. I'm not becoming someone new. I'm becoming who I already am in Christ—the charaktēr, the imprint, the exact representation of the Father's nature.

Stop. Breathe. Let that land. You were created to carry His shadow (TSELEM). Not perform His nature. Reflect it. Your gaps aren't mistakes. They're meeting places where His glory shines through your weakness. Your cracks are where His light becomes visible. Your weaknesses are windows where people see His strength, not your performance.

Heaven's Definition Synthesized

God's attributes are His revealed nature (SHEM), His manifest glory (KABOD), His consistent ways (DEREKH), His essential being (PHYSIS), His exact representation in Christ (CHARAKTĒR), and the image (TSELEM) we were created to reflect. They're not separate parts of God—they ARE God Himself revealed. God doesn't possess attributes. He IS His attributes. They're not what He has—they're who He is.

The Revolutionary Truth

God doesn't have love—He IS love (1 John 4:8). God doesn't possess holiness—He IS holy (Isaiah 6:3). God doesn't choose to be faithful—He IS faithfulness (2 Timothy 2:13). His attributes aren't qualities He sometimes displays. They're His unchanging essence. And here's what transforms everything: When you were adopted (Day 8), you didn't just join a family—you received the family DNA. "His divine power has given us everything we need for a godly life through our knowledge of Him who called us by His own glory and goodness. Through these He has given us His very great and precious promises, so that through them you may participate in the divine nature" (2 Peter 1:4).

You're not trying to become like God. You're discovering you already carry His nature through adoption. You were created as His image (TSELEM), and adoption restores what sin distorted. You're being conformed to Christ's exact representation (CHARAKTĒR) through beholding Him. Orphans perform godliness. Children reflect it.

ATTRIBUTES AS GAP-FILLERS: WHAT GOD SHOWED ME IN THE BREAKING

I need to tell you how I discovered this. Because for years, I treated my gaps like shameful secrets. My weaknesses were evidence I wasn't spiritual enough. My insufficiencies proved I was failing. Then came 2019. The year everything I'd been hiding ripped open—fear, scarcity, powerlessness, inadequacy, anxiety. Five gaps. Exposed. Raw. Humiliating. I sat in my prayer closet one morning, journaling through Psalm 23, and Holy Spirit stopped me cold at verse 1: "The LORD is my shepherd; I shall not want."

"You're reading this like a nice sentiment," He said. "But I'm showing you a pattern. Your LACK meets My SUFFICIENCY. Your weakness meets My strength. Your gaps aren't accidents, Niki. They're appointments. Meeting places where I fill what you can't provide."

And then He gave me language I'd never forget: "Your cracks are where My light shines through. Your weaknesses are windows for My glory. Your insufficiency? That's My opportunity."

I sat there stunned. For years I'd been hiding cracks, covering weaknesses, compensating for insufficiency. And God was saying they weren't problems to fix—they were display cases for His nature. Your cracks don't disqualify you. They're where His light becomes visible to a watching world. Your weaknesses aren't failures. They're windows where people see His power, not your performance. Your insufficiency isn't inadequacy. It's God's opportunity to demonstrate His all-sufficiency.

I started mapping it. Every gap I'd exposed in Days 8-12, God had a corresponding attribute designed to fill it. My orphan wound? ABBA FATHER. My scarcity crisis? JEHOVAH JIREH. My powerlessness? ADONAI. My equipment drought? HOLY SPIRIT. My destination anxiety? JEHOVAH SHAMMAH. Pattern after pattern after pattern.

Here's what transforms everything: God's attributes aren't abstract concepts—they're divine solutions to human gaps. Every lack in your life has a corresponding attribute in Him. You weren't designed to be self-sufficient. You were created with gaps—not flaws, but spaces for God to fill. Your weakness isn't a mistake; it's a meeting place. Your insufficiency isn't inadequacy; it's invitation.

Every gap in your life is a gallery where God displays His glory. Your cracks are where His light shines through. Your weaknesses are windows for His glory. Your insufficiency? God's opportunity to demonstrate all-sufficiency.

Three ways to see the same truth: Gaps become galleries. Cracks become light. Weaknesses become windows. What you've been hiding in shame, God wants to fill with glory. What you've been covering in performance, God wants to illuminate with His presence.

Watch how this works: When you are WEAK, He is EL SHADDAI [el shad-DAI]—your strength (Genesis 17:1). When you are ANXIOUS, He is JEHOVAH SHALOM [yeh-ho-VAH shah-LOME]—your peace (Judges 6:24). When you feel LOST, He is JEHOVAH ROHI [yeh-ho-VAH ro-HEE]—your shepherd (Psalm 23:1). When you face UNCERTAINTY, He is SOVEREIGN—your certainty (Psalm 103:19). When you are BROKEN, He is JEHOVAH RAPHA [yeh-ho-VAH raw-FAH]—your healer (Exodus 15:26). When you lack PROVISION, He is JEHOVAH JIREH [yeh-ho-VAH yeer-EH]—your provider (Genesis 22:14). When you need RIGHTEOUSNESS, He is JEHOVAH TSIDKENU [yeh-ho-VAH tsid-KAY-noo] (Jeremiah 23:6). When you are LONELY, He is IMMANUEL [im-man-oo-EL]—God WITH you (Matthew 1:23). When you feel INVISIBLE, He is EL ROI [el ro-EE]—the God who SEES you (Genesis 16:13).

See the pattern? Your gaps reveal which attributes you need to encounter. Your weaknesses become showcases for His strengths. Paul understood this: "My grace is sufficient for you, for My power is made perfect in weakness" (2 Corinthians 12:9). He was recognizing weakness as the very place God's power becomes most visible. What you've been hiding in shame, God wants to fill with glory. Your weakness isn't your disqualification—it's your invitation to encounter His strength.

Your chest tightens reading this. Not from anxiety. From recognition. This is YOUR gap. This is HIS attribute. This is the encounter waiting to happen.

GOD SHOWED ME SEVEN ATTRIBUTES THAT MEET EVERY HUMAN GAP

In the breaking, He revealed a pattern. Seven categories of His nature designed to fill seven kinds of human need. This isn't systematic theology I studied. This is encounter theology I lived. Watch:

ATTRIBUTE	MEANING	GAP IT FILLS	KEY SCRIPTURE	HOW IT TRANSFORMS YOU
HOLINESS qadosh [kah-DOSH]	Set apart, sacred, morally perfect	Shame, Impurity, Defilement	"Holy, holy, holy is the LORD Almighty" (Isaiah 6:3)	His holiness doesn't condemn—it cleanses. Shame is replaced with sanctification.
LOVE chesed [KHEH-sed], agape [ah-GAH-pay]	Covenant love, unconditional divine love	Rejection, Unworthiness, Feeling unloved	"God is love" (1 John 4:8)	His love never lets go. Rejection is replaced with acceptance.
JUSTICE & RIGHTEOUSNESS tsedek [TSEH-dek]	Straight, right, just	Guilt, Injustice, Condemnation	"Righteousness and justice are the foundation of Your throne" (Psalm 89:14)	His justice satisfied at the cross. Guilt is replaced with justification.
MERCY & GRACE racham [rah-KHAM], chanan [khah-NAN]	Compassion, unmerited favor	Condemnation, Hopelessness, Despair	"The LORD is compassionate and gracious" (Psalm 103:8)	Mercy withholds punishment. Grace gives blessing. Condemnation is replaced with pardon.

WEEK 2: ALIGN (7A)

FAITHFULNESS & IMMUTABILITY emunah [eh-moo-NAH]	Firmness, steadiness, unchanging	Instability, Betrayal, Uncertainty	"Great is Your faithfulness" (Lamentations 3:23)	When everything shifts, He remains. Instability is replaced with steadiness.
OMNIPOTENCE, OMNISCIENCE, OMNIPRESENCE El Shaddai [el shad-DAI]	Almighty, All-knowing, Everywhere present	Powerlessness, Confusion, Loneliness	"Nothing is too hard for You" (Jeremiah 32:17)	He is able when you're powerless. He knows when you're confused. He's present when you're alone.
SOVEREIGNTY & GOODNESS Adonai [ah-doe-NAI], tov [TOVE]	Supreme Ruler, Good	Chaos, Fear, Feeling out of control	"His kingdom rules over all" (Psalm 103:19)	His sovereignty orders chaos. His goodness ensures it works for your benefit. Fear is replaced with trust.

See the pattern? Your gaps reveal which attributes you need to encounter. Your weaknesses become showcases for His strengths. Run your finger down that table. Which gap makes you stop? That's where He's meeting you today. That's the attribute He wants you to encounter.

YOUR FIVE GAPS FROM DAYS 8-12 MEET HIS ATTRIBUTES TODAY

This week you exposed gaps you'd been hiding for years. Five days of identity alignment revealed five areas where you've been insufficient, empty, or wounded. Today you discover: Every gap you exposed has a corresponding attribute of God designed to fill it. Your gaps weren't accidents. They were appointments. Meeting places where His attributes fill your emptiness with His fullness.

Let me show you what I discovered when I stopped hiding my gaps and started encountering His attributes in them.

Day 8's Orphan Gap Meets ABBA FATHER

Five days ago, you exposed the wound you'd been hiding behind performance. That father's name in your contacts for three years. The abandonment that whispered "You're not wanted." The rejection that left you asking "Who am I? Do I belong?" The orphan identity that made you strive for approval instead of rest in acceptance.

And here's what I discovered in the breaking: God wasn't ignoring that gap. He was FILLING it. With three names I'd never truly encountered until the wound ripped open.

The first name came during worship. I was singing "Our Father" like I'd sung a thousand times, but this time I couldn't get past the first two words. "Our Father." My earthly father hadn't wanted me. So why would this Father? And then I heard it—not audible, but clear as thunder: "ABBA." Not the formal "Father" I'd been singing. The intimate, tender "Daddy" that shattered thirty years of orphan thinking. I collapsed. Sobbing. Because suddenly I wasn't singing ABOUT a Father. I was encountering THE Father.

The Aramaic ABBA isn't theological Father in heaven. It's intimate Daddy right here—present, engaged, delighted. "For you did not receive the spirit of bondage again to fear, but you received the Spirit of adoption by whom we cry out, 'Abba, Father'" (Romans 8:15). That morning in worship, I stopped reciting and started crying "ABBA" like a child who'd finally found her way home. I wasn't orphaned. I had ABBA—and He wasn't leaving.

But that wasn't all. Days later, another name emerged. I was journaling through Hagar's story—abandoned, pregnant, alone in the wilderness. And when she encountered God, she named Him EL ROI [el ro-EE]—"the God Who SEES me." "Then she called the name of the LORD who spoke to her, You-Are-the-God-Who-Sees" (Genesis 16:13). I stopped writing. That was MY story. Abandoned. Alone. Invisible. And suddenly I realized: When your earthly father didn't see you, EL ROI did. Every moment you felt overlooked, unseen, forgotten—He saw. He's been watching your whole story, recording every tear (Psalm 56:8), counting every hair on your head (Matthew 10:30). Your father may have looked away. But EL ROI never stopped seeing.

And then CHESED. I'd heard the word a hundred times—covenant love, steadfast love, loyal love. But it stayed information until the breakup. The man I'd been dating left without warning. No closure. No explanation. Just gone. And in that abandonment, CHESED became revelation. "I have loved you with an everlasting love; therefore I have continued My faithfulness to you" (Jeremiah 31:3). Human fathers fail. Human relationships fracture. But CHESED love? It NEVER lets go. It's covenant love that doesn't depend on your performance or your perfection. It's the love that pursues when you're running, holds when you're falling, stays when everyone else leaves.

Three names. One orphan wound. Complete healing. Not theology. Encounter. Your gap of rejection meets His attribute of ABBA FATHER. Your gap of invisibility meets His attribute of EL ROI. Your gap of conditional love meets His attribute of CHESED. The father wound you've been carrying? God's been waiting to fill it with Himself. Not with explanation. With encounter.

Day 9's Scarcity Gap Meets JEHOVAH JIREH

Four days ago, you exposed the fear you'd been hiding behind hustle. That 3 AM kitchen table moment. The calculator bleeding red. The "Will I have enough?" panic that's haunted you for years, making you hoard instead of give, survive instead of thrive, operate from scarcity instead of abundance.

I lived there for eighteen months. 2016-2017. The year after my divorce when the financial devastation hit. I'd wake up at 3 AM—not from God, from terror—and calculate. Mortgage plus utilities plus groceries plus gas minus income equals... not enough. Never enough. That kitchen table became my altar of anxiety. Calculator. Bills. Spreadsheet. Red numbers bleeding across white paper like wounds that wouldn't heal. "God, where's the provision? Where's the breakthrough? Where's JEHOVAH JIREH?"

And then one morning, exhausted from calculating, I heard Holy Spirit whisper: "You keep asking WHERE is Jehovah Jireh. But you should be asking WHEN I provided." I grabbed my journal. Started listing. The unexpected check that arrived the day the water bill was due. The client who prepaid for services. The friend who "just felt led" to send grocery money. Provision after provision after provision—all BEFORE I asked, BEFORE I calculated, BEFORE I panicked. And suddenly I realized: JEHOVAH

JIREH doesn't mean "The LORD Will Eventually Provide If You Panic Enough." It means "The LORD Will Provide"—future tense, guaranteed promise, already done deal.

"And Abraham called the name of the place, The-LORD-Will-Provide" (Genesis 22:14). Abraham named the place AFTER the ram appeared. Past provision. Future confidence. That 3 AM kitchen table moment when you thought you'd never make it? JEHOVAH JIREH saw it BEFORE you sat down. That calculator bleeding red? He saw your need before you calculated it. He's the God who provides BEFORE the crisis hits, not after you've exhausted every option.

But He didn't stop with provision. He went deeper. To the root beneath the scarcity. My gap wasn't just "not enough money." My gap was "I'll never BE enough to access what I need." And that's when I encountered EL SHADDAI [el shad-DAI]—the ALL-SUFFICIENT One. "I am Almighty God; walk before Me and be blameless" (Genesis 17:1). You feel insufficient. Your bank account is insufficient. Your resources are insufficient. But HE is EL SHADDAI—the ALL-SUFFICIENT ONE. What you lack, He IS. Your scarcity meets His sufficiency.

And here's what broke me open: His GENEROSITY. I'd been treating God like He was rationing resources, giving me survival portions because that's all He could spare. Then I read Ephesians 3:20: "Now to Him who is able to do exceedingly abundantly above all that we ask or think." The Greek literally says "hyper-abundantly beyond"—WAY more than you need. He's not a minimalist. He's GENEROUS. He doesn't give you survival. He gives you ABUNDANCE. Not because you earned it. Because it's His nature.

Three attributes. One scarcity wound. Complete filling. Your gap of scarcity meets His attribute of JEHOVAH JIREH. Your gap of insufficiency meets His attribute of EL SHADDAI. Your gap of fear meets His attribute of GENEROSITY. The 3 AM panic you've been carrying? God's been waiting to fill it with Himself. Not with more money first. With more of His nature.

Day 10's Powerlessness Gap Meets ADONAI

Three days ago, Day 10 ripped open the wound you'd been hiding behind religious activity. That abuse you couldn't stop. The injustice you couldn't fix. The badge you didn't know how to use. The victim mentality that kept you feeling perpetually defenseless, violated, powerless.

I know that wound. Intimately. The abuse I couldn't escape. The authority figures who violated trust. The systems that protected perpetrators while silencing victims. The powerlessness that became my identity. "Powerless" wasn't just how I felt—it became who I WAS. And for years, I accepted it. Victims stay victims, right? Until Day 10 exposed it. And Day 13 filled it.

I was reading Psalm 103:19—"The LORD has established His throne in heaven, and His kingdom rules over all"—when something shifted. I'd read this verse before. But this time, Holy Spirit asked: "Who's ruling YOUR life? The abuser who violated you? The system that failed you? Or ADONAI who's sovereign over ALL?" And I realized: I'd given my abuser more power than I'd given God. I was living under the authority of the one who hurt me instead of under ADONAI [ah-doe-NAI]—the Supreme Ruler, the Lord, the Master who rules OVER every authority that's ever hurt you.

You feel powerless. But you're not under the authority of your abuser or chaos or injustice. You're under ADONAI—the Supreme Ruler whose kingdom rules over ALL. What feels out of control to YOU is UNDER His control. The authority that violated you? ADONAI is ABOVE them. The system that failed you? ADONAI rules OVER it. You're not at the mercy of earthly authorities. You're under the protection of the HIGHEST authority.

But He went deeper. To another name I'd known about but never encountered: EL ELYON [el el-YONE]—God Most High. "I will cry out to God Most High, to God who performs all things for me" (Psalm 57:2). Every authority that's abused you? EL ELYON is ABOVE them. The perpetrator who violated you? EL ELYON is HIGHER. The system that protected them? EL ELYON is SUPREME. And when you're under the Highest authority, no earthly authority can touch you without His permission.

And then JEHOVAH NISSI [yeh-ho-VAH nis-SEE]—The LORD My Banner, The LORD My Victory. "And Moses built an altar and called its name, The-LORD-Is-My-Banner" (Exodus 17:15). You couldn't stop the abuse. You couldn't win the battle. But JEHOVAH NISSI is the LORD of your VICTORY. The battles you lost in your strength, He wins in His. Not by your might. By His banner raised over you.

And His JUSTICE. "Righteousness and justice are the foundation of Your throne" (Psalm 89:14). He SEES every wrong. He RECORDS every injustice. And He WILL make it right—if not in this courtroom, then in His. Your powerlessness meets His omnipotence. Your victimization meets His justice. Your defeat meets His victory. Four attributes. One powerlessness wound. Complete restoration.

Day 11's Equipment Gap Meets THE HOLY SPIRIT

Two days ago, Day 11 revealed the drought you'd been hiding behind religious language. That equipment room overflowing with tools you didn't know how to use. The anointing that felt dry. The empowerment that felt absent. The "What do I carry?" confusion that made you feel unqualified for the assignment God gave you.

I lived that confusion for three years. 2017-2020. Post-divorce, post-breakdown, trying to rebuild ministry while feeling perpetually unqualified. I'd watch others operate in power—prophecy flowing, healing manifest, breakthrough erupting—and wonder: "Where's MY anointing? Where's MY equipment? Why does their tool chest overflow while mine feels empty?" The comparison was crushing. The inadequacy was constant. Until Holy Spirit Himself became my revelation.

I was reading Acts 1:8—"You shall receive power when the Holy Spirit has come upon you"—when He interrupted: "Stop asking where the anointing IS. Ask who the anointing IS. You're looking for AN anointing. But the anointing is a PERSON. Me. The Holy Spirit." And suddenly I understood: I'd been treating anointing like equipment I access when I need it. But the Holy Spirit isn't equipment. He's EMPOWERMENT. The Greek dynamis [DYN-ah-mis] means explosive power, enabling force. You feel unqualified. You feel like you lack the anointing. But you have the HOLY SPIRIT—and He IS your empowerment. You're not trying to manufacture anointing. You're FILLED with the One who IS the Anointing.

But He didn't stop there. He introduced me to JEHOVAH MEKADDESH [yeh-ho-VAH meh-kah-DESH]—The LORD Who Sanctifies. The Hebrew qadash [kaw-DASH] means to consecrate, set apart, make holy. "For both He who sanctifies and those who are being sanctified are all of one" (Hebrews 2:11). JEHOVAH MEKADDESH doesn't just SET you apart—He FILLS you with what you need for the assignment. Your drought meets His SATURATION. That equipment room you thought was empty (Day 11)? It's not accumulation you need. It's accessing what the Holy Spirit has already deposited IN you.

And then GRACE. The anointing isn't earned through striving—it's received through surrender. "My grace is sufficient for you, for My power is made perfect in weakness" (2 Corinthians 12:9). Stop chasing what you already carry. The Holy Spirit isn't withheld until you qualify. He qualifies you by His presence. Three attributes. One equipment drought. Complete empowerment.

Day 12's Destination Gap Meets JEHOVAH SHAMMAH

Yesterday, you exposed the anxiety you'd been hiding behind false humility. That "WHEN will I arrive?" desperation. The comparison scrolling. The destination obsession that made you despise the journey, resent the process, and miss today's advancement while waiting for tomorrow's arrival.

I know that wound too. The "WHEN?" that became my daily prayer. "When will I arrive? When will I have the platform, the breakthrough, the vindication I've been working toward?" I'd scroll social media watching others ARRIVE while I was still ADVANCING. Their destination mocked my journey. Their harvest season reminded me of my planting season. The comparison was toxic. The destination obsession was suffocating. Until JEHOVAH SHAMMAH became my revelation.

I was reading Ezekiel 48:35—"And the name of the city from that day shall be: THE-LORD-IS-THERE"—when Holy Spirit asked: "Where are you looking for Me? At the destination? I'm not waiting for you at the finish line. I'm WITH you in the process." And I realized: JEHOVAH SHAMMAH [yeh-ho-VAH SHAM-mah] doesn't mean "The LORD Will Be There Someday When You Arrive." It means "The LORD IS There"—present tense, current reality, NOW. Not someday when you've accomplished enough. NOW. In the waiting. In the wilderness. In the process you're resenting.

You've been asking "WHEN will I GET there?" He's been answering "I AM there—in the process, in the wilderness, in the waiting." Your destination obsession meets His PRESENCE in the journey. He's not waiting at the finish line. He's WITH you in every faithful Tuesday. Every obedient moment nobody sees. Every planted seed that hasn't sprouted yet. JEHOVAH SHAMMAH—The LORD Is There. Not there at the destination. Here in the journey.

But He went deeper still. To FAITHFULNESS—He Stays UNTIL. "He will be with you. He will not leave you nor forsake you, until you have finished all the work" (1 Chronicles 28:20). The Hebrew ad [ad] means UNTIL—not "unless," not "as long as you perform well," but UNTIL completion. Your temple project may look like pain right now. Construction may seem chaotic. Timeline may feel wrong. But He's WITH you—not watching from heaven, but laboring beside you in the mess. He won't abandon you. He won't forsake you. He's committed UNTIL you finish. Not until you arrive. Until you FINISH what He started.

And His SOVEREIGN TIMING. "He has made everything beautiful in its time" (Ecclesiastes 3:11). Stop measuring your timeline against someone else's destination. Their arrival doesn't delay yours. Their harvest doesn't diminish yours. He orders your steps individually, sovereignly, perfectly. Your "WHEN?" anxiety meets His "TRUST MY TIMING" promise. Three attributes. One destination obsession. Complete rest in the journey.

THE ARCHITECTURE REVEALED

This is why Days 8-12 had to come BEFORE Day 13. You had to FEEL the gap before you could ENCOUNTER the Filler. If Day 13 came first, His attributes would be information—concepts you memorized but never experienced. Because Days 8-12 came first, His attributes are REVELATION—the Person you've encountered in your actual pain.

Your cracks are where His light shines through. And you had to see your cracks before you could see His light. Your weaknesses are windows for His glory. But you had to admit weakness before glory could shine through. Insufficiency is God's opportunity. But you had to feel insufficient before God could demonstrate His all-sufficiency.

Days 8-12 weren't random exposure. They were surgical preparation. You had to see the gap before you could behold the Filler. You had to feel the crack before you could see the light. You had to admit the weakness before you could witness the strength flowing through the window.

You didn't learn about JEHOVAH JIREH in a classroom. You MET Him at your 3 AM kitchen table. You didn't study EL ROI in seminary. You ENCOUNTERED Him when your father didn't see you but GOD did. You didn't memorize ADONAI's sovereignty. You EXPERIENCED it when powerlessness drove you to discover the authority you carry. Information became revelation. Concepts became encounters. Gaps became galleries displaying His glory.

Days 8-12 exposed your gaps—one per day, methodically, mercifully. Orphan identity. Scarcity crisis. Powerlessness wound. Equipment drought. Destination anxiety. Five days of tearing open wounds you'd been hiding. It wasn't random. It wasn't accidental. It was surgical. Because you can't encounter God's attributes in your gaps until you ADMIT you have gaps. Orphans pretend self-sufficiency. Heirs acknowledge need. You needed to see your gaps before you could behold His glory filling them.

Day 13 reveals WHO fills those gaps. Not WHAT (a concept). Not HOW (a method). WHO—the Person of God expressing specific attributes designed to fill your specific gaps. This isn't generic theology. This is personal encounter. You didn't study ABBA—you MET Him in your father wound. You didn't learn JEHOVAH JIREH—you ENCOUNTERED Him at your 3 AM table. You didn't memorize ADONAI—you EXPERIENCED Him when powerlessness drove you to authority.

Tomorrow (Day 14), your voice will declare what your eyes have seen today. You can't speak what you haven't seen. You can't declare truth you've only heard about. Days 8-12 exposed the gaps. Day 13 opened your eyes to WHO fills them. Day 14 will open your mouth to DECLARE what you've beheld. Heart received (Days 8-12). Eyes beheld (Day 13). Mouth will declare (Day 14). Heaven will manifest. This is the progression that transforms information into revelation, and revelation into declaration.

THE ARCHITECTURE: YOUR GAPS MEET HIS ATTRIBUTES

Every Gap You Exposed Has a Corresponding Attribute Designed to Fill It

DAY	GAP EXPOSED	HIS ATTRIBUTE FILLS IT	KEY SCRIPTURE	YOUR DECLARATION
DAY 8 Adoption	Orphan identity, rejection, father abandonment	ABBA FATHER — Intimate Daddy. EL ROI — God Who Sees. CHESED — Covenant love	"You received the Spirit of adoption by whom we cry out, 'Abba, Father'" (Rom 8:15)	"I am not orphaned. I have ABBA. He sees me. His CHESED love never quits."

WEEK 2: ALIGN (7A)

DAY 9 Abundance	Scarcity crisis, lack, "Will I have enough?"	JEHOVAH JIREH — The LORD Provides. EL SHADDAI — All-Sufficient. GENEROSITY — Abundant giver	"My God shall supply all your need according to His riches" (Phil 4:19)	"I am not broke. I have JEHOVAH JIREH. El Shaddai is my sufficiency."
DAY 10 Authority	Powerlessness, victim mentality, abuse	ADONAI — Sovereign Lord. EL ELYON — God Most High. JEHOVAH NISSI — Victory. JUSTICE	"His kingdom rules over all" (Ps 103:19)	"I am not powerless. I carry ADONAI's authority. El Elyon is above every power."
DAY 11 Anointing	Equipment drought, feeling unqualified, dryness	HOLY SPIRIT — Empowerment. JEHOVAH MEKADDESH — Sanctifier. GRACE — Sufficient power	"You shall receive power when the Holy Spirit has come" (Acts 1:8)	"I am not unqualified. The HOLY SPIRIT empowers me. Grace makes me sufficient."
DAY 12 Advancement	Destination obsession, "WHEN?", comparison anxiety	JEHOVAH SHAMMAH — LORD Is There. FAITHFULNESS — Stays UNTIL. SOVEREIGN TIMING	"THE-LORD-IS-THERE" (Ezek 48:35) "He will not leave... until finished" (1 Chr 28:20)	"I am not waiting alone. JEHOVAH SHAMMAH is WITH me. His timing is perfect."

Welcome to the mystery: Every gap you exposed this week was an invitation to encounter a specific attribute of God you needed to see. Your gaps weren't accidents. They were appointments. Your weaknesses aren't disqualifications. They're showcases. Every gap in your life is a gallery where God displays His glory. Every crack is where His light shines through. Every weakness is a window for His strength. And you're not closing your gaps. You're letting them become galleries where HE shines.

THE PARABLE OF THE GOVERNMENT OFFICE

There was a woman standing in line at a government service office on a Friday afternoon when the entire computer system crashed. Three hours she'd already waited. Three hours more they estimated. A woman beside her—visiting for the third time this week for the same unresolved issue—unleashed fury on the clerk. Justified fury. Lost wages. Childcare nightmares. Bureaucratic incompetence compounding into personal crisis.

Without calculation, without consulting any spiritual checklist, the woman who'd been dwelling with God that morning heard herself say: "That sounds incredibly frustrating. Can I buy you a coffee while we wait?" The angry woman stopped mid-sentence, stunned. "Why would you do that?" "Because someone bought me coffee once when I was having a terrible day, and it changed everything."

The woman softened immediately. Tears replaced rage. They talked for two hours—about divorce, about a teenage son spiraling, about fear of starting over at 47. When their numbers were finally called, the woman turned back: "Why are you different? Like... there's something about you that's just... peaceful."

Days later, a text arrived: "I went to church today. First time in years. I don't know why, but being with you made me want to be where you get that peace from."

Driving home that day, Holy Spirit whispered what would revolutionize everything: "You stopped being a window performing for people. You started being a mirror reflecting Me. You weren't displaying what they expected. You were revealing what dwelling with Me deposited. Windows perform. Mirrors reflect."

When attributes flow from identity instead of effort, people stop seeing your goodness and start seeing your God.

TESTIMONY — FROM PANIC TO PURPOSE: THE CHAYAH REVELATION

Two Crises, One Word, Five Years of Formation

2014. In the valley of my unraveling marriage, God first whispered a Hebrew word I'd never heard: CHAYAH [khah-YAH]—"to live, revive, restore, bring to life." I researched it. Journaled about it. I had INFORMATION about God's life-giving nature. **2015.** Divorce papers finalized. Identity shattered. But information without crisis is just data collecting dust. Five years later, the word came alive.

When Crisis Became Revelation

The text arrived during a team meeting—screenshots of private conversations, edited to humiliate me, sent to mutual friends by the narcissistic man I'd been dating. Below them: "Maybe work on yourself before dating again." Public humiliation. **2019.** I'd dated my way out of divorce straight into toxicity—trading one wound for a deeper one.

That night, the panic hit differently. Not just anxiety—visceral terror. My hands trembled uncontrollably. Heart hammering so violently I could feel it in my throat, taste copper on my tongue. The room tilted. Walls closed in. I collapsed onto cold bathroom tile, knees hitting hard. Mascara-streaked tears dripped onto clenched fists. Chest heaving. Gasping for air that wouldn't come. The humiliation wasn't just emotional—it was physical, pressing down like concrete, crushing the breath from my lungs.

"God, how do I avoid this in the future?" I choked out between sobs.

His answer: "Crucify your old self. Daily. And remember CHAYAH—I'm not finished with that word yet."

That's when God gave me fresh revelation of the word I'd carried for five years. This time, CHAYAH wasn't a word study. It was an encounter with the Life-Giver Himself. And the Life-Giver doesn't just comfort—He operates. Divine surgery began. Layer by layer, God worked beneath the surface. Not just addressing the toxic relationship—that was the visible symptom. He went deeper. To the roots. To the fears beneath the choices. To the panic attacks that had become my 6 PM ritual.

Every evening. 6 PM. Like clockwork. Panic would seize my chest—that crushing sensation, like an invisible hand squeezing my ribcage. Vision tunneling. Room spinning. Cold sweat. Catastrophic thoughts spiraling. I'd tried everything—breathing exercises, therapy, medication adjustments. Nothing stopped the 6 PM ambush.

Until God spoke His surgical strategy: "365: Live Fearlessly."

But before movement came revelation: "Your anxiety, anger, depression, shame, guilt, rejection—all symptoms of the same disease: FEAR. Stop treating symptoms. Let Me remove the root."

The 5:55 Strategy — God's Surgical Precision

Then came the most specific instruction: "Plan joy in your day at 5:55."

Five minutes before the panic attack.

God wasn't telling me to fight 6 PM fear when it arrived. He was teaching me to meet pain BEFORE it showed up—with His gain through faith. "The joy of the Lord is your strength" (Nehemiah 8:10).

So I started small. Every day at 5:55 PM:

Week 1: One worship song (even through tears).
Week 2: One thing I was grateful for (even if forced).
Week 3: One joke (even when nothing felt funny).
Week 4: One declaration: "Fear doesn't live here anymore. CHAYAH does."

It felt ridiculous at first. But something shifted. The 6 PM panic started arriving at 6:15. Then 6:30. Then sporadically. Then... it stopped hunting me. Because I'd stopped waiting for pain to ambush me. I was ambushing pain with praise.

But the 5:55 joy wasn't just coping—it was God's scalpel, cutting deeper:

Layer 1 (Surface): The toxic relationship—removed.
Layer 2: The desperation that attracted toxicity—addressed.
Layer 3: The low self-esteem fueling desperation—healed.
Layer 4: The rejection wound driving self-esteem issues—touched.
Layer 5 (Root): The FEAR beneath everything—"If I'm alone, I'm worthless."

God didn't just bandage the visible wound. He performed surgery on the invisible root. CHAYAH was bringing life to places I didn't even know were dead.

Character to Conduct — The Inside-Out Transformation

Three months into daily crucifixion and 5:55 joy, I realized: I hadn't opened a dating app in weeks. Not through willpower—I'd simply stopped WANTING validation from men. The gap of fear-driven desperation was being filled by CHAYAH—God's life-giving nature making me ALIVE in ways male attention never could.

Six months in: A man I would have desperately pursued a year ago showed interest. Charming. Successful. Subtly controlling. Old me would have ignored red flags. New creation me? I saw it clearly. And walked away. Peacefully. Not "I'm too damaged" but "I'm too VALUABLE to settle." Not rejection but REFLECTION—mirroring the Father who calls me daughter, not the man who wanted a project.

From Breakthrough to Movement

But God wasn't finished. "365: Live Fearlessly" stopped being just MY breakthrough—it became a MOVEMENT. Then the pandemic hit. March 2020. Fear became the global epidemic beneath the viral one. Anxiety spiked worldwide. Panic attacks became normal.

And God whispered: "Now. Launch CHAYAH globally."

In December 2020, www.chayah.club launched—a virtual gathering place for believers worldwide who needed what I'd needed: encounter with the Life-Giver Himself. Not just information about God's attributes. But revelation OF them.

Today, CHAYAH serves Christians globally—believers in every timezone setting alarms, ambushing pain with praise, encountering the Life-Giver in their gaps. What God used to resurrect one woman from panic became the strategy He used to revive thousands from fear. The Hebrew word whispered in 2014 valley became the movement launched in 2020 pandemic.

CHAYAH—to live, revive, restore, bring to life. Not just for me. For us.

The Theology — Information to Revelation

I KNEW about CHAYAH for five years. But knowing ABOUT God's life-giving nature isn't the same as ENCOUNTERING the Life-Giver Himself. The difference: Crisis + Crucifixion + Beholding = Transformation.

My gap: Fear. **His attribute:** CHAYAH—Life-Giving Power. **The filling:** He didn't just CALM my fear. He KILLED the root and PLANTED life. Layer by layer. 5:55 by 5:55.

I didn't behavior-modify into better dating choices. BEHOLDING the Life-Giver transformed my CHARACTER, and transformed character naturally produced transformed CONDUCT. This is Egypt to Royalty transformation. Egypt me panicked at 6 PM. Royalty me worships at 5:55.

God loved desperate, panicked, humiliated me. But He loved me too much to leave me that way. Old self: Crucified. New creation: Alive. Fear: Removed. CHAYAH: Reflected.

THE MIRROR VS. WINDOW: REVOLUTIONARY DISTINCTION

The government office encounter taught me what would revolutionize my understanding of attributes: "You stopped being a window performing for people. You started being a mirror reflecting Me. Windows perform. Mirrors reflect."

A WINDOW is performance-based: Transparent for others to see through, takes on colors of culture, fragile under pressure, creates gaps between who you are and who you pretend, exhausting to maintain.

A MIRROR is identity-based: Reflects the One looking at it, maintains its nature regardless of surroundings, strengthens through proper backing (relationship with God), reveals truth—His attributes filling your gaps, sustainable through dwelling.

When you're a window, you're constantly concerned with who's watching. When you're a mirror, you're only concerned with one gaze—His. And as you behold Him, you unconsciously reflect Him to others.

The Greek word katoptrizomai [kat-op-TRID-zom-ahee] in 2 Corinthians 3:18 means "to look at oneself in a mirror"—but it's reflexive. You're seeing yourself IN God. You're beholding Him and discovering you're being transformed into His image. Not through striving, but through seeing. "But we all, with unveiled face, beholding as in a mirror the glory of the Lord, are being transformed into the same image from glory to glory, just as by the Spirit of the Lord" (2 Corinthians 3:18).

Transformation comes through beholding, not becoming. Through reflection, not performance.

Three weeks after the government office, someone said: "You seem different lately. Calmer. More... like how you describe God." I hadn't been TRYING to be calm. Hours beholding His peace in prayer were doing what years of "practicing patience" couldn't. Dwelling was depositing. Gazing was transforming.

Your job isn't to be a window displaying godliness for crowds. Your job is to be a mirror reflecting the Father you've been beholding.

BIBLICAL WITNESSES OF TRANSFORMATION: WHEN BEHOLDING CREATED BECOMING

Moses — Face Shining From Proximity

"Now the man Moses was very humble, more than all men who were on the face of the earth" (Numbers 12:3). The man who murdered an Egyptian in rage became the meekest man on earth. What changed? Forty years in God's presence.

"The skin of Moses' face shone while he talked with Him" (Exodus 34:29). He didn't TRY to glow. Beholding God's glory for forty days caused him to unconsciously reflect what he'd been gazing at.

And here's the stunning part: "But Moses did not know that the skin of his face shone" (Exodus 34:29). He was unaware of his own transformation. The glow wasn't manufactured. It was reflected. Moses didn't try to shine. He gazed at glory and shone.

The Man Born Blind — When Physical Sight Becomes Spiritual Vision

"One thing I know: though I was blind, now I see" (John 9:25). Born blind. Never seen color, light, faces. Then Jesus made mud, anointed his eyes, and sent him to wash. Physical sight restored.

But watch what happens next—it's not just his EYES that opened. It's his REVELATION.

First encounter: "The man called Jesus made mud and anointed my eyes" (John 9:11). Information. Surface level.

Second encounter: "He is a prophet" (John 9:17). Deeper. Recognition of divine activity.

Third encounter: When Jesus found him again and asked, "Do you believe in the Son of Man?" The healed man replied, "Lord, I believe." And he worshiped Him (John 9:35-38). Full revelation. From information to worship. From knowing ABOUT Jesus to beholding Jesus as Lord.

Here's the twist: The Pharisees had physical sight but spiritual blindness. They studied Scripture daily. Knew theology. Memorized law. Had all the INFORMATION. But they couldn't SEE who was standing in front of them.

Jesus said: "For judgment I have come into this world, that those who do not see may see, and that those who see may be made blind" (John 9:39). The blind man SAW Jesus clearly. The religious experts remained blind.

Many have sight but no vision. Eyes open but no revelation. Physical seeing without spiritual beholding. This is Day 13's invitation: spiritual sight. Not just reading ABOUT God's attributes—SEEING them. The blind man's testimony becomes ours: "I was blind to who You really are. But now I see."

The Woman at the Well — When Shame Met Seeing

Five husbands. Living with the sixth man. Fetching water at noon to avoid the other women's eyes. She'd been hiding in shame for years. Then a Jewish man asked her for water. She deflected with theology. He responded with truth: "You have had five husbands, and the one whom you now have is not your husband" (John 4:18).

He SAW her. Completely. The thing she'd been hiding—He knew. And He didn't condemn. He offered living water.

Her gap: Shame and rejection.

His attribute: The God who SEES (El Roi [el ro-EE]) and ACCEPTS.

Watch the transformation. She came to the well hiding. She left running—not from Him but TO the city: "Come, see a Man who told me all things that I ever did. Could this be the Christ?" (John 4:29).

Information would have kept her debating theology. Revelation sent her declaring testimony.

The result? "And many of the Samaritans of that city believed in Him because of the word of the woman who testified" (John 4:39). The woman who hid at noon became the evangelist who brought a city to Jesus. Not through performance. Through reflection. She simply told what she'd seen.

Beholding precedes declaring. Seeing enables saying. Encounter creates evangelism.

Jehoshaphat — Beholding God in Overwhelming Crisis

Surrounded by three armies. Vastly outnumbered. No military solution. Jehoshaphat's response wasn't to strategize harder—it was to BEHOLD longer. "We have no power to face this vast army that is attacking us. We do not know what to do, but our eyes are on you" (2 Chronicles 20:12).

Watch the progression: Admit helplessness → Declare dependence → Fix eyes on God.

This is gap-filling in real-time. His gap: Powerlessness. God's attribute: Omnipotence. When Jehoshaphat couldn't see a way forward, he SAW God more clearly.

God's response? "The battle is not yours, but God's" (2 Chronicles 20:15).

Victory came through worship-filled beholding. They didn't fight—they sang. As they BEHELD God's glory through worship, He fought for them. The enemies destroyed each other. The battles you can't win in your strength are the exact battles God wants to win in His.

THE NAMES OF GOD: ATTRIBUTES AS INVITATIONS

Every Name Reveals an Attribute That Fills a Specific Gap. When God reveals a name, He's revealing part of His character—and inviting you to encounter that specific attribute in your specific gap.

NAME	MEANING	ATTRIBUTE	GAP IT FILLS	SCRIPTURE
EL SHADDAI [el shad-DAI]	Almighty God, All-Sufficient One	Omnipotence, Sufficiency	Insufficiency, Weakness	Genesis 17:1
JEHOVAH JIREH [yeh-ho-VAH yeer-EH]	The LORD Will Provide	Provision, Generosity	Lack, Scarcity	Genesis 22:14

JEHOVAH RAPHA [yeh-ho-VAH raw-FAH]	The LORD Who Heals	Healing, Restoration	Brokenness, Pain	Exodus 15:26
JEHOVAH SHALOM [yeh-ho-VAH shah-LOME]	The LORD Is Peace	Peace, Rest	Anxiety, Chaos	Judges 6:24
JEHOVAH TSIDKENU [yeh-ho-VAH tsid-KAY-noo]	The LORD Our Righteousness	Righteousness, Justification	Guilt, Shame	Jeremiah 23:6
JEHOVAH SHAMMAH [yeh-ho-VAH SHAM-mah]	The LORD Is There	Presence, Nearness	Loneliness, Abandonment	Ezekiel 48:35
EL ROI [el ro-EE]	God Who Sees Me	Attentiveness, Awareness	Feeling Invisible, Forgotten	Genesis 16:13
JEHOVAH NISSI [yeh-ho-VAH nis-SEE]	The LORD My Banner	Victory, Triumph	Defeat, Disgrace	Exodus 17:15
JEHOVAH ROHI [yeh-ho-VAH ro-HEE]	The LORD My Shepherd	Guidance, Care	Feeling Lost, Directionless	Psalm 23:1
IMMANUEL [im-man-oo-EL]	God With Us	Presence, Intimacy	Isolation, Separation	Matthew 1:23
EL ELYON [el el-YONE]	God Most High	Sovereignty, Supremacy	Chaos, Powerlessness	Genesis 14:18-20
EL OLAM [el o-LAHM]	Everlasting God	Eternity, Unchangeableness	Fear of Change, Instability	Genesis 21:33

When you don't know what to pray, pray His names. When you don't know which attribute you need, look at your gap—it reveals which name to call. Your gap reveals which attribute you need to encounter. Your weakness shows which aspect of His strength to behold.

FROM EGYPT TO ROYALTY: CHARACTER DETERMINES CONDUCT

Here's where everything you've learned about attributes becomes transformation you live. Because seeing God's character isn't just revelation—it's renovation. Not external behavior modification, but internal DNA recoding. This is the shift from Egypt slave mentality to Kingdom royalty identity. From performing righteousness to reflecting it.

"Therefore, if anyone is in Christ, he is a new creation; old things have passed away; behold, all things have become new" (2 Corinthians 5:17). Not "becoming new"—HAVE BECOME new. Past tense. Already done. The old self isn't limping along needing improvement. It's dead. Crucified with Christ (Romans 6:6). The new creation isn't aspirational—it's actual. Already alive. Already carrying divine DNA.

"I have been crucified with Christ; it is no longer I who live, but Christ lives in me" (Galatians 2:20). Old self crucified. Christ now living IN you. His attributes aren't something you achieve externally. They're Someone living internally, expressing Himself through your personality, choices, relationships, conduct.

God's Attributes Determine His Actions — Yours Should Too

God's attributes determine His actions. He doesn't act loving some days and cruel others. He IS love, so He consistently ACTS lovingly. He IS faithful, so He consistently DEMONSTRATES faithfulness. His character determines His conduct.

And you're made in His image (Genesis 1:26-27). Your character should determine your conduct. Your transformed nature should govern your behavior. Not through willpower alone. But through the new creation reality that Christ lives IN you, and His nature is becoming your nature through dwelling.

This is why behavior modification always fails long-term. You can white-knuckle kindness for a season. But you can only sustain conduct that flows from character. If your character hasn't changed, your conduct will eventually revert. But when character transforms through beholding God's attributes—when His nature becomes your nature through adoption and dwelling—conduct changes naturally, organically, permanently.

The Fruit of the Spirit, Not Just Gifts

Too much emphasis on gifts—prophecy, healing, miracles. Not enough on fruit—love, joy, peace, patience, kindness, goodness, faithfulness, gentleness, self-control (Galatians 5:22-23). Gifts are given instantly. Fruit grows gradually through abiding.

You can have prophetic gifts and a sharp tongue. Healing anointing and a hard heart. But fruit? Fruit reveals character. Fruit proves transformation. Fruit demonstrates that you've been WITH Jesus (Acts 4:13), not just working FOR Him.

And here's what's revolutionary: The fruit of the Spirit are God's attributes manifesting through you. Love? That's His agape flowing through you. Joy? His gladness expressed through your personality. Peace? His shalom settling your anxious mind. All HIS attributes, revealed through your conduct because your character is being transformed into His image.

You're not trying to produce fruit. You're abiding in the Vine (John 15:5), and fruit is the natural result of that union.

He Loves You As You Are—But Too Much to Leave You the Same

God's love accepts you completely as you are. Broken. Messy. Struggling. He doesn't wait for you to clean up before He embraces you. "But God demonstrates His own love for us in this: While we were still sinners, Christ died for us" (Romans 5:8). While. Still. Sinners.

But here's the other truth: He loves you too much to LEAVE you the same. Acceptance isn't approval of destructive patterns. Love that truly loves doesn't enable—it transforms. God's love is holy love. Covenant love. Chesed love. The kind that pursues, heals, refines, and restores.

You can't encounter God and remain unchanged. Moses glowed unknowingly (Exodus 34:29). The disciples spoke boldly after being with Jesus (Acts 4:13). The woman at the well left her water pot and became an evangelist (John 4:28-29).

Encounter produces transformation. Beholding creates becoming. Gazing at His attributes changes your character, and changed character transforms your conduct.

This isn't self-improvement. This is inside-out transformation. Spiritual DNA recoding. Old creation death. New creation life. This is what Paul meant: "Do not be conformed to this world, but be transformed by the renewing of your mind" (Romans 12:2). The Greek word for "transformed" is metamorphoō [met-am-or-FOH-oh]—metamorphosis. Caterpillar to butterfly. Not improved caterpillar. Different creature entirely.

That's what beholding God's attributes does. You don't become a better version of your old self. You become a new creation reflecting His nature. Egypt slave becomes Kingdom ambassador. Fear-driven becomes fearless. Panic-stricken becomes peace-filled. Performance-exhausted becomes reflection-sustained.

And it's not achieved. It's received. Not manufactured. Reflected. Not forced. Flowed. He loves you as you are. He loves you too much to leave you the same. Behold Him until you become like Him.

HOW ATTRIBUTES ACTIVATE: THE PROTOCOL OF DIVINE REFLECTION

BEHOLDING TRANSFORMS. "But we all, with unveiled face, beholding as in a mirror the glory of the Lord, are being transformed into the same image from glory to glory" (2 Corinthians 3:18). You're beholding Him and discovering you're being transformed. Not through striving, but through seeing. Spend time daily gazing at ONE attribute. Let your eyes linger. Behold until the attribute begins to fill the gap.

ABIDING PRODUCES. "Abide in Me, and I in you. As the branch cannot bear fruit of itself, unless it abides in the vine, neither can you, unless you abide in Me" (John 15:4). The Greek meno [MEN-oh] means to dwell, remain, stay. Fruit comes from abiding, not achieving. You don't vacation with a vine; you're grafted into it. Stop treating time with God like a quick visit and start treating it like dwelling. Stay. Remain. Linger. Abide in Me—not visit Me. Dwell, don't drop by.

PRESSURE REVEALS. "My brethren, count it all joy when you fall into various trials, knowing that the testing of your faith produces patience" (James 1:2-4). Pressure doesn't CREATE attributes—it REVEALS what dwelling has deposited. The squeeze reveals the juice. When pressure comes, don't panic that attributes seem absent. Pressure is revealing what's being formed.

PATIENCE TRUSTS THE TIMELINE. Moses: 40 years becoming meek. Joseph: 13 years from pit to palace. Jesus: 30 years preparation for 3 years ministry. There's no prescriptive timeline because you're not manufacturing; you're marinating. Some attributes emerge in weeks; others take decades. Trust that every day of dwelling is depositing. Every moment of beholding is transforming—even when you can't see it yet.

WHEN ATTRIBUTES SEEM ABSENT: SEVEN CHECKPOINTS

Before concluding attributes aren't working or the mirror is broken, check these seven areas:

1. Are you beholding or just Bible-studying? (Information vs. revelation problem. Moses spent 40 days beholding, not just reading. Gazing transforms; studying informs.)

2. Are you trying to be a window performing for people? (Mirror reflects naturally; window strains to display. Check your motivation: approval or reflection?)

3. Have you confused feelings with transformation? (Mother Teresa felt nothing for 50 years but reflected Christ powerfully. Transformation doesn't depend on feelings.)

4. Are you in the "dark night of the soul" season? (John of the Cross: Sometimes God withdraws feeling to deepen faith. Keep beholding even when you feel nothing.)

5. Are you expecting instant results instead of trusting the timeline? (Moses: 40 years becoming meek. Joseph: 13 years pit to palace. Transformation is slow-cooked, not microwaved.)

6. Are you focusing on one gap while God addresses a deeper root? (CHAYAH testimony: God addressed panic attacks by removing fear root. Sometimes He operates on what you can't see.)

7. Have you stopped the practices thinking you've "arrived"? (Attributes flow from abiding, not achieving. The moment you stop dwelling, reflection fades. Keep beholding.)

Final Reminder: Moses glowed and didn't know it (Exodus 34:29). You're transforming even when you can't see it. Ask others—they often see growth you miss. The mirror works even when you can't see the reflection yourself. Stalled feelings don't mean stalled transformation. Darkness doesn't mean distance. Keep beholding by faith, not by feeling. The darkness you feel might be the shadow of God standing very close.

MONTHLY ATTRIBUTE ENCOUNTER ASSESSMENT

Track your journey from information to revelation monthly. Rate yourself 0-10 in each area:

Beholding Practice: ___/10 (10 = Daily gazing at God's attributes through prayer/worship; 1 = Only crisis-driven prayers)

Information vs. Revelation: ___/10 (10 = Encountering God's character personally through experience; 1 = Only knowing about Him secondhand)

Mirror vs. Window: ___/10 (10 = Reflecting God naturally without performing; 1 = Exhausted from performing godliness for people)

Gap Awareness: ___/10 (10 = Seeing gaps as galleries for His glory; 1 = Hiding gaps in shame, pretending self-sufficiency)

Character-Based Conduct: ___/10 (10 = Behavior flows naturally from transformed character; 1 = White-knuckling good behavior through willpower)

Total Score: ___/50

Interpretation:
- **0-20:** Information-driven, window performing. Practice daily 15-minute beholding sessions. Review one attribute weekly. Focus on encountering, not just learning.

- **21-35:** Transitioning from information to revelation. Continue monthly tracking. Celebrate progress. Focus on lowest-scoring area. Ask trusted friend what attribute they see in you.
- **36-50:** Revelation-walking, mirror reflecting. Maintain quarterly check-ins. Ready to mentor others in attribute encounter. Model beholding lifestyle. Share testimonies of transformation.

Compare scores monthly. Celebrate every increase—transformation is progressive. If scores decrease, review Seven Checkpoints above. Check for performance pressure, feelings-based assessment, or impatience with timeline. Realign without shame. You're measuring progress, not perfection. The assessment itself IS advancement—awareness precedes transformation.

THE 6-DIMENSIONAL ATTRIBUTE ACTIVATION

Attributes aren't one-dimensional—they transform every area of your life:

DIMENSION	GAP TO FILL	PRACTICE	EVIDENCE
SPIRITUAL	Distance from God	Gaze at one attribute daily	That attribute emerges naturally in your character
MENTAL	Performance pressure	Replace achieving with receiving	Peace replaces striving; trust replaces anxiety
EMOTIONAL	Disconnection from feelings	Ask "Father, what are You feeling?"	Divine emotions flow through you naturally
PHYSICAL	Hidden transformation	Let countenance reflect encounters	People notice "something different" about you
FINANCIAL	Scarcity mindset	Give as He gives (generously, secretly)	Abundance flows through open hands
RELATIONAL	Surface connections	Love through His heart, not capacity	Relationships deepen; people feel truly seen

Every dimension of your life becomes a display case for His attributes when you stop performing and start reflecting.

6-DIMENSIONAL ATTRIBUTE PRAYERS: CHARACTER TO CONDUCT TRANSFORMATION

SPIRITUAL: "Father, I advance from information about You to revelation OF You. My old self is crucified. I behold Your attributes and reflect them naturally. Your attributes transform my character. My character determines my conduct. From Egypt slave mentality to Kingdom ambassador identity. In Jesus' name, spiritually transformed!"

MENTAL: "Father, I advance from orphan thinking to heir consciousness. My old patterns—performance pressure, comparison, scarcity mindsets—are crucified. I replace achieving with receiving. Your attributes fill gaps in my thinking. My character determines my thought patterns. From Egypt thinking to royalty consciousness. In Jesus' name, mentally transformed!"

EMOTIONAL: "Father, I advance from disconnection to divine alignment. My old emotional patterns—fear-driven, shame-saturated, rejection-ruled—are crucified. I don't suppress feelings—I submit them to Your character. Your joy becomes my strength. My character determines my emotional responses. From Egypt's fear to royalty's freedom. In Jesus' name, emotionally transformed!"

PHYSICAL: "Father, I advance from hidden struggle to visible reflection. My old self's destructive patterns are crucified. My body is Your temple. People notice I'm different even when I don't speak. My conduct reflects character: healthy choices flow from identity. From Egypt's bondage to royalty's wholeness. In Jesus' name, physically transformed!"

FINANCIAL: "Father, I advance from scarcity slave to abundance heir. My old self—hoarding, anxious, Egypt-minded about money—is crucified. I give as You give: cheerfully, secretly, abundantly. My character determines my financial conduct. From Egypt's poverty mentality to royalty's abundance consciousness. In Jesus' name, financially transformed!"

RELATIONAL: "Father, I advance from performance-based connections to authentic reflection. My old self—people-pleasing, approval-seeking, window mentality—is crucified. I'm a mirror reflecting You. I love with Your agape. My character determines my conduct in every relationship. From Egypt's comparison to royalty's collaboration. In Jesus' name, relationally transformed!"

COMPREHENSIVE DECLARATION: "I declare transformation across ALL six dimensions: SPIRITUALLY—I behold You and reflect You. MENTALLY—I think with renewed mind. EMOTIONALLY—I feel aligned with Your heart. PHYSICALLY—My body is Your temple. FINANCIALLY—I steward as Your heir. RELATIONALLY—I love as You love. My old self is crucified. My new creation is alive. Your attributes transform my character. My character determines my conduct. Egypt mentality is dead. Royalty identity is alive. He loves me as I am. He loves me too much to leave me the same. I am becoming who I already am in Christ. In Jesus' name, COMPLETELY transformed!"

TRANSFORMATION — FROM INFORMATION TO REVELATION

INFORMATION MINDSET	REVELATION MINDSET
Knows ABOUT God	SEES God clearly
Studies His attributes	Encounters His character
Memorizes His names	Experiences His nature
Learns His promises	Lives His presence
Accumulates theology	Beholds His glory
Tries to be godly	Reflects being with God
Performs for people (window)	Reflects for Father (mirror)
Strives to manufacture resemblance	Trusts dwelling to create likeness
Exhausted by achieving	Energized by receiving
Egypt slave mentality	Royalty ambassador identity
Old self improvement	New creation emergence

Information says "God is faithful." Revelation says "I've SEEN His faithfulness hold me when everything else let go."

MANIFESTATION — DAILY ATTRIBUTE PRACTICES

Stop waiting for transformation to arrive. Start beholding through daily actions.

THE ESSENTIAL 3:

1. GAZE AT ONE ATTRIBUTE DAILY — Choose one attribute. Read scriptures about it. Meditate. Let your eyes linger. Ask: "Father, show me this aspect of who You are."

2. IDENTIFY YOUR BIGGEST GAP — What gap are you most aware of today? That gap reveals which attribute you need to encounter.

3. REFLECT, DON'T PERFORM — In one interaction today, consciously be a mirror instead of a window.

Gaze at one attribute. Fill one gap. Be one reflection.

ADDITIONAL PRACTICES: Practice secret generosity. Pause before reacting—60-second breath prayer. Shepherd someone today. Keep one small promise perfectly. Give someone full presence. Speak one truth in love. Set 5:55 alarm (ambush pain with praise).

START HERE: If you can only do ONE thing today, text someone: "God's attributes are filling my gaps!"

THE PROPHETIC ACT — MIRROR DECLARATION

Stand before a mirror. Look at your reflection—not critically but prophetically. You're about to declare what's true even when you can't see it yet:

"I see a child of God. I carry His DNA. I am His mirror, not the world's window. The Hebrew calls me TSELEM—His image. The Greek calls me CHARAKTĒR—His exact representation.

Every gap in my life meets His corresponding attribute. My cracks are where His light shines through. My weaknesses are windows for His glory. My insufficiency is His opportunity to demonstrate all-sufficiency.

My weakness meets His STRENGTH (El Shaddai). My chaos meets His PEACE (Jehovah Shalom). My lack meets His PROVISION (Jehovah Jireh). My loneliness meets His PRESENCE (Immanuel). My guilt meets His RIGHTEOUSNESS (Jehovah Tsidkenu). My brokenness meets His HEALING (Jehovah Rapha). My invisibility meets His SEEING (El Roi). My defeat meets His VICTORY (Jehovah Nissi). My fear meets His SOVEREIGNTY (Adonai). My shame meets His HOLINESS that cleanses. My rejection meets His LOVE that never lets go.

I don't ACHIEVE these attributes—I RECEIVE them through adoption. I REVEAL them through relationship. I REFLECT them as His mirror. From this day forward: I stop being a window for people. I start being a mirror for my Father. My old self is crucified. My new creation is alive. Egypt mentality is dead. Royalty identity is reflected. He loves me as I am. He loves me too much to leave me the same. In Jesus' name, I look like my Father!"

PRAYER OF GAP-FILLING ACTIVATION

"Father, forgive me for trying to be a window when You designed me as a mirror. Thank You that every gap reveals space for Your attributes. Your chesed love never fails. Your racham compassion never ends. My weaknesses showcase Your strengths. My old self is crucified. My new creation is alive. Your attributes transform my character. My character determines my conduct.

THE DANIEL FAST: CLOSING THE GAP!

Today I receive Your attributes as gap-fillers: I am not spiritually blind—You've opened the eyes of my heart (Ephesians 1:18). Like the man born blind, I move from information to revelation. From 'a man called Jesus' to 'Lord, I believe.' Heal me from spiritual blindness. Let me see You as You truly are.

I am not weak—I carry El Shaddai's strength. I am not anxious—I reflect Jehovah Shalom's peace. I am not lacking—I display Jehovah Jireh's provision. I am not alone—I manifest Immanuel's presence. I am not guilty—I bear Jehovah Tsidkenu's righteousness. I am not broken—I demonstrate Jehovah Rapha's healing. I am not invisible—I experience El Roi's seeing. I am not defeated—I carry Jehovah Nissi's victory. I am not fearful—I trust Adonai's sovereignty.

Let my life reflect You. Let every gap become a gallery of Your glory. Let every crack become a place where Your light shines through. Let every weakness become a window for Your strength. Let every insufficiency become Your opportunity. I will behold until I broadcast. I will gaze until gaps close. I will remain until I reflect. I will abide until fruit manifests. Because children look like their Father. And I'm Your kid. From Egypt to Royalty. From slave to ambassador. From information to revelation. From performance to reflection. From old creation to new. He loves me as I am. He loves me too much to leave me the same. I am not who I was. I am becoming who I already am in Christ. In Jesus' name, Amen."

SOAP JOURNAL — DAY 13

S (Scripture): Which attribute verse spoke to your biggest gap?
O (Observation): What gap needs God's corresponding attribute? Are you functioning as a window or a mirror?
A (Application): Which name of God will you meditate on this week? Which attribute will you gaze at daily?
P (Prayer): "Father, fill my gap of _____ with Your attribute of _____. Open my eyes to SEE who You really are."

YOUR DAY 13 ACTIVATION CHALLENGE
BEFORE SLEEP TONIGHT:
1. **IDENTIFY:** Your biggest gap and God's corresponding attribute
2. **DECLARE:** Stand before a mirror and speak the Mirror Declaration
3. **CELEBRATE:** Text someone: "God's attributes are filling my gaps!"
4. **LIST:** Three attributes you've seen (not just known about) this past year
5. **ASK:** Someone close to you: "What attribute of God do you see in me?"
6. **PRACTICE:** Being a mirror in one specific situation
7. **THANK:** Him for one gap He's already filled
8. **ASSESS:** Complete your first Monthly Attribute Encounter Assessment

WHY DAY 14 MUST FOLLOW DAY 13

You can't declare what you haven't seen. You can't confess with your mouth what your eyes haven't beheld. This is why the order matters. This is why Day 13 must open your eyes before Day 14 opens your mouth.

Tomorrow you'll discover Romans 10:9-10: "With the heart one believes... and with the mouth confession is made." But heart belief requires seeing. You must BEHOLD His attributes before you can DECLARE them. Vision precedes voice. Seeing comes before saying.

The progression is purposeful:

Days 8-12: You received WHO YOU ARE (adopted, abundant, authoritative, anointed, advancing).

Day 13: Your eyes opened to WHO HE IS (His attributes filling your gaps).

Day 14: Your voice will release what your heart has received and your eyes have seen.

Heart receives. Eyes behold. Mouth declares. Heaven manifests. Shallow sight creates shallow declarations. But what your eyes have truly SEEN today becomes unshakeable foundation for what your mouth will DECLARE tomorrow.

CLOSING — FROM INFORMATION TO REVELATION

Day 13 complete. Twelve days established WHO YOU ARE. Today established WHO HE IS. And that changes everything. You can't declare with conviction what you've only heard about. But what you've SEEN becomes unshakeable foundation. Your gaps aren't accidents. They're appointments. Your weaknesses aren't disqualifications. They're invitations. You're not a window performing for crowds. You're a mirror reflecting the Father you've been beholding.

The mystery: The more you behold Him, the more you become like Him—unconsciously, naturally, supernaturally. Moses glowed and didn't know it. You're transforming and might not see it yet. But HE does. When tomorrow comes and your voice declares, it will carry the weight of what your eyes have seen today.

He loves you as you are—but He loves you too much to leave you the same. The old self that was desperate, panicked, exhausted? Crucified. The new creation that reflects His peace, provision, presence? Alive.

This isn't improvement. This is resurrection. This isn't trying harder. This is beholding longer. Your gaps reveal which attributes to encounter. The gaps you've been ashamed of are holy ground where His attributes shine brightest. Your weakness showcases His strength. Your chaos demonstrates His peace. Your fear reveals His sovereignty.

You're not closing gaps. You're letting gaps become galleries where God displays His glory. Your cracks? That's where His light shines through to a dark world. Your weaknesses? Those are windows where people see His glory, not your performance. Your insufficiency? That's His opportunity to demonstrate all-sufficiency.

When people see you, they won't see your performance. They'll catch glimpses of your Father's reflection shining through your cracks. They'll encounter the God you've been beholding through the windows of your weakness.

Because you can't encounter CHAYAH and remain unchanged. You can't behold holiness and stay defiled. You can't dwell with the Life-Giver and stay dead. Beholding transforms. Transformation proves you've been WITH Him.

"God is who He says He is. And you're beginning to look just like Him." Welcome to revelation. Welcome to being your Father's mirror. Welcome to the reality that He loves you as you are and too much to leave you the same. Your eyes are opening. What you're seeing will transform what you declare tomorrow. And what you declare tomorrow will change your world.

INFORMATION REPLACED WITH REVELATION. GAPS BECOMING GALLERIES. CRACKS BECOMING LIGHT. WEAKNESSES BECOMING WINDOWS. WINDOWS BECOMING MIRRORS. OLD SELF CRUCIFIED. NEW CREATION ALIVE. EYES OPENED. READY FOR VOICE.

TOMORROW: DAY 14 — AFFIRMATION AWAITS. VISION PRECEDES VOICE. SEEING COMES BEFORE SAYING.

END OF DAY 13. WEEK 2: ALIGN — Days 8-13 Complete Tomorrow: Day 14 — The Final Day of Week 2, Voice Activation

DAY 14 — AFFIRMATION

WHEN YOUR VOICE RELEASES WHAT YOUR EYES HAVE SEEN

> *"For with the heart one believes unto righteousness, and with the mouth confession is made unto salvation."*
> — Romans 10:10

WEEK 2 — ALIGN: Establishing Your Identity in God

Day 14 of 21. Week 2 complete. Days 8-12 established WHO YOU ARE internally—adopted, abundant, authoritative, anointed, advancing. Day 13 opened your eyes externally to WHO HE IS—His attributes, His character, His nature filling every gap. Today completes the ALIGN week with the final activation: your VOICE. Internal identity received. External vision beheld. Now your mouth declares what your heart received and your eyes have seen. This is the bridge from silent agreement to bold declaration. From believing quietly to speaking loudly. From Week 2's alignment to Week 3's propulsion. Hell muzzled me. Heaven unmutes me.

ENCOUNTER — WHERE YOU ARE

The Crisis of Silent Affirmation

The bathroom floor is cold at 3 AM. Your face, wet with tears of inadequacy, reflects in the tile. Another night of teaching others to manage emotions while drowning in your own. "It's never enough," you whisper into the darkness. "Did I say it right? Was I good enough? Do I even deserve to be here?" The declarations sit in your chest like unexploded ordnance. The affirmations echo in your mind like songs never sung. The truth you now SEE about God and yourself remains imprisoned behind your teeth. You believe it in your heart. You behold it with your eyes. But you haven't yet spoken it with your mouth.

Day 14. The final day of Week 2. Five days established who you are internally—identity anchored in your soul, provision opened in your heart, authority activated in your hands, anointing grounded in your head and spirit, advancement mobilizing your feet. Day 13 opened your eyes externally to behold His attributes filling every gap you exposed. But something remains locked in your throat. You KNOW who you are (Days 8-12). You SEE who He is (Day 13). But you haven't SAID it yet. And here's what you're discovering: Silent faith is incomplete faith. Vision without voice stays vision. What you won't declare, you won't fully carry.

The Biblical Mandate

The Scripture you've read a hundred times suddenly burns with new urgency: "For with the heart one believes unto righteousness, and with the mouth confession is made unto salvation" (Romans 10:10). Heart AND mouth. Not heart alone. Both required for full manifestation. Day 14 isn't just about positive thinking or motivational self-talk. This is the Biblical mandate to RECEIVE the Father's affirmation with your heart AND RELEASE it through your mouth. Your voice isn't optional—it's essential. Your mouth isn't just for conversation—it's for transformation. Because what you SEE in Day 13, you must SAY in Day 14. What you RECEIVE from the Father, you must DECLARE over yourself. Welcome to the day you stop agreeing silently and start declaring boldly. Welcome to the discovery that your voice is your weapon, and today you learn to fire it with Heaven's authority. "Let the redeemed of the LORD say so" (Psalm 107:2).

FOUNDATION — THE CRISIS OF SILENT AFFIRMATION

You've been a silent believer. Internally agreeing with God's truth. Privately receiving His affirmation. Quietly knowing who you are. But faith that stays silent stays dormant. Affirmation that remains internal never fully activates. Truth that's believed but never declared leaves power as potential rather than kinetic. This is the crisis of Week 2's final day: You can HEAR the Father's affirmation without ever SPEAKING it back to Him. You can RECEIVE His declarations without ever RELEASING them over yourself. You can KNOW you're loved, chosen, beautiful, and enough—but if you never SPEAK it, something remains unactivated. Faith unspoken is faith unopened. My mouth is my ministry before my platform is.

The Kadesh Barnea Tragedy

The Israelites at Kadesh Barnea proved this tragedy. Twelve spies. Same land. Same giants. Same promise. But different confession. Different declaration. Different outcome. Ten spies said: "We are not able... They are stronger than we... We were like grasshoppers in our own sight" (Numbers 13:31-33). They SPOKE fear. They DECLARED defeat. Two spies said: "Let us go up at once and take possession, for we are well able to overcome it... The LORD is with us" (Numbers 13:30; 14:9). Same circumstances. Different confession. Different fruit. God's verdict? "As I live... just as you have spoken in My hearing, so I will do to you" (Numbers 14:28-29). Their declaration determined their destination. Their confession shaped their reality. They spoke death—death manifested. They spoke defeat—defeat occurred. Not because God wanted to punish them. Because their words activated the reality they declared.

This is Day 14's revelation: Your confession doesn't create reality. But it does activate your participation in God's reality. You must RECEIVE the Father's affirmation with your heart AND RELEASE it through your mouth. Both are required. Heart belief without mouth confession keeps transformation theoretical. Internal agreement without external declaration leaves weapons undrawn, authority unused, affirmations unmade. Days 8-12 loaded the bow with identity. Day 13 aimed it by opening your eyes to His character. Day 14 fires the arrow by releasing your voice. Heart receives. Eyes behold. Mouth declares. Heaven manifests. Do not question-mark what God exclamation-pointed.

REVELATION — THE SINGULAR ACTIVATION PROTOCOL

Romans 10:9-10: Heart + Mouth = Full Manifestation

This is THE verse for Day 14. Not just about initial salvation—it's the activation protocol for how Kingdom reality manifests in every area: "If you confess with your mouth the Lord Jesus and believe in your heart that God has raised Him from the dead, you will be saved. For with the heart one believes unto righteousness, and with the mouth confession is made unto salvation." Watch the formula. Heart belief is necessary but insufficient alone. Mouth confession is required for full manifestation. Believe in heart PLUS confess with mouth EQUALS salvation activated. This isn't two separate steps—it's one complete action. Heart and mouth working together. Internal and external united. What you receive internally must be released externally. What you believe privately must be declared publicly.

Watch how this formula applies everywhere: Believe in your heart you're healed PLUS confess "I am healed" EQUALS healing manifests. Believe God provides PLUS confess "My God supplies all my needs" EQUALS provision flows. Believe you're adopted PLUS confess "I am His child" EQUALS sonship fully activates. Belief loads the bow; confession fires the arrow. This isn't "name it and claim it" heresy. This is Biblical activation. Your confession doesn't force God's hand—it aligns your mouth with His word, and that alignment releases what He's already prepared. Confession isn't pretending; it's partnering. Vision without a voice stays a vision.

The Power of Speech: Hebrew and Greek Foundations

DABAR [dah-VAR] — Word, Thing, Matter. This Hebrew word means both "word" and "thing"—because in Hebrew understanding, word and reality are connected. When God SPEAKS His dabar, reality responds: "By the word of the LORD the heavens were made" (Psalm 33:6). Your words, made in His image, carry an echo of this creative power when aligned with His words.

HOMOLOGEO [ho-mo-lo-GEH-oh] — To Say the Same Thing. This is THE New Testament word for confession. Homo (same) plus logos (word). Literally: to say the same word. When you confess Jesus as Lord, you're saying the same thing Heaven is already saying. When you declare "I am healed," you're agreeing with what God has already spoken.

RHEMA [HRAY-mah] — Spoken Word. While logos often refers to the written Word, rhema is the spoken word, the activated word: "Man shall not live by bread alone, but by every word that proceeds from the mouth of God" (Matthew 4:4). Faith comes by hearing the rhema of God (Romans 10:17). Not just reading silently—HEARING it spoken. There's power in the audible word. The rhema activates what the logos reveals. Your voice doesn't create truth. But it does activate truth in your life. Mountains move when I speak, not when I stare.

TESTIMONY — FROM SILENT PERFORMANCE TO VOCAL AFFIRMATION

The Bathroom Floor Breakdown

I was hosting a talk show alongside John when the performance finally collapsed. We'd just taught 30+ people about Managing Emotions. Comments flooded in: "Powerful!" "Life-changing!" But at 3 AM, I found myself on the bathroom floor—cold tiles pressing against my knees, tears streaming, chest heaving with sobs I'd been holding back for hours. "It's never enough," I sobbed into the phone to John, my voice breaking between gasps for air. "Did I listen enough? Did I pronounce words correctly? Was my grammar right? I teach emotional intelligence, but I'm drowning in self-condemnation and imposter syndrome." The bathroom tiles were unforgiving. The mirror reflected someone I barely recognized—a woman who'd built a ministry helping others while suffocating under the weight of never measuring up. Years of ministry. Books published. Sermons preached. Breakthrough taught. And still—August 2022, this moment, bathroom floor, 3 AM—the orphan spirit whispered I wasn't enough.

The Question That Changed Everything

John spoke life over me. Then he asked the question that would shatter everything: "When was the last time you let God affirm you without an audience?" Silence. I couldn't answer. "You'll never hear 'well done' if you're too busy earning 'well said.'" I stopped earning 'well said' and started hearing 'well done.' Three days later, after the 5 AM Live Fearlessly call ended, I sat in silence. No performance. No audience. Just me and Him. "Lord, do You even like who I'm becoming?" His response flooded my heart—not audible words, but a knowing so deep it felt like warmth spreading through my chest: "My child, I've been trying to tell you for years, but you've been too busy seeking human applause to hear Mine. I don't just love you—I LIKE you. I enjoy your laugh. I celebrate your growth. I sing over your sleeping. You've been performing for crowds when I just want you to be My kid."

The Father's Delight

Tears came again. But different tears. Not breakdown—breakthrough. When I gave my voice to God, He gave my voice authority. Then, as if reading from Song of Solomon directly to my heart: "You are altogether beautiful, my darling; there is no flaw in you" (Song of Solomon 4:7). "No flaw?" I argued internally. "But what about—" "NO FLAW," He interrupted. "Not because you're perfect, but because you're Mine. I see you through the blood of My Son." Then I heard what changed everything—not just His verdict about me, but His FEELING toward me: "The LORD your God in your midst, The Mighty One, will save; He will rejoice over you with gladness, He will quiet you with His love, He will rejoice over you with singing" (Zephaniah 3:17). He doesn't just love me. He REJOICES over me. With GLADNESS. With SINGING. Not someday when I'm fixed. NOW. While I'm still becoming. The orphan spirit lost its grip when I found my volume.

Two Courageous Decisions in Bold Humility

DECISION 1—I would RECEIVE the Father's affirmation. Stop performing for it. Just receive it. Let His delight be enough. **DECISION 2**—I would SPEAK unapologetically what He'd spoken. Out loud. Boldly. Consistently. I would declare "I am altogether beautiful" until my mouth believed what my heart was beginning to receive. I would affirm what He affirmed. I would activate through declaration what I'd received through affirmation. I'm not perfect; I'm perfectly loved—and I'll say so. The breakthrough came when I: (1) RECEIVED what He spoke, (2) RELEASED it through my mouth, (3) REPEATED it until my reality aligned with His declaration. Heart belief plus mouth confession equals identity manifested. Your Father sees your 'becoming' and calls it beautiful. Now you must say the same thing He's saying. His 'I AM' ends my 'am I?'

THE ACTIVATION PROTOCOL: BECAUSE HE IS, I AM

The Foundation of All Affirmation

When God revealed Himself to Moses, He gave a declaration: "I AM WHO I AM" (Exodus 3:14). The Hebrew YHWH [yah-WEH] (Ehyeh Asher Ehyeh [eh-YEH ah-SHER eh-YEH]) means "I AM / I WILL BE"—the self-existent, eternal, unchanging One. His nature guarantees His actions. And His actions establish your identity. Because HE IS, I AM—period. Watch the divine pattern in Exodus 6:6-8. Seven times God declares "I AM the LORD," and each declaration is followed by "I WILL": Because I AM leads to I WILL which establishes therefore you are. His character (I AM) guarantees His action (I WILL), which establishes your identity (you are). This is the foundation of all affirmation: Your "I am" flows from His "I AM."

Jesus Continues the Pattern

Jesus didn't just teach about God—He claimed the divine name. When He said "Before Abraham was, I AM" (John 8:58), He was declaring deity. His seven "I AM" statements in John's Gospel reveal how His nature meets your need:

JESUS SAYS "I AM..."	THEREFORE I AM...
"I AM the Bread of Life" (John 6:35)	I am nourished, satisfied, never lacking
"I AM the Light of the World" (John 8:12)	I am called to shine, enlightened, guided
"I AM the Door" (John 10:9)	I am welcomed, have access, belong
"I AM the Good Shepherd" (John 10:11)	I am known, protected, cared for
"I AM the Resurrection and Life" (John 11:25)	I am alive, victorious over death
"I AM the Way, Truth, and Life" (John 14:6)	I am guided, grounded, filled with life
"I AM the True Vine" (John 15:5)	I am fruitful, flourishing, connected

Each of Jesus' "I AMs" becomes YOUR "I am." Your identity flows from His identity. What He is becomes what you are. When God says 'I AM,' my doubt loses its microphone.

The Revolutionary Framework: "I AM BECAUSE HE IS"

This is Day 14's activation protocol: "I AM _____ because HE IS _____ and HE DECLARED _____." This isn't positive confession creating reality. This is agreeing with Heaven's verdict, aligning your mouth with His Word, activating through declaration what He's already established. Identity isn't invented; it's inherited and announced. I don't self-brand; I Son-brand.

Examples:

- I am STRONG because He is my Strength and He declared, "Let the weak say, 'I am strong'" (Joel 3:10).
- I am LOVED because He is Love and He declared, "I have loved you with an everlasting love" (Jeremiah 31:3).
- I am BEAUTIFUL because He is the Perfector and He declared, "You are altogether beautiful" (Song of Solomon 4:7).
- I am CHOSEN because He is Sovereign and He declared, "I chose you" (John 15:16).
- I am FREE because He is the Liberator and He declared, "If the Son makes you free, you shall be free indeed" (John 8:36).
- I am ENOUGH because He is Sufficient and He declared, "My grace is sufficient for you" (2 Corinthians 12:9).

Your identity isn't manufactured—it's received from His nature and released through your declaration. Agreement is my access.

The Comprehensive Identity Table

HE IS (Attribute)	I AM (Identity)	SCRIPTURE
Creator (Genesis 1:1)	I am created with purpose and intention	Psalm 139:13-16
Redeemer (Isaiah 47:4)	I am redeemed and free from sin	Ephesians 1:7

Love (1 John 4:8)	I am deeply loved and called to love	Romans 8:38-39
Holy (Leviticus 19:2)	I am set apart to live a holy life	1 Peter 1:15-16
Faithful (Deuteronomy 7:9)	I am secure and sustained in His promises	Lamentations 3:22-23
Shepherd (Psalm 23:1)	I am guided, provided for, protected	John 10:11
Righteous (Psalm 145:17)	I am the righteousness of God in Christ	2 Corinthians 5:21
Light (John 8:12)	I am a light in the world	Matthew 5:14
King (Psalm 47:7)	I am royalty, seated with Christ	Ephesians 2:6
Peace (Judges 6:24)	I am whole, steady, unshaken	John 14:27

Because God IS (eternal, sovereign, loving, powerful, faithful), you ARE (anchored, redeemed, victorious, whole, and free).

THE EIGHT AFFIRMATIONS YOU NEED TO HEAR AND SPEAK

1. YOU ARE LOVED. "I have loved you with an everlasting love" (Jeremiah 31:3). The Hebrew ahavah olam [ah-hah-VAH o-LAHM]—eternal love, without beginning or end. **RECEIVE:** Let Him affirm His love over you. **RELEASE:** Declare "I am loved with everlasting love." Loved isn't a feeling; it's a verdict—and I'm repeating the ruling.

2. YOU ARE HIS. "Fear not, for I have redeemed you; I have called you by your name; you are Mine" (Isaiah 43:1). Three declarations: redeemed, called, possessed. **RECEIVE:** Hear Him say "You are Mine." **RELEASE:** Declare "I belong to the King of Kings."

3. YOU ARE CHOSEN. "You did not choose Me, but I chose you and appointed you that you should go and bear fruit" (John 15:16). **RECEIVE:** Let Him affirm your chosen-ness. **RELEASE:** Declare "I am chosen for purpose." Chosen cuts through crowded—He picked me on purpose.

4. YOU ARE BEAUTIFUL. "You are all fair, my love, and there is no spot in you" (Song of Solomon 4:7). Not partially beautiful. ALTOGETHER beautiful. NO flaw. **RECEIVE:** Hear "You are altogether beautiful." **RELEASE:** Declare "I am altogether beautiful, no spot in me." Altogether beautiful—no spot, no apology.

5. YOU ARE SEEN. "Then she called the name of the LORD who spoke to her, You-Are-the-God-Who-Sees" (Genesis 16:13). El Roi [el ro-EE]—the God who sees. Your hidden battles, private victories, secret struggles—all seen, all precious. **RECEIVE:** Let Him affirm He sees you. **RELEASE:** Declare "I am fully seen and known."

6. YOU ARE HIS DELIGHT. "The LORD your God in your midst, The Mighty One, will save; He will rejoice over you with gladness, He will quiet you with His love, He will rejoice over you with singing" (Zephaniah 3:17). Your Father doesn't just tolerate you—He REJOICES over you. He SINGS over you. Not when you're perfect. NOW. **RECEIVE:** Hear "I rejoice over you with singing." **RELEASE:** Declare "My Father delights in me and sings over me." His delight isn't my destination—it's my daily reality.

7. YOU ARE BECOMING. "Being confident of this very thing, that He who has begun a good work in you will complete it" (Philippians 1:6). He sees not just who you are but who you're becoming. **RECEIVE:** Hear "Your becoming is beautiful to Me." **RELEASE:** Declare "I am becoming who He created me to be."

8. YOU ARE ENOUGH. "My grace is sufficient for you, for My strength is made perfect in weakness" (2 Corinthians 12:9). In your weakness, in your process—you are enough because He is enough in you. **RECEIVE:** Let Him affirm "You are enough." **RELEASE:** Declare "I am enough in Christ." Enough, because His grace is sufficient—so is my yes.

The Father's vocabulary about you is vastly different from your vocabulary about yourself. Start saying what He's saying. Altogether beautiful—said by God, echoed by me.

THE PARABLE OF THE SILENT HEIR

There was a man who discovered he'd been adopted by a king. Legal papers proved it. Royal blood now flowed through covenant. The inheritance was his—land, wealth, authority, position. Everything documented. Everything official. But he never spoke his identity. He KNEW he was the king's son. He BELIEVED it internally. But he never SAID it out loud. Never declared "I am the king's son." And so he lived like a peasant. He dressed in rags though robes awaited. He begged for bread though banquets were prepared. People would ask: "Who are you?" He'd shrug. "Nobody special." He KNEW he was royalty. He BELIEVED he was adopted. But he never SPOKE it. And what you don't declare, you don't activate.

One day, thieves surrounded him. In that moment of desperation, something broke. The silent heir found his voice: "I AM THE KING'S SON!" The words erupted like thunder. Everything shifted. The thieves fled—not from his appearance, but from his DECLARATION. The peasant clothes didn't change, but the ATMOSPHERE did. The legal reality he'd known internally became ACTIVATED externally through his VOICE. That day he understood: Adoption gives you position. But declaration activates your authority. Adoption wrote it; declaration unlocks it. You've been adopted by the King. The papers are signed. But until you SPEAK who you are, you'll live beneath your position. Your voice is the key that unlocks what's legally yours. Royalty sounds like something—SAY SO.

BIBLICAL WITNESSES: AFFIRMED AND ACTIVATED

TIER 1: Two Full Witnesses

MARY—Affirmed in Scandal. Young. Unmarried. Pregnant. Yet heaven sent affirmation: "Rejoice, highly favored one, the Lord is with you; blessed are you among women!" (Luke 1:28). She RECEIVED the affirmation then RELEASED agreement: "Behold the maidservant of the Lord! Let it be to me according to your word" (Luke 1:38). She didn't just hear Heaven's declaration. She SPOKE her agreement. And that vocal consent activated the miracle. Later, her Magnificat (Luke 1:46-55) became public declaration: "My soul magnifies the Lord... He has done great things for me." Mary's transformation: From questioning ("How can this be?") to declaring ("Let it be"). From private affirmation to public proclamation. Mary said yes out loud—and the Word became flesh.

THE DANIEL FAST: CLOSING THE GAP!

PETER—Affirmed After Failure. Three denials. Crushing shame. Yet Jesus pursued him with three affirmations: "Simon, son of Jonah, do you love Me?" (John 21:15). The activation came when Peter SPOKE: "Lord, You know all things; You know that I love You" (John 21:17). His CONFESSION—vocal, vulnerable, repeated—activated his restoration. Later, this same Peter who denied would DECLARE boldly: "Let all the house of Israel know assuredly that God has made this Jesus, whom you crucified, both Lord and Christ" (Acts 2:36). Peter's transformation: From denial in public to restoration in public to preaching in public. The voice that denied became the voice that declared. The mouth that cursed became the mouth that blessed. Peter denied in public, restored in public, preached in public.

TIER 2: When Affirmation Met Declaration

DAVID—Affirmed in obscurity (youngest, overlooked, smelling like sheep), yet anointed as king. He didn't just receive God's affirmation—he RELEASED declarations: "The LORD is my shepherd" (Psalm 23:1). "I will fear no evil" (Psalm 23:4). David spoke what God spoke until it manifested. David sang it before he sat on it.

GIDEON—Hiding in a winepress, threshing wheat in fear, yet the angel's greeting: "The LORD is with you, you mighty man of valor!" (Judges 6:12). MIGHTY MAN OF VALOR while hiding. The transformation came when he ACTED on what God declared and SPOKE commands over his army. Gideon's valor started as vocabulary. God's affirmation speaks to your potential while you're stuck in your present. But you must DECLARE what He's declared and ACT on what He's affirmed.

THE POWER OF THE TONGUE

Death and Life Are in Your Hand

"Death and life are in the power of the tongue, and those who love it will eat its fruit" (Proverbs 18:21). Your tongue has power—yad [yahd] in Hebrew, literally "hand." Your tongue is your hand that shapes reality. Death and life. Not "negativity and positivity." DEATH and LIFE. Your words carry power to kill or vivify. My tongue is a sword; I choose which kingdom it serves. And you will eat the fruit of whatever your tongue produces. Speak death long enough, death manifests. Speak life consistently, life emerges. The principle is reinforced: "From the fruit of their lips people are filled with good things" (Proverbs 12:14). Your words produce fruit—good or bad—and you eat what your lips produce. Speak life. Speak His promises. Speak His plans. Speak His purpose. Speak His attributes. Speak His healing. Speak His word. Speak His blessings. Because your tongue doesn't just describe reality—it helps shape it. If death and life are in my mouth, I pick resurrection.

The Biblical Pattern of Spoken Words

The Israelites proved it: "As you have spoken in My hearing, so I will do to you" (Numbers 14:28). Their DECLARATION determined their DESTINATION. Caleb spoke differently: "Let us go up at once and take possession, for we are well able" (Numbers 13:30). Same circumstances. Different confession. Different fruit. Jesus taught: "For assuredly, I say to you, whoever says to this mountain, 'Be removed and be cast into the sea,' and does not doubt in his heart, but believes that those things he says will be done, he will have whatever he says" (Mark 11:23). Notice what Jesus emphasizes: SAYS (three times). Not "whoever thinks." "Whoever SAYS to this mountain." The mountain must be ADDRESSED.

SPOKEN to. COMMANDED verbally. Your faith must have a voice. Heart belief plus verbal declaration equals mountain moves. Mountains move when I speak, not when I stare.

Spoken Words That Released Miracles

Throughout Scripture, spoken words—aligned with God's authority—released miracles, shifted atmospheres, healed bodies, raised the dead, and transformed reality: Creation began with "Let there be..." (Genesis 1:3). Moses commanded and the Red Sea parted and returned at his word (Exodus 14). Elijah declared and fire consumed the altar (1 Kings 18:36-38). Elijah spoke and drought and rain obeyed (1 Kings 17:1). Elisha commanded and leprosy was healed (2 Kings 5:10). Jesus spoke "Lazarus, come forth!" and death reversed (John 11:43). Jesus commanded "Peace, be still!" and nature obeyed (Mark 4:39). The centurion understood: "Only speak a word, and my servant will be healed" (Matthew 8:8). Jesus cast out demons: "Be quiet, and come out of him!" and deliverance occurred (Mark 1:25). Peter declared "In the name of Jesus Christ, rise and walk!" and the lame man leaped (Acts 3:6). Peter raised the dead: "Tabitha, arise" (Acts 9:40). Paul commanded "I command you in the name of Jesus Christ to come out of her" (Acts 16:18). "He sent His word and healed them, and delivered them from their destructions" (Psalm 107:20). "So shall My word be that goes forth from My mouth; it shall not return to Me void, but it shall accomplish what I please" (Isaiah 55:11). The word spoken in faith is the bridge between heaven's authority and earth's reality. Miracles manifest not just when we believe but when we declare what God has said.

THE TWO VOCABULARIES: WORTHY VS WORTHLESS

The Jeremiah 15:19 Revelation

God gave me a scripture that revolutionized my self-talk: **"If you utter worthy, not worthless words, you will be my spokesman"** (Jeremiah 15:19, NIV). The ESV says it this way: **"If you utter what is precious, and not what is worthless, you shall be as my mouth."** The NASB: **"If you extract the precious from the worthless, you will become My spokesman."**

This changed everything. My words weren't neutral—they were either **WORTHY** or **WORTHLESS**. Every declaration I made fell into one of these two categories. And God was making a promise: If I would choose worthy words over worthless words, He would make me His spokesperson. My voice would carry His authority. But if I kept speaking worthless words, I'd remain the enemy's echo.

The Jeremiah 15:19 Diagnostic

Before you speak, ask: **Is this WORTHY or WORTHLESS?**

WORTHLESS WORDS (What the enemy says):	WORTHY WORDS (What God says):
• "I'm not enough" • "I'm too broken to be used" • "I'm disqualified by my past" • "I'll never change" • "Nobody wants me"	• "I am His workmanship" (Ephesians 2:10) • "I am a new creation" (2 Corinthians 5:17) • "I am chosen and beloved" (Colossians 3:12) • "I am being transformed" (Romans 12:2)

• "I always fail" • "I'm a fraud"	• "I am accepted in the Beloved" (Ephesians 1:6) • "I am more than a conqueror" (Romans 8:37) • "I am the righteousness of God" (2 Corinthians 5:21)

Extract the Precious from the Worthless

Notice the NASB translation: **"If you extract the precious from the worthless."** This is active. Intentional. Surgical. You must SEPARATE worthy from worthless. Pull out what's precious. Discard what's worthless. This happens in your MIND before it comes out of your MOUTH.

Your thoughts produce two vocabularies: **Worthless vocabulary** flows from lies, fear, condemnation, the accuser. **Worthy vocabulary** flows from truth, Scripture, God's character, Heaven's verdict. Every morning, you have a choice: Which vocabulary will you speak today?

From Echo to Spokesperson

When you speak **WORTHLESS** words, you become the **enemy's ECHO**—repeating his accusations, magnifying his lies, amplifying his condemnation. But when you speak **WORTHY** words, you become **God's SPOKESPERSON**—declaring His truth, releasing His promises, activating His purposes.

The promise: "You will be my spokesman" (Jeremiah 15:19). Not might be. Not could be. **WILL BE.** Your choice of vocabulary determines your voice's authority. Worthless words = enemy's echo. Worthy words = God's spokesperson.

My Jeremiah 15:19 Transformation

For years, my self-talk was worthless: "You're not qualified. You messed up again. Everyone sees through you. You're a fraud." Every thought was the enemy's script. I was his echo chamber. Then God gave me Jeremiah 15:19. I realized: **I've been speaking worthless words and wondering why my voice has no power.**

I made a decision: From this day forward, I will **extract the precious from the worthless.** Before any thought becomes a word, I will ask: **Is this WORTHY or WORTHLESS?** If it's worthless—rooted in lies, fear, condemnation—I will NOT speak it. If it's worthy—rooted in Scripture, truth, God's character—I will DECLARE it boldly.

The transformation: My voice went from powerless echo to prophetic spokesperson. Not because I became perfect. Because I **changed my vocabulary.** I stopped uttering worthless words. I started speaking worthy words. And God kept His promise: **I became His spokesman.**

The Daily Practice

Every morning, I now pray: "Father, today I choose **WORTHY over WORTHLESS**. I refuse to be the enemy's echo. I choose to be Your spokesperson. I will **extract the precious from the worthless**—pulling out truth, discarding lies. I will **utter what is precious, not what is worthless.** My mouth will declare Your Word, not the enemy's accusations. My voice carries Your authority because I speak Your vocabulary. In Jesus' name, I am Your spokesman."

Then I speak my worthy declarations:
- "I am altogether beautiful, no spot" (not "I'm a mess")
- "I am more than a conqueror" (not "I always fail")
- "I am His workmanship" (not "I'm a mistake")
- "I am accepted in the Beloved" (not "Nobody wants me")

Jeremiah 15:19 became my filter, my diagnostic, my daily choice: Worthy or worthless? His spokesperson or the enemy's echo?

WHEN DECLARATIONS FEEL LIKE LIES: THE TWO LANGUAGES

Facts vs. Truth — The Critical Distinction

Here's the struggle: You're declaring something that isn't true YET in your experience, and it feels like lying. "I am healed"—but you're still sick. "I am prosperous"—but your account is overdrawn. **The Answer: Two Different Languages.**

THE LANGUAGE OF FACT describes current temporal reality. Facts are DATA. The diagnosis is fact. The bank balance is fact. The circumstances are facts. Facts are true but not necessarily TRUTH.

THE LANGUAGE OF TRUTH declares eternal spiritual reality. Truth is what God says. "By His stripes you WERE healed" (1 Peter 2:24) is TRUTH. Truth supersedes facts. Jesus prayed, "Sanctify them by Your truth. Your word is truth" (John 17:17). God's Word isn't just true—it IS truth itself. When you declare what God's Word says, you're speaking eternal, unchanging, sanctifying TRUTH that transforms temporal facts. Truth doesn't adjust to facts. Facts must bow to Truth. Facts describe; TRUTH decides.

When you declare "I am healed" while still sick, you're not denying facts. You're declaring TRUTH that will transform facts. You're speaking Heaven's language over Earth's circumstances. You're calling things that are not (YET) as though they were (Romans 4:17) because God does this, and you're made in His image. This isn't lying. This is faith speaking. Heaven's language upgrades earth's headlines. Truth greater than Facts. Faith stronger than Fear.

Three Concrete Scenarios

MEDICAL— The doctor says: "Stage 3 cancer" (FACT). God's Word says: "By His stripes you were healed" (TRUTH, 1 Peter 2:24). **YOUR DECLARATION:** "I honor the diagnosis. I will follow medical wisdom. AND I declare by His stripes I AM healed. I'm not denying the tumor—I'm prophesying that Truth will transform this fact. I speak Heaven's report over the medical report." Facts acknowledged. Truth declared.

FINANCIAL— The bank says: "Account overdrawn -$487" (FACT). God's Word says: "My God shall supply all your need" (TRUTH, Philippians 4:19). **YOUR DECLARATION:** "I acknowledge the overdraft. I will steward wisely and work diligently. AND I declare my God supplies ALL my needs according to His riches in glory. I'm not pretending—I'm declaring that Jehovah Jireh is my Provider. I speak abundance over lack." Not denial. DECLARATION.

RELATIONAL— Your emotions say: "Nobody wants me. I'm rejected" (FACT—how it feels). God's Word says: "I chose you and appointed you" (TRUTH, John 15:16). **YOUR DECLARATION:**

"I acknowledge the loneliness I feel. I will pursue healthy community. AND I declare I am CHOSEN by the King of Kings. I'm not ignoring the pain—I'm declaring that God's choice supersedes human rejection. I speak acceptance over the wound." Truth transforms facts. Facts describe current reality. Truth declares eternal reality. Your declarations activate the transformation of facts into truth.

THE PARABLE OF THE DAILY DECLARATION

The 128-Day Miracle

There was a woman diagnosed with a disease the doctors called "terminal." Six months, they said. Maybe a year if aggressive treatment worked. She underwent the chemo, the radiation, the endless appointments. But she also did something her oncologist didn't prescribe: Every morning at 5:30 AM, she stood in her bathroom, looked in the mirror, and spoke out loud: "By His stripes I AM healed. This body is the temple of the Holy Spirit. I speak LIFE to my cells. I command this disease to leave in Jesus' name." Day 1: She said it with faith blazing. Day 30: She said it with tears streaming. Day 90: She said it with trembling hands gripping the sink because the scans showed the tumor had grown. Her daughter begged her to stop "delusional positive thinking" and "face reality." But every morning at 5:30 AM, she stood before that mirror and spoke to the mountain in her body.

Day 120: The declaration felt like dust in her mouth. The symptoms were worse. The pain had intensified. She could barely stand, holding the bathroom counter with white knuckles, gasping between declarations. Her voice cracked: "By His stripes... I am... healed." It wasn't a shout anymore. It was a whisper. But it was still SPOKEN. Day 127: The morning routine felt robotic. Mechanical. She'd lost 30 pounds. Her skin was gray. She looked at the skeleton in the mirror and wondered if she was fooling herself. But something inside—something deeper than doubt—said: "Speak." So she did. "By His stripes I am healed. I will not die but LIVE and declare the works of the Lord." Day 128: Emergency scan. The tumor had been pressing on vital organs. The doctors prepared her family for the worst. But when the images appeared on the screen, the radiologist went silent. Called in another doctor. Then another. The tumor that had been growing for months was... gone. Not shrinking. GONE. No trace. No scar tissue. As if it had never existed. The doctor stood speechless. "I have no medical explanation." The woman smiled, exhausted, vindicated: "I do. I spoke to the mountain every morning for 128 days. And on day 128, the mountain moved." Mountains don't respond the first day you speak. But they do respond to the voice that refuses to stop speaking.

The Biblical Pattern: Spoken Word → Journey → Fulfillment

This woman's 128-day journey mirrors a Biblical pattern: some miracles are spoken in faith and initiated immediately, but the manifestation unfolds over time. The healing doesn't always happen the moment you declare—but the word sets the process in motion.

The Man Born Blind (John 9:1-7): Jesus anointed his eyes and said: "Go, wash in the pool of Siloam." The word was spoken first. But the healing didn't manifest instantly. The man had to walk. Find the pool. Wash. Obey before seeing evidence. "So he went and washed, and came back seeing." The miracle was spoken instantly, but the manifestation was progressive.

Ten lepers cleansed: Jesus said, "Go, show yourselves to the priests" (Luke 17:14). "And so it was that as they went, they were cleansed." Healing manifested as they walked—obedience activated the word.

Naaman's leprosy: Elisha said, "Go and wash in the Jordan seven times" (2 Kings 5:10). Healing required obedience to a spoken instruction.

Fig tree withered: Jesus said, "Let no one eat fruit from you ever again" (Mark 11:14). It looked unchanged when He spoke—but by the next day, it had withered from the roots.

Four Kingdom Truths About Delayed Manifestation

(1) MIRACLES BEGIN WITH A WORD. Your declaration sets the process in motion even when you see no immediate change.

(2) MIRACLES OFTEN REQUIRE PARTNERSHIP. The blind man had to walk, find the pool, wash. Faith isn't passive—it obeys before it sees.

(3) DELAY IS NOT DENIAL. The lack of instant change doesn't mean the word failed—the power is already in motion. The woman declared healing for 127 days before seeing change. But the word was working while she was walking.

(4) OBEDIENCE ACTIVATES THE INVISIBLE. Only when the blind man did exactly what Jesus said did the invisible become visible. Your continued declaration—even when you see no evidence—is the obedience that activates manifestation. The word works while you walk.

Some miracles break forth instantly, others unfold gradually—but every miracle begins with a word. If He spoke it, walk it out. If He promised it, stay in motion. Everyone craves a microwave miracle, but God often serves a slow-cooker breakthrough—marinated in affirmations, declarations, and persistent prayer until it's seasoned to perfection.

This is the protocol Day 14 demands: Speak when you see results. Speak when you see nothing. Speak when circumstances worsen. Because your voice isn't measuring outcomes—it's releasing Heaven's verdict. And Heaven's verdict doesn't adjust to facts; facts adjust to Heaven's verdict. "So shall My word be that goes forth from My mouth; it shall not return to Me void, but it shall accomplish what I please" (Isaiah 55:11). I am watching over My word to perform it—so I'm speaking His word.

HOW TO DECLARE POWERFULLY: THE COMPLETE FRAMEWORK

Your voice has different functions. Here's how to declare with power across every situation.

The Five Types of Biblical Declaration

(1) CONFESSION [HOMOLOGEO — ho-mo-lo-GEH-oh] — Agreeing With God. Speaking the same thing God speaks. "If we confess our sins, He is faithful and just to forgive us" (1 John 1:9). **Practice:** "I confess Jesus is Lord" or "I confess I am who God says I am." **How to apply:** Ground it in Scripture (speak what God has already said), speak it out loud (silent affirmations have limited power), use present tense ("I AM healed" not "I will be healed"). Say what God says—exactly.

(2) PROCLAMATION [NAGAD — nah-GAD] — Declaring What Is. Announcing truth publicly. "Declare His glory among the nations" (Psalm 96:3). **Practice:** "I proclaim I am healed by

His stripes" or "I declare God's provision." **How to apply:** Declare consistently (daily declarations, multiple times when battling opposition), believe while you declare (your mouth and heart must agree). Announce truth until walls learn your voice.

(3) COMMAND [EXOUSIA — ex-oo-SEE-ah] — Exercising Authority. Speaking with authority to circumstances, demons, mountains. "Whoever says to this mountain, 'Be removed'... he will have whatever he says" (Mark 11:23). **Practice:** "I command this anxiety to LEAVE" or "Mountain, BE REMOVED." **How to apply:** Persist through opposition (symptoms may scream louder when you declare—don't stop), act on what you declare (faith without works is dead, James 2:26). Authority isn't a tone; it's a transfer.

(4) THANKSGIVING [EUCHARISTEO — yoo-khar-is-TEH-oh] — Gratitude That Activates. Thanking God BEFORE manifestation. "In everything give thanks" (1 Thessalonians 5:18). Jesus thanked the Father BEFORE Lazarus rose (John 11:41). **Practice:** "Thank You that I am healed" (before symptoms disappear). Thanks is tomorrow's testimony in today's tense.

(5) PROPHECY [PROPHETEUO — pro-fay-TOO-oh] — Speaking Future Into Present. Declaring what God says will be. "Let the weak say, 'I am strong'" (Joel 3:10). When God mobilizes His people for spiritual warfare, He commands the weak to SPEAK strength—not to wait until they FEEL strong. **Practice:** "I prophesy breakthrough" or "I speak LIFE over this circumstance" or "Though I'm weak, I declare I AM STRONG in Him." Speak future on purpose.

Daily Affirmations Across Six Key Areas

IDENTITY—"I am a child of God, loved, chosen, and accepted" (John 1:12), "I am a new creation" (2 Corinthians 5:17), "I am God's masterpiece" (Ephesians 2:10).

STRENGTH—"I can do all God calls me to do through Christ" (Philippians 4:13), "My strength is renewed" (Isaiah 40:31), "I am more than a conqueror" (Romans 8:37).

PROVISION—"My God supplies all my needs" (Philippians 4:19), "I lack nothing—my Shepherd provides" (Psalm 23:1).

PROTECTION—"I dwell under the shadow of the Almighty" (Psalm 91:1-2), "Every weapon formed against me fails" (Isaiah 54:17).

PURPOSE—"God's plans for me are good" (Jeremiah 29:11), "My steps are ordered by the Lord" (Proverbs 16:9), "Everything works together for good" (Romans 8:28).

PRESENCE—"I am strong and courageous—God is with me" (Joshua 1:9), "I will not fear—God upholds me" (Isaiah 41:10), "I am never alone" (Matthew 28:20).

The Protocol Principles

When you declare, remember: **SCRIPTURE IS YOUR SCRIPT.** "I am watching over My word to perform it" (Jeremiah 1:12). God doesn't watch over your opinions—He watches over HIS WORD. Speak His word, and He guarantees the performance.

FAITH COMES BY HEARING (Romans 10:17). Your brain believes what it hears more than what it thinks. The spiritual realm activates through vocal declaration.

CONSISTENCY BREAKS RESISTANCE. One-time declaration rarely manifests breakthrough. Persistent declaration wears down opposition.

PARTNERSHIP MATTERS. Declaration plus corresponding action equals manifestation. You declare healing—then you take your medication, follow medical wisdom, and walk in obedience.

THE 6-DIMENSIONAL AFFIRMATION ACTIVATION

DIMENSION	PRACTICE	DECLARATION
SPIRITUAL	Ask "What do You want to say to me?" (10 min)	"I am a child of God, seated with Christ"
MENTAL	Replace self-criticism with His words	"I have the mind of Christ"
EMOTIONAL	Let yourself FEEL loved	"The peace of God guards my heart"
PHYSICAL	Stand like someone approved	"By His stripes I am healed"
FINANCIAL	Decide from affirmed identity	"My God supplies all my needs"
RELATIONAL	Give affirmation you've received	"I walk in love, blessed to bless"

Stand like someone Heaven has already stamped.

6-DIMENSIONAL DECLARATION PRAYERS

Stand and declare these with your AUDIBLE VOICE:

SPIRITUAL DECLARATION: "I declare over my spiritual life: I am born again, washed in the blood, sealed by the Spirit. I am a child of God, co-heir with Christ, seated in heavenly places. Because He IS, I AM. Because He is Love, I am loved. Because He is King, I am royalty. In Jesus' name!"

MENTAL DECLARATION: "I declare over my mind: I have the mind of Christ. My thoughts align with Heaven's thoughts. **I extract the precious from the worthless**—I reject worthless self-talk and speak **worthy declarations**. As Jeremiah 15:19 promises: I **utter what is precious, not what is worthless**—therefore I am God's spokesperson. My vocabulary is Heaven's vocabulary. In Jesus' name!"

EMOTIONAL DECLARATION: "I declare over my emotions: The peace of God guards my heart and mind. Anxiety has no authority here. Fear is replaced with faith. I walk in emotional health and divine alignment. From chaos to peace. In Jesus' name!"

PHYSICAL DECLARATION: "I declare over my body: By His stripes I AM healed—past tense, already done. My body is the temple of the Holy Spirit. I speak life to my body, strength to my frame. In Jesus' name!"

FINANCIAL DECLARATION: "I declare over my finances: My God supplies ALL my needs according to His riches in glory. The windows of heaven are open over my life. Provision flows. From lack to abundance. In Jesus' name!"

RELATIONAL DECLARATION: "I declare over my relationships: I walk in love because God is love and He lives in me. I attract healthy connections. From isolation to community, conflict to peace. In Jesus' name!"

COMPREHENSIVE 6-D DECLARATION: "I declare over ALL six dimensions: SPIRITUALLY—I am His child. MENTALLY—I have His mind. EMOTIONALLY—I carry His peace. PHYSICALLY—I walk in His health. FINANCIALLY—I access His provision. RELATIONALLY—I reflect His love. Because HE IS, I AM! In Jesus' name, AMEN!" Because He is—I am!

THE COMMUNITY PRACTICE: THE 3-LINE BLESSING

God often affirms us through His people. In our small groups, we practice:
- "I SEE _____ in you" (Observation)
- "I BLESS _____ in you" (Affirmation)
- "I BELIEVE God will _____ through you" (Prophetic declaration)

Tears, healing, and courage follow—every time. We become God's voice to each other, speaking what heaven sees. Practice this week: Pair up with someone—spouse, friend, child. Ask the Spirit for one Scripture and one strength you see in them. Speak it plainly. They respond: "I receive the Father's affirmation." If you don't have someone who speaks life when you're drowning—start by being that voice for someone else. Call the gold; God will handle the grime. What you receive from the Father, you can release to others.

THE PROPHETIC ACT — RECEIVING AND RELEASING

Part 1: Receiving the Father's Affirmation

Sit comfortably. Place both hands over your heart. Close your eyes. Imagine your Father standing before you. See delight in His eyes. Hear joy in His voice:

"My child, My beloved, My joy—I affirm who you ARE: Loved before time began, chosen before creation, adopted permanently, Mine forever, altogether beautiful, no flaw. I affirm who you're BECOMING: More like Me each day, stronger through struggles, wiser through wandering, beautiful through breaking. I affirm what you CARRY: My DNA in your spirit, My authority in your words, My anointing on your life, My purposes in your heart. Because I AM, you are. Because I WILL, you can. Because I HAVE, you possess. I am not waiting for you to arrive—I am celebrating your journey. You have My attention. You have My affection. You have My approval."

Take a moment. RECEIVE this. Let it sink deep. Hands on heart to receive; hands on head to renew; mouth open to release.

Part 2: Releasing Your Declaration

Now stand. Place those same hands on your head—affirmation transferred from heart to mind. Open your mouth and SPEAK:

"I AM WHO GOD SAYS I AM! Because He IS, I AM: Because He is LOVE—I am LOVED without condition. Because He is HOLY—I am SET APART for purpose. Because He is FAITHFUL—I am SECURE in every season. Because He is KING—I am ROYALTY with authority. Because He is PEACE—I am WHOLE, steady, fearless. Because He is PROVIDER—I am ABUNDANTLY SUPPLIED.

I am ADOPTED—chosen, loved, belonging forever. I am ABUNDANT—connected to Heaven's supply. I carry AUTHORITY—delegated by Jesus. I am ANOINTED—equipped with Holy

Spirit power. I am ADVANCING—moving forward in purpose. I BEHOLD His attributes—His faithfulness, goodness, power. I am AFFIRMED by the highest authority.

I am altogether beautiful. There is no spot in me. From this day forward: I will RECEIVE His affirmation. I will RELEASE His declaration. I will SPEAK what He's spoken. Death and life are in the power of my tongue. I choose LIFE. In Jesus' name, I AM AFFIRMED AND ACTIVATED!"

PRAYER OF RECEIVED AFFIRMATION AND RELEASED DECLARATION

"Father, forgive me for performing for what You freely give. I've exhausted myself earning what was already mine. Thank You that: Your 'I AM' guarantees my 'I am.' Your nature determines my identity. With the heart I believe, with the mouth I confess. My voice activates what You've established.

Today I receive: Every 'I AM' that becomes my 'I am.' Every promise rooted in Your character. Every affirmation You've been speaking. Today I release: Bold declarations over my identity. Vocal affirmations over my circumstances. Spoken commands over opposition.

Teach me to: RECEIVE Your affirmation without performing. RELEASE Your declarations with boldness. SPEAK what You've spoken until it manifests. Because You ARE, I AM. Because You WILL, I CAN. Because You HAVE, I POSSESS. No more silent faith. I am Your affirmed, activated, declaring child. In Jesus' mighty name!"

MANIFESTATION — THE ESSENTIAL 3

If you're short on time or feeling overwhelmed, start here. Before attempting the comprehensive challenge, master THE ESSENTIAL 3—simple, powerful, immediately accessible:

(1) RECEIVE (5 minutes). Sit quietly. Ask "Father, what do You want to say to me?" Write ONE thing you hear.

(2) RELEASE (2 minutes). Stand before a mirror. Speak ONE "I AM because HE IS" declaration OUT LOUD. Example: "I am LOVED because He IS Love and He declared 'I have loved you with an everlasting love.'"

(3) RECORD (2 minutes). Use your phone to record yourself saying it. Listen back. Notice how it feels to HEAR yourself declare truth.

Receive. Release. Record. Repeat. If I'll say it in the mirror, I'll live it in the marketplace.

Ready for more? Expand to the full Day 14 Challenge below. The comprehensive challenge includes these same 3 steps with greater depth PLUS 4 additional activations. Choose based on your available time and capacity tonight.

YOUR DAY 14 ACTIVATION CHALLENGE

If you have 30+ minutes and are ready for comprehensive activation, complete all 7 steps below. Steps 1-3 expand on the Essential 3 you just learned. Steps 4-7 take you deeper into full identity activation.

Before You Sleep Tonight:

(1) RECEIVE: Sit in silence for 10 minutes (instead of 5). Ask "Father, what do You want to say to me?" Write what you hear.

(2) RELEASE: Stand before a mirror. Speak the full "I AM WHO GOD SAYS I AM" declaration OUT LOUD (see Prophetic Act section above).

(3) RECORD: Use your phone to record yourself declaring your top 3 "I AM because HE IS" affirmations (instead of just 1). LISTEN to the recording.

(4) WRITE: Complete the Identity Formula for 3 areas: "I am _____ because He is _____ and He declared _____."

(5) TEXT: Someone: "God says I'm altogether beautiful with no spot! What has He been affirming about you?"

(6) SPEAK: Choose ONE 6-D Declaration Prayer. Speak it OUT LOUD.

(7) COMMIT: Set a daily alarm labeled "DECLARE" with ONE affirmation to speak when it rings.

SOAP JOURNAL — DAY 14

S (Scripture): Which "I AM" of God speaks most to your "I am"? Which declaration scripture became your weapon? Write Jeremiah 15:19 and Romans 10:10.

O (Observation): Where have you been receiving affirmation without releasing declaration? What have you believed in your heart but never confessed with your mouth? What worthless words have you been speaking that need to be replaced with worthy declarations?

A (Application): What specific affirmations will you speak daily? Which of the 5 types of declaration do you need most right now? How will you practice the Jeremiah 15:19 diagnostic (worthy vs worthless) this week?

P (Prayer): "Father, because You are _____, I am _____. I receive Your affirmation and release Your declaration. I choose to utter worthy, not worthless words. I extract the precious from the worthless. I am Your spokesman. In Jesus' name, Amen."

CLOSING — FROM SILENT AGREEMENT TO BOLD DECLARATION

Day 14 complete. Week 2 complete. The final day of ALIGN. The person who started on the bathroom floor at 3 AM, drowning in inadequacy? Now standing in affirmation and declaration. You're not performing for applause anymore. You're resting in His delight. You're not silently agreeing anymore. You're boldly declaring.

Fourteen days brought you here: Days 8-12 established WHO YOU ARE internally—identity anchored in your soul, provision opened in your heart, authority activated in your hands, anointing grounded in your head and spirit, advancement mobilizing your feet. Day 13 opened your EYES externally to behold His attributes filling every gap you exposed. Day 14 released your VOICE to declare what you've received and seen. Heart belief plus eyes opened plus mouth confession equals full activation.

What You've Learned

The 3 AM bathroom floor taught you: You can't earn what's freely given. The Father delights in you—not because you've arrived, but because you're His. The morning revelation showed you: He doesn't just love you—He LIKES you. You are altogether beautiful. There is no flaw in you. The Identity Formula gave you: "I AM because HE IS"—your identity flows from His nature. The Eight Affirmations anchored you: You are loved, His, chosen, beautiful, seen, His delight, becoming, enough. Not aspirationally. Actually. Right now.

The Biblical Witnesses proved it: Mary affirmed in scandal. Peter affirmed after failure. All received God's declaration, all released their agreement, all experienced activation. **The Jeremiah 15:19 revelation transformed your vocabulary: You learned to extract the precious from the worthless, to utter worthy words instead of worthless words, to become God's spokesperson instead of the enemy's echo.**

The Power of Your Voice

If your voice activates salvation (Romans 10:9-10), if death and life are in the power of your tongue (Proverbs 18:21), if Jesus commanded you to speak to mountains (Mark 11:23), if "as you have spoken, so I will do to you" (Numbers 14:28), if "let the weak say 'I am strong'" (Joel 3:10), then why would you spend another day receiving His affirmation without releasing your declaration? You can't just HEAR the Father's song and never sing it back. You can't just RECEIVE His affirmation and never RELEASE your agreement. You can't just BELIEVE in your heart and never CONFESS with your mouth. Heart belief is necessary. Mouth confession is required. Both together produce full manifestation.

Orphans chase applause. Children rest in delight. But sons and daughters who've heard their Father's voice? They SPEAK what He's spoken. So speak life. Speak His promises over your circumstances. Speak His plans over your confusion. Speak His purpose over your wandering. Speak His attributes over your gaps. Speak His healing over your pain. Speak His word over your doubt. Speak His blessings over your lack. Because "I am watching over My word to perform it" (Jeremiah 1:12). Your voice releases. His Word performs. Speak what He's spoken, and watch Him bring it to pass. Let the redeemed of the Lord say so—so I'm saying so.

The Complete Activation

What you SAW in Day 13, you SPOKE in Day 14. What you RECEIVED from the Father, you RELEASED through your voice. Vision plus voice equals activation. Seeing plus saying equals manifestation. Eyes opened plus mouth confessing equals full breakthrough. "Let the redeemed of the LORD say so" (Psalm 107:2). You ARE redeemed. Now SAY SO. You ARE adopted. Now DECLARE IT. You ARE beautiful, loved, chosen, enough. Now SPEAK IT. Out loud. Boldly. Persistently. Until facts align with truth. Until circumstances bow to declarations. Until your reality manifests what Heaven has already established.

Your voice is not just for answering questions. It's for declaring truth. Your mouth is not just for conversations. It's for commands. Your tongue is not just for tasting food. It's for tasting victory through declarations. Welcome to vocal affirmation. Welcome to declared identity. Welcome to activated authority. Welcome to the discovery that your voice is your weapon, and you've just learned to fire it with Heaven's authority. Because HE IS, you ARE. Because HE WILL, you CAN. Because HE SAYS, you SPEAK. And what you speak—aligned with His Word, rooted in His nature, released in faith—WILL MANIFEST.

SILENT FAITH EVICTED. VOCAL FAITH ACTIVATED. AFFIRMATION RECEIVED. DECLARATION RELEASED. HEART BELIEF + MOUTH CONFESSION = FULL MANIFESTATION.

WEEK 2 COMPLETE: ALIGN — Establishing Your Identity in God
Days 8-14: Adopted. Abundant. Authoritative. Anointed. Advancing. Attributes Beheld. Affirmation Activated.

Tomorrow: Day 15 — PRESENCE. Week 3 begins: PROPEL — Discovering Your WHY

DAY 14 COMPLETE: AFFIRMATION ACTIVATED

Heart belief established (Days 8-12). Eyes opened to His attributes (Day 13). Voice released in declaration (Day 14). Romans 10:9-10 activation protocol applied: Heart + Mouth = Full Manifestation. "I AM because HE IS" framework integrated across eight affirmations. Jeremiah 15:19 vocabulary shift: Worthy over worthless. Enemy's echo rejected. God's spokesperson activated. Five types of declaration learned: Confession, Proclamation, Command, Thanksgiving, Prophecy. Facts vs Truth distinction clarified. 128-day healing testimony demonstrates persistence. Silent Heir parable reveals declaration activates authority. Biblical witnesses: Mary, Peter, David, Gideon affirmed and activated. Eight affirmations received and released: Loved, His, Chosen, Beautiful, Seen, Delight, Becoming, Enough. Six-dimensional declaration prayers activated across spiritual, mental, emotional, physical, financial, relational. Essential 3 practice: Receive, Release, Record. Community practice: 3-Line Blessing. Prophetic act completed: Hands on heart (receive), hands on head (renew), mouth open (release). Week 2 ALIGN complete. Internal identity established. External vision opened. Vocal declaration activated. Silent faith evicted. Bold declaration released. Ready for Week 3: PROPEL.

SECTION FIVE
CHAMBER 2: TRANSFORM
WEEK 3: PROPEL (7P)
Purpose with the Holy Spirit

"For I know the thoughts that I think toward you, says the LORD, thoughts of peace and not of evil, to give you a future and a hope." — Jeremiah 29:11

You can't steward a calling you don't understand. With intimacy cultivated and identity secured, Week 3 activates your assignments. This week propels you from knowing whose you are and who you are to fulfilling why you're here—seven themes that launch you into Kingdom purpose with divine backing.
Days 15-21: Presence • Protection • Peace • Provision • Promotion • Prosperity • Purpose

---

THE 7 P'S ACCELERATION
Week 3 systematically activates your complete calling:
Presence positions you in intimacy | **Protection** secures your covering
Peace weaponizes your warfare | **Provision** resources your assignments
Promotion elevates from above | **Prosperity** equips with CHAYIL force
Purpose reveals WHO you build
Each day moves you from warfare positioning to legacy building—from surviving to thriving, from defense to offense, from receiving breakthrough to becoming breakthrough for others.
Your scars aren't disqualifications. They're credentials. Your pain points to your people. Week 3 doesn't just reveal your calling—it releases the resources to walk it out.

Turn the page to Day 15: PRESENCE.
Your assignment activation begins here.

DAY 15 — PRESENCE

From Visitor to Carrier — When You Become What You've Been Seeking

> *Not a building. Not a visit. A covenant Partner who moved in—and never moved out. I carry Presence. "And He said, 'My Presence will go with you, and I will give you rest.'" — Exodus 33:14*

WEEK 3 — PROPEL: Accelerating into Destiny

Day 15 of 21. Two weeks complete. Week 2 established your identity in seven dimensions—adoption, abundance, authority, anointing, advancement, attributes, affirmation. You know WHO you are. Today's Presence reveals WHAT you carry as you propel into destiny. This isn't about learning to be WITH Him anymore. This is about recognizing you've BECOME His dwelling place—a mobile throne room, a walking embassy of heaven.

Day 15 of 21. Week 2 revealed your Kingdom identity for your assignment. Today's Presence shatters the religious lie that's been keeping you spiritually homeless.

THE STRATEGIC CONNECTIONS
How Each Week 2 Day Connects to Day 13 (Attributes):

Day 8 → Day 13: I am adopted (identity) BECAUSE He is a faithful Father (character)
Day 9 → Day 13: I have abundance (provision) BECAUSE He is generous (nature)
Day 10 → Day 13: I have authority (power) BECAUSE He is sovereign (dominion)
Day 11 → Day 13: I am anointed (equipment) BECAUSE He is holy (consecration)
Day 12 → Day 13: I am advancing (movement) BECAUSE He has purpose (plan)
Day 13 → Day 14: My eyes see His character (Day 13) → My mouth declares what I see (Day 14)

ENCOUNTER: WHEN EMPTINESS BECOMES CAPACITY

Your ribs feel like a cage holding nothing but echoes. Hollow spaces where fullness used to live, carved out by fifteen days of desperate pressing in.

4:47 AM. Day 15. Your body doesn't just protest—it revolts against another morning of reaching for something that feels perpetually just beyond your grasp. Bones like brittle twigs. Soul scraped raw from seeking.

The glass of water sits untouched on your nightstand—always there, always room temperature, always neglected. Like your relationship with God lately. Present but not consumed. Available but not accessed. Right there, but somehow distant.

Your phone glows in pre-dawn darkness: 47 texts. 89 emails. 23 missed calls. Ministry obligations stacked like Jenga blocks—pull one out and everything collapses. People needing. Always needing. And you—running on fumes, calling it faith.

That sense of spiritual homelessness intensifies. Like you're always knocking on heaven's door but never quite getting inside. Always visiting, never dwelling. Always seeking, never finding rest.

But this morning's exhaustion runs deeper than hunger. This is the trembling when a seed finally splits open underground. What looks like destruction is actually preparation for sprouting. Everyone watching thinks the seed is dying. They don't see what's happening beneath the surface.

"You're not falling apart. You're falling open."

The journal lies open beside that untouched water, pen poised for another entry documenting the distance between you and God. Another prayer begging Him to show up, visit your situation, interrupt your crisis. The same prayer you prayed yesterday. And the day before. And the day before that.

But as you prepare to document emptiness, heaven interrupts with revolution:

"You weren't created to visit God. You were designed to carry Him."

The pen stops. The emptiness shifts from absence to capacity. The hollow spaces become room for habitation. The spiritual homelessness transforms into recognition—you've been seeking a home IN God when He's been seeking a home IN you.

"You don't visit the secret place. You ARE the secret place."

After fifteen days of pressing in, you've developed capacity to carry what others can only consume. The distance you've felt wasn't rejection—it was preparation for inhabitation. The emptiness wasn't failure—it was capacity building for divine indwelling.

"Seeds split before they sprout. You're not breaking down—you're breaking open for indwelling."

A pastor's words from years ago echo through your exhaustion: "You are restless because you have less of God."

RESTless because LESS. The formula burns in your chest. Less of Christ makes you RESTless and faithless. Full of Christ makes you RESTful and faithful.

This is your Day 15 awakening: The journey from spiritual homelessness to becoming God's home. From RESTless to RESTful. From having LESS to being FULL. From visitor to carrier. From consumer to dwelling place.

REVELATION: THE MOSES REVOLUTION THAT CHANGES EVERYTHING

Let me speak to what's been driving you to your knees every morning. That sense of spiritual homelessness. That feeling like you're always knocking on heaven's door but never quite getting inside. That RESTless anxiety from having LESS of God when you need to be FULL.

After the golden calf rebellion, God offered Israel everything. Promised Land flowing with milk and honey. Victory over every enemy. Abundant provision. Angels to guide them. Everything except one thing: His personal, manifest presence.

"I will send an Angel before you...but I will not go up in your midst" (Exodus 33:2-3).

Most would take that deal. Guaranteed success? Sign me up. But Moses refused.

"If Your Presence does not go with us, do not bring us up from here" (Exodus 33:15).

Moses chose wilderness WITH God over paradise without Him. Refused promotion minus presence. Rejected success that didn't include accompaniment.

But notice what Moses demanded. He didn't use the word you expect. He didn't say "presence" generically. He said PANIM [pah-NEEM]—literally "FACE."

"I don't want Your hand without Your face. I don't want Your gifts without Your gaze. I don't want Your power without Your presence."

Moses refused success without relationship. He rejected promotion without proximity. This is the revolutionary shift from consumer to carrier, from having LESS to being FULL, from spiritual homelessness to becoming God's dwelling place.

Watch God's response—the response that changes your Day 15 forever:

"My Presence will go WITH you, and I will give you rest" (Exodus 33:14).

Not TO you but WITH you. Not visiting but accompanying. Not observing but participating. Not destination but companionship. And notice the result: REST. Not from stopping, but from carrying. Not from sitting, but from knowing He's WITH you as you move.

This is your Day 15 revolution: Stop seeking God's hand. Start carrying His face. Stop begging God to visit your gap. Start recognizing He's already WITH you in it. Stop being RESTless from having LESS. Start being RESTful from being FULL.

"I'd rather fail with Your presence than succeed without it."

From spiritual homelessness to spiritual home. From RESTless to RESTful. From visitor to carrier.

THE PARADIGM DESTRUCTION: FROM CONSUMER TO CARRIER

This WITH understanding detonates every religious assumption about how presence works. It destroys the system that's kept you spiritually homeless, perpetually visiting what you were designed to carry, always RESTless because you're operating with LESS.

Traditional Prayer Teaches You to Be a Presence Consumer:

"God, come TO my situation"

"God, visit my problem"

"God, show up IN my crisis"

"God, let me feel Your presence today"

This creates a visiting relationship. You go TO the secret place. You seek encounters. You consume what you need. You visit presence when you're desperate, empty, or scheduled. Church becomes your filling station. Morning devotions become your daily dose. Crisis becomes your emergency room visit.

You show up at God's door when tanks are empty, get your fill, then leave until the next emergency. Like dating God instead of marrying Him. Like renting a hotel room instead of buying a home. This keeps you spiritually homeless, always seeking a place to belong but never finding permanent residence.

Heaven Operates from Revolutionary Reality:

"God goes WITH me into situations"

"God already inhabits my problems"

"God is present WITH me now"

"I don't seek encounters—I AM an encounter"

The Hebrew word "with" in Exodus 33:14 is IMMANU [ee-MAH-noo]—the same root as Emmanuel (God WITH us). It implies accompaniment, partnership, shared experience. Not observation but participation. Not visiting but dwelling. Not temporary but permanent.

God doesn't watch your battles from heaven's balcony—He enters them WITH you as the fourth Man in your fire. You don't walk INTO giants alone—He's the stone in your sling. You don't face storms solo—He's the peace in your boat. You don't enter your week hoping He shows up—He's already WITH you as you go.

"Your presence isn't a place you go—it's who you've become."

The Consumer to Carrier Transformation:

This destroys the religious system that limits you to consuming presence—getting your weekly dose at church, morning hit in devotions, emergency shot in crisis. This is what keeps you spiritually homeless and RESTless.

Day 15 reveals your true design: You weren't created to consume presence. You were created to carry it.

CONSUMERS	CARRIERS
"What can I get from presence?"	"What can I release through presence?"
Visit occasionally	Dwell continually
Take what they need	Overflow what they have
Need special locations	ARE special locations
Seek encounters	ARE encounters
Go TO the secret place	ARE the secret place

"After fifteen days of pressing in, you've developed capacity to carry what others can only consume."

You've become a mobile throne room. A walking embassy of heaven. A living sanctuary where His presence dwells. You're no longer spiritually homeless—you ARE His home. You're no longer RESTless from having LESS—you're RESTful from being FULL.

THE TESTIMONY: WHEN EMPTINESS BECAME CAPACITY

I need to tell you about the progression from spiritual homelessness to becoming God's dwelling place—a journey from RESTless to RESTful, from LESS to FULL. This is my path from visitor to carrier.

The Foundation (1987): Jamaica - Letters to an Invisible Friend

Fifteen years old. Under threadbare blankets with dying flashlight battery, writing letters to God on paper ripped from the back of my notebook. Folded seven times, hidden under my mattress because even my private prayers felt dangerous in that house.

Some letters marked "URGENT" in red crayon because a teenager's heartbreak always feels like the world ending. Writing to an invisible Friend because the visible father was absent and the present stepfather was mean.

"In Your presence is fullness of joy" (Psalm 16:11) became my lifeline when everything else felt hopeless. But I was still writing TO someone I thought was far away, somewhere up in heaven, maybe listening if He wasn't too busy.

I was a presence consumer. A visitor. Spiritually homeless, always seeking but never dwelling. RESTless because I had LESS. Begging for visits instead of recognizing I was being prepared to carry.

The Valley (2011-2015): The Visitor Season

Then 2010 began what I call my Job Season. Five years where everything unraveled systematically. Biological father died. Marriage died. Executive home lost.

And in 2012, the violation that changed everything: my private journals—ten years of intimate conversations with God, letters to the Father I never had—stolen and weaponized in divorce proceedings. My confessions twisted into evidence of instability. My fears used as proof of unfitness.

I stopped writing completely. Didn't pick up a journal for two years.

I'd gone from carrier to visitor almost overnight. From dwelling place to someone who stood at the back of the sanctuary hoping to catch a moment of what I used to live in continuously. Spiritually homeless again. Standing at church altars after service, weeping, feeling like a stranger in what used to be home.

One Sunday, broken beyond words, the pastor held me while I sobbed. Three words that diagnosed everything:

"You are restless because you have less of God."

RESTless because I had LESS. Less of Christ makes you RESTless and faithless. Full of Christ makes you RESTful and faithful.

I'd gone from carrier to consumer, from dwelling to visiting, from fullness to emptiness, from home to homeless. *"Do not cast me away from Your presence"* (Psalm 51:11) became my desperate cry. Not theology. Survival prayer.

The Desperation (July 2014): The Email to Myself

10:23 PM. Too ashamed to pray out loud, too broken to write in a journal that might be used against me, I did something desperate: I emailed a prayer request to my own address.

Listed everything broken, everything impossible, everything beyond my ability to fix. Home I was about to lose. Custody battle that seemed unwinnable. Bills I couldn't pay. Life I couldn't piece together.

Sent it to myself because there was no one else who wouldn't judge, wouldn't gossip, wouldn't use my desperation as evidence of failure.

"Where can I go from Your Spirit?" (Psalm 139:7)—even in desperation, questioning if He was still there, still WITH me.

The email became evidence that even when I couldn't feel His presence, I was still writing to Him. Still carrying capacity even when it felt empty. Still a dwelling place even when I felt homeless.

The Voice (February 2015): The Laundry Room Encounter

Rental home laundry room. Sobbing about an impossible house situation that required either divine intervention or financial destruction. Bills I couldn't pay. Timeline I couldn't meet. Options I didn't have.

Then audibly, clearly, unmistakably: "If I did it any other way, they would say they did it."

Said twice. Not in my head. In the room.

Those words didn't just promise provision—they revealed His determination to display glory through my impossible circumstances. He wasn't observing from heaven. He was WITH me in the laundry room. Participating in the problem. Strategizing the solution that would bring Him glory.

"God's presence speaks loudest when circumstances scream loudest."

Not a visit. Not a guest appearance. Partnership. God WITH me in the problem. And that's when I began to understand: I wasn't trying to get TO His presence. He was already IN me, speaking THROUGH me, moving WITH me.

Three months later—May 2015—the house situation resolved in a way that left no doubt: God did this. From homeless to home, literally and spiritually.

The Hunger (December 2017): The Face Cry

Crying out like Moses: "I don't want just Your hands but Your face!"

"He who dwells in the secret place of the Most High shall abide under the shadow of the Almighty" (Psalm 91:1) shifted from verse to vision. The longing wasn't for more encounters. It was for the face-to-face friendship Moses discovered.

From RESTless seeking to RESTful dwelling. From having LESS to being FULL. From spiritual homelessness to recognizing I AM His home.

The Download (January 2018): The GAP Birth

Daniel Fast. Seeking God's face, not just His hand. Crying out not just for breakthrough but for more of Him. And in the middle of that fast, dwelling in His presence instead of just seeking His presence, something downloaded: The GAP Strategy™.

"You shall hide them in the secret place of Your presence from the plots of man" (Psalm 31:20). Hidden IN His presence, the strategy downloaded.

What flowed from dwelling wasn't FOR me—it was THROUGH me for thousands. This 21-day journey you're on right now? It was birthed from dwelling in His presence during a Daniel Fast, just like you're doing on Day 15.

This is what separates visitors from carriers: Visitors consume for themselves. Carriers release for others.

The Continuing Evolution (Now): The Marriage Dynamic

Married. In ministry. Walking in more breakthrough than I've ever experienced. And STILL learning daily to prioritize presence over performance. Still discovering how to:
- Seek God's face FIRST before seeking solutions
- Include husband and family IN that presence rather than choosing between them
- Release FROM that foundation in ministry and marketplace
- Remember I don't GO to the secret place—I AM the secret place

"Presence isn't a destination you reach but a journey you deepen continuously."

This ongoing journey reveals the truth: *"And lo, I am with you always, even to the end of the age"* (Matthew 28:20) isn't just promise—it's process requiring daily choice to carry instead of consume, to dwell instead of visit, to be RESTful (FULL) instead of RESTless (LESS).

From spiritual homelessness to becoming His home. From visitor to carrier. From RESTless to RESTful. This is the journey Day 15 begins for you.

HEBREW REVELATION: YOUR PRESENCE ADDRESS

These Hebrew words aren't academic definitions—they're your spiritual address, the dimensions where you actually live. They define your home when you're no longer spiritually homeless, your fullness when you're no longer operating with LESS.

THE 5 CORE TERMS: Your Primary Address
PANIM [pah-NEEM] — The Face That Transforms Everything

Used 2,100+ times in Scripture. Literally means "face." When Moses demanded PANIM, he declared: "I don't want Your power without Your face. I don't want Your hand without Your gaze."

Jacob wrestled all night for this: *"I have seen God face to face, and my life is preserved"* (Genesis 32:30).

PANIM means God's face turned TOWARD you, not away. Face-to-face friendship, not distant deity. This is what shifts you from RESTless to RESTful—knowing His face is constantly toward you, His gaze fixed on you.

When you carry PANIM, people see His face IN your face. Moses came down from the mountain with face so radiant people couldn't look directly at him (Exodus 34:29). That's what carrying the Face does—it marks your countenance with His glory.

SHEKINAH [sheh-kee-NAH] — The Glory That Unpacked Its Bags

From SHAKAN [shah-KAHN], meaning to settle permanently, to unpack bags, to take up permanent residence. The SHEKINAH that filled the tabernacle until Moses couldn't enter (Exodus 40:34-35) now lives IN you.

God has unpacked His bags in your spirit. You're not a hotel room He visits occasionally—you're His permanent address. His home. This is the ultimate answer to spiritual homelessness: You ARE His home, and He IS your home.

The dwelling is permanent. You're not waiting for His next visit. He's moved in permanently. From visitor to resident. From homeless to home.

KAVOD [kah-BODE] — The Weight That Changes Atmospheres

Literally "weight," "heaviness," "substance." Often translated "glory" but that misses the physicality. This is presence with mass, with weight, with tangible substance.

When KAVOD shows up, you FEEL it. The air thickens. Your knees weaken. The atmosphere shifts. This isn't abstract theology—this is weighty, substantial presence that changes everything around you.

It made Moses' face shine so brightly people couldn't look directly at him (Exodus 34:29). You don't just carry presence—you carry atmosphere-changing weight. When you enter a room FULL of Christ, the KAVOD enters with you. RESTless atmospheres become RESTful through the weight you carry.

RUACH [ROO-akh] — The Breath That Creates Worlds

Spirit. Wind. Breath. The RUACH that hovered over chaos in Genesis 1:2. The breath God breathed into Adam's nostrils, transforming sculpted dust into living soul (Genesis 2:7).

Without RUACH, Adam was sculpted dust. With it, he became living soul breathing God's breath.

RUACH is presence in motion, creating life wherever you breathe. When you're FULL of RUACH instead of operating with LESS, you release life everywhere you go. The same breath that animated Adam animates you.

EMMANUEL [em-man-oo-EL] — God WITH Us Always

The ultimate presence revelation. Not God ABOVE us (transcendent but distant). Not God FOR us (helpful but separate). God WITH us—intimate, accessible, participating, never leaving.

"Behold, the virgin shall be with child, and bear a Son, and they shall call His name Immanuel, which is translated, God with us" (Matthew 1:23).

EMMANUEL means partnership. Shared experience. Divine accompaniment that never leaves. This is what destroys spiritual homelessness forever—knowing you're never alone, never abandoned, never without Him.

He doesn't watch your journey from heaven—He walks it WITH you. Doesn't observe your struggles from the throne—He enters them WITH you. This is the promise that shifts you from RESTless (feeling alone) to RESTful (knowing He's WITH you always).

THE 7 SECONDARY TERMS: Expanding Your Understanding

While the five core terms above establish your primary address, these seven additional terms expand and deepen your understanding of mobile presence theology:

MISHKAN [mish-KAHN] — Portable dwelling place. The tabernacle that MOVED with Israel, establishing that presence isn't stationary but mobile. You're not a temple tied to one location—you're a tabernacle that carries presence everywhere.

IMMANU [ee-MAH-noo] — The root of Emmanuel, meaning "with us." The "with" in Exodus 33:14 that promises accompaniment, not just visitation.

SKENOO [skay-NO-oh] — Greek for "tabernacled." Used in John 1:14: "The Word became flesh and dwelt [tabernacled] among us." Jesus didn't build a temple—He BECAME the mobile dwelling.

PAROUSIA [par-oo-SEE-ah] — From para ("beside") + ousia ("being") = "being alongside." His active arrival in every location you enter.

ENOIKEO [en-oy-KEH-oh] — EN ("in") + OIKEO ("to dwell") = to inhabit from within. The ultimate mobile theology: When God dwells WITHIN you, presence goes wherever YOU go.

YHWH SHAMMAH [yah-WEH sham-MAH] — "The Lord Is There." Wherever you go, His presence goes. When you arrive, the Lord is there—because He's in YOU.

SHAKAN [shah-KAHN] — The verb form: to settle, to dwell permanently. What God does in you isn't temporary—it's permanent residence.

"These aren't just words—they're your address. You live at the intersection of PANIM, SHEKINAH, KAVOD, RUACH, and EMMANUEL. You're no longer spiritually homeless. You ARE His home, and He IS yours."

Before I arrive, He's already there. Wherever I go, God goes—with me, in me, around me. I'm not tied to a building; I'm a Mishkan on the move. He dwells within (enoikeō), walks beside (parousia), covers my back—YHWH Shammah. Not a one-night stand, but a covenant Partner. Presence isn't a place I visit; it's the Person I carry.

THE PROGRESSION: A BRIEF GLIMPSE FROM EDEN TO YOU

While your primary focus is the shift from homeless to home, from RESTless to RESTful, understanding the biblical progression shows you're not discovering something new—you're stepping into God's eternal plan:

Eden — God walked WITH humanity in the cool of the day (Genesis 3:8). Face-to-face fellowship. No distance. No homelessness.

Tabernacle — God chose a PORTABLE dwelling (Exodus 25:8) that MOVED with Israel. Mobile presence, not stationary. They CARRIED God with them. This foreshadowed YOU.

Temple — Permanent structure but tied to one location. People had to GO TO Jerusalem. This created spiritual homelessness for anyone not in Jerusalem.

Exile — Temple destroyed, but God promised: *"I will put My Spirit within you"* (Ezekiel 36:27). From external to internal. From location-based to person-based.

Incarnation — Jesus "tabernacled" among us (John 1:14). God went mobile again, walking presence in human form.

Church Age — *"Do you not know that you are the temple of God?"* (1 Corinthians 3:16). YOU became the fulfillment. Not a temple tied to Jerusalem—a mobile tabernacle carrying presence everywhere.

The distinction matters: You're not Solomon's temple (permanent, stationary, location-based). You're Moses' tabernacle (portable, mobile, person-based). From Eden to you, God's plan was always mobile presence, always WITH-ness, always ending spiritual homelessness by dwelling IN His people.

BIBLICAL CHAMPIONS: YOUR INHERITANCE OF PRESENCE

Every biblical encounter creates pathways you can walk. Their ceiling becomes your floor. Their journey from spiritual homelessness to dwelling, from RESTless to RESTful, becomes your blueprint.

Moses: From Burning Bush to Face-to-Face Friend

Eighty years old, hiding in desert obscurity when presence interrupted: "Moses! Moses!" (Exodus 3:4). When God says your name twice, transformation is imminent.

Forty years later: *"So the Lord spoke to Moses face to face, as a man speaks to his friend"* (Exodus 33:11).

Moses progressed from burning bush encounter to face-to-face friendship. From consumer to carrier. From seeking God's hand to carrying God's face. From RESTless wanderer to RESTful friend.

Moses took forty years. You're making that journey in twenty-one days because what took him decades can be compressed into consecrated moments.

David: Choosing Dwelling Over Palace

Even as king, David understood priority: *"For a day in Your courts is better than a thousand. I would rather be a doorkeeper in the house of my God than dwell in the tents of wickedness"* (Psalm 84:10).

He brought the ark to Jerusalem BEFORE building his palace. Presence before position. Dwelling before achievement. Being RESTful in God's presence over RESTless pursuit of success.

David chose to be spiritually home in God's presence rather than physically home in his palace. His priority reveals the secret: Presence over performance. Face over favor.

Mary of Bethany: Choosing Feet Over Performance

Martha served—RESTless activity, constantly doing. Mary sat at Jesus' feet—RESTful presence, simply being.

"But one thing is needed, and Mary has chosen that good part, which will not be taken away from her" (Luke 10:42).

What Martha accomplished faded with the meal. What Mary received at His feet remains eternal. This is the choice: Consumer (taking what you need from serving) or Carrier (receiving what flows from dwelling).

Mary wasn't spiritually homeless, running around seeking fulfillment. She was spiritually home, seated at His feet. RESTful, not RESTless. FULL, not operating with LESS.

Upper Room: From Hiding to World-Changing

120 believers waiting in one accord. Spiritually homeless after Jesus ascended—what do we do now? Where do we go? Then:

"And suddenly there came a sound from heaven, as of a rushing mighty wind...And they were all filled with the Holy Spirit" (Acts 2:1-4).

Cowards became world-changers when presence filled the space. They went from RESTless hiding to RESTful power. From having LESS (Jesus physically gone) to being FULL (Holy Spirit dwelling within).

From spiritual homelessness to becoming God's mobile dwelling places, carrying presence into every nation.

"Their extraordinary is your ordinary. Their once-in-a-lifetime is your daily lifestyle."

THE CARRIER LIFESTYLE: FIVE DAILY RHYTHMS

Your transformation from visitor to carrier isn't one-time event—it's sustainable daily rhythms. Not religious obligations. Carrier maintenance. These five rhythms structure your day around dwelling, not visiting. They keep your capacity full so you can keep releasing presence.

RHYTHM	WHEN	WHAT	RESULT
1. AWAKEN	Every morning first thing	Recognize identity + Fill capacity (30 min) + Listen for direction	Start day FULL, knowing who you are and what you're carrying
2. RELEASE	Throughout day	Overflow from fullness into every situation	Impact from presence carried wherever you go
3. PAUSE	Three times daily	60-sec Selah: Remember + Check + Refill if needed	Maintain carrier awareness and fullness all day
4. SACRED SPACE	Consistent location	Designated filling station where you refill capacity	Physical place trains spirit to receive consistently
5. RESET	Weekly Sabbath (24 hours)	Stop producing, deep capacity refilling, complete rest	Sustained carrier lifestyle without burnout

Rhythm 1: AWAKEN — Morning Carrier Activation

Every morning, before your phone, before your feet hit the floor, you activate carrier identity and fill your capacity. This isn't earning God's attention. This is maintaining carrier capacity so you can release all day.

The Practice:

RECOGNIZE: Declare before rising: "I am not visiting God's presence today. I am carrying God's presence today. I don't go TO the secret place—I AM the secret place. I don't seek encounters—I AM an encounter. Presence dwells in me. I am a mobile throne room, a walking embassy of heaven."

FILL: Set alarm 30 minutes earlier. No phone for first 30 minutes. Spend time in Scripture—not just reading but FILLING. Ask: "What am I carrying today? What have I depleted? What needs refilling?" Read until something FILLS you (not just informs you). Pray from fullness (releasing) not emptiness (begging).

LISTEN: After filling, sit in silence with journal ready. Ask: "Father, what am I carrying today? Where do You want me to release it? Who needs what I'm carrying?" Don't force it. Don't manufacture words. Write what comes. Sometimes He speaks immediately. Sometimes He's silent, teaching you to walk by faith. Sometimes you'll recognize the answer later when you "randomly" encounter someone who needs exactly what you're carrying.

The Goal: Start your day knowing you're FULL—full of Him, full of presence, full of carrier capacity—and clear on where He's sending you. Then release all day from that fullness.

Practical Application: Write the RECOGNIZE declaration on an index card. Read it every morning for 21 days until it rewires your consciousness. Keep your journal by your filling location with pen ready.

Rhythm 2: RELEASE — Overflow Throughout Your Day

As you move through your day, you're not trying to GET filled—you're releasing FROM the filling you received in Rhythm 1. You're overflowing what you received this morning into every situation you encounter.

The Practice:

In **conversations**: Speak from fullness, not anxiety

In **work**: Minister from presence, not striving

In **problems**: Face them carrying solution, not seeking solution

In **relationships**: Bring presence into connection, not demands

In **decisions**: Release wisdom dwelling in you, not panic

In **crisis**: Overflow peace you're carrying, not fear you're feeling

The Shift: From "I need to get filled" to "I'm releasing what I carry." From consumer mode to carrier mode. From spiritual homelessness to being His home that travels.

The Goal: Live all day from morning fullness. You're not begging God to show up at 2 PM—you're recognizing He's been WITH you since you awakened, dwelling IN you since salvation.

Remember: You don't walk INTO situations alone hoping God joins you. You carry God INTO situations, releasing His presence from the dwelling place you are.

Rhythm 3: PAUSE — The Selah Check Throughout Day

Selah appears 74 times in Psalms. Scholars debate exact meaning, but consensus: pause, rest, reflect. It's a musical notation meaning "stop and let that sink in." David understood carriers need regular pauses to remember what they're carrying.

The Practice:

Set three alarms throughout your day labeled **"Selah"**:
- Mid-morning (around 10 AM)
- Afternoon (around 2 PM)
- Evening (around 6 PM)

When they sound, stop for **60 seconds**:

REMEMBER: "I am carrying presence RIGHT NOW. He is WITH me right now. I am His dwelling place right now. I'm not waiting to GET to God—He's already IN me."

CHECK: "Is my capacity depleted? Have I shifted back to visitor mentality? Am I operating RESTless (LESS) or RESTful (FULL)?"

REFILL if needed: If depleted, pause longer. Breathe deeply. Reconnect to Source. Remember who you are. Brief filling before continuing.

The Goal: Maintain carrier awareness all day. Don't forget at 2 PM what you knew at 6 AM. Keep recognizing you're carrying presence. The alarm isn't to remind God to show up—it's to remind YOU He never left.

The Shift: From "I need to pray more throughout the day" (visitor) to "I'm pausing to remember I'm carrying presence right now" (carrier).

Rhythm 4: SACRED SPACE — Your Filling Station

Jacob woke from his dream and declared: *"Surely the LORD is in this place, and I did not know it"* (Genesis 28:16). Then he set up a stone as memorial. Carriers need designated filling stations—not because God's only there, but because you REMEMBER He's there.

The Practice:

DESIGNATE: Choose one space in your home as your filling station. A chair. A corner. A room if possible. Nothing fancy required—just consistent. This is where you do Rhythm 1 (Awaken) every morning.

TRAIN YOUR SPIRIT: "When I sit here, I'm refilling." Consistency creates association. Your spirit learns: This space = filling time. Not the only place God is. But the place you consistently refill.

MAINTAIN: Keep this space uncluttered. Bible, journal, pen ready. No phone. No distractions. This isn't a ritual—it's practical carrier maintenance.

The Goal: Not "the only place God is" but "the place I consistently refill." Gas stations don't manufacture gas—they're just where you go to get filled. Your sacred space doesn't manufacture presence—it's just where you consistently refill carrier capacity.

The Shift: From "This is where I go to meet God" (visitor) to "This is where I refill my carrier capacity" (carrier). From seeking God in one location to recognizing you CARRY God from this location into every other location.

Rhythm 5: RESET — Weekly Sabbath Maintenance

God modeled it at creation (Genesis 2:2). Jesus practiced it during ministry (Mark 6:31). The early church honored it despite persecution. Sabbath isn't suggestion—it's command. Because God knows: Carriers who never rest eventually deplete completely.

The Practice:

ONE FULL DAY per week, 24 hours, STOP:
- Don't produce content
- Don't answer work emails
- Don't do ministry
- Don't hustle, strive, or perform

INSTEAD:
- Rest deeply. Sleep late if needed.
- Take a walk. Read a book. Play with kids.
- Enjoy a long meal. Watch something life-giving.
- Refill your soul through what restores, not what depletes.

This isn't laziness—it's maintenance. Even carriers need weekly deep refilling. Your car needs daily gas (Rhythm 1) and weekly maintenance (Rhythm 5). Your carrier capacity needs daily filling and weekly saturation.

The Goal: Weekly deep refilling. Not just daily sips but weekly saturation. God managed the universe without you for six days. He can handle one more. Carriers who skip Sabbath eventually crack under the weight of what they're carrying.

The Shift: From "I'm taking a break from God-stuff" (visitor) to "I'm doing weekly carrier capacity maintenance" (carrier). From guilt about resting to recognition that rest IS the work of maintaining capacity for sustained release.

The Metric: If you skip Sabbath, you'll notice depletion by midweek following. If you honor Sabbath, you'll notice sustained capacity throughout the next week. This isn't optional—it's essential for carrier lifestyle.

HOW THE FIVE RHYTHMS WORK TOGETHER

Morning: Rhythm 1 (AWAKEN) fills your capacity
All Day: Rhythm 2 (RELEASE) overflows what you received
Throughout Day: Rhythm 3 (PAUSE) maintains awareness and refills as needed
Consistently: Rhythm 4 (SACRED SPACE) provides reliable filling station
Weekly: Rhythm 5 (RESET) deep maintenance prevents burnout

Not religious obligation. Carrier maintenance.

You can't release what you haven't received. Can't carry what you've depleted. Can't overflow what you've emptied.

Fill daily. Release continually. Pause regularly. Refill consistently. Reset weekly.

This is sustainable carrier lifestyle.

ACTIVATION: THE SIX DIMENSIONS OF PRESENCE

DIMENSION	VISITOR MINDSET	CARRIER REALITY	YOUR DECLARATION
SPIRITUAL	Seeking encounters occasionally	Living as His dwelling place	"My spirit is His permanent home!"
MENTAL	Trying to find God's will	Thinking FROM His presence	"Mind of Christ thinks through me!"
EMOTIONAL	RESTless anxiety seeking peace	RESTful security in His face	"His PANIM is my joy!"
PHYSICAL	Exhausted from spiritual seeking	Energized by RUACH breath	"His presence is my strength!"

FINANCIAL	Worried about provision	Kingdom solutions flow through dwelling	"Presence provides supernatural wisdom!"
RELATIONAL	Feeling alone in struggles	Never alone—EMMANUEL always WITH me	"EMMANUEL goes with me everywhere!"

Presence transforms every dimension when you shift from visitor to carrier, from RESTless (LESS) to RESTful (FULL), from spiritually homeless to being His home.

FOCUS AREA PRESENCE PRAYERS

Choose your primary breakthrough area and declare:

For SPIRITUAL Focus: "Father, I reject spiritual homelessness from church hurt and toxic theology that made me a visitor instead of a carrier. I receive SHEKINAH—Your glory DWELLS in me permanently! I AM the secret place, not a project to fix but a temple You inhabit. Transform me from RESTless seeking (LESS) to RESTful dwelling (FULL). Therefore I carry Your presence into [specific place/situation] this week, knowing my spirit is Your permanent home."

For MENTAL Focus: "Father, I reject anxiety from trying to figure out Your will while social media shows everyone else 'hearing clearly' and my mind spirals with overthinking. I receive PANIM—Your face turned toward me NOW, guiding every thought. Transform my mind from RESTless confusion (LESS) to RESTful clarity (FULL). Therefore I make [specific decision] TODAY from the Mind of Christ dwelling in me, not from fear or comparison."

For EMOTIONAL Focus: "Father, I reject depression and trauma that made me believe I'm one breakdown away from losing You—that Your presence depends on my emotional stability. I receive PANIM—Your face doesn't turn away in my therapy sessions, dark nights, or trigger moments. Transform my emotions from RESTless anxiety (LESS) to RESTful peace (FULL). Therefore I carry the Healer INTO [specific emotional struggle] today, not seeking peace by visiting You but releasing peace from dwelling."

For PHYSICAL Focus: "Father, I reject burnout culture that glorifies exhaustion and hustle mentality that says rest is weakness—the physical toll of RESTless striving (LESS). I receive RUACH—Your breath ANIMATES my body as Your dwelling place requiring sacred stewardship, not grinding harder. Transform my physical strength from exhaustion to sustaining power (FULL). Therefore I rest TODAY as a sacred act, trusting that You sustain me from presence, not despite absence."

For FINANCIAL Focus: "Father, I reject financial anxiety from inflation, debt, and paycheck-to-paycheck living—visiting You only in crisis while operating from RESTless scarcity (LESS). I receive Kingdom solutions flowing through continuous dwelling—You are the Provider I carry, not the emergency I visit. Transform my finances from worry to provision (FULL). Therefore I make [specific financial decision] TODAY from dwelling, not desperation, carrying heaven's wisdom into this impossible budget."

For RELATIONAL Focus: "Father, I reject the loneliness epidemic and relational PTSD from betrayal—feeling spiritually homeless even in crowded rooms, scrolling at 2 AM wondering if anyone truly sees me. I receive EMMANUEL—You're WITH me in every conversation, conflict, and lonely moment.

Transform my relationships from RESTless isolation (LESS) to RESTful companionship (FULL). Therefore I love [specific person] from overflow today, not depletion, carrying You into this connection that exhausts me."

RESISTANCE REALITY CHECK: BREAKING THE LIES
What hell is whispering right now to keep you spiritually homeless, RESTless, and operating with LESS:

LIE #1: PERFORMANCE PRESSURE
Hell whispers: "You need to DO more to sense His presence. Pray longer. Fast harder. Worship better. THEN God will show up."

Heaven's Response: "Presence isn't earned through performance but received through positioning. You ARE the secret place. I don't dwell in you because of what you DO—I dwell in you because of who I AM. My presence is gift, not wage. Stop being RESTless through performance. Be RESTful through positioning."

Break it: "I reject performance pressure! Presence is my inheritance, not my achievement! I shift from RESTless to RESTful!"

LIE #2: LOCATION LIMITATION
Hell whispers: "God only shows up in special places—church buildings, prayer closets, worship conferences. You need to GO somewhere to encounter Him. You're spiritually homeless until you find the right location."

Heaven's Response: "You ARE the special place. His SHEKINAH has unpacked its bags in your spirit. The temple isn't a building you visit—it's the body you inhabit. You're not spiritually homeless—you ARE His home."

Break it: "I reject location limitation! I AM the temple! I'm no longer spiritually homeless—I AM His dwelling place!"

LIE #3: TIMING RESTRICTION
Hell whispers: "God only visits during certain times—early morning quiet time, Sunday services, special seasons. You need to wait for the 'right moment' to encounter Him."

Heaven's Response: "EMMANUEL means ALWAYS WITH you. Not sometimes. Not when you feel spiritual. ALWAYS. My presence doesn't operate on your schedule—it transcends all timing. You're never without Me. Never RESTless because you're always FULL."

Break it: "I reject timing restriction! You're WITH me 24/7/365! I'm RESTful because I'm FULL of You always!"

LIE #4: WORTHINESS WORRY
Hell whispers: "You're not good enough to carry His presence. Look at your failures, your struggles, your imperfections. You're spiritually homeless because you're not worthy."

Heaven's Response: "Presence isn't about YOUR goodness but MY grace dwelling in you permanently. Did I wait for you to be perfect before I saved you? I chose WEAK vessels to display My power. Your weakness doesn't create spiritual homelessness—it creates opportunity for My strength to be made perfect."

Break it: "I reject worthiness worry! His grace makes me His dwelling! Not my goodness—His!"

LIE #5: VISITOR MENTALITY

Hell whispers: "You need to go TO God's presence. Visit Him when you need something. Seek encounters when you're desperate. You're spiritually homeless—keep seeking, keep visiting, maybe one day you'll find home."

Heaven's Response: "Stop seeking encounters—you ARE one. Stop visiting presence—you CARRY it. I didn't visit the earth temporarily through Jesus—I TABERNACLED among you. And now? I've pitched My tent IN you. You're not spiritually homeless. You ARE My home."

Break it: "I reject visitor mentality! I don't visit presence—I CARRY presence! I'm not spiritually homeless—I AM His dwelling! From RESTless to RESTful! From LESS to FULL!"

"Your presence isn't based on your performance—it's based on His promise to dwell in you. From homeless to home. From RESTless to RESTful."

THE CARRIER DECLARATION

Stand in your identity. Feel His nearness. End your spiritual homelessness. Shift from RESTless to RESTful. Declare:

"I declare I am no longer spiritually homeless—I AM HIS HOME!

I live in PANIM—face-to-face intimacy with God! His face is turned toward me always!

SHEKINAH glory doesn't visit me—it DWELLS in me permanently! God has unpacked His bags in my spirit!

KAVOD weight shifts atmospheres through my presence! When I enter FULL of Christ, RESTless spaces become RESTful!

RUACH breath animates my destiny and creates life! I breathe His presence into every situation!

EMMANUEL means never alone—God is always WITH me! From homeless to home! From visitor to carrier!

I stop seeking God's hand—I seek His face!

I stop being RESTless from having LESS—I'm RESTful from being FULL!

I don't seek encounters—I AM an encounter!

I don't visit presence—I CARRY it everywhere!

Like Moses, I choose His face over His favors!

Like David, I choose dwelling over performance!

Like Mary, I choose His feet over my service!

When I enter a room, God enters with me!

When I speak, His presence speaks through me!

When I rest, He rests WITH me!

I am not spiritually homeless—I AM HIS HOME!

He is not a visitor in my life—He is my PERMANENT RESIDENT!

I don't consume presence—I RELEASE it!

From RESTless to RESTful! From LESS to FULL! From homeless to home!

I activate The Carrier Lifestyle—Five Daily Rhythms:

Rhythm 1: I AWAKEN each morning—recognize, fill, listen

Rhythm 2: I RELEASE all day—overflow from fullness

Rhythm 3: I PAUSE three times daily—remember, check, refill
Rhythm 4: I maintain SACRED SPACE—consistent filling station
Rhythm 5: I RESET weekly—Sabbath deep maintenance
I AM A PRESENCE CARRIER! I AM HIS DWELLING PLACE!
Amen!"

BREAKTHROUGH PRAYER

"Father God, PANIM who turns Your face toward me, SHEKINAH who has made me Your permanent dwelling,

Forgive me for being spiritually homeless when You've been offering to make me Your home. For being a presence consumer instead of presence carrier. For visiting what I was meant to inhabit. For seeking Your hand while ignoring Your face. For being RESTless from having LESS when You've been offering to make me RESTful through being FULL.

Thank You that Moses' journey from burning bush to face-to-face friendship creates the pathway for mine. Thank You that his forty-year progression can be walked in these twenty-one days of consecration.

Thank You that PANIM, SHEKINAH, KAVOD, RUACH, EMMANUEL aren't just Hebrew words but my spiritual address—where I actually live and move and have my being. My permanent home, ending spiritual homelessness forever.

Thank You that presence isn't earned through performance but received through positioning. That I don't visit the secret place—I AM the secret place. That You don't visit me occasionally—You dwell in me permanently.

Right now, I choose the revolutionary shift:
- From consumer to carrier
- From visitor to dweller
- From seeking Your hand to seeking Your face
- From going TO encounters to BEING encounters
- From visiting presence to carrying presence
- From RESTless performance to RESTful positioning
- From spiritual homelessness to being Your home
- From having LESS to being FULL

Transform every dimension through Your indwelling:

SPIRITUAL: My spirit is Your permanent home—no more homelessness
MENTAL: Mind of Christ thinks through me—RESTful, not RESTless thoughts
EMOTIONAL: Your face is my peace and joy—FULL, not operating with LESS
PHYSICAL: Your RUACH energizes my body—strength from dwelling, not striving
FINANCIAL: Presence provides supernatural solutions—provision flows from dwelling
RELATIONAL: EMMANUEL means never alone—always WITH me

Your presence goes WITH me into every situation. I carry heaven's embassy wherever I go. I am no longer spiritually homeless. I AM Your home. You ARE my home. From RESTless to RESTful. From LESS to FULL. From visitor to carrier. From homeless to home.

I activate The Carrier Lifestyle—Five Daily Rhythms. I commit to awaken, release, pause, maintain sacred space, and reset weekly. I will maintain my capacity through these sustainable rhythms for sustained carrier lifestyle.

In Jesus' mighty name, the visiting ends and carrying begins. I am spiritually home because You dwell in me. Amen."

PROPHETIC ACT: THE CARRIER COMMISSIONING

Visitors sit. Carriers stand and move. So this prophetic act isn't about sitting in a chair—it's about standing and stepping forward into carrier identity.

What You Need:
- Open space to stand and walk
- Your journal
- 10 minutes uninterrupted

The Act:

STEP 1: STAND IN VISITOR POSITION. Stand in one spot. This represents visitor mentality—stationary, waiting, seeking, consuming. Say out loud: "This is where I've been standing. Visiting. Seeking. Consuming. Going TO presence instead of carrying presence."

STEP 2: RECOGNIZE THE SHIFT. Place your hand over your heart. Feel it beating. That rhythm is His presence dwelling in you right now. Say out loud: "I recognize the shift. I am not a visitor. I am a carrier. Presence doesn't just visit me—presence DWELLS in me. I am His mobile home."

STEP 3: RECEIVE THE COMMISSION. Lift both hands as if receiving something being placed in them. Say out loud: "Father, I receive my commission as a carrier. You're commissioning me to carry Your presence everywhere I go. I am a mobile throne room, a walking embassy of heaven. Commission me now."

(Pause 30 seconds. Receive.)

STEP 4: STEP FORWARD INTO CARRIER IDENTITY. Take five deliberate steps forward. Each step represents one dimension of carrier life.
- **Step 1:** "I carry PANIM—Your face!"
- **Step 2:** "I carry SHEKINAH—Your dwelling!"
- **Step 3:** "I carry KAVOD—Your weight!"
- **Step 4:** "I carry RUACH—Your breath!"
- **Step 5:** "I carry EMMANUEL—God WITH me always!"

STEP 5: WALK YOUR SPACE. Walk around your room, declaring: "Everywhere I go, presence goes. Every room I enter, heaven enters. Every conversation I have, He's WITH me. Every problem I face, I bring solution. I am a carrier—mobile, not stationary. Walking, not sitting. Releasing, not just consuming."

STEP 6: WRITE YOUR COMMISSION. Sit with your journal. Write: "Today, Day 15, I recognize I am a carrier. I will carry presence into these specific places this week:

1. _____
2. _____"

Be specific. Where is God commissioning you to CARRY His presence in the next seven days?

Why This Works: Prophetic acts create spiritual shifts. The woman touched Jesus' hem—healing activated. Naaman dipped seven times—leprosy left. You step forward from visitor position to carrier position—identity shifts. "The commissioning isn't theoretical. It's activated through physical obedience."

THE FIERY FURNACE DECLARATION — CARRIERS IN CRISIS

You've declared carrier identity in normal circumstances. But what about when you're in the fire? Day 15 of your fast, halfway through, and perhaps you're facing your own furnace—crisis that feels like it might consume you.

Carriers don't just carry presence in comfort. They carry presence INTO crisis. Shadrach, Meshach, and Abednego proved it. Three young men, one impossible situation, one revolutionary declaration:

"Our God whom we serve is able to deliver us...But if not...we will not serve your gods" (Daniel 3:17-18).

Even-if faith. Never-the-less conviction. And when they were thrown into the fire, they weren't alone: *"Look!...I see four men loose, walking in the midst of the fire...and the form of the fourth is like the Son of God"* (Daniel 3:25).

The fourth Man wasn't OUTSIDE the fire watching. He was IN the fire WITH them. EMMANUEL in the furnace. And when they emerged, *"the fire had no power...the hair of their head was not singed nor were their garments affected, and the smell of fire was not on them"* (Daniel 3:27).

That's carrier theology in crisis: You don't just survive the fire—you don't even smell like smoke when you emerge. Because the Presence you're carrying protects what's carrying Him.

Stand and declare over your crisis:

"Enemy, you miscalculated. You thought this trial would break me. You thought this fire would consume me. But you forgot—I'm not just in the fire. I'm CARRYING PRESENCE into the fire. The fourth Man isn't with me—He's IN me!

You can turn up the heat seven times hotter (Daniel 3:19). You can add more fuel to the flames. But I'm not visiting presence that might leave—I'm CARRYING presence that never departs!

I declare my even-if faith: Even if deliverance doesn't come on my timeline—I'm still a carrier! Even if the answer delays—I'm still carrying presence! Even if circumstances don't change—I still carry the Changer! Even if healing takes longer—I carry the Healer! Even if breakthrough isn't immediate—I carry the Breakthrough!

And I declare my never-the-less conviction: Nevertheless, I believe He's able! Nevertheless, I trust He's faithful! Nevertheless, I know He's present! Nevertheless, I will not bow! Nevertheless, I'm STILL a carrier!

I will stumble seven times but rise eight (Proverbs 24:16)! Every time I fall, the Presence I carry LIFTS me! Every time I'm knocked down, EMMANUEL raises me! I am not defined by how many times I fall but by WHO I'm carrying when I rise!

I will not break down—I am breaking OUT and breaking THROUGH! Out of limitations! Through every barrier! Because the Presence I carry is my battering ram!

When I emerge from this fire: I will not look like what I've been through! I will not smell like the smoke I walked through! I will not bear the scars the flames should have left!

Because carriers don't just survive crisis—they emerge UNTOUCHED by what should have destroyed them. The Presence you're carrying PROTECTS what's carrying Him!

'When you walk through the fire, you shall not be burned, nor shall the flame scorch you' (Isaiah 43:2). Not burned. Not scorched. Not consumed. REFINED. STRENGTHENED. TRANSFORMED.

So come, fire. Do your worst. The fourth Man is already WITH me. Actually, He's IN me. I'm not visiting presence that might leave—I'm CARRYING presence that NEVER departs!

I won't even look like what I've been through! Because carriers don't just survive—they THRIVE! They emerge marked by presence, not by pain! In Jesus' mighty name, I am a carrier IN the fire, and I will emerge as a carrier FROM the fire! Amen!"

CLOSING: FROM HOMELESS TO HOME, FROM RESTLESS TO RESTFUL

You awakened feeling spiritually homeless—ribs like a cage holding nothing but echoes. Hollow spaces where fullness used to live. Soul scraped raw from seeking. That sense that you're always knocking on heaven's door but never quite getting inside.

RESTless because you had LESS.

Tonight you rest knowing the truth that changes everything: You ARE God's home, and He is eternally WITH you. The emptiness wasn't failure—it was capacity building. The distance wasn't rejection—it was preparation for inhabitation. The spiritual homelessness was the last stage before discovering you ARE His dwelling place.

Day 15's revolutionary gift: Recognition that you don't visit God's presence—you carry it.

"When a seed is buried, before a single sprout appears, the whole seed bursts open. You're not falling apart. You're falling open."

Seeds split before they sprout. What looked like destruction was actually preparation for breakthrough. What felt like dying was actually preparation for dwelling.

But the deeper transformation is this: You've shifted from RESTless to RESTful. From LESS of Christ to FULL of Christ. From spiritual homelessness to being His home.

That altar moment years ago—when a pastor's arms held me as I sobbed and three simple words diagnosed everything—created the formula that determines everything:

"You are restless because you have less of God."

Less of God makes you RESTless and faithless.

Full of Christ makes you RESTful and faithful.

This is your daily diagnostic. The question that determines your reality. The shift that changes everything.

Moses took forty years to progress from burning bush to face-to-face friendship. You're making that journey in twenty-one days because what took him decades can be compressed into consecrated moments when you recognize you're carrying, not just visiting.

"God doesn't want servants who visit. He wants friends who dwell."

You've received Day 15's signature framework: **The Carrier Lifestyle—Five Daily Rhythms:**

1. **AWAKEN** (morning: recognize, fill, listen)
2. **RELEASE** (all day: overflow from fullness)
3. **PAUSE** (three times daily: remember, check, refill)

4. **SACRED SPACE** (consistent filling station)
5. **RESET** (weekly Sabbath maintenance)

These aren't religious obligations. They're carrier maintenance. You can't release what you haven't received. Can't carry what you've depleted. Can't overflow what you've emptied.

Tomorrow: Day 16 PROTECTION begins. You'll discover that dwelling in presence automatically activates divine protection. The same presence you're learning to carry becomes impenetrable fortress surrounding you. Carriers are automatically protected by what they carry.

The shifts you've chosen today—from consumer to carrier, visitor to dweller, RESTless to RESTful, homeless to home—don't happen once. They're daily decisions that compound into lifestyle transformation.

Even now, years into ministry and marriage, I'm still learning to prioritize presence. Still discovering how to seek God's face first, include family in that presence, release from that foundation. This continuous growth is the secret—not arrival but evolution. Not perfection but progression. Not one-time decision but daily recognition.

Which dimension needs your carrier declaration tonight? Where do you need to shift from visitor to carrier? Where are you operating RESTless (with LESS) instead of RESTful (FULL)? Which of the Five Daily Rhythms will you activate first tomorrow morning?

Check yourself right now: RESTful or RESTless? Your answer determines everything.

Are you FULL of Christ (RESTful and faithful) or operating with LESS of Christ (RESTless and faithless)? This diagnostic cuts through every religious pretense, every spiritual performance, every attempt to appear more mature than you are.

The same God who spoke face-to-face with Moses as a friend, who filled Solomon's temple with uncontainable glory, who promised EMMANUEL—God WITH us always—that same God has made you His permanent dwelling place.

You are no longer spiritually homeless. You ARE His home.

"You don't visit the secret place. You ARE the secret place."

"Stop seeking encounters—you ARE one. Stop visiting presence—you CARRY it."

"From homeless to home. From RESTless to RESTful. From LESS to FULL. From visitor to carrier."

Not a building. Not a visit. A covenant Partner who moved in—and never moved out. I carry Presence.

Your hands reaching for that glass of water—no longer neglected but received. Like His presence. Always there. Always available. Always WITH you. You drink deeply, knowing you're not just consuming water. You're practicing carrier theology.

Receive. Be filled. Dwell. Carry.

Week 3 Continues: PROPEL into Destiny - Presence EMBODIED

Tomorrow: Day 16 PROTECTION begins. Dwelling presence becomes divine defense. Carrying God means His protection goes WITH you everywhere. What you carry automatically protects you.

FADE OUT: Your hands closing the journal, not documenting distance but declaring identity: "I am no longer spiritually homeless. I AM HIS HOME. From RESTless to RESTful. From LESS to FULL. Check: I am RESTful because I am FULL."

WEEK 3: PROPEL (7P)

THE PRESENCE CARRIER AWAKENING IS COMPLETE.
SOAP JOURNAL — DAY 15
S (Scripture): Write Exodus 33:14. Circle "WITH you." Underline "My Presence will go." Add Psalm 91:1 about dwelling in the secret place.

O (Observation): Are you trying to visit God's presence or recognizing you carry it? Are you spiritually homeless or dwelling in Him? Are you operating as consumer or carrier today? Where have you been seeking His hand instead of His face? Most important: Are you RESTful (FULL of Christ) or RESTless (LESS of Christ)? Which of the Five Daily Rhythms resonates most? Which rhythm will you activate first?

A (Application): Practice declaring "I don't visit the secret place—I AM the secret place" throughout today. Practice the diagnostic: "Am I RESTful or RESTless right now?" Choose one dimension for carrier transformation. Activate Rhythm 1 (AWAKEN) tomorrow morning. Set three Selah alarms for Rhythm 3 (PAUSE). Designate your sacred space for Rhythm 4. Text someone: "Day 15. Learning I don't visit God's presence—I carry it. From homeless to home. From RESTless to RESTful."

P (Prayer): "Father, I choose Your face over Your hand. Transform me from presence consumer to presence carrier, from visitor to permanent dweller, from spiritually homeless to being Your home, from RESTless to RESTful, from LESS to FULL. SHEKINAH glory lives in me. Your presence goes WITH me everywhere. I activate The Carrier Lifestyle—Five Daily Rhythms. I am no longer homeless—I AM Your home. In Jesus' name."

TODAY'S BREAKTHROUGH MARKER: How did shifting from "seeking God's presence" to "carrying God's presence" change your approach to challenges today? How did recognizing you're no longer spiritually homeless but ARE His home transform your identity? Where did you catch yourself being RESTless (operating with LESS) and shift to RESTful (FULL of Christ)? Which Daily Rhythm will you implement first? What specific place will you carry presence into this week?

TOMORROW'S EXPECTATION: Based on today's presence foundation, how will carrying God's dwelling create automatic divine protection in every situation? If you ARE His home and He dwells in you permanently, what does that mean for your safety?

DAY 15 COMPLETE: PRESENCE CARRIER ACTIVATED
SPIRITUAL HOMELESSNESS ENDED. FROM RESTLESS TO RESTFUL. FROM LESS TO FULL. FROM VISITOR TO CARRIER. FROM HOMELESS TO HOME. THE CARRIER LIFESTYLE: FIVE DAILY RHYTHMS ACTIVATED. SHEKINAH DWELLING ACTIVATED. PANIM FACE-TO-FACE. READY FOR PROTECTION.

DAY 16 — PROTECTION

From Fighting to Dwelling Under the Shadow: Orphans build walls. Sons dwell under wings.

> *"He who dwells in the secret place of the Most High shall abide under the shadow of the Almighty."*
> — Psalm 91:1

WEEK 3 — PROPEL: Accelerating into Destiny

Day 16 of 21. You've learned you're a carrier (Day 15)—now discover what automatically activates when you dwell. Protection isn't what you earn through fighting. It's what flows from where you position yourself. Today, heaven shifts you from orphan defending to son dwelling.

ENCOUNTER: WHEN THE FEATHER OUTWEIGHS THE FORTRESS

4:30 AM. Day 16 of your fast. Your hands are bloody from building walls that never stop the attacks. Not literal blood. The invisible kind. Soul-scraped, marrow-deep exhaustion from sixteen days of fasting combined with years of defending yourself against threats that know your address, your vulnerabilities, your breaking points.

The fortress you've constructed—brick by prayer brick, stone by fasting stone—towers around you. Impressive architecture. Years of spiritual construction. Walls to keep threats out. Barriers to block attacks. Fortifications to survive what's targeting you.

Yet the attacks keep coming. Penetrating somehow. Finding cracks. Exploiting weaknesses. Every wall you built to keep threats out has locked you in. You're not just protected—you're imprisoned. Defending has become your identity. Fighting has become your lifestyle. Exhaustion has become your normal.

On your nightstand sits the journal—pages filled with battle plans, defensive strategies, warfare prayers. Beside it, something you haven't noticed in sixteen days of frantic fortification. A single feather. Small. Almost weightless. Resting on top of all your defensive documentation like a whisper interrupting a war strategy meeting.

You don't remember it appearing. Don't know how long it's been there. But something about its presence—fragile, light, almost laughable next to your war plans—arrests your attention.

One feather versus years of walls.

Heaven speaks through the contradiction: "Orphans build walls. Sons dwell under wings."

The feather didn't build itself into a fortress. It simply fell from the place where you're supposed to be positioned: under the shadow of wings that never fail.

You've been exhausting yourself constructing barriers when you could have been resting under feathers.

"He shall cover you with His feathers, and under His wings you shall take refuge" (Psalm 91:4).

The fortress you built? Orphan thinking. Performance protection. Defending through your effort, your vigilance, your constant fighting.

The feather on your journal? Son reality. Positional protection. Covered through His provision, His watchfulness, His constant presence.

Same threats. Different approach. Orphans fight for protection. Sons rest in protection. Orphans perform. Sons position.

Protection isn't about how hard you fight—it's about where you dwell.

This is your Day 16 awakening: The shift from fighting to dwelling. From walls to wings. From performance to position. From orphan exhausted to son rested.

One fragile feather outweighs all your fortifications.

REVELATION: THE PROTECTION PARADIGM THAT CHANGES EVERYTHING

Let me speak to the exhaustion threatening to break you. That sense that you're one attack away from collapse. That feeling like you're constantly defending, constantly vigilant, constantly fighting battles that never seem to end.

You're not failing. You're just operating from the wrong position.

The Orphan vs. Son Protection Paradigm

ELEMENT	ORPHAN (Fighting/Defending)	SON (Dwelling/Protected)
POSITION	Outside the secret place, exposed	Inside the secret place, hidden
POSTURE	Standing in my own strength	Resting under His wings
MINDSET	"I must defend myself"	"He defends me while I dwell"
WEAPONS	Self-constructed walls	Divine armor (Ephesians 6:10-18)
STRATEGY	Fight harder, pray longer, perform better	Position correctly, dwell consistently
LOCATION	Battlefield (exhausting)	Secret place (restful)
OUTCOME	Exhaustion from constant vigilance	Rest while Keeper watches (Psalm 121:3-4)
SECURITY	Dependent on my performance	Secured by His covenant
COVERING	Walls I build (crumble under pressure)	Wings He provides (Psalm 91:4)
PROTECTION TYPE	Reactive (respond after attack)	Proactive (shadow covers before attack)
CONFIDENCE	"If I fight hard enough..."	"He who is in me is greater" (1 John 4:4)
IDENTITY	Defender (self-reliant)	Dwelling (God-dependent)
RESULT	Vulnerability despite effort	Security through position

Here's what makes you an orphan or son—it's not your activity but your motivation:
ORPHANS and **SONS** both pray. Both fast. Both seek God. Both face battles.
The difference?
ORPHANS pray and fast to **EARN** protection through performance.
SONS pray and fast to **POSITION** themselves in the secret place where protection is automatic.

Fasting and prayer are not performance—they're positioning. They're not payment for protection—they're posture in the secret place where protection flows naturally.

This is why you're fasting today—Day 16 of 21 days. Not to earn God's favor. Not to perform your way into protection. But to position yourself in the dwelling place where His shadow automatically covers.

Daniel's 21-Day Fast: The Positioning Model

When Daniel fasted 21 days (Daniel 10), watch the timeline:

Day 1: Daniel prays. *"From the first day that you set your heart to understand...your words were heard"* (Daniel 10:12).

Days 2-21: Spiritual warfare in the heavenlies. The prince of Persia withstands the angel bringing Daniel's answer.

Day 21: Breakthrough manifests. Michael arrives. Victory accomplished.

Here's the revelation: God heard Daniel's prayer on **Day One**. The answer was released **immediately**. Spiritual warfare delayed manifestation for 21 days. Daniel's 21-day fast wasn't **earning** the answer—it was **positioning** him in the secret place while heaven fought the battle.

Applied to you: From Day One of your fast, heaven heard. The answer is in motion. Spiritual forces may be delaying manifestation, but your fasting isn't earning the breakthrough—it's positioning you in the dwelling place where protection covers you while the battle rages.

Sons fast and pray not to earn protection but to position themselves in the secret place.

Same activities. Radically different motivations.

Protection flows from position, not performance.

THE THREE PROTECTION TYPES: UNDERSTANDING GOD'S METHODS

Many believers struggle when protection doesn't look like they expected. "Why did God protect Peter but not Stephen?" "Why prevention sometimes, survival other times, and martyrdom occasionally?"

Understanding the three protection types resolves the tension:

Protection Type 1: FROM (Complete Prevention)

Promise: "This won't touch you"

Biblical Examples:
- Peter walks free from prison (Acts 12:6-11) — chains fall, guards sleep, gates open
- Hebrew boys emerge untouched from furnace (Daniel 3:27) — no smell of smoke
- David protected from Saul's spear (1 Samuel 18:11) — twice it missed

Testimony: Jamaica 2020 — Death came calling, one word ("Jesus") stopped it, baby slept through it

Application: Sometimes God prevents the attack from ever reaching you. Complete protection. Total deliverance. No damage.

Protection Type 2: THROUGH (Supernatural Survival)

Promise: "This touches but doesn't take you"

Biblical Examples:
- Daniel survives lion's den (Daniel 6:22) — lions present but mouths shut
- Paul bitten by viper (Acts 28:5) — venom touches but doesn't kill

- Job loses everything (Job 1-2) — Satan touches possessions and body but not life

Testimony: Canada 3-year attack — Attacks continued but couldn't reach soul, ministry grew during assault, dwelling conquered what fighting couldn't

Application: Sometimes God allows the trial but supernaturally sustains you through it. The fire burns around but not within. Survival against odds.

Protection Type 3: UNTO (Graduation Through Glory)

Promise: "This graduates you to glory"

Biblical Examples:
- Stephen stoned (Acts 7:55-56) — sees heaven opened while stones fly
- James beheaded (Acts 12:2) — first apostle martyred, church explodes
- Joseph's pit (Genesis 37-50) — betrayal becomes pathway to palace

Application: Sometimes what looks like failure is actually graduation. God protects your eternal destiny while allowing temporary vessel damage. Death becomes promotion. Suffering becomes glory.

All three are protection. All three are love. All three flow from dwelling.

The question isn't "Which protection type is best?" The question is "Am I dwelling in the secret place where God determines which type I need?"

Through. Not stuck in. Through.

BIBLICAL FOUNDATION: THE THREE PROTECTION PSALMS

Three Psalms form your complete protection theology. Not multiple methods—one position with three perspectives:

Psalm 91: WHERE to Dwell

"He who dwells in the secret place of the Most High shall abide under the shadow of the Almighty" (v.1).

The foundation: Secret place dwelling activates shadow covering. Position determines protection.

The progression: Dwell → Abide → Shadow covers. Not occasional visits but continuous habitation.

The promise: Verses 3-13 detail comprehensive protection from every threat—plague, terror, arrow, pestilence, lion, serpent.

The condition: Verse 1. Dwelling isn't optional add-on—it's foundational requirement.

Psalm 23: WHO You're With

"The Lord is my shepherd...though I walk through the valley of the shadow of death, I will fear no evil; for You are with me" (v.1,4).

The comfort: Not protection FROM valleys but protection THROUGH valleys. Not absence of danger but presence of Protector.

The confidence: "I will fear no evil" — not because threats don't exist but because He's WITH me in them.

The companionship: "You are with me" — same theology as Day 15. EMMANUEL. God WITH us always.

Psalm 121: HOW LONG He Watches

"He who keeps you will not slumber. Behold, He who keeps Israel shall neither slumber nor sleep" (v.3-4).

The vigilance: Your Keeper never sleeps. While you rest, He watches. While you dwell, He defends.

The scope: "The Lord shall preserve you from all evil; He shall preserve your soul" (v.7). Comprehensive coverage.

The duration: "The Lord shall preserve your going out and your coming in from this time forth, and even forevermore" (v.8). Permanent protection for dwelling sons.

Together they answer:
- **WHERE:** Secret place (Psalm 91)
- **WHO:** The Lord WITH you (Psalm 23)
- **HOW LONG:** Forever, never sleeping (Psalm 121)

Position correctly. He handles the rest.

THE TESTIMONY: FROM WALLS TO WINGS

I need to tell you about the progression from orphan fighting to son dwelling—a journey from exhaustion to rest, walls to wings.

Jamaica 2020: When Death Came Calling

My baby Nick, only weeks old, lying beside me as I studied. Nine days earlier, a woman sent a message: "You have 9 days to live." I dismissed it. Kept living. Yet God was preparing protection.

Day 9 arrived. Suddenly, I felt myself falling—spiritually plummeting into darkness. My body went numb. Cold spreading from fingertips inward. I knew: I was dying.

In that terrifying descent, only one word surfaced: "Jesus."

Whispered in my mind. One word. Five letters. Everything.

Instantly—the falling stopped. Like spiritual brakes engaging.

My phone rang. My Christian friend, breathless: "A pastor just prayed and stopped mid-prayer. He said the spirit of death just came to your house. We're pleading the blood right now."

Death had come calling. Day 9, exactly as promised. But one name—Jesus—activated NATSAL [nah-TSAL]: violent rescue.

My baby never even stirred. He slept through death's arrival and departure.

That's protection Type 1: FROM. Complete prevention. The attack came but couldn't touch. I wasn't fighting—I was dwelling. And from that dwelling position, one word released supernatural deliverance.

Canada 2021-2024: Three Years Under Attack

Three years later, different battle. Public attack. Ministry questioned. Character assassinated. Online campaign against everything we'd built. Relentless. Calculated. Exhausting.

Year One: Fighting in flesh

I spent months defending publicly. Every attack, I countered. Every lie, I corrected. Building walls with words. Constructing defenses with explanations. The more I fought, the worse it became.

I was performing protection—exhausting myself through effort.

One night, my son found me broken on the floor—the same baby who'd slept through death in Jamaica, now a young man watching his mother crumble under assault.

His question pierced me: "Mom, where's your Bible?"

As he read Psalm 91 over me, the Lord spoke: "Are you dwelling or defending?"

I'd abandoned the secret place for the battlefield. Stopped being son, started being orphan. Trading wings for walls. Trading rest for fight.

Year Two: Positioned in spirit

Daily at 4:30 AM, I established new discipline. Not new warfare prayers. New positioning practice.

"I dwell in the secret place of the Most High. I abide under the shadow of the Almighty. No weapon formed against me shall prosper."

Not fighting. Dwelling. Not performing. Positioning.

The shift was immediate. Attacks continued but couldn't reach my soul. Like arrows hitting invisible shield. Truth emerged without my voice defending it. Ministry grew during the assault. Doors opened while opposition raged. Peace ruled while storms surrounded.

I wasn't working harder—I was positioned correctly.

Year Three: Victory manifested

The campaign eventually ended. Not because I fought it to conclusion. It simply collapsed under the weight of dwelling truth versus fighting lies.

Ministry expanded nationally. Reputation restored with increased credibility. Platforms multiplied. Three years of opposition couldn't penetrate one secret place consistently occupied.

That's protection Type 2: THROUGH. The attack came and stayed. But dwelling position meant it touched circumstances while missing soul. I survived what should have destroyed. Not because I fought better but because I positioned correctly.

The generational circle:

The baby who slept through death in Jamaica became the man who read God's Word over crisis in Canada. From protected infant to protecting intercessor.

What God protects in you flows through you to the next generation.

HEBREW VOCABULARY: YOUR PROTECTION ADDRESS

Six Hebrew terms define your dwelling protection. Not academic study—your spiritual coordinates.

CHACAH [khah-SAH] — *To flee for protection, to take refuge urgently*

Used in Psalm 91:4: "Under His wings you shall take refuge [CHACAH]." The picture: small bird fleeing predator, diving under mother's wing just in time. Urgent refuge. Last-second safety. This is instinctive protection—you don't think, you run to the covering that never fails.

SETHER [SAY-ther] — *Secret hiding place, concealment*

Psalm 91:1: "He who dwells in the secret place [SETHER]." Not public visibility but hidden security. The place where enemies can't find you because you're concealed in Him. Your secret location isn't geographic—it's positional. Hidden in Christ.

TSINNAH [tsin-NAH] — *Large shield, wall-sized protection*

Psalm 91:4: "His truth shall be your shield [TSINNAH]." Not small shield blocking single arrows—massive wall-sized protection covering entire body. When you dwell in truth, you're protected by what He says, not by what circumstances show.

MAGEN [mah-GANE] — *God Himself as shield, divine protection*

Genesis 15:1: "I am your shield [MAGEN]." Not just God providing shield—God BEING your shield. The Protector becomes the protection. You're not holding defensive weapon—you're surrounded by divine Person who shields completely.

SHAMAR [shah-MAR] — *To keep, guard, watch over with intent*

Psalm 121:3-4: "He who keeps [SHAMAR] you will not slumber." Active guarding. Intentional watching. Your Keeper never sleeps, never takes breaks, never misses threats. While you rest in dwelling, He maintains vigilance over covering.

NATSAL [nah-TSAL] — *To snatch away, violently rescue*

Psalm 91:3: "He shall deliver [NATSAL] you from the snare of the fowler." Not gentle removal but violent rescue. When death came calling in Jamaica, one word—Jesus—activated NATSAL. Snatched from danger. Violently rescued. Often happens when you're resting, not striving.

These six terms aren't vocabulary—they're your protection coordinates. When you dwell (SETHER), you're urgently covered (CHACAH), massively shielded (TSINNAH), divinely surrounded (MAGEN), constantly watched (SHAMAR), and violently rescued when needed (NATSAL).

All six activate from one position: dwelling.

BIBLICAL CHAMPIONS: YOUR INHERITANCE OF PROTECTION

Four champions model dwelling protection. Their legacy becomes your reality.

Daniel: The Den That Couldn't Consume

Thrown into lions' den for praying (Daniel 6). *"My God sent His angel and shut the lions' mouths"* (v.22). Morning check reveals: *"No injury was found on him, because he believed in his God"* (v.23).

Daniel didn't fight lions. He dwelled in God. Position activated protection. Mouths shut not because Daniel defended but because he dwelled.

Hebrew Boys: The Fire That Couldn't Burn

Shadrach, Meshach, Abednego thrown into furnace (Daniel 3). Emerged completely untouched—not singed hair, affected garments, or smell of smoke (v.27). The fourth Man walked WITH them in flames.

They didn't fight fire. They dwelled in presence. EMMANUEL in furnace. Protection Type: FROM. Complete prevention of damage despite being in danger.

David: The Keeper Who Never Sleeps

"I will both lie down in peace, and sleep; for You alone, O Lord, make me dwell in safety" (Psalm 4:8). David faced Saul's pursuit, Absalom's rebellion, constant threats. Yet slept peacefully because he knew: dwelling position means the Keeper watches while son rests.

Orphans stay awake guarding themselves. Sons sleep while Father guards them.

Peter: The Prison That Couldn't Hold

Arrested, chained between soldiers, scheduled for execution (Acts 12:6). Yet sleeping so soundly angels had to strike him awake (v.7). Chains fell, guards slept, gates opened. Protected FROM execution while sleeping through rescue.

NATSAL while resting. This is dwelling protection—heaven works while sons sleep.

"Their extraordinary is your ordinary. Their den is your dwelling place. Their protection is your inheritance."

THE TEN-LAYER PROTECTION SYSTEM

When you dwell in the secret place, ten layers activate simultaneously. Not earned sequentially—received positionally.

1. PRESENCE PROTECTION
"Fear not, for I am with you" (Isaiah 41:10) — EMMANUEL theology. He's WITH you always, in every battle, never leaving.

2. ANGELIC PROTECTION
"He shall give His angels charge over you" (Psalm 91:11) — Assigned angels guard dwelling sons.

3. PERIMETER SECURITY
"I will be a wall of fire all around" (Zechariah 2:5) — 360-degree protection, front guard (Isaiah 45:2), rear guard (Isaiah 52:12).

4. NAME PROTECTION
"The name of the Lord is a strong tower" (Proverbs 18:10) — Jesus stops every assignment. One word activated deliverance in Jamaica.

5. BLOOD PROTECTION
"When I see the blood, I will pass over you" (Exodus 12:13) — Death passes over what the Blood marks. Applied by dwelling, not performing.

6. COVENANT PROTECTION
"No weapon formed against you shall prosper" (Isaiah 54:17) — Not absence of weapons but failure of weapons. Attacks come but cannot succeed against covenant sons.

7. OFFENSIVE AUTHORITY
"I give you authority to trample on serpents and scorpions" (Luke 10:19) — Not just defensive but offensive. You don't just survive—you trample. Bronze wall enemies cannot breach (Jeremiah 1:18).

8. TRUTH PROTECTION
"His truth shall be your shield" (Psalm 91:4) — What He says outweighs what circumstances show. TSINNAH—wall-sized shield of divine truth.

9. FAITH PROTECTION
"Above all, taking the shield of faith" (Ephesians 6:16) — Quenches fiery darts. Active protection through active trust.

10. DIVINE EQUIPMENT
"Put on the whole armor of God" (Ephesians 6:11) — Belt, breastplate, shoes, shield, helmet, sword. Complete spiritual armor for complete spiritual warfare.

All ten layers activate from one position: dwelling in the secret place.

You're not earning protection through performance. You're receiving protection through positioning.

Shadow already exists. Tree is planted. Protection is available. Your fasting positions you underneath it.

ACTIVATION: THE SIX DIMENSIONS OF PROTECTION

DIMENSION	ORPHAN (Fighting)	SON (Dwelling)	EVIDENCE OF SHIFT
SPIRITUAL	Exhausting myself through warfare	Resting in covering warfare	Peace during spiritual attack
MENTAL	Defending every thought anxiously	Shielded by truth (TSINNAH)	Clarity despite mental assault
EMOTIONAL	Reacting to every attack emotionally	Emotions covered under wings	Stability through emotional storms
PHYSICAL	Fighting illness through performance	Body protected through dwelling	Supernatural health/healing
FINANCIAL	Defending resources anxiously	Provision flows from position	Increase during opposition
RELATIONAL	Building walls to keep people out	Wings cover all relationships	Restored connections, healed bonds

Protection transforms every dimension when you shift from orphan fighting to son dwelling.

FOCUS AREA PROTECTION PRAYERS

Choose your primary breakthrough area and declare:

For SPIRITUAL Focus: "Father, I reject orphan mentality that exhausts me through constant spiritual warfare. I reject building walls when You offer wings. I receive CHACAH—urgent refuge under Your covering. Transform me from fighting to dwelling. I take my position in SETHER—the secret place where ten layers activate automatically. Therefore, I stop defending and start dwelling in [specific spiritual battle], knowing protection flows from position, not performance."

For MENTAL Focus: "Father, I reject defending every anxious thought, building mental walls against every attack. I receive TSINNAH—Your truth as wall-sized shield covering my entire mind. Transform my thinking from orphan defending to son dwelling. Mind of Christ guards my thoughts from dwelling position. Therefore, I release [specific mental battle] under Your wings, knowing Your truth shields me automatically when I dwell correctly."

For EMOTIONAL Focus: "Father, I reject reacting emotionally to every attack, exhausting myself through emotional defense. I receive covering under Your wings—emotions protected not through my performance but through my position. Transform my emotions from RESTless fighting to RESTful dwelling. SHAMAR watches over my heart while I rest. Therefore, I bring [specific emotional wound] under Your covering, knowing dwelling protects what fighting cannot."

For PHYSICAL Focus: "Father, I reject orphan thinking that says I must fight every physical threat through my effort. I receive NATSAL—violent rescue even while I'm resting. Transform my body from battlefield to dwelling place. Your presence inhabits my physical form. Therefore I position my body under Your shadow regarding [specific health battle], knowing You protect the temple You inhabit."

For FINANCIAL Focus: "Father, I reject anxiety that makes me defend resources through walls of fear. I receive provision that flows from dwelling position. Transform my finances from orphan scarcity to son abundance. When I dwell correctly, You defend my provision. Therefore I release [specific financial pressure] under Your wings, knowing dwelling activates provision protection automatically."

For RELATIONAL Focus: "Father, I reject building relational walls to keep people out, exhausting myself through self-protection. I receive MAGEN—You as my shield in every relationship. Transform my connections from orphan defending to son dwelling. EMMANUEL means You're WITH me in every interaction. Therefore I bring [specific relationship] under Your covering, knowing Your wings protect me in connections I cannot control."

RESISTANCE REALITY CHECK: BREAKING THE LIES

What hell whispers to keep you building walls instead of dwelling under wings:

LIE #1: "PROTECTION REQUIRES CONSTANT FIGHTING"

Hell whispers: "If you stop defending, you'll be destroyed. Rest means vulnerability. Let your guard down and attacks will penetrate."

Heaven's Response: "Peter was sleeping between soldiers the night before execution (Acts 12:6). Rest while I work. SHAMAR never sleeps—I watch while you rest. Dwelling isn't passivity—it's positioned security."

Break it: "I reject exhausting vigilance! Protection flows from dwelling, not defending! From walls to wings!"

LIE #2: "YOUR FASTING EARNS PROTECTION"

Hell whispers: "Fast harder to earn God's favor. Pray longer to convince Him to protect you. Your performance determines your covering."

Heaven's Response: "Daniel's prayer was heard Day One (Daniel 10:12). Your fasting isn't earning the answer—it's positioning you in the secret place while I fight the battle. From Day One, heaven heard. Protection flows from position, not performance."

Break it: "I reject performance protection! Fasting is positioning, not earning! I dwell in automatic covering!"

LIE #3: "YOU'RE UNPROTECTED WHEN ATTACKS COME"

Hell whispers: "If God was protecting you, this wouldn't be happening. Attacks prove absence of covering. Trials mean God's abandoned you."

Heaven's Response: "Three protection types: FROM (prevention), THROUGH (survival), UNTO (graduation). All three are protection. Hebrew boys were IN fire yet untouched. I protect through trials, not just from trials. Shadow covers before attack arrives."

Break it: "I reject the lie that trials mean no protection! I'm covered FROM, THROUGH, and UNTO! Wings never fail!"

LIE #4: "DWELLING IS PASSIVE WEAKNESS"

Hell whispers: "Real warriors fight. Dwelling is retreat. Positioning is excuse for not engaging. Sons who rest are cowards who quit."

Heaven's Response: "David slept peacefully while enemies pursued (Psalm 4:8). Peter slept between soldiers (Acts 12:6). Dwelling isn't weakness—it's positioned strength. I give offensive authority to trample (Luke 10:19). You're not just defended—you're dangerous."

Break it: "I reject calling dwelling weakness! Positioned sons terrify their terror! I trample from dwelling place!"

LIE #5: "ONE FEATHER CAN'T OUTWEIGH YOUR WALLS"

Hell whispers: "Your fortifications are necessary. That fragile feather is no match for real threats. Walls are wisdom. Wings are wishful thinking."

Heaven's Response: "One feather proves position. Walls you build crumble under pressure. Wings I provide never fail. The fragile proves the powerful. Weakness displays My strength (2 Corinthians 12:9). Stop building what I never asked you to construct."

Break it: "I reject trusting my walls over Your wings! One fragile feather outweighs all my fortifications! Position defeats performance!"

"Protection isn't absence of battle—it's assurance of victory. From orphan walls to son wings."

THE DWELLING DECLARATION

Stand in your position. Feel His shadow. Declare your covering:

"I declare I am no longer an orphan building walls—I am a SON dwelling under wings!

I reject exhausting myself through constant defending. I reject building fortifications through my performance. I reject the lie that protection requires my vigilance. I stop fighting for covering and start resting IN covering!

I dwell in SETHER—the secret place of the Most High! I urgently flee to CHACAH—refuge under Your wings! I'm shielded by TSINNAH—wall-sized protection of Your truth! I'm surrounded by MAGEN—You Yourself as my shield! I'm watched by SHAMAR—Keeper who never sleeps! I'm rescued by NATSAL—violently snatched from danger!

TEN LAYERS activate from ONE position: **Layer 1:** PRESENCE—You're WITH me always (Isaiah 41:10). **Layer 2:** ANGELS—Assigned and guarding (Psalm 91:11). **Layer 3:** PERIMETER—Wall of fire, front guard, rear guard (Zechariah 2:5). **Layer 4:** NAME—Jesus stops every assignment. **Layer 5:** BLOOD—Death passes over what Blood marks. **Layer 6:** COVENANT—No weapon prospers (Isaiah 54:17). **Layer 7:** AUTHORITY—I trample serpents (Luke 10:19). **Layer 8:** TRUTH—What You say shields me (Psalm 91:4). **Layer 9:** FAITH—Shield quenches darts (Ephesians 6:16)**Layer 10:** ARMOR—Fully equipped for warfare (Ephesians 6:11)

Like Daniel, my dwelling shuts lions' mouths!

Like Hebrew boys, fire cannot burn what dwells in presence!

Like David, I sleep while Keeper watches!

Like Peter, I rest while heaven rescues!

I am not unprotected—I'm just repositioning!

From orphan exhaustion to son rest!

From walls I build to wings He provides!

From defending through performance to dwelling in position!

Protection Type 1: FROM—Some attacks prevented completely
Protection Type 2: THROUGH—Some trials survived supernaturally
Protection Type 3: UNTO—Some suffering graduates to glory

All three are protection! All three flow from dwelling!

My fasting isn't earning covering—it's positioning me IN covering! From Day One, heaven heard! The answer is in motion! While I dwell, heaven fights!

I am a DWELLING SON, covered by WINGS that never fail! Amen!"

BREAKTHROUGH PRAYER

"Father God, CHACAH where I urgently flee, MAGEN who shields me completely,

Forgive me for building walls You never asked me to construct. For exhausting myself defending what You promised to cover. For orphan thinking that trusts my fortifications over Your wings. For fighting for protection instead of resting IN protection.

Thank You that one fragile feather outweighs all my walls. That position defeats performance. That dwelling activates what fighting cannot achieve.

Thank You for the three protection types—FROM, THROUGH, UNTO. That all three are love. All three are covering. All three flow from dwelling in the secret place.

Thank You that Daniel's 21-day fast models mine. Day One, You heard. The answer released. While spiritual warfare delays manifestation, my fasting positions me where Your shadow automatically covers.

Right now, I stop building and start dwelling:
SPIRITUAL: I position myself in SETHER—no more exhausting warfare, just dwelling security
MENTAL: TSINNAH shields my thoughts—truth outweighs circumstances
EMOTIONAL: Your wings cover my heart—SHAMAR watches while I rest
PHYSICAL: My body is Your temple—NATSAL rescues even while I sleep
FINANCIAL: Dwelling activates provision—covenant protection over resources
RELATIONAL: EMMANUEL in every connection—You're WITH me in relationships

Transform me from orphan to son. From walls to wings. From defending to dwelling. From performance to position. From exhaustion to rest.

Activate all ten layers right now. Presence, angels, perimeter, Name, Blood, covenant, authority, truth, faith, armor—all covering me because I dwell correctly.

I am not unprotected. I'm just repositioning. From fighting to dwelling. From battlefield to secret place. From orphan exhausted to son rested.

In Jesus' mighty name, the walls come down and the wings cover me completely. I dwell under the shadow of the Almighty. Amen."

GENERATIONAL BREAKTHROUGH PRAYER

"Father, I break every curse that made my family orphans instead of sons. Every generational pattern of defensive living, wall-building, constant fighting. Every cycle that said 'you must defend yourself because no one else will.'

I declare: That pattern stops with me. My children will not inherit orphan anxiety. My lineage will not continue exhausting vigilance. The walls end here. The wings begin now.

Like the baby who slept through death in Jamaica and became the man reading Scripture over crisis in Canada—what You protect in me flows through me to the next generation. From protected to protector. From covered to covering.

I decree over my children: They will dwell, not defend. Rest, not fight. Position, not perform. They will know they're sons, not orphans. They will run to CHACAH—urgent refuge—instead of building walls. They will sleep under SHAMAR—watchful Keeper—instead of staying awake in anxiety.

Ten layers cover not just me but my lineage. Presence, angels, perimeter, Name, Blood, covenant, authority, truth, faith, armor—all protecting the next generation because I positioned correctly in this generation.

From orphan curse to son blessing. From walls to wings. From generation to generation, we dwell under Your shadow.

In Jesus' name, generational protection established. Amen."

MEMORIAL 1: PSALM 91 BIBLE ACTIVATION

This isn't just reading—it's establishing permanent record. You'll create a memorial in your Bible you'll reference for years.

What You Need: Your Bible, opened to Psalm 91. Pen (not pencil—this is permanent). 15 minutes uninterrupted.

Step 1: Read Psalm 91 Aloud. Stand. Read all 16 verses aloud. Let each promise sink in. This is your dwelling address. Your protection coordinates.

Step 2: Write in the Margins

Top of the page: Write today's date and "The day I stopped building walls and started dwelling under wings"

Left margin: List what you're currently fighting: Spiritual attacks. Mental battles. Emotional wounds. Physical threats. Financial pressures. Relational conflicts. Be specific. Name them. This is what you're bringing under His wings today.

Right margin: Write what you're: Praying for. Fasting out of (what you're leaving). Fasting into (what you're entering). Your root fear (what drives the wall-building).

Bottom of the page: Sign and date

Step 3: Speak the Name and the Blood. With your hand on the page, declare: "In the name of Jesus—every attack listed in these margins is stopped. The Name that delivered me stops every assignment against me. I plead the Blood of Jesus over everything written here. The Blood that marked doorposts in Egypt marks my dwelling today. Death passes over what the Blood covers."

Step 4: Make the Dwelling Declaration. Place both hands on Psalm 91. Declare: "I reject building walls through my effort. I choose dwelling under wings through Your provision. These margins list my orphan fighting. This psalm declares my son dwelling. From this day forward, I don't defend through performance—I rest in position. I am a dwelling son covered by wings that never fail."

Step 5: Personalize Verses 14-16. In the margin beside verses 14-16, rewrite them with YOUR name: *"Because [Your Name] has set their love upon Me, therefore I will deliver them; I will set them on high, because they* *have known My name. [Your Name] shall call upon Me, and I will answer them; I will be with them in trouble; I will deliver them and honor them. With long life I will satisfy [Your Name], and show them My salvation."*

Step 6: Listen and Respond. Sit in silence for 3 minutes. Ask: "Holy Spirit, what are You saying about my protection?" Write what you hear in the margin. Date it. This becomes prophetic word you'll reference.

Step 7: Seal the Memorial. At the bottom, write your final statement: "On [date], I stopped being orphan and started being son. From walls to wings. From fighting to dwelling. This page is my memorial. Every time I open here, I remember: protection flows from position, not performance."

Sign it. Date it.

Keep your Bible open to this page on your nightstand tonight. Let it be the last thing you see before sleeping and first thing you see upon waking. You're establishing dwelling as your new default.

This memorial becomes permanent testimony. Years from now, you'll open to Psalm 91 and see your handwriting, the date, the battles you were fighting, and God's faithfulness to cover you when you stopped building walls and started dwelling under wings.

MEMORIAL 2: THE FEATHER

This is your daily reminder that position defeats performance, that one fragile feather outweighs all your fortifications.

Your Assignment: Within 24 hours, find a feather. Yard, park, store, anywhere. When you find it, receive it as prophetic symbol: "Orphans build walls. Sons dwell under wings."

Place it where you'll see it daily: Beside your Bible. On your desk. In your car. By your mirror.

Every morning, practice this: Touch the feather. Speak: "This reminds me: I don't build walls—I dwell under wings. I don't defend through performance—I rest under feathers. One fragile feather outweighs all my fortifications. Protection flows from position, not performance. I am a dwelling son covered by wings that never fail."

In crisis moments: When attacks come, hold the feather. Remember: "The One whose wing this represents covers me completely. I don't fight—I dwell. I don't defend—I rest. His wings never fail. His shadow never moves. I am positioned correctly."

The feather becomes your physical anchor: Every time you see it, remember the Day 16 shift from walls to wings, orphan to son, fighting to dwelling.

"One fragile feather outweighs all my fortifications."

CLOSING: FROM EXHAUSTION TO REST

You awakened with bloody hands from building walls that never stopped attacks. Sixteen days of fasting combined with years of defending yourself through orphan effort. Exhausted. Ready to collapse.

Tonight you rest knowing the truth that changes everything: Protection flows from position, not performance.

The feather that appeared on your journal—fragile, weightless, almost laughable next to your war plans—wasn't mockery. It was mercy. Heaven's gentle interruption of your exhausting self-defense: "Stop building walls. Start dwelling under wings."

Day 16's revolutionary gift: The shift from orphan fighting to son dwelling.

"Orphans build walls. Sons dwell under wings."

You've marked your Bible. Listed your battles in the margins of Psalm 91. Spoken the Name and the Blood over every threat. Declared dwelling over defending. Your permanent memorial is established.

You've found your feather (or will within 24 hours). Your daily reminder that one fragile piece of evidence outweighs years of fortifications. Position defeats performance.

But the deeper transformation is this: You've stopped exhausting yourself trying to earn through performance what God freely gives through positioning.

This is the fasting theology that resolves everything: Daniel's 21-day fast wasn't earning the answer—it was positioning him in the secret place while heaven fought. Your 16-day fast isn't convincing God to protect you—it's positioning you where His shadow automatically covers.

From Day One, heaven heard. The answer is in motion. Spiritual warfare may be delaying manifestation, but your dwelling position means you're covered while the battle rages.

Three protection types—all from dwelling: FROM: Some attacks prevented completely. THROUGH: Some trials survived supernaturally. UNTO: Some suffering graduated to glory.

All three are protection. All three are love. All three flow from secret place dwelling.

The baby who slept through death in Jamaica. The three years of attacks that couldn't reach my soul in Canada. Different protection types. Same dwelling position. From protected infant to protecting intercessor. What God protects in you flows through you to the next generation.

Tomorrow: Day 17 PURPOSE begins. You'll discover that the same dwelling position that activated protection also activates purpose. Where you dwell determines what you carry and where you're sent.

The shifts you've chosen today—from walls to wings, orphan to son, fighting to dwelling—aren't one-time declarations. They're daily repositioning that compounds into lifestyle transformation.

Which dimension needs dwelling breakthrough tonight? Where are you still building walls instead of resting under wings? Where are you performing for protection instead of positioning in covering?

Touch your feather right now. Or if you haven't found it yet, imagine holding it. Feel how light it is. How fragile. How completely insufficient it would be as defensive weapon.

Yet that's the point. One fragile feather proves the power of position over performance. You don't need heavy walls when you have His wings. You don't need exhausting fortifications when you have His covering.

The same God who shut lions' mouths for dwelling Daniel, who protected Hebrew boys in fire, who let David sleep peacefully while enemies pursued, who freed Peter from prison while he slept—that same God covers you when you stop building and start dwelling.

You are no longer an orphan defending yourself. You are a son dwelling in covering.

"Protection flows from position, not performance."

"One fragile feather outweighs all my fortifications."

"From walls to wings. From orphan to son. From fighting to dwelling."

Orphans build walls. Sons dwell under wings.

Your hands—once bloody from building walls—now gently hold a feather. The contrast is everything. Heavy fortress construction versus weightless wing fragment. Exhausting self-defense versus effortless divine covering.

The walls can come down now. The wings were always there.

Position correctly. He handles the rest.

Week 3 Continues: PROPEL into Destiny - Protection ACTIVATED

Tomorrow: Day 17 PURPOSE begins. Dwelling position activates divine assignments. Where you position determines what you carry and where you're sent. Protected sons discover purpose.

FADE OUT: Your hands closing around the feather, no longer building but receiving: "I don't build walls—I dwell under wings. Protection flows from position, not performance. I am a dwelling son covered by wings that never fail."

THE PROTECTION PARADIGM SHIFT IS COMPLETE.
SOAP JOURNAL — DAY 16

S (Scripture): Write Psalm 91:1. Circle "dwells" and "shadow." Underline "secret place." Add Psalm 91:4 about feathers and wings.

O (Observation): Are you building walls (orphan) or dwelling under wings (son)? Are you fighting for protection or resting in protection? Where have you been performing instead of positioning? Most important: Is your fasting earning covering or positioning you IN covering? Which protection type do you need most today—FROM, THROUGH, or UNTO?

A (Application): Complete Psalm 91 Bible Activation (Memorial 1) within 24 hours. Find your feather (Memorial 2) and place where you'll see it daily. Choose one Focus Area prayer and declare it. Practice touching feather each morning and declaring position over performance. Stop building one specific wall today and instead dwell under His wings. Text someone: "Day 16. Learning orphans build walls, sons dwell under wings. From fighting to dwelling. From walls to wings."

P (Prayer): "Father, I stop building walls through my effort. I start dwelling under wings through Your provision. Transform me from orphan fighting to son dwelling. CHACAH, SETHER, TSINNAH, MAGEN, SHAMAR, NATSAL—all covering me from dwelling position. Ten layers activate because I dwell correctly. From walls to wings. From orphan to son. In Jesus' name."

TODAY'S BREAKTHROUGH MARKER: What wall did you stop building today? What wing covering did you start trusting? How did shifting from fighting to dwelling change your approach to current attack? Where did you choose position over performance? Did you complete the Psalm 91 Bible Activation? Did you find your feather?

TOMORROW'S EXPECTATION: Based on today's protection foundation, how will dwelling position activate divine purpose? If you're covered while you dwell, what assignments might God release that you couldn't carry while building walls?

DAY 16 COMPLETE: PROTECTION ACTIVATED

FROM WALLS TO WINGS. FROM ORPHAN TO SON. FROM FIGHTING TO DWELLING. FROM PERFORMANCE TO POSITION. PSALM 91 MEMORIAL ESTABLISHED. FEATHER REMINDER ACTIVATED. TEN LAYERS COVERING. THREE PROTECTION TYPES RECEIVED. READY FOR PURPOSE.

DAY 17 — PEACE

Your Weapon of Rest: Orphans fight for peace. Heirs fight with peace.

> *"And the peace of God, which surpasses all understanding, will guard your hearts and minds through Christ Jesus."*
> *— Philippians 4:7*

WEEK 3 — PROPEL: Accelerating into Destiny

Day 17 of 21. Yesterday's Protection covered you completely. Today's Peace shatters everything you thought you knew about spiritual warfare.

THE STRATEGIC CONNECTIONS

Day 16's Protection covered you completely. Seven layers activated from one position: dwelling in the secret place. Today reveals what happens when you're fully covered—supernatural calm becomes your warfare strategy. Protected hearts produce peaceful warfare. When you know you're CHACAH [khah-SAH] under wings, SETHER [SAY-ter] in hiding place, MAGEN [mah-GEHN] surrounded by God Himself—anxiety loses its power. Yesterday you learned: don't fight for protection, fight from protection. Today you discover: don't fight for peace, fight with peace. Day 14's Affirmation showed what you believe about yourself. Day 17's Peace demonstrates what you affirm in calm manifests in chaos. Authority from peace creates Kingdom order; authority from panic creates chaos. Week 2 gave you identity. Day 16 covered you with protection. Today weaponizes your rest.

ENCOUNTER: WHEN REST BECOMES RESISTANCE

Your chest constricts like a vise. Breath shallow, heart hammering against ribs like a prisoner desperate for escape. 4:30 AM. Day 17. The alarm shatters silence but can't shatter the warfare tension gripping your soul. Mind already calculating strategies for conflicts you haven't faced yet. The bitter metallic taste of anxiety coating your tongue. Muscles aching from spiritual warfare waged with human weapons instead of heaven's strategy. Seventeen days of pressing in, and you're still fighting like an orphan instead of warring like an heir. "Orphans fight for peace. Heirs fight with peace." You've grown in intimacy, aligned with identity, discovered presence goes with you, learned protection covers you completely. But this morning, exhaustion whispers its seductive lie: "How much longer can you keep fighting like this?"

Here's what heaven is downloading: You've been fighting wrong. Not wrong battles—wrong weapons. The journal lies open, pen poised for another battle report. Another strategy session with anxiety. Another negotiation with chaos. But as you prepare to document desperation, heaven interrupts with revolution: "Peace isn't what you achieve after winning. It's how you win." The pen stops. The chest loosens. The warfare paradigm explodes. "The enemy fears nothing more than a believer who refuses to be moved from peace."

REVELATION: THE WARFARE REVOLUTION

Let me speak directly to that knot strangling your stomach. That situation suffocating your sleep. That racing mind calculating outcomes you can't control. You've been programmed with hell's lie: Peace comes after problems resolve. After enemies retreat. After storms pass. After wars end. Heaven is detonating that deception with revolutionary truth: Peace isn't the absence of war. Peace is your warfare. When God whispers SHALOM over your Day 17 exhaustion, He's not offering rest from battle. He's handing you the weapon that wins battles through rest.

The Biblical Definition

Peace in Scripture is far more than absence of conflict—it is divinely established wholeness, harmony, safety, rest, and flourishing that flows from God's presence and rule. It means being reconciled to God, at rest within yourself, in harmony with others, and living under His Kingdom order. Biblical peace operates in four dimensions simultaneously: Vertical (reconciliation with God), Internal (calmness and stability in heart and mind), Horizontal (unity and harmony in relationships), and External (divine order manifested in circumstances). This isn't wishful thinking. This is covenant reality. Peace is both positional—your reconciled state before God through Christ—and experiential—the ongoing condition of rest, security, and assurance in daily life. The peace you crave is not merely absence of chaos; it's contentment, calmness, and freedom despite disruption and trouble. This peace is not passive. It is divine weapon, heavenly armor that extinguishes the fiery arrows of worry and doubt.

SHALOM: Nothing Missing, Nothing Lacking, Nothing Broken

SHALOM [shah-LOME]—that ancient word pulsing through Scripture 237 times like a heartbeat—means something that will revolutionize your approach to every conflict. It comes from the root shalam, meaning to make whole, restore, or repay. SHALOM means nothing missing, nothing lacking, nothing broken. Not after the storm passes—in the storm itself. "Peace doesn't avoid the fight. Peace transforms how you fight." SHALOM is covenantal—tied to God's promises, blessings, and presence dwelling among His people. It implies restored order, flourishing in every dimension—spiritual, physical, emotional, relational, and societal. When the Aaronic blessing declares "The Lord lift up His countenance upon you and give you shalom" (Numbers 6:26), it's not wishing you calm feelings. It's pronouncing complete wholeness over your entire existence. Isaiah understood this: "The work of righteousness will be shalom, and the effect of righteousness, quietness and assurance forever" (Isaiah 32:17). Peace isn't circumstantial—it's positional. From your position dwelling in the secret place, covered by protection, peace becomes the most violent weapon in your spiritual arsenal.

EIRENE: Joined Back Together

When Jesus said "Peace I leave with you, My peace I give to you; not as the world gives do I give to you" (John 14:27), He used the Greek word EIRENE [ay-RAY-nay]. Derived from the verb eiro meaning "to join" or "bind together," EIRENE means being joined back into unity—peace with God, inner tranquility, and harmony among people. EIRENE carries the idea of things woven together into wholeness—restoring what was broken and bringing order where there was chaos. It describes both reconciliation and the state of calm that flows from God's reign. It's the fruit of the Spirit (Galatians 5:22), showing peace is a product of divine indwelling. When Paul writes "the peace of God, which surpasses all understanding, will guard your hearts and minds through Christ Jesus" (Philippians 4:7), he uses PHROUREO [froo-REH-o]—military garrison. Your peace is an armed garrison, executing heaven's protection protocol around your mind and emotions. When you're peaceful in chaos, you're not being passive. You're being violently aggressive against the kingdom of darkness. Peace isn't passive—it's violently active against chaos. It doesn't ignore the diagnosis—it dominates it.

The Critical Distinction

The orphan mindset says: "I must fight harder to earn peace. My performance determines my calm. If I pray enough, fast enough, warfare enough—then God will give me peace." This is exhausting striving that treats spiritual disciplines as payment for peace. The son mindset says: "I fast and pray not to earn peace but to position myself where peace reigns. Fasting and prayer are not performance—they're posture. They're how I access the Prince of Peace." This is strategic positioning that treats spiritual disciplines as intimacy with the Peace-Giver. Same activities, radically different motivations.

THE ORPHAN VS. HEIR PEACE PARADIGM

ELEMENT	ORPHAN (Fighting FOR Peace)	HEIR (Fighting WITH Peace)
IDENTITY	"I must earn peace through performance"	"Peace is my inheritance through position"
MINDSET	"Peace comes after victory"	"Peace is how I achieve victory"
STRATEGY	Fight harder, pray longer, try more	Dwell deeper, rest stronger, position correctly
WEAPONS	Human effort, anxiety-driven warfare, panic prayers	SHALOM, EIRENE, weaponized rest, Kingdom authority
SOURCE	My strength, my vigilance, my effort	His sufficiency, His watching, His presence
POSTURE	Standing in my own strength (exhausting)	Resting under His wings (restful)
AUTHORITY	"I must create peace through spiritual gymnastics"	"I speak TO storms FROM peace position"
MOTIVATION	Fear of what happens if I don't fight hard enough	Confidence in the One who never sleeps
VIEW OF PEACE	Goal to achieve, reward to earn, feeling to create	Weapon to wield, position to occupy, Person to carry
BATTLE APPROACH	Reactive—respond to every attack with panic	Proactive—peace deployed before attack arrives
RELATIONSHIP WITH GOD	God as last resort, 911 emergency service	God as first priority, 24/7 companionship
EMOTIONAL STATE	Anxious vigilance, exhausted defending, frantic striving	Supernatural calm, confident security, violent rest
TRUST PLACEMENT	"If I fight correctly, I'll finally have peace"	"Because He fights for me, I already have peace"
HOW THEY FIGHT	For peace—trying to achieve it through warfare	With peace—deploying it as warfare strategy
WHEN THEY REST	After the battle ends, after enemies retreat	During the battle—rest itself is the weapon
PEACE LOCATION	Outside looking in—trying to reach peace	Inside looking out—releasing peace from position
WARFARE CRY	"I need peace! Where is it?"	"I have peace! Deploy it!"
RESULT	Vulnerability despite effort, exhaustion, burnout	Security through position, supernatural endurance

Daniel's 21-Day Fast: The Positioning Model

The shift from orphan to heir is not a change in activity—it's a change in motivation and position. Heirs fast and pray just like orphans do. But motivation transforms everything. Daniel's 21-day fast reveals this pattern: "Then he said to me, 'Do not fear, Daniel, for from the first day that you set your heart to understand, and to humble yourself before your God, your words were heard; and I have come because of your words. But the prince of the kingdom of Persia withstood me twenty-one days'" (Daniel 10:12-13). Watch carefully. God heard Daniel's prayer on Day One. The answer was released immediately. Spiritual warfare delayed manifestation for 21 days. Daniel's 21-day fast wasn't earning the answer—it was positioning him in the secret place while heaven fought the battle. Daniel fought with peace, not for it. He dwelt in God's presence while angelic armies waged war he never saw.

This is why you're fasting today—Day 17 of 21 days. Your fasting isn't earning God's favor. It's positioning you in the secret place where His peace automatically covers. From Day One, heaven heard. The answer is in motion. Your dwelling through fasting and prayer is strategic positioning that releases peace as weapon, not desperate performance that begs for peace as reward. Jesus Himself taught: "This kind does not go out except by prayer and fasting" (Matthew 17:21). Not because God demands payment through spiritual disciplines, but because certain spiritual realities require positioning in the peace-filled intimacy that fasting and prayer create. Heaven's voice thunders with authority: "Your calm in crisis prophesies the outcome. Your rest in battle announces which kingdom wins." This isn't denial. This isn't passivity. This is weaponized rest that makes hell tremble and heaven celebrate. You don't create peace to speak to storms. You speak to storms from peace position.

THIS IS HOW PSALM 91 CHANGED ME

For three days, you've been learning a truth that changes everything: Psalm 91 isn't a prayer you pray when crisis comes—it's the address where you already live. Day 15 taught you the five daily rhythms of dwelling. Day 16 revealed the seven layers of protection activated from that dwelling place. Today unveils what dwelling in the secret place creates: automatic peace that functions as warfare.

"I used to visit God's presence when I was in crisis. Like showing up at a shelter when it's storming, then leaving when the sun comes out. But dwelling is different. Dwelling means: This is where I LIVE now. I don't visit the secret place when terror comes. I already live there, so terror has to break through covering to reach me—and it can't. I don't run to the shadow when arrows fly. I already abide under the shadow, so arrows hit the covering before they hit me. The breakthrough wasn't learning to be braver. It was learning to live in a different location."

This is the peace positioning Daniel mastered. This is what fighting WITH peace looks like. You're not running TO peace when crisis hits—you're releasing peace FROM where you already dwell. The secret place isn't your emergency shelter. It's your permanent address. And when you live there, peace becomes your automatic atmosphere, not your desperate prayer. Day 15's five rhythms positioned you. Day 16's seven-layer protection covered you. Day 17's weaponized peace flows from that positioning and covering. From the secret place, under the shadow, covered by wings—peace doesn't have to be achieved. It's already your atmosphere. You're not fighting for it. You're fighting with it.

BIBLICAL FOUNDATION: PEACE AS VIOLENCE AGAINST DARKNESS

Jesus: The Master of Weaponized Peace

"But He was in the stern, asleep on a pillow. And they awoke Him and said to Him, 'Teacher, do You not care that we are perishing?'" (Mark 4:38). Experienced fishermen panicking. Waves crashing. Boat filling. Death imminent. Jesus? Asleep on a pillow during the storm. Not exhaustion—exhibition. Not denial—demonstration. When awakened, He spoke two words that rewrote warfare forever: "Peace, be still!" Jesus didn't calm the storm from panic—He commanded it from peace. The storm submitted because Peace Himself spoke. That same peace dwells in you now. Jesus demonstrated what Daniel practiced and what Psalm 91 promises: when you dwell in peace position, storms submit to your command. He wasn't running to peace in crisis—He was releasing peace from position. The boat was His secret place. The pillow was His shadow. The storm couldn't reach Him until it passed through His Father's covering. And when He spoke, He spoke not TO peace but FROM peace.

Gideon: From Hiding to JEHOVAH-SHALOM

Seven years of Midianite oppression. Israel hiding in caves. Gideon threshing wheat in a winepress—wrong tool, wrong place, but the only hidden place available. The Angel appears: "The Lord is with you, you mighty man of valor!" Gideon argues from fear. But after the encounter, heaven speaks eight words that revolutionize warfare: "Peace to you; do not fear; you shall not die" (Judges 6:23). God doesn't give peace as reward for victory. He is peace as strategy for winning. Watch Gideon's response: He builds an altar and calls it JEHOVAH-SHALOM—The Lord is Peace. Not the Lord gives peace. The Lord is peace. In the middle of national oppression, personal fear, family poverty—Gideon discovers God is peace. The transformation: Man hiding in winepress becomes warrior whose 300 defeat thousands. Your hiding place becomes your war room. Your fear becomes fuel. Your weakness becomes weapon. Gideon's altar became his secret place. JEHOVAH-SHALOM became his covering. And from that position, 300 defeated thousands because peace positioned them for God's intervention.

The Names of God That Reveal Peace

Each name of God is a doorway into a different dimension of peace. As YHWH SHALOM, He brings identity—peace is part of His nature, not something He occasionally distributes. As SAR SHALOM (Prince of Peace from Isaiah 9:6), He brings authority—where He reigns, peace reigns. As JEHOVAH RAAH (The Lord My Shepherd from Psalm 23), He brings rest—"He leads me beside still waters." As EL SHADDAI (God Almighty), He brings provision—peace thrives when we trust God's provision and stop striving. As JEHOVAH TSIDKENU (The Lord Our Righteousness from Jeremiah 23:6), He brings reconciliation—peace is impossible without righteousness. As EL ROI (The God Who Sees), He brings assurance—knowing we are seen brings deep peace. As EMMANUEL (God With Us), He brings presence—where He is, peace abides. As PARAKLETOS (The Comforter), He brings internal calm through Holy Spirit's abiding presence. Peace is not something God gives apart from Himself—it is who He is and how He reveals Himself.

The Seven Dimensions of Peace

Peace operates in seven interconnected dimensions: First, peace with God through reconciliation—"Therefore, having been justified by faith, we have peace with God through our Lord

Jesus Christ" (Romans 5:1). Second, peace of God as internal calm—"And the peace of God, which surpasses all understanding, will guard your hearts and minds through Christ Jesus" (Philippians 4:7). Third, peace from God as divine gift—"Grace to you and peace from God our Father and the Lord Jesus Christ" (Romans 1:7). Fourth, peace in God's presence as safety—"You will keep him in perfect peace, whose mind is stayed on You, because he trusts in You" (Isaiah 26:3). Fifth, peace through obedience as blessing—"Oh, that you had heeded My commandments! Then your peace would have been like a river" (Isaiah 48:18). Sixth, peace between people as harmony—"For He Himself is our peace, who has made both one, and has broken down the middle wall of separation" (Ephesians 2:14). Seventh, peace over circumstances as authority—"Peace, be still!" (Mark 4:39). All seven activate from one reality: Christ dwelling in you. Peace is not fragile—it's fierce. It's not passive—it's powerful. It doesn't ignore storms—it silences them.

BIBLICAL CHAMPIONS: WARRIORS WHO WEAPONIZED PEACE

Daniel sealed with hungry lions for an entire night didn't fight them. He rested in God's protection while surrounded by predators. "My God sent His angel and shut the lions' mouths, so that they have not hurt me" (Daniel 6:22). Daniel slept so peacefully that the king called at dawn to check if he was still alive. Peace made predators powerless. Paul and Silas beaten, bleeding, chained in maximum security responded at midnight with singing hymns. Peace produced praise that triggered earthquake that opened every prison door. When you sing in your prison, earth itself responds to heaven's frequency. Stephen stoned to death watched his face shine like an angel while stones crushed his body. He saw heaven opening, died with prayer for his killers. Peace that transcends even martyrdom. David hunted by his own son Absalom wrote: "I lay down and slept; I awoke, for the Lord sustained me. I will not be afraid of ten thousands of people" (Psalm 3:5-6). Your peace in persecution becomes prophecy of protection. The Hebrew boys facing fiery furnace declared: "Our God whom we serve is able to deliver us...But if not, let it be known to you, O king, that we do not serve your gods" (Daniel 3:17-18). Peace that doesn't require rescue to remain intact. Fourth man appears when peace refuses to panic. Their pattern becomes your pathway: Peace works everywhere, against any enemy, through any storm.

THE TESTIMONY: WHEN PEACE BECAME OUR FAMILY'S WEAPON

The Hospital Crisis

I need to tell you about the day heaven taught me that peace deployed from one location creates victory in another—even across continents. My mother had come to Canada during my divorce—this woman who'd raised me alone, who'd taught me to write letters to God in childhood darkness. She came to hold me through adult darkness. Then chronic illness struck with devastating precision. Without permanent resident status, every day in a Canadian hospital would financially destroy what divorce hadn't already taken. I flew with her back to Jamaica for treatment. On that plane, watching her struggle for breath, fear crushing our faith, I received something from heaven. Not a healing promise—a warfare strategy. "My child, teach her to speak life when death is speaking loudest." I taught her one declaration: "I shall not die, but live, and declare the works of the Lord" (Psalm 118:17). She repeated it like learning a new language—the language of life when death was screaming. Peace in crisis becomes evangelism without words.

The Medical Verdict

In Jamaica, her condition worsened. Hospital fluorescent lights making everything look like endings. The medical team gathered our family—when they gather family, you know what's coming. They delivered their verdict with practiced gentleness, statistics wrapped in sympathy, timelines measured in weeks rather than years. This testimony reflects our family's unique experience and should never replace professional medical care. Each person's healing journey is unique, and outcomes vary greatly. While we pursued every available medical treatment under qualified doctors' supervision, I understood we needed resources beyond what medicine alone could provide. In that moment, with my mother barely able to form words, I asked: "Mom, what's the declaration?" The room went silent. Machines beeping our countdown. Then, like a warrior summoning strength from realms unseen, she whispered: "I shall not die..." When you speak from peace instead of to it, your words carry heaven's authority. Pause. Deeper breath. Voice gaining strength: "...but live..." Eyes opening wider, voice carrying authority that made medical staff step back: "...to declare the works of the Lord." Something shifted in that room. Peace had entered—not as feeling but as force. Not as surrender but as sword.

The Distance Battle

Days later, alone in my Canadian bedroom, separated by thousands of miles from my mother's Jamaican hospital bed, I faced the powerlessness of distance. On my knees, carpet pressing into bone, I cried out: "How do I fight this battle when I can't even be there?" The response came as correction, not comfort: "Don't ask how to fight. Ask with what. Your peace is that weapon. Right now, anxiety is attacking your mother's body. Fear is accelerating her symptoms. But watch what happens when My peace enters her battlefield. Distance is irrelevant when you're wielding the right weapon. From your bedroom in Canada, release My peace to that hospital room in Jamaica." Everything shifted. I stopped begging for healing and started deploying peace. Peace deployed from one location creates victory in another. Geography cannot limit spiritual weapons.

The Peace Protocol

From Canada, I covered my mother in Jamaica with peace like artillery: When anxiety attacked at 3 AM, "Be anxious for nothing" (Philippians 4:6). When fear whispered death, "Fear not, for I am with you" (Isaiah 41:10). When storms raged in her body, "Peace, be still!" (Mark 4:39). When sleep eluded, "I will both lie down in peace, and sleep" (Psalm 4:8). This wasn't positive thinking—this was JEHOVAH-SHALOM speaking through human vessels. A warrior's peace is not kept—it's wielded. While acknowledging that medical outcomes vary greatly and that faith expressions manifest differently for each person, what followed demonstrated peace as spiritual technology. Where deterioration was predicted, improvement occurred. Where statistics suggested decline, recovery emerged. Where medical protocols expected certain timelines, supernatural acceleration happened. The medical team noted in her records: "unusual peace," "remarkable calm," "faith-driven stability." One doctor documented that her lack of stress seemed to positively affect her physical response to treatment in ways they couldn't medically explain. My mother remains with us today—living testimony that peace deployed strategically creates measurable transformation. Some families pass down property. We pass down peace. Not as heirloom to display, but as weapon to deploy. But hear this with absolute clarity: My mother's physical healing testified to God's power, but even if her body had failed, our peace would have testified to His presence. This is the revolution: Peace wins whether the body heals or goes home to heaven. Whether God raises up or calls home. Whether miracles manifest in time or eternity. Peace isn't validated by physical outcomes—it's vindicated by Kingdom authority over chaos. The victory isn't measured by what happened to her body. It's measured by what happened to fear when peace entered the room. Death lost its voice when SHALOM took the floor.

The Father's Lap

I will never forget the day peace found me in a different way. I was driving alone, tears streaking my cheeks, my heart barely holding itself together. I wasn't praying eloquent prayers or quoting Scripture—I was just talking to God from the deepest place of my pain. I whispered through sobs, "Lord, I can't do this anymore." And in that still, small voice, He spoke: "Come and sit on My lap." It startled me. The Almighty God—the Creator of heaven and earth—inviting me into something so intimate, so tender. But I pulled over, closed my eyes, and in my spirit I climbed into His arms. "Tell Me everything," He said. So I did. I told Him about the brokenness. The betrayal. The divorce papers. The empty bank account. The friends who disappeared. The shame. The loneliness. The depression. Every symptom. Every wound. Every fear. It felt like I was sitting in a doctor's office—except the Great Physician Himself was taking the chart. For every pain I confessed, He spoke a healing word: "Where does it hurt?" He asked. "My heart is shattered." "I will bind up your wounds." "I feel like a failure." "I am your Restorer." "I'm so alone." "I am your closest Friend. You are never alone." "I feel hopeless." "I am your Comforter." I wept as He replaced every lie with truth, every wound with a promise. And then He handed me a report—not written on paper but sealed on my heart: Diagnosis: Complete. You are healed. You are delivered. You are restored. You are renewed. "Do not fear the pain of this process," He said. "You are just passing through. I am your Great Physician. I am your Shepherd. I am the light in your darkness." When that divine appointment ended, I stepped out of His embrace still surrounded by the same circumstances—but something had changed. I had peace. Unexplainable. Unshakeable. Irreversible peace. There wasn't a single tear He hadn't seen, a single word He hadn't answered. And as I continued to pour out my heart, He kept pouring in His presence: "You've had little strength, but you never let go. Because of that, I've opened a door no man can shut. You're coming out of this valley. You will live again. And not just you—your children too." In that moment, I realized: peace isn't the absence of pain—it's the presence of a Person. And His presence spoke louder than every storm.

THE FIVE FUNCTIONS OF PEACE

Peace isn't passive—it's the most aggressive force in the spiritual realm. **Peace guards territory**: "And let the peace of God rule in your hearts" (Colossians 3:15). The word "rule" means umpire, arbitrate, govern. Peace becomes decision-maker and boundary-keeper over your inner world. When peace leaves a decision, stop. When peace affirms a direction, move. **Peace disarms accusations**: "Great peace have those who love Your law, and nothing causes them to stumble" (Psalm 119:165). When accusations can't destabilize you, they lose power. **Peace confuses chaos**: "For God is not the author of confusion but of peace" (1 Corinthians 14:33). Your peace literally scrambles enemy strategy. Chaos expects panic—when it meets peace, its operating system crashes. **Peace attracts presence**: "The Lord will bless His people with peace" (Psalm 29:11). Peace creates atmosphere for increase. Where peace rules, God's presence multiplies exponentially. **Peace prophesies victory**: Your calm in crisis declares the outcome before it manifests. When you carry peace, you carry heaven's atmosphere into earth's chaos.

THE DANIEL FAST: CLOSING THE GAP!

ACTIVATION: THE SIX DIMENSIONS OF WEAPONIZED PEACE

DIMENSION	WITHOUT PEACE	WITH WEAPONIZED PEACE	YOUR ACTIVATION
SPIRITUAL	Anxious warfare	Rest as violent resistance	"I fight with peace, not for it!"
MENTAL	Thought spirals	Peace-guarded strategic mind	"Peace patrols every thought!"
EMOTIONAL	Reactive patterns	Peace-ruled responses	"Peace arbitrates my emotions!"
PHYSICAL	Stress manifesting	Peace healing at cellular level	"Peace speaks to my symptoms!"
FINANCIAL	Panic decisions	Peace-led supernatural wisdom	"Provision follows my peace!"
RELATIONAL	Conflict cycles	Peace shifting atmospheres	"My peace changes every room!"

FOCUSED DIMENSION PEACE PRAYERS

For Spiritual Peace: "Father, I'm exhausted from anxious warfare that never ends. The enemy wants me to believe that if I let my guard down, I'll lose ground. But today I discover: my rest is my most violent weapon. I reject fighting for peace. I position myself to fight with peace. When spiritual attack comes, I don't panic—I release SHALOM. JEHOVAH-SHALOM—You are my peace. My spiritual warfare transforms today. I don't fight harder—I rest deeper. My peace is violence against darkness. In Jesus' name, I am spiritually at peace. Amen."

For Mental Peace: "Father, my mind is a battlefield. Racing thoughts at 3 AM. Intrusive worries that won't stop. Mental exhaustion from calculating outcomes I can't control. But today I learn: The battlefield may be my mind, but victory is won in the spirit. I reject anxiety as my default. I receive PHROUREO—the armed garrison of Your peace standing guard over my mind. Every anxious thought must pass through the peace checkpoint. 'You will keep him in perfect peace, whose mind is stayed on You' (Isaiah 26:3). I fix my focus on You. Perfect peace guards my thoughts. In Jesus' name, I am mentally at peace. Amen."

For Emotional Peace: "Father, I'm bleeding emotionally from wounds others can't see. Betrayal broke something deep. Rejection taught me to build walls. Now I'm numb when I should be alive. But today I learn: SHALOM offers a third option—emotionally whole while remaining tender. I reject emotional shutdown as my only defense. 'Peace I leave with you, My peace I give to you' (John 14:27). Your peace transforms how I process what I feel. Where grief has tried to define me—SHALOM restores me. Where betrayal broke me—peace makes me whole again. Not numb. Whole. In Jesus' name, I am emotionally at peace. Amen."

For Physical Peace: "Father, my body feels like it's failing me. Chronic pain. Symptoms that terrify me. Physical exhaustion from fighting battles I can't see but constantly feel. Sleep eludes me. Stress manifests in my body. I'm tired of being tired. 'I will both lie down in peace, and sleep' (Psalm 4:8). Today I receive Your peace not just spiritually but physically. Peace that heals at cellular level. Peace that speaks to symptoms: 'Peace, be still!' SAR SHALOM—Prince of Peace—reign over my physical body. I don't just pray for healing—I release peace as the atmosphere where healing thrives. In Jesus' name, I am physically at peace. Amen."

For Financial Peace: "Father, I'm drowning in financial fear. Bills I can't pay. Debt crushing me. Panic every time I check my account. Financial stress is stealing my peace, and without peace, I make panic decisions. 'Be anxious for nothing, but in everything by prayer...let your requests be made known to God' (Philippians 4:6). I refuse to let financial anxiety be my counselor. You are JEHOVAH-JIREH—my Provider. When I rest in You as source, resources find me. I decree that provision follows my peace. My financial breakthrough doesn't come from frantic striving—it flows from peaceful positioning. In Jesus' name, I am financially at peace. Amen."

For Relational Peace: "Father, relationships have become minefields. People I trusted destroyed me. I'm afraid to let anyone close because everyone who got close eventually left. I've built walls to protect myself, isolated to prevent pain. But isolation isn't peace—it's prison. 'Blessed are the peacemakers, for they shall be called sons of God' (Matthew 5:9). I'm not just a peace-keeper avoiding conflict—I'm a peacemaker carrying Kingdom atmosphere. I reject isolation as protection. I receive peace-positioned relationships. Where toxic relationships tried to kill what You're building—Your peace exposes them. Where divine connections are destined—Your peace attracts them. My peace changes every room I enter. In Jesus' name, I am relationally at peace. Amen."

RESISTANCE REALITY CHECK: BREAKING THE LIES

Peace Passivity: Hell whispers: "If I'm peaceful, I'm not fighting hard enough." Heaven's Response: "Peace is your weapon against darkness. Rest is resistance. Your calm terrifies hell more than your panic ever could." Break it: "I reject peace passivity! My rest is violent resistance against chaos!"

Circumstance Dependency: Hell whispers: "I can't be peaceful until things change." Heaven's Response: "Peace doesn't require change—it creates change through spiritual authority. SHALOM operates in the storm, not after it." Break it: "I reject circumstance dependency! My peace doesn't wait for change—it commands it!"

Performance Pressure: Hell whispers: "I need to feel peaceful to have peace." Heaven's Response: "Peace is position, not emotion. Declare it whether you feel it or not. You're positioned in Christ—peace is your inheritance." Break it: "I reject performance pressure! Peace is my position in Christ, not my feeling!"

Crisis Panic: Hell whispers: "This situation is too big for peace to handle." Heaven's Response: "No storm is bigger than the One who sleeps through storms. If Jesus could rest in a boat filling with water, you can rest in your crisis." Break it: "I reject crisis panic! My peace is bigger than this storm!"

Your peace isn't based on your circumstances—it's based on your position in Christ.

THE FIVE HEBREW WORDS FOR PEACE: YOUR COMPLETE ARSENAL

Heaven wants you armed with comprehensive peace vocabulary. The Hebrew language contains not one but five distinct words for peace—each revealing a different dimension of the SHALOM God releases into your warfare.

1. SHALOM [shah-LOME] — Complete Wholeness

Nothing missing, nothing lacking, nothing broken. SHALOM is the comprehensive peace that addresses every dimension of your existence simultaneously. When you declare SHALOM over a situation, you're prophesying complete restoration, not partial repair. This is the foundation word, the mother of all peace declarations. "The Lord lift up His countenance upon you, and give you shalom" (Numbers 6:26). SHALOM is God's signature—His completeness stamped on your chaos.

2. SHALEV [shah-LEHV] — Secure Tranquility

SHALEV comes from the same root as SHALOM but emphasizes the emotional and psychological dimensions—secure, at ease, carefree, undisturbed. This is the peace that quiets anxious thoughts, settles racing minds, and brings supernatural security to internal chaos. "I will both lie down in peace [SHALOM], and sleep; for You alone, O Lord, make me dwell in safety [BETACH]" (Psalm 4:8). SHALEV is what happens internally when SHALOM rules externally. When anxiety attacks at 3 AM, SHALEV is the weapon that restores secure tranquility to your thought life. This is peace that makes you mentally unshakable.

3. SHAQAT [shah-KAHT] — Undisturbed Rest

SHAQAT means to be quiet, at rest, undisturbed—even in the midst of storms. This is the peace Jesus demonstrated sleeping on a pillow during the storm (Mark 4:38). SHAQAT doesn't deny the storm exists; it refuses to be moved by the storm's presence. "He makes wars cease to the end of the earth" (Psalm 46:9)—the Hebrew carries the idea of causing rest (SHAQAT) by silencing conflict. When circumstances rage around you but your spirit remains unmoved, that's SHAQAT. This is peace that makes you circumstantially immovable. While SHALEV quiets your mind, SHAQAT anchors your spirit.

4. BETACH [BEH-takh] — Confident Security

BETACH emphasizes trust, security, safety, and confidence—especially in dangerous situations. This word appears when Scripture describes dwelling safely despite surrounding threats. "So Israel dwelt in safety [BETACH], the fountain of Jacob alone, in a land of grain and new wine" (Deuteronomy 33:28). BETACH is what enabled Daniel to sleep with lions, Hebrew boys to stand before fire, David to face Goliath. This is peace-as-confidence that says, "I am secure not because danger doesn't exist, but because God is my security." When you're surrounded by predators but sleep like Daniel, that's BETACH. This is peace that makes you dangerously confident.

5. EIRENE [ay-RAY-nay] — Joined-Together Harmony

Though this is Greek rather than Hebrew, it completes your peace arsenal by emphasizing reconciliation and unity. EIRENE joins back together what was broken apart—relationships restored, divisions healed, harmony established. "For He Himself is our peace [EIRENE], who has made both one, and has broken down the middle wall of separation" (Ephesians 2:14). Where the Hebrew words address your relationship with God and your internal state, EIRENE addresses your relationships with others. This is peace that makes you a relational healer.

How the Five Work Together

Watch how these five peace dimensions create comprehensive transformation: SHALOM restores what's broken (comprehensive wholeness), SHALEV quiets what's anxious (mental security), SHAQAT anchors what's shaken (spiritual stability), BETACH emboldens what's fearful (confident trust), EIRENE reconciles what's divided (relational harmony). You don't need to choose one—you deploy all five simultaneously. When you pray the activation prayer that follows, you're releasing a five-dimensional peace arsenal that addresses broken areas, anxious thoughts, stormy circumstances, dangerous situations, and divided relationships. Together with PHROUREO (the armed garrison guarding your mind from Philippians 4:7), you now possess six peace weapons that create comprehensive coverage. Nothing missing. Nothing lacking. Nothing broken. The enemy thought he could attack one dimension while you defended another. But when you deploy all five Hebrew peace words plus the Greek garrison, you're covered completely. Your peace isn't fragile—it's fierce. Not passive—powerful. Not singular—comprehensive.

PROPHETIC ACTIVATION: RELEASE YOUR PEACE ARSENAL

Stand in the center of your home. Take three deep breaths. Feel His peace within you like loaded ammunition. Now speak with authority: "I release the peace of God into this atmosphere! Peace, invade every room! Peace, dominate every door! Peace, patrol every thought! Peace, govern every decision! Where chaos has tried to rule—peace, seize dominion! Where anxiety has camped—peace, execute eviction! Where confusion has clouded—peace, detonate clarity! Where warfare has wearied—peace, win this battle! I am a carrier of Kingdom peace! My calm is warfare! My rest is resistance! My SHALOM is authority against darkness! Peace of God—rule with absolute authority!" Now walk through each room, releasing peace like perfume, deploying it like artillery. Your peace has an assignment—let it work.

MEMORIAL: THE PEACE STONE

This is your daily reminder that peace is your weapon, not your reward. Position creates peace; performance begs for it. Within 24 hours, find a smooth stone—yard, park, riverbank, anywhere. When you find it, receive it as prophetic symbol: "I fight WITH peace, not FOR it." Optional: Use a marker to write "SHALOM" on one side or keep it unmarked as reminder of peace's simplicity. Place it where you'll see it daily: beside your Bible, on your desk, in your car, by your mirror. Every morning, touch the stone and speak: "This stone is solid. My peace is more solid. SHALOM—nothing missing, nothing lacking, nothing broken. I don't fight FOR peace today—I fight WITH peace. My calm is warfare. My rest is resistance. Prince of Peace, reign through me."

The Peace Pause (3x Daily)

Set three alarms throughout your day labeled "Peace Check" for mid-morning, afternoon, and evening. When alarm sounds, ask yourself: "Am I fighting FOR peace or WITH it?" If fighting FOR, stop, breathe, touch your peace stone if nearby, and reposition from orphan to heir. If fighting WITH, continue from peace position, knowing you're weaponizing rest. In crisis moments, when attacks come, hold the stone and remember SHAQAT—undisturbed rest even in storms. Declare: "This stone remains solid regardless of circumstances. My peace remains solid regardless of storms. I am positioned in SHALOM. Peace, speak to this situation: Be still!" The stone becomes your physical anchor reminding you of the Day 17 shift from fighting FOR peace to fighting WITH peace.

WEEKLY PRACTICE: THE FATHER'S LAP

Once per week, schedule a "Divine Appointment" with the Great Physician. Find a quiet place, close your eyes, and in your spirit imagine climbing into the Father's lap just as the testimony described. Say: "Father, I'm here. I'm climbing into Your arms. I need to tell You everything." Then tell Him—every wound, every fear, every pain, every symptom. Don't filter. Don't perform. Just pour out. Listen as He responds to each one and write what He says in your journal. This isn't one-time experience—it's ongoing

THE DANIEL FAST: CLOSING THE GAP!

relationship. The Father's lap is always available. His invitation never expires. Over time, you'll create a record of Divine Appointments—a journal of healing conversations where the Great Physician replaced lies with truth, wounds with promises. Peace isn't the absence of pain—it's the presence of a Person.

PEACE DECLARATION

Stand and declare with authority: "Today, I choose peace—not as the world gives, but as Heaven decrees. I declare that the Prince of Peace reigns in every corner of my heart and every circumstance of my life. I will not be shaken by what I see, because I am anchored in the One who never changes. I decree that my mind is guarded by the shalom of God—wholeness, wellness, harmony, and rest—from the top of my head to the soles of my feet. Nothing missing. Nothing lacking. Nothing broken. Anxiety has no authority here. Fear has no legal right to speak. Chaos must bow to Christ. I speak to every storm within and around me: 'Peace, be still.' I command every lie of the enemy to be silenced and every accusation to crumble under the weight of God's truth. I am not abandoned—I am accompanied. I am not defeated—I am delivered. I am not overwhelmed—I am overshadowed by His peace. I declare that my heart is not a battlefield but a sanctuary. The war ends here. The striving ceases now. The Prince of Peace lives in me—and His presence is my portion. I prophesy that doors of restoration are opening before me. I decree that wounds of the past are being healed, that labels of failure are being rewritten by grace. I announce that peace will follow me into every room, every decision, every relationship, and every assignment. I have SHALOM—nothing missing, nothing lacking, nothing broken! I have SHALEV—secure tranquility guarding my mind! I have SHAQAT—undisturbed rest in every storm! I have BETACH—confident security in danger! I have EIRENE—peace binding everything together! I have PHROUREO—armed garrison guarding my mind! If Jesus could sleep through storms, so can I! If Daniel could rest with lions, so can I! If Paul could sing in prison, so can I! If the Hebrew boys could be calm in fire, so can I! I don't fight for peace—I wield it as weapon! My peace confuses hell! My rest disrupts darkness! My calm prophesies victory! Like my spiritual mother, I shall not die but live to declare God's works! I fight with peace! I am armed with SHALOM! I align my words with Heaven's verdict: I am whole. I am healed. I am restored. I am renewed. I am at peace—body, soul, and spirit—in Jesus' name. Amen!"

ACTIVATION PRAYER: PRINCE OF PEACE, REIGN IN ME

"Abba Father, I come before You not as a warrior trying to win a battle, but as a child climbing into the arms of a loving Father. You are Jehovah Shalom—the Lord my Peace—and I surrender every storm, every struggle, and every secret wound into Your hands. Prince of Peace, I invite You into every room of my soul. Walk into the places barricaded by fear. Breathe into the corners of my mind clouded by anxiety. Sit upon the throne of my heart where chaos once reigned, and establish Your Kingdom of calm. Lord, I release to You the weight I was never meant to carry—the betrayals, the disappointments, the loneliness, the loss, the shame. I place them all at Your feet. Speak into my pain the same words You spoke over the sea: 'Peace, be still.' Where there is confusion, release Your clarity. Where there is grief, pour out Your comfort. Where there is turmoil, usher in Your stillness. Where there is striving, anchor me in Your sufficiency. Today, I renounce every agreement I made with fear. I break partnership with anxiety, torment, and restlessness. I silence the voice of the accuser that says I am unworthy of peace. I align myself with Your truth: I am loved. I am held. I am secure. I am safe. Jesus, teach me to trust Your timing. Teach me to rest even when I don't have the answers. Teach me to abide in Your presence, where peace is not a passing feeling but a permanent reality. Let Your peace guard my heart and mind like a fortress—immovable, unshakable, unstoppable. I declare that peace will govern my thoughts, guide my decisions, guard my relationships, and fill my home. Peace will become the atmosphere I carry into every room. Right now, I receive peace as warfare strategy that destroys every assignment against me: SHALOM over every broken area—complete wholeness now! Nothing missing, nothing lacking, nothing broken! SHALEV quieting every anxious thought—supernatural security now! SHAQAT bringing rest to every storm—unmoved peace now! BETACH providing security in danger—confident trust now! EIRENE binding together what division tried to break—restoration now! PHROUREO standing guard over heart and mind—armed protection now! I receive the divine exchange: my pain for Your goodness, my anxiety for Your assurance, my confusion for Your counsel, my condemnation for Your covering, my old name for Your new identity, my chaos for Your calm, my brokenness for Your wholeness. Prince of Peace, reign over my life. Be the stillness in my storm. Be the calm in my chaos. Be the anchor when everything else is shifting. Today and every day, I choose to rest in Your perfect peace. In the mighty name of Jesus, Amen."

CLOSING: FROM FIGHTING FOR TO FIGHTING WITH

You awakened fighting for peace through human effort. Tonight you rest armed with peace as heaven's weapon. Day 17's revolutionary gift: Peace isn't what you achieve after victory—it's how you achieve victory. The same peace that governed my mother's recovery across continents can dominate your current battle. The same JEHOVAH-SHALOM that transformed Gideon's fear can transform your fight. The same invitation to sit on the Father's lap is extended to you today. Scripture demonstrates that peace-filled believers consistently see supernatural outcomes. Jesus slept through storms before commanding them. Daniel rested with lions before being delivered. Paul sang in prison before earthquakes opened doors. Hebrew boys remained calm before the fourth man appeared. While spiritual experiences vary among individuals and outcomes differ in each situation, the principle remains: peace positions you for God's intervention.

Tomorrow begins Day 18: Provision—discovering that peaceful hearts become provision portals. When you rest in God as source, resources find you like magnets drawn to peace. But tonight, you're different. You're not anxious about tomorrow's battles. You're not worried about next week's challenges. You're not panicked about circumstances beyond your control. Your peace has an assignment—let it work. Which dimension needs your peace deployed today? Which storm needs your calm commanded? Which battle needs your rest weaponized? Your diagnostic remains simple: Are you fighting for peace or with it? Stop fighting for peace. Start fighting with it. Your rest is resistance. Your calm is warfare. Your SHALOM is authority against darkness. Touch your peace stone. Remember the shift. Deploy the arsenal.

Three days of positioning complete: Day 15 taught you to dwell in five daily rhythms. Day 16 covered you with seven layers of protection. Day 17 weaponized your peace from that dwelling position. The secret place isn't where you visit—it's where you live. The shadow isn't where you run—it's where you abide. The peace isn't what you achieve—it's what you deploy. From dwelling comes protection. From protection comes peace. From peace comes tomorrow's provision. The foundation is laid. The covering is activated. The weapon is loaded.

Week 3 Continues: PROPEL into Destiny - Peace WEAPONIZED. Tomorrow: Day 18 Provision begins. Peaceful positioning creates provision portals. What flows from rest cannot be earned through striving. Your hand closing around the peace stone, no longer fighting for but releasing from: "I fight WITH peace. My calm is warfare. My rest is resistance. I am armed with SHALOM—nothing missing, nothing lacking, nothing broken." The peace warfare revolution is complete.

SOAP JOURNAL — DAY 17

S (Scripture): Write Philippians 4:7 and Mark 4:39. Circle "peace of God" and "Peace, be still." Underline the phrase that stands out most.

O (Observation): Am I fighting FOR peace or WITH peace? What would change if I shifted today? Where in my life is God inviting me to weaponize rest instead of anxious striving? What does "nothing missing, nothing lacking, nothing broken" reveal about God's heart for me? Which of the five Hebrew peace words (SHALOM, SHALEV, SHAQAT, BETACH, EIRENE) do I need most today? How does understanding dwelling (Day 15), protection (Day 16), and peace (Day 17) as connected change my approach to warfare?

A (Application): Choose one dimension (spiritual, mental, emotional, physical, financial, or relational) and pray that focused prayer daily this week. Find your peace stone within 24 hours. Set three "Peace Check" alarms. Schedule your first Father's Lap Divine Appointment. Walk through your home once, releasing peace into each room. Practice touching your stone each morning and declaring: "I fight WITH peace today." Review Day 15's five rhythms and Day 16's protection—peace flows from this positioning.

P (Prayer): "Prince of Peace, I've been fighting FOR peace when You've already given me peace to fight WITH. Today I receive peace as my weapon, not my reward. Transform my rest into resistance and my calm into warfare. I am armed with SHALOM, SHALEV, SHAQAT, BETACH, and EIRENE. In Jesus' name, Amen."

Today's Breakthrough Marker: How did discovering peace as weapon change your approach to current spiritual battles? What happened when you climbed into the Father's lap (or imagined it)? Which dimension experienced the greatest shift through targeted prayer? Did you find your peace stone? Which of the five Hebrew peace words resonated most? How does the connection between Days 15-16-17 (dwelling → protection → peace) transform your understanding of Psalm 91?

Tomorrow's Expectation: Based on today's weaponized peace foundation, how will rest as resistance create provision breakthrough in every dimension? If peace positions you for God's intervention, what provision might manifest from peaceful positioning? How might the three-day foundation (dwelling, protection, peace) prepare you for provision?

Day 17 Complete: Peace Weaponized. Fighting for peace ended. Fighting with peace begun. Shalom activated across six dimensions—nothing missing, nothing lacking, nothing broken. Peace deployed as weapon, not feeling. Rest positioned as resistance. Five Hebrew words mastered (Shalom, Shalev, Shaqat, Betach, Eirene) plus Phroureo garrison. Peace stone memorial established. Peace pause 3x daily activated. Father's lap weekly practice scheduled. Orphan-to-heir paradigm shifted. Six focused prayers activated. Eight names of God revealed. Psalm 91 transformation testimony integrated—dwelling creates automatic peace. Three-day foundation complete: Day 15 positioning through rhythms, Day 16 covering through protection, Day 17 weaponizing through peace. Ready for provision.

DAY 18 — PROVISION

From Orphan Panic to Heir Confidence

> *"And my God shall supply all your need according to His riches in glory by Christ Jesus."* — Philippians 4:19

WEEK 3 — PROPEL: Accelerating into Destiny

Day 18 of 21. Yesterday's Peace weaponized your warfare. Today's Provision shatters the lie that's kept you begging when you should be stewarding.

THE STRATEGIC CONNECTIONS: HOW PEACE PREPARED YOU FOR PROVISION

Day 17's Peace taught you to fight with peace, not for it. Calm in crisis prophesies outcomes. Rest became resistance. SHALOM [shah-LOME] meant nothing missing, nothing lacking, nothing broken—not after the storm, but in the storm itself. Today reveals what happens when peace positions you for provision. Peaceful hearts become provision portals. When anxiety leaves, abundance flows. When panic dies, stewardship thrives. Day 14's Affirmation declared your identity. Day 17's Peace weaponized your rest. Today's Provision demonstrates that identity determines approach, and approach determines outcome. You cannot receive heir-level provision with orphan-level thinking. Week 2 gave you identity. Day 16 covered you with protection—CHACAH [khah-SAH] under wings, SETHER [SAY-ter] in hiding place, MAGEN [mah-GEHN] surrounding you completely. Day 17 weaponized your rest. Today transforms how you approach provision.

ENCOUNTER: WHEN IDENTITY DETERMINES DESTINY

Your hands tremble around the water glass. Not from cold—from terror. 4:30 AM. Day 18. The kitchen table has become a courtroom where bills serve as prosecutors and your bank balance testifies against your faith. Numbers glowing like accusations on your phone screen. The metallic taste of financial anxiety coating your tongue like poison. But it's deeper than money. Time hemorrhaging before you can capture it. Energy depleted by decisions that shouldn't matter. Dreams suffocating under the weight of "not enough." Eighteen days of pressing in, and you're still thinking like an orphan instead of living like an heir. The journal lies open, pen poised for another poverty report. Another desperate prayer that sounds more like begging than believing. But as ink prepares to document lack, heaven detonates your scarcity with revelation: "What if thieves don't break into empty houses? What if they break into houses full of treasures?" The pen stops. The kitchen shifts from courtroom to throne room. Bills become opportunities for stewardship instead of evidence of failure. "What if you're not poor? What if you're so spiritually rich that hell mobilized its best thieves?" "You're not poor. You're dangerous. And hell knows it." Your spine straightens with remembered identity. Orphan panic dies in the presence of heir confidence.

REVELATION: THE IDENTITY REVOLUTION THAT CHANGES EVERYTHING

Listen with every cell in your body: After eighteen days of consecration, heaven is exposing the warfare strategy that's been sabotaging your supply. This isn't about your faith level. Not about hidden sin. Not about working harder or praying longer. The attacks on your provision are strategic warfare against your spiritual wealth. Heaven's voice thunders with revelation that shatters every poverty lie: "Your empty bank account doesn't diminish your spiritual account. You're not failing—you're threatening darkness." "Every attack on your natural provision confirms your spiritual wealth." Consider the biblical pattern: Paul carried world-changing revelation with a thorn. Jesus held all authority with nowhere to lay His head. Elijah called down fire while fed by ravens. Hell only robs houses full of treasure. "Why would the enemy attack your finances if you carried nothing valuable? Why contest your resources if you posed no threat to his kingdom?" The intensity of the battle reveals the treasure. You're not poor. You're so spiritually rich that hell mobilized its best thieves.

The Identity Distinction. The way you approach provision reveals whether you know whose child you are. Orphans panic. Heirs plan. Orphans hoard. Heirs steward. Orphans beg. Heirs receive. Orphans scramble. Heirs rest. Scripture thunders with kingdom mathematics: "Now I say that the heir, as long as he is a child, does not differ at all from a slave...but when the fullness of the time had come, God sent forth His Son...to redeem those who were under the law, that we might receive the adoption as sons" (Galatians 4:1, 4-5). You're not a slave begging for scraps. You're an adopted heir learning to steward family resources. Heaven's voice silences every poverty lie with supernatural authority: "Identity determines approach. Approach determines outcome. You cannot receive heir-level provision with orphan-level thinking." This doesn't mean faithful people never face financial storms. Jesus had nowhere to lay His head yet carried all authority. Paul knew both abundance and need while advancing the Kingdom. The widow of Zarephath faced genuine lack until obedience unlocked supernatural supply. "God's faithfulness isn't measured by your bank account—it's demonstrated through every season of trust."

The Biblical Definition: What Is Provision? Provision is not a momentary transaction—it is the manifestation of God's nature, covenant, and Kingdom order. It is the divine act of God supplying, sustaining, and equipping His people with everything they need—materially, spiritually, physically, emotionally, and missionally—to fulfill their calling, advance His Kingdom, and live in wholeness. It is more than financial blessing—it is the fullness of divine sufficiency for every good work. "And God is able to make all grace abound toward you, that you, always having all sufficiency in all things, may have an abundance for every good work" (2 Corinthians 9:8). Provision literally means "for the vision"—what God supplies to resource what He calls you to. God's provision is proactive, abundant, and purposeful. He sees, prepares, and supplies before the need even exists.

The Hebrew Revelation: JEHOVAH-JIREH. From YIREH, meaning "to see." When Abraham lifted the knife over Isaac, heaven interrupted with rams in thickets and revelation in names: "And Abraham called the name of the place, The-Lord-Will-Provide; as it is said to this day, 'In the Mount of the Lord it shall be provided'" (Genesis 22:14). JEHOVAH-JIREH [yeh-ho-VAH yir-EH] means "The Lord will see to it." God's provision is foresight plus supply—He sees needs before they arise and provides ahead of time. You've been begging for drops when positioned for rivers. God doesn't provide because you panic. He provides because He sees your need before you recognize it yourself. "And my God shall supply all your need according to His riches in glory by Christ Jesus" (Philippians 4:19). The word "supply" is PLĒROŌ—filled to overflowing, pressed down, running over. Not barely enough but abundantly sufficient.

The Hebrew Revelation: EL SHADDAI. When God revealed Himself as EL SHADDAI [el shah-DYE] (Genesis 17:1), the Hebrew contains "shad"—breast. He's not distant supplier but intimate nourisher. The All-Sufficient One who is more than enough—overflowing abundance. You don't beg for provision any more than an infant begs for milk. You receive what loving faithfulness supplies. "The Lord is my shepherd; I shall not want" (Psalm 23:1).

The Greek Revelation: NATHAN. "Every good gift and every perfect gift is from above, and comes down from the Father of lights" (James 1:17). NATHAN [NAH-than] means "to give, bestow, grant." God's nature is generous. His character is giving. But heaven whispers the question that determines everything: "Do you love Me or just what I give?" If provision never came, would the Provider be enough? Your answer determines whether you receive crisis handouts or covenant wealth. "I want to be your Provider, not just your provision." God gives not because you deserve but because He delights in generous children who love Him more than His gifts.

THE FRAMEWORK: FROM ORPHAN PANIC TO HEIR CONFIDENCE

ELEMENT	ORPHAN (Panic/Scarcity)	HEIR (Confidence/Abundance)	BIBLICAL BASIS
MINDSET	"There's never enough"	"God is enough, always"	"My God shall supply all your need" (Phil 4:19)
APPROACH	"I have to grab what I can"	"I steward what He gives"	"Moreover it is required in stewards that one be found faithful" (1 Cor 4:2)
COMPARISON	"Others have more blessing"	"My portion is perfect for my purpose"	"The Lord is the portion of my inheritance" (Ps 16:5)
TRUST	"God forgot about me"	"God sees my need before I ask"	"Your Father knows the things you have need of before you ask Him" (Matt 6:8)
STEWARDSHIP	"I need to hoard everything"	"Generous giving creates generous flow"	"Give, and it will be given to you" (Luke 6:38)
FOCUS	"Survival mindset dominates"	"Kingdom stewardship mentality"	"Seek first the kingdom of God" (Matt 6:33)

The difference between orphan panic and palace heir confidence isn't your circumstances—it's your identity. Palace thinking creates palace provision. You were born to think Kingdom, not scramble for rations.

THE TESTIMONY: WHEN HEAVEN TAUGHT STEWARDSHIP THROUGH STRANGERS

The Empty Tank and Impossible Interview

I need to tell you about the day God used a wrong number to teach me the difference between provision and divine positioning. Contract expired. Account emptied. Pride shattered beyond repair. I sat in my car staring at an interview address forty-five minutes away, gas gauge resting on E like a death sentence. Not enough fuel to arrive, definitely not enough to return home. This interview was my only lead after weeks of desperate searching. Three friends. Three desperate texts: "Need $50 for gas. Interview today. Will pay back." Two ignored me. The third's number had changed. My text launched into digital darkness, landing in some stranger's phone like a message in a bottle thrown into an ocean of impossibility. Sometimes God uses wrong numbers to connect you with right people. The response stunned me into tears: "I don't know you as I just changed my phone. I don't have a lot of money but I will send you $41.10." $41.10? Such an odd, specific amount. But desperation doesn't negotiate with precision. The money transferred instantly. I got gas, prayed over my reflection in the rearview mirror, and drove toward what felt like my final chance. The moment I walked into that conference room, something shifted. Wisdom flowed from sources I didn't naturally possess. Words carried authority that exceeded my experience. The conversation felt divinely choreographed. Driving home, my phone exploded with destiny: Contract secured. Six-figure opportunity born from a $41.10 seed. But heaven wasn't finished with the lesson.

The Prophetic Code Hidden in Provision

That evening, drowning in gratitude, I heard heaven whisper: "Look up 41.10." My hands trembled opening Scripture to Isaiah 41:10: "Fear not, for I am with you; be not dismayed, for I am your God. I will strengthen you, yes, I will help you, I will uphold you with My righteous right hand." That stranger hadn't just sent money—they'd sent prophecy encoded in provision. The "wrong number" had been heaven's perfect connection. When God provides, He often sends both supply and scripture—the provision and the promise wrapped together. That night, still amazed by divine precision, heaven delivered the life-altering perspective shift: "Do you understand why that stranger could hear My voice so precisely? They loved Me more than money. When I whispered '41.10,' they didn't calculate—they obeyed." Obedience to God's voice matters more than the size of your account. Then came the identity revolution: "You think provision is about accumulation. I think provision is about circulation. You want to receive. I want you to become a conduit." God doesn't fill dead-end rivers. He flows through tributaries that water other gardens. This testimony demonstrates God's creative provision, though I recognize each person's financial journey contains unique complexities and challenges beyond spiritual practices alone.

BIBLICAL PATTERNS: HOW HEAVEN PROVIDES

Scripture reveals eight consistent patterns of God's provision—not formulas to manipulate but principles that position you to receive. These aren't isolated miracles but repeated realities demonstrating how JEHOVAH-JIREH operates across generations.

Pattern One: Provision Before the Need—He Sees Ahead. Abraham climbed Mount Moriah with his promised son, a knife, and a command that made no logical sense. Every step up that mountain was warfare against orphan thinking. Logic screamed abandonment. Circumstances testified failure. But Abraham walked in heir confidence, telling his servants, "The lad and I will go yonder and worship, and we will come back to you" (Genesis 22:5). Isaac asked the question that pierced heaven: "Look, the fire and the wood, but where is the lamb for a burnt offering?" (Genesis 22:7). Abraham's response became prophetic declaration: "My son, God will provide for Himself the lamb" (Genesis 22:8). The knife raised. Heaven watching obedience that trusted Provider over provision. Then—"Abraham! Abraham!...Do not lay your hand on the lad" (Genesis 22:11-12). "Then Abraham lifted his eyes and looked, and there behind him was a ram caught in a thicket by its horns" (Genesis 22:13). The ram wasn't wandering nearby. It was caught—positioned, prepared, provided before Abraham arrived. JEHOVAH-JIREH had seen the need before Abraham recognized it and supplied before the crisis peaked. "And Abraham called the name of the place, The-Lord-Will-Provide" (Genesis 22:14). God provides before the need. Your current crisis has already been addressed in heaven's provision protocol. Obedience positions you to see what foresight prepared. "I am not the sacrifice; The Lord indeed will provide!"

Pattern Two: Provision in Impossible Places—Deserts Become Supply. The wilderness had no grocery stores. The desert offered no water fountains. Logic declared death inevitable. But Israel discovered what orphan thinking cannot comprehend: God provides where nothing exists. "Then the Lord said to Moses, 'Behold, I will rain bread from heaven for you'" (Exodus 16:4). Rain bread from heaven? The environment declared impossible, but heaven operated by different economics. Every morning, dew evaporated to reveal manna. Daily bread. Supernatural supply. When thirst threatened death, Moses struck rock at God's command. "He brought streams out of the rock and caused waters to run down like rivers" (Psalm 78:16). Water from stone. Refreshment from impossibility. Your wilderness isn't evidence of abandonment—it's the environment where supernatural provision becomes undeniable. Lack doesn't limit supply when JEHOVAH-JIREH is your source.

Pattern Three: Provision Through Obedience—Faith Activates Supply. The widow of Zarephath gathered sticks for her final meal. Three years of drought. No rain. No crops. No hope. Flour enough for one cake, oil enough for one more day, then death for her and her son. Then Elijah appears with heaven's impossible demand: "Do not fear; go and do as you have said, but make me a small cake from it first, and bring it to me; and afterward make some for yourself and your son" (1 Kings 17:13). Feed the prophet first—before her dying son, before her final meal. She faced the choice every heir must make: Will I trust Provider or provision? She chose purpose over panic. Kingdom over comfort. "So she went away and did according to the word of Elijah; and she and he and her household ate for many days. The bin of flour was not used up, nor did the jar of oil run dry, according to the word of the Lord" (1 Kings 17:15-16). Daily bread. Supernatural supply. She gave what she couldn't afford to give and received what she couldn't afford to lose. "My jar of flour will not be used up, and my jug of oil will not run dry until the day the Lord sends His rain." Years later, another widow faced debt threatening to enslave her sons. Elisha asked, "What do you have in the house?" Her answer revealed orphan thinking: "Your maidservant has nothing in the house but a jar of oil" (2 Kings 4:2). Nothing but oil. She focused on lack instead of seed. Elisha commanded radical obedience: "Go, borrow vessels from everywhere...then pour into all those vessels" (2 Kings 4:3-4). She obeyed. Poured. Watched impossibility become reality. The oil multiplied until vessels ran out. Supply wasn't limited by the jar—it was limited by her preparation. What you make room for, God makes provision for.

Pattern Four: Provision Through Positioning—From Gleaning to Possessing. Ruth's story reveals provision through positioning: gleaning to possessing, stranger to heir, widow to wife. As a Moabite widow with no inheritance, she loyally followed Naomi to Bethlehem and positioned herself in Boaz's field to glean—gathering leftover grain, provision for the poor. "Please let me go to the field, and glean heads of grain after him in whose sight I may find favor" (Ruth 2:2). Positioning does something powerful. Boaz noticed her character, loyalty, work ethic. He commanded his workers: "Let her glean even among the sheaves...Also let grain from the bundles fall purposely for her" (Ruth 2:15-16). Ruth came for leftovers. Boaz ensured abundance. The story doesn't end with gleaning—it ends with possessing. Boaz marries Ruth. She becomes co-owner of the estate where she once gathered scraps. From gleaning to possessing. From poverty to wealth. From no future to the lineage of King David and Jesus Christ. "God is transitioning me from gleaning to possessing. Where I'm gathering leftovers today, I'll own the estate tomorrow." This is provision through positioning—being in the right place with the right heart attracts the right provision. Your current gleaning season is preparation for your possessing season.

Pattern Five: Provision Through Unexpected Sources—God Is Creative. Drought declared. No rain for three and a half years by Elijah's prophetic word. The prophet himself faced the famine he'd pronounced. Then heaven demonstrated creativity that defies natural law: "Then the word of the Lord came to him, saying, 'Get away from here and turn eastward, and hide by the Brook Cherith...And it will be that you shall drink from the brook, and I have commanded the ravens to feed you there'" (1 Kings 17:2-4). Ravens? Unclean birds. Scavengers. The least likely supply source. Yet: "The ravens brought him bread and meat in the morning, and bread and meat in the evening" (1 Kings 17:6). God's provision doesn't always come through conventional means. Centuries later, Jesus demonstrated the same creative provision. Peter worried about temple tax. Then heaven interrupted with specific instruction: "Go to the sea, cast in a hook, and take the fish that comes up first. And when you have opened its mouth, you will find a piece of money; take that and give it to them for Me and you" (Matthew 17:27). A coin in a fish's mouth. Provision with precision and timing from completely unexpected source. Your provision may not look like you expected. It might come through "ravens"—unlikely people, unexpected opportunities, impossible timing. Trust the Provider's creativity, not your limited imagination.

Pattern Six: Provision Through Multiplication—Little Becomes Much. Five thousand men. Plus women and children. Perhaps fifteen thousand hungry people on a hillside with evening approaching. The disciples calculated impossibility: "Send the multitudes away, that they may go into the villages and buy themselves food" (Matthew 14:15). Orphan thinking: Send them away because we don't have enough. Jesus responded with heir confidence: "They do not need to go away. You give them something to eat" (Matthew 14:16). The disciples protested with orphan mathematics: "We have here only five loaves and two fish" (Matthew 14:17). Only. That word reveals everything. Orphan thinking focuses on lack. Heir thinking recognizes seed. "He said, 'Bring them here to Me'" (Matthew 14:18). Jesus didn't create bread from nothing. He multiplied what they already had. Provision often starts with surrendering the little you're holding. "And He took the five loaves and the two fish, and looking up to heaven, He blessed and broke and gave the loaves to the disciples; and the disciples gave to the multitudes. So they all ate and were filled, and they took up twelve baskets full of the fragments that remained" (Matthew 14:19-20). Everyone ate. Everyone filled. Twelve baskets leftover—one for each disciple who said "only." Kingdom mathematics: When placed in God's hands, the little you have becomes more than enough.

Pattern Seven: Provision for Purpose—God Funds His Mission. Before Israel left Egypt, God positioned provision for the journey ahead. "Now the children of Israel had done according to the word of Moses, and they had asked from the Egyptians articles of silver, articles of gold, and clothing. And the Lord had given the people favor in the sight of the Egyptians, so that they granted them what they requested. Thus they plundered the Egyptians" (Exodus 12:35-36). Four hundred years of slavery ended with supernatural wealth transfer. The oppressors supplied the oppressed. Egypt's gold built Israel's tabernacle. Enemy provision funded Kingdom purpose. Where there is vision, there is provision. Centuries later, Nehemiah stood before a pagan king with a burdened heart for Jerusalem's broken walls. He requested timber, letters of safe passage, resources for reconstruction. The king's response demonstrated divine provision through strategic relationships: "And the king granted them to me according to the good hand of my God upon me" (Nehemiah 2:8). Divine provision often flows through strategic relationships and favor. When God calls you to build, He positions people to supply. Your assignment comes with its provision protocol.

Pattern Eight: Provision Through Jesus—The Ultimate Supply. A Samaritan woman came to Jacob's well for physical water. Jesus offered spiritual provision that transcended natural need: "Whoever drinks of this water will thirst again, but whoever drinks of the water that I shall give him will never thirst. But the water that I shall give him will become in him a fountain of water springing up into everlasting life" (John 4:13-14). The greatest provision is not material goods but God Himself. "I am the bread of life. He who comes to Me shall never hunger, and he who believes in Me shall never thirst" (John 6:35). When Jesus taught His disciples to pray, He included: "Give us this day our daily bread" (Matthew 6:11). Not weekly bread. Not monthly provision. Daily. Because provision is relational—it flows from trust and intimacy with the Father. "He who did not spare His own Son, but delivered Him up for us all, how shall He not with Him also freely give us all things?" (Romans 8:32). If God gave you Jesus, everything else is already included.

THE SIX DIMENSIONS OF PROVISION TRANSFORMATION

Provision isn't just financial—it transforms every dimension of your existence when you shift from orphan panic to heir confidence. Watch how identity determines approach across all six areas simultaneously:

DIMENSION	ORPHAN (Panic/Scarcity)	HEIR (Confidence/Abundance)	YOUR ACTIVATION
SPIRITUAL	Begging for encounters	Blessed with every spiritual blessing (Eph 1:3)	"I receive spiritual supply!"
MENTAL	Exhausted from figuring out	Wisdom given liberally (James 1:5)	"I receive divine wisdom!"
EMOTIONAL	Emotionally bankrupt	Perfect peace, satisfied soul (Isaiah 26:3)	"I receive emotional security!"
PHYSICAL	Physically depleted	Strength renewed like eagles (Isaiah 40:31)	"I receive physical vitality!"
FINANCIAL	Poverty panic, hoarding	Supply according to His riches (Phil 4:19)	"I receive financial provision!"
RELATIONAL	Toxic/draining connections	Iron sharpens iron (Prov 27:17)	"I receive divine connections!"

The Pattern: Orphan thinking produces scarcity in all areas. Heir identity releases abundance across all dimensions simultaneously. You don't beg for provision in six separate areas—you receive from one identity position, and JEHOVAH-JIREH supplies comprehensively.

THE SIX DIMENSIONS WHERE PROVISION FLOWS

Provision isn't just financial—it's foundational to every dimension of your existence. God provides in spiritual realms, mental capacity, emotional security, physical strength, financial resources, and relational connections because you need wholeness, not just wealth.

For Spiritual Provision: "Father, I've been spiritually hungry while seated at Your table. Begging for encounters when You've prepared divine appointments. But today I discover: You are not just Provider—You are provision itself. 'His divine power has given to us all things that pertain to life and godliness' (2 Peter 1:3). I reject spiritual poverty mentality. I reject the lie that encounters are rare. 'Blessed be the God and Father of our Lord Jesus Christ, who has blessed us with every spiritual blessing in the heavenly places in Christ' (Ephesians 1:3). Today I receive JEHOVAH-JIREH as my spiritual supplier. You see my need for fresh manna before I recognize hunger. Where I've been begging for drops—rivers open. Where I've been rationing revelation—abundance flows. I am not spiritually bankrupt. I am blessed with every spiritual blessing. In Jesus' name, I am spiritually provided for. Amen."

For Mental Provision: "Father, my mind is exhausted from trying to figure out what only You can reveal. Mental fatigue from calculating outcomes I can't control. But today I learn: You don't just give wisdom—You are wisdom. 'If any of you lacks wisdom, let him ask of God, who gives to all liberally and without reproach' (James 1:5). I reject the lie that I must have all the answers. I reject confusion when Kingdom wisdom is available. Today I receive EL SHADDAI as my mental nourisher. You feed my mind with strategies that exceed my experience. 'For the Lord gives wisdom; from His mouth come knowledge and understanding' (Proverbs 2:6). Where I've been mentally exhausted—supernatural energy flows. Where I've been confused—clarity breaks through. My mind is nourished by EL SHADDAI. I don't scramble for answers—I receive revelation as heir. In Jesus' name, I am mentally provided for. Amen."

For Emotional Provision: "Father, I've been emotionally bankrupt while positioned for supernatural security. Running on empty when You offer fullness. But today I discover: You don't just calm emotions—You are my emotional security. 'You will keep him in perfect peace, whose mind is stayed on You, because he trusts in You' (Isaiah 26:3). I reject emotional instability as my identity. I reject anxiety as my default. Today I receive JEHOVAH-SHALOM as my emotional provider. You supply peace that surpasses understanding. 'The Lord will guide you continually, and satisfy your soul in drought, and strengthen your bones; you shall be like a watered garden' (Isaiah 58:11). Where anxiety attacked—peace defends. Where insecurity dominated—confidence rises. I don't beg for emotional stability—I receive it as inheritance. In Jesus' name, I am emotionally provided for. Amen."

For Physical Provision: "Father, my body feels the weight of provision battles. Physical exhaustion from fighting lack. But today I learn: You don't just heal bodies—You provide strength for the journey. 'The Lord will guide you continually...and strengthen your bones' (Isaiah 58:11). I reject sickness as my portion. I reject physical exhaustion as inevitable. Today I receive JEHOVAH-RAPHA as my physical provider. 'For I am the Lord who heals you' (Exodus 15:26). Where exhaustion attacked—energy flows. Where sickness threatened—healing manifests. 'Those who wait on the Lord shall renew their strength; they shall mount up with wings like eagles' (Isaiah 40:31). I don't beg for physical health—I receive it as covenant promise. In Jesus' name, I am physically provided for. Amen."

For Financial Provision: "Father, I'm drowning in financial fear. Bills that testify against my faith. Accounts that accuse my trust. But today I discover: The intensity of the financial attack reveals the treasure I carry. Hell only robs houses full of wealth. My empty bank account doesn't diminish my spiritual account. I reject the lie that financial lack defines my worth. I reject poverty as my portion. Today I receive JEHOVAH-JIREH as my financial provider. 'And my God shall supply all your need according to His riches in glory by Christ Jesus' (Philippians 4:19). Not according to my account—according to His riches. I am not an orphan scrambling for scraps. I am an heir stewarding family resources. 'Seek first the kingdom of God and His righteousness, and all these things shall be added to you' (Matthew 6:33). Where lack dominated—abundance flows. 'Give, and it will be given to you: good measure, pressed down, shaken together, and running over' (Luke 6:38). I don't hoard—I circulate. I don't panic—I plan. In Jesus' name, I am financially provided for. Amen."

For Relational Provision: "Father, relationships have cost me more than they've contributed. People who drained instead of deposited. But today I learn: You don't just send people—You provide divine connections that sharpen, strengthen, and supply. 'Two are better than one, because they have a good reward for their labor' (Ecclesiastes 4:9). I reject toxic relationships as normal. I reject isolation as protection. Today I receive You as my relational provider. 'Iron sharpens iron, so a man sharpens the countenance of his friend' (Proverbs 27:17). Where isolation dominated—divine connections emerge. Where toxic relationships drained—Kingdom partnerships deposit. You led Ruth to Boaz. You connected David with Jonathan. You positioned Elijah with Elisha. You provide relationships that resource destiny. In Jesus' name, I am relationally provided for. Amen."

RESISTANCE REALITY CHECK: BREAKING THE LIES

Understanding these attacks helps you respond with truth instead of terror. But before you break these enemies, you must ask yourself the questions that expose their root: Do I cherish the gift more than the Giver? Has the provision claimed precedence over the Provider in my life? Would I, like Abraham, be willing to surrender my greatest treasure in obedience and devotion to God, my Provider? These questions aren't condemnation—they're calibration. They position your heart to receive provision with the right priorities.

LIE #1: ORPHAN PANIC / CONDEMNATION Hell whispers: "You're unworthy because you're struggling financially. There's never enough, you have to grab what you can get." Heaven's Response: "I'm qualified by Christ's blood, not my bank balance. I provide according to My riches, not your limitations. You're My heir, stewarding family resources." Break it now: "I reject orphan panic and condemnation! I am an heir stewarding family resources! Romans 8:1—there is no condemnation in Christ Jesus! Philippians 4:19—God supplies according to His riches!"

LIE #2: COMPARISON TRAP Hell whispers: "Others are more blessed because they're more faithful. Others have more because they deserve more." Heaven's Response: "Your portion is perfect for your purpose. Stay in your lane, trust My timing. My gifts match My calling on your life. Don't measure My faithfulness by comparing your chapter to someone else's." Break it now: "I reject comparison! My portion matches my purpose! Psalm 16:5—the Lord is the portion of my inheritance and my cup! My story is custom-designed for my destiny!"

LIE #3: PROVISION ANXIETY / CONFUSION Hell whispers: "What if God doesn't come through this time? Maybe He forgot about you. Maybe He doesn't care anymore." Heaven's Response: "I've never failed you yet. I know your needs before you ask. My track record speaks—count the times I came through when logic said impossible. I see and supply before you recognize the need." Break it now: "I reject provision anxiety and confusion! God's faithfulness is my foundation! Matthew 6:8—He knows my needs before I ask! His past faithfulness predicts His future provision!"

LIE #4: STEWARDSHIP FEAR / COMPROMISE Hell whispers: "What if you give and then don't have enough? Hoard what you have. Just compromise this once—bend the rules, use worldly methods." Heaven's Response: "You can't out-give Me. Generous hearts always receive generous supply. Integrity in the process protects provision in the outcome. Character maintained brings long-term provision sustained." Break it now: "I reject stewardship fear and compromise! Generosity creates circulation! Luke 6:38—give and it will be given! Integrity positions me for sustained provision, not just temporary gain!"

Your provision anxiety is just identity confusion. Remember whose child you are. The intensity of the attack reveals the treasure you carry. Your attacks prove your anointing. Your battles confirm your significance.

PROPHETIC ACTIVATION: THE GENEROUS SEED

Within 24 hours, find a seed—from an apple, orange, garden packet, anywhere. This small seed contains forests. When you find it, hold it in your palm. Feel its weight. So small, yet containing potential for multiplication beyond measure. Now speak with authority, releasing the provision principles that break orphan thinking and activate heir confidence:

"This seed represents what I currently hold. It looks insufficient. Logic says hoard it. Fear says protect it. But JEHOVAH-JIREH says plant it! 'Now may He who supplies seed to the sower, and bread for food, supply and multiply the seed you have sown' (2 Corinthians 9:10). God doesn't just give bread to eat—He gives seed to plant! I am not just a consumer—I am a sower! 'He who refreshes others will himself be refreshed' (Proverbs 11:25). The more I pour out, the more flows in! 'Give, and it will be given to you: good measure, pressed down, shaken together, and running over will be put into your bosom' (Luke 6:38). Generosity creates circulation! Circulation attracts supply! Isaac planted in the year of famine—the worst possible time by natural logic. 'Then Isaac sowed in that land, and reaped in the same year a hundredfold; and the Lord blessed him' (Genesis 26:12). Same year! Hundredfold! In famine! When you plant in faith, God multiplies in the same season! Job prayed for his friends when he was the one in crisis. 'And the Lord restored Job's losses when he prayed for his friends. Indeed the Lord gave Job twice as much as he had before' (Job 42:10). Blessing others during your own battle positions you for double restoration! 'Bring all the tithes into the storehouse, that there may be food in My house, and try Me now in this,' says the Lord of hosts, 'If I will not open for you the windows of heaven and pour out for you such blessing that there will not be room enough to receive it' (Malachi 3:10). Test Me! God invites you to test His faithfulness in generosity! I am not an orphan hoarding scraps—I am an heir circulating blessing! This seed goes into Kingdom ground! Where I plant in faith, God multiplies in harvest! I break orphan panic! I break hoarding mentality! I release this seed as declaration: I trust the Provider more than the provision! From gleaning to possessing! From pit to palace! From lack to abundance! My jar of flour will not run out! The Lord indeed will provide!"

Now complete your prophetic act by choosing ONE of three options:

Option 1 - Plant the Seed Literally: In soil, pot, or garden—plant it with intention. Nurture it. Water it. Watch it grow. Every time you see the plant emerging, remember: What I sow in obedience, God multiplies in harvest. This isn't magic—it's Kingdom mathematics. The seed becomes living testimony to divine multiplication.

Option 2 - Give Sacrificially: Keep the seed as your memorial (instructions below), but give away some of the money you were keeping, planning, or hoarding. Not recklessly—strategically. Ask God: "Who needs what I'm holding?" Then give it. Not from abundance, but from obedience. The widow gave her last. Ruth gave her loyalty before seeing provision. Abraham gave his promised son. What you release in faith, God replaces with increase.

Option 3 - Bless Someone Tangibly: Keep the seed as your memorial (instructions below), but immediately bless someone. Buy coffee for the person behind you. Purchase a gift card for someone in need. Serve someone who can't repay you. Pray for someone's breakthrough. Refresh others and watch God refresh you. When you water others, heaven waters you.

Let your chosen action break orphan thinking and activate heir confidence. Provision follows generosity because circulation attracts supply. Dead-end rivers stagnate. Flowing tributaries stay fresh. You're not the reservoir—you're the river. Let it flow.

MEMORIAL: THE PROVISION SEED (DAILY PRACTICE)

If you chose Option 2 or 3 above, you have your seed for this memorial. If you planted your seed (Option 1), find a second seed to serve as your daily reminder. Place your seed in a small clear container, envelope, or jar beside your Bible, your peace stone from Day 17, or on your desk where you'll see it daily. This seed represents the Kingdom principle: God gives seed to the sower, not just bread to the eater. You're not just consuming—you're cultivating.

Every morning, look at the seed and declare: "I am not an orphan hoarding what I have. I am an heir circulating what God gives. This seed reminds me: What I plant in faith, God multiplies in harvest. JEHOVAH-JIREH sees my need before I ask. EL SHADDAI nourishes abundantly. From gleaning to possessing. From pit to palace. I am not the sacrifice—The Lord indeed will provide!"

THE WEEKLY GENEROSITY CHECK

Once per week, do one act of generosity despite current circumstances. This isn't about the amount—it's about the obedience. The widow gave two mites. The stranger gave $41.10. Ruth gave loyalty. Abraham gave his promised son. What you release in faith, God replaces with increase.

Choose one: buy someone's coffee or meal; send $5-$20 to someone in need (ask God who and how much); give away something you were keeping; serve someone without expecting return; pray specifically for someone's breakthrough; share resources, skills, or time sacrificially.

Why weekly generosity? Because generosity breaks orphan thinking. When you give from lack, you prove you trust the Provider more than the provision. This isn't earning favor—it's positioning for flow. Circulation attracts supply. Stagnant water spoils. Flowing rivers stay fresh. "He who refreshes others

THE DANIEL FAST: CLOSING THE GAP!

will himself be refreshed" (Proverbs 11:25). Track these acts in your journal under "Generosity Log." Date it. Note what you gave. Watch how provision follows generosity. Not as transaction, but as Kingdom principle proven across generations. Isaac sowed in famine, reaped hundredfold same year. Job prayed for friends in crisis, received double restoration. The widow fed Elijah first, flour never ran out.

Your seed, whether planted in soil or kept in a jar, becomes your memorial. Every time you see it—growing in the garden or resting beside your Bible—remember: I'm not an orphan scrambling for scraps. I'm an heir stewarding family resources. The Provider sees before I ask. The Nourisher supplies before I'm empty. From gleaning fields to owning estates. From prison pits to palace authority. This is my testimony: The Lord indeed will provide.

THE STEWARD'S DECLARATION

Stand and declare with authority: "I am not an orphan scrambling for scraps—I am an heir stewarding family resources! JEHOVAH-JIREH sees my needs before I recognize them! EL SHADDAI nourishes like a faithful parent! The Lord is my Shepherd; I lack nothing! With God at my side, I lack nothing! He will provide all that I need! I shall not be found wanting! Like Abraham—trusting provision before seeing supply! I am not the sacrifice; The Lord indeed will provide! Like the widow—generous in lack, supplied in need! My jar of flour will not be used up! My jug of oil will not run dry until the Lord sends His rain! Like Ruth—from gleaning to possessing, from the field to the estate! God is transitioning me from gathering scraps to owning the harvest! Like Elijah—fed by ravens when logic declared death! God's provision comes through unexpected sources! Like the multitudes—watching little become much in Jesus' hands! What I surrender, He multiplies! Like Isaac—sowing in famine, reaping hundredfold same year! Like Job—blessing others in crisis, receiving double restoration! I seek first His Kingdom—everything else follows! I give generously—it shall be given unto me! I steward faithfully—increase comes through integrity! From orphan panic to heir confidence! From begging to receiving! From hoarding to stewarding! From pit to palace, from pain to promise, from trials to triumph! I am an heir of the King! Amen!"

BREAKTHROUGH PRAYER

"JEHOVAH-JIREH, faithful Provider, EL SHADDAI who nourishes, forgive me for thinking like an orphan when You've made me an heir. For panic when You call for trust. For hoarding when You designed me for generous circulation. Forgive me for times when the gift became more precious than the Giver, when provision claimed precedence over the Provider in my life. Thank You that my identity doesn't change with my circumstances. That You see my needs before I recognize them. That Your provision flows according to Your riches, not my limitations. You have been my Provider in the past, You are my Provider in the present, and You will be my Provider in the future, unknown though it may be. This past-present-future faithfulness anchors my trust in every season. Right now, I receive heir-level confidence. Spiritual encounters that satisfy soul-deep. Mental wisdom transforming thoughts. Emotional peace anchored in Your character. Physical strength for service and calling. Financial resources for Kingdom and family. Relational connections that sharpen and strengthen. Like Abraham, I trust Your YIREH—You see and provide. I am not the sacrifice; The Lord indeed will provide! Like Israel, I receive manna in wilderness. Like the widow, I give from lack and receive from abundance. My jar of flour will not be used up! My jug of oil will not run dry! Like Ruth, I transition from gleaning to possessing. God is moving me from gathering leftovers to owning the estate! Like Elijah, I'm fed by unexpected sources. Like the multitudes, I watch You multiply what I surrender. Like Isaac, I sow in famine and reap hundredfold! Like Job, I bless friends and receive double! Like Nehemiah, I receive favor for Kingdom purpose. Like Joseph, I go from pit to palace, from pain to promise, from trials to triumph! I don't beg for provision—I receive from position. I don't hoard resources—I circulate blessing. Transform me from orphan to heir, from panic to confidence, from grasping to stewarding. In Jesus' name, the scrambling ends and stewarding begins. Amen."

CLOSING: FROM PANIC TO CONFIDENCE

You awakened approaching provision like an orphan begging for scraps. Tonight you rest knowing you're an heir stewarding family resources. Day 18's transformative gift: Identity determines approach, and approach determines outcome. The $41.10 experience demonstrated God's creative provision—both supply and scripture, money and message encoded together. While recognizing that each person's financial journey contains unique complexities, this experience revealed divine faithfulness in unexpected ways. But the deeper revolution transcends any single testimony: You're not an orphan scrambling for survival. You're an heir learning stewardship. This doesn't mean faithful people never face financial challenges. Scripture shows us provision patterns that work in every season—rams in thickets, manna in wilderness, flour that doesn't run out, ravens that feed prophets, coins in fish mouths, multiplied loaves, Ruth's elevation from gleaning to possessing, Isaac sowing in famine and reaping hundredfold, Job blessing friends and receiving double, Joseph's journey from pit to palace, favor with kings. God's faithfulness isn't measured by your bank account—it's demonstrated through every season of trust.

Tomorrow begins Day 19: Purpose—discovering that faithful stewardship positions you for divine assignment. When God trusts your heart with little, He prepares to trust you with much. But tonight, the question remains: Which dimension needs your declaration? Which area requires the shift from orphan thinking to heir confidence? Your diagnostic remains supernatural: Am I approaching this like an orphan or an heir? Orphans panic about provision. Heirs rest in the Provider's faithfulness. Stop begging for what already belongs to you. Start stewarding what's been yours all along. Touch your provision seed. Remember the eight patterns. Declare the Ruth testimony: from gleaning to possessing. Declare the Joseph testimony: from pit to palace. Declare the Isaac testimony: sowing in famine, reaping hundredfold same year. Declare the Job testimony: blessing others in crisis, receiving double restoration. You are not an orphan scrambling. You are an heir positioned. The Provider sees before you ask. The Nourisher supplies before you're empty.

Four days of foundation built: Day 15 positioned you through dwelling. Day 16 covered you through protection. Day 17 weaponized you through peace. Day 18 resources you through provision. The secret place becomes the supply place. The shadow becomes the source. The peace becomes the portal. The provision flows from position. Provision flows from position, not performance. Week 3 Continues: PROPEL into Destiny—Provision Stewarded. Tomorrow: Day 19 Purpose begins. Faithful stewardship unlocks divine assignment. What you manage with little determines what God trusts you with much.

THE DANIEL FAST: CLOSING THE GAP!

SOAP JOURNAL — DAY 18

S (Scripture): Write Philippians 4:19 and Genesis 22:14. Circle "supply all your need" and "The-Lord-Will-Provide." Underline the phrase that stands out most to you.

O (Observation): Am I approaching provision like an orphan or an heir? Do I cherish the gift more than the Giver? Has provision claimed precedence over the Provider in my life? Which provision pattern speaks to my current situation—provision before need (Abraham's ram), in impossible places (manna/water from rock), through obedience (widow's flour), through positioning (Ruth: gleaning to possessing), unexpected sources (ravens/coin in fish), multiplication (five loaves), for purpose (Nehemiah's favor), or through Jesus (ultimate supply)? Am I trusting the Provider or just the provision?

A (Application): Choose one dimension (spiritual, mental, emotional, physical, financial, or relational) and pray that focused prayer daily this week. Find your provision seed within 24 hours and place it where you'll see it daily. Declare "I am not the sacrifice; The Lord indeed will provide!" Complete the Prophetic Activation—do one of the three actions (plant seed, give sacrificially, bless someone). Schedule your first weekly Generosity Check and create your Generosity Log in your journal. Touch your seed daily and declare: "From gleaning to possessing. From pit to palace. From sowing in famine to reaping hundredfold."

P (Prayer): "JEHOVAH-JIREH, I've been fighting for provision with orphan panic. Today I receive heir confidence. You see my needs before I ask. From pit to palace, from gleaning to possessing, from lack to abundance—I am positioned and provided for. I trust the Provider more than the provision. In Jesus' name, Amen."

Today's Breakthrough Marker: How did shifting from orphan panic to heir confidence change your approach to provision? Which biblical pattern resonated most deeply? Did the Ruth story (gleaning to possessing), Joseph story (pit to palace), Isaac story (sowing in famine, reaping hundredfold), or Job story (blessing in crisis, double restoration) speak to your current season? Did you complete the Prophetic Activation? Did you find your provision seed? Which of the three generosity actions will you take this week?

Tomorrow's Expectation: Based on today's stewardship foundation, how will faithful provision management prepare you for divine promotion? If God trusts you with little, what might He trust you with much? How does understanding provision prepare you for understanding purpose?

Day 18 Complete: Provision Stewarded. Orphan panic ended. Heir confidence activated. Eight biblical patterns revealed (provision before need, impossible places, through obedience, through positioning, unexpected sources, multiplication, for purpose, through Jesus). Six dimensions declared. Hell robs full houses—I am that house. Identity determines approach. "I am not the sacrifice; The Lord indeed will provide!" Gift vs Giver examined. From gleaning to possessing. From pit to palace. From sowing in famine to reaping hundredfold. From praying for friends to receiving double. JEHOVAH-JIREH sees and supplies. EL SHADDAI nourishes abundantly. Provision seed memorial established. Weekly Generosity Check activated. Prophetic activation completed. Stewardship positioned. Generosity circulating. Four-day foundation complete: Dwelling (Day 15), Protection (Day 16), Peace (Day 17), Provision (Day 18). Three more days ahead. Ready for purpose.

DAY 19 — PROMOTION

Divine Elevation for the Positioned

> *"For promotion comes neither from the east nor from the west nor from the south. But God is the Judge: He puts down one and exalts another."* — Psalm 75:6-7

WEEK 3 — PROPEL: Accelerating into Destiny

Day 19 of 21. Yesterday's Provision transformed your approach from orphan panic to heir confidence. Today's Promotion unveils the most revolutionary truth about divine elevation you'll ever encounter—not what you climb toward, but what descends from heaven's throne.

THE STRATEGIC CONNECTIONS: HOW PROVISION PREPARED YOU FOR PROMOTION

Day 18's Provision taught you that identity determines approach, and approach determines outcome. You discovered you're not an orphan scrambling for scraps but an heir stewarding family resources. Eight biblical patterns demonstrated JEHOVAH-JIREH's consistent character. From Abraham's ram to Ruth's gleaning-to-possessing, you learned God provides before the need. Today reveals what happens when provision positions you for promotion. Faithful stewardship of little qualifies you for authority over much. What you manage in obscurity prepares you for influence in prominence. When peace weaponizes you and provision resources you, promotion elevates you. Week 2 taught you advancement—the process of elevation. Day 12 through Day 14 prepared you with the anointing for the assignment. Today you discover promotion—the event, the divine appointment where preparation meets opportunity and heaven's timing aligns with earth's readiness. Day 14's Affirmation declared your identity. Day 17's Peace weaponized your rest. Day 18's Provision resourced your calling. Today's Promotion positions you where character, calling, and consecration collide with destiny.

ENCOUNTER: WHEN HEAVEN REWRITES YOUR STORY

Your body doesn't wake. It resurrects. 4:30 AM. Day 19. Nineteen days of Daniel fasting have carved you into something unrecognizable. The person who started this fast checking LinkedIn notifications, measuring worth by titles, exhausting themselves climbing corporate ladders—that person died somewhere around Day 14. What remains is this strange hybrid of weakness and power. This vessel emptied of ambition but filled with something that makes hell tremble and heaven celebrate. You move to your prayer corner in practiced silence. No phone. No scrolling to see who got promoted while you fasted. Those concerns feel like artifacts from another lifetime, relics from someone you used to be. Your knees find the familiar groove in the carpet—that spot worn smooth by nineteen days of desperate seeking. But as you settle into position, a memory ambushes you with surgical precision. The conference room. Two years ago. The announcement that shattered everything you thought you understood about merit, fairness, and divine justice. Someone else's name where yours belonged. The position you'd earned through three years of excellence, given to someone with half your experience but twice your connections. The metallic taste of being overlooked still burns your throat. But nineteen days of fasting have taught you something that corporate America never could: Sometimes what looks like rejection is actually divine redirection.

"God," you whisper into darkness, Hannah's ancient prayer rising through your lips like incense, "The Lord makes poor and makes rich; He brings low and lifts up. He raises the poor from dust and lifts the beggar from the ash heap, to set them among princes." "I've been the beggar in this story too long. Show me how You make owners from beggars, employers from employees, influencers from the overlooked." Silence stretches like eternity. Then heaven detonates your resignation with revelation that will redefine everything: "What if you were never overlooked? What if you were looking in the wrong direction?"

REVELATION: THE MISSING DIRECTION

Your spine straightens as truth crashes through every doubt: "You were looking east for opportunity. West for position. South for connections. But promotion doesn't come from east, west, or south." The psalmist mapped supernatural GPS with surgical precision: "For promotion comes neither from the east nor from the west nor from the south" (Psalm 75:6). Three directions named with deliberate exclusion. One direction omitted with prophetic purpose. NORTH—the dwelling place of God's throne. Isaiah saw it: "I will exalt my throne above the stars of God... on the farthest sides of the north" (Isaiah 14:13). The psalmist confirmed: "Beautiful in elevation... Mount Zion on the sides of the north" (Psalm 48:2). Heaven's voice thunders with authority that silences every competing narrative: "Notice what's missing? NORTH. Where My throne sits. Promotion descends vertically from My throne, not horizontally from human tables." "You weren't overlooked. You were positioned for elevation that bypasses every protocol, transcends every system, and makes impossible things inevitable."

The Biblical Definition: What Is Promotion?

Promotion is not a position to pursue—it's a posture to steward. It is the divine elevation of a person into greater influence, authority, responsibility, and impact in alignment with God's purpose and timing, not for self-exaltation. Promotion in Scripture is more than job title or career advancement. It is God's strategic placement of people for Kingdom purpose, impact, and stewardship. It is the act of God elevating a person as a reward for humility, faithfulness, obedience, and purpose alignment. Promotion is not a prize for ambition—it is a position for assignment. It is not a sign of status—it is a tool for stewardship. When God promotes, it is not just an elevation; it's an awakening, a paradigm shift that nourishes your spirit, fosters deeper connection with Him, and opens your heart to receive the wisdom of His word. The phrase "God is the Judge" uses SHAPHAT [shah-FAHT]—He decides, He vindicates, He positions. Your promotion isn't up for committee vote, board approval, or human consensus. It's up to God alone. "But God is the Judge: He puts down one, and exalts another" (Psalm 75:7). Week 2 taught you advancement—the progressive process of elevation, the journey where anointing develops for assignment. Today you discover promotion—the event, the divine appointment where God places His prepared vessel in strategic position for Kingdom advancement. Advancement prepares you with the anointing. Promotion positions you with the appointment.

The Hebrew Revelation: RUM

The Hebrew crashes like thunder through twenty centuries of striving: RUM [room]—to be lifted by another's strength, to be raised, exalted, elevated. This word thunders through Scripture 190 times because God loves lifting beggars to thrones. You don't RUM yourself. You are RUM-ed by God. Hannah sang it after barrenness broke: "The Lord lifts up! He raises the poor from dust and lifts the beggar from the ash heap!" (1 Samuel 2:7-8). RUM means rising from dust to dynasty. You're shifting from renter to owner, employee to employer, follower to leader, overlooked to overbooked. But here's what changes everything: You don't lift yourself. Another lifts you. Biblical promotion isn't climbing a ladder—it's being lifted by the Lord who owns every ladder, every building, every corporation, and every throne.

The Hebrew Revelation: NASA

This word appears 650 times in Scripture. NASA [nah-SAH] means "to carry, bear up, lift, raise"—carried beyond your ability to reach, elevated past where credentials qualify, positioned where résumés can't secure and connections can't guarantee. Joseph testified with certainty born of supernatural transportation: "God will surely carry [NASA] you up" (Genesis 50:24). Stop exhausting yourself climbing. NASA means God's carrying you where human effort cannot reach.

The Greek Revelation: HUPSOŌ

When James wrote "Humble yourselves in the sight of the Lord, and He will lift you up [HUPSOŌ]" (James 4:10), he used the word HUPSOŌ [hoop-SO-oh] that means "to exalt, lift to the highest rank, raise to dignity." This is divine elevation connected to God's glory, not human achievement. Every time you chose serving over spotlight, HUPSOŌ activated in heaven's database. Hidden faithfulness becomes public platform. Secret service becomes visible authority. The humble get lifted—not because they deserve it, but because God delights in elevating those who decrease so He can increase. Promotion is not achieved—it's received. It's not the result of manipulation, competition, or ambition—but of God's sovereign choice and timing.

THE FRAMEWORK: KINGDOM PRINCIPLES THAT GOVERN PROMOTION

PRINCIPLE	DESCRIPTION	SCRIPTURE	RESULT
Humility	Humbling yourself positions you for exaltation	James 4:10; 1 Peter 5:6	God lifts you in due time
Obedience	Faithful obedience opens doors to elevation	Deuteronomy 28:1	God sets you "high above"
Faithfulness	Stewarding small things qualifies you for greater	Matthew 25:21	Greater authority entrusted
Character	Integrity sustains what favor opens	Psalm 37:5-6	Promotion without downfall
Timing	Waiting on God's season prevents premature elevation	Ecclesiastes 3:1	Promotion in due season
Purpose	God promotes for Kingdom assignments, not ambition	Esther 4:14	Elevated "for such a time"
Service	Serving others is the pathway to authority	Matthew 23:11-12	The greatest is the servant

The difference between worldly ambition and Kingdom promotion isn't your circumstances—it's your posture. Kingdom law operates backwards from corporate culture: Service leads to stewardship. Stewardship builds trust. Trust qualifies for elevation. Excellence in one dimension positions you for promotion in all dimensions. Faithfulness in little qualifies you for authority over much.

THE TESTIMONY: WHEN DEMOTION BECAME DIVINE STRATEGY

The Headhunter's Humiliating Offer

I need to tell you about the day heaven taught me that sometimes going backwards is the only way to go forward in God's economy. The call that would redefine everything came on a Tuesday afternoon that felt like the end of my world. "They're offering you the Senior Manager position." I sat in my car—the one symbol of success I still clutched like a life preserver—staring at what felt like professional suicide. I'd interviewed for Senior Director. This was demotion dressed as opportunity. Director to Senior Manager. Less money, less prestige, less everything that corporate culture teaches you to worship. My comfortable commute replaced by two hours door-to-door via train. Every fiber of my being screamed: "This is humiliation." The headhunter's voice echoed through the phone like a death sentence, each word a nail in my professional coffin. I could see it already—the questions from colleagues, the pity in their eyes, the whispered conversations: "Did you hear? She went backwards. Must have done something wrong." But nineteen days of fasting had taught me to listen for heaven's voice beneath hell's accusations. Somewhere beneath the shame, beneath the panic, beneath the logical arguments against accepting less—a whisper: "What if I'm positioning you?" "For what?" The question tore from my throat, raw with desperation and confusion. "Everyone will ask why I'm going backward. How do I explain accepting less to people who measure everything by more?"

The Wrestling Match with Pride

Three days I wrestled. Three days pride and obedience fought to the death in my spirit. Three days of heaven and hell warring over one decision that would determine the trajectory of my destiny. I made lists. Pros and cons. Financial calculations. Career trajectory projections. Every logical analysis screamed "NO!" But every time I prayed, peace flooded the "yes." Pride whispered its seductive logic: "You've worked too hard to go backwards. What will people think? This will ruin your reputation. This makes no sense." But somewhere deeper than pride, louder than fear, stronger than shame—heaven's persistent whisper: "Trust Me. This demotion is divine positioning. Sometimes I take you down to lift you higher than you could climb." Finally, with ego bleeding on obedience's altar, with every logical argument surrendered to supernatural peace, I accepted. Senior Manager. The title felt like a scarlet letter, but the peace felt like heaven's approval. The answer that would save my life came wrapped in contradiction: "Sometimes I demote you to promote you. Sometimes backward is forward in My economy. Sometimes what looks like professional death is resurrection in disguise."

The Divine Mathematics of Protection

Six months later, my phone exploded with devastating news that revealed divine precision I couldn't have imagined. Former colleagues texting in panic: Company restructuring. Director position—eliminated. Entire leadership level—dissolved. Every Director—packaged out with minimal severance, careers shattered, families devastated. The same role I'd coveted, the promotion I'd thought I deserved—

obliterated. Everyone at that level—gone. I sat in my "lesser" office, trembling at divine precision that took my breath away. The demotion had been evacuation before explosion. The humiliation had been salvation in disguise. God hadn't withheld promotion—He'd prevented devastation. What I'd seen as rejection had been protection. What felt like going backward had positioned me forward. The shame I'd carried for six months transformed into awe. God saw the earthquake coming and moved me to safer ground before it struck. But heaven wasn't finished with His backwards mathematics.

When Professional Death Birthed Eternal Purpose

Valley's deepest floor arrived like scheduled devastation. Divorce finalized with soul-crushing precision. Home sold by court order. Custody battle draining every resource like spiritual hemorrhaging. Then the final blow that should have destroyed me: "Your position is being eliminated." This time I recognized the pattern. This time I asked different questions: "What are You positioning me for now, Lord?" "Your CHAYAH moment." CHAYAH means resurrection life—God breathing life into dead things. The business I'd registered in 2011—Nikimac—lay dormant for four years. Zero clients. Zero income. Zero hope by human standards. But CHAYAH specializes in what looks permanently dead. Within weeks of surrendering to His backwards plan—updating website, expanding services, trusting Him with my reputation in shambles—my phone rang with destiny. Contract secured. First corporate client. The rate exceeded my Director salary. Position elimination birthed Chayah Club—breathing life into thousands globally. Professional death became purpose birth. The demotion I'd resisted had been divine positioning for multiplication I couldn't imagine. Every backwards step had been forward progress in heaven's GPS system. When heaven demotes you, it's positioning you for promotion no human title could contain, no corporate structure could limit, no earthly system could define. This testimony demonstrates how God can transform devastating setbacks into divine positioning, though I recognize each person's career journey contains unique complexities beyond spiritual practices alone.

BIBLICAL CHAMPIONS: THE PROMOTION PATTERN THAT NEVER FAILS

Scripture reveals a consistent pattern across generations: Hidden faithfulness leads to divine positioning, which results in supernatural elevation that creates generational impact. These aren't isolated miracles but repeated realities demonstrating how divine promotion operates.

Joseph: Prison to Palace Through Thirteen Years of Preparation

Seventeen with dreams that seemed delusional. Thirty when they became undeniable. Thirteen years of systematic breaking that felt like cosmic cruelty but was actually divine preparation for unprecedented authority. Sold into slavery by jealous brothers who couldn't tolerate his father's favor. "Now Israel loved Joseph more than all his children... and he made him a tunic of many colors" (Genesis 37:3). But favor doesn't protect you from process—it prepares you through it. Potiphar's house became Joseph's first training ground. "The Lord was with Joseph, and he was a successful man... And his master saw that the Lord was with him and that the Lord made all he did to prosper in his hand. So Joseph found favor in his sight, and served him" (Genesis 39:2-4). Watch this carefully: Excellence in obscurity. Integrity in isolation. Joseph served like the master's son, not a purchased slave. He stewarded another man's house with supernatural faithfulness that attracted divine attention and human favor. Then betrayal struck again. Potiphar's wife's false accusation landed him in prison—from favored servant to forgotten prisoner. But here's what hell's attacks couldn't destroy: Joseph's character. "The Lord was with Joseph and showed him mercy, and He gave him favor in the sight of the keeper of the prison... because the Lord was with him; and whatever he did, the Lord made it prosper" (Genesis 39:21, 23). Prison couldn't change what pit hadn't destroyed. Joseph served in shackles with the same excellence he'd demonstrated in palaces. He managed prisoners with the same integrity he'd managed households. Character developed in hiddenness prepares you for authority in prominence.

Two more years of forgotten faithfulness. The cupbearer Joseph helped forgot him the moment he was restored. "Yet the chief butler did not remember Joseph, but forgot him" (Genesis 40:23). Sometimes promotion's greatest preparation is learning to serve without recognition, to excel without applause, to remain faithful when forgotten. Then one conversation with Pharaoh changed everything: "See, I have set you over all the land of Egypt" (Genesis 41:41). Twenty-four hours from prisoner to prime minister. Thirteen years of preparation culminated in one day of elevation. When heaven's timing aligned with earth's need, readiness met opportunity with explosive results. Your thirteen years of preparation are about to culminate in your twenty-four hours of elevation. Excellence positioned him. Character sustained him. Faithfulness qualified him. Timing elevated him. Where you've faced trials, you are divinely equipped. Your challenges are stepping stones leading to your appointed season of promotion.

David: From Overlooked to Unforgettable

Hidden in fields while brothers were showcased for the prophet. Eight sons standing before Samuel, but God saw past the lineup to the one left behind with sheep. "Are all the young men here?" Samuel asked. Then Jesse's admission that exposed everything wrong with human assessment: "There remains yet the youngest, and there he is, keeping the sheep" (1 Samuel 16:11). Not worth calling inside. Too young to consider. Hidden in fields doing work nobody celebrated. But God operates by different promotion protocols than human recognition systems. "The Lord said, 'Arise, anoint him; for this is the one!'" (1 Samuel 16:12). Private anointing preceded public platform by years. David returned to sheep after Samuel's oil ran down his face. Back to obscurity after heaven's declaration. Back to hiddenness after destiny's confirmation. Because anointing happens in secret before authority manifests in public. Goliath provided the platform, but sheep had provided the preparation. Lions and bears in wilderness trained him for giants in valleys. "Your servant has killed both lion and bear; and this uncircumcised Philistine will be like one of them" (1 Samuel 17:36). Excellence in what others overlook positions you for impact in what everyone watches. "Do you see a man who excels in his work? He will stand before kings; he will not stand before unknown men" (Proverbs 22:29). Your hidden years weren't wasted—they were warfare training for the kingdom you're about to influence. Sheep-keeping faithfulness prepared David for king-making authority. You are being shaped in seclusion for your forthcoming elevation and legendary promotion.

Esther: Positioned for National Transformation

Orphan to queen through circumstances that looked coincidental but were completely orchestrated. "Esther had neither father nor mother... And when her father and mother died, Mordecai took her as his own daughter" (Esther 2:7). Nothing in her background suggested royalty. Nothing in her circumstances predicted promotion. But God specializes in beggar-to-royalty transformation that makes impossible things inevitable. "The king loved Esther more than all the other women, and she obtained grace and favor in his sight... So he set the royal crown upon her head and made her queen" (Esther 2:17). Favor positioned her. Character sustained her. Purpose elevated her beyond personal comfort into national deliverance. Then Mordecai's revelation exposed promotion's true purpose: "Yet who knows whether you have come to the kingdom for such a time as this?" (Esther 4:14). Your promotion serves others' salvation. Position isn't reward—it's responsibility for generational transformation. Esther's elevation saved a nation. Your promotion will serve purposes greater than personal advancement. When God lifts you, He positions you where your authority advances His covenant and impacts generations you'll never meet. You are created, destined, and positioned for such a time as this.

Daniel: Excellence Makes You Undeniable

Exiled in Babylon, far from home and heritage. But excellence transcends geography, culture, and circumstance. "Then this Daniel distinguished himself above the governors and satraps, because an excellent spirit was in him; and the king gave thought to setting him over the whole realm" (Daniel 6:3). Three kingdoms, multiple governments, different cultures—none could deny his excellence. When you're excellent where planted, promotion hunts you down across kingdoms, cultures, and centuries. "So Daniel prospered in the reign of Darius and in the reign of Cyrus the Persian" (Daniel 6:28). Governments changed but Daniel's influence remained. Leaders shifted but his authority endured. Because promotion rooted in character and excellence sustains through every transition. You remain steadfast in trials, knowing faithfulness paves the way for unparalleled promotion. Your unwavering faith will open doors of favor and elevation that human networking cannot unlock.

Moses: When "Too Late" Becomes "Right Time"

Eighty years old when heaven interrupted his retirement with destiny. Forty years in palace preparing for something he didn't understand. Forty years in wilderness being prepared by Someone who understood everything. When human ambition was buried, God appeared: "Come now, therefore, and I will send you to Pharaoh that you may bring My people, the children of Israel, out of Egypt" (Exodus 3:10). Your wilderness wasn't waste—it was waiting room. Character developed in hiddenness serves purposes revealed in elevation. Moses' eighty years positioned him for the promotion that would liberate nations. Their pattern becomes your promise: Hidden faithfulness leads to divine positioning. Divine positioning results in supernatural elevation. Supernatural elevation creates generational impact. Your current situation is not your final destination. God is using your private struggles to shape your public victories.

THE FIVE HEBREW WORDS FOR PROMOTION: YOUR ELEVATION VOCABULARY

Before you pray the dimensional prayers and declarations, heaven wants you armed with comprehensive promotion vocabulary. The Hebrew and Greek languages contain multiple words for elevation—each revealing a different dimension of how God lifts His people. You've already encountered RUM, NASA, and HUPSOŌ. Now discover the complete arsenal heaven downloaded into ancient language to equip modern believers for supernatural promotion.

1. RUM [room] — Lifted by Another's Strength

You know this one intimately now—to be lifted by another's strength, to be raised, exalted, elevated. RUM thunders through Scripture 190 times because God loves lifting beggars to thrones. You don't RUM yourself. You are RUM-ed by God. Hannah sang it after barrenness broke: "The Lord lifts up! He raises the poor from dust and lifts the beggar from the ash heap!" (1 Samuel 2:7-8). RUM means rising from dust to dynasty. You're shifting from renter to owner, employee to employer, follower to leader, overlooked to overbooked. Biblical promotion isn't climbing a ladder—it's being lifted by the Lord who owns every ladder.

2. NASA [nah-SAH] — Carried Beyond Ability

NASA appears 650 times in Scripture, meaning "to carry, bear up, lift, raise"—carried beyond your ability to reach, elevated past where credentials qualify, positioned where résumés can't secure and connections can't guarantee. Joseph testified with certainty born of supernatural transportation: "God will surely carry [NASA] you up" (Genesis 50:24). NASA is what happens when God picks you up and places you in positions human effort could never reach. Stop exhausting yourself climbing. NASA means God's carrying you where human effort cannot reach. This is promotion as divine transportation—you're not walking to the next level, you're being carried there.

3. GADAL [gah-DAHL] — Magnified to Greatness

GADAL means "to become great, to be magnified, to grow up." When God uses GADAL, He's not just lifting you—He's enlarging you. "The Lord has done great [GADAL] things for us, and we are glad" (Psalm 126:3). This is promotion that doesn't just change your position—it changes your capacity. God makes you bigger on the inside so you can handle what He's positioning you for on the outside. GADAL is what happened to David: "So David became greater and greater [GADAL], for the Lord God of hosts was with him" (2 Samuel 5:10). Your promotion isn't just about a better title—it's about becoming a greater person. GADAL means you're not the same person in a higher position; you're a transformed person prepared for greater responsibility.

4. CHAYAH [khah-YAH] — Resurrected from Death

CHAYAH means "to live, to have life, to revive, to restore to life." This is the promotion word for dead dreams, buried callings, forgotten promises, and abandoned destinies. When everyone says "it's over," CHAYAH says "it's resurrection time." Ezekiel witnessed it in the valley of dry bones: "So I prophesied as He commanded me, and breath came into them, and they lived [CHAYAH], and they stood upon their feet, an exceedingly great army" (Ezekiel 37:10). CHAYAH is God's specialty—breathing resurrection life into what looks permanently dead. That business idea from 2011. That ministry vision from your twenties. That calling you buried after disappointment. CHAYAH means God is about to resurrect what you wrote off as finished. Your CHAYAH moment is coming—resurrection of dead dreams, revival of buried callings, restoration of forgotten promises.

5. HUPSOŌ [hoop-SO-oh] — Exalted to Highest Rank

Though this is Greek rather than Hebrew, it completes your promotion arsenal by emphasizing divine exaltation connected to God's glory. HUPSOŌ means "to exalt, lift to the highest rank, raise to dignity." "Humble yourselves in the sight of the Lord, and He will lift you up [HUPSOŌ]" (James 4:10). This is the promotion that comes through humility, not through self-promotion. Every time you chose serving over spotlight, HUPSOŌ activated in heaven's database. Hidden faithfulness becomes public platform. Secret service becomes visible authority. HUPSOŌ is what Jesus demonstrated: "Therefore

God also has highly exalted [HUPSOŌ] Him and given Him the name which is above every name" (Philippians 2:9). The humble get lifted—not because they deserve it, but because God delights in elevating those who decrease so He can increase.

Plus: SHAPHAT [shah-FAHT] — Judged and Positioned

SHAPHAT means "to judge, vindicate, govern, execute judgment." When Psalm 75:7 says "But God is the Judge [SHAPHAT]: He puts down one, and exalts another," it's declaring that your promotion isn't up for committee vote or human consensus—it's up to God alone. SHAPHAT means God examines, evaluates, vindicates, and positions. He's the ultimate Judge who sees hidden faithfulness, rewards secret service, and elevates based on character not connections. When people overlook you, SHAPHAT sees you. When systems pass you by, SHAPHAT positions you. Your promotion is in the hands of the righteous Judge who never makes mistakes.

How the Six Work Together as Complete Arsenal

Watch how these six promotion dimensions create comprehensive transformation: RUM lifts you by another's strength (you don't self-promote). NASA carries you beyond ability (supernatural transportation). GADAL magnifies you to greatness (internal capacity increases). CHAYAH resurrects dead dreams (what died comes alive). HUPSOŌ exalts through humility (serving leads to authority). SHAPHAT vindicates and positions (God is the Judge). You don't need to choose one—you deploy all six simultaneously. When you pray the declarations that follow, you're not just asking for "promotion." You're releasing a six-dimensional elevation arsenal that addresses lifting by divine strength, supernatural transportation, internal magnification, dead dream resurrection, humble exaltation, and divine positioning. Together they create comprehensive coverage. Nothing missing. Nothing lacking. Nothing broken. The enemy thought promotion came through human systems you couldn't access. But when you understand RUM, NASA, GADAL, CHAYAH, HUPSOŌ, and SHAPHAT, you're positioned for elevation that bypasses every protocol, transcends every system, and makes impossible things inevitable. Now you're ready to pray the dimensional prayers and declarations with full understanding of the arsenal you're releasing.

THE SIX DIMENSIONS OF DIVINE ELEVATION

Promotion isn't just positional—it transforms every dimension of your existence when you shift from horizontal striving to vertical positioning. Watch how looking to NORTH (God's throne) instead of east/west/south (human systems) determines approach across all six areas simultaneously:

DIMENSION	HORIZONTAL STRIVING (East/West/South)	VERTICAL POSITIONING (NORTH)	ACTIVATION
SPIRITUAL	Positioning for recognition/platform	Serving with excellence in hiddenness (Matt 23:11)	"I am promoted from NORTH!"
MENTAL	Limited by credentials/education	Wisdom that makes me undeniable (Dan 6:3)	"I receive supernatural strategy!"

EMOTIONAL	Wounded by rejection/overlooking	Healed wounds become authority (Ps 147:3)	"My wounds become platform!"
PHYSICAL	Confined to current small space	Enlarged territory through faithfulness (Isa 54:2)	"My territory is enlarging!"
FINANCIAL	Compromise/shortcuts for advancement	Integrity in little qualifies for much (Matt 25:21)	"I am financially elevated!"
RELATIONAL	Networking/using people for gain	Character attracts divine connections (Prov 18:16)	"Strategic connections emerge!"

The Pattern: Horizontal striving (east/west/south) produces frustration in all areas. Vertical positioning (NORTH) releases supernatural elevation across all dimensions simultaneously. You don't climb ladders in six separate areas—you are lifted by the Lord from one position, and promotion descends from His throne comprehensively.

THE SIX DIMENSIONS WHERE PROMOTION FLOWS

Promotion isn't just positional—it's foundational to every dimension of your existence. God elevates in spiritual authority, mental wisdom, emotional influence, physical platform, financial resources, and relational connections because you need wholeness, not just position.

For Spiritual Promotion: "Father, I've been begging for authority while neglecting faithfulness in hidden places. Measuring spiritual influence by platform size instead of character depth. Envying others' public ministry while avoiding private obedience that qualifies for Kingdom authority. But today I discover the revolutionary truth: Spiritual promotion doesn't come from east, west, or south—from networking, visibility, or self-promotion. It descends from NORTH, from Your throne, through humility and hidden faithfulness. I reject the lie that spiritual authority comes through positioning myself for recognition. I reject measuring worth by who knows my name instead of how I serve in secret. I reject pursuing platform before character is prepared for it. 'Humble yourselves in the sight of the Lord, and He will lift you up' (James 4:10). Today I receive spiritual promotion as RUM—rising by Your strength, not my striving. As NASA—carried to spiritual authority beyond human effort. As GADAL—magnified in Kingdom capacity. As CHAYAH—dead callings resurrecting by Your breath. As HUPSOŌ—lifted by grace into greater Kingdom impact. I decree that spiritual promotion flows according to hidden faithfulness, not public visibility. Where I've served in obscurity—authority is being prepared. Where I've remained faithful without recognition—influence is being positioned. Where I've stewarded small assignments excellently—greater responsibility approaches. Like Joseph who served excellently in Potiphar's house before governing Egypt—I excel in current assignment. Like David who protected sheep faithfully before leading nations—I steward hidden responsibilities. Like Daniel who maintained integrity in exile before influencing kingdoms—I guard character in obscurity. Spiritual authority is being released over my life, my family, my sphere. Not authority born of ambition but authority earned through faithful service in places nobody celebrates. In Jesus' name, I am spiritually promoted. Amen."

For Mental Promotion: "Father, my mind has been limited by human wisdom when positioned for supernatural strategy. Relying on education alone when You offer revelation. Depending on experience when You provide divine insight that transcends credentials. But today I learn: Mental promotion doesn't come from degrees, connections, or human recognition—it descends from NORTH, from wisdom that makes you undeniable across kingdoms, cultures, and circumstances. I reject the lie that wisdom comes only through traditional education. I reject limiting my thinking to what I've learned instead of what You can reveal. I reject measuring intelligence by credentials when positioned for supernatural understanding. 'If any of you lacks wisdom, let him ask of God, who gives to all liberally and without reproach, and it will be given to him' (James 1:5). Today I receive mental promotion as GADAL—magnified understanding that exceeds natural capacity. As supernatural success through divine strategy. I decree that mental promotion flows from seeking Your wisdom, not just human knowledge. Where I've been limited by education—revelation breaks through. Where I've relied on experience—supernatural strategy emerges. Where I've depended on credentials—divine insight positions me. Like Solomon who received wisdom that attracted world leaders—I receive supernatural understanding. Like Joseph who interpreted dreams no Egyptian could explain—divine revelation flows through me. Like Daniel who possessed wisdom that distinguished him across kingdoms—excellence in understanding makes me undeniable. My mind is being elevated into greater wisdom, sharper discernment, supernatural strategy that positions me for influence beyond human qualification. In Jesus' name, I am mentally promoted. Amen."

For Emotional Promotion: "Father, I've been emotionally wounded by rejection, overlooking, and delayed promotion. Carrying bitterness from being passed over. Nursing resentment from watching less qualified people advance while I remained hidden. But today I discover: Emotional promotion isn't about avoiding pain—it's about transforming wounds into authority. Your healing becomes platform. Your restored emotions become influence that helps others heal. I reject emotional instability keeping me from promotion. I reject bitterness disqualifying me from elevation. I reject resentment blocking me from the very advancement I desire. I reject wounds becoming weapons that hurt others instead of healed scars that help them. 'He heals the brokenhearted and binds up their wounds' (Psalm 147:3). Today I receive emotional promotion as emotional healing that creates authority to minister to others' wounds. As influence born not from avoiding pain but from being healed through it. I decree that emotional promotion flows from healed wounds, not hidden bitterness. Where rejection wounded me—healing positions me to help others rejected. Where overlooking hurt me—restoration equips me to see the overlooked. Where disappointment crushed me—renewed hope empowers me to encourage the disappointed. I am bent but unbroken, stretched to my limit but not torn. I am assailed from all sides, yet I remain undeterred. I may be puzzled and unsure, not knowing the way forward, but I refuse to succumb to despair. Despite persecution and false accusations, I am never abandoned by God. Like Joseph who forgave brothers who sold him—emotional healing positioned him to save nations. Like David who honored Saul even when hunted—character under pressure prepared him for throne. Like Esther who leveraged pain of being orphan—past wounds became platform for national deliverance. My emotions are being healed, stabilized, and positioned for influence that comes through helping others navigate what I've overcome. In Jesus' name, I am emotionally promoted. Amen."

For Physical Promotion: "Father, my physical platform has felt limited by circumstances, location, or resources. Confined to small spaces when positioned for enlarged territory. Restricted to current assignment when prepared for greater reach. But today I learn: Physical promotion isn't about where I am—it's about faithfulness in that place. Excellence in small spaces positions you for influence in large places. Faithfulness in hidden assignments qualifies you for visible platforms. I reject the lie that my current space limits my future influence. I reject dissatisfaction with present assignment that prevents preparation for coming promotion. I reject despising small beginnings that God uses to develop character for large platforms. 'Enlarge the place of your tent, and let them stretch out the curtains of your dwellings; do not spare; lengthen your cords, and strengthen your stakes' (Isaiah 54:2). Today I receive physical promotion as enlarged territory, expanded influence, increased reach that serves Kingdom purposes. I decree that physical promotion flows from excellence in current space, not escape from it. Where I've been faithful in small platform—larger territory is being prepared. Where I've served excellently in obscurity—visible influence approaches. Where I've stewarded limited resources well—multiplication is loading. Like Joseph who managed Potiphar's household before governing Egypt—current excellence positions future expansion. Like David who pastured sheep before ruling nations—faithfulness in small field prepared him for large kingdom. Like the widow whose small offering was noticed by Jesus—God sees excellence in small spaces. My physical platform is being enlarged, my territory expanded, my influence increased for Kingdom advancement. In Jesus' name, I am physically promoted. Amen."

For Financial Promotion: "Father, I've been financially anxious while positioned for supernatural provision. Comparing my resources to others' abundance. Measuring worth by account balance instead of character quality. Striving for increase through human methods instead of stewarding what You've given faithfully. But today I discover: Financial promotion doesn't come from east, west, or south—from connections, manipulation, or self-promotion. It descends from NORTH, through faithful stewardship of little that qualifies you for authority over much. I reject the lie that financial promotion comes through compromise. I reject shortcuts that damage character for temporary increase. I reject comparing my portion to others' prosperity when my assignment requires different resources. 'Moreover it is required in stewards that one be found faithful' (1 Corinthians 4:2). Today I receive financial promotion as RUM—rising from lack to abundance through faithful stewardship. As resource multiplication that serves Kingdom purposes, not personal comfort. I decree that financial promotion flows from integrity in little, not striving for much. Where I've been faithful with limited resources—multiplication approaches. Where I've stewarded small income excellently—greater provision is positioned. Where I've given generously from lack—abundance prepares to flow. Like Joseph whose integrity in Potiphar's house positioned him to manage Egypt's economy—faithfulness in small creates capacity for large. Like the widow who gave her last to the prophet—obedience in lack unlocked supernatural supply. Like the faithful servant in Jesus' parable—'You were faithful over a few things, I will make you ruler over many things' (Matthew 25:21). My finances are being elevated, my resources multiplied, my stewardship expanded for Kingdom advancement and generational blessing. In Jesus' name, I am financially promoted. Amen."

For Relational Promotion: "Father, my relationships have felt limited by who I know instead of who You're positioning me to meet. Striving to network for advancement instead of serving excellently where planted. Trying to connect with influential people instead of becoming someone worth connecting with through character and faithfulness. But today I learn: Relational promotion doesn't come from networking—it comes from becoming. When you're excellent, connections find you. When you're faithful, doors open that networking couldn't unlock. When you're positioned by God, relationships align that human effort couldn't create. I reject the lie that advancement depends on who I know. I reject using relationships for personal gain instead of serving Kingdom purposes. I reject pursuing connections for what they can do for me instead of what I can contribute through them. 'A man's gift makes room for him, and brings him before great men' (Proverbs 18:16). Today I receive relational promotion as NASA—carried into relationships beyond my ability to network. As divine connections that serve mutual Kingdom advancement, not personal exploitation. I decree that relational promotion flows from character that attracts, not connections I chase. Where I've been faithful in current relationships—strategic connections are being prepared. Where I've served without expecting return—divine relationships approach. Where I've honored authority even when overlooked—favor with influencers is positioning. Like Ruth whose loyalty to Naomi positioned her in Boaz's field—faithfulness in current relationships opens doors to strategic connections. Like Esther who found favor with the king—character creates connections networking cannot. Like Daniel whose excellence attracted attention across kingdoms—when you're excellent, influential people notice. My relational sphere is being elevated, strategic connections emerging, divine relationships forming that advance Kingdom purposes beyond personal advancement. In Jesus' name, I am relationally promoted. Amen."

MEMORIAL: THE NORTH COMPASS (DAILY REMINDER)

Within 24 hours, create your NORTH compass memorial. Take your journal or a small card and draw a simple compass rose with four directions: N, E, W, S. Circle NORTH in bold. Write above it: "My promotion comes from here." Place this compass where you'll see it daily—beside your provision seed from Day 18, your peace stone from Day 17, in your Bible, on your desk. Every morning, look at the compass and declare: "My promotion doesn't come from east, west, or south—it descends from NORTH. I stop looking horizontally for human approval. I start positioning vertically for divine appointment. I am RUM—lifted by God's strength. I am NASA—carried beyond ability. I am GADAL—magnified for greatness. I am CHAYAH—resurrected from death. I am HUPSOŌ—exalted through humility. I am SHAPHAT—positioned by the Judge. The Lord lifts me from NORTH!" This compass becomes your daily reminder: Stop networking. Start serving. Stop climbing. Start positioning. Stop striving for recognition. Start stewarding for Kingdom impact. Hidden faithfulness leads to divine positioning. Divine positioning results in supernatural elevation. Supernatural elevation creates generational impact. Your four memorials now work together as complete arsenal: Day 17's peace stone reminds you that rest weaponizes warfare. Day 18's provision seed declares that God gives seed to sowers, not just bread to eaters. Day 19's NORTH compass positions you to look up instead of sideways. These memorials are prophetic anchors—visual reminders that transformation happened, is happening, and will continue happening as you steward what heaven downloaded.

BREAKING THE FOUR ENEMIES OF PROMOTION

Understanding these attacks helps you respond with truth instead of terror. Each enemy has a lie it whispers and a truth that shatters it. Comparison Poison whispers: "Others are getting promoted while you're stuck. They're less qualified but better connected. They started after you but advanced faster. Something's wrong with you." This lie makes you measure your timeline against someone else's assignment, your portion against another's purpose. But heaven thunders back: "Your assignment is unique. Your timing is specific. Their elevation doesn't delay yours—it demonstrates Mine is coming." "The Lord is the portion of my inheritance and my cup" (Psalm 16:5). God doesn't compare children. He customizes portions for purposes. Your manna matches your mission. Timing Torment whispers: "You've waited too long—you're too old, too young, too inexperienced, too overlooked. The window closed while you were preparing. Opportunity passed while you were faithful. It's too late for your breakthrough." But truth declares: "He knows my season and my timing is perfect in His hands." "To everything there is a season, a time for every purpose under heaven" (Ecclesiastes 3:1). Moses was eighty. David was a teenager. Joseph waited thirteen years. Timing that looks wrong to human eyes is often precisely right in heaven's purposes. Qualification Questioning whispers: "You don't have the right credentials, connections, background, education, or experience. Look at what others have that you lack. You're not qualified for promotion." But scripture silences doubt: "My excellence will open doors that credentials cannot. My character will create connections that networking cannot." "Do you see a man who excels in his work? He will stand before kings" (Proverbs 22:29). God qualifies the called. Your faithfulness in hidden places prepares you for influence in prominent places. Positioning Panic whispers: "Nothing's happening. Maybe you misheard God. Perhaps you imagined the promises. Possibly you were never really called to anything greater. Forget the dreams—they were delusion." But heaven responds with certainty that quiets every doubt: "Hidden preparation is happening. When My timing aligns with your readiness, elevation will be undeniable." Challenges often prepare ordinary individuals for exceptional promotions, breakthroughs, and legendary destinies. What feels like preparation taking too long is actually development going deep enough. Your current positioning is preparation for promotion you can't yet see, influence you can't yet imagine, impact you can't yet comprehend. The intensity of the delay often reveals the magnitude of the coming promotion. Hell wouldn't fight advancement that doesn't threaten his kingdom. Your battles confirm your significance. Your delays develop your character.

RESISTANCE REALITY CHECK: BREAKING THE LIES

Comparison Trap. Hell whispers: "Others less qualified are getting promoted while you remain stuck." Heaven's response: "Your assignment is unique. Your timing is specific. Their elevation doesn't delay yours—it demonstrates Mine is coming." Break it now: "I reject comparison! My portion matches my purpose! Psalm 16:5—the Lord is my inheritance!"

Timing Anxiety. Hell whispers: "You've waited too long. You're too old or too young. The opportunity passed." Heaven's response: "Moses was 80. David was a teenager. Joseph waited 13 years. My timing always aligns with My purposes." Break it now: "I reject timing anxiety! God's season is perfect! Ecclesiastes 3:1—there is a time for every purpose!"

Qualification Doubt. Hell whispers: "You don't have the right credentials, connections, or background." Heaven's response: "I qualify the called. Your excellence will open doors that credentials cannot. Your character will create connections that networking cannot." Break it now: "I reject qualification doubt! God positions the faithful! Proverbs 22:29—excellence brings me before kings!"

Positioning Panic. Hell whispers: "Nothing's happening. Maybe you misheard God." Heaven's response: "Hidden preparation is happening. When My timing aligns with your readiness, elevation will be undeniable." Break it now: "I reject positioning panic! Preparation precedes promotion! My current positioning prepares coming elevation!"

WEEK 3: PROPEL (7P)

Your current positioning is preparation for promotion you can't yet see, influence you can't yet imagine, impact you can't yet comprehend.

THE STEWARD'S DECLARATION

Stand with prophetic authority. Feel the confidence of one positioned by heaven, not striving for human tables. Declare: "I am not climbing ladders—I am being lifted by the Lord! My promotion doesn't come from east, west, or south—it descends from NORTH where heaven's throne determines earth's elevation! I am RUM—rising by Your strength, not my striving! I am NASA—carried to heights impossible through human effort! I am GADAL—becoming greater through Your magnification! I am CHAYAH—dead dreams resurrecting by Your breath! I am HUPSOŌ—lifted by grace, positioned by faithfulness! I am SHAPHAT—positioned by the righteous Judge! Like Joseph—from forgotten to elevated overnight! From prison to palace in twenty-four hours! Like David—from overlooked to unforgettable! From shepherd to king! Like Moses—from wilderness to world leadership! From exile to influence! Like Daniel—from captive to counselor! From overlooked to undeniable! Like Esther—from orphan to authority! From nothing to nations! Every overlooked season was ordained preparation! Every setback was sovereign setup! Every demotion was divine protection! Every delay developed character for coming platform! Every rejection redirected me toward purpose! I don't network for advancement—I serve with excellence! I don't strive for recognition—I steward for Kingdom impact! I don't chase promotion—I attract it through positioning! Humility positions me! Faithfulness qualifies me! Excellence makes me undeniable! My promotion serves Kingdom purposes! My authority advances divine covenant! My influence impacts generations! I am positioned and promoted by heaven's design! Amen!"

BREAKTHROUGH PRAYER

"Father of elevation, Lord of impossible promotion, like Hannah who prayed 'The Lord lifts the beggar from the ash heap to set them among princes,' I surrender my promotion timeline to Your sovereignty. Nineteen days have positioned me for this revelation: promotion comes not from east, west, or south—but from NORTH, Your throne. 'For promotion comes neither from the east nor from the west nor from the south. But God is the Judge: He puts down one, and exalts another' (Psalm 75:6-7). Your Word declares with unshakeable authority: 'The Lord makes poor and makes rich; He brings low and lifts up. He raises the poor from the dust and lifts the beggar from the ash heap, to set them among princes' (1 Samuel 2:7-8). 'Humble yourselves in the sight of the Lord, and He will lift you up' (James 4:10). 'He removes kings and raises up kings' (Daniel 2:21). Today I receive divine positioning for supernatural promotion. I am RUM—rising by Your strength, not my striving! I am NASA—carried to heights impossible through human effort! I am GADAL—becoming greater through Your magnification! I am CHAYAH—dead dreams resurrecting by Your breath! I am HUPSOŌ—lifted by grace, positioned by faithfulness! I am SHAPHAT—positioned by the Judge who never errs! Every overlooked season was ordained preparation. Every setback was sovereign setup. Every demotion was divine protection. Every delay developed character for coming platform. Every rejection redirected me toward purpose. Like Joseph—from forgotten to elevated overnight! Like David—from overlooked to unforgettable! Like Moses—from wilderness to world leadership! Like Daniel—from exile to influence across kingdoms! Like Esther—from orphan to authority over nations! I am positioned and promoted by heaven's design! My elevation serves Kingdom purposes! My authority advances divine covenant! My influence impacts generations! Promotion flows from the NORTH! In Jesus' mighty name, Amen."

CLOSING: FROM STRIVING TO RECEIVING

You awakened questioning your worth after nineteen days of pressing in. Tonight you rest knowing you're divinely positioned for supernatural promotion that serves something greater than personal advancement. Day 19's transformative gift: Divine elevation comes from God's throne, not human tables, systems, connections, or qualifications. The demotion-to-promotion testimony demonstrates God's backwards mathematics—what looks like professional suicide is often resurrection in disguise. While career challenges have complex causes, this experience reveals how heaven can transform even devastating setbacks into divine positioning. When heaven demotes you, it's positioning you for promotion no human title could contain, no earthly system could define, no corporate structure could limit. But the deeper lesson transcends career considerations: You're not climbing ladders. You're being lifted by the Lord who owns every ladder, every building, every throne. This doesn't mean faithful people never face workplace challenges or professional setbacks. Scripture shows Joseph in prison, David hiding in caves, Daniel in exile. But it does mean God specializes in beggar-to-royalty transformation that makes impossible things inevitable. Those most overlooked are often most ordained. Your current positioning is preparation for promotion you can't yet see.

Tomorrow begins Day 20: Prosperity—discovering how divine promotion releases Kingdom stewardship. When God elevates, He equips. When He positions, He provisions. When He promotes, He empowers with resources that serve purposes greater than personal comfort. Which dimension needs your positioning declaration tonight? Which area requires the shift from horizontal striving to vertical receiving? Your elevation protocol remains supernatural: Excel where planted. Serve in hiddenness. Trust heaven's timing. Prepare for promotion that transcends human systems. Stop climbing. Start positioning. Stop networking. Start serving. Stop striving for recognition. Start stewarding for Kingdom impact. The same God who lifted Joseph from dungeon to dynasty, David from pasture to palace, and Moses from desert to national leadership lifts you from current position to divine destiny that impacts generations. My promotion doesn't come from east, west, or south—it descends from NORTH where heaven's throne determines earth's elevation. Week 3 continues: Propel in Destiny—Promotion positioned. Tomorrow: Day 20 Prosperity begins.

SOAP JOURNAL — DAY 19

S (Scripture): Write Psalm 75:6-7 and 1 Samuel 2:7-8. Underline where promotion comes from and circle "The Lord lifts up."

O (Observation): Where have I been looking horizontally (east, west, south) instead of vertically (north) for promotion? Which enemy of promotion resonates most—comparison, timing anxiety, qualification doubt, or positioning panic? How has faithful service in hiddenness prepared me for influence in prominence? Which of the six Hebrew/Greek words speaks most to my current season?

A (Application): Choose one dimension and pray that focused prayer daily this week. Identify one area to stop self-promoting and start excelling. Celebrate one person's promotion instead of envying it. Create your NORTH compass memorial within 24 hours and place it with your other memorials. Declare the six-word arsenal (RUM, NASA, GADAL, CHAYAH, HUPSOŌ, SHAPHAT) when tempted to compare or strive.

P (Prayer): "Father, I trust Your NORTH promotion over east/west/south striving. Position me like David—from overlooked to influential. Like Joseph—from forgotten to elevated. I am RUM, NASA, GADAL, CHAYAH, HUPSOŌ, SHAPHAT—lifted by You. In Jesus' name, Amen."

Today's Breakthrough Marker: How did shifting from horizontal striving to vertical positioning change your approach to current assignment? Which biblical champion's pattern resonated most deeply with your season? Did you create your NORTH compass memorial? Which of the six promotion words (RUM, NASA, GADAL, CHAYAH, HUPSOŌ, SHAPHAT) speaks most powerfully to where you are right now?

Tomorrow's Expectation: Based on today's promotion positioning, how will divine elevation prepare you for Kingdom prosperity that serves purposes greater than personal comfort? How does understanding that promotion comes from NORTH prepare you for stewarding what flows from heaven's throne?

Day 19 Complete: Promotion Positioned. Horizontal striving ended. Vertical receiving activated. NORTH promotion revealed. Six dimensions declared. RUM, NASA, GADAL, CHAYAH, HUPSOŌ, SHAPHAT integrated. Joseph, David, Esther, Daniel, Moses patterns revealed. Comparison, timing, qualification, positioning enemies broken. Demotion-to-promotion testimony expanded. Backwards-is-forward economics demonstrated. Hidden faithfulness leads to divine positioning. Divine positioning results in supernatural elevation. Supernatural elevation creates generational impact. Six Hebrew/Greek words mastered. Promotion not prize for ambition but position for assignment. Challenges prepare ordinary for exceptional. Bent but unbroken language added. NORTH compass memorial created. Four memorials working together: peace stone + provision seed + NORTH compass = complete arsenal. Two more days ahead. Ready for prosperity.

DAY 20 — PROSPERITY

Armed with Kingdom Force for Divine Assignment

> "But you shall remember the Lord your God, for it is He who gives you power to get wealth, that He may establish His covenant." — Deuteronomy 8:18

WEEK 3 — PROPEL: Accelerating into Destiny

Day 20 of 21. Yesterday's Promotion revealed divine elevation for the positioned. Today's Prosperity unveils the most revolutionary understanding of biblical abundance you'll ever encounter—not what religion fears or culture corrupts, but what heaven designed for Kingdom conquest.

THE STRATEGIC CONNECTIONS: HOW PROMOTION PREPARED YOU FOR PROSPERITY

Day 19's Promotion taught you that divine elevation comes from NORTH—from God's throne, not human tables. You discovered you're not climbing ladders but being lifted by the Lord. RUM (rising by another's strength), NASA (carried beyond ability), HUPSOŌ (humble get lifted)—heaven's vocabulary of vertical receiving replaced horizontal striving. Today reveals what happens when promotion positions you for prosperity. Faithful stewardship of influence qualifies you for increased resources. What heaven elevates, heaven equips. When God promotes you, He arms you with Kingdom force for the assignment He reveals. Week 2 taught you advancement—the process developing anointing for assignment. Day 19 unveiled promotion—the event positioning you where character, calling, and consecration collide. Today you discover prosperity—the equipment, the comprehensive Kingdom force that enables you to fulfill what heaven assigned. Day 18's Provision resourced your calling. Day 19's Promotion elevated your platform. Today's Prosperity arms you with comprehensive force for Kingdom conquest that transforms generations.

ENCOUNTER: WHEN HEAVEN REWRITES EVERYTHING

Your alarm doesn't sound. Your spirit does. 4:30 AM. Day 20. Twenty days of Daniel fasting have prepared ground in the Spirit—debris cleared, vision clarified, intimacy deepened, identity aligned, momentum building toward destiny. The Father honors what He already planted, bringing His deposit into the open. The person who started this fast worried about bills, checked bank balances with dread, accepted poverty as spiritual—that old mindset died somewhere around Day 14. What remains is someone discovering that prosperity isn't what religion taught or culture corrupted. It's something else entirely. Something dangerous. Something that makes hell tremble and heaven celebrate.

You sit on the edge of your bed, feet touching cold floor, remembering. Your grandmother working herself to death—literally. Chronic illness claiming her far too soon, body breaking under decades of financial strain she wore like cross to bear. Your mother following similar patterns, always stretching to make ends meet, faithful yet financially constrained, noble in poverty but never free. The generational pattern playing on repeat like inherited curse nobody questioned. Poverty passed down like heirloom nobody wanted but everyone accepted. But patterns can be broken by those who understand Kingdom force.

"God," you whisper into darkness, voice raw from twenty days of seeking, "when does someone in our family actually prosper? When do we stop surviving and start thriving for Your Kingdom? When does the pattern break?" The answer comes not gentle but forceful, like thunder splitting sky: "When you understand prosperity isn't money—it's comprehensive Kingdom force. When you realize I don't make you wealthy—I make you dangerous with resources for divine assignment." Your spine straightens as revelation crashes over you like wave you can't resist: "You think prosperity is about bank accounts. I'm talking about equipped capability. Kingdom architecture. Resources as stewardship responsibility for covenant purposes. You're not getting rich—you're getting armed for Kingdom conquest that impacts nations." The truth detonates through every cell, demolishing both prosperity gospel and poverty theology with prophetic precision: "Every generation before you had wealth wrong—either feared it as evil or worshipped it as god. But Kingdom prosperity makes resources weapons for covenant advancement. You're about to become the first in your bloodline to carry comprehensive force that transforms generations through excellent stewardship."

REVELATION: THE ARCHITECTURE THAT CHANGES WEALTH FOREVER

Twenty days of pressing into presence have prepared you for revelation that transcends both accumulation theology and poverty spirituality. Heaven unveils not just prosperity principles but comprehensive Kingdom architecture.

The Biblical Definition: What Is Prosperity?

Prosperity is not a number in a bank account—it's the divine state of thriving and flourishing in spirit, soul, body, relationships, resources, and purpose. It is God's covenant desire for His people to live fruitful, impactful, and generous lives that advance His Kingdom and reflect His glory. God's definition of prosperity is about thriving, not just surviving. It's about reaching the full potential of what He has planned for us—wholeness, flourishing, success, and divine well-being that results from living in covenant alignment with God. This encompasses spiritual vitality, emotional peace, physical health, relational favor, material provision, and generational blessing. True prosperity is a prosperous soul, a healthy body, a peaceful mind, a joyful spirit, a loving heart, and a life that radiates His glory. Prosperity is not marked by what you own but by what you are in the eyes of God. Material wealth is temporary, but spiritual wealth is eternal. Yet biblical prosperity includes both—not wealth instead of spirituality, but resources serving Kingdom purposes through spiritual maturity. This is God's original intent in Eden: "Be fruitful and multiply" (Genesis 1:28). This is His ongoing promise in Christ: "I have come that they may have life, and that they may have it more abundantly" (John 10:10). Prosperity is total-life abundance, multidimensional flourishing that reflects Heaven's economy on earth.

The Hebrew and Greek Revelation

When John prayed "Beloved, I pray that you may prosper in all things and be in health, just as your soul prospers" (3 John 1:2), he used EUODOŌ [yoo-oh-deh-OH]—to prosper, succeed, progress forward in every dimension. Not just financial increase but comprehensive advancement in all things. SHALOM [shah-LOME] means peace, wholeness, well-being, prosperity—complete flourishing where nothing is missing, nothing is broken. Your finances whole. Your health whole. Your relationships whole. Your purpose funded. Total prosperity across every dimension. TSALACH [tsah-LAKH] means to succeed, advance, break out, prosper—used when "the Lord was with Joseph, and he was a successful man...and the Lord made all he did to prosper" (Genesis 39:2-3). Forward movement and thriving in purpose. CHAYIL [khah-YEEL] means force, strength, capability, excellence, influence, and yes—resources, all combined for Kingdom purposes. When Deuteronomy 8:18 says God gives you "power to get wealth," the word is CHAYIL. Not money—Kingdom capability. Not riches—divine influence. Not comfort—conquest equipment. BERAKA [beh-rah-KAH] means blessed to bless—Abraham's promise: "I will bless you...and you shall be a blessing" (Genesis 12:2). Biblical blessing flows through you to advance Kingdom purposes in others' lives. RABAH [rah-BAH] means multiplication beyond mathematics: "I will multiply your descendants" (Genesis 22:17). Your seed becomes harvest that defies calculation, resources multiplying for Kingdom advancement. PERISSEUO [per-is-SYOO-oh] means abundance that overflows: "I have come that they may have life, and that they may have it more abundantly" (John 10:10). Your cup overflows into others' empty spaces, creating margin for mission. Heaven's vocabulary doesn't reduce prosperity to money—it expands prosperity to comprehensive Kingdom force across every dimension of existence.

THE TESTIMONY: WHEN HEAVEN PLANTED SEED THAT BECAME ARCHITECTURE

2013: The Sanctuary of Broken Dreams. I need to tell you about the twelve-year journey that transformed desperation into stewardship, survival into Kingdom architecture, begging into equipped capability that now serves nations. Spring 2013. Divorce proceedings draining every resource like spiritual hemorrhaging. Sitting in a church sanctuary in Mississauga, Ontario, Canada with my two boys, trying to hold together what was left of our family while everything else disintegrated. Every Sunday, same pew, same desperate questions burning holes through my faith: How do I provide for my children? How do I rebuild from nothing? Is there escape from this generational cycle of noble poverty? The boys fidgeting beside me, unaware their mother was drowning financially while trying to appear spiritually strong. Corporate clothes from better days now camouflaging current poverty, professional wardrobe hiding personal devastation. Smiling while suffocating under weight of lack and hopelessness nobody could see. Every bill a testimony against my faith. Every bank balance check an accusation that God had forgotten me. Every month stretching resources that shouldn't stretch, exhausted from performing financial miracles with mathematical impossibilities. Then that Sunday morning, heaven interrupted my desperation with teaching that would begin twelve-year transformation from survival to stewardship, from poverty mentality to Kingdom architecture.

The Word That Shattered Everything. "Stop praying for money. Start praying for CHAYIL." The sanctuary went silent. Everyone leaning forward, sensing we were about to receive something that would change everything. The teaching opened Deuteronomy 8:18, and I watched as the Hebrew text was unpacked like treasure being delivered: "But you shall remember the Lord your God, for it is He who gives you power to get wealth, that He may establish His covenant." "That word 'power'?" The voice paused for effect, letting anticipation build. "It's CHAYIL. Not money—force. Not riches—Kingdom capability. Not comfort—comprehensive influence that serves divine purposes." My pen couldn't write fast enough as revelation unpacked what would become my survival manual, my transformation blueprint, my twelve-year journey from seed to architecture: "CHAYIL isn't about getting rich. It's about getting armed. God doesn't make you wealthy for comfort—He equips you with comprehensive force for Kingdom assignment." Seven CHAYIL dimensions were taught that day—Wisdom, Worship, Favor, Honor, Power, Wealth, Influence—and I wrote furiously, tears streaming down my face because I was hearing something I'd never heard before: Prosperity serves purpose. Resources enable stewardship. Wealth arms Kingdom advance.

The Prayer That Rewrote My Bloodline. That night changed everything. Alone in my rental house, in my bedroom, after tucking my boys into beds while praying I would have the upcoming rent by the due date, after checking accounts that testified lack, after wrestling with fear that tomorrow would be worse than today—I discarded every poverty-mentality prayer I'd ever prayed. No more begging for breakthrough. No more apologizing for needing provision. No more accepting lack as badge of spirituality. "God," I prayed with new authority born of revelation, "I don't just want money—I want CHAYIL. Not survival but Kingdom influence. Not barely making it but comprehensive force that transforms my bloodline forever. Manifest CHAYIL on me and my boys—Wisdom, Worship, Favor, Honor, Power, Wealth, Influence for Your glory, not my comfort. Make me dangerous with resources. Arm me for Kingdom stewardship." The shift was immediate. Not in my bank account—that required faithful stewardship over time, excellence in small things before authority over much. But in my approach to resources, opportunity, and Kingdom assignment. Everything changed when I stopped begging for breakthrough and started positioning for stewardship responsibility.

Walking Out the Seed Revelation. The results didn't happen overnight. It wasn't magic—it was stewardship applied with excellence over time. Heaven doesn't reward desperation—it rewards diligence. God doesn't bless panic—He blesses positioning. CHAYIL Wisdom started downloading during prayer—strategies for business, approaches to opportunities, Kingdom thinking that created pathways where none existed. CHAYIL Favor began opening doors that credentials couldn't unlock, relationships forming that networking couldn't create. CHAYIL Provision manifested through management consulting opportunities that exceeded my qualifications, contracts secured that defied my damaged credit and broken circumstances. In my July 2013 email to myself, I asked for CHAYIL glory to be manifested in my life. Within months, mortgage approved despite financial devastation. Within a year, income restored beyond what I'd lost. Within two years, everything stolen being returned for Kingdom purposes, but with interest—spiritual, relational, and financial. But the most profound transformation wasn't financial—it was generational. My boys watching their mother shift from fear-based survival to faith-based stewardship. Learning that provision isn't luck—it's alignment with Kingdom purpose. That wealth isn't accumulation—it's stewardship responsibility that serves others' breakthrough.

2015-2023: Revelation Deepens Into Architecture. As I continued stewarding CHAYIL principles with excellence, God began expanding my understanding beyond the original seven dimensions. What that Sunday teaching planted as seed, Holy Spirit was developing into comprehensive system. He showed me prosperity isn't one-dimensional—it's multifaceted architecture. Not just about having wealth or influence but about building sustainable system that impacts generations through excellent stewardship. It's progressive revelation that matures over time through faithful application. The Holy Spirit started teaching that prosperity is divine flow beginning in God, belonging to God, existing to serve God's mission across every dimension of existence. Not accumulation theology or poverty spirituality but Kingdom stewardship that transforms lives, territories, and generations.

THE DANIEL FAST: CLOSING THE GAP!

2024-2025: The Complete Architecture Revealed. Early in 2025, after more than a decade of stewarding seed revelation with increasing excellence, God completed the picture. What started as seven CHAYIL dimensions in 2013 matured into comprehensive Kingdom Prosperity Architecture—one foundation and ten pillars operating together as integrated system. That Sunday morning in 2013 didn't just teach CHAYIL—it planted seed that Holy Spirit cultivated into comprehensive architecture over twelve years of faithful stewardship. What heaven downloaded through anointed teaching, Holy Spirit matured through consistent application. What began as survival prayer became Kingdom system now serving thousands globally. Twelve years ago, CHAYIL was lifeline pulling me from financial despair. Today, those same principles—refined, expanded, matured through Holy Spirit and faithful application—have become global framework for Kingdom wealth and excellent stewardship. What started as "God, help me survive" became "God, make me conduit of Your abundance for others' breakthrough." What began with widow's desperation is now blueprint for impact, destiny, and legacy serving multiple generations. I am no longer chasing provision—I am stewarding comprehensive prosperity. I am no longer praying for resources—I am armed with Kingdom force. And I am no longer building wealth for comfort—I am building capacity for conquest that transforms nations through excellent stewardship.

THE KINGDOM PROSPERITY ARCHITECTURE: FOUNDATION AND TEN PILLARS

After twenty days of fasting, heaven reveals biblical prosperity operates not as isolated concept but as comprehensive architecture—one foundation establishing purpose, ten pillars working together creating sustainable Kingdom force.

ELEMENT	MEANING	SCRIPTURE	PURPOSE
FOUNDATION: Covenant & Lordship	Divine Ownership	Matthew 6:33	All prosperity begins in God, belongs to God, serves God's mission. Not accumulation for comfort but arming for Kingdom assignment.
1. Grace (Charis)	Divine Empowerment	1 Cor 15:10; 2 Cor 9:8	Empowers what human strength cannot achieve, opening doors effort alone never could.
2. Wisdom (Chokmah)	Divine Strategy	Prov 4:7; James 1:5	Orders steps, clarifies path, equips with Heaven's strategies for effective stewardship.
3. Valor (Chayil)	Comprehensive Capability	Prov 31:10; 1 Sam 16:18	Equips with skill, courage, integrity, strength to manage and multiply what God entrusts.
4. Advancement (Tsalach)	Breakthrough Success	Gen 39:2; Ps 1:3	Transforms resistance into testimony, propelling into new levels of impact and influence.
5. Wholeness (Shalom)	Nothing Missing, Nothing Broken	3 John 1:2; Ps 23:1	Aligns every area—finances, health, relationships, calling—into complete flourishing harmony.
6. Holistic Wellness (Euodoō)	Soul-First Prosperity	3 John 1:2; Rom 12:2	Ensures inner health produces external abundance, spiritual vitality manifesting in every dimension.

WEEK 3: PROPEL (7P)

7. Righteousness (Tsedaqah)	Justice & Generosity	Ps 112:9; Prov 21:3	Grounds prosperity in integrity, ensuring fair dealings, open-handed generosity, wealth reflecting God's character.
8. Blessing (Beraka)	Conduit of Favor	Gen 12:2; Deut 28:2	Positions as vessel through whom God's favor flows—blessing families, cities, nations beyond yourself.
9. Multiplication (Rabah)	Seed to Harvest Increase	Gen 22:17; Deut 1:11	Expands impact of every seed planted, transforming small beginnings into exponential Kingdom harvests.
10. Overflow (Perisseuo)	More-Than-Enough Supply	John 10:10; 2 Cor 9:8	Creates margin for mission, funding every good work, resourcing breakthrough far beyond personal needs.

The Divine Sequence: Foundation of Covenant and Lordship establishes purpose → Grace empowers capability → Wisdom orders strategy → Valor deploys comprehensive skill → Advancement breaks through resistance → Wholeness sustains flourishing → Holistic Wellness aligns dimensions → Righteousness governs with integrity → Blessing flows to others → Multiplication expands impact → Overflow funds mission beyond yourself. This produces: Impact that transforms lives. Destiny that fulfills calling. Legacy that blesses generations. Prosperity is not the goal—stewardship is. God doesn't make you rich to be comfortable. He makes you dangerous with resources so you can transform lives, territories, and generations through excellent stewardship of comprehensive Kingdom force.

BIBLICAL CHAMPIONS: KINGDOM STEWARDS WHO CHANGED HISTORY

Scripture reveals consistent pattern across generations: Those who stewarded excellently what God provided created impact transcending their lifetimes. These aren't isolated examples but repeated realities demonstrating how Kingdom prosperity operates through faithful stewardship.

Solomon: Wisdom Attracts Overwhelming Resources for Kingdom Building. Young king facing overwhelming assignment. God appears offering anything. Solomon requests understanding heart to serve his people well (1 Kings 3:9). Watch God's response that revolutionizes prosperity theology: "Because you have asked this thing, and have not asked long life for yourself, nor have asked riches for yourself, nor have asked the life of your enemies, but have asked for yourself understanding to discern justice, behold, I have done according to your words...And I have also given you what you have not asked: both riches and honor" (1 Kings 3:11-13). Solomon asked for wisdom to serve assignment. God gave CHAYIL to fulfill it—666 talents of gold yearly, silver common as stones in Jerusalem, trade routes spanning continents, influence attracting world leaders from distant nations seeking his wisdom. But notice Solomon's stewardship sequence revealing proper priorities: First built God's temple (seven years), then his palace (thirteen years). Kingdom before comfort. Purpose before personal. Assignment before accumulation. "So King Solomon surpassed all the kings of the earth in riches and wisdom. Now all the earth sought the presence of Solomon to hear his wisdom, which God had put in his heart" (1 Kings 10:23-24). Wisdom attracted resources. Resources enabled Kingdom building. Kingdom impact attracted nations. When you seek wisdom for Kingdom assignment, comprehensive prosperity pursues you with resources you never requested. Stewardship excellence positions you for increased capability. This is divine sequence: Wisdom first, wealth follows, stewardship determines sustainability.

Joseph: Environmental Excellence Makes Every Place Prosper. Joseph demonstrates that Kingdom force isn't location-dependent—it's character-rooted. Potiphar's house prospered because of Joseph. Prison thrived under his stewardship. Egypt survived seven-year famine through his wisdom. Environmental CHAYIL works everywhere because excellence transcends circumstances. "The Lord was with Joseph, and he was a successful man; and he was in the house of his master the Egyptian. And his master saw that the Lord was with him and that the Lord made all he did to prosper in his hand" (Genesis 39:2-3). Watch this carefully: Joseph's stewardship excellence in another man's house positioned him for managing Egypt's entire economy. Faithfulness in small qualifies for authority over much. Excellence in obscurity prepares for influence in prominence. Then prison: "But the Lord was with Joseph and showed him mercy, and He gave him favor in the sight of the keeper of the prison...because the Lord was with him; and whatever he did, the Lord made it prosper" (Genesis 39:21, 23). Same excellence. Different environment. Consistent prosperity because character-rooted capability transcends location. Finally Egypt: "See, I have set you over all the land of Egypt" (Genesis 41:41). Twenty-four hours from prisoner to prime minister because thirteen years of excellent stewardship in hidden places prepared him for visible authority over nations. "The Lord blessed the Egyptian's house for Joseph's sake; and the blessing of the Lord was on all that he had in the house and in the field" (Genesis 39:5). Your comprehensive force doesn't just bless you—it prospers every environment you steward with excellence. This is environmental CHAYIL.

The Proverbs 31 Woman: Marketplace Excellence Serves Multiple Generations. "Who can find a virtuous [CHAYIL] wife? For her worth is far above rubies" (Proverbs 31:10). She embodies comprehensive Kingdom prosperity through marketplace excellence serving family, employees, and community. She creates wealth through diligent enterprise: "She considers a field and buys it; from her profits she plants a vineyard" (Proverbs 31:16). Strategic thinking generating Kingdom resources. She manages international business: "She is like the merchant ships, she brings her food from afar" (Proverbs 31:14). Global influence through excellent stewardship. She employs others, providing livelihood beyond her household: "She perceives that her merchandise is good, and her lamp does not go out by night" (Proverbs 31:18). Creating employment, generating economic impact, establishing legacy through marketplace presence. She ministers to the poor while building wealth: "She extends her hand to the poor, yes, she reaches out her hands to the needy" (Proverbs 31:20). Prosperity enabling generosity. Resources serving others' breakthrough. Wealth circulating instead of accumulating. Her legacy transcends her lifetime: "Her children rise up and call her blessed; her husband also, and he praises her" (Proverbs 31:28). Generational impact. Family blessed. Community transformed. This is CHAYIL—comprehensive capability creating sustainable prosperity through excellent stewardship that serves multiple generations.

Isaac: Supernatural Harvest in Natural Famine. Isaac sowed during famine when logic declared impossibility. "Then Isaac sowed in that land, and reaped in the same year a hundredfold; and the Lord blessed him. The man began to prosper, and continued prospering until he became very prosperous" (Genesis 26:12-13). Notice the progression: Prosper. Continued prospering. Became very prosperous. This is RABAH—multiplication beyond mathematics. Advancement through seasons. Sustained increase because obedience in difficulty positions you for breakthrough in impossibility.

Abraham, Isaac, Job: All demonstrated that faithfulness through trials leads to greater abundance. "And the Lord restored Job's losses when he prayed for his friends. Indeed the Lord gave Job twice as much as he had before" (Job 42:10). Not just restoration—multiplication. Not barely recovering—flourishing beyond previous levels. Their pattern becomes your promise: Obedience positions. Excellence attracts. Faithfulness sustains. Stewardship multiplies. Generosity circulates. Legacy blesses generations beyond your lifetime.

THE SIX DIMENSIONS OF KINGDOM STEWARDSHIP

Prosperity isn't just financial—it transforms every dimension when you shift from accumulation mentality to stewardship excellence. Watch how approaching resources as Kingdom force (not personal security) creates comprehensive flourishing:

DIMENSION	ACCUMULATION (Personal Security)	STEWARDSHIP (Kingdom Force)	ACTIVATION
SPIRITUAL	Platform-chasing for recognition	Presence depth creating authority	"I steward spiritual authority!"
MENTAL	Limited by past education	Wisdom downloaded for current assignments	"I receive divine strategies!"
EMOTIONAL	Wounded, isolated, bitter	Healing becomes platform for ministry	"My wounds become testimony!"
PHYSICAL	Exhausted from striving	Health sustained for long-term impact	"I steward physical vitality!"
FINANCIAL	Hoarding for personal security	Circulating for Kingdom advancement	"I steward for conquest!"
RELATIONAL	Networking for personal gain	Covenant partnerships for mutual Kingdom impact	"I steward divine connections!"

The Pattern: Accumulation mindset (personal security) creates anxiety across all areas. Stewardship excellence (Kingdom force) releases comprehensive prosperity serving covenant purposes. You're not getting rich in six separate areas—you're being armed with comprehensive force from one foundation (Covenant & Lordship), and resources flow through all dimensions simultaneously to advance God's mission.

THE SIX DIMENSIONS WHERE KINGDOM PROSPERITY FLOWS

Prosperity isn't just financial—it's foundational to every dimension of your existence. God prospers in spiritual authority, mental wisdom, emotional wholeness, physical health, financial resources, and relational connections because you need comprehensive force, not isolated increase.

For Spiritual Prosperity: "Father, I've been measuring spiritual wealth by what I see instead of what I carry. Envying others' platforms while neglecting intimacy developing Kingdom authority. Pursuing visibility when You're developing capability in hidden places. But today I discover: Spiritual prosperity isn't about platform size—it's about presence depth. Not recognition but relationship. Not ministry fame but Kingdom effectiveness through sustained intimacy and obedient stewardship. I reject measuring spiritual prosperity by external metrics. I reject pursuing platform before character qualifies for it. I reject visibility without sustainability, recognition without responsibility, influence without intimacy. 'Blessed be the God and Father of our Lord Jesus Christ, who has blessed us with every spiritual blessing in the heavenly places in Christ' (Ephesians 1:3). Today I receive spiritual prosperity as comprehensive blessing—intimacy with You, authority for Kingdom purposes, wisdom for assignments, favor for breakthrough, anointing for impact. I decree that spiritual prosperity flows from presence cultivated in secret places. Where I've invested in intimacy—authority develops for public ministry. Where I've stewarded small assignments faithfully—greater Kingdom responsibility approaches. Where I've remained hidden developing character—visible influence emerges at appointed time. Like David anointed privately before ruling publicly—hidden preparation precedes public promotion. Like Joseph excellent in obscurity before managing Egypt—faithful stewardship in small qualifies for authority over much. Like Jesus thirty years hidden before three years visible—sustained preparation produces sustainable impact. Spiritual prosperity manifesting: Deep intimacy fueling Kingdom authority. Sustained presence producing lasting impact. Character developed qualifying for increased responsibility. Anointing flowing for generational breakthrough. In Jesus' name, I am spiritually prosperous. Amen."

For Mental Prosperity: "Father, my mind has been limited by past education when positioned for present revelation. Relying on previous knowledge when You offer fresh strategies. Thinking within natural boundaries when available for supernatural breakthrough beyond human wisdom. But today I learn: Mental prosperity isn't about information accumulated—it's about wisdom received. Not degrees earned but revelation downloaded. Not past learning but present insight for current assignments and future advancement. I reject limiting my thinking to natural wisdom. I reject dependence on credentials when positioned for divine strategies. I reject educational ceiling preventing revelation breakthrough when You offer wisdom transcending human understanding. 'If any of you lacks wisdom, let him ask of God, who gives to all liberally and without reproach, and it will be given to him' (James 1:5). Today I receive mental prosperity as comprehensive wisdom—strategic thinking creating Kingdom solutions, divine insight solving impossible problems, supernatural understanding navigating complex situations. I decree that mental prosperity flows from seeking Your wisdom daily. Where natural knowledge ends—supernatural strategy begins. Where human wisdom fails—divine insight prevails. Where educational credentials fall short—revelation wisdom opens doors. Like Solomon whose wisdom attracted world leaders—divine understanding creates influence credentials cannot. Like Joseph interpreting dreams Egyptians couldn't explain—revelation downloads solutions human wisdom cannot access. Like Daniel possessing understanding distinguishing him across kingdoms—Heaven's strategies produce undeniable results. Mental prosperity manifesting: Wisdom creating wealth through excellent decisions. Understanding producing breakthrough in impossible situations. Strategic thinking generating Kingdom solutions. Divine insight positioning for sustained success. In Jesus' name, I am mentally prosperous. Amen."

For Emotional Prosperity: "Father, I've been emotionally bankrupt while positioned for supernatural wholeness. Carrying wounds that drain energy meant for Kingdom advancement. Nursing bitterness consuming resources intended for others' blessing. Operating from brokenness preventing sustainable stewardship excellence. But today I discover: Emotional prosperity isn't about avoiding pain—it's about healing creating authority. Your restoration becoming my ministry. Wounds transformed into wisdom serving others' breakthrough through testimony of Your faithfulness. I reject emotional instability preventing excellent stewardship. I reject bitterness blocking generosity that blesses others. I reject brokenness disqualifying me from comprehensive prosperity You designed. I reject wounds remaining weapons instead of becoming testimonies. 'He heals the brokenhearted and binds up their wounds' (Psalm 147:3). Today I receive emotional prosperity as comprehensive wholeness—joy fueling generous stewardship, peace enabling wise decisions, stability creating sustainable impact, healing qualifying for ministry to others' brokenness. I decree that emotional prosperity flows from Your healing touch. Where wounds drained—wholeness restores. Where bitterness blocked—generosity flows. Where brokenness limited—healing positions for increased stewardship. Where pain isolated—restoration connects for Kingdom relationships. Like Joseph forgiving brothers who betrayed him—emotional healing positioned national salvation. Like David honoring Saul while being hunted—character under pressure prepared for throne. Like the woman who washed Jesus' feet with tears—past brokenness became worship offering and testimony of transformation. Emotional prosperity manifesting: Joy sustaining generous stewardship. Peace producing wise resource management. Wholeness enabling sustainable Kingdom impact. Healing becoming ministry to others' wounds. In Jesus' name, I am emotionally prosperous. Amen."

For Physical Prosperity: "Father, my body has felt the weight of stewardship battles. Physical exhaustion from managing resources without margin. Health compromised by stress of financial pressure. Energy depleted preventing sustained excellence in Kingdom assignments You've entrusted. But today I learn: Physical prosperity isn't about comfort—it's about capability for sustained stewardship. Health enabling long-term Kingdom impact. Strength supporting multi-generational influence. Energy sustaining excellence across years of faithful management. I reject accepting physical limitation as permanent. I reject sickness preventing stewardship assignments. I reject exhaustion blocking excellent management of Kingdom resources. I reject treating my body carelessly when it's temple carrying comprehensive force for divine purposes. 'Beloved, I pray that you may prosper in all things and be in health, just as your soul prospers' (3 John 1:2). Today I receive physical prosperity as comprehensive wellness—health sustaining Kingdom service, strength enabling sustained excellence, vitality supporting long-term stewardship, energy maintaining generous impact. I decree that physical prosperity flows from stewarding health excellently. Where exhaustion drained—supernatural energy restores. Where sickness limited—divine healing manifests. Where physical weakness prevented—strength renews for sustained Kingdom assignments. Like Caleb at 85 saying 'I am as strong this day as on the day Moses sent me'—sustained vitality enables long-term impact. Like Moses whose 'eyes were not dim nor his natural vigor diminished' at 120—physical strength supports generational influence. Like Jesus sustaining ministry demands through prayer and rest—wise health stewardship enables sustained effectiveness. Physical prosperity manifesting: Health supporting Kingdom assignments. Strength enabling sustained excellence. Energy maintaining generous stewardship. Vitality creating long-term impact capacity. In Jesus' name, I am physically prosperous. Amen."

For Financial Prosperity: "Father, I've been anxious about provision while positioned for comprehensive stewardship. Comparing my portion to others' abundance. Measuring worth by account balance instead of faithful management. Operating from accumulation mentality instead of circulation stewardship for Kingdom advancement. But today I discover revolutionary truth: Financial prosperity isn't about accumulation for comfort—it's about stewardship for Kingdom conquest. Resources arming divine assignments. Wealth enabling generous impact. Money becoming ammunition for covenant advancement serving multiple generations. I reject accumulation theology hoarding for personal security. I reject poverty mentality accepting lack as spirituality. I reject comparison measuring my stewardship against others' assignments. I reject fear-based resource management instead of faith-based generous stewardship. 'And my God shall supply all your need according to His riches in glory by Christ Jesus' (Philippians 4:19). Today I receive financial prosperity as comprehensive stewardship force—resources funding Kingdom purposes, wealth enabling generous impact, provision sustaining excellent management, multiplication creating exponential advancement. I decree that financial prosperity flows from excellent stewardship of current resources. Where lack dominated—abundance manifests through faithful management. Where poverty limited—comprehensive force positions for increased responsibility. Where fear controlled—faith-based stewardship attracts divine provision. Where accumulation mindset reigned—circulation stewardship blesses others. Like Solomon stewarding wisely and receiving overwhelming resources—excellence attracts increased capability. Like Joseph managing excellently and prospering every environment—faithful stewardship creates environmental blessing. Like the Proverbs 31 woman creating wealth through marketplace diligence—Kingdom business generates sustainable prosperity. 'The blessing of the Lord makes one rich, and He adds no sorrow with it' (Proverbs 10:22). Financial prosperity manifesting: Resources multiplying through excellent stewardship. Wealth creating generous impact beyond personal needs. Provision enabling Kingdom assignments. Money becoming force for covenant advancement. In Jesus' name, I am financially prosperous. Amen."

For Relational Prosperity: "Father, relationships have felt transactional instead of transformational. Connections pursued for personal gain instead of mutual Kingdom advancement. Networking replacing authentic relationship building for divine purposes and generational impact. But today I learn: Relational prosperity isn't about quantity of connections—it's about quality of covenant relationships. Not networking for advancement but authentic partnerships for Kingdom purposes. Not using people but serving together for mutual breakthrough and generational blessing. I reject transactional relationship approaches. I reject using connections for personal gain without serving Kingdom purposes. I reject isolation preventing collaborative impact when positioned for partnership multiplication. I reject superficial networking instead of deep covenant relationships. 'A man who has friends must himself be friendly, but there is a friend who sticks closer than a brother' (Proverbs 18:24). Today I receive relational prosperity as comprehensive connection force—covenant partnerships multiplying Kingdom impact, authentic friendships providing mutual support, strategic relationships enabling collaborative advancement, generational connections blessing multiple families. I decree that relational prosperity flows from authentic Kingdom relationships. Where isolation limited—divine connections emerge. Where transactional approaches failed—covenant partnerships form. Where superficial networking disappointed—deep friendships provide mutual support. Where individual effort strained—collaborative stewardship multiplies impact. Like Ruth and Naomi's covenant loyalty opening doors to Boaz—authentic relationships create strategic positioning. Like David and Jonathan's friendship sustaining through adversity—covenant connections provide sustained support. Like Paul and Timothy's partnership advancing Kingdom mission—generational mentorship multiplies impact beyond individual capacity. Relational prosperity manifesting: Covenant partnerships multiplying Kingdom effectiveness. Authentic friendships providing mutual encouragement. Strategic connections enabling collaborative advancement. Generational relationships blessing families beyond my lifetime. In Jesus' name, I am relationally prosperous. Amen."

WEEK 3: PROPEL (7P)

MEMORIAL: THE STEWARDSHIP LEDGER (WEEKLY ACCOUNTABILITY)

Within 24 hours, create your Stewardship Ledger. Take a page in your journal or notecard and create three columns labeled: **RECEIVED | STEWARDED | MULTIPLIED**. This becomes your weekly accountability tool for excellent Kingdom stewardship. Every Sunday evening or Monday morning, conduct your stewardship review:

RECEIVED: What did God entrust this week? List opportunities, resources, relationships, wisdom, favor, time, influence, responsibilities. Acknowledge everything as coming from His hand. "Every good gift and every perfect gift is from above, and comes down from the Father of lights" (James 1:17).

STEWARDED: How did I manage what He gave? Evaluate your stewardship honestly—excellent, mediocre, wasted, or multiplied. This isn't condemnation but calibration. Where you stewarded excellently, celebrate and continue. Where you were mediocre, identify what would raise it to excellence. Where you wasted opportunities, repent and redirect. "Moreover it is required in stewards that one be found faithful" (1 Corinthians 4:2).

MULTIPLIED: What Kingdom impact resulted? Document how your stewardship blessed others, advanced covenant purposes, transformed lives, or positioned for increased responsibility. This tracks the fruit of faithful management and builds testimony of God's faithfulness through your stewardship.

Place this Ledger with your other memorials: Day 17's peace stone (weaponized rest), Day 18's provision seed (generous circulation), Day 19's NORTH compass (vertical positioning). These four memorials now work together as your complete arsenal: Peace Stone weaponizes rest for spiritual warfare through SHALOM. Provision Seed declares generous circulation over accumulation. NORTH Compass positions you to receive from God's throne vertically. Stewardship Ledger creates accountability for excellent Kingdom management. Every Sunday, review your Ledger and declare: "I am not accumulating for comfort—I am stewarding for Kingdom conquest. What God entrusts, I manage excellently. What I steward faithfully qualifies me for increased responsibility. My comprehensive force serves covenant purposes impacting generations." The Ledger creates sustainable accountability structure for stewardship excellence while honoring what God provides through grateful recognition of His consistent generosity and faithful provision.

BREAKING THE FOUR ENEMIES OF KINGDOM PROSPERITY

Understanding these attacks helps you respond with truth instead of terror. Each enemy whispers lies designed to prevent comprehensive stewardship force from manifesting through your life.

Accumulation Temptation whispers: "Now you can focus on getting wealthy for yourself. Build your empire. Secure your future. Accumulate resources protecting you from ever experiencing lack again." This lie makes prosperity about personal security instead of Kingdom stewardship. But heaven thunders back: "Comprehensive force serves Kingdom purposes, not personal comfort. Resources are stewardship responsibility, not personal reward. I don't make you rich—I make you dangerous with resources for covenant advancement." Excellence in stewardship positions you for increased responsibility, not comfortable retirement.

Poverty Spirit Attack whispers: "Who are you to think you deserve abundance? Godly people struggle financially. Spirituality means accepting lack. Wanting resources proves you're not truly spiritual."

This lie makes poverty badge of honor instead of position for breakthrough. But truth declares: "This isn't about deserving—it's about stewarding. Excellence in small things qualifies for greater Kingdom responsibility. God delights in prosperity of His servants who steward excellently for His purposes" (Psalm 35:27). Faithfulness positions. Excellence attracts. Stewardship qualifies.

Religious Condemnation whispers: "Wanting resources means you're not spiritual. Pursuing prosperity proves worldliness. Money is evil—avoid it completely." But heaven responds: "Comprehensive force includes spiritual authority, wisdom, and resources—all serving Kingdom advancement together. Money isn't evil—love of money is (1 Timothy 6:10). I give power to get wealth to establish covenant (Deuteronomy 8:18). Resources become weapons for Kingdom conquest through excellent stewardship."

Timing Anxiety whispers: "When will breakthrough manifest? You've been faithful but nothing's changing. Maybe prosperity isn't for you. Perhaps you're doing something wrong." But truth silences panic: "Focus on faithful stewardship of current opportunities. Excellence attracts increased responsibility according to My timing. Joseph was 30 when promoted after 13 years preparation. David was anointed privately years before ruling publicly. Your faithful stewardship today qualifies for tomorrow's increased capability." The intensity of testing often reveals magnitude of coming stewardship responsibility. Hell wouldn't fight prosperity that won't threaten his kingdom. Your battles confirm your significance for Kingdom advancement.

RESISTANCE REALITY CHECK: BREAKING THE LIES

Accumulation Mindset. Hell whispers: "Now focus on building wealth for personal security and comfortable retirement." Heaven's response: "Comprehensive force serves Kingdom purposes, not personal comfort. You're not accumulating—you're stewarding for covenant advancement." Break it now: "I reject accumulation theology! I steward for Kingdom conquest! My resources serve covenant purposes!"

Poverty Spirit. Hell whispers: "Godly people struggle financially. Spirituality means accepting lack." Heaven's response: "God delights in prosperity of servants who steward excellently. This is about positioning for Kingdom responsibility, not proving spirituality through poverty." Break it now: "I reject poverty spirit! God arms me with resources for His purposes! Psalm 35:27—He delights in my prosperity!"

Religious Condemnation. Hell whispers: "Wanting resources proves you're not truly spiritual." Heaven's response: "Comprehensive force includes spiritual authority AND resources—all serving Kingdom together. Money becomes ammunition for covenant advancement through excellent stewardship." Break it now: "I reject religious condemnation! Resources serve Kingdom purposes! Deuteronomy 8:18—power to get wealth establishes His covenant!"

Timing Panic. Hell whispers: "Nothing's changing despite your faithfulness. Maybe prosperity isn't for you." Heaven's response: "Excellence in current stewardship positions for future responsibility. Joseph waited 13 years. David was anointed years before ruling. My timing perfects your character for coming capability." Break it now: "I reject timing panic! Faithful stewardship today qualifies for tomorrow! My excellence attracts increased responsibility!"

Your stewardship excellence today positions for increased Kingdom responsibility tomorrow. Focus on faithful management of current opportunities while trusting divine timing for expanded capability.

THE STEWARD'S DECLARATION

Stand with Kingdom authority. Declare over your stewardship with confidence born of twenty days pressing into presence: "I am not accumulating for comfort—I am stewarding for Kingdom conquest! These hands carry comprehensive force for divine assignments! Not getting rich—getting armed for covenant advancement! I am positioned on Foundation of Covenant and Lordship! All prosperity begins in God, belongs to God, serves God's mission! Grace empowers what I cannot achieve! Wisdom orders my strategies! Valor deploys comprehensive capability! Advancement breaks through resistance! Wholeness sustains flourishing! Holistic Wellness aligns dimensions! Righteousness governs through integrity! Blessing flows to others! Multiplication expands impact! Overflow funds Kingdom mission! Like Solomon—wisdom attracts overwhelming resources for Kingdom building! Like Joseph—excellent stewardship prospers every environment! Like Proverbs 31—marketplace excellence serves multiple generations! Like Isaac—supernatural harvest in natural famine! Every dimension prospering: Spiritual authority deepening! Mental wisdom expanding! Emotional wholeness enabling generosity! Physical health sustaining service! Financial resources multiplying! Relational connections strengthening! TSALACH [tsah-LAKH] breakthrough manifesting! SHALOM [shah-LOME] wholeness across all dimensions! BERAKA [beh-rah-KAH] blessing flowing through me! RABAH [rah-BAH] multiplication defying calculation! PERISSEUO [per-is-SYOO-oh] abundance overflowing for Kingdom purposes! I don't accumulate—I circulate for Kingdom advancement! I don't hoard—I steward with excellence! I don't get rich—I get dangerous with resources! My comprehensive force serves covenant purposes! My resources fund divine assignments! My stewardship impacts generations! I am armed with Kingdom prosperity architecture! Amen!"

BREAKTHROUGH PRAYER

"Father of abundance, Lord of Kingdom resources, after twenty days positioning my heart for comprehensive stewardship force, I surrender every dimension to Your Kingdom purposes. 'Beloved, I pray that you may prosper in all things and be in health, just as your soul prospers' (3 John 1:2). Today, I receive comprehensive prosperity—not accumulation for comfort but stewardship for conquest. Your Word declares: 'The Lord has pleasure in the prosperity of His servant' (Psalm 35:27). 'And my God shall supply all your need according to His riches in glory by Christ Jesus' (Philippians 4:19). 'The blessing of the Lord makes one rich, and He adds no sorrow with it' (Proverbs 10:22). I repent for accepting poverty as piety, fearing wealth as evil, worshipping money as god, accumulating for security, comparing my portion to others, operating from lack mentality instead of stewardship excellence. Today I receive Kingdom Prosperity Architecture: Foundation of Covenant and Lordship establishing purpose! Grace empowering capability! Wisdom ordering strategy! Valor deploying comprehensive force! Advancement breaking through! Wholeness sustaining! Holistic Wellness aligning! Righteousness governing! Blessing flowing! Multiplication expanding! Overflow funding mission! Like Solomon—wisdom brings overwhelming resources! Like Joseph—excellent stewardship prospers everywhere! Like Proverbs 31—marketplace diligence serves generations! Like Isaac—supernatural harvest in natural famine! Today I declare the pattern of divine shifting over my life: You are shifting me from imprisonment to prosperity, just as You did for Joseph! From orphanhood to royalty, just as You did for Esther! From shepherd's obscurity to king's authority, just as You did for David! From barrenness to fruitfulness, just as You did

THE DANIEL FAST: CLOSING THE GAP!

for Sarah, Rachel, and Hannah! From pain to purpose, just as You did for Jabez! From death to resurrection life, just as You did for Lazarus and through Jesus Christ! I proclaim and claim my truth, transformation, and transition! Every generational pattern of lack breaks now! Every limitation lifting! Every restriction removing! I am moving from barely surviving to abundantly thriving for Kingdom purposes! I am not getting rich—I am getting armed for Kingdom conquest! My prosperity serves Your covenant advancement! My stewardship impacts generations for Your glory! Comprehensive force activated across six dimensions! Spiritual authority! Mental wisdom! Emotional wholeness! Physical health! Financial resources! Relational connections! In Jesus' mighty name, Kingdom prosperity architecture fully operational! The shifting is happening now! Amen!"

CLOSING: FROM ACCUMULATION TO STEWARDSHIP

You awakened wondering when your family would experience biblical prosperity. Tonight you rest knowing you're armed with comprehensive Kingdom force through architecture serving multiple generations. Day 20's transformative gift: Biblical prosperity is Kingdom architecture stewarded excellently for divine purposes, not personal accumulation for comfortable security. The twelve-year journey from 2013 CHAYIL seed to 2025 Kingdom Prosperity Architecture demonstrates how Holy Spirit cultivates revelation through faithful stewardship over extended time. When anointed teaching plants seed that Holy Spirit matures through consistent application, survival prayer becomes Kingdom system serving thousands globally. This isn't about getting rich for comfort—this is about getting armed for Kingdom assignment that transforms lives, territories, and generations through comprehensive stewardship force. But the deeper lesson transcends financial considerations: You're not accumulating for security—you're stewarding for covenant advancement impacting multiple generations. God shifts His positioned servants from imprisonment to prosperity, obscurity to influence, barrenness to fruitfulness, pain to purpose, death to resurrection life. This doesn't mean faithful stewards never face financial challenges or that proper stewardship guarantees abundance. Scripture shows faithful people experiencing various seasons requiring trust through difficulty. But it does mean God provides what we need for His purposes when we steward excellently whatever He entrusts, positioning us for increased Kingdom responsibility. Excellence in stewardship attracts increased stewardship opportunity. Faithfulness in little qualifies for authority over much. Tomorrow unveils Day 21: Purpose—discovering how comprehensive prosperity force serves your ultimate Kingdom assignment. When God arms you with resources, He reveals what you're building for His glory that blesses generations beyond your lifetime.

The six dimensions activated today—spiritual, mental, emotional, physical, financial, relational—work together as comprehensive force for Kingdom influence through excellent stewardship. Which dimension needs your stewardship excellence today? Which area requires shift from accumulation mentality to circulation stewardship for others' breakthrough? Where is God shifting you from limitation to abundance for Kingdom purposes? Your prosperity protocol remains foundational: Steward excellently whatever God provides for Kingdom advancement through comprehensive force impacting generations. You're not getting rich for comfort—you're getting armed for Kingdom conquest. I don't accumulate—I steward for covenant advancement. The same God who gave Solomon wisdom and wealth for temple building, blessed Joseph's stewardship in every environment, honored the Proverbs 31 woman's marketplace excellence, and produced supernatural harvest through Isaac's obedience, arms you with comprehensive prosperity architecture for Kingdom purposes impacting multiple generations through

WEEK 3: PROPEL (7P)

faithful stewardship. Week 3 Continues: Propel in Destiny—Prosperity stewarded. Tomorrow: Day 21 Purpose begins. Comprehensive force finds ultimate expression in Kingdom assignment serving others' breakthrough and God's glory across generations.

SOAP JOURNAL — DAY 20

S (Scripture): Write Deuteronomy 8:18 and 3 John 1:2. Circle "power" (CHAYIL [khah-YEEL]) and "prosper in all things." Underline "establish His covenant."

O (Observation): How does Kingdom Prosperity Architecture transform understanding from accumulation to stewardship? Which of the ten pillars resonates most with current season? Where is God shifting you from one pattern to another? What current opportunities require excellent stewardship positioning for increased Kingdom responsibility? How does the 12-year testimony (2013-2025) demonstrate progressive revelation through faithful application?

A (Application): Choose one dimension for focused stewardship excellence this week. Identify one way to use current resources for Kingdom advancement beyond personal needs. Recognize one area where God is shifting you from limitation to abundance. Develop one skill or capability for greater Kingdom influence through excellent stewardship. Create your Stewardship Ledger and conduct first weekly review this Sunday.

P (Prayer): "Father, arm me with Kingdom Prosperity Architecture for covenant stewardship. I choose circulation over accumulation, excellence over mediocrity, stewardship over ownership. Shift me from every limitation into Your abundance for Kingdom purposes. My comprehensive force serves Your covenant advancement impacting generations through faithful management of everything You entrust. In Jesus' name, Amen."

Today's Breakthrough Marker: How did shifting from accumulation theology to Kingdom Prosperity Architecture change your approach to current resources, opportunities, and generational impact through excellent stewardship? Where do you see God shifting you from one pattern to another? Which pillar of the architecture do you need most right now?

Tomorrow's Expectation: Based on today's comprehensive prosperity activation, how will Kingdom stewardship force serve the ultimate assignment God reveals in Day 21 Purpose for His glory and others' breakthrough? What is God building through you that will outlast your lifetime?

Day 20 Complete: Prosperity Stewarded. Accumulation mentality ended. Stewardship architecture activated. Foundation: Covenant and Lordship established. Ten pillars integrated: Grace [CHARIS khah-RISS], Wisdom [CHOKMAH khokh-MAH], Valor [CHAYIL khah-YEEL], Advancement [TSALACH tsah-LAKH], Wholeness [SHALOM shah-LOME], Holistic Wellness [EUODOŌ yoo-oh-deh-OH], Righteousness [TSEDAQAH tseh-dah-KAH], Blessing [BERAKA beh-rah-KAH], Multiplication [RABAH rah-BAH], Overflow [PERISSEUO per-is-SYOO-oh]. Six dimensions declared: Spiritual, Mental, Emotional, Physical, Financial, Relational. Twelve-year testimony expanded: 2013 CHAYIL seed → 2025 Kingdom Architecture. Biblical champions deepened: Solomon, Joseph, Proverbs 31, Isaac. Four enemies broken: Accumulation, poverty spirit, religious condemnation, timing anxiety. Stewardship Ledger memorial created. Divine shifting pattern declared: Imprisonment→Prosperity. Orphanhood→Royalty. Obscurity→Authority. Barrenness→Fruitfulness. Pain→Purpose. Death→Life. Comprehensive force armed for Kingdom conquest. One more day ahead. Ready for purpose.

DAY 21 — PURPOSE

Claimed for Your Assignment

> *"In Him also we have received an inheritance, a destiny—we were claimed by God as His own, having been predestined according to the purpose of Him who works everything in agreement with the counsel and design of His will."* — Ephesians 1:11

WEEK 3 — PROPEL: Accelerating into Destiny

Day 21 of 21. Yesterday's Prosperity revealed Kingdom stewardship architecture. Today's Purpose unveils the most revolutionary truth of your entire journey—not what you seek, but who you're destined to build.

HOW PROSPERITY ARMED YOU FOR PURPOSE

Day 20's Prosperity taught you biblical abundance is Kingdom force stewarded for divine purposes, not personal accumulation. You discovered comprehensive prosperity architecture—one foundation and ten pillars working together creating sustainable Kingdom force. Today reveals what happens when prosperity arms you for purpose. Faithful stewardship positions you for ultimate assignment. What heaven equips, heaven reveals. When God arms you with Kingdom force, He unveils who you're building for His glory.

Day 18's Provision resourced your calling. Day 19's Promotion elevated your platform. Day 20's Prosperity armed you with comprehensive force. Today's Purpose reveals who receives everything heaven positioned you to steward.

ENCOUNTER: THE FINAL AWAKENING

The Twenty-First Dawn

Your body doesn't wake. Your spirit ignites. 4:30 AM. Day 21. Twenty-one days of fasting have positioned ground in the Spirit—debris cleared, vision clarified, intimacy deepened, identity aligned, momentum building. The Father honors what He planted, bringing His deposit into the open.

The purpose-seeker who started this fast desperately asking "What's my calling?" has died somewhere between Day 17 and yesterday. What remains understands something that will shatter every assumption you've carried: Purpose isn't something you find. It's something you've always been.

Your prayer corner holds twenty journal entries bleeding the same question: "What's my purpose?" Every page desperate. The handwriting growing more urgent, more pleading, more broken. This morning, the question itself breaks.

The Wrong Question

"God," you whisper into pre-dawn silence, voice raw from twenty-one days of seeking, "after everything—identity, inheritance, positioning—I still don't understand my PURPOSE. What am I supposed to DO?"

The silence that follows isn't absence. It's preparation. Then His voice detonates through your bones: "Wrong question."

Your eyes snap open. Your heart stops. Then pounds like thunder. "You keep asking WHAT. Purpose isn't WHAT you do—it's WHO you build. You keep seeking an assignment. You ARE the assignment—positioned to pull others from where you escaped."

The Revolutionary Revelation

The revelation explodes through every cell: "Look at your scars. Now look at their wounds. Perfect match. Your worst season wasn't preparing you for something—it was preparing you for SOMEONE. Many someones. They have your former face. They're praying your old prayers. Stuck where you escaped. And you? You're their predestined builder."

The words hang like lightning striking ground that will never be the same. "You haven't been searching for purpose. Purpose has been searching for you."

REVELATION: YOUR DIVINE DOCUMENTATION

Ephesians 1:11 contains your spiritual birth certificate, Kingdom social security number, heavenly passport. Paul packed eternity into one sentence. Every word Spirit-chosen, every phrase pregnant with power to transform civilizations.

"IN HIM" — Your Permanent Position

Before anything else, notice your location: IN HIM. Not trying to reach Him. Not hoping to find Him. Already IN HIM. This changes everything that follows. Your inheritance, destiny, choosing—all happen IN HIM. You're not outside begging for admission. You're INSIDE discovering what's already yours. When heaven looks at you, it doesn't see struggle—it sees POSITION. "For I know the thoughts that I think toward you, says the Lord, thoughts of peace and not of evil, to give you a future and a hope" (Jeremiah 29:11).

"WE HAVE RECEIVED" — Past Tense Power

Not "will receive someday." Not "might receive if good enough." HAVE RECEIVED. Done. Completed. Sealed. KLEROŌ [klay-ro-OH] means to obtain by lot, to inherit. In ancient times, "lot" wasn't luck—it was DIVINE DECISION. "The lot is cast into the lap, but its every decision is from the Lord" (Proverbs 16:33). Your inheritance wasn't random. It was divinely determined before time began, already deposited in heavenly accounts with your name on it.

"AN INHERITANCE, A DESTINY" — Your Double Portion

INHERITANCE (kleronomia [klay-ron-om-EE-ah]) — What you receive from eternity past. Your spiritual DNA. Kingdom bloodline. Everything Jesus purchased becoming yours. "For we are His workmanship, created in Christ Jesus for good works, which God prepared beforehand that we should walk in them" (Ephesians 2:10).

DESTINY (kleros [KLAY-ross]) — What you release to eternity future. Your assignment. Your portion. Your specific part in God's master plan that only you can fulfill. "For David, after he had served the purpose of God in his own generation, fell asleep" (Acts 13:36). You're both HEIR and HEIR-MAKER. Receiving from eternity past, depositing into eternity future.

"CLAIMED BY GOD AS HIS OWN" — The Ultimate Identity

CLAIMED. Past tense. Done. Finished. Not auditioning—already cast. Not hoping—already chosen. Picture a father at the orphanage pointing with absolute authority: "That one. That's MINE." No negotiation. No uncertainty. CLAIMED. Before your first breath, before your first cry, before your first mistake—CLAIMED. "Before I formed you in the womb I knew you; before you were born I sanctified you; I ordained you a prophet to the nations" (Jeremiah 1:5). You were WANTED before you were BORN.

"PREDESTINED (CHOSEN, APPOINTED BEFOREHAND)"

PREDESTINED. Before failure, chosen. Before falling, appointed. Before your worst season, selected for your greatest work. PROORIZŌ [pro-or-IZ-oh]—marked out beforehand, predetermined, horizon already set. This isn't about losing free will—it's about discovering you were WANTED, CHOSEN, APPOINTED before the foundation of the world. "He has saved us and called us with a holy calling, not according to our works, but according to His own purpose and grace" (2 Timothy 1:9). Your mistakes didn't disqualify you—they were INCLUDED in the plan.

"ACCORDING TO THE PURPOSE OF HIM"

According to HIS purpose—not yours to create, His to reveal. Not yours to manufacture, His to unveil. Not yours to discover, His to declare with thunder. God doesn't make mistakes. He makes MASTERPIECES. You're His masterpiece with PROTHESIS [PROTH-es-iss]—preset purpose awaiting activation. "The counsel of the Lord stands forever, the plans of His heart to all generations" (Psalm 33:11).

"WHO WORKS EVERYTHING"

WHO WORKS EVERYTHING. Victories. Defeats. Promotions. Betrayals. Successes. Failures. Joy. Pain. EVERYTHING working toward this moment. ENERGEŌ [en-air-GEH-oh]—actively energizing, effectually working, divinely orchestrating every detail of your story. "And we know that all things work together for good to those who love God, to those who are the called according to His purpose" (Romans 8:28). Nothing wasted. Nothing random. Everything working. Your setbacks were setups. Your delays were developments. Your confusion was preparation. My past may have been riddled with pain, but God will not allow my suffering to be in vain.

"IN AGREEMENT WITH THE COUNSEL AND DESIGN OF HIS WILL"

Three witnesses in Heaven agreeing on your purpose: Father, Son, Holy Spirit. Trinity-level consensus. Heaven's board meeting concluded: You're supposed to be here. Your life has meaning. Your purpose is backed by divine agreement that cannot be overturned. "I am God, and there is none like Me...My counsel shall stand, and I will do all My purpose" (Isaiah 46:9-10). What was decided in eternity cannot be changed in time.

I declare over you: You are not an accident—you are an APPOINTMENT. Not random—PREDETERMINED. Not hoping—WALKING IN IT.

HEAVEN'S VOCABULARY OF DESTINY

These aren't vocabulary lessons—they're prophetic detonations:

MATSAH [mah-TSAH] — **Found Treasure.** Purpose isn't created—it's discovered. Like buried treasure waiting excavation. "Counsel in the heart of man is like deep water, but a man of understanding will draw it out" (Proverbs 20:5).

QARA [kah-RAH] — **Called by Name.** "I have called you by your name; you are Mine" (Isaiah 43:1). Not number. Not category. By NAME. Before your parents chose your name, Heaven knew your nature.

CHAPHETS [khah-FETS] — Divine Delight. "Yet it pleased the Lord to bruise Him" (Isaiah 53:10). God delights in your purpose like a father watching his child take first steps. "For it is God who works in you both to will and to do for His good pleasure" (Philippians 2:13).

YAATS [yah-ATS] — Eternal Counsel. "The counsel of the Lord stands forever" (Psalm 33:11). Counseled in eternity. Your purpose was planned in heavenly boardrooms. What was decided there cannot be changed here.

PROTHESIS [PROTH-es-iss] — Predetermined Purpose. "Called according to His purpose" (Romans 8:28). Pre-positioned purpose seeking expression through your availability. Not something you achieve—something you become.

KALEO [kah-LEH-oh] — Divine Summons. "Called to be an apostle" (Romans 1:1). Not suggestion—command. Not invitation—commission. "You did not choose Me, but I chose you and appointed you that you should go and bear fruit" (John 15:16).

TELOS [TEL-oss] — Completion Point. "Christ is the end of the law" (Romans 10:4). Your completion point where every thread connects. Everything has been moving toward this moment.

THE PURPOSE PARADIGM

Twenty-one days of seeking have revealed the pattern that governs every calling:

YOUR WORST SEASON → YOUR DIVINE WORK → YOUR TEMPLE ASSIGNMENT

Where most broken → What qualifies you → Who you build

PREDESTINED PAIN → PREDETERMINED PURPOSE → PREAPPOINTED PEOPLE

Not random → Not generic → Not theoretical

Your worst season wasn't wasted—it was your qualification exam. The places where you bled are where you'll bring healing. The areas where you broke are where you'll build others. The wounds that nearly destroyed you will become wells watering others' drought.

THE 4 P'S — IDENTIFYING YOUR TEMPLE

Heaven has given you a diagnostic system:

PAIN → PURPOSE

The wound that hurt you becomes the well that heals others. "Blessed be the God and Father of our Lord Jesus Christ, the Father of mercies and God of all comfort, who comforts us in all our tribulation, that we may be able to comfort those who are in any trouble, with the comfort with which we ourselves are comforted by God" (2 Corinthians 1:3-4).

Divorced? Build marriages in crisis. Betrayed? Build both betrayed AND betrayers. Abandoned? Build the forsaken. Addicted? Build the bound. Bankrupt? Build financial freedom.

PASSION → PEOPLE

Your holy tears point to your holy tribe. When Nehemiah heard about Jerusalem's broken walls, he "sat down and wept, and mourned for many days" (Nehemiah 1:4). When Jesus saw the multitudes, He "was moved with compassion" (Matthew 9:36).

Cry at custody battles? Single parents are your assignment. Weep over addiction? Addicts and families need you. Break over betrayal? Both sides need what you carry.

PROVISION → PLATFORM

Where God keeps supplying, He keeps assigning. "And God is able to make all grace abound toward you, that you, always having all sufficiency in all things, may have an abundance for every good work" (2 Corinthians 9:8).

Legal favor? Build through justice. Business success? Build through marketplace. Prophetic words? Build through activation.

PATTERNS → CONFIRMATION

What repeats, confirms. "By the mouth of two or three witnesses every word shall be established" (2 Corinthians 13:1). "I have set before you an open door, and no one can shut it" (Revelation 3:8).

Same stories, different faces? They find you without advertising. Open without prompting. Trust without history. When all four P's align, your temple assignment becomes undeniable.

THE DIVINE PROGRESSION

Purpose flows through four essential stages:

STAGE	FOCUS	SCRIPTURE	KEY TRUTH
Purpose	Who You ARE	Jeremiah 1:5	Your spiritual DNA, established before birth
Process	How You're SHAPED	Hebrews 10:36	Character development through pressure and trials
Destiny	What You DO	Esther 4:14	Purpose activated at appointed time
Legacy	What You LEAVE	Proverbs 13:22	Purpose multiplied through others beyond your lifetime

Purpose — Who You ARE

Your spiritual DNA, established before birth. Not what you do but who you're designed to be. "Before I formed you in the womb I knew you; before you were born I sanctified you" (Jeremiah 1:5). Your purpose existed in God's mind before time began. Woven into your design like DNA into cells—inseparable from essence. You don't create purpose. You discover what was always there.

Process — How You're SHAPED

The character-developing bridge between purpose recognition and destiny fulfillment. Heaven molds you through pressure, tests you through trials, qualifies you through faithful obedience. God uses what you resist to develop what you need. The process isn't punishment—it's preparation. Not rejection—refinement. "For you have need of endurance, so that after you have done the will of God, you may receive the promise" (Hebrews 10:36).

Moses needed forty years in wilderness. David needed years running from Saul. Joseph needed thirteen years of breaking. The process qualifies you for what purpose positions you to receive.

Destiny — What You DO

Purpose activated through faithful service in appointed season. When heaven's timing aligns with your readiness, when character development meets divine opportunity—destiny activates. "Yet who knows whether you have come to the kingdom for such a time as this?" (Esther 4:14). Right person, right preparation, right positioning, right moment.

Legacy — What You LEAVE

Purpose multiplied through others beyond your lifetime. Kingdom influence that transcends your years and continues through those you built. "A good man leaves an inheritance to his children's children" (Proverbs 13:22). Not just financial but spiritual legacy. David fought wars so Solomon could build in peace. Your faithful stewardship in difficulty creates others' platform in blessing.

The Divine Formula

PURPOSE + PROCESS = READINESS
READINESS + GOD'S TIMING = DESTINY ACTIVATION
DESTINY + OTHERS = LEGACY MULTIPLICATION
PURPOSE × PROCESS × DESTINY × LEGACY = KINGDOM TRANSFORMATION

You're not stuck—you're being shaped. You're not forgotten—you're being formed. You're not abandoned—you're being aligned for activation that will impact generations.

THE PROCESS OF TRANSFORMATION: FROM WHEAT TO FLOUR

Heaven reveals purpose through process using nature's most powerful metaphor—transformation through pressure that produces something far more valuable than original form. The transformative process of wheat milling serves as powerful metaphor for personal growth. Once separated and cleansed of impurities, wheat undergoes milling to become valuable flour, ready to fulfill purpose. This mirrors believers separated from the world, cleansed from sin, shaped through trials to fulfill God's divine purpose.

I am like a wheat grain. The experiences I face—challenging or comforting—shape, refine, and prepare me for divine destiny. In this process of life's milling—suffering, redemption, salvation—I taste God's unconditional love. His saving grace enables me to comfort others facing similar pain.

The Wheat's Journey

The wheat must be separated from chaff (what looks like substance but has no value), cleansed of impurities (what contaminates and prevents usefulness), crushed through milling (what breaks down to release potential), and refined into flour (what transforms into something valuable). Each stage feels destructive but produces what the wheat was always meant to become. The crushing isn't the end—it's the activation. What seemed like breaking point becomes breakthrough moment.

THE PATTERN OF TRANSFORMATION THROUGH PRESSURE

THE CATERPILLAR → THE BUTTERFLY. The caterpillar enters chrysalis seemingly entombed, body breaking down—complete destruction of original structure. But this "death" births metamorphosis. Beauty manifesting from what seemed ugly. As Maya Angelou observed: "We delight in the beauty of the butterfly, but rarely admit the changes it has gone through to achieve that beauty." Your transformation may feel like complete breakdown. You're not dying—you're metamorphosing. What dissolves in darkness reforms as glory.

CARBON → DIAMOND. Carbon buried deep underground endures intense heat and crushing pressure for thousands of years. Extreme conditions that should destroy instead crystallize, transforming ordinary element into most valuable gem. What was common becomes precious. Same element, completely different value—all through pressure. Your pressure isn't punishment—it's production. Heaven isn't crushing you to destroy but to crystallize purpose.

OYSTER → PEARL. When irritant enters oyster's shell causing pain, the oyster doesn't expel it. Instead, it coats the irritant layer by layer with nacre, transforming source of pain into object of beauty. The very thing that hurt becomes what makes it valuable. Your irritants—betrayals, disappointments, losses—aren't destroying your value. They're creating it. What wounded you is becoming what makes you priceless.

OLIVES → FINEST OIL. Olives must be crushed to release oil within. The pressure that bruises releases anointing. Multiple pressings produce oil of increasing purity. First pressing—good oil. Second pressing—better oil. Third pressing—finest oil reserved for holy purposes. Your repeated pressings aren't abandonment. They're proof of selection for holy use. The more you're pressed, the finer the oil.

THE SEED PRINCIPLE: NOT BURIED BUT PLANTED

I am a seed, not buried, but intentionally planted by God. He carefully tends to me, nourishing and nurturing me to flourish and yield abundant harvest. My transformation may be akin to seed planted in soil. It may seem like the end as it's buried, but it's the start of new beginning. In darkness, the seed breaks open, and from it springs forth new life—process that seems destructive but births something beautiful.

Like the seed, I too am going through process that might feel like breaking, but it's not my breaking point—it's my inflection point, my breakthrough moment. I'm being transformed to serve higher purpose. Isaiah 66:9 (NCV) declares transformative truth: "In the same way I will not cause pain without allowing something new to be born," says the Lord.

I am teeming with promise, pregnant with unique purpose and divine destiny. The pain I've been feeling is akin to labor pain. I am on the brink of giving birth to new season! The pain isn't termination—it's transition. Not conclusion—but commencement. Not death—but delivery of what heaven planted before I knew I was pregnant with purpose.

The Divine Truth About Process. The wheat milling, diamond refining, butterfly metamorphosis, pearl formation, olive pressing, and seed germination all indicate profound truth: Beauty, value, and purpose often come from pressure, heat, and transformation. Though drastically changed, each element becomes precisely what it was destined to be. The crushing wasn't cruelty—it was cultivation. The pressure wasn't punishment—it was preparation.

My pleasant and painful life experiences aren't random or meaningless. They're part of divine process molding, shaping, refining, and preparing me for purpose I was created for. In the hands of the Master Potter, I'm becoming the person He envisioned (Jeremiah 18:1-6). The process may be challenging and sometimes painful, but I trust His craftsmanship. Amid pressures, heat, crushing, and refining, I'm emerging as vessel fit for His use, ready to fulfill divine destiny. His grace is sufficient, for His strength is made perfect in my weakness (2 Corinthians 12:9).

With assurance of His word, I boldly declare: "I am who God says I am. I am becoming what He destined me to be! I am not buried—I am PLANTED!"

THE TESTIMONY: WHEN PURPOSE FOUND ME THROUGH FIRE

I need to tell you about the day purpose died so it could resurrect with unstoppable power.

The Building Season. Several years ago, I ran a women's empowerment coaching program. Undercharged to keep it accessible. Poured everything out—late-night crisis calls, personalized strategies, celebrating their victories as my own because I genuinely believed this was my purpose, my calling, my life's work. The breakthroughs were real and beautiful: Women leaving toxic relationships after years of bondage. Businesses launching from pure faith and desperate courage. Leadership promotions manifesting through rebuilt confidence. Deep healing happening in real-time as lies were replaced with truth, shame with identity, fear with faith.

I thought I'd found purpose. I thought this was it—my calling crystallized, my assignment clarified, my reason for breathing finally understood. I poured everything into building these women. Every resource. Every strategy. Every late night. Everything. Then betrayal arrived with surgical precision that would teach me what I thought I knew about purpose was merely the seed of what God intended to grow.

The Systematic Destruction. One woman joined with hidden agenda. Not seeking transformation—planning theft. Studying my materials to steal. Recording my methods to replicate. Plotting while pretending, scheming while smiling, planning destruction while receiving healing. I didn't see it. Couldn't see it. Was too busy building to notice someone was studying the blueprint to steal the building.

Behind my back, she recruited MY women. Secret conversations poisoning wells I'd spent years digging. Seeds of doubt disguised as prayer requests. Promises of "better" if they followed her instead. Systematic undermining wrapped in spiritual language. The coordination was military-level. The timing, surgical. The devastation, complete.

Then came the exodus. Synchronized. Same day. Same hour. Same devastating precision that left me gasping. My phone became a funeral procession: "Canceling membership." "Ending subscription." "No longer need coaching." Each message another nail in the coffin of everything I thought I was building. The exodus wasn't random—it was orchestrated. The betrayal wasn't accidental—it was planned. My only income—gone in coordinated destruction that left me financially devastated and spiritually shattered.

But the cruelest cuts came through social media. Women I'd helped heal from toxic relationships posted toxic messages about me. Those I'd helped launch businesses used their new platforms to destroy mine. Those I'd promoted to leadership led the charge against my character. She launched her program before year's end—MY materials, MY methods, MY former clients as founding members. Everything I'd poured out now being used to build her platform while mine lay in ruins.

The Dark Night That Became Dawn. I sat on my bedroom floor, laptop showing zero members where dozens had been, sobbing until my ribs ached and my throat was raw from crying out to God with questions that felt like accusations. "God, I healed them and they used healing to hurt me! I lifted them and they used elevation to crush me! HURT PEOPLE HURT PEOPLE even after healing! I'm DONE with women's ministry. DONE building people who become my destruction. DONE trusting. DONE serving. DONE."

The silence that followed wasn't absence. It was God letting me die so I could resurrect differently, letting my understanding of purpose break completely so He could rebuild it with eternal foundation instead of earthly assumptions. Then His voice, gentle but firm: "My child, even Jesus had Judas among the twelve. Even I have children who betray Me daily. Even My Son was crucified by those He came to save. Watch what I do with betrayal—I reveal your true temple, not just those you thought you were building."

"My true temple? These betrayers who destroyed everything?" "Your temple includes both: those betrayed like you AND those who betray because they're still broken. You'll build victims AND victimizers. Both wounded AND wounders. Those hurt by others AND those who hurt others. This is why you needed yesterday's CHAYIL—resources for both sides of brokenness, wisdom for both faces of your temple."

The Resurrection Revelation. The revelation that would change everything: "These scars aren't disqualifications. They're credentials." Let that sink into your bones like it sank into mine that night. Your wounds aren't why you can't build—they're why you must. Your scars aren't evidence of failure—they're proof of qualification. Your betrayal wasn't the end of your purpose—it was the completion of your preparation.

"When a woman says, 'My sisters betrayed me,' you'll say with authority born of experience, 'Mine too. Let's heal together.' When another whispers, 'I was the betrayer. Can God still use me?' you'll say with compassion forged through fire, 'There's redemption for both sides. I'm building you anyway.'"

"Your temple includes those who hurt you and those hurt like you. Both victims and victimizers. Both wounded and wounders. Purpose required crucifixion before resurrection. You had to die to applause to live for anyway. You had to lose the approval of people to gain the assignment from heaven."

"Your battle scars have morphed into beauty marks and stars, qualifying you to minister, serve, empathize, be compassionate, love, heal, and lead others."

The Return and Rebuilding. For years, I stayed away. Wounds too fresh. Trust shattered. Heart too broken to risk building again. But after the pandemic broke everyone open, after collective suffering exposed universal need, He called me back—differently: "Start Unstoppable Women of Word. Not programs but My Word. Not coaching but Kingdom revelation. Show them Tamar's pain had purpose. Hagar's rejection had redemption. Even Eve's failure had future. Build with Scripture, not systems. Foundation that cannot be stolen because it's already freely given."

The Temple Revealed. Today, Unstoppable Women of Word reaches globally. Women betrayed by sisters find healing through understanding Leah and Rachel's complicated sisterhood. Women betrayed by narcissistic lovers find freedom through recognizing Tamar's resilience and Bathsheba's redemption. Women who were the betrayers themselves find restoration through comprehending Rahab's transformation and the Samaritan woman's second chance.

My temple has BOTH faces because "You intended to harm me, but God meant it for good to accomplish what is now being done, the saving of many lives" (Genesis 50:20). Both victims needing validation and victimizers needing redemption. Both those betrayed like me and those who betrayed like her. Both wounded hearts and wounding hearts still broken underneath their weapons.

Sometimes your temple crucifies you before receiving resurrection through you. Sometimes those you're called to build will break you before they're ready to be built. Sometimes your greatest pain becomes your primary qualification. Moses knew—those he delivered wanted to stone him. He built anyway. David knew—those he served tried to kill him. He built anyway. Jesus knew—those He healed would crucify Him. He built anyway.

Your worst season qualifies you for your greatest work. "The most powerful warrior in the Kingdom isn't the one who wins a debate — it's the one who wins a soul."

BIBLICAL CHAMPIONS: BUILDERS FROM BROKENNESS

Scripture reveals consistent pattern: Heaven selects builders whose breaking prepared them for building others through identical struggles.

Moses: From Murderer to Deliverer of Millions

"He killed the Egyptian and hid him in the sand" (Exodus 2:12). Murderer at forty. Forgotten in wilderness for forty years. His impulsive murder taught him premature deliverance costs lives. His exile taught him patience with process. Eighty years of preparation for forty years of purpose. When God appeared in the burning bush, Moses argued his disqualification: "Who am I that I should go to Pharaoh?" (Exodus 3:11). But God's response revealed divine purpose paradigm: "I will certainly be with you" (Exodus 3:12).

His murder didn't disqualify him—it qualified him. Because when you've taken life and been forgiven, you understand grace that delivers murderers. When you've run from justice and been restored, you comprehend mercy that pursues the guilty. "Come now, therefore, and I will send you to Pharaoh that you may bring My people, the children of Israel, out of Egypt" (Exodus 3:10). The murderer became deliverer. The fugitive became leader. His worst season positioned him for his greatest work.

Moses' temple: Enslaved people needing deliverance. But also stubborn people who would complain, rebel, build golden calves, and threaten to stone him. He built them anyway because his breaking taught him to build broken people who would break him again.

Joseph: From Pit to Provider for His Betrayers

"They hated him and could not speak peaceably to him" (Genesis 37:4). Thirteen years of systematic breaking that felt like cosmic cruelty but was actually divine preparation for unprecedented authority and impossible grace. Seventeen with dreams that seemed delusional. Betrayed by brothers who threw him in pit. Sold into slavery by those who should have protected him. Falsely accused after faithful service. Forgotten in prison by cupbearer he helped. Every step down preparing him for climb up that would position him to save those who destroyed him.

"You intended to harm me, but God meant it for good to accomplish what is now being done, the saving of many lives" (Genesis 50:20). This is purpose paradigm crystallized: Your betrayers become your temple. Those who meant harm become those you feed during famine. Joseph's breaking taught him: Pit prepares you for palace. Slavery teaches stewardship. Prison develops character for power. Being forgotten qualifies you to remember others. Betrayal positions you to bless betrayers.

His temple: Not just hungry Egyptians needing grain. His brothers needing forgiveness. His father needing reunion. His betrayers needing salvation from famine they couldn't survive without the one they betrayed.

Paul: From Persecutor to Planter Among Former Enemies

"He made havoc of the church, entering every house, and dragging off men and women, committing them to prison" (Acts 8:3). Chief enemy became chief apostle. Most violent persecutor became most effective planter. His persecution gave him credibility with persecutors. His transformation gave him testimony among the transformed. When he wrote "I am the chief of sinners" (1 Timothy 1:15), he meant it literally—he had murdered believers and felt their blood on his hands.

"He is a chosen vessel of Mine to bear My name before Gentiles, kings, and the children of Israel. For I will show him how many things he must suffer for My name's sake" (Acts 9:15-16). Chosen not despite his violence but through it. Selected not around his sin but through his redemption from it. Paul's breaking taught him: Persecutors can become planters. Murderers can become missionaries. Chief of sinners can become chief apostle. Nobody's beyond redemption. Nobody's too broken for purpose.

His temple: Gentile converts needing foundation. Jewish believers needing bridge. Church leaders needing instruction. But also persecutors still pursuing believers—people exactly like he'd been. He built both sides because his transformation qualified him to speak to both tribes with authority nobody else carried.

The Woman at the Well: From Shame to City Evangelist

"You have had five husbands, and the one whom you now have is not your husband" (John 4:18). Most avoided became most effective. Her shame became her credential. Her mess became her message. She came at noon to avoid people who whispered. She'd been married five times, divorced five times, living with a man who wouldn't marry her. Despised, gossiped about, rejected, isolated. The kind of woman respectable people avoided.

Then Jesus met her at the well, knowing everything, and instead of condemning her shame, He revealed her purpose. "Go, call your husband and come here" (John 4:16). Not to expose her—to equip her. Not to shame her—to send her. "Come, see a Man who told me all things that I ever did. Could this be the Christ?" (John 4:29). Her shame became her invitation. Her scandal became her credential. The same rejection that isolated her from the city positioned her to reach the city nobody else could reach.

Her temple: Other broken women hiding shame. Men and women tangled in complicated relationships. People religious folks avoided. She built them because her breaking qualified her to reach those still breaking. Their pattern is your promise: Your worst season qualifies you for your greatest work. Your breaking prepares you for building. Your scars become credentials for others' healing.

THE SIX DIMENSIONS OF PURPOSE ACTIVATION

Purpose isn't just missional—it transforms every dimension when you shift from seeking activity to serving people. Watch how recognizing your temple assignment (not finding your calling) creates comprehensive clarity:

DIMENSION	SEEKING ACTIVITY (Confusion)	SERVING PEOPLE (Clarity)	ACTIVATION
SPIRITUAL	"What's my calling?" endless seeking	Building assigned temple revealed through scars	"I build my temple!"

MENTAL	Comparing my purpose to others' assignments	Recognizing pain points to people	"My scars reveal my temple!"
EMOTIONAL	Wounds feel like disqualifications	Scars become credentials for building	"My wounds are credentials!"
PHYSICAL	Exhausted from purpose anxiety	Energized by temple clarity	"I steward strength for building!"
FINANCIAL	Anxious about resources for unknown calling	Stewarding provision for known assignment	"Resources fund my temple!"
RELATIONAL	Isolated by fear of betrayal again	Building both victims AND victimizers	"I build both sides!"

The Pattern: Seeking activity (endless confusion) produces anxiety across all areas. Serving people (temple clarity through scars) releases comprehensive purpose activation. You're not finding calling in six separate areas—you're building assigned temple from one revelation (your scars match their wounds), and purpose flows through all dimensions simultaneously to advance Kingdom construction.

Now activate what the table reveals through targeted prayer in each dimension:

THE SIX DIMENSIONS WHERE PURPOSE FLOWS

Purpose isn't just missional—it's foundational to every dimension of your existence.

For Spiritual Purpose. Father, I've been seeking assignment while neglecting character development. Pursuing platform while avoiding process. Wanting to build others while my own foundation remains unstable. But today I discover: Spiritual purpose isn't about how many I lead—it's about who I become through leading. Not platform size but presence depth. Not ministry recognition but Kingdom effectiveness through sustained intimacy.

I reject seeking purpose before character qualifies me. I reject pursuing assignment while avoiding process. I reject measuring purpose by external metrics when You measure by internal maturity. "For we are His workmanship, created in Christ Jesus for good works, which God prepared beforehand that we should walk in them" (Ephesians 2:10). Today I receive spiritual purpose as comprehensive calling—not just what I do but who I become through faithful obedience in obscurity.

I decree that spiritual purpose flows from character developed in secret. Where I've remained faithful without recognition—authority prepares to manifest. Where I've served in obscurity—influence positions for emergence. Like Moses forty years in wilderness before leading exodus—hidden preparation precedes public purpose. Like David years with sheep before ruling nations—character in obscurity qualifies for authority over many. Like Jesus thirty years hidden before three years visible—sustained development produces sustainable impact.

Spiritual purpose manifesting: Deep intimacy producing Kingdom authority. Character development qualifying for increased assignment. Faithful obscurity positioning for purposeful prominence. In Jesus' name, my spiritual purpose is clear. Amen.

For Mental Purpose. Father, my mind has been confused about calling. Comparing my purpose to others' assignments. Measuring my value by what I haven't discovered instead of what You've already revealed. But today I learn: Mental purpose isn't about discovering what—it's about recognizing who. Not finding perfect calling but building assigned people.

I reject confusion that keeps me seeking instead of serving. I reject comparison measuring my purpose against others' assignments. I reject anxiety about what I haven't discovered while ignoring who I'm positioned to build. "Do not be conformed to this world, but be transformed by the renewing of your mind, that you may prove what is that good and acceptable and perfect will of God" (Romans 12:2). Today I receive mental purpose as comprehensive clarity—understanding purpose isn't what I do but who I build.

I decree that mental purpose flows from renewed understanding. Where confusion dominated—clarity breaks through. Where comparison paralyzed—recognition activates. Where seeking prevented serving—building begins. Like Nehemiah recognizing his temple through tears over broken walls—holy grief reveals holy assignment. Like Esther understanding "for such a time as this"—positioning clarifies purpose.

Mental purpose manifesting: Confusion replaced with clarity. Comparison dissolved by recognition. Seeking transformed into building. In Jesus' name, I know my purpose. Amen.

For Emotional Purpose. Father, I've been emotionally wounded by my worst season. Carrying pain from betrayal. Nursing bitterness from being used. Operating from brokenness that feels like permanent disqualification. But today I discover: Emotional purpose isn't about avoiding pain—it's about transforming wounds into wells. Your healing of my emotions becomes qualification for ministry to others' brokenness. Scars I wanted hidden become credentials for building both victims and victimizers.

I reject believing my wounds disqualify me. I reject hiding scars that could heal others. I reject thinking my worst season was waste instead of preparation. "Blessed be the God and Father of our Lord Jesus Christ, the Father of mercies and God of all comfort, who comforts us in all our tribulation, that we may be able to comfort those who are in any trouble, with the comfort with which we ourselves are comforted by God" (2 Corinthians 1:3-4). Today I receive emotional purpose as comprehensive healing—my wounds becoming wells, my scars becoming credentials.

I decree that emotional purpose flows from redeemed pain. Where wounds hurt—wells prepare to water others' drought. Where betrayal broke—healing positions me for building both betrayed and betrayers. Like Joseph forgiving brothers who sold him—emotional healing positioned national salvation. Like Jesus on cross saying "Father, forgive them"—ultimate wound became ultimate qualification.

Emotional purpose manifesting: Wounds becoming wells. Scars becoming credentials. Pain becoming preparation. Worst season qualifying for greatest work. In Jesus' name, my emotions serve my purpose. Amen.

For Physical Purpose. Father, my body has felt exhausted from the journey. Physical weariness from years of preparation. Health compromised by stress of process. But today I learn: Physical purpose isn't about comfort—it's about capability for sustained building. Health enabling long-term temple construction. Strength supporting multi-generational impact.

I reject accepting physical limitation as permanent. I reject exhaustion preventing temple building. I reject treating my body carelessly when it's vessel carrying purpose for others' breakthrough. "The Lord will fulfill His purpose for me; Your love, O Lord, endures forever" (Psalm 138:8). Today I receive physical purpose as comprehensive strength—health sustaining temple building, vitality supporting sustained service.

I decree that physical purpose flows from stewarding health excellently. Where exhaustion drained—supernatural strength restores. Where sickness limited—divine healing manifests. Like Caleb at

85 still strong for conquering territory—sustained vitality enables long-term purpose. Like Paul pressed but not crushed—endurance maintains purpose activation through difficulty.

Physical purpose manifesting: Health supporting temple building. Strength sustaining faithful service. Energy maintaining excellent stewardship. In Jesus' name, my body serves my purpose. Amen.

For Financial Purpose. Father, I've been financially anxious about provision while positioned for purpose. Worried about resources for building. Measuring capability by current finances instead of future stewardship. But today I discover: Financial purpose isn't about accumulation—it's about stewardship for temple building. Yesterday's CHAYIL prosperity arming me for today's purpose activation. Resources enabling construction of assigned people.

I reject financial anxiety preventing purpose activation. I reject scarcity mentality limiting temple construction. I reject fear-based resource management instead of faith-based generous building. "And my God shall supply all your need according to His riches in glory by Christ Jesus" (Philippians 4:19). Today I receive financial purpose as comprehensive provision—resources funding temple building, wealth enabling generous impact.

I decree that financial purpose flows from faithful stewardship. Where anxiety dominated—provision manifests. Where scarcity limited—abundance positions for building. Like Solomon receiving overwhelming resources for temple building—yesterday's prosperity enables today's purpose. Like Macedonian churches giving beyond ability—generosity serves purpose beyond personal capacity.

Financial purpose manifesting: Resources funding temple building. Yesterday's CHAYIL arming today's construction. Provision enabling purpose. In Jesus' name, finances serve my purpose. Amen.

For Relational Purpose. Father, relationships have felt complicated by betrayal. Connections broken by those who hurt me. Isolation from protecting myself instead of building assigned temple. But today I learn: Relational purpose isn't about avoiding pain—it's about building both sides of brokenness. Connections serving temple construction. Relationships enabling collaborative impact.

I reject isolation preventing temple building. I reject fear blocking authentic connections for purpose. I reject protecting myself from risk while people wait for building. "Yet who knows whether you have come to the kingdom for such a time as this?" (Esther 4:14). Today I receive relational purpose as comprehensive connection—partnerships multiplying temple construction, authentic relationships enabling sustained building.

I decree that relational purpose flows from authentic Kingdom partnerships. Where isolation limited—divine connections emerge for building. Where fear blocked—authentic relationships form for purpose. Like Nehemiah building with partnerships despite opposition—collaborative effort completes purpose. Like Ruth and Naomi's covenant loyalty—authentic connections advance generational purpose.

Relational purpose manifesting: Partnerships multiplying temple construction. Authentic relationships enabling sustained building. Collaborative stewardship advancing purpose. In Jesus' name, relationships serve my purpose. Amen.

BREAKING THE FOUR ENEMIES OF PURPOSE

Understanding these attacks helps you respond with truth instead of terror.

Purpose Confusion whispers: "You still don't know your calling. Everyone else has clear purpose while you remain confused." This lie keeps you seeking instead of serving. But heaven thunders: "Purpose isn't what you do—it's who you build. Your scars reveal your temple. Your pain points to your people. Look at your wounds, then look at their faces. Perfect match."

Assignment Anxiety whispers: "What if you choose wrong? What if you build the wrong people?" This lie paralyzes through fear of mistakes. But truth declares: "Your temple finds you. Pain reveals people. Passion exposes tribe. Provision shows platform. Patterns confirm assignment. The 4 P's eliminate guesswork."

Qualification Doubt whispers: "Your worst season disqualified you. Your scars prove you're broken, not qualified." This lie makes wounds into disqualifications. But scripture silences doubt: "These scars aren't disqualifications—they're credentials. Moses murdered, then delivered. Joseph was betrayed, then blessed betrayers. Paul persecuted, then planted. Your worst season qualified you for your greatest work."

Temple Panic whispers: "What if they betray you again? What if your temple crucifies you?" This lie prevents building through fear of repetition. But heaven responds: "Sometimes your temple crucifies you before receiving resurrection through you. Moses' temple wanted to stone him—he built anyway. David's temple tried to kill him—he built anyway. Jesus' temple crucified Him—He built anyway."

The intensity of these attacks reveals the significance of your temple assignment. Hell wouldn't fight building that doesn't threaten his kingdom.

THE SOVEREIGN SHIFT: YOU'RE BUILDING, BUT I'M MAKING YOU

As you complete this 21-day journey, heaven reveals the divine exchange: "You are building them, but I AM MAKING YOU." Like Nehemiah, you've been building while battling—sword in one hand, trowel in the other. Every brick laid under warfare. Every wall raised through resistance. But watch what heaven declares: "I AM closing the GAP!"

Every gap. The gap between who you were and who you're created to be. Between questioning and knowing. Between seeking and serving. Between confusion and clarity. Between preparation and activation.

The David to Solomon Hope. Your season of constant spiritual warfare—fighting for every promise, gathering materials through battle—has been preparation, not punishment. You're not building in battle forever. David fought wars so Solomon could build in peace. David conquered enemies so Solomon could receive tribute from them. Your warfare wasn't waste—it was preparation for what you're about to build.

The CHAYIL you received yesterday? Kingdom force for influence. Resources for building. Wisdom for wealth management. Power for purpose fulfillment. Comprehensive prosperity arming you for comprehensive temple construction. What David couldn't build because of warfare, Solomon built in wisdom. Your season of battle is transitioning to season of building. Your warfare is positioning you for temple construction in relative peace as wisdom replaces weapons, as strategies replace struggles.

This isn't guaranteed prosperity—it's available grace. This isn't promised wealth—it's potential stewardship for those who've pressed through consecration. This isn't automatic transition—it's accessible shift for those positioned through faithful endurance. The gap between seasons can close through faith. The shift from warfare to building can activate through obedience.

The Divine Exchange. While you serve others' breakthrough, God develops your character. While you steward resources for Kingdom advancement, He prepares you for greater assignment. While you build your temple, He makes you into builder qualified for generational impact. War wounds become wisdom wells. Battle scars become building credentials. Warfare experience becomes wealth strategy. Fighting faith becomes flourishing favor.

Your temple may start small—few people, limited resources, humble beginning. But faithful stewardship of small temple qualifies for authority over large influence. Excellence in obscurity positions for impact in prominence. The gap is closing. The shift is activating. You're moving from seeking purpose to serving people, from asking "what's my calling?" to building "who's my temple?"

THE MYLES MUNROE WARNING: DON'T DIE WITH YOUR PURPOSE UNACTIVATED

Before we proceed to activation, heaven issues solemn warning through voice of the late Dr. Myles Munroe:

"The wealthiest place in the world is not the gold mines of South America or the oil fields of Iraq or Iran. They are not the diamond mines of South Africa or the banks of the world. The wealthiest place on the planet is just down the road. It is the cemetery. There lie buried companies that were never started, inventions that were never made, bestselling books that were never written, and masterpieces that were never painted. In the cemetery is buried the greatest treasure of untapped potential."

The cemetery is filled with people who knew their temple but never built. Recognized their purpose but never activated. Identified their people but never served. Understood their assignment but never obeyed. They took their potential to the grave. They buried their purpose with their bodies. They left their temple unbuilt, their people unserved, their assignment unfulfilled.

Why? Fear of failure. Fear of betrayal. Fear of rejection. Fear of inadequacy. Fear that kept them seeking instead of serving, planning instead of building, preparing instead of activating. But you're different. Twenty-one days have stripped away excuses. The gap is closed. The temple is visible. The purpose is clear. The people are waiting.

Dr. Munroe also declared: "The greatest tragedy in life is not death, but a life without a purpose." You now know your purpose. You've identified your temple. You recognize your people. The 4 P's have confirmed your assignment. Heaven has spoken. The question isn't whether you have purpose—it's whether you'll activate it. The question isn't whether your temple exists—it's whether you'll build it. The question isn't whether people are waiting—it's whether you'll serve them.

May I never leave my potential untapped but instead strive to fulfill my divine purpose and live life to the fullest by His grace and all for the glory of God. Don't become another statistic in the cemetery of untapped potential. Don't let fear prevent what heaven predestined. Don't die with your music still inside you, your temple unbuilt, your purpose unactivated. The wealthiest place shouldn't be the cemetery. Let it be your life—lived fully, purpose activated, temple built, people served, assignment completed. BUILD.

THE BUILDER'S DECLARATION

Stand with prophetic authority. Declare over your purpose:

I was CLAIMED for this assignment before I understood it! Before I was born, predestined for this purpose! Before I drew breath, positioned for this temple! I am not accident—I am APPOINTMENT!

My worst season was my qualification exam! My scars are credentials, not disqualifications! My pain points to my purpose! My wounds reveal my work! These aren't marks of failure—they're certificates of preparation!

Purpose isn't something I find—it's something I've always been! I haven't been searching for calling—calling has been searching for me! These people aren't random—they're preappointed! This temple isn't theory—it's reality!

I am the builder of the broken! I am the healer of the hurt! I build those betrayed like me AND those who betray because they're broken! I serve both victims and victimizers! Both wounded and wounders! Both sides of brokenness!

Like Moses—murderer became deliverer! Like Joseph—betrayed then blessed betrayers! Like Paul—persecutor became planter! Like woman at well—shame became credential! Their pattern is my promise!

I am not buried—I am PLANTED! My pain is labor pain giving birth to new season! My battle scars have become beauty marks and stars! My transformation is complete: wheat to flour, carbon to diamond, caterpillar to butterfly, irritant to pearl, olive to oil, seed to harvest!

Every dimension aligned for purpose: Spiritual authority building! Mental clarity recognizing! Emotional healing serving! Physical strength sustaining! Financial resources funding! Relational partnerships multiplying!

The 4 P's confirmed: My PAIN reveals purpose! My PASSION exposes people! My PROVISION shows platform! My PATTERNS confirm assignment!

Purpose → Process → Destiny → Legacy activated! David season transitioning to Solomon building! Warfare positioning for wisdom construction! Battle scars becoming building credentials!

I don't accumulate—I build! I don't seek—I serve! I don't question—I construct! My temple is gathering! My people are appearing! My purpose is clear!

The gap is CLOSED! The shift is HERE! The building BEGINS! I refuse to take my potential to the cemetery! I will not die with my purpose unactivated! I am their predestined builder! Amen!

BREAKTHROUGH PRAYER

Father of purpose, God who claims and commissions, after twenty-one days stripping me to essence and revealing eternal assignment, I stand in recognition of divine calling. "In Him also we have received an inheritance, a destiny—we were claimed by God as His own, having been predestined according to the purpose of Him who works everything in agreement with the counsel and design of His will" (Ephesians 1:11).

Your Word declares: "Before I formed you in the womb I knew you; before you were born I sanctified you" (Jeremiah 1:5). "For we are His workmanship, created in Christ Jesus for good works, which God prepared beforehand that we should walk in them" (Ephesians 2:10). "The Lord will fulfill His purpose for me" (Psalm 138:8).

I am not accident—I am APPOINTMENT. Not random—PREDETERMINED. Not hoping—WALKING IN IT. I was WANTED before I was BORN. I receive the revelation that transforms everything: Purpose isn't WHAT I do—it's WHO I build. I'm not seeking assignment—I AM the assignment, positioned to pull others from where I escaped. My worst season wasn't preparing me for something—it was preparing me for SOMEONE.

I accept my temple assignment revealed through the 4 P's: My PAIN points to purpose. My PASSION reveals people. My PROVISION shows platform. My PATTERNS confirm assignment. My temple includes both: Those stuck where I escaped. Those betrayed like me AND those who betray because they're still broken. Both wounded AND wounders. Both victims AND victimizers. I build both sides because my scars qualify me for comprehensive healing.

These scars aren't disqualifications—they're credentials. My wounds aren't marks of failure—they're certificates of preparation. My worst season qualified me for my greatest work. My battle scars have become beauty marks and stars. Like Moses—from murderer to deliverer. Like Joseph—from betrayed to blessing betrayers. Like Paul—from persecutor to planter. Like woman at well—from shame to city evangelist. Their pattern is my promise.

I am not buried—I am PLANTED! My pain is labor pain birthing new season! My transformation complete: wheat to flour, carbon to diamond, caterpillar to butterfly, irritant to pearl, olive to oil, seed to harvest! You are building them, but You are MAKING me! While I serve their breakthrough, You develop my character! The gap is CLOSED! The shift is ACTIVATED! The temple is VISIBLE! The building BEGINS!

Purpose → Process → Destiny → Legacy operational! David warfare transitioning to Solomon wisdom! Battle season positioning for building elevation! Everything working together for this assignment! I refuse to take my potential to the cemetery! I will not die with my purpose unactivated! I will not let fear prevent what heaven predestined! The wealthiest place will not be my grave—it will be my life lived fully for Your glory!

In Jesus' mighty name, IT IS FINISHED. IT IS BEGINNING. The 21-day journey complete. The lifetime construction commencing. I am their predestined builder. Amen!

A WORD FROM YOUR FATHER

Beloved, I speak directly to your heart in this moment of purpose activation:

Understand this: I did not bring you into existence with the expectation of perfection but rather with the aspiration for unwavering faithfulness. Cherish My perfect love, enjoy My everlasting peace, and trust in the excellence of My promises. I have intricately woven a divine purpose into your being, a unique mission you alone can fulfill within My grand design. This purpose existed before your first breath, developed through every season, and now positions for activation at appointed time.

Today, I extend My hand towards you, beckoning you to step courageously onto the path of purpose I have carved for you. Do not fear the journey; I am with you, guiding your every step. Do not fear the betrayal; I am your shield, protecting your heart while you serve. Do not fear the pain; I am your strength, sustaining you through process that prepares for destiny.

Embrace your divine calling, and let your life become a testimony of My transformative love and power. I have chosen you for such a time as this, and in your hands, My purpose will unfurl, touching the world with My goodness. Your temple may crucify you before receiving resurrection through you. Your people may wound you while you're healing them. Your assignment may break you while building you into what I need you to become.

But I am closing every gap. Between who you were and who you're created to be. Between preparation and activation. Between warfare and building. Between seeking and serving. Your David season transitions to Solomon wisdom. Your battle scars become building credentials. Your worst season becomes qualification for greatest work. Your wounds become wells. Your pain becomes purpose. Your scars become credentials for comprehensive healing ministry.

Trust in Me, and live out the magnificent purpose I have entrusted to you. Build your temple. Serve both sides of brokenness. Don't take your potential to the cemetery. Don't die with your music still inside. The gap is closed. The shift is activated. The temple is visible. Your people are waiting. BUILD.

I am with you always, even to the end of the age.

~ Your Father

THE CINEMATIC CLOSING: YOUR COMMISSION

"Be strong and do the work" (1 Chronicles 28:10). The camera pans across your journal. Twenty-one entries of desperate seeking. Then closes on today's final entry: Names. Faces. Your temple assignment written in permanent ink. You began Day 1 asking "What's my purpose?" Tonight you hold something more powerful than answers—you hold people. Real faces. Your temple assignment. Your predestined building project. But more than identification—you hold ACTIVATION.

The Revolution Complete. Twenty-one days closed every gap between who you were and who you're created to be, between questioning purpose and knowing assignment, between seeking calling and serving people, between purpose anxiety and Kingdom authority, between buried and planted, between confusion and clarity, between warfare and building.

The revolution is complete: PURPOSE hasn't been hiding—it's been searching for you. Your mistakes didn't disqualify—they were INCLUDED. You were WANTED before you were BORN. Your worst season qualified you for your greatest work. These scars aren't disqualifications—they're credentials.

The pattern is eternal: Moses murdered, then delivered murderers. Joseph was betrayed, then blessed betrayers. David was rejected, then received rejecters. Paul persecuted, then planted among persecutors. Woman at well carried shame, then reached city. Wheat was crushed, then fed multitudes. Carbon was pressured, then adorned royalty. Caterpillar dissolved, then pollinated gardens. Irritant wounded, then became pearl. Olive was pressed, then anointed kings. Seed was buried, then multiplied into harvest. You were wounded, now you heal the wounded.

Your temple includes both: those who hurt you and those hurt like you. Both victims and victimizers. Both wounded and wounders. You build both sides because your comprehensive breaking qualified you for comprehensive building. You are not buried—you are PLANTED. Your pain is labor pain birthing new season. Your battle scars have become beauty marks and stars. Your transformation is complete through process that seemed destructive but was actually developmental.

The Generational Declaration. As you break this fast tomorrow, you break more than dietary restriction. You break generational limitation. You break family patterns. You break bloodline bondage.

You break purpose confusion. You break assignment anxiety. You break the curse of untapped potential being buried in cemeteries instead of activated in lives.

You are the first in your lineage to understand purpose as assignment, not achievement. To build those who broke you instead of building walls. To turn scars into credentials instead of hiding wounds. To see pain as preparation instead of punishment. To build your temple with both sides of brokenness. To serve both victims and victimizers with equal grace. To refuse to take your potential to the cemetery. To activate purpose instead of dying with it unbuilt.

The Final Charge. Thunder rolls across the pages of your story. Lightning illuminates faces waiting for your building. The storm of your season is ending. The construction of your calling begins. Consider your list of names. They're waiting. Consider your season—it's shifting. Consider the gap—it's CLOSED. Consider your temple—it's gathering. Consider your scars—they're credentials. Consider your pain—it points to people. Consider your purpose—it's clear. Consider Dr. Munroe's warning—the cemetery shouldn't be the wealthiest place. Consider your Father's voice—He's beckoning you to build.

The fasting is finished. The building begins. Twenty-one days of preparation. A lifetime of construction.

BUILD ANYWAY. BUILD IN BLESSING. BUILD WITH CHAYIL. BUILD THE BROKEN. BUILD BOTH SIDES. BUILD BEYOND BETRAYAL. BUILD YOUR TEMPLE. DON'T TAKE YOUR POTENTIAL TO THE CEMETERY. BUILD.

Credits roll across scenes of transformation: Day 1's confusion becoming Day 21's clarity. Week 1's intimacy building Week 2's identity. Week 3's purpose activating eternal assignment. Broken hearts becoming building blueprints. Wounded healers becoming warrior builders. Seekers becoming servants. Questions becoming construction. Wheat becoming flour. Carbon becoming diamond. Caterpillar becoming butterfly. Irritant becoming pearl. Olive becoming oil. Seed becoming harvest. Buried becoming planted. Pain becoming labor. Scars becoming beauty marks and stars. Warriors becoming builders. The cemetery losing another potential deposit. The Kingdom gaining another activated builder.

The final frame freezes on your hands holding that list of names—your temple assignment, your predestined building project, your eternal purpose crystallized in human faces waiting for builder they don't know has been prepared specifically for them through every crushing, pressing, breaking season that wasn't destruction but transformation.

FADE TO BLACK.
TEXT APPEARS:
"THE DANIEL FAST: CLOSING THE GAP"
"COMPLETE"
"THE BUILDING BEGINS NOW"
"DON'T TAKE YOUR PURPOSE TO THE CEMETERY"
"BUILD"
THE END
THE BEGINNING

You are claimed for this assignment. You are equipped for this construction. You are commissioned for this temple. The gap is closed. The purpose is clear. Your people are waiting. The cemetery will not have your potential. BUILD.

THE DANIEL FAST: CLOSING THE GAP!

SOAP JOURNAL — DAY 21

S (Scripture). Write Ephesians 1:11 in full. Circle "claimed" and "predestined." Add Genesis 50:20, 2 Corinthians 1:3-4, and Isaiah 66:9.

O (Observation). How does being CLAIMED before birth transform everything about purpose? What does the 4 P's reveal about your temple assignment? Where do you see your worst season qualifying you for your greatest work? Who keeps appearing in your pain, passion, provision, and patterns? How does "purpose isn't what but who" revolutionize your understanding? What does the wheat to flour metaphor reveal about your process? How does "I am not buried, I am planted" reframe your painful seasons? What does Dr. Munroe's cemetery warning speak to your heart?

A (Application). Write specific names of people stuck where you escaped. Include both those betrayed like you AND those who betrayed (if applicable). Identify which of the 4 P's most clearly reveals your temple. Consider this message: "God put you on my heart during my 21-day fast. I've been where you are. You're going to make it. There's purpose in your pain." Plan first concrete step for temple construction after breaking the fast. Commit to not taking your potential to the cemetery—activate purpose instead of dying with it unbuilt.

P (Prayer). "Father, thank You that I was CLAIMED for this temple assignment before I understood it. My scars are credentials, not disqualifications. My pain points to purpose. These people are my preappointed assignment. Purpose isn't what I do but who I build. I am not buried—I am PLANTED. My pain is labor pain birthing new season. My battle scars have become beauty marks and stars. The gap is closed. The building begins. I refuse to take my potential to the cemetery. In Jesus' name, Amen."

TODAY'S BREAKTHROUGH MARKER

How did discovering you're "their predestined builder" transform your understanding of purpose from seeking activity to serving people? What shifted when you recognized your scars as credentials instead of disqualifications? How does "I am not buried, I am planted" reframe your painful seasons? What does Dr. Munroe's cemetery warning provoke in your spirit about purpose activation?

BEYOND DAY 21: YOUR TEMPLE CONSTRUCTION TIMELINE

Day 22 (Tomorrow): Break fast with breakthrough consciousness. Your body transitions from fasting to feeding, but your spirit remains positioned in revelation. The physical fast ends but spiritual alignment continues.

Day 23-30: Your 10-year legacy vision. 3-year target. Annual goals. Quarterly milestones.

Day 60: Initial multiplication begins manifesting. Names on your list start responding. Divine appointments accelerate. Resources for building begin appearing through unexpected sources.

Day 90: Temple construction becomes visible. Small group forming. Initial healing happening. Building momentum establishing patterns that will define your lifetime assignment.

Year 1: Generational impact becomes undeniable. Your temple grows beyond initial faces. Others join construction. Multiplication activates as those you build begin building others. Legacy foundation established.

You don't return to who you were Day 1. You can't. That person died between seeking and serving, between questioning and building, between confusion and clarity, between buried and planted.

WEEK 3: PROPEL (7P)

What remains is builder equipped with comprehensive force for temple construction across generations who refuses to take potential to cemetery. The wealthiest place will not be your grave. It will be your life—lived fully, purpose activated, temple built.

DAY 21 COMPLETE: PURPOSE ACTIVATED

Wrong question rejected. Right revelation received. Purpose isn't WHAT but WHO. Scars are credentials. Battle scars are beauty marks and stars. Pain points to people. Temple identified through 4 P's. Ephesians 1:11 exegesis complete.

Twelve biblical words revealed through destiny declaration:

"Purpose isn't something I hunt for—it's the position I take in partnership with God. While I was still in the womb—before I drew breath, before the first wound, before any achievement or title—He had inscribed purpose within me and ordered my steps: I was *KLEROŌ*—obtained as His own, given *KLERONOMIA*—inheritance; my *KLEROS*—destiny—*PROORIZŌ*—predestined, set by *PROTHESIS*—His purpose. Even now He *ENERGEŌ*—actively works—so my *MATSAH*—found treasure—becomes testimony; He *QARA*—called me by name—with *CHAPHETS*—divine delight—according to *YAATS*—eternal counsel—by *KALEO*—divine summons—toward *TELOS*—the completion point in Christ."

Divine progression revealed: Purpose → Process → Destiny → Legacy. Transformation metaphors integrated: wheat to flour, caterpillar to butterfly, carbon to diamond, oyster to pearl, olive to oil, seed to harvest. Revolutionary language activated: "I am not buried, I am planted." "Pain is labor pain" birthing new season. Maya Angelou butterfly wisdom added. Betrayal-to-building testimony vulnerably told. Biblical champions pattern demonstrated: Moses (murderer to deliverer), Joseph (betrayed to blessing betrayers), Paul (persecutor to planter), Woman at Well (shame to evangelist). Six-dimensional purpose framework applied. Six dimension prayers activated. Four enemies broken: confusion, anxiety, doubt, panic. David-to-Solomon transition declared: warfare resources become building materials. Myles Munroe cemetery warning urgently delivered: potential must not die unactivated. God's direct voice prophetically spoken. Builder's Declaration powerfully consolidated. Breakthrough Prayer comprehensively prayed. Father's personal message lovingly delivered. Gap CLOSED. Temple VISIBLE. Cemetery warned against. Building BEGINS NOW. 21-day journey COMPLETE. Lifetime construction COMMENCING. Potential will NOT be buried. Purpose ACTIVATED.

SECTION SIX
CHAMBER 3: INTEGRATE
THE LIFESTYLE THAT LASTS

Days 22-90+ | Sustainable Transformation

"Therefore, if anyone is in Christ, he is a new creation; old things have passed away; behold, all things have become new."
— 2 Corinthians 5:17

Day 22 is where most people lose everything. You can't live on breakthrough memories—you need breakthrough maintenance. Chamber 3 transforms the 21-day catalyst into daily architecture that sustains what emotion ignited but discipline must maintain.

Chayah [khah-YAH] = Fully alive. Not surviving. Not maintaining. **Thriving.**

THE INTEGRATION ARCHITECTURE
STAGE 3.1: BREAKING THE FAST (DAY 22)
How to reintroduce food without reintroducing chaos. Your Day 22 strategy determines whether breakthrough becomes lifestyle or fades into memory. The most dangerous day of your transformation journey—make it your launching pad, not your collapse point.

STAGE 3.2: ARCHITECTING THE CHAYAH LIFESTYLE (DAYS 23-90+)
Vision architecture and daily rhythm sustaining transformation:

10-year legacy vision → 3-year targets → Annual goal setting → Quarterly milestone review → Daily rhythm: 8F

The **8F daily framework:** Faith • Fasting • Fitness • Food • Focus • Finances • Fellowship • Fun

The Chayah Blueprint™ guides you through architecting your complete vision (Days 23-30), then executing your first 90 days and beyond. You steward the 8F ingredients. God multiplies the 6D results—spiritual, mental, emotional, physical, financial, relational wellness.

THE INTEGRATION REALITY
Without Chamber 3: Breakthrough evaporates by Day 30. The fast "worked" temporarily but failed permanently.

With Chamber 3: What 21 days catalyzed, 90 days consolidates, and lifestyle perpetuates. By Day 90, breakthrough becomes your new normal.

This is the difference between event and identity, between temporary intensity and permanent infrastructure.

STAGE 3.1
DAY 22 - BREAKING THE FAST
"FROM SACRED DISCIPLINE TO SACRED LIVING"

The toast looked like betrayal. Day 22. 8:00 AM. Kitchen counter bathed in morning light that felt too bright, too normal, too ordinary for what this moment meant. I sat there, fully dressed but spiritually naked. Twenty-one days of victory behind me. One piece of bread in front of me. Golden. Innocent. Mocking. The butter had softened to room temperature, spreading like liquid temptation. The smell of yeast and wheat—once comforting—now felt like the aroma of compromise. My dandelion tea sat untouched, steam rising like incense carrying my fears to heaven. "Just eat it," my stomach whispered, cramping with familiar hunger. "Don't you dare," my spirit screamed back, knowing what hung in the balance. My hand trembled—not from hunger but from terror. This wasn't breakfast. This was warfare. The war between who I was and who I'd become. Between temporary victory and permanent transformation. I've guided thousands through this exact moment. I know the statistics like a battlefield surgeon knows casualties. Most people who experience genuine breakthrough during intensive spiritual seasons will begin sliding backward today. Not through dramatic moral failure. Through casual resumption of unconscious living. Welcome to the most dangerous day of your transformation journey.

THE SACRED THRESHOLD

You stand between two worlds. Behind you: 21 days of the most intensive spiritual partnership most people ever experience. Ahead: the rest of your life, waiting to see if this breakthrough becomes lifestyle or fades into memory like every other "spiritual high" you've ever had. Day 22 isn't graduation day—it's the first day of forever. Research from University College London reveals the cruel irony: it takes an average of 66 days for new behaviors to become automatic (Lally et al., 2009). Yet most people quit their transformation on Day 22—surrendering with 44 days left until permanence, right when the miracle was about to become unstoppable. The voice that called you into this fast now speaks over your first meal: "This doesn't end your discipline—it begins your stewardship."

FROM INTENSITY TO INFRASTRUCTURE

Here's what separates the 5% who multiply breakthrough from the 95% who lose it: understanding that Day 22 requires a completely different strategy than Day 1. The first 21 days ran on intensity. Desperation drove you. Crisis motivated you. The structure of the fast sustained you—clear boundaries, daily content, consecutive momentum, a visible finish line on Day 21. You could sprint because you knew exactly when the sprint ended. Starting today, you need infrastructure. Not motivation—systems. Not willpower—rhythms. Not intensity—sustainability. Think of it this way: Intensity is rocket fuel. Infrastructure is orbit. The rocket burns hot and fast to escape gravity, but once you reach space, you don't keep burning fuel—you establish orbit that sustains without constant thrust. Your 21 days were the burn. Today you establish the orbit. Intensity creates breakthrough. Infrastructure sustains it. You're not abandoning discipline—you're architecting sustainability. You're not lowering standards—you're building systems that last. You're not compromising breakthrough—you're creating the framework that multiplies it for decades. Tomorrow's Stage 3.2 provides the complete architecture for converting intensity into infrastructure—the 8F framework that turns breakthrough into lifestyle.

HONOR THE TEMPLE GOD TRANSFORMED

Before we go further, if you experienced health improvements during your fast—blood pressure changes, blood sugar stabilization, medication adjustments—consult your healthcare provider before resuming normal eating patterns. Your body adapted. Your chemistry shifted. Your temple transformed. Prolonged fasting creates significant metabolic changes: improved insulin sensitivity, reduced inflammation markers, enhanced autophagy (cellular cleanup), and optimized hormone production (Patterson & Sears, 2017). Honor these changes with professional guidance. This isn't paranoia. This is stewardship of the miracle God gave you.

THE GENTLE RETURN PROTOCOL

Before you touch food, place both hands on your heart and speak these words aloud: "Father, for 21 days, food was my sacrifice. Today it becomes my sacrament. This meal doesn't end my fast—it begins my feast. Not feast of flesh, but feast of fulfillment. I break this fast but not this fellowship. I am Chayah—fully alive, completely Yours."

Your First Sacred Meal Sets the Trajectory

Morning: Eat slowly and reverently, stopping at 80% fullness. Choose gentle foods: cooked grains, steamed vegetables, mild proteins. Avoid processed foods, high sugar, and excessive portions. Chew each bite 20 times—taste how transformation changes everything.

Midday: Add one element you've missed: eggs, yogurt, different proteins. Keep Daniel-fast vegetables as your foundation and hydrate generously as your body recalibrates.

Evening: Prepare a simple, nourishing meal. Journal how food feels in your transformed body. Resist celebration overeating—tomorrow you can expand again.

WHEN THE PENDULUM SWINGS WILD

Some of you won't eat one piece of toast mindfully. You'll demolish an entire pizza desperately. I know because I've done it. Six years ago, Day 22 of my most powerful Daniel Fast, I sat in my car outside a pizza shop at 11:47 AM. Engine running. Shame burning. Air conditioning blasting cold guilt across my face. The parking lot smelled like asphalt and failure. Twenty-one days of discipline about to be destroyed in twenty minutes. "You're stronger than this," I whispered to my reflection in the rearview mirror. My reflection whispered back: "No, you're not. But grace is." By 2 PM, I was curled in bed. Cramping stomach. Shame tears. Convinced I'd ruined everything God had done. That voice lies.

The 24-Hour Grace Protocol

If you completely break on Day 22, you've joined the statistical majority, not the spiritual minority. This doesn't reveal character failure—it reveals why framework matters more than willpower.

Hours 1-6: Stop and breathe. Don't compound failure with punishment eating. Grace is bigger than your biggest binge.

Hours 6-12: Hydrate generously and rest without shame—recovery, not revenge.

Hours 12-24: Eat one simple Daniel meal. Not punishment—proof you still remember your strength.

Day 23: Return to gentle Daniel protocol this day only. Remember who you became, then resume integration.

"For a righteous man may fall seven times and rise again" — *Proverbs 24:16*. The righteous FALL. Multiple times. They RISE. That's what makes them righteous—not perfection but persistence through grace. Your Day 22 disaster doesn't disqualify you. It qualifies you to help others through theirs.

THE EMPTY HOUSE WARNING

Jesus warned about this exact threshold: *"When an unclean spirit goes out of a man, he goes through dry places, seeking rest, and finds none. Then he says, 'I will return to my house from which I came.' And when he comes, he finds it empty, swept, and put in order. Then he goes and takes with him seven other spirits more wicked than himself"* — *Matthew 12:43-45*. Your twenty-one days swept house clean. Demons fled. Strongholds fell. Patterns broke. But here's what most people miss: a clean empty house invites worse problems than a dirty occupied one. The fast evicted what didn't belong. Starting tomorrow, you must fill every room with what does. Scripture warns: *"As a dog returns to his vomit, so a fool repeats his folly"* — *Proverbs 26:11*. The dog doesn't return because the vomit became appetizing—it returns because it forgot why it was expelled. Day 22 matters more than Day 1—it determines whether your house stays clean or becomes seven times worse than when you started. The fast cleaned house. The lifestyle keeps it full. This is why tomorrow's Stage 3.2 isn't optional—it's essential. The 8F Architecture you'll receive provides the infrastructure that fills what intensity emptied. Without it, you're maintaining a clean house with no occupants, and spiritual nature abhors that vacuum.

REVIEW YOUR TRANSFORMATION TIMELINE

Before you measure your miracle, retrieve all 21 days of your GAP Strategy SOAP Journal entries. You completed SOAP journaling every single day for three weeks—**S**cripture, **O**bservation, **A**pplication, **P**rayer. That daily discipline created documented evidence of your transformation, not vague feelings or distant memories. Pull out every entry. Spread them across your table. This is your testimony in ink.

The Three-Week Progression: Your journey followed a deliberate architecture: Week 1 (GROW) answered *Whose You Are*—establishing intimacy with God. Week 2 (ALIGN) answered *Who You Are*—solidifying identity in Christ. Week 3 (PROPEL) answered *Why You Are*—activating destiny with the Holy Spirit. Review your entries through this lens and watch the documented transformation unfold.

WEEK	SCRIPTURE	OBSERVATION	APPLICATION	PRAYER
Week 1: GROW *Whose You Are* (Intimacy)	Surface verses	Noticed God's character	Tentative: "I'll try to trust..."	Raw desperation, begging
Week 2: ALIGN *Who You Are* (Identity)	Deeper identity passages	Saw yourself through God's eyes	Declarative: "I am His beloved"	Partnership, declaring from identity

| Week 3: **PROPEL** *Why You Are* (Purpose) | Mission-aligned | Revealed Kingdom purposes | Commissioning: "My pain → their pathway" | Breakthrough declarations over assignments |

This isn't vague testimony—"I feel closer to God" or "I think I've changed." This is systematic documentation and transformation with 21 pieces of evidence. Pull out all 21 entries now. Don't rely on memory. Let the documentation speak.

What Your Journal Proves: Read your Day 1 entry—notice the tentative hope or desperate pleas, whatever GAP scores you recorded. Then read Day 7—observe how your observations deepened, how your language shifted, how your scores changed. Continue to Day 14—watch declarative statements replacing questions, identity solidifying in your own words. Finally, Day 21—see the mission language, activated purpose, and whatever transformation your scores document. Your gap checkboxes documented which dimensions closed when. Review which gaps you marked as closing across all 21 days. Your breakthrough markers across 21 days—"today's anchor" and "tomorrow's expectation"—create a timeline of progressive victory documented in your own hand.

MEASURE YOUR MIRACLE

What doesn't get measured doesn't get sustained. You must document what God accomplished before amnesia steals your testimony. The Daniel Fast promised to close the gap. Your three weeks of daily documentation proved it happening in real time. Now let's measure the full impact.

The GAP Closure Assessment: Your journal tracked three core dimensions daily: Intimacy with God (GROW), Identity Security (ALIGN), Purpose Clarity (PROPEL). You rated each dimension 1-10 for all 21 days. Now consolidate that journey into Day 1 versus Day 22 comparison.

GAP DIMENSION	DAY 1	DAY 22	GAIN
Intimacy with God (GROW) — *Whose You Are*	___	___	+___
Identity in Christ (ALIGN) — *Who You Are*	___	___	+___
Destiny with Holy Spirit (PROPEL) — *Why You Are*	___	___	+___
TOTAL GAP CLOSURE	___/30	___/30	+___ points

This is the core transformation. Your 21 entries documented the journey from Day 1 scores to Day 22 scores. Week 1 observations revealed God's character, growing intimacy. Week 2 application statements proved identity solidifying—language shifted from "I hope" to "I am." Week 3 prayers activated purpose—declarations replaced petitions. Closing the gap with God, your identity in Christ, and your destiny with the Holy Spirit changes everything. This breakthrough becomes the engine that drives transformation across every area of your life.

Your 6D Life Transformation Assessment: When you close the gap spiritually, breakthrough cascades into every dimension of life. Your three weeks of gap checkboxes documented this progression. Rate your satisfaction on a 1-10 scale based on what your journal proves:

DIMENSION	DAY 1	DAY 22	GAIN
Spiritual	___	___	+___
Mental	___	___	+___
Emotional	___	___	+___
Physical	___	___	+___
Financial	___	___	+___
Relational	___	___	+___
TOTAL LIFE IMPACT	___/60	___/60	+___ points

Your observations didn't stay theoretical—they cascaded into every area of life. Review your application sections across all 21 days. How did growing intimacy with God (Week 1) affect your mental clarity? How did aligning with your identity (Week 2) shift your emotional patterns? How did activating your destiny (Week 3) change your physical energy, financial decisions, relational dynamics? Write this down. Date it. You'll need this testimony later. What you don't measure, you can't multiply.

THE DANIEL PRINCIPLE: YOUR BEFORE AND AFTER TEST

Remember the original Daniel? He and his friends faced this exact moment. After refusing the king's rich food and wine, after choosing vegetables and water instead, they stood for examination. *"And at the end of ten days their features appeared better and fatter in flesh than all the young men who ate the portion of the king's delicacies"* — *Daniel 1:15*. The test proved what obedience produces: transformation visible to everyone. Daniel didn't just survive his consecration—he thrived through it. His countenance revealed what his discipline created. Now it's your turn.

Look at your GAP scores: Day 1 versus Day 22. The difference isn't just numbers—it's testimony documented through 21 days of entries. Your intimacy with God deepened—your Week 1 observations prove it. Your identity in Christ solidified—your Week 2 application statements prove it. Your destiny with the Holy Spirit activated—your Week 3 prayers prove it. Then look at your 6D scores: spiritual breakthrough cascaded into mental clarity, emotional freedom, physical vitality, financial peace, and relational restoration. Like Daniel, your obedience produced visible transformation. Your face carries different light. Your body radiates different energy. Your spirit manifests different authority. The king's court noticed Daniel's transformation. Your community will notice yours. This measurement isn't vanity—it's verification that partnership with Heaven produces results the world's best cannot match. Daniel's vegetable diet outperformed the king's delicacies. Your consecration season outperformed the world's self-help strategies. The before and after test isn't about comparison with others—it's about documentation that God's way works. Daniel used his results to gain influence. You'll use yours to multiply transformation.

CELEBRATE YOUR BREAKTHROUGH PUBLICLY

Your Chayah Club family has prayed with you, struggled with you, and overcome with you for 21 days. Today they deserve to celebrate what God did through their prayers. Share your breakthrough:

THE DANIEL FAST: CLOSING THE GAP!

"Day 22 - GAP CLOSED! Day 1: ___/30 → **Day 22: ___/30 = + points! Week 1 (GROW): Intimacy transformed. Week 2 (ALIGN): Identity solidified. Week 3 (PROPEL): Destiny activated. Total life impact: +** points across 6D (___/60 → ___/60). Like Daniel after his test, my 21 days of documented obedience produced visible transformation. Biggest breakthrough: ___. **Hardest day: Day. Most powerful truth: ''** Not the same person who started. Ready for Stage 3.2: Architecting the Chayah Lifestyle!"

LIVING FROM REST, NOT FOR IT

The Christian life isn't striving toward rest—it's operating from it. *"Abide in Me, and I in you. As the branch cannot bear fruit of itself, unless it abides in the vine, neither can you, unless you abide in Me" — John 15:4*. The branch doesn't strain for grapes. It stays connected. Fruit becomes the inevitable outcome of abiding, not the exhausting result of effort. Your transformation practices—like the journaling you maintained for 21 consecutive days—aren't spiritual gymnastics performed for God's approval. They're positions of connection maintained for Heaven's overflow. When you drift—and you will—don't spiral into performance anxiety. Just return to the vine. Return to your journal. Return to daily Scripture, Observation, Application, Prayer. Religion says perform for acceptance. Relationship says abide in acceptance. Connection produces transformation. Striving produces exhaustion. This is the infrastructure difference. Intensity says "maintain perfection or lose everything." Infrastructure says "return to the system when you drift." Intensity creates all-or-nothing pressure. Infrastructure creates grace-filled sustainability. You're not abandoning discipline—you're building systems that catch you when you stumble and restore you when you fall.

STAND IN YOUR MIRROR

Stand up right now. Go to your mirror. Look at the person you've become. Feel the transformation in your bones. Speak these words over your reflection with authority: "I am not who I was 22 days ago. That person needed a fast. This person has become a faster. That person struggled with discipline. This person completed 21 consecutive days of documentation—proof I can sustain daily habits. That person lived from emptiness. This person overflows from fullness documented in 21 days of breakthrough entries. This meal doesn't end my partnership with heaven—it deepens it. What God downloaded in 21 days, I'll live out for 21 years. From sacred discipline to sacred living—the transformation multiplies. From intensity to infrastructure—the breakthrough becomes lifestyle. I choose never to be the same again. I am Chayah—fully alive, completely His, forever changed."

BECOME A FASTER, NOT A FINISHER

The most dangerous words you could speak today: "I completed a fast." Completed suggests finished. Finished implies done. Done means returning to normal. You didn't complete a fast. You discovered fasting. You didn't finish something. You started everything. You're not someone who fasted. You're someone who fasts. This identity shift determines whether transformation becomes lifestyle or remains a one-time event. Tomorrow's Stage 3.2 will guide you in choosing your sustainable fasting rhythm—monthly intensives, weekly disciplines, or quarterly seasons. Your 21 days of consecutive discipline proved you can maintain daily practice. That consistency becomes your foundation for ongoing fasting rhythms integrated into the complete 8F Architecture (Faith, Fasting, Fitness, Food, Focus, Finances, Fellowship, Fun). Don't choose based on today's enthusiasm—choose based on sustainable commitment to growth. A sustainable practice beats an unsustainable performance every time.

THE SACRED CEREMONY

Don't you dare let Day 22 pass without marking this moment.

Morning Ritual: Play worship music that moved you during the fast. Light a candle representing the light God ignited in you. Read aloud your Day 1 entry, then your Day 21 entry. Burn or bury a written list of what you're leaving behind forever.

Evening Commitment: Choose one breakthrough practice you'll maintain daily—will you continue journaling? Text your celebration to three people who need hope. Schedule Stage 3.2 planning sessions for Days 23-30. Write a letter to yourself to open on Day 365.

Three Written Commitments - Before sleep tonight, write these:
1. **Stewardship Commitment:** "I will honor my body's transformation through wise eating choices and appropriate medical consultation if needed."
2. **Growth Commitment:** "I will continue growing in my strongest breakthrough dimension: _____. I will maintain daily spiritual practice."
3. **Community Commitment:** "I will celebrate my breakthrough with my Chayah Club family and commit to Stage 3.2 accountability together."

Sacred ceremony separates casual resumption from intentional continuation. What gets honored gets sustained. What gets ignored gets abandoned.

THE BRIDGE PRAYER

Place your hands on your heart and pray with me: "Father of transformation, Lord of sustainable change, thank You that these 21 days weren't an event but an initiation into lifestyle transformation. Thank You for the discipline that documented my journey through GROW, ALIGN, and PROPEL. As I cross the bridge from fasting to feasting, from discipline to stewardship, from intensity to infrastructure, guard my heart from the lie that normal eating means normal living. This food I receive as sacrament, not just sustenance. This body I honor as Your temple, not just my vessel. This life I live as Your dwelling place, not just my existence. What You've done in me through 21 days of documented breakthrough, multiply through me for years to come. What You've taught me through Scripture observations, let me teach others. What You've healed in me through vulnerable applications, use to heal generations. The intensity season is complete. The infrastructure season has just begun. Tomorrow I begin architecting the Chayah Lifestyle—the complete framework for staying fully alive in every dimension. In Jesus' mighty name, Amen."

THE TOAST GOES DOWN

The toast went down slowly. Thoughtfully. Reverently. Each bite tasted different—not just because my palate had changed, but because my entire relationship with nourishment had transformed. The butter carried the weight of stewardship. The wheat whispered of covenant. The simple act of chewing had become an act of worship. Victory. Not because I ate perfectly, but because I ate purposefully. Not because I felt strong, but because I chose strength when I felt vulnerable.

Most transformations die on Day 22. Yours is just being born. You're not the same person who started this journey hungry for breakthrough. You're the person who partnered with heaven for 21 days, documented transformation through daily practice, and discovered that sustainable transformation isn't about perfect discipline—it's about sacred stewardship of what God downloads. The trembling stops. The confidence builds. The integration begins.

Tomorrow starts Stage 3.2: Architecting the Chayah Lifestyle—where breakthrough becomes systematic living, where intensity converts to infrastructure, where vision becomes permanent reality. The 8F Architecture you'll receive provides the complete framework for filling the house that fasting cleaned. Without it, you risk the empty house syndrome Jesus warned about. With it, you build the lifestyle that lasts. Tonight, sleep as the person you've become, not the person you used to be. The bridge has been crossed. Sacred living has begun. The sprint ended. The orbit established. From intensity to infrastructure. From breakthrough to lifestyle. From 21 days to 21 years. Someone needs to see you succeed beyond Day 22. Someone needs proof that breakthrough can become lifestyle. Your sustained transformation is their permission to begin.

END OF STAGE 3.1: DAY 22 - BREAKING THE FAST
Continue to Stage 3.2: Architecting the Chayah Lifestyle
DAY 22 COMPLETE. THE MOST DANGEROUS DAY SURVIVED. FROM INTENSITY TO INFRASTRUCTURE. FROM SACRED DISCIPLINE TO SACRED LIVING. READY FOR THE 8F ARCHITECTURE.

STAGE 3.2
ARCHITECTING THE CHAYAH LIFESTYLE
THE COMPLETE SUSTAINMENT ARCHITECTURE FOR STAYING FULLY ALIVE

The person in the mirror looked like a fraud. Day 25. 11:47 PM. Bathroom vanity, fluorescent lights humming their clinical judgment overhead. The faucet dripped steadily—one drop every three seconds, counting down to my inevitable failure. Three days ago, I was invincible—Day 22 victory celebration still fresh, breakthrough measurements documented, community cheering my transformation. Tonight, I could feel it starting. The slow fade. The gradual drift. The whisper that sounds like wisdom: "You don't have to be so intense anymore. You've had your breakthrough. Time to be normal again." I pressed my palms against the cold porcelain sink, feeling the weight of expectation pressing down on my shoulders. My reflection stared back—eyes that had seen God move, now clouded with familiar doubt. The taste of fear, metallic and bitter, filled my mouth. "What if this was just another spiritual high that fades by February?" I've guided thousands through breakthrough seasons. I know the statistics like a trauma surgeon knows mortality rates. Most people lose significant ground by Day 45—not through dramatic moral failure but through casual resumption of unconscious living, through lack of systematic sustainment planning. I opened my eyes and looked at my reflection again—really looked. "Not you," I whispered fiercely to the person I'd become. "Not this time. Not ever again." Welcome to the most critical stage of your transformation journey—architecting permanence from breakthrough.

TWO PATHS THROUGH STAGE 3.2

Choose your pathway based on where you are right now:

PATH 1: DEEP DIVE (RECOMMENDED) - Complete all 5 days using the comprehensive journal-mining process (Days 23-30). This path creates the most robust architecture for permanent transformation. Time investment: 3-4 hours total over 7 days.

PATH 2: ESSENTIAL LAUNCH - If overwhelmed or needing immediate structure, complete Days 23-24 (Legacy Vision) + Day 30 (Daily Mastery) only. Return to Days 25-29 by Day 60 when ready for deeper architecture. Time investment: 60-90 minutes now, complete later.

Both paths work. Choose based on capacity, not guilt.

THE CHAYAH REVELATION

CHAYAH [khah-YAH]—Hebrew for "fully alive, revived, flourishing." Not just breathing. Not surviving. Not maintaining. Fully alive in every dimension—spiritually connected, mentally clear, emotionally free, physically vital, financially secure, relationally rich, joyfully abundant. The Chayah Lifestyle is the systematic framework that architects this "fully alive" state permanently. While others hope breakthrough will naturally sustain itself, you engineer its multiplication through strategic life planning.

THE DANIEL FAST: CLOSING THE GAP!

I learned this the hard way. Five years ago, after my most powerful 21-day season, I measured incredible breakthrough—a +23 point transformation across all dimensions. I celebrated. I testified. I moved on. By Day 60, I was back at baseline. By Day 90, I was lower than when I started. The devastation nearly destroyed my faith in spiritual transformation. That failure birthed the architecture you're about to receive. The missing piece that separates temporary inspiration from permanent transformation.

THE GAP TAX YOU JUST STOPPED PAYING

Every day your spiritual, identity, or purpose gaps stay open, you pay an invisible cost—what I call the Gap Tax. It's the price of living below God's design for your life. **Spiritual Gap Tax:** Anxiety instead of peace. Powerlessness instead of authority. Prayer feels like obligation. Scripture feels distant. You're spiritually breathing but not thriving. **Identity Gap Tax:** Performance treadmill that never stops. Comparison that steals joy. Exhaustion from trying to prove your worth. You're constantly earning what you already possess. **Purpose Gap Tax:** Drift without direction. Distraction without discernment. Working hard but not on what matters. Busy but not fruitful. You're surviving but not fulfilling calling.

Your 21-day fast closed the gaps. The Gap Tax stopped. You felt it immediately—peace replaced anxiety, clarity replaced confusion, power replaced powerlessness. The freedom was undeniable. But here's what most people miss: gaps don't stay closed automatically. Without systematic infrastructure, they reopen slowly. The Gap Tax resumes—quietly at first, then devastatingly. The Chayah Lifestyle eliminates the Gap Tax permanently through systematic daily practices that keep what your fast closed, closed.

FROM INTENSITY TO INFRASTRUCTURE

Here's what separates the 5% who multiply breakthrough from the 95% who lose it: understanding that Day 22 requires a completely different strategy than Day 1. The first 21 days ran on intensity. Desperation drove you. Crisis motivated you. The structure of the fast sustained you—clear boundaries, daily content, consecutive momentum, a visible finish line on Day 21. You could sprint because you knew exactly when the sprint ended. Starting Day 23, you need infrastructure. Not motivation—systems. Not willpower—rhythms. Not intensity—sustainability.

INTENSITY = ROCKET FUEL | INFRASTRUCTURE = ORBIT

INTENSITY (ROCKET FUEL)	INFRASTRUCTURE (ORBIT)
Burns hot and fast to escape gravity	Sustains indefinitely without constant thrust
Requires massive energy output	Efficient energy usage
Depletes quickly	Stable and predictable
Can't sustain indefinitely	Can maintain for decades
Gets you TO the breakthrough	Keeps you IN the breakthrough
Temporary thrust	Permanent systems
Daily heroics	Daily habits
Gritted teeth	Strategic rhythms
White knuckles	Wise stewardship
Exhausts eventually	Energizes continually

Your 21 days were the burn that escaped gravity—the rocket fuel that closed the gap. The next 90 days establish the orbit that sustains forever—the infrastructure that keeps the gap closed without daily desperation. You can't keep burning rocket fuel—you'll exhaust. Infrastructure creates sustainable orbit. The practices that worked during the fast won't sustain lifestyle without adaptation. Daily SOAP journaling during 21 days? That was intensity. Continuing journaling three times weekly with monthly deep dives? That's infrastructure. Fasting from all food until 6 PM for 21 days? Intensity. Choosing weekly 24-hour fasts with quarterly intensive seasons? Infrastructure. You're not abandoning discipline—you're architecting sustainability. You're not lowering standards—you're building systems that last. You're not compromising breakthrough—you're creating the framework that multiplies it for decades.

THE HEART-BREAKING TRUTH

Most people think the battle is won on Day 22. The real battle begins on Day 23. Your breakthrough created a target. Hell noticed. The enemy of your soul isn't impressed by your 21-day victory—he's planning your Day 45 defeat. Research from habit formation studies confirms what I've observed: the period between Days 22-66 represents the highest risk for transformation collapse (Lally et al., 2009). Most people quit when they're two-thirds of the way to permanent change. *"When an unclean spirit goes out of a man, he goes through dry places, seeking rest, and finds none. Then he says, 'I will return to my house from which I came.' And when he comes, he finds it empty, swept, and put in order. Then he goes and takes with him seven other spirits more wicked than himself"* — Matthew 12:43-45. Your 21 days swept house. Without systematic architecture, you're building an invitation for worse oppression than you started with. This isn't paranoia. This is pastoral protection from someone who has watched too many victories turn into devastating defeats.

THE CAKE MODEL: UNDERSTANDING YOUR CONTROL

Most people confuse what they control with what they experience. The Cake Model eliminates this confusion permanently. Think of transformation like baking a cake. You have ingredients you control daily and results you experience over time.

8F INPUT BEHAVIORS (Ingredients You Control Daily): Faith (prayer, worship, Scripture—the flour that provides foundation); Fasting (spiritual discipline rhythms—the yeast that creates growth catalyst); Fitness (exercise, sleep, movement—the protein that builds strength); Food (nutrition, eating patterns—the nutrients that fuel performance); Focus (mental and emotional health practices—the sugar that brings mental sweetness); Finances (money stewardship systems—the salt that provides stability); Fellowship (relationships, community—the milk that adds richness); Fun (joy, recreation, sabbath—the vanilla that gives flavor).

6D OUTPUT SATISFACTION (Results You Experience): When you faithfully manage the eight ingredients daily, you experience satisfaction across six life dimensions: Spiritual, Mental, Emotional, Physical, Financial, and Relational.

Here's the revelation that saved my transformation: You can't directly control how the cake tastes, but you absolutely control what ingredients you put in daily. Skip ingredients, get poor results. Use quality ingredients consistently, get excellent results. You steward the ingredients. God multiplies the results.

YOUR JOURNAL: THE BLUEPRINT FOR ARCHITECTURE

Before we design your 5-day sustainment architecture, retrieve your GAP Strategy SOAP Journal one more time. You're not just reviewing it for nostalgia—you're mining it for architectural blueprints. Your 21 days of Scripture, Observation, Application, and Prayer entries contain the raw materials for building permanent lifestyle transformation: Week 1 observations revealed what ingredients created spiritual breakthrough; Week 2 applications documented what daily practices shifted your identity; Week 3 prayers declared what assignments require systematic support. Your daily GAP scores across 21 days show which ingredients need strengthening. Your gap checkboxes demonstrate which life dimensions respond to which daily practices. Your breakthrough markers—"today's anchor" and "tomorrow's expectation"—create momentum timeline for ongoing victories. The discipline you maintained for 21 consecutive days isn't just proof you can journal—it's proof you can architect and sustain daily lifestyle habits. You showed up every single day for three weeks to document Scripture revelation, observe God's work, apply truth to life, and pray breakthrough. That consistency becomes your foundation for the 8F Chayah Lifestyle ahead. What you documented during your fast, you now architect into permanent systems. Your journal isn't a relic of the past 21 days—it's the blueprint for the next 21 years.

THE 5-DAY SUSTAINMENT ARCHITECTURE

DAYS 23-24: 10-YEAR LEGACY VISION

Two years ago, sitting in my car after another failed attempt at sustained transformation, engine ticking as it cooled, I heard Holy Spirit whisper: "Stop thinking about personal improvement. Start thinking about generational warfare." That's when everything changed. Your breakthrough wasn't personal improvement—it was generational warfare. You didn't just break patterns for yourself. You broke them for your bloodline. The question that changes everything: "Will my transformation die with me, or multiply through generations?"

Now retrieve your journal and read through all 21 days of prayer entries. Don't skim—read every prayer you wrote over three weeks. Notice recurring themes: What did you ask God for repeatedly in Week 1? What did you declare consistently in Week 2? What assignments emerged in Week 3? Those patterns in your prayers aren't random—they're prophetic direction for your legacy. Read your Day 15, 17, and 21 prayers from PROPEL week. What Kingdom assignments appeared? What nations did you pray for? What generations did God burden you to impact? Those aren't fleeting thoughts—those are legacy seeds planted through intercession.

Now review your 21 days of application statements. Notice how your language evolved. Early applications said "I will try to trust more" or "I hope to walk in identity." Later applications declared "Peace is my inheritance through position" or "I lead from overflow, not emptiness" or "My pain becomes their pathway." Those mature application statements contain theology for legacy building. The truths you applied to your life become truths you'll multiply through others' lives. Your observations across 21 days revealed God's character—His faithfulness, His love, His power, His purposes. Those observations about God inform what you'll believe about His capacity to use your life for generational impact. Your breakthrough markers show what momentum looks like. Your "tomorrow's expectation" statements created forward motion every single day. That same principle—declaring tomorrow's breakthrough today—becomes the foundation for declaring your 10-year legacy now.

Write your 10-year legacy declarations across each dimension, informed by your journal discoveries: Spiritual Multiplication (What prayer movements will birth through your intimacy overflow? Review Week 1 GROW prayers—what burden for prayer did God give you?); Emotional Healing Legacy (What family emotional patterns die with your healing journey? Review Week 2 ALIGN observations—what generational wounds did you identify?); Physical Vitality Impact (How will your energy transformation serve your enlarged calling? Review your physical breakthrough markers—what vitality shift occurred?); Financial Kingdom Influence (What Kingdom resources will you steward through wise financial living? Review entries where financial breakthroughs appeared—what stewardship revelations came?); Relational Multiplication (What communities will you build from relational abundance? Review observations about relationships—what healing happened?).

Complete this declaration, informed by your documented discoveries: "Through my Chayah Lifestyle, God will multiply my transformation into: ___ leaders raised and equipped for Kingdom impact, ___ families transformed through my example, ___ ministries or movements funded through my stewardship, ___ communities served from my overflow, ___ generational patterns broken permanently, ___ nations touched through my obedient living." Legacy thinking changes how you live today. When you know your transformation will impact generations, you architect sustainability differently. Your 21 days aren't just personal breakthrough documentation—they're generational warfare ammunition.

DAYS 25-26: 3-YEAR TARGET & ANNUAL GOALS

Your 10-year vision provides direction. Your 3-year target creates the bridge. Your 1-year goals create momentum. But here's what I learned through painful trial and error: vague hopes create vague results. Specific targets create specific actions. *"Write the vision and make it plain on tablets, that he may run who reads it"* — *Habakkuk 2:2.*

Pull out your Day 22 GAP Closure Assessment and 6D Life Transformation Assessment. Those scores—documented through 21 days of tracking—become your baseline for annual target setting. Review your 21 days of daily GAP scores. Which dimension showed most growth? That's your strength to leverage. Which dimension grew slowest? That's your priority for focus. Your journal entries explain why. If Identity Security (ALIGN) showed dramatic growth, read your Week 2 applications—what daily practices created that shift? Replicate those. If Purpose Clarity (PROPEL) lagged, read your Week 3 prayers—what obstacles appeared? Address those systematically.

Create your annual target chart. List each of the six dimensions: Spiritual, Mental, Emotional, Physical, Financial, Relational. Record your Day 22 score for each (out of 10). Then set your 365-day target for each dimension. For every dimension scoring below 8/10, ask three questions informed by your journal: (1) What specific daily ingredients need strengthening? Review entries where this dimension showed breakthrough—what practices created that? (2) What systems need creation or overhaul? Look at gap checkboxes across 21 days—which days did this dimension close? What was different those days? (3) What professional help do I need? Your observations might have revealed needs you can't meet alone—counselor, financial advisor, fitness trainer, mentor.

I remember staring at my financial score—a devastating 3/10—and realizing I needed more than prayer. I needed a financial advisor, a budget system, and the humility to learn stewardship from scratch. My entries from the fast revealed the depth of financial chaos through observations I couldn't ignore. Those honest observations became the catalyst for seeking professional help. Your journal holds similar revelations. The observations you wrote—especially the vulnerable, painful ones—expose what needs systematic attention beyond daily prayer. Review your 21 days of observations. What patterns did you observe about yourself that need professional intervention? Mental health struggles? Physical health concerns? Financial illiteracy? Relational dysfunction? Your honest observations become your roadmap for annual target planning. Dreams with deadlines become destinies. Destinies shared become legacies.

DAYS 27-28: QUARTERLY VICTORIES

Annual goals can feel overwhelming. Quarterly victories create unstoppable momentum. Choose 3-5 breakthrough victories for the next 90 days that move you toward annual targets across your weakest dimensions. Your journal provides the blueprint. Review all 21 days of "tomorrow's expectation" statements. Those daily momentum declarations show what progressive victory looks like: Day 1 expectation: "Tomorrow I hope to pray longer" | Day 21 expectation: "Tomorrow I declare breakthrough over assignments." That progression—from hoping to declaring—took 21 days. Your quarterly victories replicate that pattern over 90 days.

Choose spiritual milestones informed by Week 1 GROW entries. What prayer rhythms emerged during the fast? Establishing unshakeable morning prayer rhythm (30+ minutes daily) might be one victory. What Scripture engagement patterns worked? Your Scripture selections across 21 days show what passages brought breakthrough—build on those. Choose physical victories informed by breakthrough markers tracking your body's response. Review gap checkboxes—which days did Physical Gap close? What was different? If your journal shows Physical Gap closed on days you exercised before 9 AM, your quarterly victory becomes "Exercise 6-9 AM, 5 days/week for 90 days." If sleep quality improved when you journaled before bed, your victory becomes "Evening wind-down routine with journaling, 90 consecutive nights." Translate documented breakthrough patterns into measurable 90-day targets.

Financial breakthroughs include creating detailed budgets with 90-day adherence, paying off specific debt amounts or increasing savings, and establishing emergency fund milestones. Your observations about financial stress and applications about stewardship create the "why" behind these goals. If your journal reveals anxiety about month-end bills, your quarterly victory might be "Build $1,000 buffer in checking account by Day 90." If observations show guilt about impulse purchases, your victory becomes "30-day rule for purchases over $50—90-day adherence." Your documented financial pain points become specific quarterly targets. Relational growth means planning and executing monthly quality time commitments, addressing and resolving specific relationship conflicts documented in entries, and developing new meaningful friendships. If your journal shows marriage tension around communication, your quarterly victory might be "Weekly date night with 30-minute check-in conversation, 12 consecutive weeks." If observations reveal isolation, your victory becomes "Attend or host fellowship gathering twice monthly for 90 days." Let your documented relational breakthroughs and struggles guide your specific targets.

TESTIMONY: QUARTERLY ARCHITECTURE IN ACTION - Peter implemented the quarterly victory framework after his Daniel Fast. His journal showed prayer created breakthrough, so his Q1 victory was establishing a 30-minute morning prayer habit before 7 AM. He faced obstacles—kids waking early, work emergencies, travel disruptions. But his journal had documented 21 days of consistency despite obstacles, proving he could adapt. By Day 90, he'd completed 82 of 90 days—missing only during a family crisis week. His next quarterly review showed intimacy score rising from 7/10 to 9/10. He celebrated the 82-day victory publicly, which inspired three friends to launch their own quarterly frameworks. The architecture works when you work it. One 90-day season changes everything.

Every 90 days, conduct a quarterly review just like you reviewed entries for Day 22 assessment: Assess current satisfaction levels against targets using same 1-10 scale you used in daily tracking; Analyze which daily ingredients drove strongest improvements—your applications documented what worked; Adjust systems based on what's working—your 21 days of trial and observation revealed what's sustainable versus unsustainable for you; Advance to next quarter's victory targets—your "tomorrow's expectation" pattern continues; Announce victories with your accountability community—just like sharing breakthroughs. The quarterly rhythm becomes your sustained transformation engine.

DAY 29: MONTHLY MOMENTUM

Quarterly milestones guide direction. Monthly actions create traction. Break your quarterly milestones into weekly actions for Month 1 (Days 31-60), using your journal as guide. Your 21 days of applications documented what daily actions created breakthrough. Now systematize those into weekly structure. Each monthly planning session becomes your opportunity to translate quarterly targets into immediate action steps that build momentum one week at a time.

For spiritual growth informed by Week 1 GROW: Week 1 establishes morning prayer space and time consistency—replicate what worked during the fast. Your entries show when you prayed, how long, what obstacles you overcame. If your journal shows 6 AM prayer worked best, block that time for Week 1. Week 2 begins systematic Scripture reading with application—your 21 days of Scripture selections show which passages brought revelation. If Psalms opened your heart during the fast, start Month 1 with systematic Psalms reading. Week 3 connects with accountability partners or mentors—your observations about community's impact on breakthrough inform who you need. Week 4 plans and executes first post-fast intensive day—return to the discipline with monthly one-day fasts.

For physical transformation informed by gap checkboxes and breakthrough markers: Week 1 designs and begins sustainable fitness routines. Review which days Physical Gap closed during the fast—what movement happened those days? If walking 30 minutes closed the gap on Day 8, 12, and 19, establish that as Week 1's daily target. Week 2 implements meal planning and preparation systems. Your Daniel Fast proved you can maintain eating discipline—extend principles (whole foods, mindful eating) into sustainable plan. If Sunday meal prep supported your fast success (check your observations), dedicate Sunday afternoons Week 2-4 to batch cooking. Week 3 optimizes sleep schedule and environment. Your observations probably mentioned sleep quality improving—systematize what created that. Week 4 schedules and completes health screenings. Your observations might have noted physical symptoms needing attention—address them professionally this week.

On the last day of every month, conduct your monthly calibration: Celebrate victories that build momentum—what worked this month like it worked during the fast? Write these down specifically. Calibrate what adjustments are needed—review your applications' evolution for pattern of adaptation. Your journal shows you adjusted prayer times when obstacles arose; apply that flexibility monthly. Connect with accountability community to share progress—mimic the vulnerability you practiced in entries. Commit to next month's specific targets—use "tomorrow's expectation" principle at monthly scale. Write Month 2's focus areas informed by Month 1's data, just like Day 8's focus built on Day 7's breakthrough. Monthly momentum creates quarterly milestones. Quarterly milestones achieve annual goals. Annual goals build legacy vision. The monthly rhythm prevents drift while allowing course correction.

DAY 30: DAILY MASTERY

Vision inspires. Goals focus. Milestones motivate. Actions create progress. But daily habits determine destiny. After five years of failed transformation attempts, I finally understood: I was majoring in inspiration and minoring in daily ingredient mastery. Your 21 days of journaling proved you can master daily habits. You completed Scripture, Observation, Application, Prayer every single day for three weeks. That wasn't motivation—that was discipline. That wasn't inspiration—that was consistency. You tracked daily GAP scores, marked gap checkboxes, wrote breakthrough markers, maintained vulnerability in observations, documented applications honestly, prayed breakthrough declarations—all daily for 21 consecutive days. If you can sustain that discipline for 21 days, you can sustain 8F lifestyle architecture for 365 days and beyond. The consistency you demonstrated during the fast becomes the foundation for the lifestyle you're architecting now.

Design your personalized 8F Chayah Lifestyle, informed by what your journal revealed works for you:

INGREDIENT	DAILY PRACTICES INFORMED BY JOURNAL
Faith	Continue with the **365: Live Fearlessly** framework and daily SOAP journaling (Scripture, Observation, Application, Prayer). Maintain the practices your entries proved most effective: reading God's Word, worship, declarations, and specific prayer minutes. Throughout the day, sustain constant conversation with God—documenting the moments when you sensed His presence most powerfully.
Fasting	Your 21-day consecutive discipline proved your capacity. Choose your sustainable rhythm based on where grace meets capacity: **Awakening Level** (Monthly 1-day fasts—establishing foundation rhythm, perfect for building fasting muscle memory); **Foundation Level** (Weekly 24-hour fasts—deepening consistency, creates regular touchpoints that compound); **Acceleration Level** (Weekly plus quarterly 21-day intensives—pursuing advanced transformation, combines sustainable rhythm with periodic depth); **Consecration Level** (Annual corporate fasts plus personal intensive seasons—called to leadership and multiplication, positions you to lead others); **Multiplication Level** (Leading while living the lifestyle—raising up others in fasting culture, your sustainable practice becomes

	their permission to begin). Start where grace meets capacity. Grow as strength develops. A sustainable practice beats an unsustainable performance every time.
Fitness	Your gap checkboxes showed when Physical Gap closed. Replicate what worked on breakthrough days through daily movement. Build on energy patterns you observed through weekly structure.
Food	Your Daniel Fast proved discipline capacity. Extend mindful eating you practiced through daily framework. Maintain water intake that worked through hydration excellence.
Focus	Your observations documented mental and emotional shifts. Continue reflection practice through daily mind renewal. Extend vulnerability through emotional regulation.
Finances	Your entries revealed financial revelations. Apply financial observations through daily stewardship. Implement applications through weekly systems. Address needs through monthly planning.
Fellowship	Your observations showed relational impact. Replicate what strengthened relationships through daily connection. Build on relational observations through weekly investment.
Fun	Your breakthrough markers captured joy returning. Notice what brought joy during fast through daily delight. Systematize sabbath rhythms through weekly recreation.

Create your daily 8F scorecard using the same discipline as daily tracking. Each evening, rate your daily performance on a 1-5 scale across all eight ingredients: Faith, Fasting, Fitness, Food, Focus, Finances, Fellowship, Fun. Your daily total out of 40 points tracks ingredient consistency just like daily GAP scores out of 30 tracked spiritual consistency. You proved for 21 days you can track daily. Now extend that discipline to 8F tracking. Your journal demonstrated you can maintain daily documentation and self-assessment. That proven capacity becomes your advantage for daily 8F mastery. Master the inputs, trust God for multiplied outputs. Download the 8F Daily Scorecard template and quarterly review worksheets at danielfastclub.com/chayah-tools for printable tracking resources that extend your journaling practice into comprehensive lifestyle management.

WHEN YOU DRIFT (BECAUSE YOU WILL)

You're going to drift. Not might. Will. You'll miss days. You'll forget to track. You'll score 15/40 when you promised 30+. This doesn't disqualify you. It qualifies you to demonstrate grace.

THE RECOVERY RATIO

Most people quit because they think one failure = total failure. The truth: Your recovery speed matters more than your perfection rate. **Recovery Ratio = How fast you return ÷ How long you drifted.** Drifted 1 day, returned Day 2 = 1:1 ratio (Excellent); Drifted 1 week, returned Week 2 = 7:7 ratio (Good); Drifted 1 month, returned Month 2 = 30:30 ratio (Acceptable); Drifted 3 months, never returned = ∞ ratio (Failure). *"For a righteous man may fall seven times and rise again"* — *Proverbs 24:16*. The righteous

FALL. Multiple times. They RISE. That's what makes them righteous—not perfection but persistence through grace.

THE 68% RULE

Perfect consistency: 100% of days = IMPOSSIBLE | Excellent consistency: 80%+ of days = SUSTAINABLE | Good consistency: 70%+ of days = PROGRESS | Winning consistency: 68%+ of days = BREAKTHROUGH. If you steward your 8F inputs 250+ days out of 365 (68%), you're WINNING. Translation: 365 days in a year; 68% = 248 days of faithful stewardship; You can miss 117 days and still win; That's 3+ months of "off days" built into success. Stop aiming for 100%. Start celebrating 68%+. This grace-filled framework acknowledges reality: sickness happens, crises emerge, seasons shift, life disrupts plans. The 68% Rule builds in margin for being human while maintaining trajectory for transformation.

THE CHAYAH BLUEPRINT: YOUR COMPLETE ARCHITECTURE TOOL

You've just completed Days 23-30—architecting your Legacy Vision, Annual Goals, Quarterly Victories, Monthly Momentum, and Daily Mastery. Now it's time to consolidate everything into one strategic operating system. The Chayah Blueprint is your vision-to-execution map. It connects your 21-day Daniel Fast breakthrough (Day 22 scores) to lifelong transformation (10-year legacy). Without this map, breakthrough becomes memory. With this map, breakthrough becomes lifestyle.

You have three options: (1) Fill out the blueprint below using what you created in Days 23-30; (2) Download the fillable PDF version at danielfastclub.com/chayah-blueprint; (3) Access digital tracking tools at danielfastclub.com/chayah-tools (includes automated scorecard, quarterly reviews, and progress dashboards). Once completed, post your Blueprint where you'll see it daily: Bathroom mirror. Office wall. Phone lock screen. Refrigerator door. This isn't just a planning document—it's your covenant with destiny.

THE CHAYAH BLUEPRINT: YOUR VISION-TO-EXECUTION MAP

Name: _____ | Date Created: _____ | Last Updated: _____

MY ANCHOR SCRIPTURE (Foundation for Everything)
Scripture & Reference: _____
Why this verse: _____

MY VISION & VOW
Personal Vision Statement: _____
My Vow Statement: _____

10-YEAR LEGACY VISION (Who I'm Becoming)

DIMENSION	LEGACY (10-YEAR)
Spiritual	
Mental	
Emotional	
Physical	
Financial	
Relational	

THE LIFESTYLE THAT LASTS

3-YEAR MILESTONE HORIZON (Evidence I'm On Track)

DIMENSION	MILESTONE (3-YEAR)
Spiritual	
Mental	
Emotional	
Physical	
Financial	
Relational	

ANNUAL GOALS (This Year's Targets)

DIMENSION	DAY 22	ANNUAL GOAL (SMART)	METRIC	DEADLINE
Spiritual	___/10			Month ___
Mental	___/10			Month ___
Emotional	___/10			Month ___
Physical	___/10			Month ___
Financial	___/10			Month ___
Relational	___/10			Month ___

QUARTERLY VICTORIES (Next 90 Days)

Quarter: ___ Q___ (_____ to _____)

#	VICTORY	METRIC	8F	DUE	STATUS
1					On Track / At Risk / Off Track
2					On Track / At Risk / Off Track
3					On Track / At Risk / Off Track
4					On Track / At Risk / Off Track
5					On Track / At Risk / Off Track

MONTHLY FOCUS (This Month's Priority)

Month: _____ | Primary Focus: _____

WEEK	ACTION
Week 1	
Week 2	
Week 3	
Week 4	

DAILY 8F COMMITMENTS (My Non-Negotiables)

INGREDIENT	MINIMUM	MY COMMITMENT
Faith	Word + worship + declaration + prayer. Guided lesson such as the 365: Live Fearlessly	
Fasting	1 rhythm/week	
Fitness	30 min movement + sleep	
Food	Plate plan + hydration	
Focus	1 focus block (30-90 min)	
Finances	5-min check + autopay	
Fellowship	1 meaningful connection	
Fun	15-30 min restorative joy	

Weekly 8F Target: 192+ points (24/day average = 68% consistency)

THE DANIEL FAST: CLOSING THE GAP!

BREAKTHROUGH BARRIERS (What's Blocking Progress)

BARRIER	IMPACT	ACTION	OWNER	BY WHEN
	H/M/L		Me	
	H/M/L		Me	
	H/M/L		Me	

ACCOUNTABILITY CIRCLE

Inner Circle (3-5 Truth-Tellers): 1. _____ 2. _____ 3. _____ 4. _____ 5. _____
Growth Circle (People I'm Discipling): 1. _____ 2. _____ 3. _____
Cohort Partners (If Applicable): 1. _____ 2. _____ 3. _____ 4. _____ 5. _____

MILESTONE DATES (Mark Your Calendar)

EVENT	DATE	STATUS	NOTES
Weekly Alignment	Every _____	Scheduled / Pending	
Monthly Momentum	Last day of month	Scheduled / Pending	
Quarterly Recalibration	Day ___ (90 days)	Scheduled / Pending	
Day 90 Celebration	_____	Scheduled / Pending	
Multiplication Launch (invite 3)	Day ___	Scheduled / Pending	

MY CHAYAH DECLARATION

"I am Chayah—fully alive, completely His. My ceiling becomes someone else's floor. I steward my 8F ingredients daily. God multiplies the results. My breakthrough won't die with me. I am building legacy, not just having testimony."

Signed: _____ Date: _____

Download the full playbook with templates: Chayah.Club/playbook

HOW TO USE THIS BLUEPRINT

STEP 1: FOUNDATION (Complete Once) - Start with your Anchor Scripture—the verse that grounds your entire transformation journey. Write your personal vision statement (who you're becoming) and vow statement (your irreversible commitment). These three elements create your foundation.

STEP 2: LONG-TERM VISION (Annual Review) - Define your 10-year legacy vision across all six dimensions. This is who you're becoming, not what you're doing. Then work backward to 3-year milestones—tangible evidence you're on track. Update annually.

STEP 3: ANNUAL TARGETS (Year Start + Day 22) - After completing your 21-day Daniel Fast, transfer your Day 22 scores into the Annual Goals table. For each dimension, create one SMART goal (Specific, Measurable, Achievable, Relevant, Time-bound) with clear success metrics and deadlines.

STEP 4: QUARTERLY EXECUTION (Every 90 Days) - Break annual goals into quarterly victories—5 specific wins per quarter. Assign each to one of the 8F ingredients. Track status weekly: On Track (green), At Risk (yellow), Off Track (red). Recalibrate every 90 days.

STEP 5: MONTHLY PRIORITIES (Start of Each Month) - Choose one primary focus for the month. Break it into 4 weekly actions—one specific action per week that moves you toward your monthly focus. Keep it simple, keep it actionable.

STEP 6: DAILY DISCIPLINE (Every Single Day) - Your Daily 8F Commitments are your non-negotiables. These aren't aspirations—they're minimums. Write your specific commitment for each ingredient. Score yourself daily (3 points per ingredient, 24 points total). Weekly target: 192+ points = 68% consistency.

STEP 7: BARRIERS & ACCOUNTABILITY (Weekly Review) - Identify what's blocking progress. Rate impact (High/Medium/Low). Assign action, owner, and deadline. Don't just name problems—solve them. Engage your Inner Circle weekly, Growth Circle monthly, Cohort Partners for specific projects.

STEP 8: MILESTONE TRACKING (Calendar Integration) - Schedule all recurring rhythms immediately: Weekly Alignment (same day/time each week), Monthly Momentum (last day of month), Quarterly Recalibration (every 90 days), Day 90 Celebration, Multiplication Launch. What gets scheduled gets done.

STEP 9: DECLARATION & SIGNATURE (Monthly Renewal) - Read your Chayah Declaration aloud monthly. This isn't motivation—it's identity declaration. Sign and date each time you review. Your signature is covenant, not a suggestion.

MAINTENANCE SCHEDULE: Daily: Score 8F ingredients (2 minutes) | Weekly: Review Quarterly Victories status + Breakthrough Barriers (15 minutes) | Monthly: Update Monthly Focus + read Declaration (30 minutes) | Quarterly: Complete full recalibration + adjust Annual Goals (2 hours) | Annually: Refresh 10-year vision + 3-year milestones + restart after next Daniel Fast (3-4 hours).

This blueprint is your strategic operating system. It connects your 21-day Daniel Fast breakthrough (Day 22 scores) to lifelong transformation (10-year legacy). Without this map, breakthrough becomes memory. With this map, breakthrough becomes lifestyle.

INTEGRATION WITH YOUR 21-DAY FAST

BEFORE YOUR FAST (Day -7 to Day 0): Complete the Foundation section (Anchor Scripture, Vision, Vow) during Stage 1.1: I DECIDE preparation. This grounds your fast in long-term vision, not short-term emotion.

DURING YOUR FAST (Days 1-21): Use your Daily 8F Commitments as your baseline discipline. Your SOAP Journal documents spiritual transformation. Your 8F scoring tracks behavioral consistency. Both feed into your Day 22 assessment.

IMMEDIATELY AFTER YOUR FAST (Day 22): Transfer your final GAP scores into the Annual Goals table. Compare Day 1 vs Day 22 across all six dimensions. This documented proof becomes your baseline for the next 90 days.

ONGOING LIFESTYLE (Days 23+): Your Quarterly Victories break annual goals into 90-day sprints. Your Monthly Focus creates immediate action. Your Daily 8F Commitments maintain consistency. Your Accountability Circle keeps you from drifting.

NEXT FAST (90-180 days later): Return to this blueprint before your next 21-day fast. Update your 10-year vision if needed. Refresh your 3-year milestones based on progress. Set new Annual Goals based on your last Day 22 scores. Repeat the cycle.

This creates the transformation loop: **21-day fast → Day 22 baseline → 90-day execution → quarterly recalibration → next 21-day fast.** Each fast compounds the previous one. Each quarter builds on the last. Your ceiling becomes someone else's floor through documented, measurable, reproducible transformation. Your blueprint connects Chamber 1 (Preparation) + Chamber 2 (21-Day Fast) + Chamber 3 (Daily Lifestyle) + Chamber 4 (Multiplication) into one integrated system.

YOUR BLUEPRINT IS NOW COMPLETE

Take a moment to look at what you've created. This single page contains: Your spiritual foundation (Anchor Scripture, Vision, Vow); Your 10-year trajectory across all 6 dimensions; Your measurable annual goals informed by Day 22 scores; Your next 90 days broken into specific victories; Your monthly focus with weekly actions; Your daily 8F minimums with 68% consistency target; Your breakthrough barriers with resolution plans; Your accountability circle—inner truth-tellers and growth disciples; Your milestone dates scheduled in your calendar; Your Chayah Declaration signed as covenant. This is the infrastructure that keeps the rocket in orbit. Your 21 days of intensity created the thrust. This blueprint creates the sustainable trajectory. Your journal built the content. The Blueprint organizes it for action. Your signature makes it covenant.

Read your Chayah Declaration aloud right now: *"I am Chayah—fully alive, completely His. My ceiling becomes someone else's floor. I steward my 8F ingredients daily. God multiplies the results. My breakthrough won't die with me. I am building legacy, not just having testimony."*

Sign it. Date it. Own it.

THE CHAYAH LIFESTYLE COVENANT

"Father, I thank You for these transformative days. You have been faithful through every step. When I was weak, You were strong. When I wanted to quit, You sustained me. *'Being confident of this very thing, that He who has begun a good work in you will complete it until the day of Jesus Christ'* — Philippians 1:6. You have shown me that transformation is possible—not through my strength, but through Yours. *'I can do all things through Christ who strengthens me'* — Philippians 4:13. Thank You for teaching me daily discipline—daily Scripture revelation, honest observation, practical application, breakthrough prayer. That practice taught me vulnerability, consistency, and systematic transformation. I commit to stewarding what You have given me: To seek You first in all things, continuing daily spiritual practice; To honor my body as Your temple, applying what 21 days of observations taught me; To live from abundance, not scarcity, based on identity applications I wrote and declared; To build community that reflects Your love, extending the vulnerability I practiced in entries; To use my breakthrough to serve others, multiplying what You revealed through 21 days of prayer declarations. *'Trust in the Lord with all your heart, And lean not on your own understanding; In all your ways acknowledge Him, And He shall direct your paths'* — Proverbs 3:5-6. I choose to stay fully alive—CHAYAH—not through perfect performance, but through daily surrender to You. Help me remember that every day is a new beginning, every breath a fresh mercy, just like every entry was fresh encounter with You. *'Through the Lord's mercies we are not consumed, Because His compassions fail not. They are new every morning; Great is Your faithfulness'* — Lamentations 3:22-23. Transform my breakthrough into a lifestyle that honors You and blesses others. What I documented in 21 days, multiply through decades of faithful living. In Jesus' mighty name, Amen."

CELEBRATE YOUR ARCHITECTURE PUBLICLY

Your Chayah Club family has walked every step of this journey with you. Share your victory: "I've completed Stage 3.2: Architecting the Chayah Lifestyle! My 21 days of journaling became the blueprint for my future. I reviewed all my prayer entries—recurring themes became my 10-year legacy vision. I analyzed my application statements—theology I wrote becomes beliefs I build on. I tracked which practices closed which gaps—that data informed my annual targets. My quarterly victories reflect patterns from my breakthrough markers. My monthly momentum extends disciplines my entries proved work. My daily 8F mastery builds on consistency I maintained for 21 days. This isn't just personal transformation—it's generational warfare. What God revealed in my journal, I'm architecting into permanent lifestyle. What I documented through Scripture, Observation, Application, and Prayer over 21 days, I'll live out through systematic daily habits for decades. I've completed my Chayah Blueprint and signed my Declaration: 'I am Chayah—fully alive, completely His. My ceiling becomes someone else's floor.' Ready for Stage 4: Multiplication Model!"

THE JOSHUA PROMISE

After 40 years in wilderness preparation and crossing Jordan breakthrough, Joshua faced his greatest challenge: not conquering the Promised Land, but living in it consistently. *"Only be strong and very courageous, that you may observe to do according to all the law which Moses My servant commanded you; do not turn from it to the right hand or to the left, that you may prosper wherever you go. This Book of the Law shall not depart from your mouth, but you shall meditate in it day and night, that you may observe to do according to all that is written in it. For then you will make your way prosperous, and then you will have good success"* — Joshua 1:7-8. Your 21-day fast was wilderness preparation. Your Day 22 was crossing Jordan. Days 23-30 are establishing your Promised Land lifestyle. The Promised Land isn't a destination—it's a lifestyle of sustained victory through systematic partnership with heaven. Your journaling taught you to meditate on God's Word daily, observe what He's doing, apply truth practically, and pray breakthrough—that's Joshua 1:8 lived out. Continue that discipline. The Law didn't depart from Joshua's mouth because he reviewed it constantly. Your journal doesn't disappear into a drawer—it remains active reference, ongoing practice, daily discipline extending into lifestyle.

THE WARNING AND THE PROMISE

WARNING FOR DAYS 35-45: The greatest danger isn't dramatic failure—it's gradual fade. Without systematic architecture, most people slowly drift back toward baseline by Day 45. Your 21 days of discipline created muscle memory for daily spiritual practice. Don't abandon that now: Continue journaling even in abbreviated form; Stay connected to accountability; Keep measuring progress using same 1-10 scale you used for 21 days; Maintain your structured approach informed by what your journal revealed works.

But here's the promise from Philippians 1:6: *"Being confident of this very thing, that He who has begun a good work in you will complete it until the day of Jesus Christ."* God isn't interested in temporary breakthrough. He's committed to permanent transformation. Your Chayah Lifestyle partners with His faithfulness to ensure completion. The discipline He taught you during 21 days wasn't for 21 days—it was training for lifestyle.

THE ARCHITECTURE IS COMPLETE

You now possess what separates sustainable transformation from temporary inspiration. The missing piece every other program lacks: Baseline Measurement (Day 0 honest assessment through first entry); Transformation Catalyst (21-day GAP Strategy with daily documentation); Breakthrough Celebration (Day 22 victory measurement consolidating 21 entries); Sustainment Architecture (Days 23-30 systematic planning informed by documented discoveries); Ongoing Framework (Chayah Lifestyle daily living extending discipline into 8F mastery); Complete Blueprint (Your vision-to-execution map signed as covenant).

The Chayah Lifestyle minimizes transformation failure by providing systematic sustainment architecture that keeps breakthrough fully alive permanently. Your breakthrough has been documented through 21 entries, measured through Day 22 assessments, architected through Days 23-30 planning, and consolidated into your signed Chayah Blueprint. Your journal isn't finished—it continues as ongoing tool for daily Faith ingredient and monthly intensive seasons. What you learned through 21 days of Scripture, Observation, Application, Prayer becomes foundation for decades of systematic spiritual growth.

Tomorrow, someone else needs to see what systematic transformation looks like. Someone needs to see your journal and Blueprint and understand that sustainable breakthrough requires daily documentation, honest observation, practical application, consistent prayer, and strategic architecture. Tomorrow, your ceiling becomes someone else's floor. Your 21 entries and signed Blueprint become their permission to begin.

END OF STAGE 3.2: ARCHITECTING THE CHAYAH LIFESTYLE
Continue to Stage 4: The Multiplication Model™
DAYS 23-30 COMPLETE. BLUEPRINT SIGNED. ARCHITECTURE ESTABLISHED. FROM ROCKET FUEL TO ORBIT. FROM INTENSITY TO INFRASTRUCTURE. FROM GAP TAX TO GAP-FREE LIVING. READY FOR MULTIPLICATION.

SECTION SEVEN
CHAMBER 4: MULTIPLY
THE LEGACY THAT OUTLIVES YOU

Day 91+ | From Personal Victory to Institutional Legacy

"And the things that you have heard from me among many witnesses, commit these to faithful men who will be able to teach others also." — 2 Timothy 2:2

Success without successor is failure. Legacy without multiplication is memory. Your breakthrough wasn't just for you—it was downloaded to equip others through you. Chamber 4 transforms personal transformation into generational impact through The Multiplication Model™.

THE MULTIPLICATION ARCHITECTURE
STAGE 4: THE MULTIPLICATION MODEL™ (LEGACY LIVING)

The **C1-C5 Framework** for building institutional legacy:

C1: COMMITMENT — Lock your legacy through 3-3-3-3 testimony. Your credential isn't your degree, it's your deliverance.

C2: COMMON VISION — Identify your cultural mountain and brand your mission. Your pain becomes their pathway.

C3: CHANGE PROCESS — Distill breakthrough into 4-Week Launch. Complexity impresses, simplicity transforms.

C4: COMMUNITY — Build Three Circles: Inner truth-tellers, Growth disciples, Movement reach.

C5: COMMISSIONING — Release through 90-Day Multiplication Cycles. Disciples make disciples.

When your ceiling becomes someone else's floor, you've created legacy. When your absence doesn't stop the movement, you've achieved multiplication.

THE MULTIPLICATION REALITY

Without Chamber 4: Your breakthrough dies with you. Transformation remains personal testimony, never becoming reproducible framework. Your valley prepared you for a mountain no one else will climb.

With Chamber 4: Four generations multiply: you heard, you commit, they teach, others learn. Your survival becomes their strategy. Your scars become their sermon.

This is biblical multiplication—not optional ministry but definitional discipleship.

Turn the page to Stage 4: The Multiplication Model™.
Someone's coloring holes in their shoes right now.
They're wrong about their future. You're their proof.

STAGE 4
THE MULTIPLICATION MODEL™ (LEGACY LIVING)
"WHEN YOUR CEILING BECOMES SOMEONE ELSE'S FLOOR"

Jamaica. The marker trembled in my fourteen-year-old hand like a prayer before persecution. Dark brown marker. A few cents from the corner store. The only thing standing between me and the laughter that kills teenage souls in my high school's unforgiving hallways. I pressed the tip against worn leather, coloring each hole with desperate precision. The leather cracked under pressure, releasing the musty smell of poverty that followed me everywhere. My fingers cramped from gripping hope too tightly. Not for fashion. For survival. "Nice shoes, Niki," a classmate had sneered last week, pointing at my feet during lunch. "You get those from the ragman?" The laughter followed me down the hallway, echoing off concrete walls like a verdict I couldn't appeal. Today I'd make sure the holes were hidden. My mother's voice echoed from the kitchen: "Niki, you ready for school?" "Coming, Mommy," I called back, hiding the evidence of our reality behind my back. That marker in my hand—it wasn't just coloring leather. It was coloring my future. Painting over shame. Covering what I thought disqualified me. Those marked-up shoes carried me from shame to scholarship. From poverty to purpose. From colored markers to global multiplication. Today, someone else holds a marker. Different country, different decade, same desperation. They're wrong about their future. And you're their proof.

THE MATHEMATICS ONLY HEAVEN CALCULATES

Thirty years later, His equation defies every earthly logic. Colored shoes became doctoral robes. Company with no clients serves organizations across continents. Director position lost birthed CEO calling. Five o'clock morning prayers alone sparked global movements. Divorce that broke me led to marriage that restored me. Each loss became gain. Each ending, a beginning. Each valley, a classroom for someone else's victory. Born Nicola McFadden—the go-getter. Survived as Nicola Chambers—the overcomer. Now Dr. Nicola McFadden-Marvin—the multiplier. Each name marks elevation. Each valley carved capacity for someone else's climb. Your valley wasn't a wasteland—it was a classroom. Your pain wasn't pointless—it was your curriculum. What you sacrifice for Kingdom, God returns with interest.

THE VALLEY PREPARATION PRINCIPLE

Your decade in the wilderness wasn't punishment. It was preparation. Moses spent forty years tending sheep before liberating nations. Joseph endured thirteen years in slavery before governing Egypt. David hid in caves for fifteen years before ruling Israel. *"For I know the thoughts that I think toward you, says the Lord, thoughts of peace and not of evil, to give you a future and a hope"* — Jeremiah 29:11. Every crisis downloaded content. Every breakdown built framework. Every failure forged what thousands would follow. The length of your valley doesn't determine your worth—your faithfulness in it determines your impact. What feels like wasted time to you is required preparation for them. The person you became in the valley is exactly who someone needs to meet on their mountain.

THE DIVINE FORMULA COMPLETES

Remember the equation from your journey? Purpose plus process equals readiness—your 21-day breakthrough. Readiness plus God's timing equals destiny activation—your Chayah Lifestyle. Destiny plus others equals legacy multiplication—this moment. Stage 4 operationalizes that final equation. Your activated destiny meets others who need your process. *"The things that you have heard from me among many witnesses, commit these to faithful men who will be able to teach others also"* — 2 Timothy 2:2. Four generations in one verse. You heard. You commit. They teach. Others learn. This isn't optional discipleship—this is biblical multiplication. Let God close the gap between your pain and His purpose. Let God close the gap between your valley and your calling. Let God close the gap between your breakthrough and others' breakthrough.

THE MULTIPLICATION MODEL™: C1-C5 FRAMEWORK

Transform personal victory into institutional legacy through five systematic components. Each builds on the previous, creating infrastructure that transforms movements from inspiration to institution. Success without successor is failure. Legacy without multiplication is memory. You don't need a perfect story—you need a reproducible process.

C1: COMMITMENT - LOCK YOUR LEGACY

"Write the vision and make it plain on tablets, that he may run who reads it. For the vision is yet for an appointed time" — Habakkuk 2:2-3. Your breakthrough becomes movement when commitment crystallizes into permanent legacy. Three months after my most powerful breakthrough season, I sat in my car, air conditioning humming against August heat. The euphoria had faded. The disciplines had relaxed. "God," I whispered, gripping the steering wheel, "how do I keep this alive?" That's when He downloaded the framework you're about to receive.

Your transformation needs two anchors: testimony that connects and theology that endures. Most people share either raw story (emotional but unsustainable) or rigid doctrine (accurate but unapproachable). Your multiplication requires both. **Create your 3-3-3-3 Testimony**—the testimony that becomes theology for others.

Three sentences about desperation: Where you were, what broke you, why you needed rescue. "I was a single mother drowning in legal battles, paying spousal support from disability income, watching generational patterns claim my bloodline like inherited poison."

Three sentences about transformation: What God did, how breakthrough came, when everything shifted. "During my 21-day Daniel Fast, God closed the gap between who the world said I was and who He designed me to be—intimacy deepened, identity solidified, destiny activated."

Three sentences about multiplication vision: Who you'll serve, what you'll build, how others will benefit. "I'm building Chayah Club to serve people trapped in the same cycles I broke, creating reproducible frameworks so no one stays stuck where God never intended them to stay."

Three beliefs anchoring everything: Core truths you'll never compromise, Kingdom principles defining your movement. "Transformation requires systematic architecture. Daily disciplines determine destiny. Personal breakthrough births corporate deliverance."

Tonight, text one person: "God did something in me during this fast. I want to share it with you. When can we talk?" Don't edit. Don't overthink. Don't wait for perfect confidence. Your multiplication begins with one conversation. Your credential isn't your degree—it's your deliverance. That person you're thinking of right now? They're not coincidence. They're assignment.

C2: COMMON VISION - WE GREATER THAN ME

"Where there is no vision, the people perish" — *Proverbs 29:18*. Individual vision inspires. Common vision builds movements. Recently, one woman booked a Zoom meeting, tears streaming down her face, tissues crumpled in her lap. "I keep trying to help everyone," she sobbed. "But I'm scattered, exhausted, and seeing no real change." "Which mountain calls to you?" I asked gently. She paused, breath catching. "Family," she whispered. "I want to break these generational patterns forever." "Then that's where your multiplication begins," I replied. "Your pain becomes their pathway."

God positions you for influence on one of eight cultural mountains—the spheres where society's values are shaped and futures are formed. **Religion** transforms how people worship and relate to God. **Family** shapes how households function and generational patterns flow. **Education** determines what knowledge gets transferred and how minds develop. **Government** influences laws, justice, and societal structures. **Media** controls narratives, information, and public consciousness. **Arts** creates culture through entertainment, beauty, and creative expression. **Business** generates wealth, employment, and economic systems. **Technology** advances innovation, connectivity, and human capability. Which mountain makes your heart beat faster? Where does righteous anger rise when you see brokenness? That's not random emotion—that's prophetic assignment.

Brand your mountain using this framework: "We become people who _____ so that _____." Fill in the blanks with your specific calling. My mission: "We become people who transform valleys into victories so that no one stays stuck where God never intended them to stay." Your mission might be: "We become people who heal family trauma through Christ-centered counseling so that generational curses die and blessings multiply." Or: "We become people who teach biblical financial stewardship so that Kingdom resources fund Kingdom purposes rather than perpetual debt." Or: "We become people who create redemptive media so that culture reflects Heaven's values rather than hell's agenda."

"He comforts us in all our troubles so that we can comfort others. When they are troubled, we will be able to give them the same comfort God has given us" — *2 Corinthians 1:4*. Your comfort becomes their comfort. Your breakthrough becomes their blueprint. Your mountain becomes your mission field. Aligned vision creates concentrated power. Scattered vision creates exhausted people. Choose your mountain. Brand your mission. Build your movement.

C3: CHANGE PROCESS - MAKE IT SIMPLE

"My people are destroyed for lack of knowledge" — *Hosea 4:6*. Create curriculum from your crucible. Your proven process becomes their pathway. Marcus called me frustrated after his first attempt at sharing his breakthrough. "I overwhelmed them with everything I learned," he confessed, voice tight with disappointment. "They looked confused, then checked their phones. I lost them." "Can your twelve-year-

old nephew follow what you shared?" I asked. Silence. "Definitely not," he admitted. "Then we need to simplify."

Here's what I learned through painful trial and error: complexity impresses experts but confuses beginners. Simplicity serves everyone. Your 21-day journal contains everything they need—but they can't digest 21 days in one conversation. **Distill your breakthrough into a 4-Week Launch** that makes transformation accessible without losing power.

Week One: Share Story, Cast Vision — Tell your 3-3-3-3 testimony and invite them into the journey. You're not teaching yet—you're opening hearts. "This is where I was. This is what God did. This is what's possible for you." Watch their faces. When their eyes widen, when they lean forward, when they whisper "that's me"—that's when you know vision has landed.

Week Two: Teach Foundation Framework — Introduce the core system—GAP Strategy (GROW, ALIGN, PROPEL) and why it works. Use simple language. Draw pictures. Make them repeat it back. "So intimacy comes first, then identity, then purpose?" Yes. Exactly. They've got it.

Week Three: Start Day 1 Together — Don't send them home to start alone. Do Day 1 with them. Show them how to select Scripture, write observations, create applications, pray breakthrough. Document your first day together. They'll reference this moment for months.

Week Four: Navigate Crisis Days — Around Day 7-10, someone will want to quit. Expect it. Prepare for it. Teach them the 24-Hour Grace Protocol from Stage 3.1. Show them Peter's testimony—82 out of 90 days is still victory. Normalize struggle. Celebrate persistence.

"Let the little children come to Me, and do not forbid them" — *Matthew 19:14*. Jesus made profound truth accessible to children. If children can't understand your framework, it's not simple enough. *"God has chosen the foolish things of the world to put to shame the wise"* — *1 Corinthians 1:27*. The person holding a brown marker in Jamaica became Dr. Nicola because God specializes in using the unlikely. Your simple process—the one that feels too basic to share—is exactly what someone needs. Complexity impresses. Simplicity transforms.

C4: COMMUNITY - THREE CIRCLES DEEP

"As iron sharpens iron, so a man sharpens the countenance of his friend" — *Proverbs 27:17*. Isolation kills breakthrough. Community multiplies it exponentially. Build three circles, each serving different purposes, each essential for sustainable multiplication.

Your Inner Circle includes three to five people who know your worst moments and speak truth when everyone else speaks flattery. These are not your followers—these are your truth-tellers. My inner circle includes my husband John, my sons Nick and Matt, and my accountability sister Mary. They've seen me curled in bed with pizza shame. They've heard me whisper "I'm a fraud" at 11:47 PM. They've watched me almost quit this book at 2 AM. And they said: "Not you. Not this time. Get up." Your inner circle doesn't cheer your every decision—they challenge your compromises. They don't attend your events—they pray through your crises. They don't promote your brand—they protect your soul. Who has earned the right to speak into your darkest moments? Invite them into systematic accountability, not casual friendship.

Your Growth Circle contains twelve to fifteen people experiencing real transformation through your complete multiplication model. They become your proof that the ecosystem works—from crisis to calling to commission. These are the people you're actively discipling, mentoring, coaching through their 21 days and beyond. You meet with them regularly, answer their panicked texts at Day 9, celebrate their Day 22 victories, help them architect their lifestyle, watch them multiply into others. This circle validates your process. When someone asks "does your system really work?" you don't give theory—you introduce them to your Growth Circle. Let them hear the testimonies. Let them see the transformation. Let them meet the proof.

Your Movement Circle extends through digital platforms, speaking engagements, published content, and organic reach—thousands benefiting from your overflow without requiring direct time investment from you. This is where your 3-3-3-3 testimony reaches people you'll never meet personally. Your books, podcasts, social media, video teachings, blog posts—these create Movement Circle impact. Someone in Malaysia reads your story at 3 AM and texts a friend: "This is exactly what we need." Your multiplication just went international without you booking a flight.

TESTIMONY: WHEN MERCY SAID NO — FROM CRISIS TO INSTITUTIONAL LEGACY

K. joined the Daniel Fast as a single mother in the United States—broken and broke, struggling to make ends meet. For twenty years she'd battled one question: "Why am I still alive?" Mental trauma, grief, isolation, and loss had convinced her that her life had no meaning, no purpose. But even in darkness, she kept seeking God with her daughter by her side. This wasn't just another church fasting event for her. The Daniel Fast became her identity fast—21 days to close the gap between who the world said she was and who God designed her to be. Week One, she encountered God's character through GROW. Week Two, she discovered her identity through ALIGN. Week Three, she activated her purpose through PROPEL. This wasn't temporary motivation. This was permanent transformation from crisis to calling.

Despite her financial struggle, she planted a seed in the Chayah Club community believing blessings would follow. After the 21-day fast ended, she didn't return to normal. She shifted into the 365: Live Fearlessly—daily rhythms that sustained her transformation beyond the intensive season. Every day, new devotionals. Every day, deeper alignment. Every day, fearless living becoming her new normal. The ecosystem held her breakthrough when motivation faded. In the months that followed, God began orchestrating her next season. The right worship songs. The right scriptures. The right people. Then came the prophetic word: "Go back to the land of your ancestors, where there is milk and honey. I am doing a new thing." She quit her job, packed up with her daughter, and returned to the Caribbean to reunite with her husband—fearless, confident, and full of faith. That's C1 (Commitment) and C2 (Common Vision) activated.

When she reached out about launching her business, I didn't just offer prayer and encouragement. I took her through the complete multiplication model—the full architecture that supports transition from individual transformation to institutional legacy. Together, we developed her brand strategy—not surface positioning but Kingdom identity translated into marketplace language. We built her business model—not generic templates but customized frameworks aligned with her prophetic assignment. We created her complete website infrastructure. We planned her book publishing—her testimony becoming theology for others. And I coached her for speaking engagements—equipping her to multiply her message across platforms. This is C3 (Change Process), C4 (Community), and C5 (Commissioning) in action.

One year after joining the Daniel Fast, K. launched her business. The same date she once mourned her brother's death now celebrates her company's birth. One year from identity fast to institutional legacy. One year from "Why am I still alive?" to "I know exactly why God kept me alive." From broken and broke to business builder with brand strategy, website infrastructure, book in development, and speaking platform—impacting two nations. The Daniel Fast closed her gap. The 365 lifestyle sustained her rhythms. Now her multiplication closes others' gaps. The enemy wanted her dead. But Mercy said no. When the enemy thought he won, he realized that God never loses a battle. This is the ultimate comeback. Individual breakthrough became institutional legacy. Personal transformation became reproducible framework. Crisis became calling. Calling became commission. One woman's valley became vehicle for others' victory. Our God is intentional. And K. is living proof that when Mercy says no to death, purpose rises to life—and when you have an ecosystem that supports your transition from individual transformation to institutional legacy, multiplication happens beyond measure.

"We don't fix people here," I tell new group leaders. "We witness their transformation." No one performs, everyone progresses. No one compares, everyone encourages. No one pretends, everyone grows. "Bear one another's burdens, and so fulfill the law of Christ" — Galatians 6:2. Communities don't grow through marketing gimmicks. They multiply through authentic transformation stories. Your three circles create multiplication infrastructure that outlasts your personal energy.

C5: COMMISSIONING - RELEASE TO REPRODUCE

"Go therefore and make disciples of all the nations, baptizing them in the name of the Father and of the Son and of the Holy Spirit, teaching them to observe all things that I have commanded you" — Matthew 28:19-20. The ultimate test of multiplication: Can your movement continue without you? Can your breakthrough become someone else's blueprint? Can your ceiling become their floor?

Commission using a 90-Day Multiplication Cycle that mirrors their transformation timeline. **Days 1-30:** They experience breakthrough through your direct leadership—you're walking them through their 21-day intensive, celebrating their Day 22, helping them architect Days 23-30. You're present, available, coaching every step. **Days 31-60:** They share testimony and attract their first followers—now they're texting friends about their breakthrough, inviting coworkers into the next intensive, becoming living proof that transformation works. You're still available but less directive. They're leading from overflow. **Days 61-90:** They launch their first group with your support—they're facilitating Week 1 (share story), Week 2 (teach framework), Week 3 (start Day 1 together), Week 4 (navigate crisis) for 3-5 people. You observe, provide feedback, troubleshoot obstacles. **Day 91 and beyond:** They commission the next generation—their first followers are now ready to launch their own groups. Your spiritual grandchildren emerge. Multiplication compounds.

"Are you sure I'm ready?" one woman asked before launching her first group, hands trembling exactly like mine had holding that brown marker decades ago. Fear pooled in her eyes. Doubt weighted her voice. "I still struggle sometimes. What if I fail them?" I took her hands. "I was terrified too," I admitted. "But remember what Jesus told His disciples." I opened to John 14:12 and read slowly: *"Most assuredly, I say to you, he who believes in Me, the works that I do he will do also; and greater works than these he will do, because I go to the Father."* God doesn't call the equipped—He equips the called. Your struggle doesn't disqualify you—it qualifies you to help others through theirs. The woman who needed a brown marker to hide shame now equips others to walk in confidence. Multiplication isn't optional for disciples—it's definitional. If you're not reproducing, you're not discipling. Jesus didn't say "make converts." He said "make disciples." Disciples make disciples. That's how two thousand years later, we're still multiplying His message.

THE 5B INSTITUTION TEST

You've built legacy when you pass the 5B Institution Test—five markers that prove your movement transcends your personal presence. **Belief** guides without your voice—people quote your frameworks in conversations you're not part of, using your language to explain transformation to others. **Brand** stands without your face—when someone asks "where did you learn this?" they say the movement name, not just your personal name. **Business** runs without your hands—systems execute automatically, products deliver value, services maintain quality whether you're present or traveling. **Bible studies** teach without your presence—your curriculum gets facilitated by others in cities you've never visited, impacting people you'll never meet. **Building** continues without your permission—multiplication happens organically as second and third generation disciples launch their own circles.

When your absence doesn't stop the movement, you've achieved true multiplication. When people implement your process without needing your approval, you've built institution. When your ceiling becomes someone else's floor, you've created legacy.

THE VULNERABILITY MOMENT

Few months ago, I almost quit. I lay in my bed at two o'clock in the morning, exhausted but unable to sleep, as I continued rewriting this book. The deadline loomed. My determination to articulate what the Spirit was saying felt overwhelming. "Who am I kidding?" I whispered to John in the darkness, staring at ceiling shadows that seemed to mock my ambition. "These people need real leaders, not someone who colored holes in her shoes with a dark brown marker from the corner store." The shame tried to creep back. The lie tried to resurrect.

John turned toward me, his voice gentle but firm, cutting through the darkness with truth. "Nicky, that's exactly why they need you. They don't need perfection—they need permission." The next morning, a woman texted: "Because of your story, I finally left my abusive relationship. Your scars gave me courage." I read that text three times. Let the tears come. Understood again what God has been teaching me for three decades: *"My grace is sufficient for you, for My strength is made perfect in weakness"* — 2 Corinthians 12:9.

They don't need your authority—they need your authenticity. They don't need your perfection—they need your process. They don't need your credentials—they need your scars. The thing you're most ashamed of is exactly what qualifies you to help them. The valley that almost destroyed you prepared you for their mountain. Stop hiding the marker. Start sharing the story.

JESUS' MULTIPLICATION STRATEGY

Jesus spent three years with twelve disciples—His strategy wasn't mass evangelism but multiplication through discipleship. *"Come, follow Me, and I will send you out to fish for people"* — Matthew 4:19. First He called them to Himself—intimacy before activity, relationship before commission. *"Come to Me, all you who labor and are heavy laden, and I will give you rest"* — Matthew 11:28. You came broken. He gave rest. That was your "come to Me" season—your 21 days, your Day 22, your architecture planning. Now He commissions: *"Go therefore and make disciples of all the nations"* — Matthew 28:19. You're healed. Now heal others. You're delivered. Now deliver others. You're transformed. Now transform others. The Great Commission isn't just evangelism—it's multiplication through discipleship. Make disciples who make disciples who make disciples. Four generations in Matthew 28:19-20, just like four generations in 2 Timothy 2:2. This is biblical pattern, not contemporary strategy.

YOUR MULTIPLICATION STARTS TONIGHT

TONIGHT: Write three names of people who need what you've received. Don't overthink it. Who came to mind while reading this chapter? That's not coincidence—that's assignment.

THIS WEEK: Share your 3-3-3-3 testimony with those three people. Invite them into the next intensive.

THIS MONTH: Gather your first three for the 21-day journey. Launch using the 4-Week framework: Week 1 (story), Week 2 (foundation), Week 3 (Day 1 together), Week 4 (navigate crisis).

NEXT 90 DAYS: Walk them through the complete C1-C5 framework. Watch them transform. Document their breakthroughs. Celebrate their Day 22. Help them architect their lifestyle.

DAY 91 AND BEYOND: Watch them multiply into their own three. Your spiritual grandchildren emerge.

Don't wait for perfect credentials. I started with colored shoes and a brown marker. Don't wait for a platform. Jesus started with twelve unknown men in an obscure region. Don't wait for confidence. Moses said "send someone else" and God used him anyway. Don't wait for opportunity. Create it by saying yes to one person. And God is asking the question He's asked every generation: *"Whom shall I send, and who will go for Us?"* — Isaiah 6:8.

Someone's coloring holes in their shoes right now. Literally or metaphorically, they're hiding shame, covering wounds, painting over pain they think disqualifies them. They're wrong about their future. God is calling you to be their proof. His hand isn't too short to use your story. Your valley wasn't too deep for His purpose. Your pain isn't disqualifying—it's your credential. Your scars aren't shame—they're your sermon. *"But we have this treasure in earthen vessels, that the excellence of the power may be of God and not of us"* — 2 Corinthians 4:7.

Your purpose is clear. Your process is proven. Your destiny is activated. The marker in your hand might be coloring holes today. Tomorrow it's writing history. The valley you survived is preparing you for the mountain you'll climb. The breakthrough you received is waiting to be multiplied through others. Will you answer?

THE MULTIPLICATION COVENANT

Stand. Feel the weight of destiny settling on your shoulders like a mantle you were born to wear. This is not heavy burden—this is glorious assignment. Declare over your future, your calling, your legacy:

"Father, my breakthrough won't die with me. Let God close the gap between my pain and His purpose. Let God close the gap between my valley and my calling. Let God close the gap between my breakthrough and others' breakthrough. My survival becomes their strategy. My healing becomes their hope. My ceiling becomes their floor.

I commit to The Multiplication Model: Lock my legacy through unwavering commitment—my 3-3-3-3 testimony is ready to share. Build common vision that unites and multiplies—I know my mountain and my mission. Create simple processes others can follow—complexity impresses, simplicity transforms. Cultivate transformational community through three circles—inner truth-tellers, growth disciples, movement reach. Commission others to reproduce and release—multiplication is biblical mandate, not optional ministry.

They don't need my perfection—they need my process. They don't need my credentials—they need my scars. The holes in my story become holy ground for others to walk on. The valleys that almost destroyed me become classrooms for their victory. Purpose times process times destiny times legacy equals generational impact. It starts now. It starts with one. It multiplies through faithfulness. In Jesus' mighty name, Amen."

CELEBRATE YOUR MULTIPLICATION PUBLICLY

Share your commitment with your Chayah Club family: "Multiplication activated! My valley season prepared me for this mountain moment. My breakdown built framework others will follow. My 21-day breakthrough becomes their blueprint. Someone needs my story—not the perfect version I wish happened, but the messy, honest, colored-marker version that actually did. Someone needs proof their valley has purpose. My ceiling becomes their floor. My scars become their sermon. Ready to multiply breakthrough beyond myself. Who's first?"

THE CINEMATIC ENDING

Thirty years from today, you sit where I sit now. Gray touches your temples like wisdom made visible—not the gray of age but the silver of refinement. Hands weathered by faithful service show the cost and the crown of multiplication. Eyes bright with satisfaction only multiplication brings, the kind that comes from seeing your spiritual children raising spiritual grandchildren. The numbers tell your story, not for pride but for proof: Souls saved and lives transformed—dozens becoming hundreds becoming thousands. Leaders raised and equipped—generations prepared for Kingdom impact you'll never fully witness. Families restored and healed—redemption flowing forward through bloodlines and backward through generations. Communities transformed—your mountain shaped by Kingdom influence that outlasts your lifetime. Nations touched—ripples reaching shores you'll never see, languages you'll never speak, people you'll never meet.

Someone approaches your office. Young. Broken. Desperate. The same desperation you remember from your own mirror moment, your own valley season, your own brown marker days. "I heard what God did in your life," they whisper, voice trembling with hope and fear competing for dominance. "Could He do it in mine?" Their eyes search yours for permission to believe impossible things.

You smile. Not the polite smile of religious performance. The knowing smile of someone who has walked this path, fallen multiple times, risen through grace, and watched multiplication compound beyond comprehension. Remember this moment. Your first yes to multiplication thirty years ago—the text you sent, the person you called, the courage you chose when fear screamed louder. That decision birthed everything sitting before you now.

"Let me tell you about The Divine Formula," you say gently, opening your desk drawer with hands that no longer tremble. You pull out a frame. Behind glass, preserved with intentionality: one weathered brown Crayola marker, the label faded from three decades, the tip worn flat from pressing hope into leather. "And how your ceiling can become someone else's floor."

The young person stares at the marker, confused. "Why do you keep that?" You lift the frame, let light catch the glass, see your younger self reflected back. "Because I used to think this marker was my shame. Now I know it was my preparation. I colored holes in shoes because I couldn't afford new ones. Today I color futures for people who think they can't afford breakthrough. The thing I hid became the thing I share. The valley I survived became the mountain I climb. Your pain isn't pointless—it's your curriculum."

Their tears fall. Your story gave permission. The colored shoes story multiplies through another generation. *"And the things that you have heard from me among many witnesses, commit these to faithful men who will be able to teach others also"* — 2 Timothy 2:2. Four generations in one verse. You heard. You committed. They're teaching. Others will learn.

Live like legends. Leave legacies. Your legacy lives forever. Not because you were perfect. Because you were faithful. Not because you had credentials. Because you had scars. Not because you avoided valleys. Because you let God transform your valleys into someone else's victory.

The Divine Formula is complete. The Multiplication Model is activated. Your legacy living starts now. Let God close the gap.

JOIN THE MULTIPLICATION

Your Chayah Club family awaits. Not as spectators observing from safe distance, but as co-laborers in the greatest multiplication movement of our generation. We've walked together—from Day 0 baseline through 21 days of breakthrough, from individual transformation to lifestyle architecture, now to legacy multiplication that outlasts our individual lifetimes. Your story isn't finished. It's just beginning. The best chapters are ahead. The greatest multiplication is coming. Come multiply with us at **Chayah.Club**. Because someone's coloring holes in their shoes right now. Someone's hiding shame they think disqualifies them. Someone's painting over pain they think God can't use. They're wrong about their future. And you're their answer. Your valley prepared you. Your breakthrough equipped you. Your multiplication begins now.

THE DIVINE FORMULA IS COMPLETE. THE MULTIPLICATION MODEL™ IS ACTIVATED. YOUR LEGACY LIVING STARTS NOW.

Let God close the gap.

END OF STAGE 4: THE MULTIPLICATION MODEL™. CHAMBER 4 COMPLETE. FROM PERSONAL VICTORY TO INSTITUTIONAL LEGACY. FROM COLORED MARKERS TO GLOBAL MULTIPLICATION. FROM YOUR CEILING TO THEIR FLOOR. READY TO MULTIPLY.

REFERENCES

Bennett, M. P., Zeller, J. M., Rosenberg, L., & McCann, J. (2003). The effect of mirthful laughter on stress and natural killer cell activity. *Alternative Therapies in Health and Medicine, 9*(2), 38–45. https://pubmed.ncbi.nlm.nih.gov/12652882/

Bloomer, R. J., Kabir, M. M., Canale, R. E., Trepanowski, J. F., & Farney, T. M. (2010). Effect of a 21-day Daniel Fast on metabolic and cardiovascular parameters in men and women. *Lipids in Health and Disease, 9*, 94. https://doi.org/10.1186/1476-511X-9-94

Blumenthal, J. A., Babyak, M. A., Moore, K. A., Craighead, W. E., Herman, S., Khatri, P., … Krishnan, K. R. (1999). Effects of exercise training on older patients with major depression. *Journal of the American Medical Association, 282*(11), 1038–1045. https://doi.org/10.1001/jama.282.11.1038

Collins, J. J. (1993). *Daniel: A commentary on the book of Daniel.* New Haven, CT: Yale University Press.

Cotman, C. W., Berchtold, N. C., & Christie, L. A. (2007). Exercise builds brain health: Key roles of growth-factor cascades and inflammation. *Trends in Neurosciences, 30*(9), 464–472. https://doi.org/10.1016/j.tins.2007.06.011

Gershon, M. D. (1998). *The second brain: A groundbreaking new understanding of nervous disorders of the stomach and intestine.* New York, NY: HarperCollins.

Hölzel, B. K., Carmody, J., Vangel, M., Congleton, C., Yerramsetti, S. M., Gard, T., & Lazar, S. W. (2011). Mindfulness practice leads to increases in regional brain gray-matter density. *Psychiatry Research: Neuroimaging, 191*(1), 36–43. https://doi.org/10.1016/j.pscychresns.2010.08.006

Holt-Lunstad, J., Smith, T. B., & Layton, J. B. (2010). Social relationships and mortality risk: A meta-analytic review. *PLOS Medicine, 7*(7), e1000316. https://doi.org/10.1371/journal.pmed.1000316

Lally, P., Van Jaarsveld, C. H. M., Potts, H. W. W., & Wardle, J. (2009). How are habits formed? Modelling habit formation in the real world. *European Journal of Social Psychology, 40*(6), 998–1009. https://doi.org/10.1002/ejsp.674

Moll, J., Krueger, F., Zahn, R., Pardini, M., de Oliveira-Souza, R., & Grafman, J. (2006). Human fronto-mesolimbic networks guide decisions about charitable donation. *Nature Neuroscience, 9*(9), 1288–1295. https://doi.org/10.1038/nn1760

Nobel Prize Committee for Physiology or Medicine. (2016). *The Nobel Prize in Physiology or Medicine 2016: Yoshinori Ohsumi.* NobelPrize.org. https://www.nobelprize.org/prizes/medicine/2016/press-release/

Sapolsky, R. M. (2004). *Why zebras don't get ulcers: The acclaimed guide to stress, stress-related diseases, and coping* (3rd ed.). New York, NY: Henry Holt and Company.

Trepanowski, J. F., & Bloomer, R. J. (2010). The Daniel Fast: A spiritual and nutritional intervention. *Nutrition Journal, 9*, 82. https://doi.org/10.1186/1475-2891-9-82

Waldinger, R. J., & Schulz, M. S. (2016). The Harvard Study of Adult Development: Lessons from 75 years of study of human development. *Harvard Review of Psychiatry, 24*(3), 75–83. https://doi.org/10.1097/HRP.0000000000000114

www.ingramcontent.com/pod-product-compliance
Lightning Source LLC
Chambersburg PA
CBHW060307240426
43661CB00059B/2689